Theory
and Practice of
Group Counseling
SECOND EDITION

The recent books that Jerry Corey has authored or co-authored (all published by Brooks/Cole Publishing Company) include:

- *Issues and Ethics in the Helping Professions, 2nd Edition* (1984, with Marianne Schneider Corey and Patrick Callanan)
- *I Never Knew I Had a Choice, 2nd Edition* (1983, in collaboration with Marianne Schneider Corey)
- *Case Approach to Counseling and Psychotherapy* (1982)
- *Casebook of Ethical Guidelines for Group Leaders* (1982, with Marianne Schneider Corey and Patrick Callanan)
- *Groups: Process and Practice, 2nd Edition* (1982, with Marianne Schneider Corey)
- *Group Techniques* (1982, with Marianne Schneider Corey, Patrick Callanan, and J. Michael Russell)
- *Theory and Practice of Counseling and Psychotherapy, 2nd Edition* (and *Manual*) (1982)

Theory and Practice of Group Counseling

SECOND EDITION

Gerald Corey
California State University
Fullerton

Diplomate in Counseling Psychology,
American Board of Professional Psychology

Brooks/Cole Publishing Company
Monterey, California

Brooks/Cole Publishing Company
A Division of Wadsworth, Inc.

Printed in the United States of America

10   9   8   7   6   5

Library of Congress Cataloging in Publication Data

Corey, Gerald F.
    Theory and practice of group counseling.

    Bibliography: p.
    Includes index.
    1. Group counseling.   2. Small groups.   I. Title.
BF637.C6C576   1984   616.89′152   84-5026
ISBN 0-534-03223-0

Sponsoring Editor: *Claire Verduin*
Editorial Associate: *Pat Carnahan*
Production Editor: *Fiorella Ljunggren*
Manuscript Editor: *William Waller*
Permissions Editor: *Carline Haga*
Interior and Cover Design: *Vernon T. Boes*
Typesetting: *Graphic Typesetting Service, Los Angeles, California*
Printing and Binding: *R. R. Donnelley & Sons Co., Crawfordsville, Indiana*

To the people in my long-term family group:
Marianne, Heidi, and Cindy

GERALD COREY, Professor and Coordinator of the Human Services Program at California State University at Fullerton and a licensed psychologist, received his doctorate in counseling from the University of Southern California. He is a Diplomate in Counseling Psychology, American Board of Professional Psychology; is registered as a National Health Service Provider in Psychology; and is a Fellow of the American Psychological Association (Counseling Psychology). Jerry is a member of the American Association for Counseling and Development, the American Group Psychotherapy Association, the American Orthopsychiatric Association, the Association for Humanistic Psychology, the Association for Specialists in Group Work, the National Association of Human Services Educators, the Western Association for Counselor Education and Supervision, and the Western Psychological Association.

Jerry has a special interest in teaching courses in group counseling and theories of counseling. With his colleagues Marianne Schneider Corey, Patrick Callanan, and J. Michael Russell, he regularly gives presentations at state and national professional conventions, conducts in-service training workshops, offers week-long residential personal-growth groups, and conducts occasional workshops in Mexico and Europe.

Jerry was the recipient of the Association for Specialists in Group Work's 1984 Professional Career Award for Distinguished Service in the Field of Group Work. In June of 1984, he received the Distinguished Faculty Member Award from the School of Human Development and Community Service of California State University, Fullerton.

❖

PREFACE

Group counseling is an increasingly popular form of therapeutic intervention in a variety of settings. Although there are many textbooks on the market that deal with groups, very few of them present an overview of various theoretical models and describe how these models apply to group counseling. The purposes of this book are to outline the basic elements of group process, present an overview of the key concepts and techniques of ten theoretical approaches to group counseling, attempt an integration of these approaches, and deal with some ethical and professional issues special to group work.

Theory and Practice of Group Counseling is written in a clear and simple style, so that students with little background in counseling theory will have no difficulty understanding the theoretical concepts and their relationship to group practice. The book focuses on the *practical applications* of the theoretical models to group work. This updated and considerably expanded second edition devotes more space to helping readers develop their own synthesis of various aspects of these approaches. It also has two detailed chapters on the stages of a group's development, providing a guide for group leaders in the practice of counseling.

Part One presents an overview of the various types of groups; ethical and professional issues in group work; the stages in the evolution of a group, from its formation to its termination and follow-up; and some basic issues in group membership and group leadership.

Part Two examines ten theoretical approaches to group counseling. Here the chapters follow a common organizational pattern, so that students can easily compare and contrast the various models. A typical chapter introduces the rationale for the model and its unique characteristics; discusses the model's key concepts and their implications for group process, as well as the model's basic procedures and techniques; defines the role and functions of the group leader according to the approach being discussed; and, when applicable, describes the stages of development of that particular group process. Applications of each model to group work with families is a new feature of this second edition. Each of these theory chapters also contains my own evaluation of the approach under discussion. In this edition, Questions for Reflection and Discussion have been added to help students review basic issues. Annotated lists of reading suggestions at the end of these chapters are offered to stimulate students to expand on the material and broaden their learning through further reading.

In the two chapters in Part Three, I have applied the ten models to a group in action in order to illustrate how practitioners of different orientations would view a particular group and how they might deal with certain typical themes that emerge in groups. The aim of these illustrative samples of group work is to make the theoretical perspectives come alive and provide some flavor of the differences and similarities among the approaches. The final chapter compares and contrasts the various group approaches with respect to the goals of group counseling, the role and functions of the group leader, the degree of structuring and division of responsibility in groups, and the use of techniques. The chapter concludes with a description of an "integrated eclectic model of group counseling," which utilizes concepts and techniques from all the other models examined and which should help students attempt their own personal integration. I strongly recommend that students read Part Three, Chapters 16 and 17, early in the course, because it provides a useful overview and synthesis.

This book is for graduate and undergraduate students in any field involving human services—from counseling psychology to social work. It is especially suitable for students enrolled in any of the courses under the general designation of "Theory and Practice of Group Counseling." The book is also for practitioners who are involved in group work or who are training paraprofessionals to lead various types of groups. Others who may find this book useful are psychiatric nurses, ministers, social workers, psychologists, marriage and family counselors, and mental-health professionals and paraprofessionals who lead groups as a part of their work.

A second edition of *Manual for Theory and Practice of Group Counseling* is available to help students gain maximum benefit from this book and actually experience group process and group techniques. The manual includes questions, suggested activities for the whole class and for small groups, ideas for self-directed groups, summary charts, self-inventories, study guides, group techniques, and examples of cases with open-ended alternatives for group-counseling practice. An *Instructor's Resource Manual* is also available.

I want to express my appreciation to several people who helped me in many ways as I was writing this book. My greatest thanks go to my wife, Marianne Schneider Corey, who has offered help, criticism, advice, and encouragement, and to my close friends and colleagues J. Michael Russell, Patrick Callanan, Mary Moline, and Helga Kennedy, who have contributed greatly to my views of group process and to my group-leadership style. The six of us regularly co-lead groups. The ideas and experiences that we have shared have profoundly influenced and greatly enhanced my skills as a group practitioner.

Others who have reviewed chapters or the entire manuscript and who have offered helpful and constructive criticism are William H. Blau of Day Treatment Center, Norwalk, California; Raymond Corsini; Albert Ellis of the Institute for Rational-Emotive Therapy; Donna Evans of the University of Maine at Orono; William Fischer of Duquesne University; Sandra Garfield of the Psychodrama Institute West Coast, Los Angeles; George M. Gazda of the University of Georgia; William Glasser of the Institute for Reality Therapy; Robert Goulding of the Western Institute for Group and Family Therapy, Watsonville, California; Reese House of Western Oregon State College; Arthur Lange of the University of California at Irvine; Thomas McGovern of Virginia Commonwealth University; Beverly Palmer of California State University at Dominguez Hills; Kathleen Ritter of California State College, Bakersfield; Sheldon Rose of the University of Wisconsin-Madison; Max Rosenbaum; Joseph Scalise of Nicholls State University; Harold Silverman of Wright State University; Treva Sudhalter; Warren Valine of Auburn University; Molly Vass of the University of Wyoming; John K. Wood of the Center for Studies on Person-Centered Therapy; David Zimpfer of Kent State University; and Joseph Zinker of the Cleveland Institute of Gestalt Therapy. To all of them I express my appreciation and gratitude. I also thank the student reviewers, who provided me with realistic viewpoints and reactions: Dennis Casarez, Chuck Geddes, Doug Hall, Carol Harrison, Sandy Jacobs, Larisa Lamb, Victoria Le Beau, Gladys Lorenzo, Andrea Mark, Kate McNamara, Bonnie Nelson, and Anne Rose. I am especially indebted to Joanna Doland, who also prepared the indexes for the book.

Once again, I am very appreciative of the constant support and encouragement I received from Claire Verduin of Brooks/Cole. Finally I want to thank Fiorella Ljunggren, also of Brooks/Cole, and Bill Waller for their superb production and editing jobs. Their contribution, well beyond the call of duty, has added much to this book.

Gerald Corey

CONTENTS

PART TWO
Theoretical Approaches to Group Counseling 131

PART ONE

Basic Elements of Group Process: An Overview

1

INTRODUCTION

Many of you who are in the human-services field will find that you are expected to use group approaches in your work with various types of clientele and for a variety of purposes. In a state mental hospital, for example, you may be asked to design and lead groups for different kinds of patients, or for those who are about to leave the hospital and be reintegrated into the community, or for the patients' families. Some of the group approaches commonly used in mental-health hospitals are insight groups, remotivation groups, assertion-training groups, and recreational/vocational-therapy groups, as well as specific kinds of groups such as reality-therapy, transactional-analysis, and Gestalt groups or one of the many forms of behavior modification done in a group setting.

If you work in a community mental-health center, a college counseling center, or a day-treatment clinic, you will be expected to provide therapeutic services in a wide range of group settings. A sample of groups commonly offered in these community facilities includes consciousness-raising groups for women (and for men), groups for alcoholics and for their families, groups for adolescents with drug habits, crisis-oriented groups for people in some immediate difficulty, groups for senior citizens, and groups for parents who are trying to communicate more effectively with their children.

The school is the setting for special groups designed to deal with the students' educational, vocational, personal, or social problems. If you work in a school, you may be asked to form a test-anxiety-reduction group, a career-exploration group, a group aimed at teaching interpersonal skills, or some type of self-awareness or personal-growth group.

In sum, for almost any need you can think of, you can find some type of group approach designed to help people meet that need. One of the main reasons for the popularity of the group as a primary therapeutic tool in many agencies and institutions is that the group approach is frequently more effective than individual approaches. This is due to the fact that group members can practice new skills both in the group and in their everyday interactions outside of it. There are practical considerations, too, such as cost and distribution of the available counselors and therapists.

The problem, however, is that even people with an advanced degree in one of the helping professions often have had very little exposure to the theory and techniques of group work. Many of these professionals find themselves in the role of group leaders as part of their job requirements without adequate preparation and training. It is not surprising that some of them—literally thrust into a group and expected to be responsible for providing the necessary leadership—panic and don't know where to begin. Although this book is not intended as an exclusive means of preparing competent group leaders, it is aimed at giving you some preparation for coping with the demands of group leadership.

ABOUT THIS BOOK

Theory and Practice of Group Counseling (second edition) is designed to introduce you to some basic issues and key concepts of group leadership and membership and to show you how groups function. The text is also designed to provide you with a good overview of a variety of theoretical models underlying group counseling, so that you can see the connection between theory and practice. In writing the chapters that describe these models, I've selected what I consider to be some of the more significant aspects of each theoretical approach. I have worked toward simplicity, clarity, and conciseness, and I have chosen a common format for the chapters, which should enable you to make comparisons among the various models.

From this text you will learn only some of the essentials of the therapies explored. The text is *not* designed to make you an expert in any one group approach. Its aim is to provide you with an understanding of some of the significant commonalities and differences among these theoretical models. My hope is that you will become sufficiently motivated to select some approaches and learn more about them by doing additional reading (which is suggested after each chapter) and by actually experiencing some of these group approaches as a participant. The ultimate goal is for you to develop a sufficient basis to be able to achieve your own theoretical perspective and personal style of group leadership.

This is basically a survey book. Instead of merely focusing on the theoretical aspects of the models selected, the book presents key concepts and deals with how these concepts are applied to group work. The goals of group process, the role and functions of the group leader, and specific techniques and procedures applicable to the group in action are some of the areas of focus. In brief, the book aims at a synthesis between theory and practice and at a balanced view of how group leaders can draw on various theoretical models in their actual practice of group work.

The remainder of Part One treats the basic elements of group process and practice that you'll need to know regardless of the types of group you may lead or the theoretical orientation you may hold. In Chapter 2 you are introduced to important ethical and professional issues that you will inevitably encounter as you lead groups. The emphasis is on the rights of group members and the responsibilities of group leaders. Chapter 3 deals with basic concerns of *group leadership,* such as the personal characteristics of effective leaders, the problems group leaders face, the different styles of group leadership, and the range of specific skills required for effective leading of groups. In Chapters 4 and 5 you are introduced to the major developmental tasks confronting a group as it goes through its various *stages,* from its formation to its termination, evaluation, and follow-up. The central characteristics of the stages that make up the life history of a group are examined, with special attention paid to the major functions of the group leader at each stage. These chapters also focus on the functions of the members of a group and the possible problems that are associated with each stage in the group's evolution.

Part Two offers an overview of ten major theoretical approaches to group counseling. These models have been selected to present a balanced perspective of the theories that underlie group practice. More specifically, the psychoanalytic model was selected because it is the theory from which most other approaches have developed. Even though, as group counselors, you may find some of the psychoanalytic techniques limited, you can still draw on psychoanalytic concepts in your work. The Adlerian approach to groups is included because there appears to be a resurgence of interest in Adlerian concepts and procedures in group counseling. The inclusion of psychodrama is based on my belief that the action-oriented methods of role playing can be integrated into most forms of group work. The relationship-oriented therapies—which include the existential approach, the person-centered approach, and the Gestalt approach—are important because they stress the experiencing of feelings and interpersonal relationships in group practice. Transactional analysis is included because of its current popularity and because it provides a cognitive structure for group work and can be integrated into a variety of other group approaches. The behavioral-cognitive therapies—behavior therapy, rational-emotive therapy, and reality therapy—stress action methods and behavior change and have been selected to present the cognitive and behavioral methods of group work.

To facilitate your task of comparing and contrasting these ten theories and to provide a framework that will help you integrate the theoretical models, the chapters follow a common outline. These chapters present the key concepts of each theory and their implications for group practice; outline the role and functions of the group leader according to the particular theory; discuss how each theory is applied to group practice, including working with family groups; and describe the major techniques employed under each theory. Illustrative examples make the use of these techniques more concrete. Each chapter contains my evaluation of the approach under discussion—an evaluation based on what I consider to be its major strengths and weaknesses—and a brief description of how I incorporate aspects of that approach into my own style of group leadership. Near the end of these chapters are questions for reflection and discussion. Throughout the book I encourage you to look for ways of selectively borrowing from each approach, so that you'll be able to develop a personal style of group leadership that fits the person you are. It is important that you do further readings in each of the theories, especially those that are of special interest to you. The annotated reading suggestions at the end of these chapters will help you select useful material.

Part Three focuses on the practical application of the theories and principles covered in Parts One and Two. To make such applications more vivid and concrete, Chapter 16 follows a group in action and discusses how the various therapeutic approaches apply to the case. In this way you'll get some idea of how practitioners with differing orientations work with the same group and with the same themes. This comparative view will also demonstrate some of the techniques of group leading in action. Chapter 17 is designed to help you pull together the various methods and approaches and look for commonalities and differences among them. This chapter also presents my own eclectic approach, which integrates concepts and techniques from the various theories.

I invite you to keep an open mind, yet to read critically. By being an active learner and by raising questions, you'll gain the necessary foundation for becoming an effective group leader. A *Manual for Theory and Practice of Group Counseling* (second edition) has been designed as a supplement to the textbook, so that you can actually experience the techniques that you are studying. Your active involvement in the manual's exercises and activities will make what you read in this textbook come alive for you.

OVERVIEW OF THE COUNSELING GROUP

The focus of this book is on group *counseling*. There are other types of therapeutic groups, and most of them share some of the goals, procedures, techniques, and processes of counseling groups. They differ, however, with respect to goals, the role of the leader, the kind of people in the group, and the emphasis given to issues such as prevention, remediation, treatment, and development. To make these similarities and differences clear, the discussion of group counseling in this section is followed by brief descriptions of group psychotherapy, encounter groups, T-groups (or laboratory-training groups), structured groups, and self-help groups.

Group counseling has preventive as well as remedial aims. Generally, the counseling group has a specific focus, which may be educational, vocational, social, or personal. The group involves an interpersonal process that stresses conscious thoughts, feelings, and behavior. Often counseling groups are problem oriented; their content and focus are determined largely by the members, who are basically well-functioning individuals who don't require extensive personality reconstruction and whose concerns relate to the developmental tasks of the life span. Group counseling tends to be growth oriented in that its focus is on discovering internal resources of strength. The participants may be facing situational crises and temporary conflicts, or they may be trying to change self-defeating behaviors. The group provides the empathy and support necessary to create the atmosphere of trust that leads to the sharing and exploration of these concerns. Group counseling is often carried out in institutional settings, such as schools, university counseling centers, community mental-health clinics, and other human-services agencies.

The group counselor uses verbal and nonverbal techniques as well as structured exercises. Common techniques include reflection (mirroring the verbal and nonverbal messages of a group member), clarification (helping members understand more clearly what they are saying or feeling), role playing, and interpretation (connecting present behaviors with past decisions). Other common techniques used in group counseling are described in more detail in Chapter 3. Basically, the role of the group counselor is to facilitate interaction among the members, help them learn from one another, assist them in establishing personal goals, and encourage them to translate their insights into concrete plans that involve taking action outside of the group. Counselors perform this role largely by teaching the members to focus on the here and now and to identify the concerns they wish to explore in the group.

Goals

Ideally, group members decide for themselves the specific goals of the group experience. Some of the general goals shared by most counseling groups in most settings with most populations are:

- to learn how to trust oneself and others
- to foster self-knowledge and the development of a unique sense of identity
- to recognize the commonality of the participants' needs and problems
- to increase self-acceptance, self-confidence, and self-respect in order to achieve a new view of oneself
- to find alternative ways of dealing with normal developmental problems and of resolving certain conflicts
- to increase self-direction, autonomy, and responsibility toward self and others
- to become aware of one's choices and to make choices wisely
- to make specific plans for changing certain behaviors and to commit oneself to follow through with these plans
- to learn more effective social skills
- to become more sensitive to the needs and feelings of others
- to learn how to confront others with care, concern, honesty, and directness
- to move away from merely meeting others' expectations and to learn to live by one's own expectations
- to clarify one's values and decide whether and how to modify them

Rationale

There are a number of advantages to group counseling as a vehicle for assisting people to make changes in their attitudes, beliefs about themselves and others, feelings, and behaviors. One is that participants can explore their styles of relating with others and learn more effective social skills. Another is that the group process provides a situation in which the members can discuss their perceptions of one another and receive valuable feedback on how they are experienced in the group.

In many ways the counseling group provides a re-creation of the participants' everyday world, especially if the membership is diverse with respect to age, interest, background, socioeconomic status, and type of problem. It is this kind of diversity that makes the group a microcosm of society. The group process provides a sample of reality, for the struggles and conflicts that people experience in the group situation are no different from those that they experience outside of it. The diversity that characterizes most groups also results in unusually rich feedback for the participants, who can see themselves through the eyes of a wide range of people.

The group offers support and understanding, which foster the members' willingness to explore the problems they brought with them to the group. The participants achieve a sense of belonging, and through the cohesion that develops, they learn ways of being intimate, caring, and challenging. In this supportive atmosphere, members can experiment with alternative behaviors. They can practice these behaviors in the group, where they receive encouragement as well as suggestions on how to apply what they learn in the group to their lives outside of it.

Ultimately, it is up to the members themselves to decide what changes they want to make. They can compare the perceptions they have of themselves with the perceptions others have of them and then decide what to do with this information. In essence, the members get a clearer glimpse of the kind of person they would like to become, and they come to understand what is preventing them from becoming that person.

Value for Special Populations

Group counseling can be designed to meet the needs of special populations such as children, adolescents, college students, and the elderly. Special counseling groups with these and other populations are described in the book *Groups: Process and Practice* (Corey & Corey, 1982), which offers suggestions on how to set up these groups and on what techniques to use for dealing with the unique problems of each of them. Here I'd like to discuss in brief the value of counseling groups for these special populations.

Counseling groups for children.   Counseling groups for children can be for preventive or for remedial purposes. In the school setting, group counseling is often suggested for children who display behaviors or attributes such as excessive fighting, inability to get along with peers, violent outbursts, chronic tiredness, lack of supervision at home, and neglected appearance. Small groups can provide children with the opportunity to express their feelings about these and related problems. Identifying children who are developing serious emotional and behavioral problems is extremely important. If these children can receive psychological assistance at an early age, they stand a better chance of coping effectively with the developmental tasks they must face later in life.

Counseling groups for adolescents.   The adolescent years can be extremely lonely ones, and it is not unusual for an adolescent to feel that there is no one there to help. Adolescence is also a time of deep concerns and key decisions that can affect the course of one's life. Dependence/independence struggles, acceptance/rejection conflicts, identity crises, the search for security, pressures to conform, and the need for approval are all part of this period of life. Many adolescents are pressured to perform and succeed, and they frequently experience severe stress in meeting these external expectations.

Group counseling is especially suited for adolescents because it gives them a place to express conflicting feelings, explore self-doubts, and come to the realization that they share these concerns with their peers. A group allows adolescents to openly question their values and to modify those that need to be changed. In the group, adolescents can learn to communicate with their peers, can benefit from the modeling provided by the leader, and can safely experiment with reality and test their limits. Another, unique value of group counseling for adolescents is that it offers them a chance to be instrumental in one another's growth. Because of the opportunities for interaction available in the group situation, the participants can express their concerns and be heard, and they can help one another on the road toward self-understanding and self-acceptance.

Counseling groups for college students.   Counseling groups are a valuable vehicle for meeting the developmental needs of the many college students who feel that the college or university is preoccupied with their intellectual development to the exclusion of their emotional and social growth. It was during the years I spent working in the counseling centers at two universities that I became aware of the need for groups on campus. At those universities the existing groups were designed for the relatively healthy students who were experiencing developmental crises. The main purpose of these groups was to offer the participants an opportunity for growth and a situation in which they could deal with issues concerning career decisions, male/female relationships, identity problems, educational plans, isolation feelings on an impersonal campus, and other concerns related to becoming an autonomous person.

Many university and college counseling centers now offer a wide range of structured groups to meet the diverse needs of the students, a few of which are assertion groups, consciousness-raising groups for women and men, groups for minorities, groups for the physically handicapped, stress-reduction groups, groups for middle-aged returning students who are considering career and life-style changes, and test-anxiety-reduction groups. These structured groups will be examined briefly in the next section.

Counseling groups for the elderly.   Counseling groups can be valuable for the elderly in many of the same ways that they are of value to adolescents. As people grow older, they often experience isolation, and many of them, seeing no hope of meaning—let alone excitement—in their future, may resign themselves to a useless life. Like adolescents, the elderly often feel unproductive, unneeded, and unwanted by society. Another problem is that many older people buy into myths about aging, which then become self-fulfilling prophecies—for example, the misconception that old people can't change or that, once they retire, they will be doomed to depression. Counseling groups can do a lot to help older people challenge these myths and deal with the developmental tasks that they, like any other age group, must face in such a way that they can retain their integrity and self-respect. The group situation can assist people in breaking out of their isolation and offer the elderly the encouragement necessary to seek for and find meaning in their lives so that they can live fully and not merely exist.

OTHER TYPES OF GROUPS

Group Psychotherapy

A major difference between group *therapy* and group *counseling* lies in their goals. Whereas counseling groups focus on growth, development, enhancement, prevention, self-awareness, and releasing blocks to growth, therapy groups focus on remediation, treatment, and personality reconstruction. Group psychotherapy is a process of reeducation that includes both conscious and unconscious awareness and both the present and the past. Some therapy groups are primarily designed to correct emotional and behavioral disorders that impede one's functioning. The goal may be a minor or a major transformation of personality structure, depending on the theoretical orientation of the group therapist. Because of this goal, therapy groups tend to be of relatively long duration. The people who make up the group may be suffering from severe emotional problems, deep neurotic conflicts, or psychotic states, and some may exhibit socially deviant behavior. Therefore, many of these individuals are in need of remedial treatment rather than developmental and preventive work. In general, the goal of a therapy group is the achievement of interpersonal and intrapsychic adequacy (Shapiro, 1978).

Group therapists are typically clinical or counseling psychologists, psychiatrists, and psychiatric social workers. They use a wide range of verbal modalities (which group counselors also use), and some employ techniques to induce regression to earlier experiences, to tap unconscious dynamics, and to help members reexperience traumatic situations so that catharsis can occur. As these experiences are relived in the group, members become aware of and gain insight into past decisions that interfere with current functioning. The group therapist assists members in developing a corrective emotional experience and in making new decisions about the world, others, and themselves. Working through unfinished business from the past that has roots in the unconscious is a primary characteristic of group therapy. This focus on past material, unconscious dynamics, personality reconstruction, and development of new patterns of behavior based on insight also accounts for the longer duration of group therapy.

Group psychotherapy, like group counseling, may be based on one of several therapeutic models. Many therapy groups employ psychoanalytic concepts and procedures, such as working with dreams, focusing on past experiences, trying to uncover the unconscious, and symbolically reliving unfinished significant relationships. Others—for example, behavior-therapy groups and rational-emotive-therapy groups—use techniques aimed at cognitive and behavioral changes. Many therapy groups are characterized by an eclectic approach; that is, concepts and techniques from several theoretical perspectives are incorporated into the practice of the group.

Encounter Groups

Encounter groups (sometimes known as personal-growth groups) offer an intense group experience designed to assist relatively healthy people in achieving better contact with themselves and others. The ground rules of encounter groups are that participants be open and honest in the group setting, that they avoid intellectualization, and that they talk instead about their feelings and perceptions. The emphasis is on eliciting emotions and on expressing these emotions fully; therefore, confrontations within the group are encouraged. Encounter groups focus on the here and now and on teaching people to live in the present.

Most people who join an encounter, or personal-growth, group seek increased intimacy with others and intend to explore blocks within themselves that keep them from realizing their full potential. Their goal is to feel more alive, become more spontaneous, be more aware of their total experience, and overcome feelings of isolation.

Although the original encounter groups used mainly verbal techniques, such groups now use a wide range of nonverbal modalities designed to foster interaction; touching, the use of fantasy, encounter games, sensory-awakening exercises, massage, meditation, and centering are just a few of them. These groups are usually time-limited; they often meet for a weekend or longer in a residential setting away from the distractions of daily living. During this time the participants are encouraged to become increasingly aware of their feelings and to engage in risk-taking behavior to discover different dimensions of themselves.

In sum, some of the goals of encounter groups are:

- to become aware of hidden potentials, to tap unused strengths, and to develop creativity and spontaneity
- to become more open and honest with selected others
- to decrease game playing, which prevents intimacy
- to become freer of "oughts," "shoulds," and "musts" and to develop internal values
- to lessen feelings of alienation and fears of getting close to others
- to learn how to ask directly for what one wants
- to learn the distinction between having feelings and acting on them
- to increase one's capacity to care for others
- to learn how to give to others
- to learn to tolerate ambiguity and to make choices in a world where nothing is guaranteed

Marathon groups. The marathon group is a variation and an intensification of the encounter-group experience. The group meets for a sustained period of time—anywhere from 24 hours to a week or more—and it's not unusual for the group to function almost nonstop, breaking only for meals and perhaps for a short nap. In this format the process of opening up appears to be accelerated by continuous contact and by fatigue-produced lowering of inhibitions and defenses. Marathon-group members are encouraged to become aware of the masks they wear in daily life, to discover genuine aspects of themselves beyond the social facades, and to risk giving up some of these pretenses as they reenter their day-to-day lives.

Other encounter-group variations. Encounter groups vary according to structure and format. For example, Carl Rogers (1970) describes the process of the "basic encounter group" as something that evolves through the decisions of the members of that group. He provides very little structure or direction other than to create a climate of trust and acceptance. Rogers avoids using structured group exercises, because he thinks that the group members have the capacity to move forward in constructive directions without using group techniques. Rogers' view of the basic encounter group is dealt with in some detail in Chapter 10.

Very different from Rogers' is the "open encounter group" described by Schutz (1967, 1971)—a group characterized by structure and by the group leader's initiating encounter games as catalysts. In his books *Joy* and *Here Comes Everybody*, Schutz describes specific techniques that are designed to create intense feelings and interaction. These techniques include breaking into and out of a circle, arm wrestling, nonverbal exercises, touching, and guided fantasy.

The encounter-group movement reached its peak during the 1960s and was perhaps the major vehicle of the human-potential movement, which stressed maximizing one's potential, living fully and spontaneously, overcoming barriers that hinder personal expression and contact with others, and striving for interpersonal honesty. The encounter-group movement has become more and more diversified by encompassing many approaches to personal growth, such as *psychosynthesis* (a psychological and educational approach for harmonizing the diverse elements of one's inner life); *Rolfing*, or *structural integration* (a method of deep manipulation of the muscular-skeletal system aimed at balancing the major segments of the body); *massage* (for relaxation, release of tension, and balance of energy flow); *bioenergetics* (an approach that focuses on understanding conflicts through the body);*yoga;* and *meditation.* Encounter techniques are often used in conjunction with some of the above approaches to human growth.

In examining the current status and future of encounter groups, Gazda (1978) sees a decline in the enthusiasm generated by this type of group experience. But, although Gazda predicts that the encounter-group movement will slow down considerably, he also believes that encounter techniques will be applied to group counseling and group psychotherapy and that the result will be an intensification and acceleration of the traditional processes of group counseling and psychotherapy. Gazda also predicts that encounter techniques will be incorporated into systematic human-relations-training groups.

T-Groups

T-groups—also referred to as training groups, laboratory-training groups, or sensitivity-training groups—focus more on group process than on personal growth. (*Group process* refers to the stages of development of a group and the characteristics of each stage.) Since these groups are aimed at interpersonal self-study, participation is meant to lead to improved interpersonal skills. Besides being taught how to observe their own processes, the participants also learn how groups function and how the participant can develop a leadership role. The goal is to become capable of applying what one has learned about group dynamics and interpersonal relationships to the settings in which one lives and works.

What are the distinguishing features of the laboratory approach? Golembiewski and Blumberg (1977) describe three of these features as follows:

1. *The T-group is a learning laboratory.* Personal change is *not* the main goal. The group's aim is to provide feedback and support for testing whether change will help people get what they want from their relationships with others. The T-group is a laboratory for interpersonal learning in these senses:
   * It attempts to create a miniature society.
   * It stresses inquiry, exploration, and experimentation with behavior.
   * It is focused on helping people learn *how* to learn.
   * It attempts to create a safe atmosphere conducive to learning.
   * It places the responsibility of determining what is to be learned on the members, even though a trainer is usually available for guidance.

2. *The T-group provides an opportunity for learning how to learn.* Typically, people join these groups with the vague goal of becoming more sensitive. Thus, the initial stages are characterized by ambiguity, since most members have no clear idea of what is to be learned (and how to go about it). Participants come to realize that any member in the group who can provide data for learning is a teacher. They learn that the only real answers are those provided by themselves and not by an authority figure or by the trainer.

3. *In the T-group, paying attention to the here and now is the grist for the learning mill.* Participants are discouraged from picking a "there-and-then" topic for discussion—that is, a topic external to what is going on in the group at the present moment. This practice can create frustration and anxiety in the initial stages of development of a T-group. Eventually, however, participants learn that what is happening now and how they feel about it are what matters.

Systematic human-relations training. An extension and adaptation of the laboratory approach is represented by what is called *systematic human-relations training*. This approach has its origins in Carkhuff's (1969a, 1969b) pioneering skill-development training for counselors, which focused on the level of skill that counselors demonstrated in perceiving and responding with genuineness, concreteness, self-disclosure, confrontation, and immediacy. Carkhuff also developed scales to evaluate the level of functioning of counselor skills in areas such as attending and responding, acquiring accurate empathy, responding with warmth and respect, and being aware of nonverbal behavior. Building on Carkhuff's model of skill development, Gazda, Asbury, Balzer, Childers, and

Walters (1977) have developed a systematic human-relations-development program for educators. Finally, Egan (1976, 1977) has translated the Carkhuff model for people interested in systematic training in the skills of interpersonal living.

Egan's approach to human-relations training in groups borrows many elements from the laboratory approach to learning. The major features of Egan's human-relations training in groups are experiential learning, a small group, feedback to and from others, a climate of experimentation, psychological safety, and here-and-now focus. Leadership is provided by the members of the group, because the trainer is actually both leader and member. The core of Egan's human-relations-training model is the contract, which spells out the goals and the procedures of the training group. This contractual approach consists of:

- working cooperatively to achieve the goals of the group
- actively listening to others
- responding to others concretely
- talking about oneself in personal ways
- giving feedback to others
- sharing oneself during the laboratory
- asking for feedback on one's interpersonal style
- dealing with feelings that arise from participation in the group

Structured Groups

Structured groups, or groups characterized by some central theme, seem to be gaining in popularity. Many college and university counseling centers offer a variety of special groups for particular populations, in addition to unstructured personal-growth groups and counseling groups. Below, for example, is a sample list of some of the structured groups offered by the Counseling-Psychological Services Center at the University of Texas at Austin:

- Mid-life transitions: Values and life decisions
- Gaining control of your life-style and "work-style"
- Stress-management workshop
- Depression-management training
- Managing relationships/ending relationships
- Type A stress group
- Strategies for building self-confidence for graduate women
- Eating disorders (binge/purge syndrome)
- Learning to cope with speech anxiety
- Developing assertive behavior
- Women in transition: Shifting gears
- Perfectionism: The double-edged sword
- The aftermath of suicide: A special kind of grief
- Jealousy: Taming the green-eyed monster
- Students with an alcoholic parent

The above list gives you some idea of the scope of topics for structured groups. These groups help people develop specific skills, understand certain themes, or go through difficult life transitions. Although specific topics do vary according to the interests of the group leader and the clientele, such groups have a common denominator of providing members with increased awareness of some life problem and tools to better cope with it. Typically, the sessions are two hours each week, and the groups tend to be relatively short-term. They may last for only four or five weeks, up to a maximum of one semester.

Members are generally asked to complete a questionnaire at the beginning of the group that pertains to how well they are coping with the particular area of concern. Structured exercises and homework assignments are typically introduced as ways of teaching new skills, and another questionnaire is often used at the final session to assess the members' progress. A contract is frequently drawn up as a way of helping members pinpoint specific goals that will guide their participation in the group and stimulate them to practice new skills outside of the group.*

Self-Help Groups

In the past decade there has been a burgeoning of self-help groups that allow people with a common interest to create a support system that protects them from psychological stress and gives them the incentive to begin changing their lives. These self-help groups serve a critical need for certain populations that is not met by professional mental-health workers or by other educational, religious, or community institutions (Cole, 1983; Lieberman, 1980; Lieberman & Borman, 1979).

In his comparison of contemporary healing groups, Lieberman (1980) categorizes them along a continuum. On one end of the continuum is *group psychotherapy*, which involves professionally led groups that often employ the medical model of treating a psychological disorder. On the other end is the *self-help movement*, which consists of organizations of people with similar emotional, physical, or behavioral problems or a common concern or affliction. Examples of these groups are Weight Watchers, Mended Hearts, Recovery, Inc., Alcoholics Anonymous, and so forth. Lieberman mentions that there are perhaps as many as 216 of these organizations. Such self-help groups are led by people who are struggling with the same issues as the members of the group, and by intention they are not professionally led. However, they do use professionals as guest speakers and consultants at times. The self-help movement's focus is limited to group members who have a common problem or life predicament, distinguishing them from traditional group therapies.

Typically, self-help groups meet in a community setting such as a school or a church. The members share their experiences, learn from one another, offer suggestions for new members, and provide support and encouragement for people who sometimes see no hope for their future.

Differences between the self-help group and others. With most of the groups that we have described (counseling groups, psychotherapy groups, encounter groups, T-groups), a basic assumption is that the group represents

---

*Those interested in more information about structured groups and workshops can write to Clearinghouse for Structured Group Programs, Office of Counseling and Student Development, Roosevelt Hall, University of Rhode Island, Kingston, RI 02881.

a *social microcosm*. These groups attempt to reflect in some way all of the dimensions of the members' real social environment. The therapeutic factor that accounts for change in the participants is the group process as a sample of the interpersonal conflicts that members confront in their daily lives.

In contrast, self-help groups are not a social microcosm. The interactions of members within the group are not viewed as the primary catalyst for change. Instead, attention is placed on providing an accepting and supportive climate in the group itself. The group becomes a means of helping people modify their beliefs, attitudes, and feelings about themselves. Self-help groups stress a common identity based on a common life situation to a far greater extent than do most other groups.

Sources of change.   Both Cole (1983) and Lieberman (1980) describe the factors associated with individual change in self-help groups. These sources of change can be viewed from emotional, cognitive, and behavioral perspectives.

Self-help groups provide for *emotional nurturing*. People who are attracted to these groups are often in great need of understanding and acceptance. They are likely to feel alone with their problem, often feel needless guilt, and may feel that others do not care about them. In the group setting they can find warmth, empathy, and encouragement. Most important, seeing fellow members who are finding their way instills hope in them. Before these people become a part of the group, they may feel demoralized and lost; once they become involved, they often find ways of participating actively in their own care and finding creative solutions to their problems. By witnessing other members in the group who are successfully coping with their life situation and making constructive life changes, they begin to believe that there is hope for an improved future for themselves also. This sense of communion is a most important factor fostering individual change in the self-help group.

Cognitive factors are also critical if individual change is to occur. Members are able to compare their thinking and their basic assumptions about life with those of others who are struggling with a common problem. By doing so they are provided with a new frame of reference for understanding their situation and for doing something different. For example, an alcoholic wife and mother may be convinced that she could control her drinking patterns and be a social drinker like her other friends. She is likely to deceive herself into thinking that she does not really have a drinking problem. If she attends Alcoholics Anonymous meetings, she may learn how to view her drinking from a different perspective as she hears fellow alcoholics tell their stories. Through the group experience, she may be motivated to take an honest look at her present condition and thus begin to do something that could bring about change for her and others.

Self-help groups also offer *behavioral strategies* for change. There is an emphasis on publicly committing oneself to a course of action, on mutual help, and on exchanging coping strategies. For example, the woman mentioned above learns to refuse that first drink, to live each day as it comes, and to call a fellow alcoholic when she desperately craves a drink. She learns to talk to another concerned person who has traveled the same road as she instead of continuing the path of self-destruction by drinking to avoid life's problems. Self-help groups offer a variety of ways to experiment with new behavior, and any small steps are reinforced by the other members.

The future of self-help groups. It appears that people have an increasing interest in banding together to find ways of helping themselves. Although I think that professionally led counseling and therapy groups still serve a vital role and are here to stay, I see it as a healthy sign that people are seeking other methods. So does Cole (1983):

> Although [self-help groups were] never intended to replace professional health care, patient response to them has been so overwhelming that they must be reckoned with. It is to be hoped that, in this consumer era, more professionals will become aware of the value inherent in self-help group membership [p. 150].

It seems to me that many self-help groups serve a unique function, one that cannot always be met in professionally led counseling and psychotherapy groups. Further, I see the possibility that people will seek either individual counseling or group therapy or both and at the same time be actively involved in a self-help group. Combining forces can promote the autonomy and growth of the client.

MISCONCEPTIONS ABOUT GROUPS

Before discussing the group process and its development, we need to consider some common misconceptions about groups. Although I call them "misconceptions," there is some element of truth in most of them. Thus, these views need to be investigated and evaluated so that we can separate myths from facts.

1. "Groups are antiintellectual." This view is based on the fact that, in some groups, thinking is seen as a "head trip" intended to avoid genuine feelings. Although there is some truth to this notion, I hasten to add that group process doesn't have to be antiintellectual. In my view, the best groups are those that don't contrast thinking and feeling but, instead, help members to integrate thinking/feeling/behaving/experiencing. I also believe that you will learn more and retain more of what you learn if you devote some effort to thinking and conceptualizing. Making some sense out of what you are being exposed to in a group is quite valuable.

2. "Groups foster impulsiveness." Some attack the groups because they see them as encouraging people to act impulsively, even irresponsibly. Groups don't necessarily foster impulsiveness. There is a distinction between acting spontaneously while, at the same time, retaining a sense of responsibility and "doing one's own thing." In my view, groups should teach people how to overcome unnecessary blocks to spontaneity and yet remain responsible individuals who act on more than passing whims. Genuine freedom implies acceptance of responsibility and accountability for one's actions; being the slave of one's impulses is the antithesis of being free.

3. "A group is a place to get emotionally high." From my viewpoint, if you leave a group feeling high, you might consider it a fringe benefit; but I surely don't see getting high as the main reason for participating in a group. In fact, some group participants may encounter periods of depression after the high they experienced in a group, particularly when they don't find in their daily lives the kind of support they received when they were in the group. Whereas in the group situation they most likely received positive feedback and encouragement for their efforts to change, outside of it they may encounter resistance when they dare to be different. Thus, the temporary letdown members often experience when they discover that they cannot conquer the world as they had hoped is something they need to be prepared for.

4. "Sick people are the only ones who can benefit from a group." It is a myth that counseling, individually or in groups, is aimed mainly at treating individuals with serious psychological disorders. Many people feel a sense of shame in admitting that they are involved in a group, because they have come to associate groups with the cure of emotional disorders. Although it is true that some groups are aimed at helping a disturbed population function more effectively, there are *many* groups geared toward developmental purposes—groups designed to assist people in recognizing and using their fullest capabilities. Thus, for those who are already functioning relatively well, the group can provide tools to remove blocks that stand in the way of even better functioning. Most of us could benefit from honest feedback concerning how others see us and from learning additional interpersonal skills.

5. "Groups are a cure-all." There are surely limitations to what you can learn in a group. The group can be a very important source of learning and an adjunct to other means of growth, but it is an error to think of groups as the only way of becoming more of the person you would like to be.

6. "The aim of the group is to make you feel close to everyone in the group." It is true that a genuine bond of intimacy and cohesion characterizes most effective groups, and the resulting closeness should not be discounted as artificial. However, although real intimacy results from the participants' shared struggling and risking, intimacy is the by-product and not the central goal of the group.

7. "Groups are basically destructive. They are places where people tear you down and then don't rebuild you." If this occurs, it is the product of inept leadership. In a group, people can learn that their defenses are not always justified and that they can choose to eliminate unnecessary walls that separate them from others. I surely don't support the type of attack group that strives for a careless stripping away of all defenses. But I do believe that the members of a group can be encouraged to trust themselves and others enough to believe that, if they open themselves up, they can find a wealth of resources and strengths.

8. "Group participation leads to selfishness and to a disregard for others." When you are in a group, you are asked to think about your own needs, but this is not an indication that groups endorse a selfish and uncaring attitude. Instead, when you learn how to take care of yourself, you increase the proba-

bility of your being able to care for others more genuinely. Caring for oneself is *not* the same as disregarding others.

9. "What occurs in a group is artificial and unreal." This view implies that what goes on in a group has little connection with the "real world." When this view is justified, the basic purpose of the group is lost. Groups do contain some degree of artificiality, at least in the sense that they are structured experiences. However, in many important respects groups can be far more real than much of the reality you experience in your day-to-day living. In effective groups, people shed many of their pretenses, and their interactions reflect the members' commitment to openness and honesty. How "real" your group is depends on how determined you are to use what you do in your group sessions to change your everyday life.

10. "Groups make you miserable." Some are convinced that those who expose themselves to any type of counseling run the risk of becoming even more unhappy, because they discover problems that they were not aware of before. For a time this may be true. As you get new insights into yourself, you are bound to experience some discomfort. Seeing yourself as others sometimes see you may be painful, yet it is a prerequisite for personal growth and change. I don't believe, however, that awareness of problems and shortcomings needs to result in a prolonged state of discouragement and unhappiness. You can make choices to change some of the aspects of yourself and of your environment that are causing most difficulties.

11. "Groups practice brainwashing." Successful group participation will help you acquire an increased ability to look within yourself for the source of ultimate answers. It is a myth that dispensing cheap advice or indoctrinating members with a particular philosophy of life is a common group practice. When that happens, it is clearly an abuse of the group's power. A group experience that substitutes one unquestioned style of life for another is not of much value in helping people become more self-directed. An effective group will challenge you to reexamine your own philosophy but will not pressure you to blindly accept a new set of dictates about the way you "should be."

2

ETHICAL AND PROFESSIONAL ISSUES IN GROUP PRACTICE

INTRODUCTION

In my view, those who seek to be professional group leaders must be willing to question the level of their ethical and professional standards. This chapter deals with the ethics of group work, education and training standards for group leaders, and the maintaining of competence through continued education. Some other professional issues treated here are confidentiality, psychological risks of groups, controversial issues in group work, the impact of the group leader's values, personal relationships with clients, and specific ethical guidelines for group leaders.

As a responsible group practitioner, you must clarify your thinking about the ethical and professional issues that are discussed in this chapter—for example, when to break confidentiality, how to determine whether you are qualified to lead a certain group, how to deal with subgrouping and extragroup socialization, and how to determine when certain activities are high risk. Professional and ethical standards for group leaders have been established by, among others, the American Group Psychotherapy Association (1978), the Association for Specialists in Group Work (1980, 1983), the American Association for Counseling and Development (1981), the American Psychological Association (1973, 1981), the American Association for Marriage and Family Therapy (1975), the National Association of Social Workers (1979), the American Psychiatric Association (1970), and the National Training Laboratory Institute (1969).

Although you are obligated to be familiar with, and bound by, the ethical codes of your specialization, many of these codes offer only general guidelines. Thus, you will be challenged to develop your own ethical and professional standards. It is my hope that you will begin to develop an ethical awareness and that you will reflect on ethical issues *before* you actually begin to lead groups. It is also my hope that, as you practice your profession, you will continue to interpret and translate general ethical guidelines into appropriate, specific principles that will govern your practice.

THE RIGHTS OF GROUP PARTICIPANTS

My experience has taught me that those who enter groups are frequently unaware of their basic rights, as well as their responsibilities, as participants. I believe that it is your function as a group leader to help prospective group members learn what these rights and responsibilities are. Therefore, this section offers a detailed list of group participants' rights.

Keep in mind, however, that there are exceptions to these rights, for there are many variables that determine their range. For example, group members who voluntarily join a counseling group have a right to leave the group if they decide that the group doesn't offer what they need. But this right does not apply to members of involuntary groups consisting of people in correctional institutions. In that case, participation in a group may be an integral part of the rehabilitation program, and it is mandatory. The eventual release of these individuals may be partially contingent on their cooperation and progress in the group. Although the rights listed below primarily concern members of voluntary groups, many of them apply to both voluntary and involuntary participants. Even when group participation is mandatory, participants do have certain rights, and they should be clearly aware of these rights. For example, if full confidentiality cannot be guaranteed, group members have a right to know what the limits of confidentiality are.

If the matter of member rights is discussed openly during the pregroup interview and at the initial session, the members are likely to be far more cooperative and active as participants. A leader who does this as a matter of policy demonstrates honesty and respect for the members and encourages the trust necessary for group members to extend themselves by being open and active. Such a leader has obtained the *informed consent* of the participants. People have the basic right to know what they are getting into before they make a commitment to become a part of any group.

Issues before joining a group. The following is a list of what group participants have a right to expect *before* they make the decision to join a group:

- a clear statement regarding the purpose of the group
- a description of the group format, procedures, and ground rules
- a pregroup interview to determine whether this particular group with this particular leader is at this time appropriate for one's needs

- an opportunity to seek information about the group, to pose questions, and to explore concerns
- a statement describing the education, training, and qualifications of the group leader
- information concerning fees and expenses and whether the fee includes a follow-up session; also, information about length of group, frequency and duration of meetings, group goals, and types of technique being employed
- information about the psychological risks involved in group participation
- knowledge of the limitations of the confidential character of the group— that is, of circumstances in which confidentiality must be broken because of legal, ethical, or professional reasons
- clarification of what services can and cannot be provided within the group
- help from the group leader in developing personal goals
- a clear understanding of the division of responsibility between leader and participants
- a discussion of the rights and responsibilities of group members

Issues during the group.   Following is a list of what members have a right to expect during the course of the group:

- instructions concerning what is expected of the participants
- the freedom to leave the group if it doesn't appear to be what one expected or what one wants or needs at this time
- notice of any research involving the group and of any tape recording or audiovisual taping of group sessions
- if tape recording does take place, the right to stop it if it restricts member participation
- assistance from the group leader in translating group learning into action in everyday life
- opportunities to discuss what one has learned in the group and to bring some closure to the group experience, so that the participant is not left with unnecessary unfinished business
- a consultation with the group leader should a crisis arise as a direct result of participation in the group, or a referral to other sources of help if further help is not available from the group leader
- the exercise of reasonable safeguards on the leader's part to minimize the potential risks of the group
- respect for member privacy with regard to what the person will reveal as well as to the degree of disclosure
- freedom from undue group pressure concerning participation in group exercises, decision making, disclosure of private matters, or acceptance of suggestions from other group members
- observance of confidentiality on the part of the leader and other group members
- freedom from having values imposed by the leader or other members
- the opportunity to use group resources for growth
- the right to be treated as an individual

It should be stressed that participation in groups carries certain responsibilities as well as rights. Some of these responsibilities include attending regularly, being prompt, taking risks, being willing to talk about oneself, giving others feedback, maintaining confidentiality, and asking for what one needs.

Three Important Freedoms

The rights of group members can be illustrated by taking as examples the right to leave the group at any time, the right to use group resources, and the right to be free from coercion.

Freedom of exit. One of the ethical guidelines of the Association for Specialists in Group Work (ASGW) states: "Group leaders shall inform members that participation is voluntary and that they may exit from the group at any time" (1980). This topic should be discussed during the initial session, and the leader's attitudes and policies about the freedom to leave a group should be clarified from the outset. Corey, Corey, Callanan, and Russell (1982a) take the position that clients have a responsibility to the leaders and other members to explain why they want to leave. There are a number of reasons for such a policy. For one thing, it can be deleterious to members to leave without having been able to discuss what they considered threatening or negative in the experience. If they simply leave when they become uncomfortable, they are likely to be left with "unfinished business," and so are the remaining members. It can surely damage the cohesion and trust in a group, for the remaining members may think that they in some way "caused" the departure. It is a good practice to tell members that, if they are even thinking of withdrawing, they should bring the matter up for exploration in a session. Although it is not ethical to use undue pressure to keep a person in a group, it is critical that members at least be invited to discuss their departure. At times they can be challenged in a constructive way to take an honest look at why they feel like leaving the group.

Freedom to use group resources. Members have a right to expect that they will be able to make optimum use of the resources within a group. At times, however, certain members may monopolize the group's time or engage in long-winded storytelling, leaving little time for serious members who want time to work on their concerns. The ASGW's guideline here is: "Group leaders shall insure to the extent that it is reasonably possible that each member has the opportunity to utilize group resources and interact within the group by minimizing barriers such as rambling and monopolizing time" (1980).

Although the group leader does not have to assume complete responsibility for intervening with members who are disrupting the group, the leader should notice the situation and work with the group in such a way that one member does not sap the energy of the group and make it difficult for others to do productive work. I see it as the leader's function to teach rambling members to become aware of the ways they present themselves to others in the group. Without being sharp or overly critical, a leader can help members learn how to be specific and to avoid getting lost in the details of a story.

Freedom from coercion and undue pressure. Members can reasonably expect to be respected by the group and not to be subjected to coercion and undue group pressure. On this matter the ASGW's (1980) guideline is: "Group leaders shall protect member rights against physical threats, intimidation, coercion, and undue peer pressure insofar as it is reasonably possible."

On the one hand, some degree of group pressure is inevitable, and it is even therapeutic in many instances. People in a group are confronted with some of their self-defeating beliefs and behaviors, and to some extent there are pressures to admit what they are doing and determine whether they want to remain the way they are. Further, there is pressure in sessions to speak up, to make personal disclosures, to take certain risks, to share one's reactions to the here-and-now events within the group, and to be honest with the group.

On the other hand, members can easily be subjected to needless anxiety if they are badgered to behave in a certain way or pressured into making decisions that the group wants them to make. Members may also be pressured to take part in communication exercises or nonverbal exercises designed to promote interaction. It is essential that leaders be sensitive to the values of members who decline to participate in certain group exercises. Leaders must make it genuinely acceptable for members to abstain by mentioning this option periodically whenever it is appropriate.

THE ISSUE OF CONFIDENTIALITY

Confidentiality is a central ethical issue in group counseling. Not only are you as a leader required to keep the confidences of group members; you have the added responsibility of impressing on the members the necessity of maintaining the confidential nature of whatever is revealed in a group.

I think it is a good practice to remind participants from time to time of the danger of inadvertently revealing confidences. I have found that members rarely gossip maliciously about others in their group. However, people do tend to talk more than they should outside the group and can unwittingly offer information about fellow group members that should not be revealed. If the maintenance of confidentiality within the group seems to be a matter of concern, the subject should be discussed fully in a group session. Clearly there is no way to ensure that group members will respect the confidences of others. You can discuss the matter, express your feelings about the importance of maintaining confidentiality, have members sign contracts agreeing to it, and even impose some form of sanction on those who break confidentiality; ultimately, however, it is up to the members to respect the need for confidentiality and to maintain it.

In his article "Confidentiality in Group Counseling," Plotkin (1978) calls confidentiality the "ethical cornerstone" of the client/counselor relationship. He maintains that, since group members are a "necessary and customary" part of a group counselor's procedures, they have the same obligation as the counselor to maintain the confidential character of their group. Plotkin offers the following suggestion to group leaders:

Group leaders are well advised to rethink the contracts they enter into with their clients. These contracts should specify in writing, at a minimum, the therapist's duty to maintain the confidentiality of the relationship and should include those situations in which the law or ethics may require the therapist to reveal certain confidences. They should also spell out the client's obligations to maintain the confidentiality of any group sessions in which he or she participates [p. 14].

In the ASGW's *Ethical Guidelines for Group Leaders* (1980) there are two principles related to the issue of confidentiality: "Group leaders shall protect members by defining clearly what confidentiality means, why it is important, and the difficulties involved in enforcement" and "Group leaders shall inform members about recording of sessions and how tapes will be used."

With respect to the use of videotapes and audiotapes of group sessions, certain steps are necessary to protect the rights of group members and to ensure confidentiality. Members have the right to know of any recordings that might be made and what they will be used for, and their written permission should be secured before any recording of a session. If the tapes will be used for research purposes or will be critiqued by a supervisor or other students in a group-supervision session, then the members have a right to be informed; they also have the right to deny permission.

Exceptions to Confidentiality

The American Association for Counseling and Development (AACD) specifies exceptions to the general norm of confidentiality regarding all group members' disclosures: "When the client's condition indicates that there is a clear and imminent danger to the client or others, the counselor must take reasonable personal action or inform responsible authorities. Consultation with other professionals must be used where possible" (1981).

In basic agreement with the AACD position is that of the American Psychological Association (APA):

[Psychologists] reveal . . . information to others only with the consent of the person or the person's legal representative, except in those unusual circumstances in which not to do so would result in clear danger to the person or to others. Where appropriate, psychologists inform their clients of the legal limits of confidentiality [1981].

Of course, it is imperative that those who lead groups learn the state laws that will have an impact on their practice. Counselors are legally required to report clients' threats to harm themselves or others. This requirement also covers cases of child abuse or neglect, incest, or child molestation. Taking an extreme case, if one of your group members convincingly threatens to seriously injure another person, you may have to consult your supervisor or other colleagues, warn the intended victim, and even notify the appropriate authorities. The threat need not involve others; clients may exhibit bizarre behavior, like having "visions" or "hearing voices" telling them to maim themselves—behavior that may require you to take steps to have them temporarily hospitalized.

If you lead a group at a correctional institution, you may be required to act as more than a counselor; for instance, you may have to record in a member's file certain behaviors that he or she exhibits in the group. At the same time, your responsibility to your clients requires you to inform them that you are recording and passing on certain information. Generally speaking, you will find that, if you are candid about your actions, you have a better chance of gaining the cooperation of group members than if you hide your disclosures and thereby put yourself in the position of violating their confidences.

Another delicate problem related to confidentiality involves group counseling with children and adolescents. Do parents have a right to information that is disclosed by their children in a group? The answer to that question depends on whether you are looking at it from a legal, ethical, or professional viewpoint. Before any minor enters a group, it is a good practice to routinely require written permission from the parents. It is useful to have this permission include a brief statement concerning the purpose of the group, along with comments regarding the importance of confidentiality as a prerequisite to accomplishing such purposes and your intention not to violate any confidences. Clearly, it may be useful to give the parents information about their child, but this can be done without violating confidences. One useful practice to protect the privacy of what goes on in the group is to provide feedback to parents in a session with the child and one or both of the parents. In this way the child will have less cause to doubt the group leader's integrity in keeping his or her disclosures private.

The APA has a general guideline for leaders of groups composed of minors: "When working with minors or other persons who are unable to give voluntary, informed consent, psychologists take special care to protect these persons' best interests" (1981).

THE ISSUE OF PSYCHOLOGICAL RISKS IN GROUPS

Since groups can act as powerful catalysts for personal change, they can also pose definite risks for group members. The nature of these risks—which include group pressure, hostile and destructive confrontations, breaches of confidences, invasion of privacy, scapegoating, physical injury, and emotional harm—and what the leader can do about them are the subjects of this section. At the outset, I'd like to say that it is unrealistic to expect that a group will not involve risk, for all meaningful learning in life involves taking risks. However, it is the responsibility of the group leader to ensure that prospective group members are aware of the potential risks and to take every precaution against them. The ASGW's ethical guidelines specify that "group leaders shall stress the personal risks involved in any group, especially regarding potential life-changes, and help group members explore their readiness to face these risks" (1980). A minimal expectation is that group leaders discuss with members the advantages and disadvantages of a given group, that they prepare the members to deal with any problems that might grow out of the group experience, and that they be alert to the fears and reservations that members might have.

Following are some of the problems that group leaders must warn members about and must work to minimize:

1. Members should be made aware of the possibility that participating in a group (or any other therapeutic endeavor) may disrupt their lives. As members become increasingly self-aware, they may make changes in their lives that, although constructive in the long run, may create crisis and turmoil along the way. For example, changes that a wife makes in her life as a result of what she gains in a group may evoke resistance, even hostility, in her husband, with a resulting strain on their marriage.

2. The group as a whole may pressure an individual member to "let it all hang out," to tell more than the member wishes to tell about himself or herself. If the pressure is successful, the individual's privacy may be invaded.

3. A variety of group pressures—including demands to be honest, to take risks, to make decisions, to expose one's thoughts and feelings about oneself and others, and to try new behavior—can in certain instances violate the individual's freedom to choose his or her actions and impinge on the individual's responsibility for such actions.

4. Occasionally an individual member may be singled out as the scapegoat of the group. Other group members may "gang up" on this person, making him or her the object of hostility or other forms of negativity. Clearly, the group leader can and should take firm steps to eliminate such occurrences.

5. Confrontation, a valuable and powerful tool in any group, can be misused, especially when it is employed to destructively attack another. Here, again, leaders (and members as well) must be on guard against behavior that can pose a serious psychological risk for group participants.

6. As discussed in the preceding section, there is an ever-present risk that confidences shared in a group may not be maintained.

7. Physical injury that may occur as a result of useful group activity, such as certain "encounter games" that involve releasing pent-up feelings of anger and aggression, is a definite risk in some groups. Because some of these "encounter games" involve shoving, pushing, holding down, wrestling, and so forth, they can lead to violent outbursts and physical violence. Clearly, group leaders should instigate such exercises with great care and only when they are quite sure that the participants will not act out of control. If the leader has any question about the members' tendencies toward physical violence, he or she may be advised to have members release their aggressive feelings symbolically—say, by beating a pillow.

On this issue of the risks involved in using physical techniques, several guidelines for preventing negative consequences are described by Corey, Corey, Callanan, and Russell (1982a):

- If leaders introduce physical techniques, they should protect the person and the other members from harm; they should also be prepared to deal with unforeseen directions the exercise might take.
- For safety reasons, it is best not to introduce physical techniques that involve the whole group.
- Such techniques should not be used unless the leader knows the members quite well and has established a relationship based on trust.

- Leaders who introduce such techniques should have the experience and training to deal with the intense reactions that can follow.
- Beginning group leaders should either avoid using physical techniques or do so only when direct supervision is available or when they are co-leading with an experienced therapist.
- It is unwise to goad or push members into participating in physical exercises. Members can be invited to participate, but they should have the clear option to decline.

As indicated earlier, one cannot eliminate psychological risks in groups, but one can minimize them. One way is to use a contract approach, wherein the leaders specify the nature of their responsibilities and the members specify their commitment to the group by stating what they are willing to explore and do in the group. If members and leaders function within the framework of a contract that delineates expectations, there is less chance for members to be exploited or to leave a group feeling that they have had a negative experience.

Another safeguard against unnecessary risk is the ability of leaders to sincerely recognize the boundaries of their competence and to restrict themselves to working only with those groups for which their training and experience have properly prepared them. Even if they have a license or certification that *legally* permits them to conduct any kind of therapy group with any population, responsible group leaders realize that they are *ethically* and *professionally* restricted to working within the limits of their background of training. For example, a group leader may be experienced and very skilled in working with children and adolescents in groups yet be unprepared to lead a group of adult psychotics, regardless of what his or her credentials may say.

Ultimately, it is the group leader who is responsible for minimizing the inevitable psychological risks that attend all group activity. To best assume this responsibility, the leader must be willing to undergo the supervised practice and course work that will be described later in this chapter.

CONTROVERSIAL ISSUES

There are a number of controversial issues related to group practice that warrant special attention. As a group leader, I believe, you need to think through these issues and clarify your position on each of them.

Socializing among Group Members

One issue concerns the question of whether socializing among group members hinders or facilitates group process. Yalom (1975) writes that a therapy group teaches people *how* to form intimate relationships but does not *provide* these relationships. Yalom also points out that members meeting outside of the group have a responsibility to bring information about their meeting into the group. I take the position that any type of subgrouping or out-of-group socialization that interferes with the functioning of the group is counterproductive and should be discouraged, particularly if participants discuss issues relevant to the group away from the group and avoid bringing up the same issues in the group itself.

Leaderless and Self-Directed Groups

Another issue relates to the questions of whether group members have the capacity to direct themselves without a formal or trained leader and what the advantages and disadvantages of a leaderless group may be. Many self-help and peer groups are basically self-directed, wherein certain members assume leadership functions. These groups operate on the assumption that, since the primary resources of healing lie within the group itself, a formal leader is unnecessary.

Mullan and Rosenbaum (1978) describe a version of a leaderless group known as the *alternate session*—meetings without the leader. The purpose of the practice, according to Mullan and Rosenbaum, is to promote the therapeutic process by fostering support and increasing interaction among the members. Yalom (1975) agrees that there is value in occasional or regularly scheduled leaderless meetings as adjuncts to traditional therapist-led groups. In his view, such sessions can lessen dependence on the leader by fostering self-responsibility within the group. Yalom warns, however, that proper timing is essential and that the group should develop cohesiveness before these leaderless meetings are begun.

Dinkmeyer and Muro (1979) are of the opinion that leaderless groups can be useful—especially for helping counselors who are in training to learn firsthand how small groups function. They add that the leaderless approach may be less useful for leaders who work with "normal" people in developmental groups. Gazda (1978) maintains that the practice of allowing therapy and quasitherapy groups to meet without the presence of a professional leader should be discouraged until there is more supportive research evidence.

The Use of Structured Exercises

In my opinion, there is no question about the validity of structured exercises. I have, however, some questions about *which* exercises to use, *when* to use them, and *why* to use a particular exercise. In their eagerness to get a group moving and keep it moving, some group leaders try one exercise after another in a hit-or-miss attempt at finding ways of constructively intervening in a group. I agree with Gazda (1978) when he criticizes the use of structured group experiences without a rationale or an explanation of the purpose of the exercise in terms of the goals and processes of a group. According to Gazda, exercises that relate to the overall plan of the group and are appropriately applied in a timely fashion can be a powerful tool for positive change; lacking proper application, they can be quite harmful.

Group leaders should be careful not to overuse structured exercises. It is the nature of these exercises to foster interaction among group members, and members can quickly become overly dependent on them. If, each time that members encounter an impasse, they are rescued with some kind of exercise, they will not learn to struggle on their own and draw on their own responses to get through the impasse. A typical misuse of structured exercise occurs when the group energy level is low and the members seem to have little investment in the group. If the leader continually plugs in an exercise as a kind of psychological pep pill, the group members will never make the effort to take a look at what is producing this boredom and apathy. Indeed, in this case, the exercise can encourage avoidance behaviors in the members.

Nonverbal exercises have a great potential for enhancing the group process when used wisely and a great potential for harm when used unwisely. Some typical nonverbal activities include falling backward and trusting to be caught by a partner, breaking into and breaking out of a circle, fighting with bataccas (soft, felt-covered clubs), beating a pillow, holding a person down, arm wrestling, lifting and rocking a person, massaging, facial caressing, touching palms, dancing, sculpting, and milling around and making contact with eyes closed.

I deem it important that the group leader give members an opportunity to share their reactions to, and to discuss the meaning of, the exercise. It is also important that participants verbalize what they have learned as a result of the experience.

I think that structured exercises can be very useful, especially during the initial and the final stages of a group. At the beginning of a group I use certain structured exercises designed to assist members in focusing on their personal goals, in dealing with their expectations and fears, and in building trust. These exercises consist of asking members to work in dyads, triads, and small groups on some selected topic—for example, what they hope to get from the group. During the closing phase of a group, I rely on some behavior-rehearsal exercises, use contracts, suggest homework assignments, and use a variety of other procedures designed to help consolidate learning and facilitate its generalization.

In spite of my positive view of exercises, I must caution that overuse of techniques and exercises can short-circuit certain processes that members must experience if they are to develop autonomy as a group. Generally, I don't use techniques to actually stir up the members' desire to work. But once participants commit themselves to work—particularly when they have clearly identified issues to explore and have shown a willingness to penetrate their problems more deeply—I have found that a technique or an exercise can help them deepen their explorations and lead to new awareness and action.

Sexuality in Groups

In my view, group participants should be encouraged to speak about and explore their sexual feelings as openly as they express and explore their other feelings. Sensuality, touching, and physical displays of affection, which often occur in groups, are an important part of the group process. If, however, group participants are invited to discuss their fears and desires related to sex, I believe that it is especially important that sexual intercourse between members or between leader and members be avoided. Clearly, the issue of sexual intercourse is far more pressing in marathon groups, where people live together for anywhere between 36 hours and a week or longer, than it is in groups that meet weekly for two hours. For residential and marathon groups, Corey and Corey (1982) have observed not only that participants tend to feel safer about expressing their sexual feelings if there is a policy of no sexual intercourse but also that such a policy prevents the participants from avoiding significant personal issues by seeking sexual relationships with each other.

Even in groups that meet weekly, some members become sexually and emotionally involved with each other outside of the group. Although it is not the role of the leader to monitor all the activities of members when they are away from the group, it may be useful to discourage such relationships and to caution members about the problems that these relationships can create. At best, sexual or romantic relationships—like any form of subgrouping—can have the effect of reducing openness among members and can interfere with interactions in the group.

Schutz (1971) doesn't discuss sexual relationships between members in ethical terms. It is his policy to hold members of his residential encounter groups responsible for following certain rules of openness and honesty. And, as long as these rules are observed, whatever happens between the members is seen as a source of growth and self-understanding.

Gazda (1978) takes the position that sexual relationships between the leader and group members are unethical. Also, he considers it unethical for group leaders to either encourage or condone sexual relationships between group members. Beyond the ethical aspects, Gazda makes the practical observation that professional liability insurance does not protect psychologists and counselors against suits arising from situations involving sexual relationships in the therapy.

The Impact of the Leader's Values on the Group

In all controversial issues related to the group process, the group leader's values play a central role. For instance, your sexual values or views on touching will influence the position you take on some of the issues that have been discussed above. More specifically, your awareness of how your values influence your leadership style is in itself a central professional issue. Sometimes group counselors are taught to be neutral and are urged to attempt to keep their values separate from their leadership function. I take the position that it is neither possible nor desirable for counselors to be scrupulously neutral with respect to values in the therapeutic relationship. Whereas I don't see the proper function of counselors as persuading clients to accept a certain value system, I do think it critical that counselors be clear about their own values and how these values influence their therapeutic work and, ultimately, the directions taken by their clients. Since counselors' values inevitably affect their counseling, counselors must be willing to express their values openly when such an expression is relevant and appropriate to the work of the group.

I'd be inclined to expose my values in those situations where there were conflicts between a member's values and my own. It does not seem therapeutic to feign acceptance or to pretend that no difference of opinion exists. Expressed values are less likely to interfere with the process of a group than values that are concealed.

In my view, the crux of the ethical concern is leaders who use their groups as a forum for advancing their personal agenda or seek to meet their own needs at the expense of the welfare of the members. The ASGW's guideline here is: "Group leaders shall refrain from imposing their own agendas, needs, and values on group members" (1980). The critical word in this rule is *imposing*. I see a real difference between *imposing* and *exposing* one's values. In the case of imposing a leader's values, the members' integrity is not respected, for they are not seen as capable of discovering a meaningful set of values and acting on them by themselves. In the case of exposition of leader values, in contrast, the members are free to challenge their own thinking against the background of the leader's beliefs, but they can still make their own choices without being burdened with guilt that they are not meeting the leader's expectations. In short, it is the group leader's function to challenge members to find their own values, rather than doing the deciding for them. Ethical practice requires that leaders help the participants clarify and define their own values.

THE ETHICS OF GROUP LEADERS' ACTIONS

Almost all of the professional organizations have gone on record as affirming that professionals should be aware of prevailing community standards and of the possible impact of conformity to or deviation from these standards on rendering their services effectively. These organizations explicitly state that professionals will avoid exploitation of the therapeutic relationship, that they will not damage the trust that is necessary for a relationship to be therapeutic, and that they will avoid dual relationships if such relationships would interfere with the primary therapeutic aims. Typically, the ethical codes caution against attempting to blend social or personal relationships with professional ones. They also explicitly state that sexual intimacies with clients are unethical. Three examples of these guidelines follow:

- "Dual relationships with clients that might impair the member's objectivity and professional judgment (e.g., as with close friends or relatives, sexual intimacies with any client) must be avoided and/or the counseling relationship terminated through referral to another competent professional" (AACD, 1981).
- "A therapist will attempt to avoid relationships with clients which might impair professional judgment or increase the risks of exploiting clients. Examples of such relationships include: treatment of family members, close friends, employees, or supervisees. Sexual intimacy with clients is unethical" (American Association for Marriage and Family Therapy, 1975).
- In providing psychological or counseling services to clients, professionals (clinical mental-health counselors, psychologists) must not violate or diminish the legal and civil rights of their clients (American Mental Health Counselors Association, 1980; APA, 1981).

The last guideline implies that professionals who work with groups must be familiar with the legal aspects of group work. Group leaders need to keep familiar with the laws of their state as they affect their professional practice. Those leaders who work with groups of children and adolescents, especially, must know the law as it pertains to matters of confidentiality, parental consent, the right to treatment or to refuse treatment, informed consent, and other legal rights of clients. Such awareness not only protects the group members but also protects group leaders from malpractice suits arising from negligence or ignorance.

The major mental-health professions have prohibitions against any type of relationship that is likely to impair one's ability to function in a professionally therapeutic manner. In addition, it is clear that, if a client/therapist relationship does develop into a relationship that could potentially be countertherapeutic, then ethical practice calls for a termination of the professional relationship and a referral to another professional.

THE ISSUE OF THE GROUP LEADER'S COMPETENCE

Determining One's Own Level of Competence

The issue of whether one is competent to lead a specific group or type of group is an ongoing question that faces all professional group leaders. Questions that you are likely to struggle with include:

- Am I qualified to lead this specific group?
- What criteria can I use to determine my degree of competence?
- Perhaps I am "technically qualified," but do I have the practical training or experience necessary to conduct this group?
- How can I recognize my limits?
- If I am not as competent as I'd like to be, what specifically can I do?

These and similar questions do not admit of simple answers and do require considering several factors. Different groups require different leader qualities. For example, you may be fully competent to lead a group of relatively well-adjusted adults or of adults in crisis situations yet not be competent to lead a group of seriously disturbed people. You may be well trained for, and work well with, adolescent groups, yet you may not have the skills or training to do group work with younger children. You may be successful leading groups with alcoholics or drug addicts yet find yourself ill prepared to work successfully with family groups. In short, you need specific training and supervised experience for each type of group you intend to lead; competence in *some* areas of group work does not imply competence in *all* areas.

Degrees, licenses, and credentials may be necessary but are not sufficient in themselves; all they indicate is a certain background of content and experience, which usually means that you have completed a *minimum* number of hours of training and experience. (Obviously, the quality of training and experience indicated by credentials varies greatly.)

There are numerous paths that can lead one to become a qualified group leader. Most practitioners have had their formal training in one of the branches of the mental-health field, including psychiatric social work, clinical psychology, nursing, psychiatry, counseling psychology, marriage and family counseling, educational psychology, and pastoral psychology. Generally, however, those who seek to become group practitioners find that formal education, even at the master or doctoral level, doesn't give them the practical grounding they require to effectively lead groups. Thus, they find it necessary to take a variety of specialized group-therapy training workshops.

In its *Professional Standards for Training of Group Counselors*, the ASGW (1983) sets out *knowledge competencies*, *skill competencies*, and suggested supervised clinical group *experience* for leaders.* In the area of *knowledge competencies*, the ASGW takes the position that the qualified group leader has demonstrated specialized knowledge in the following aspects of group work:

- the major theories of group counseling, including their differences and common concepts
- the basic principles of group dynamics and the key ingredients of group process
- one's own strengths and weaknesses, values, and other personal characteristics that have an impact on one's ability to function as a group leader
- ethical and professional issues special to group work
- updated information on research in group work
- the facilitative and debilitative roles and behaviors that group members may assume
- the advantages and disadvantages of group work and the situations in which it is appropriate or inappropriate as a form of therapeutic intervention
- the characteristics of group interaction and counselor roles involved in the stages of a group's development

In the area of *skill competencies*, the ASGW contends that qualified group leaders should be able to demonstrate a mastery of the following skills:

- being able to screen and assess the readiness of clients to participate in a group
- having a clear definition of group counseling and being able to explain its purpose and procedures to group members
- diagnosing self-defeating behaviors in group members and being able to intervene in constructive ways with members who display such behaviors
- modeling appropriate behavior for group members
- interpreting nonverbal behavior in an accurate and appropriate manner
- using skills in a timely and effective fashion
- intervening at critical times in the group process
- being able to make use of major techniques, strategies, and procedures of group counseling
- promoting therapeutic factors that lead to change both in a group and within an individual
- being able to use adjunct group procedures such as homework
- being able to work effectively with a co-leader
- knowing how to effectively bring a group session to a close and how to terminate a group
- using follow-up procedures to maintain and support group members
- using assessment procedures to evaluate the outcomes of a group

*Adapted from *Professional Standards for Training of Group Counselors* (ASGW, 1983) and reproduced by permission of the ASGW, a division of the American Association for Counseling and Development, 5999 Stevenson Avenue, Alexandria, VA 22304.

In the area of *clinical practice*, the ASGW specifies the following types of supervised experience in group work:

- critiquing of group tapes
- observing group counseling sessions
- participating as a member in a group
- co-leading groups with supervision
- practicum experience—leading a group alone with critical self-analysis of performance as well as a supervisor's feedback
- internship—practice as a group leader with on-the-job supervision

In addition to formal academic study, workshops, and supervised experience, I think it's important that practitioners participate as *members* in a variety of groups and, if at all possible, that they also undergo individual therapy. Being a member in a variety of groups can prove to be an indispensable part of training for group leaders, for it allows them to feel what it is like to be a working member of a group. By experiencing their own resistances, fears, and uncomfortable moments in a group; by being confronted; and by struggling with their problems in a group context, practitioners can receive practical experience concerning what is needed to build a trusting and cohesive group. Furthermore, I believe that being a group member is something that one should do from time to time, whether the aim is to continue professional training, to achieve personal growth, or both.

To summarize, I believe that everyone who leads groups needs to struggle continually and sincerely with the issue of his or her competence. It is important that you keep evaluating your competence and that you keep questioning it. Ask yourself, for example:

- What techniques can I skillfully employ?
- What kinds of client do I work with *best* in groups?
- With whom do I work *least* well?
- How far can I go with clients?
- When and how should I refer clients?
- When do I need to consult with other professionals?
- How can I continue to upgrade my professional leadership abilities?

The Role of Continuing Education in Maintaining Competence

The education and training of a group leader is an ongoing process—one that does not terminate when the diploma or license is granted. I believe that continuing education is mandatory for anyone who seeks to develop both as a person and as a group leader. Corey, Corey, and Callanan (1984) suggest several ways of maintaining a high level of competence:

- Develop or upgrade your skills by working with colleagues who have specialized or more advanced knowledge and experience in areas where you need further training.
- Learn new skills by attending conferences and conventions, especially those workshops that are designed for the in-service training of group leaders.

- Take advanced courses in areas you don't know too well, as well as special-interest courses offered through continuing education at various colleges, to keep abreast of current developments in your field.
- Attend workshops that combine didactic and experiential learning, along with some supervised practice.

Most professional organizations are currently attempting to make continuing education a requirement for relicensure. It is my hope, however, that you will take the initiative in updating, developing, and refining your knowledge and techniques rather than relying on mandates to motivate you.

ETHICAL GUIDELINES FOR GROUP LEADERS

Group leaders soon learn that the task of developing and maintaining a sense of professional and ethical responsibility is unending. As you gain practical experience, you also learn that you are continually being required to reexamine basic ethical issues. The intent here is not to provide you with ready-made answers concerning ethical practice; rather, the aim is to offer you some general ethical guidelines, with the hope that they will stimulate you to design your own code of ethical and professional conduct. This code will require much honest thinking and evaluating on your part.

What follows are some ethical guidelines for responsible group leadership throughout the course of a group's life. These issues will be discussed in greater detail in Chapters 4 and 5 when we consider leader tasks appropriate to the stages of group development.

Considerations before the group begins:

1. Take responsibility for getting the training and supervision you need to do a competent job of leading groups. Avoid undertaking a project that is clearly beyond the scope of your training and experience.
2. Develop a means of screening that will allow you to differentiate between suitable and unsuitable applicants. Also, be able to explain to prospective participants the expectations you have of them, the techniques that are likely to be employed, and the ground rules that will govern the group.
3. The importance of confidentiality cannot be overstressed. (It is a good practice to discuss this topic with members before they enter a group, during the group sessions when it is relevant, and before the group comes to an end.)
4. The psychological risks of participating in a group can be explored with prospective group members during the screening interview and again during the group sessions when it is appropriate.

Considerations during the early stages of a group's development:

1. Clarify and, if necessary, redefine the purpose of your group. Ensure that your techniques and methods are appropriate for these purposes.
2. Be aware of the impact of your personal values on group members. Make sure that you understand your basic values and how these values affect you as a leader.

3. Be alert for symptoms of psychological debilitation in group members, which may indicate that participation in the group should be discontinued. Be able to put such clients in contact with appropriate referral resources.
4. Protect the rights of individual group members. This entails, among other things, ensuring that members reveal in the group only what they choose to share, blocking any group pressure that would violate the rights of an individual member to determine his or her actions, and stopping any scapegoating that would deprive individual members of their dignity.
5. Develop and manifest a genuine respect for the members of your groups. This implies not only that you refrain from exploiting members for your own psychological needs but also that you respect the members' capacity to direct their own life.
6. Keep yourself informed about research findings related to group process and be able to apply this information to increase the effectiveness of your groups.

Considerations during the later stages of a group's development:

1. Frequently question yourself about the modeling you provide for your group members. Are you demonstrating honest and direct behavior in the group? Are you willing to do in your own life what you are encouraging your members to do in their life?
2. Be concerned about promoting the independence of the members from the group as efficiently as possible.
3. Do not attempt a technique unless you are trained in its use or under supervision by an expert familiar with the intervention.
4. Consider setting aside time at the end of each group session to encourage members to express their thoughts and feelings about the session. Part of your task as a leader is to help members develop self-evaluation skills.
5. Help participants deal with potentially negative reactions from others in their attempts to apply their group learning to their daily life. Help them deal with any regression they might experience, and encourage them to develop a support system outside of the group that will increase their chances of maintaining any behavioral changes they have made in the group.

Considerations after the termination of a group:

1. Consider arranging for a follow-up session with the group so that the members can see how they've done and so that you can evaluate the effectiveness of the group as an agent of change.
2. Consider private postgroup interviews with members to discuss with them the progress they have made in reaching their personal goals. Such a practice is a preventive measure against the tendency of some members to discount the value of a group experience. Be prepared to make appropriate referrals for further growth experiences.
3. Develop methods of evaluation to determine the effectiveness of a group. Accountability is a way to refine your leadership techniques and to develop your style of leadership.

3

GROUP LEADERSHIP

INTRODUCTION

This chapter focuses on the influence of the group leader, as a person and as a professional, on group process. After discussing the personal characteristics of effective leaders, the chapter analyzes the skills and techniques that are necessary for successful leadership and the specific functions and roles of group leaders. The purpose of this chapter is to give you enough information about these crucial topics to allow you to fully benefit from the discussion in the next two chapters of the stages in a group's development.

The topics covered in this chapter also represent an important prelude to the theory chapters in Part Two. Those chapters discuss and compare the various therapeutic approaches and highlight their basic similarities and differences in areas such as the group leader's role, the goals of groups, and the practical applications of techniques.

THE GROUP LEADER AS A PERSON

The techniques group leaders use cannot be divorced from the leader's personal characteristics. Leaders who are too concerned with techniques and don't pay enough attention to their own powerful influence as a person run the risk of becoming mere technicians. In my opinion, group leaders have an impact on group process not only through the skillful use of group techniques but also through their personal characteristics and behaviors. Thus, I don't agree with those leaders who attribute the success or failure of a group mainly to the characteristics of the participants or to the specific techniques being used to get the group moving. These are no doubt important variables, but I don't see them, by and of themselves, as determining the outcome of a group.

It is my belief that group leaders can acquire extensive theoretical and practical knowledge of group dynamics and be skilled in diagnostic and technical procedures yet be ineffective in stimulating growth and change in the members of their groups. Leaders bring to every group their personal qualities, values, and life experiences. In order to promote growth in the members' lives, leaders need to live growth-oriented lives themselves. In order to foster honest self-investigation in others, leaders need to have the courage to engage in self-appraisal themselves. In order to inspire others to break away from deadening ways of being, leaders need to be willing to seek new experiences themselves. In short, the most effective group direction is found in the kind of life the group members see the leader demonstrating and not in the words they hear the leader saying.

Surely I am not implying that group leaders must be self-actualized beings who have successfully worked through all of their problems. The issue is not whether leaders do or do not have personal problems but whether they are willing to make serious attempts to live the way group members are encouraged to live. More important than being a finished product is the willingness to continually look at oneself to see whether one's life reflects life-giving values. The key to success as a group leader is the commitment to the never-ending struggle to become more effective as a human being.

Personality and Character

The following are some personal characteristics that I see as vitally related to effective group leadership, since their presence or absence can facilitate or inhibit the group process. I hope you'll keep these descriptions in mind to evaluate your own personal characteristics in terms of effective and ineffective group leadership. Although the following discussion is based on my own experience and observations and reflects my own views, its emphasis on the personal characteristics of the therapist is shared by a number of writers, including Arbuckle (1975), Bugental (1965), Carkhuff and Berenson (1977), Corlis and Rabe (1969), Jourard (1968, 1971), Kottler (1983), May (1961), Rogers (1951, 1961, 1969, 1970, 1980), Truax and Carkhuff (1967), and Yalom (1975).

Presence.   Being emotionally present means being moved by the joy and pain others experience. If leaders are in touch with their own emotions, they can become more emotionally involved with others. Although this doesn't necessarily imply talking about the life experiences associated with these feelings, the ability to draw on these experiences makes it easier for the leader to empathize with and be compassionate toward the group members.

Personal power.   Personal power involves self-confidence and awareness of one's influence on others. It should be stressed that it does *not* mean domination and exploitation of others, which are abuses of power. Truly powerful leaders use the effect they have on group participants to encourage them to get in contact with their own unused power, not to foster their dependency. Personal power is always accompanied by self-confidence and by the recognition that one doesn't need to keep others in an inferior position to maintain one's own power.

Courage.   Effective group leaders are aware that they need to exhibit courage in their interactions with group members and that they cannot hide behind their special role as counselors. Leaders show courage by taking risks in the group and admitting mistakes, by being occasionally vulnerable, by confronting others with care and revealing their own reactions to those they confront, by acting on intuitions and beliefs, by sharing with the group their thoughts and feelings about the group process, and by being willing to share their power with the group members.

Willingness to confront oneself.   Courage applies not only to the ways in which leaders deal with the group members but also to the ways in which they deal with themselves. One of their central tasks is to promote self-investigation in their clients. Since group counselors cannot expect participants to do something that they themselves are not prepared to do, they must show that they are willing to question themselves. Self-confrontation can take the form of posing and answering questions such as the following:

- Why am I leading groups? What am I getting from this activity?
- Why do I behave as I do in a group? What impact do my attitudes, values, biases, feelings, and behavior have on the people in the group?
- What needs of mine are served by being a group leader? and to what degree?
- Do I ever use the groups I lead to satisfy my personal needs at the expense of the members' needs?

Self-confrontation is an ongoing process, and there are no simple answers to the questions above. The main issue is the *willingness* of group leaders to continually raise questions in order to determine how honest they are with themselves about their motivations for being group leaders.

Self-awareness.   Self-awareness is a concomitant of the willingness to confront oneself. This essential characteristic of effective leadership includes awareness of self, of one's needs and motivations, of personal conflicts and problems, of defenses and weak spots, of areas of unfinished business, and of the potential influence of all of these on the group process. For example, it is possible to use one's role as a group leader to win approval from group members. Group leaders have the power to control the sessions so that their needs for external confirmation can continually be reinforced through the group. If leaders depend primarily on the group members to give them validation as persons and professionals, they can create the dangerous situation of a group whose members devote more of their efforts to pleasing the leader than to working on themselves. Leaders who care are leaders who avoid using group members to meet their own personal needs and to bolster their own egos. (For a discussion of the importance of self-awareness in group leaders, see Levine, 1979, pp. 55–56.)

Sincerity.   One of the leader's most important qualities is a sincere interest in the well-being of others and in their ability to develop in constructive ways. Since sincerity involves being direct, it also involves telling members what they don't necessarily want to hear. For a group leader, caring means challenging the members to look at parts of their lives that they might want to deny and discouraging any form of dishonest behavior in the group.

Authenticity.   This characteristic is closely related to sincerity. Effectiveness demands that the leader be an authentic, real, congruent, and honest person. Such a person does not live by pretenses and does not hide behind masks, defenses, sterile roles, and facades. Authenticity also entails the willingness to appropriately disclose oneself and share feelings and reactions to what is going on in the group.

Sense of identity.   If group leaders are to help others discover who they are, they need to have a clear sense of their own identity. This means knowing what one values and living by internally derived standards and not by what others expect of one. It also means being aware of one's own limitations, strengths, needs, fears, motivations, and goals. Finally, it means knowing what one is capable of becoming, what one wants from life, and how one is going to get what one wants.

Belief in group process.   I think that the leader's deep belief in the value of group process is essential to the success of the group. Why should group members believe that the group experience will be of value to them if the leader is without enthusiasm or doesn't believe in the therapeutic power of the group? While I am not suggesting that leaders should be uncritical about groups or that they should regard groups as the *only* way of achieving personal growth, I do see it as essential that they believe in the value of therapeutic work.

Enthusiasm.   If group leaders lack enthusiasm for what they are doing, it is unlikely that they will inspire group members and provide them with an incentive to work. This is not to say that practitioners should adopt a "cheer-leading" style. What I'm suggesting is that leaders need to show that they enjoy their work and like being with their groups. A leader without enthusiasm tends to become routinized. Even more importantly, the leader's lack of enthusiasm is generally reflected in the members' lack of excitement about coming to group sessions and in their resistance to doing significant work.

Inventiveness and creativity.   The capacity to be spontaneously creative and to approach a group with fresh ideas says a lot about the potential effectiveness of a leader. Leaders need to avoid getting trapped in ritualized techniques and preprogrammed presentations that are void of life. It may not be easy to approach each group with new ideas, especially if one does a lot of group work. Inventive and creative leaders are willing to be open with themselves and with others in the group, open to new experiences, and open to life-styles and values that differ from their own.

Stamina.   Since group leading can be physically and psychologically taxing, leaders must find ways to remain vital throughout the course of the group. Thus, they need to be aware of their own energy level and to have sources of psychological nourishment. The demands of their profession make it imperative that they take good care of themselves, or they may find themselves "burnt out," with little to give to anyone.

Being centered.   The leader's personal life is a critical variable in being able to lead well. Leaders need to find their own ways of getting centered and avoiding the fragmentation that typically accompanies a busy life. Remaining creative in one's personal life is the best way to stay alive as a therapist.

Other Views and a Concluding Comment

The issue of the personal characteristics associated with effective group leadership has been the object of attention on the part of a number of authors. Shapiro (1978), for example, describes the "ideal personality for a group therapist" in terms of honesty, integrity, patience, courage, flexibility, warmth, empathy, intelligence, timing, and self-knowledge. But he also emphasizes that, although these qualities are necessary conditions for effective group leadership, by themselves they are not sufficient. Group leaders need to develop a counseling style and a method of leading that suit their personalities. They also need knowledge of theory and of group dynamics as well as the skills for applying this knowledge in practice.

Research on the leader's characteristics necessary for establishing a therapeutic relationship has been done by Carkhuff (1969a, 1969b), Carkhuff and Berenson (1977), and Truax and Carkhuff (1967). These researchers have identified empathy, genuineness, respect, and concreteness as the "primary core of the facilitative dimension." In summarizing the research on characteristics of group leaders, Bednar and Kaul (1978) observe that relatively little research has been done in the area. They conclude: "Despite the nearly universal agreement that leader characteristics are important determinants of the group process and outcomes, the literature does not reflect much empirical interest in the topic" (p. 786).

My own conclusion is that the personal dimensions described in the preceding pages are essential and that, without them, techniques and skills are of little value. Yet they are not sufficient for successful leadership. Specialized knowledge and skills, as identified by ASGW's (1983) *Professional Standards for Training Group Counselors* and described in the last chapter, are central to effective group leadership. Later in this chapter we will examine these skills and competencies in greater detail.

SPECIAL PROBLEMS AND ISSUES FOR BEGINNING GROUP LEADERS

Through my work in training, supervising, and providing in-service workshops for group leaders, I have come across a number of issues that have special relevance for beginning leaders. Although these issues must be faced by all group leaders regardless of their experience, they are especially significant for those who are relatively inexperienced.

If you have just begun your career as a group leader, you may wonder whether you have what it takes to be an effective leader. Or perhaps you have discovered that there is a gap between your formal academic training and the actual work you are expected to do when you conduct a group. It is well to keep in mind that these and other concerns are rarely resolved once and for all. As you gain experience, you may put these issues into a new perspective, yet from time to time you'll probably find yourself still struggling with doubts and anxieties about your adequacy and the impact you have on your groups.

Initial Anxiety

It is very likely that, before you lead your first group, you will experience some anxiety about getting the group started and about keeping it moving. In other words, you will probably ask yourself the following or similar questions with a certain degree of trepidation:

- Do I know enough to lead a group yet?
- What do the participants really expect of me?
- Will I be able to get the group started? how?
- Should I take an active role, or should I wait for the group to start on its own?
- Should I have an agenda, or should I let the group members decide what they want to talk about?
- What techniques shall I use during the early stages of the group?
- Will the group members want to come back?
- What if nobody wants to participate?

When I supervise and train beginning leaders, I encourage them to recognize that to have these doubts and concerns is perfectly normal and that moderate anxiety can be beneficial because it can lead to honest self-appraisal. Anxiety, however, can be counterproductive if it begins to feed on itself and is allowed to freeze one into inactivity. Therefore, I encourage beginning leaders to voice their questions and to explore them in the course of the supervised-training sessions. Their very willingness to do this can allay some unnecessary anxiety, for the trainees discover that their peers share their same concerns. Frequently students say that their peers appear to be so much more knowledgeable, skilled, talented, and self-confident than they themselves are. When they hear their peers express anxieties and feelings of inadequacy, these students realize that those who appear to be extremely self-confident also struggle with self-doubts about their adequacy as group leaders. The interchanges that occur when trainees are willing to openly discuss their anxieties offer invaluable opportunities for personal and professional growth. Exploring these feelings with peers and a supervisor can help the beginning leader distinguish between realistic and unrealistic anxiety and thus defuse unwarranted and counterproductive anxiety.

Self-Disclosure

Regardless of their years of experience, many group leaders struggle with the problem of self-disclosure. For beginning leaders, the issue is of even greater concern. Although *what* to reveal and *when* are factors in determining the appropriateness of self-disclosure, the issue centers on *how much*. And it is not uncommon to err on either extreme—disclosing too little or disclosing too much.

Too little self-disclosure.   If you try very hard to maintain stereotyped role expectations and keep yourself mysterious by hiding behind your professional facade, you can lose your personal identity in the group and allow very little of yourself to be known. The reasons for functioning in a role (rather than as a person who has certain functions to perform) are many. One may be the fear of appearing unprofessional or of losing the respect of the members. Another may be the need to keep a distance or to maintain a "doctor/patient" relationship.

In addition to being unwilling to share your personal life, you may also be hesitant to disclose how you feel in the group or how you feel toward certain members. As a way of avoiding sharing your own reactions to what is occurring within the group, you might limit your interventions to detached observations. Such "professional" aloofness may be expressed by making interpretations and suggestions, asking questions rather than making personal statements, acting as a mere coordinator, providing one structured exercise after another to keep the group moving, and clarifying issues. Although these functions are important, I think that they can be carried out without keeping you from revealing what you are presently experiencing in the group.

In my opinion, the most productive form of sharing is disclosure that is related to what is going on in the group. For instance, if you have a persistent feeling that most members are not very motivated and are not investing themselves in the session, you are likely to feel burdened by the constant need to keep the meetings alive all by yourself, with little or no support from the participants. Disclosing how you are affected by this lack of motivation is generally very useful and appropriate.

Too much self-disclosure.   At the other end of the continuum are the problems associated with excessive self-disclosure. Most beginning group leaders (and many experienced ones) have a strong need to be approved of and accepted by the group members. It's easy to make the mistake of "paying membership dues" by sharing intimate details to prove that you are just as human as the members. There is a fine line between appropriate and inappropriate self-disclosure. It is a mistake to assume that "the more disclosure, the better." It is also inappropriate to "let it all hang out" without evaluating the reasons for your disclosures, the readiness of the members, the impact that your sharing of intimate details is likely to have on them, and the degree to which your disclosures are relevant to the here-and-now process of the group.

You may be tempted to submit to group pressure to share more of yourself. Members often say to leaders "We don't know much about you. Why don't you say more about yourself? For example, tell us about your hang-ups. *We* talk about ourselves, and now we'd like to see you come down to our level and open up too!" The members can exert more subtle, but no less strong, pressures for you to "become a member" of the group you are leading. Out of your attempt to avoid getting lost in a professionally aloof role, you may try too hard to be perceived as a friend and a fellow group member. If you decide to share personal concerns, it should be for the benefit of your clients. The place to *explore* these concerns (and thus serve your own needs) is a group in which you are a participant yourself. Group leading is demanding work, and you can make this work even more difficult by confusing your role and functions with those of the participants.

Facilitative and appropriate self-disclosure is an essential aspect of the art of group leading. It is not necessary to disclose details of your past or of your personal life in order to make yourself known as a person or to empathize with the participants. A few words can convey a great deal, and nonverbal messages—a touch, a look, a gesture—can express feelings of identification and understanding. Appropriate disclosure does not take the focus away from the client and is never a contrived technique to get the group members to open up. Your sensitivity to how people respond to your disclosures can teach you a lot about their timeliness and value. Timeliness is a truly critical factor, for what might be inappropriate to disclose during the early stages of a group could be very useful at a later stage.

Learning what constitutes valuable self-disclosure does require experience. Only experience can teach you how to be yourself and how to effectively express feelings of identification and understanding. Only experience can teach you how to overcome the need to prove your humanness at the risk of failing to be authentic or serving your own needs instead of those of the group members.

I think that Kottler (1983) makes an excellent point about the abuse of self-disclosure: "Group leaders who like to hear themselves talk, who, because of ego deficiencies, attempt to impress clients with their prowess, or who use group time to meet their own needs are acting unethically" (p. 10). He suggests that leaders ask themselves: Whom will I help by my sharing? How will it help them? This kind of self-monitoring can ensure that leaders use disclosure to promote client change.

THE GROUP LEADER AS A PROFESSIONAL

Group-Leadership Skills

It would be a mistake to assume that anyone with certain personal qualities and a desire to help will be an effective group leader. Successful leadership requires specific group-leadership skills and the appropriate performance of certain functions. Like most skills, leadership skills need to be learned and practiced, although they cannot be divorced from the leader's personality.

Active listening.   Active listening involves paying total attention to the speaker and being sensitive to what is being communicated at the verbal as well as nonverbal levels. Active listening also involves being attuned to underlying messages—that is, to what is *not* being directly expressed.

Like any skill, active listening can be developed to varying levels. Thus, your ability to hear what is being communicated improves as your expertise improves. Many leaders make the mistake of focusing too intently on the *content*, and, in doing so, they don't pay enough attention to the *way* in which group members express themselves. Being a skilled group leader entails picking up the rich cues provided by members through their style of speech, body posture, gestures, voice quality, and mannerisms. (The topic of active listening will be dealt with in greater detail in Chapter 10, since attending and listening are key concepts of the person-centered approach to group work.)

Restating.   In a sense, restating is an extension of listening. It means recasting what someone said into different words so that the meaning is clearer to both the speaker and the group. Effective restating zeroes in on the core of a person's message, brings into sharper focus the meaning of what was said, and thus eliminates ambiguity. By capturing the essence of a member's message and reflecting it back, the leader helps the person continue the self-exploration process on a deeper level.

Restating is not an easy skill to master. Some group leaders, for example, confine themselves to simply repeating what was said, adding little new meaning and not really clarifying the message. Others overuse the technique, with the result of sounding mechanical and repetitive. The value of accurate and concise restating is twofold: it tells the participants that they are being understood, and it helps them see more clearly the issues they are struggling with and their own feelings and thoughts about these issues.

Clarifying.   Clarifying, too, is an extension of active listening. It involves responding to confusing and unclear aspects of a message by focusing on underlying issues and helping the person sort out conflicting feelings. Often members say that they are not clear with regard to how they feel about something; for example, they have ambivalent feelings, or they are feeling many things at once. Clarification can help the participants sort out their feelings so that they can focus more sharply on what they are actually experiencing. The same procedure applies to thinking. At one time or another, group participants will say that their thoughts are muddled and they are not sure what they are really thinking. Clarification can help sort out these thoughts. In clarifying, the group leader stays within the individual's frame of reference but, at the same time, helps the client put things into perspective; this, in turn, may lead to a slightly deeper level of self-exploration on the part of the client.

Summarizing. The skill of pulling together the important elements of a group interaction or part of a session is known as summarizing. It is a technique that is particularly useful when a transition from one topic to another needs to be made. Rather than merely proceeding from issue to issue, it is valuable to pull together some of their common elements for the purpose of enhancing meaning and continuity.

Summarizing is especially needed at the end of a session. It is a mistake for a group leader to end a session abruptly, with little attempt to pull the session together. One of the leader's functions is to help members reflect on and make sense of what occurred in their group. Summarizing encourages participants to think about what they have learned and experienced in a session and about ways of applying what they have gained to their everyday lives. At the end of the session group leaders may offer their own brief summary or ask each member in turn to summarize what has taken place, what the highlights of the session were, and how they responded to the interaction.

Questioning. Questioning is probably the technique that novice group leaders tend to overuse most. Bombarding members with question after question does not lead to productive outcomes and may even have a negative impact on the group interaction. There are several problems with the ineffective use of questioning. Members feel violated, as if they had been subjected to the "third degree." The questioner probes for personal information while remaining safe and anonymous behind the interrogation. Also, a low-level questioning style on the leader's part provides a poor model for the members, who soon begin to imitate the leader's ineffective questioning style when they deal with one another.

Not all questioning is inappropriate. It is closed questions, which require a mere "yes" or "no" response, that are generally fruitless. And so are "why" questions, because they usually lead to intellectual ruminating. Instead, open questions—questions that open up alternatives and new areas of self-investigation—can be of real value. "*What* are you experiencing right now?" and "*What* is happening with your body at this moment?" and "*How* are you dealing with your fear in this group?" are questions that can help the participants become more focused and feel their emotions more deeply. Therefore, it is important that leaders ask questions that, instead of merely probing endlessly, are meant to explore issues in greater depth.

Interpreting. The leader interprets when he or she offers possible explanations for a participant's behavior, feelings, or thoughts. By offering tentative hypotheses concerning certain patterns of behavior, interpreting helps the individual see new perspectives and alternatives. Interpreting requires a great deal of skill. Interpreting too soon, presenting an interpretation in a dogmatic way, and encouraging the members to become dependent on the leader to provide meanings and answers are some of the common mistakes. Timing is especially important. Interpretations not only have to be made at a time when the person is likely to be willing to consider them but also need to be expressed in a tentative way that gives the person a chance to assess their validity. Although an interpretation may be technically correct, it might be rejected if the leader is not sensitive to the client's willingness or unwillingness to accept it. (We will return to the topic of interpreting in Chapters 6 and 7.)

Confronting.   Confrontation can be a powerful way of challenging members to take an honest look at themselves. If it is handled poorly, it also has the potential of being detrimental both to the person being confronted and to the group process. Many beginning leaders shy away from confrontation, because they fear its possible repercussions—blocking the group interaction, hurting someone, or becoming the target of retaliation. The problem with confrontation is that it can easily be seen as an uncaring attack. That's why skilled group counselors confront only when they care about the person, and they do so in a way that gives the person ample opportunity to consider what is being said. Skillful confrontation specifies the behavior or the discrepancies between verbal and nonverbal messages that are being challenged, so that no labeling can possibly occur.

It is useful for leaders to bring their own reactions into the act of confrontation. Thus, skilled counselors would not say "George, you are a boring person." Instead, they might say "George, I find it difficult to pay attention to what you say. I'm aware that I get impatient and that I tend to tune you out. I really don't like this, and I'd like to be able to attend to what you are saying." (Confrontation is a skill we will discuss in more detail in Chapter 10.)

Reflecting feelings.   Reflecting feelings is the skill of responding to the essence of what a person has communicated. The purpose is to let members know that they are being heard and understood. Although reflection entails mirroring certain feelings that the person has expressed, it is not merely a bouncing-back process. Reflection is dependent on attention, interest, understanding, and respect for the person. When reflection is done well, it fosters further contact and involvement; feeling understood and achieving a clearer grasp of one's feelings are very reinforcing and stimulate the person to seek greater self-awareness.

Supporting.   Supporting means providing group members with encouragement and reinforcement, especially when they are disclosing personal information, when they are exploring painful feelings, and when they are taking risks. A leader can provide support by being fully present at the appropriate time. This full presence is what Ivey and Authier (1978) refer to as *attending behavior,* and it requires a combination of skills: listening actively to what is being said, being psychologically present with the client, and responding in a way that encourages the client to continue working and to move forward. Full attention can be communicated in a variety of ways—through eye contact, posture, or gestures and by staying with a client on a single theme.

The essence of this skill is knowing when it will be facilitative and when it will be counterproductive. Some group leaders make the mistake of being overly supportive, of supporting without challenging, or of supporting too soon. I like

Egan's (1973) caution about the blending of support and confrontation: "Confrontation without support is disastrous; support without confrontation is anemic" (p. 132). If leaders limit themselves to a style that is almost exclusively supportive, they deprive the members of potentially valuable challenges. Leaders who offer support too quickly when someone is exploring painful material tend to defuse the intensity of the experience and pull group members away from their feelings.

Support is particularly appropriate when people are faced with a crisis, when they are venturing into new territory, when they are trying to rid themselves of unconstructive behavior and establish new behaviors, and when they are attempting to implement what they are learning in the group to situations in their daily lives. (We will return to this topic in Chapter 10.)

Empathizing.   The core of the skill of empathy lies in the leader's ability to sensitively grasp the subjective world of the participant and yet retain his or her own separateness. In order to empathize effectively, a leader must care for and respect the group members. A background that includes a wide range of experiences can help the leader identify with others. (Empathy, too, is discussed in more detail in Chapter 10.)

Facilitating.   Facilitating is aimed at enhancing the group experience and enabling the members to reach their goals. Facilitation skills involve opening up clear and direct communication among the participants and helping them assume increasing responsibility for the direction of the group. Since facilitating is a vital tool in the person-centered approach, it will be explored in more depth in Chapter 10. Here we briefly consider some specific ways in which group leaders can facilitate group process. They are:

- focusing on resistances within the group and helping members realize when they are holding back and why
- encouraging members to openly express their feelings and expectations
- teaching members to focus on themselves and their feelings
- teaching members to talk directly and plainly to one another
- actively working to create a climate of safety that will encourage members to take risks
- providing support for members as they try new behaviors
- fostering a member-to-member, rather than member-to-leader, interactional style
- encouraging open expression of conflict
- assisting members in overcoming barriers to direct communication
- helping members integrate what they are learning in the group and find ways to apply it to their everyday lives
- helping members achieve closure by taking care of any unfinished business in the group

Initiating.   Dyer and Vriend (1977) use the term *initiating* to refer to the leader's ability to bring about group participation and to introduce worthwhile focal material to the group. They describe two kinds of initiating: (1) getting a group started and (2) exploring new terrain after concluding a phase of work with a group member. Good initiating skills on the leader's part keep the group from floundering without direction. These skills include using catalysts to get members to focus on meaningful work, knowing how to employ various techniques that promote deeper self-exploration, and providing links among the various themes being explored in the group. Whereas appropriate leader direction can give the group a focus and keep it moving, too much direction can lead to passivity on the part of members.

Goal setting.   Productive goal setting is at the core of group counseling. Note that group leaders do not set goals for the clients; they help group members select and clarify their own specific goals. Although goal setting is especially important during the initial stages of a group, throughout the group's life leaders need to encourage the participants to take another look at their goals, to modify them if necessary, and to determine how effectively they are accomplishing them. Leaders who don't develop the intervention skills of challenging members to formulate concrete goals often find that their groups are characterized by aimless and unproductive sessions.

Evaluating.   Evaluating is an ongoing process that continues for the duration of a group. After each session the leader needs to assess what is happening in the group as a whole and within individual members. Leaders must also teach participants how to evaluate themselves and how to appraise the movement and direction of their group. For example, if at the end of a session most participants agree that the session was superficial, they can be challenged to find the reasons for the unsatisfactory outcome and to decide what they are willing to do to change the situation.

Giving feedback.   A skilled group leader gives specific and honest feedback based on his or her observation of and reaction to the members' behaviors and encourages the members to give feedback to one another. One of the great advantages of groups is that the participants can tell other members their reactions to what they observe. The purpose of feedback is to provide a realistic assessment of how a person appears to others. The skill involved in productive feedback relates to the ability to present the feedback so that it is acceptable and worthy of serious consideration. Feedback that is specific and descriptive rather than global and judgmental is the most helpful.

Suggesting.   Suggestion is a form of intervention designed to help participants develop an alternative course of thinking or action. It can take many forms, a few of which are giving information and advice, giving "homework assignments," asking members to think of experiments they might try inside and outside of the group, and encouraging members to look at a situation from a different perspective. Giving information and providing appropriate suggestions for alternative plans of action can hasten the progress members make in a group. Suggestions need not always come from the leader, for members can make suggestions for others to consider.

The overuse of persuasion, suggestions, and advice entails some dangers. One is that members can be led to falsely believe that simple and neat solutions exist for complex problems. Another is that members may remain dependent on other people to suggest what they should do in the face of future problems; instead of growing toward autonomy, they come to look to others for answers and direction. There is a fine line between suggesting and prescribing, and the skill consists in knowing when and how suggestions enhance an individual's movement toward independence.

Protecting. Without assuming a parental attitude toward the group, leaders need to be able to safeguard members from *unnecessary* psychological or physical risks associated with being in a group. Although the very fact of participating in a group does entail certain risks, leaders can step in when they sense that psychological harm may result from a series of group interactions. For example, intervention is called for when a member is being treated unfairly or when an avalanche of feelings from the group is directed toward one person.

It takes skill for a leader to warn members of the possible dangers inherent in group participation without "setting them up" by implanting unnecessary fears about these risks. If leaders are overprotective, the members' freedom to experiment and learn for themselves is unduly restricted. If leaders fail to be protective enough, members may suffer from negative outcomes of the group experience.

Disclosing oneself. When leaders reveal some personal information, they usually have an impact on the group. The skill consists of knowing what, when, how, and how much to reveal. If the leader shares appropriately, the effects on the group are likely to be positive, because the members may imitate his or her willingness and try to make themselves known. If leaders share too much of themselves too soon, the effects are likely to be adverse, because the members may not be able yet to handle such openness comfortably. The most productive disclosure is related to what is taking place within the group. The skill involved in appropriate self-disclosure lies in the ability to present the information in such a way that the members are encouraged to share more of themselves.

Modeling. Group members learn by observing the leader's behavior. If leaders value honesty, respect, openness, risk taking, and assertiveness, they can foster these qualities in the members by demonstrating them in the group. From a leader who shows respect by really listening and empathizing, members learn a direct and powerful lesson in *how* respect is shown behaviorally. In short, one of the best ways leaders can teach more effective skills of interpersonal relating is by direct example.

Dealing with silence. Silence can have many different meanings. In a group session, silence may mean that members don't want to be in the group or that they are bored; it can also indicate that participants are passively waiting for the leader to do something to keep them moving or that they are quietly thinking of what is occurring in the group. Silence may follow a highly emotional experience and signal that members are trying to deal with the feelings elicited by it. Silence may also indicate fear or lack of trust. Thus the leader must be able to differentiate among the many kinds of silence and deal with each according to its nature.

When a group falls silent, many beginning leaders, not knowing what to do, tend to intervene rather quickly to overcome the discomfort they feel. A better course is to let the group remain silent for a while and then explore with them the meaning of the silence.

At times I've suggested to leaders in training that they announce to the group that they (the leaders) will be silent for a certain period of time (say, 45 minutes), thus allowing the group to function knowing that the leader will not intervene. This seems especially useful when a group has become so dependent on the leader to initiate and direct that, when this direction is lacking, silence follows. The announcement by the leader that he or she will not intervene can mobilize the participants to look at their own resources for initiating action. On the other hand, it is possible for this technique to be misused if the leader communicates an unspoken attitude of challenge for the group to prove autonomy—an attitude that could be interpreted as competitive or hostile.

Blocking.   Blocking refers to the leader's intervention to stop counterproductive behaviors within the group. It is a skill that requires sensitivity, directness, and the ability to stop the activity without attacking the person. The focus should be on the specific behavior and not on the person as a whole, and labeling should be avoided. For example, if a member is invading another member's privacy by asking probing and highly personal questions, the leader will point to this behavior as unhelpful, without referring to the person as a "peeping Tom" or an "interrogator." Some of the behaviors that need to be blocked are:

1. *Scapegoating.* If several people "gang up" on an individual and begin dumping their feelings on the person in an accusatory manner, the leader may intervene and ask the members involved to turn their attention to what is going on inside them.
2. *Group pressure.* Group leaders need to be aware of subtle or not-so-subtle attempts on the part of some members to pressure others to take a specific course of action or to make certain changes. It is one thing to offer feedback and another to *demand* that others change and accept standards imposed by the group.
3. *Questioning.* Members who habitually interrogate others or ask too many closed questions can be invited to try to make direct statements instead of asking questions.
4. *Storytelling.* If lengthy storytelling occurs, the leader may intervene and ask the person how the story relates to present feelings and events.
5. *Gossiping.* If a member talks *about* another member in the room, the leader can ask the member to speak directly to the person being spoken about.

Other behaviors that group leaders need to watch for and block when necessary include making excuses to justify failure to make changes, breaking confidences, invading a member's privacy, perpetually giving advice, offering support inappropriately, and making inaccurate or inappropriate interpretations. Whatever the behavior, blocking must be carried out gently and sensitively.

Terminating.   Group leaders must learn when and how to terminate their work with individuals as well as groups. The skills required in closing a group session or ending a group successfully include providing members with suggestions for applying what they've learned in the group to their daily lives, preparing the participants to deal with the problems they may encounter outside of the group, providing for some type of evaluation and follow-up, suggesting sources of further help, and being available for individual consultation should the need arise.

Terminating work with an individual takes skill. The person should not be left hanging, and premature closure should be avoided, since it would result in no further self-investigation on the part of the member. Some leaders end up working too long with a given member, simply because they don't know how to wrap up a piece of work comfortably.

An Integrated View of Group-Leadership Skills

It is not unusual for beginning group counselors to feel somewhat overwhelmed when they consider all the skills that are necessary for effective group leadership. If you, too, feel overwhelmed and somewhat discouraged, think about what it was like when you were learning to drive a car. If you had tried to think of all the rules and all the dos and don'ts simultaneously, you would have become frustrated and incapable of responding appropriately. The same applies to developing specific leadership skills. By systematically learning certain principles and practicing certain skills, you can expect to gradually refine your leadership style and gain the confidence you need to use these skills effectively. Participating in a group as a member is one way of developing these skills, for you can learn a lot through observing and actively participating in groups led by experienced people. Of course, you also need to practice these skills by leading groups under supervision. Feedback from group members, your co-leader, and your supervisor is essential to the refinement of your leadership skills. Seeing yourself in action on a videotape playback can be a powerful source of feedback that allows you to note the specific areas that are most in need of strengthening.

Like all skills, group-leadership skills exist in degrees, not on an all-or-nothing basis. They may be developed only minimally, or they may be highly refined and used appropriately. But, through training and supervised experience, these skills can be constantly improved. Table 3-1 presents an overview of the group-leading skills discussed in the preceding pages.

Table 3-1. Overview of Group-Leadership Skills

Skills	Description	Aims and Desired Outcomes
Active listening	Attending to verbal and nonverbal aspects of communication without judging or evaluating.	To encourage trust and client self-disclosure and exploration.
Restating	Saying in slightly different words what a participant has said to clarify its meaning.	To determine whether the leader has understood correctly the client's statement; to provide support and clarification.
Clarifying	Grasping the essence of a message at both the feeling and the thinking levels; simplifying client statements by focusing on the core of the message.	To help clients sort out conflicting and confused feelings and thoughts; to arrive at a meaningful understanding of what is being communicated.
Summarizing	Pulling together the important elements of an interaction or session.	To avoid fragmentation and give direction to a session; to provide for continuity and meaning.
Questioning	Asking open-ended questions that lead to self-exploration of the "what" and "how" of behavior.	To elicit further discussion; to get information; to stimulate thinking; to increase clarity and focus; to provide for further self-exploration.
Interpreting	Offering possible explanations for certain behaviors, feelings, and thoughts.	To encourage deeper self-exploration; to provide a new perspective for considering and understanding one's behavior.
Confronting	Challenging participants to look at discrepancies between their words and actions or body messages and verbal communication; pointing to conflicting information or messages.	To encourage honest self-investigation; to promote full use of potentials; to bring about awareness of self-contradictions.
Reflecting feelings	Communicating understanding of the content of feelings.	To let members know that they are heard and understood beyond the level of words.
Supporting	Providing encouragement and reinforcement.	To create an atmosphere that encourages members to continue desired behaviors; to provide help when clients are facing difficult struggles; to create trust.
Empathizing	Identifying with clients by assuming their frames of references.	To foster trust in the therapeutic relationship; to communicate understanding; to encourage deeper levels of self-exploration.

Table 3–1. *Overview of Group Leadership Skills* *(continued)*

Skills	Description	Aims and Desired Outcomes
Facilitating	Opening up clear and direct communication within the group; helping members assume increasing responsibility for the group's direction.	To promote effective communication among members; to help members reach their own goals in the group.
Initiating	Taking action to bring about group participation and to introduce new directions in the group.	To prevent needless group floundering; to increase the pace of group process.
Goal setting	Planning specific goals for the group process and helping participants define concrete and meaningful goals.	To give direction to the group's activities; to help members select and clarify their goals.
Evaluating	Appraising the ongoing group process and the individual and group dynamics.	To promote deeper self-awareness and better understanding of group movement and direction.
Giving feedback	Expressing concrete and honest reactions based on observation of members' behaviors.	To offer an external view of how the person appears to others; to increase the client's self-awareness.
Suggesting	Offering advice and information, direction, and ideas for new behavior.	To help members develop alternative courses of thinking and action.
Protecting	Safeguarding members from unnecessary psychological risks in the group.	To warn members of possible risks in group participation; to reduce these risks.
Disclosing oneself	Revealing one's reactions to here-and-now events in the group.	To facilitate deeper levels of interaction in the group; to create trust; to model ways of making oneself known to others.
Modeling	Demonstrating desired behavior through actions.	To provide examples of desirable behavior; to inspire members to fully develop their potential.
Dealing with silence	Refraining from verbal and nonverbal communication.	To allow for reflection and assimilation; to sharpen focus; to integrate emotionally intense material; to help the group use its own resources.
Blocking	Intervening to stop counterproductive behavior in the group.	To protect members; to enhance the flow of group process.
Terminating	Preparing the group to end a session or finalize its history.	To prepare members to assimilate, integrate, and apply in-group learning to everyday life.

Note: The format of this chart is based on Edwin J. Nolan's article "Leadership Interventions for Promoting Personal Mastery," *Journal for Specialists in Group Work*, 1978, 3(3), 132–138.

SPECIAL SKILLS FOR OPENING AND CLOSING GROUP SESSIONS

In training and supervising group leaders, I have found that many of them lack the necessary skills to open and close a group session effectively. For example, some simply select one member and focus on that person while the rest of the group sit passively back. Because of the leader's anxiety to "get things going," any member who raises a question is likely to receive attention, without any attempt to involve the other participants in the interaction. The problem is that, when a group session begins poorly, it may be difficult to accomplish any sustained work during the rest of the meeting.

The way each session is closed is as important as the way it is initiated. I have observed group leaders who simply allow the time to elapse and then abruptly announce, "Our time is up; we'll see you all next week." Because of the leader's failure to summarize and offer some evaluation of the session, much of the potential value of the meeting is lost. The effective opening and closing of each session ensure continuity from meeting to meeting. Continuity makes it more likely that participants will think about what occurred in the group when they are outside of it and that they will try to apply what they have learned to their everyday lives. Also, continuity, together with encouragement and direction from the leader, facilitates the members' task of assessing their own level of participation at each session.

Procedures for Opening a Group Session

With groups that meet on a weekly or other regular basis, group leaders can follow a number of procedures to open the session.

1. Participants can be asked to briefly state what they want to get from the session. I prefer a quick "go around" in which each group member identifies issues or concerns that could be explored during the session. Before focusing on one person, it is a good procedure to give all members a chance to at least say what they want to bring up during the meeting. In this way a loose agenda can be developed, and, if a number of people are concerned with similar issues, the agenda will allow the repeated involvement of several members.

2. It is useful to give people a chance to express any thoughts that they might have had about the previous session or to bring up for consideration any unresolved issues from an earlier meeting. Unresolved issues between members themselves or between members and leader can make progressing with the current agenda most difficult, since the hidden agenda will interfere with productive work until it has surfaced and been dealt with effectively.

3. Participants can be asked to report on the progress or difficulties they experienced during the week. Ideally, they have been experimenting with other ways of behaving outside of the group, they are getting involved in carrying out "homework assignments," and they are working on concrete plans that are action oriented. Even if not all of these desirable activities have taken place, time can be profitably used at the beginning of a session to share successes or to bring up specific problems.

4. The group leader might want to make some observations about the pre-

vious meeting or discuss some thoughts that occurred to him or her since the group last met.

Procedures for Closing a Group Session

Before closing a session, time should be allowed for integrating what has occurred, for reflecting on what has been experienced, for talking about what the participants may do between now and the next session, and for discussing other summary matters. The leader may also find it useful to check with the group around the midpoint of the session and say something like "I'm aware that we still have an hour left before we close today. So I want to check with you to see if there are any matters you want to bring up before we close" or "I'd like each of you to give me an idea of how you feel about this session. So far, have you gotten what you wanted from it?" Although these assessments in the middle of a session don't have to be made routinely, doing so from time to time can encourage members to evaluate their progress. If they are not satisfied with either their own participation or what is going on in the session, there is still time to change the course of the group before it ends.

In a similar fashion, group members can be encouraged to assess their direction after they have been together for about 50 percent of the group's lifetime. A comment along the following lines may motivate the participants to think about what they can do now to enhance the value of their group experience: "We have been working together for 15 weeks, and in 15 more weeks we'll have our final session. I'd like to go around and have each of you say something about how you'd feel if *this* were the last meeting. What have you gotten from the group so far? What do you want to be able to say about your experience when the group terminates? In what ways would you like to see the next 15 weeks be the same as, or different from, the past 15?"

Generally members do not automatically evaluate the degree of their investment in the group or the extent of the gains they have made. The leader can do a great deal to guide participants into reflecting on the time limitations of their group and on whether they are satisfied with their participation. Members also need guidance in appraising how fully their goals are being achieved and how effectively the group is operating. If this periodic appraisal is done well, members have a chance of formulating plans for changes in the group's direction before it is too late. Consequently, it is less likely that they will leave the group feeling that they didn't get what they had hoped for when they joined.

In sum, the leader's closing skills bring unity to the group experience and help consolidate the learning that has occurred during a session. The following is a list of the steps group leaders can take toward the end of each weekly session to assist members in evaluating their participation and in bridging the gap between the group and their daily existences.

1. Group leaders should strive to close the session without closing the issues raised during the session. Although the anxiety that results from "leaving people hanging" may be counterproductive, it is not therapeutic to wrap up an issue too quickly. Many leaders make the mistake of forcing resolution of problems prematurely. Being task oriented, they feel uncomfortable about allowing mem-

bers the time they need to explore and struggle with personal problems. In such instances, the leader's intervention has the effect of resolving quite superficially what may be complex matters that need to be fully explored if members are to resolve their conflicts adequately. It is good for people to leave a session with unanswered questions, so that they will be motivated to think more about their concerns and come up with some tentative solutions on their own. Leaders need to learn the delicate balance between bringing temporary closure to an issue at the end of a session and closing the issue completely. The following comment, for example, indicates that the leader knows how to achieve such a balance: "I'm aware that the matter you worked on today has not been fully resolved. I hope, however, that you'll give further thought to what we *did* explore and to what you *did* learn about yourself today. I look forward to working further with you on this issue in future sessions."

2. Summarizing can be effective at the end of each session. It is helpful to ask members to summarize both the group process and their own progress toward their goals. Comments can be made about common themes and issues that have emerged. The group leader can add summary comments, especially as they pertain to group process, but it is even better to teach members how to integrate what they have learned for themselves.

3. Participants can be asked to tell the group how they perceived the session, to offer comments and feedback to other members, and to make a statement about their level of investment in the session. By doing this regularly, members share in the responsibility of deciding what they will do to change the group's direction if they are not satisfied with it. For example, if participants report week after week that they are bored, they can be asked what they are willing to do to relieve their boredom.

4. It is helpful to focus on positive feedback, too. Individuals who got involved should be recognized and supported for their efforts by both the leader and other participants.

5. Members can report on their homework assignments, in which they tried to put into practice some of their new insights; they can briefly discuss what they are learning about themselves through their relationships in the group context; and they can make plans about applying what they have learned to problem situations outside the group.

6. Participants can be asked whether there are any topics or problems that they would like to put on the agenda for the next session. Besides linking sessions, this procedure prompts the participants to think about ways of exploring these concerns in the next meeting—that is, to work between sessions.

7. Group leaders may want to express their own reactions to the session and make some observations. These reactions and comments about the direction of the group can be very useful in stimulating thought and action on the part of the members.

In summary, the kinds of leader interventions that I have described illustrate that careful attention to the opening and closing of group sessions enhances and facilitates learning during a particular session. It has the effect of challenging members to recognize their role in determining the outcomes of the group, and it reminds them of their responsibility for taking active steps to maintain an effective group.

CO-LEADING GROUPS

As a group practitioner, you are very likely to work at times with a co-leader. In my opinion, the co-leadership style has many advantages and a few disadvantages. Here are some of the advantages:

- Group members can benefit from the insights of two therapists; the leaders may have different perspectives on any given situation.
- Two leaders can complement each other; a group can benefit from the combined strengths of the co-leading team.
- If one of the leaders is female and the other is male, they can re-create some of the original dynamics involved in the members' relationships with their parents; the opportunities for role playing are various.
- Co-leaders can serve as models for the participants with respect to how they relate to each other and to the group.
- The co-leaders can provide each other with valuable feedback; they can discuss what happened in the group and consult and plan together.
- Each leader can grow from observing, working with, and learning from the other.
- The participants have the opportunity of getting feedback from two leaders instead of one; occasional differing feedbacks may inject vitality into the group and offer opportunities for reflection and further discussion.

Most of the disadvantages of the co-leading model arise when the co-leaders fail to create and maintain an effective working relationship. I believe that the central factor in determining the quality of this relationship is *respect*. The two leaders will surely have their differences in leadership style, and they can't always agree or share the same perceptions or interpretations. But, if there is mutual respect, they will be open and direct with each other, they will trust each other, they will work cooperatively instead of competitively, and they will be secure enough to be free of the constant need to "prove" themselves.

The choice of a co-leader is an important one, because, if the co-leaders are incompatible, their group will surely suffer. An ongoing power struggle can have the effect of dividing the group. If the co-leaders don't work as a harmonious team, the group may follow their example and become extremely fragmented. If the co-leaders evidence even subtle ongoing friction, they are providing a poor model of interpersonal relating. This friction can lead to unexpressed hostility within the group, which interferes with effective group work. Productive work is blocked because of the tensions generated by the conflicts between the co-leaders.

In my view, it is essential that co-leaders get together regularly to give each other specific feedback and to discuss any matter that may affect their work—for example, how they feel about working together, how they see their group, and how they may enhance each other's contribution. Ideally, they will arrange to spend some time together before and after each group session, so that they can plan for the session or discuss what has gone on in the group, share their perceptions, and iron out any difficulties that arise between them.

In the next two chapters I suggest specific issues that co-leaders might talk about in their meetings at each of the various stages of a group: the initial stage, the transition period, the working phase, the final phase, and the period after the termination of a group.

I prefer the co-leadership model both for leading groups and for the training and supervising of leaders. In training workshops, professionals and university students continually tell my colleagues and me how they value working with a partner. This is especially true if they are leading a group for the first time. It is typical for beginning group leaders to experience self-doubt, anxiety, and much trepidation. Facing a group for the first time with a co-leader whom you trust and respect can make what might seem like an onerous task a delightful learning experience.

WORKING WITHIN A SYSTEM

Most groups that you lead will be under the auspices of some type of institution—a school system, a community mental-health organization, a state mental hospital, a clinic or hospital, or a local or state rehabilitation agency. When conducting groups in an institutional setting, one quickly discovers that mastering group-leadership theory and practice doesn't guarantee successful groups. Being able to deal effectively with institutional demands and policies may at times be as important as being professionally competent. On the basis of my experience and of discussions with other professionals who have worked within a variety of systems, I offer some information on what I consider to be important dynamics within institutions that you need to be aware of if you hope to survive in a system.

The Challenge of Doing Group Work in an Institutional Setting

A common problem among those who regularly do group work in an institutional setting is the constant struggle to retain dignity and integrity in a system where the administrators are primarily concerned with custodial care or with putting out "crisis fires" and are relatively indifferent to the pursuit of genuine group therapy or counseling. Another common problem besetting counselors in an institution relates to demands that they function as leaders of groups that they are unequipped or ill equipped to handle. This problem is intensified by the fact that few institutions provide the training needed for the type of group leadership they demand and burden the counselors they employ with such a work load that these counselors don't have the time to attend any sort of in-service continuing education during their regular working hours. Thus, many institutional counselors are forced to take courses or attend workshops on their own time and at their own expense.

I have touched on a couple of problems of working within an institutional system, and there are more. The point I wish to make is that the problems exist and it is up to you to deal with them and to work within the system while, at the same time, maintaining your professional standards and integrity. Ultimately, the responsibility for conducting successful groups is yours. Beware of blaming external factors for failures in your group-counseling programs. Watch out for statements that absolve you of responsibility and lead you to a sense of personal powerlessness:

- My administrator is not sympathetic toward my attempts to develop groups.
- The bureaucratic structure hampers my development of innovative and meaningful programs.
- I'm prevented from doing any *real* counseling because of office policies.
- The system doesn't reward us for our efforts.
- We don't have the funds to do what is necessary.
- The people in this community are not receptive to the idea of any type of group therapy; they won't come for help even when they need it.

I'm *not* implying that these complaints don't reflect real obstacles. I know from personal experience how taxing and draining any battle with a bureaucracy can be. There are times when the hassle of merely trying to get a group started in some institutions may overwhelm us to the point of questioning whether the effort is worth it. My point is that, whatever the external obstacles, it is our responsibility to face them and not allow them to render us powerless.

Professional impotency of any kind is a condition that feeds on itself. When counselors abdicate their own power, they assume the role of victims, or they develop the cynical attitude that all their proposals and efforts are doomed— that nothing they do matters or makes any difference. So, by way of summary and restatement, when we surrender our power by placing *all* the responsibility for the failure of our programs outside of ourselves, we are in jeopardy of having our work devitalize us when it should be having the opposite effect.

STYLES OF GROUP LEADERSHIP

I indicated at the beginning of this book that my goal is to help you develop a leadership style that is your own and that expresses your uniqueness as a person. I believe that, if you attempt to copy someone else's style, you can lose much of your potential effectiveness as a group leader. Surely you will be influenced by supervisors, co-leaders, and leaders of groups and workshops that you attend as a participant. But it is one thing to be influenced by others— most leaders borrow from many resources in developing their style of group leadership—and another to deny your own uniqueness by copying others' therapeutic styles, which may work well for them but may not be suited to you.

In essence, there are as many methods of group counseling as there are leaders; and even those leaders who subscribe to a primary therapeutic model, such as behavior therapy or transactional analysis, show considerable variance in the way they lead groups. As a group leader, you bring your background of experiences and your personality, value systems, biases, and unique talents and skills to the group you lead. You also bring to it your theoretical preferences. You may advocate an approach that emphasizes thinking or one that stresses experiencing and expressing feelings or one that focuses on action-oriented methods. On the other hand, your approach to group may be an eclectic one that integrates the thinking/feeling/acting dimensions. Regardless of the kind of approach you favor, your theoretical preferences will no doubt influence your style, especially with regard to the aspects of the group inter-action on which you choose to focus. As you study in Part Two the ten chapters on theoretical models of group counseling, you will become aware of the com-monalities and differences among these models and of the ways in which the various perspectives can shape your style as a group leader.

Shapiro (1978) describes two types of group-leadership styles: the intraper-sonally oriented and the interpersonally oriented. These two leadership styles can be best understood as ranging on a continuum from strict intrapersonal to strict interpersonal style. Those group leaders who are *intrapersonally ori-ented* tend to deal with group members in a one-to-one manner. This has often been referred to as individual counseling (or therapy) in a group situation. The focus is on intrapsychic concerns, or the conflicts and dynamics that exist within the individual. There is an interest in one's past, in the development of insight, and on the resolution of internal conflicts. In sum, the style of the intrapersonal leader focuses on the individual rather than on the group's dynamics or on the process of interaction among members.

At the other end of the continuum are those group leaders with an *inter-personal orientation.* They focus on the interactions among the members and on the relationships that are formed in the group. They are less interested than their intrapersonal counterparts in the individual's past, unconscious processes, and intrapsychic conflicts. This style of leadership emphasizes the here and now, the interactions among members, the group as a whole, the ongoing group dynamics, and the obstacles to the development of effective interper-sonal relationships within the group.

I agree with Shapiro's contention that successful group leaders are able to incorporate *both* approaches into their style of leadership. Shapiro also stresses that effective group leaders have an orientation that fits their own personality, regardless of whether it leans toward the interpersonal or toward the intra-personal pole. A crucial aspect of a leader's style is knowing when and to what degree each of these two orientations is appropriate with certain members or with a particular group. Learning how to integrate the best features of each orientation into a style that is personally your own is an ongoing process that depends heavily on your actual experience in the practice of leading groups.

4

EARLY STAGES IN THE DEVELOPMENT OF A GROUP

INTRODUCTION

This chapter and the next one are meant to be a road map of the stages through which a group progresses. This map is based on my own experience, as well as on the experience and writings of others, and describes what I consider to be the essential issues that characterize the development of a group.

A point that needs to be clarified right away is that the stages described in this chapter don't correspond to discrete and neatly separated phases in the life of a real group. There is considerable overlap between the stages, and groups don't conform precisely to some preordained time sequence that theoretically separates one phase from the next. Also, the content of the group process varies from group to group, and different aspects of the process may be stressed depending on the theoretical orientation of the leader, the purpose of the group, and the population that makes up the group. In spite of these differences, however, there does seem to be some generalized pattern in the evolution of a group, and it is to the stages that make up this pattern that this chapter addresses itself.

Regardless of your theoretical preference or preferences as a group leader, you must have a clear grasp of the stages of group development. This understanding, by making you aware of the factors that facilitate group process and of those that interfere with it, will maximize your ability to help the members of your group reach their goals. By learning about the problems and potential crises of each stage, you learn *when* and *how* to intervene. As you gain a picture of the systematic evolution of groups, you become aware of the developmental tasks that must be successfully met if a group is to move forward, and you can predict problems and intervene therapeutically. Finally, knowledge of the developmental sequence of groups will give you the perspective you need to lead group members in constructive directions by reducing unnecessary confusion and anxiety.

Several authors have discussed the stages of group-process development, and from these descriptions it is clear that, whereas the specific *content* of groups varies considerably, the trends and *process* are very similar. In other words, regardless of the nature of the group and the leader's theoretical orientation, there are some generalized trends that become apparent in most groups that meet over a period of time. Gazda (1978) observes that the stages through which counseling groups progress are most clearly visible in closed groups—those that maintain the same membership for the duration of the group. Schutz (1973b) writes about three stages: inclusion, control, and affection. Mahler (1969) describes in detail five stages: the formation, involvement, transition, working, and ending stages. Gazda's (1978) four stages are similar to Mahler's: exploratory, transition, action, and termination stages. In describing the process of the basic encounter group, Rogers (1970) identifies 15 stages, which can be summarized under four or five stages typically listed. J. L. Shapiro (1978) outlines four general phases (preparation, learning the ground rules, therapeutic intervention, and termination), but within this framework he identifies 37 stages that are descriptive of an optimally functioning and closed group that is led by a competent leader. He remarks, however, that his is an *ideal* model and that not all groups complete these stages successfully. He also emphasizes that successful completion of each stage is a prerequisite for dealing with the stages that follow.

Adlerian group counselors speak of four stages: establishment of a therapeutic relationship based on trust, interpretation of dynamics, development of insight, and reorientation (Dinkmeyer, Pew, & Dinkmeyer, 1979). Much of Levine's (1979) text is devoted to an analysis of the four phases of the dynamics of group development: the parallel-relations phase, the inclusion phase, the mutuality phase, and the termination phase. Hansen, Warner, and Smith (1980) write about five stages: initiation of the group, conflict and confrontation, development of cohesiveness, productivity, and termination. Yalom (1975) identifies three stages. The initial stage is characterized by orientation, hesitant participation, and the search for meaning; the second, by conflict, dominance, and rebellion. The third stage—the stage of cohesion—is marked by an increase of morale, trust, and self-disclosure.

This chapter begins with a focus on concerns related to the formation of a group—leader preparation, announcing a group, screening and selecting members, and preparing the members for a successful experience. *Stage 1* is the *orientation phase*—a phase of exploration during the initial sessions. *Stage 2*, the *transition stage*, is characterized by dealing with conflict, defensiveness, and resistance. In the following chapter we will continue with *stage 3*, called the *working stage*. This phase is marked by action—dealing with significant personal issues and translating insight into action both in the group and outside of it. *Stage 4*, the *consolidation stage*, occurs during the final phases of a group. The focus here is on applying what has been learned in the group and putting it to use in everyday life. I will conclude with an examination of post-group concerns, including follow-up and evaluation. The description of these stages is based on models presented by various writers as well as on my own observations of the ways groups evolve.

PREGROUP ISSUES: FORMATION OF THE GROUP

If you want a group to be successful, you need to devote considerable time to planning. In my view, planning should begin with the drafting of a written proposal. The issues that need to be dealt with in the proposal include the basic purposes of the group, the population to be served, a clear rationale for the group—namely, the need for and justification of that particular group—ways to announce and recruit for membership, screening and selection of members, size and duration of the group, frequency and time of meetings, group structure and format, methods of preparing members, open versus closed group, voluntary versus involuntary membership, and follow-up and evaluation procedures.

Leader Preparation

It cannot be overstressed that leader preparation at this formative phase is crucial to the outcome of a group. Thus, leaders will spend time wisely by thinking about what kind of group they want and by getting themselves psychologically ready for the group. If your expectations for the group are unclear and if the purposes and structure of the group are vague, the members will surely engage in an unnecessary amount of floundering.

Group leaders need to decide the basis for the homogeneity of their groups. By *homogeneous* I mean a group composed of people who, for example, are similar in ages, such as a group for children, for adolescents, or for the elderly. Other homogeneous groups are those based on a common interest or problem. Thus, there are groups designed for people with a weight problem or for those who are overdependent on drugs or alcohol, as well as consciousness-raising groups for women or for men. Some groups taking place in a school setting are especially designed for children and adolescents with learning difficulties or for those who have serious problems adjusting to the school environment.

For a given population with certain needs, a group composed of homogeneous members is more functional than one composed of people from different populations. Consider, for example, a group for adolescents. Such a group can focus exclusively on the unique developmental problems adolescents face, such as those related to interpersonal relationships, sexual development and identity, and the struggle toward autonomy. In a group designed for and composed exclusively of adolescents, the participants are encouraged to express many feelings that they have kept to themselves; through interaction with others of their same age, they can share their concerns and receive support and understanding.

While homogeneous membership can be more appropriate for certain target populations with definite needs, heterogeneous membership has some definite advantages for many types of personal-growth groups. A heterogeneous group, by representing a microcosm of the social structure that exists in the everyday world, offers the participants the opportunity to experiment with new behavior, develop social skills, and get feedback from many diverse sources. If a simulation of everyday life is desired, then it is well to have a range of ages, backgrounds, and interests and concerns.

Announcing a Group and Recruiting Members

How a group is announced influences the way it will be received by potential members and the kind of people who will be attracted to it. In announcing a group, it is imperative that you say enough to give prospective members a clear idea about the group's rationale and goals. The written announcement of the formation of a group could include:

- the type of group
- the purpose of the group
- times and place of meetings
- procedure for joining
- a statement of what the members can expect from the leader(s)
- a statement of the group leader's qualifications and background
- guidelines for determining who is suitable for the group
- fees being charged

Care must be taken to avoid making "promises" about the group's outcomes and raising unwarranted expectations on the part of the participants. Also to be avoided are commercial presentations; a simple and professional announcement designed to give people an accurate picture of the group should be employed.

Although printed announcements have their value if they can reach the population they are intended for, they have their limitations. Regardless of how specific you are in these announcements, people—at least some of them—are likely to misunderstand them. Because of this risk, I am in favor of making direct contact with the population that is most likely to benefit from the group. For example, if you are planning a group at a school, it is a good idea to make personal visits to several classes to introduce yourself and tell the students about the group. You could also distribute a brief application form to anyone who wanted to find out more about the group.

Screening and Selecting Group Members

The ethical guidelines of the Association for Specialists in Group Work (1980) state:

> The group leader shall conduct a pre-group interview with each prospective member for the purposes of screening, orientation, and, insofar as possible, shall select group members whose needs and goals are compatible with the established goals of the group; who will not impede the group process; and whose well-being will not be jeopardized by the group leader.

In keeping with the spirit of this guideline the leader, after recruiting potential members, must next determine who (if anyone) should be excluded. Careful
screening will lessen the psychological risks of inappropriate participation in
a group (discussed in Chapter 2). During the screening session, the leader can
spend some time exploring with potential members any fears they have about
participating in a group. The leader can help them make an assessment of their
readiness for a group and discuss the potential life changes that might come
about as a result of being in a group. The efforts the leader devotes to member
selection and orientation can result in a group that is motivated and ready to
work and contribute.

The following questions will also help you screen and select group members:
How can you decide who is most likely to benefit from the group you plan to
create? Who is likely to be disturbed by group participation or become a negative influence for the other members?

It is my position that screening should be a two-way process. Therefore, the
potential members should have an opportunity at the private screening interview to ask questions to determine whether the group is right for them. I believe
that group leaders should encourage prospective members to be involved in
the decision concerning the appropriateness of their participation in the group.

Of course, there is always the possibility that the leader has real reservations
about including some people who are quite determined to join the group.
Ultimately it is the group leader's task to make the decision. It is a difficult
decision, and I recognize that screening and selection procedures are subjective. Yet there are certain guidelines that can help a leader make this and other
decisions wisely. I find that it is often difficult to determine which candidates
will benefit from a group. During the private interview people are often vague
about what they hope to get from the group. They may be frightened, tense,
and defensive, and they may approach the personal interview as they would
a job interview, especially if they are anxious about being admitted to the group.
It is not uncommon in my experience to find people actually trying to be vague
in their answers and attempting to say what they think I expect of them—not
unlike a job interview. This is especially true if there are more applicants than
you can accept.

The basic criterion for the selection of group members is whether they will
contribute to the group or whether they will be counterproductive. Some people
can quite literally drain the energy of the group so that little is left for productive
work. Also, the presence of certain people can make group cohesion difficult
to attain. This is especially true of individuals who have a need to monopolize
and dominate, of hostile people or aggressive people with a need to act out,
and of people who are extremely self-centered and who seek a group as an
audience. Others who should generally be excluded from most groups are
people who are in a state of extreme crisis, who are suicidal, who have sociopathic personalities, who are highly suspicious, or who are lacking in ego
strength and are prone to fragmented and bizarre behavior. It is difficult to say
categorically that a certain kind of person should be excluded from all types
of groups, for a guiding principle is that the type of group should determine
who should be accepted. Thus, an alcoholic might be excluded from a per-

sonal-growth group but be an appropriate candidate for a homogeneous group of individuals who suffer from addiction problems—be it addiction to alcohol, to other drugs, or to food.

If the private screening session is an opportunity for the leader to evaluate the candidate and determine what he or she wants from the group experience, it is also a chance for the prospective members to get to know the leader and develop a feeling of confidence. The manner in which this initial interview is conducted has a lot to do with establishing the trust level of the group. This is why during the interview I stress the two-way exchange, hoping that members will feel free enough to ask questions that will help them determine whether they want to join this group at this particular time. Some questions I consider are: Does this person appear to want to do what is necessary to be a productive group member? Has the decision to join the group been made by the person, or has it been influenced by someone else's opinion? Does the candidate have clear goals and an understanding of how a group might help him or her attain them? Is the individual open and willing to share something personal?

The selection of members to ensure optimum group balance often seems an impossible task. Yalom (1975) proposes that cohesiveness be the main guideline in the selection of participants. Thus, the most important thing is to choose people who are likely to be compatible, even though the group may be a heterogeneous one.

Practical Concerns in the Formation of a Group

Open versus closed group. Whether the group will be open or closed may be in part determined by the population and the setting. But, regardless of whether the group will be an open or a closed one, the issue needs to be discussed and decided at the initial session. There are some distinct advantages to both kinds of groups. In the closed group no new members are added once the group gets under way for the predetermined duration of its life. This practice offers a stability of membership that makes continuity possible and fosters cohesion. A problem with closed groups is that, if too many members drop out, the group process is drastically affected.

In an open group new members replace those who are leaving, and this can provide for new stimulation. A disadvantage of the open group is that new members may have a difficult time in becoming a part of the group, because they are not aware of what has been discussed before they joined. Another disadvantage is that the changing of group membership can have adverse effects on the cohesion of the group. Therefore, if the flow of the group is to be maintained, the leader needs to devote time and attention to preparing new members and helping them to become integrated into the existing group.

Voluntary versus involuntary membership. Should groups be composed only of members who are there by their own choice, or can groups function even when they include involuntary members? The ASGW (1980) and Gazda (1978) maintain that people should not be coerced to join a group—either by superiors or by the group leader—that they should have the "freedom of exit" from the group, and that they should be removed from the group if the leader determines that they are being harmed by the experience. For sensitivity-training groups, Lakin (1972) believes, membership should be voluntary. He argues that, if people are to enter into the interactional aspects of a group, they must be there by choice and feel free from negative evaluation if they choose not to participate. Schutz (1971) will not accept anyone in his encounter groups who is not there voluntarily. He has found that involuntary group members often block the group process, for they are unwilling to participate. In its guidelines for psychologists who conduct growth groups, the American Psychological Association (1973) cautions: "Entering into a growth group experience should be on a voluntary basis; any form of coercion to participate is to be avoided" (p. 933).

Obviously, there are a number of advantages to working with a group of clients who are willing to invest themselves in the group process. The most important criterion for inclusion in a group, according to Yalom (1975), is motivation. He maintains that, in order to benefit from the group experience, a person must be highly motivated, especially in the case of group therapy. Attending a group because one has been "sent" there by someone greatly curtails the chances for success. Yalom believes that people with a deeply entrenched unwillingness to enter a group should not be accepted. However, he thinks that many of the negative attitudes that involuntary candidates have about groups can be changed by adequately preparing members for a group.

In line with Yalom's view, I have found that many involuntary members learn that a group-counseling experience can help them make some of the changes they want to achieve. In many agencies and institutions, practitioners are expected to lead groups with an involuntary clientele. It is therefore important for these counselors to learn how to work within such a structure rather than holding on to the position that they can be effective only with a voluntary population. If, by presenting the group experience in a favorable light, the leader can help involuntary members to see the potential benefits of the experience, the chances of productive work taking place will be increased. The key to successful participation here lies in thorough member orientation and preparation, as well as in the leader's belief that group process has something to offer to these prospective members.

Group size.　　The desirable size for a group depends on factors such as the age of the clients, the type of group, the experience of the group counselors, and the type of problems explored. Another element to be taken into consideration is whether the group has one leader or more. For ongoing groups with adults, about eight members with one leader seems to be a good size. Groups with children may be as small as three or four. In general, the group should have enough people to afford ample interaction so that it doesn't drag and yet be small enough to give everyone a chance to participate frequently without, however, losing the sense of "group."

Frequency and length of meetings.　　How often should groups meet? and for how long? These issues, too, depend on the type of group and, to some extent, on the experience of the leader. Generally, once a week is a typical format for most counseling groups. With children and adolescents, it is usually better to meet for more frequent and shorter sessions. For adults who are relatively well functioning, a two-hour group each week is long enough to allow for some intensive work and yet not so long that fatigue sets in and results in diminishing returns.

Group duration.   In my opinion, it is wise to set a termination date at the outset of a closed group, so that members have a clear idea of the time limits within which the group operates. Some psychoanalytically oriented groups run between 200 and 300 sessions, or between 2½ and 3 years (Mullan & Rosenbaum, 1978). In private practice, groups can run for 30 to 50 weeks. Many college and high school groups typically run for the length of a semester (about 15 weeks). In general, the duration varies from group to group, depending on the type of group and the population. The group should be long enough to allow for cohesion and productive work, yet not so long that the group seems to drag on interminably.

Meeting place.   Another pregroup concern is the setting. Privacy, a certain degree of attractiveness, and a place that allows for face-to-face interaction are crucial. Since a poor setting can set a negative tone that will adversely affect the cohesion of the group, an effort should be made to secure a meeting place that will make it possible to do in-depth work.

For more detailed information on these practical concerns I suggest Gazda's *Group Counseling: A Developmental Approach* (1978), Shapiro's *Methods of Group Psychotherapy and Encounter: A Tradition of Innovation* (1978), and Yalom's *The Theory and Practice of Group Psychotherapy* (1975).

The Uses of a Pregroup Meeting or the Initial Session

Preparation of group members.   After the group membership has been established, another question needs to be raised: What is the group leader's responsibility in preparing members to get the maximum benefit from their group experience? My bias is that systematic preparation is essential, and that it begins at the private screening interview and continues during the first few sessions. Preparation consists essentially of exploring with members issues such as expectations, fears, goals, misconceptions, the basics of group process, psychological risks associated with group membership and ways of minimizing them, the values and limitations of groups, guidelines for getting the most from the group experience, and the necessity of confidentiality. This preparation can be done through a preliminary meeting of all those who will be joining a group.

In addition to the private interview with each person before the group is formed, I also use the initial session as a group-screening device. The initial session is a good place to talk about the purposes of the group, to let members know how they will be using group time, to explore many of the possible issues that might be considered in the group, to discuss the ground rules and policies, and to begin the getting-acquainted process. My experience as a group leader has taught me that many of the people who show up for the first session opt not to return because of a number of reasons. For example, they may not like the leader or some members of the group; they may find out that the group is not what they had expected; or they may not be willing to share their personal experiences and feelings with others in the group. Because I prefer to have people decide early if they are ready for a group and willing to become active members, I encourage the participants to consider the first session as an opportunity to help them make such a decision.

The structuring of the group, including the specification of norms and procedures, should be accomplished early in the group's history. Although some of this structuring will have been accomplished or at least begun at the private intake session, it will be necessary to continue this process the first time the group actually meets. In fact, structuring is an ongoing process, one that will be a vital part of the early phases of your group.

Other writers endorse the idea of systematic preparation for group participation. Egan (1976) uses a skills-contract approach in his human-relations-training groups. He describes research that suggests that lack of structure during the initial phase of a group intensifies the members' fears and unrealistic expectations. Egan's approach to group work is based on the assumption that participants will learn more from a group experience if they have a clear understanding of what the group's goals are and how the group functions. Thus, in Egan's approach to group work, members learn the basics of human-relations training. They learn that the group is a laboratory where experimentation and new behavior are encouraged, that the focus is on the here and now, that sharing of oneself is expected, that giving and receiving feedback are a basic part of the process, and that members are encouraged to apply the skills they acquire in their group to action programs designed for change outside of the group. Egan's (1976) view of systematic preparation is summed up in his words to his readers: "The more clearly you understand the experience before you embark upon it, the more intelligently you will be able to give yourself to it and the more valuable it will be to you" (p. 3).

Another advocate of systematic preparation for group members is Yalom (1975). His preparation includes explaining his theory of group work, exploring misconceptions and expectations, predicting early problems and stumbling blocks, discussing how the participants can best help themselves, talking about trust and self-disclosure, and exploring the risks associated with experimenting with new behavior. Yalom also discusses matters such as the goals of group therapy, confidentiality, and extragroup socialization.

While I strongly believe in the value of systematic and complete preparation of group members, I also see problems in the extreme of overpreparation. For example, I typically ask members to talk early in the group about any fears or reservations they might have. I also explore a few common risks of participating in a group. In this particular area, however, if the leader becomes overspecific, the members may end up developing concerns or even fears that they never had before and that may become self-fulfilling prophecies. Also, too much structure imposed by the leader can stifle any initiative on the part of the members. The risks inherent in overpreparation should be balanced against those that accompany insufficient preparation. Excessive floundering and useless conflict during the group's later stages are often the result of the fact that some basic skills and understanding of group process have never really been acquired.

Teaching members about group process. In the following section I'll give you some ideas for orienting members to become active group participants. Of course, you would not want to bombard the members with *all* of these points in one preliminary session, but you can begin teaching them ways to get the most from a group. Teaching members about how groups function begins at this time and continues throughout the group's four stages.

I suggest that, as you read over the guidelines for group members in the next section, you ask yourself questions such as:

- What would I most want to emphasize to members about group process?
- How can I bring to the attention of members certain issues at each of the various stages of a group's development that will have meaning to them at the time?
- How can I avoid the extremes of giving members too much information about group process, thus overwhelming them, or not providing enough direction or information, leading to floundering and wasting of valuable time?

Guidelines for Group Members

I begin my orientation program by discussing with the group members the importance of their own preparation for group work and the level of their investment in the group. I stress that what participants get out of this experience is in direct proportion to their investment in it.

The guidelines that follow are those that I use myself when I prepare participants for the group experience. As I said earlier, you can use these guidelines to decide your own approach—one that suits your own leadership style and your personality and that is appropriate for the kinds of groups you lead. Note that the following suggestions are directed to the *members* and *not* to the leader.

1. *Examine and decide your level of commitment.* If you are not willing to invest yourself, you will not gain enough from the group to be able to apply what you have learned to your outside life. Begin by deciding for yourself what you want from your group experience, and think about how you can best accomplish your personal goals.

2. *Clarify your personal goals.* It is likely that you will come to the group with unclear and abstract goals. When I ask people what they hope to accomplish or what they want for themselves from the group, the answers I hear most frequently are:

- I'd like to get in touch with my feelings.
- I want personal growth, and I'd like to become self-actualized.
- I want feedback on how I come across to others.

- I want to be more self-confident.
- I hope to become more assertive.
- I'd like to be more spontaneous.
- I'd like to be a happy person.
- I want to relate to others more successfully.

The trouble with these goals—all worthwhile and shared by most of us—is that they are so abstract and general that they are almost meaningless. In a sense they are clichés of what we think we should want; after all, who wants to think of himself or herself as someone who is not in touch with feelings, not interested in personal growth, and not able to be spontaneous? To be meaningful, these goals must be clarified and made concrete.

3. *Consider making specific contracts.* After you have decided on some personal goals, you can refine them and make them more specific by making a contract with yourself. I help members draw realistic and meaningful contracts by asking them to think about questions such as the following:

- What do you hope you'll be able to say about yourself when you leave this group?
- What are the specific changes that you *most* want to make in your life?
- What are some specific steps you can take to make these changes? How will you know when you have actually made these changes?

Basically, a contract is a clear statement concerning the behavior you want to change and the steps you are willing to take to bring about these changes. Take, for example, someone who says "I'd like to be more assertive." What does this statement mean in concrete terms, and how will the individual know whether the goal has been attained? If you can break down a general goal into definite and observable subgoals, you have some specific points of reference to evaluate the degree of your changes. Using the example above, let's say that you are someone who is unwilling to speak out in class for fear of saying something stupid. One positive step you can take to test and gradually overcome this fear is to decide to contribute some comments to at least one class on a regular basis. Even if you express your ideas only once during each class session, you have moved in the direction in which you say you want to go. So, you first make a contract to get in touch with your instructors privately to discuss with them your unassertive behavior in their classes. After you have achieved this goal, you make a contract to express your ideas in class at least once each session.

4. *Focus on issues you need to bring up in the group.* You can make best use of the time you have in your group by developing an agenda. The agenda can include topics you'd like to bring up for discussion, things you need to say to other members or to the leader, and new activities in your everyday life that you want to share with your group. Often people float aimlessly in a group session because they have not given much thought to the issues they need to deal with.

5. *Be flexible.* Preparing an agenda is very useful. However, if carried to excess, adherence to an agenda can become quite limiting. Thus, you need to be willing to work on other issues that may come up through spontaneous interaction in the group.

6. *Prepare yourself by reflecting, reading, and writing.* Reading and writing can be useful adjuncts to a group experience. For example, to help group members see patterns in their behavior, I encourage them to keep an ongoing journal in which they write in a free-flowing style. Journals generally include the members' reactions to the group sessions, descriptions of their everyday experiences, and notes to themselves concerning issues they need to bring up in future sessions. Reading books that deal with relevant personal issues is also extremely helpful, because it can provide new perspectives and allow the person to see new alternatives.

7. *Be aware of self-fulfilling prophecies.* When you present yourself to others in a predetermined manner—that is, as a certain kind of person—eventually people begin to see you and respond to you as if you were indeed that person. Such responses confirm your view of yourself and make change in self-perception difficult. For example, if you see yourself as a rescuer—someone who typically rushes in to help others feel better whenever they express pain or sadness—you may be tempted to announce this perception of yourself to the group. A more productive course of action would be to refrain from structuring the situation and creating certain expectations in others. Instead, you can pay attention to your behavior in the group and make a conscious effort to show other sides of yourself to the other members.

8. *Use the group to practice new behaviors.* The group should not be considered as an end in itself but, rather, as a means to help you make the changes you desire in your everyday life. For example, if you feel that you lack vitality, you may look to your group to find some sources of emotional excitement. More importantly, you can explore the ways in which you don't feel as alive as you'd like and then begin to experiment, in and out of group, with things you could do to feel more alive. In my view, a group provides opportunities for developing and practicing social skills that can be used outside the group situation.

9. *Realize that time is limited.* One way to get the most from a group is to avoid postponing the risk taking involved in letting others know you. Sometimes group members say that they need to sit back, observe, and get to know the others before attempting to drop their masks. It is well to remind yourself that, the longer you wait, the more difficult it becomes to be a participating member. By the end of the group you may realize with disappointment that the time and the opportunity have slipped by because you failed to keep in mind that time was limited.

10. *Become actively involved.* You'll get far more from your group if you strive to take the initiative and if you express what is going on within you. If you remain a passive observer, you might learn vicariously from others, but this form of learning can hardly be compared to the valuable direct learning that results from sharing yourself with others.

11. *Decide for yourself what you will share with others.* Related to the matter of becoming an active and contributing participant is the issue of deciding for yourself what and how much you are willing to disclose of yourself. In making that decision, however, you must keep in mind that the others in your group can care for you only when they know who you are. If you want the other

members to become something other than strangers and if you hope to establish meaningful relationships, it is up to you to take the steps that make it possible for others to know you on a deeper level.

12. *Realize that your contribution is vital in creating trust in your group.* When you join a group, you may think that trust will occur automatically. Thus, you may hope that the leader will do something to establish trust, so that it is safe for you to disclose yourself, or you may wait for others to prove that they are trustworthy. If enough people wait for someone else in the group to "make trust happen," chances are that the group will be characterized by a good bit of holding back.

I don't think that you need to reveal your innermost feelings or some especially sensitive personal experience. Being an open person in a group does *not* mean being an open book. What I think is essential is that you reveal to your group persistent feelings that you have while participating in the group experience. This means that, if you feel negative, instead of sitting on your negative feelings, you let others know what these feelings are. In my experience, when members withhold negative feelings, they become increasingly mistrustful and detached from the group. As a result, the flow of group process becomes blocked.

13. *Become aware of the ways in which you might sabotage yourself in the group.* I routinely ask participants in the early stages of a group to talk about the ways in which they might sabotage their own efforts to get involved in the group or to make changes. Similarly, you can reflect on the things you do that can get in your way as a group member. Consider, for example, how you typically react when you are threatened. Do you tend to close up and become silent? If so, it is likely that, when you get anxious in the group, you will adopt this type of response. As you can easily imagine, this very behavior is counterproductive if you hope to change your way of responding to people or situations that are threatening. If you develop awareness of how you respond in certain circumstances, you can talk about it in the group and decide to behave in a different way.

14. *Be willing to discover positive as well as negative sides of yourself.* A common fear that people have as they enter a group is that they will discover negative aspects of themselves and that the other members will discover these aspects too. In other words, they are afraid of seeing themselves and being seen by others as unloving and unlovable, empty, selfish, and even worthless. Time and again, I find that people discover beautiful sides of themselves when they risk being open. If you keep yourself hidden for fear that others will see your weaknesses and deficiencies, you also keep others from seeing your talents, your wit and humor, your compassion and tenderness, and your strength.

15. *See the group as a vehicle for growth.* If you believe that groups are primarily for people suffering from severe emotional and behavioral problems, this misconception will get in your way and hinder your work in the group. Groups offer opportunities for growth by helping you see how you block your strength and effectiveness and how you can modify this pattern. Even if you are not trying to solve some major problems in your life right now, you can benefit from a group experience by willing to be open to that experience.

16. *Keep in mind that change takes effort and time.* If you expect to see instant

changes as a result of your participation in the group, you are not being realistic. I tell people in my groups that personal change may be slow and subtle and that they can anticipate occasional setbacks. Expectations of rapid and dramatic changes are unrealistic because you have been developing your personality for years, and you cannot radically change it overnight and with little effort. As a matter of fact, not only are such expectations unrealistic, but they may also keep you from appreciating the changes that you do make. Your defenses have been a part of you for a long time, and it is unlikely that you will give them up easily. Change entails sustained work and commitment, and it is a never-ending process. You can greatly contribute to the success of your efforts by concentrating on the process itself rather than striving to become your ideal "finished product."

17. *Think of ways of applying what you are learning in the group to your everyday life.* Perhaps one of the most important guidelines for getting the most from your group is to focus on ways of applying what you learn in the group to your daily life outside of it. I continually stress this guideline and encourage the members of my groups to use group time to practice new behaviors. I ask participants to pay attention to the constant feedback they get when they are together and then decide for themselves what they want and can do with this feedback.

Using feedback successfully entails the capacity to listen carefully to what others are saying and the ability to be discriminating—that is, neither accepting feedback wholesale nor rejecting it without careful reflection. If you keep receiving similar feedback from many people in your group (or even in different groups), it is likely that such feedback is accurate and valid.

Ultimately, it is of course up to you to make the necessary choices concerning the actions you will take. I cannot stress enough the necessity of making some concrete choices that lead to action beyond the group. But they must be *your* choices and *your* action program if they are to have significance for you. Groups can provide you with new insights and opportunities for practice, but the ultimate test of the value of the experience is the degree to which you make your own decisions and actually apply them to your life outside the group.

Pregroup Issues for Co-Leaders

Teamwork is essential.   If you are co-leading a group, the central issue at this early stage is that you and your co-leader have equal responsibility in forming the group and getting it going. Both of you need to be clear as to the purpose of the group, what you hope to accomplish with the time you have, and how you will meet your objectives. Cooperation and basic agreement between you and your co-leader will be essential in getting your group off to a good start.

This cooperative effort might well start with a meeting to develop a proposal, and ideally both of you would present your joint proposal to whoever has the authority to accept it. You and your co-leader will be a team when it comes to matters such as announcing and recruiting for membership; conducting screening interviews and agreeing on whom to include and exclude; agreeing on basic ground rules, policies, and procedures—and presenting them to the members as a co-leading team; and sharing in the practical matters that must be handled to implement a group.

It may not always be possible to share equally in all the responsibilities of planning and implementing a group. While it is *ideal* that both leaders interview the applicants, time constraints may make this impractical. Tasks might have to be divided, but as much as possible both co-leaders should be involved in what is necessary to make a group a reality. If one leader does a disproportionate share of the work, the other leader can easily develop a passive role in the leadership of the group once it begins.

Getting together with your co-leader. If co-leaders do not know each other, or if they don't have much sense of how they each work professionally, they are likely to get off to a poor start. Simply walking into a group cold, without any initial planning or getting acquainted with your co-leader, is to invite future problems. I have a few suggestions that co-leaders can consider before the initial session:

1. Make the time at least to get to know something about each other personally and professionally before you begin leading together.
2. Talk about your theoretical orientation and how each of you perceives groups. What kind of group work has each of you had? What ways will your theory and leadership style influence the direction the group takes?
3. Does either of you have any concerns or reservations about leading with the other? What might get in the way of your teamwork? How can you use your separate talents productively as a team? How can your differences in leadership style have a complementary effect and actually enhance the group?
4. For the two of you to work together well as a team, you should be in agreement on the ethical aspects of group work. What does each of you consider to be unethical practice, and are you together on actions that are unethical?

Summary of Pregroup Stage

Member functions and possible problems. Before joining a group, members must possess the knowledge necessary for making an informed decision concerning their participation. Members should be active in the process of deciding if a group is right for them. Following are some issues that pertain to the role of members at this stage.

- Members should know all the specifics about a group that might have an impact on them.
- Members need to learn how to screen the group leader to determine if this group with this particular leader is appropriate for them at this time.
- Members need to be involved in the decision to include or exclude them from the group.
- Members need to prepare themselves for the upcoming group by thinking about what they want from the experience and how they can attain their goals.

Some possible problems that can arise with members are:

- being coerced into a group
- not having adequate and full information about the nature of the group and thus not knowing what they are getting themselves into
- being passive and giving no thought to what they want or expect from the group

Leader functions.   The main tasks of group leaders during the formation of a group include:

- developing a clearly written proposal for the formation of a group
- presenting the proposal to the proper authorities and getting the idea accepted
- announcing the group in such a way as to inform prospective participants
- conducting pregroup interviews for screening and orientation purposes
- making decisions concerning selection of members
- organizing the practical details necessary to launch a successful group
- getting parental permission, if appropriate
- preparing psychologically for leadership tasks, and meeting with co-leader (if appropriate)
- arranging for a preliminary group session for the purposes of getting acquainted, presenting ground rules, and preparing the members for a successful group experience
- making provisions for informed consent and exploring with participants the potential risks involved in a group experience

---

STAGE 1: INITIAL STAGE—ORIENTATION AND EXPLORATION

Characteristics of the Initial Stage

The initial stage of a group is a time of orientation and exploration—determining the structure of the group, getting acquainted, and exploring the members' expectations. During this phase, members learn how the group functions, define their own goals, clarify their expectations, and look for their place in the group. At the initial sessions, members tend to keep a "public image"; that is, they present the dimensions of themselves they consider socially acceptable. This phase is generally characterized by a certain degree of anxiety and insecurity about the structure of the group. Members are tentative, because they are discovering and testing limits and are wondering whether they will be accepted.

Typically, members bring to the group certain expectations, concerns, and anxieties, and it is vital that they be allowed to express them openly. At this time the leader needs to clear up the participants' misconceptions and, if necessary, demystify their ideas of groups. I see this initial phase as akin to the first few days one spends in a foreign land, having to learn the rudiments of a new language and different ways of expressing oneself.

Primary Tasks of the Initial Stage: Inclusion and Identity

Finding an identity in the group and determining the degree to which one will become an active group member are the major tasks of the initial stage. Schutz (1973a) says that this phase involves deciding whether to be in or out of the group, maintaining one's individuality within the group, and making commitments.

The following questions are the kind members often ask themselves at the initial sessions:

- Will I be in or out of this group?
- How much do I want to reveal of myself?
- How much do I want to risk?
- How safe is it to take risks?
- Can I really trust these people?
- Do I fit and belong in here?
- Whom do I like, and whom do I dislike?
- Will I be accepted or rejected?
- Can I be myself and, at the same time, be a part of the group?

Fried (1972) calls attention to the need for group members to resist group pressure that could lead them to relinquish their uniqueness. She stresses the importance of remaining an autonomous and separate human being and not getting lost by fusion in the group. Fried's caution relates to the members' right to maintain their own rhythm and to the need for the members to achieve and maintain a sense of individuation.

The Foundation of the Group: Trust

Most writers agree that establishing trust is vital to the continued development of the group. Without trust, group interaction will be superficial, little self-exploration will take place, constructive challenging of one another will not occur, and the group will operate under the handicap of hidden feelings.

It is a mistake to assume that people will "naturally" trust one another as soon as they enter a group. And why should they trust without question? How do they know that the group will offer a more accepting and safer climate than society at large? My view is that people make a decision whether or not to trust a group. Such a decision depends in part on the leader's ability to demonstrate that the group can be a safe place in which to be oneself and reveal who and what one is. Also, by encouraging members to talk about any factors that inhibit their trust, the leader supports the therapeutic atmosphere necessary for openness and risk taking on the part of the members.

Ways of establishing trust. The manner in which leaders introduce themselves can have a profound effect on the group's atmosphere. Is the leader enthusiastic, personable, psychologically present, and open? To what degree does the leader trust himself or herself? To what degree does the leader show trust and faith in the group? I have often heard members comment that it felt good to be trusted by their leaders.

The leader's success in establishing a basic sense of trust and security depends in large part on how well he or she has prepared for the group. Careful selection of members and efforts to make sure that the group is appropriate for them are very important, and so is the way in which the leader presents the ground rules of the group. Leaders who show that they are interested in the welfare of individual members and of the group as a whole engender trust. Talking about matters such as the rights of participants, the necessity of confidentiality, and the need for respecting others demonstrates that the leader has a serious attitude toward the group. If leaders care, chances are that the members will also care enough to invest themselves in the group to make it successful.

These comments, however, should not be interpreted to mean that trust building is the exclusive province of group leaders. True, leaders can engender trust by their attitudes and actions, but the level of trust also depends in large part on the members—individually and collectively.

Members usually bring to the group some fears as well as hopes. Participants will trust the group more if they are encouraged to expose their fears, because talking about them is likely to reveal that the fears are shared by others. If one member, for example, is concerned about not being able to express herself effectively and someone else expresses the same concern, almost invariably a bond is established between the two.

Silences and awkwardness are characteristically part of the beginning session. The more unstructured the group, the greater the anxiety and ambiguity about how one is to behave in a group. The members are floundering somewhat as they seek to discover how to participate in the group. As the sessions progress, the members generally find it easier to raise issues and participate in the discussion. More often than not, these issues tend to be safe ones (at the beginning), and there is some talking about other people and there-and-then material. This is one way that the members go about testing the waters. It is as though they were saying "I'll show a part of myself—not a deep and sensitive one—and I'll see how others treat me."

Another characteristic aspect of this initial phase is the tendency for some participants to jump in and try to give helpful advice as problems are brought up. It is the leader's task to make sure that these "problem-solving interventions" do not become a pattern, since they will cause enough irritation in other members to precipitate a confrontation with those who are quick to offer remedies for everyone's troubles.

The group's atmosphere of trust is also affected by the negative feelings that members often experience at the initial stage toward certain other members or toward the leader and over the fact that the group is not proceeding the way they would like to see it proceed. This is an important turning point in a group, and trust can be lost or enhanced depending on the manner in which negative feelings are dealt with. If conflict is brought out into the open and negative feelings are listened to nondefensively, there's a good chance that the situation producing these feelings can be changed. Members need to know and feel that *it is OK* to have and express negative feelings. Only then can the group move ahead to a deeper level of work. The members feel secure enough to take greater risks and are able to focus on struggles that are personally significant and to express here-and-now feelings.

As members reveal more of themselves to one another, the group becomes cohesive; in turn, this emerging cohesion strengthens the trust that exists in the group and creates the right atmosphere for members to try new ways of behaving in the group. When the members trust one another, they also trust the feedback they receive, which they can use as they try to carry these newly acquired behaviors into their daily lives.

Role of the Group Leader at the Initial Stage

Modeling. When you lead a group, you set the tone and shape the norms as a model-setting participant as well as a technical expert (Yalom, 1975). It is important that you state your own expectations for the group openly during the first session and that you create a trusting climate by modeling interpersonal honesty and spontaneity. This means that you need to be aware of your own behavior and of the impact you have on the group and that you practice the skills that create a therapeutic milieu.

To be effective, a leader must be able and willing to be psychologically present in the group and to be genuine. A genuine leader is one who is congruent, who does not resort to various roles to maintain artificial distance, and who is willing to do what he or she expects the members to do. Genuineness implies a level of enthusiasm and involvement in one's work as a leader. How can you expect the participants to get involved and believe in the potential of your group if you don't believe in what you are doing or if you are apathetic?

Gazda (1978) encourages group leaders to tell the group something about themselves and to model the facilitative dimensions of empathy, warmth, respect, regard, and genuineness. With regard to empathy—both cognitive and affective—you can create a therapeutic situation by being able to see and understand the world from the internal vantage point of the members. Another key characteristic is your sensitivity in attending and responding not only to what is said but also to the subtle messages conveyed beyond words. This applies to individual members as well as to the group as a whole. Finally, the people who make up your group need to sense that you have respect and positive regard for them.

All of these comments acquire special meaning if you keep in mind that, at the initial stage, the participants depend very much on you. They turn to you for direction and structure and often focus so much on you that they neglect their own resources. This situation, which exists in most groups, requires that you be constantly aware of your own need to be seen as an authority figure and to keep tight control on the group. If you are not aware of these needs in yourself, you may keep the members of your group from becoming autonomous.

Assisting in identifying goals. Another of your main tasks as a group leader is to help the participants get involved. You can do a lot to motivate, inspire, and challenge people to *want* to get the most from their group. At this stage you do it mostly by helping them to identify, clarify, and develop meaningful goals. There are *general group goals*, which vary from group to group because they depend on the purpose of the group, and there are *group-process goals*, which apply to most groups. Egan (1976) has described several of them: self-exploration, experimentation, staying in the here and now, making oneself known to others, challenging oneself and others, taking risks, giving and receiving feedback, listening to others, responding to others honestly and concretely, dealing with conflict, dealing with feelings that arise in group, deciding what to work on, acting on new insights, and applying new behavior in and out of group.

In addition to establishing these group-process goals, you need to help members establish their own goals. Typically, people during the early stages of a group have vague ideas about what they want from a group experience. These vague ideas need to be translated into specific and concrete goals with regard to the desired changes and to the efforts the person is actually willing to make to bring about these changes. It is during the initial phase that this process needs to take place if the members are to derive the maximum benefit from the group. As I said earlier, you can do much to promote this process by assuming the responsibility of practicing and modeling the skills and attitudes that are necessary for effective group interaction.

One of the leader's basic tasks, and a most challenging one, is to bring hidden agendas out into the open. For example, some members may have hidden goals that are at cross-purposes with group goals. They may have an inordinate need to be the center of attention, or they may sabotage intimacy in a group because of their uncomfortableness in getting close to others. A leader's function is to do what is needed to make these hidden agendas explicit. If such personal goals remain hidden, they are bound to undermine the effectiveness of the group.

The division of responsibility.   A basic issue that group leaders must consider is responsibility for the direction and outcome of the group. If a group proves to be nonproductive, is this due to a lack of leader skill, or does the responsibility rest with the group members?

One way of conceptualizing the issue of responsibility is to think of it in terms of a continuum. At one end is the leader who assumes a great share of the responsibility for the direction and outcomes of the group. These leaders tend to have the outlook that, unless they are highly directive, the group will flounder. Such leaders tend to see their role as that of the expert, and they actively intervene to keep the group moving in ways they deem productive. A disadvantage of this form of responsible leadership is that it robs the members of the responsibility that is rightfully theirs; if members are perceived by the leader as not having the capacity to take care of themselves, they soon begin to live up to this expectation by being irresponsible, at least in the group.

Leaders who assume an inordinate degree of responsibility not only undermine members' independence but also burden themselves. If people leave unchanged, they see it as their fault. If members remain separate, never forming a cohesive unit, such leaders view this as a reflection of their lack of skill as leaders. If the group is disappointed, these leaders feel disappointed and tend to blame themselves, believing that they didn't do enough to create a dynamic group. This style of leadership is draining, and leaders who use it may eventually lose the energy required to lead groups.

At the other end of the responsibility continuum is the leader who proclaims, "I am responsible for me, and you are responsible for you. If you want to leave this group with anything of value, it is strictly up to you. I can't do anything for you—make you feel something or take away any of your defenses—unless you allow me to." When people are together for a period of time in an intensive group, they need some protection, and I feel that it is irresponsible for the leader not to provide it.

Ideally, each leader will discover a balance, accepting a rightful share of the responsibility but not usurping the members' responsibility. This issue is central because a leader's approach to other issues (such as structuring and self-disclosure) hinges on his or her approach to the responsibility issue. The leader's personality is involved in the determination of how much responsibility to assume and what, specifically, this responsibility will include.

Structuring.   Like responsibility, structuring exists on a continuum. At one end are T-group leaders who typically do nothing at the onset of the group except wait for one of the members to assume the leadership. The entire T-group experience is often characterized by this lack of structure so that the participants will define their own structure. This style frequently results in negative feelings on the part of group members, who eventually attack the facilitators for not doing "what they're supposed to do."

At the opposite end of the continuum are the leaders who operate with a very structured program. They use structured exercises to open sessions, and they employ exercises throughout the group—to heighten experiencing; to focus members on a particular theme or problem area; and to elicit certain feelings, such as anger, closeness, or even extreme loneliness or rage.

In brief, some degree of structuring is essential in a group. However, the structuring should not be so tight that it robs the group members of the responsibility of providing their own structure. Ultimately, the type and degree of structuring you employ will depend upon the population of your group.

Co-Leader Issues at the Initial Stage

If you are working with a co-leader, discussing the issues of division of responsibility and structuring is essential for group unity. If you and your co-leader don't agree on the balance of responsibility, your disagreement is bound to have a negative effect on the group.

For example, if you assume the majority of the responsibility to ensure that the group continues to move, while your co-leader assumes almost no responsibility on the ground that the members must decide for themselves what to do with group time, then the members will sense this division and are bound to be confused by it. Similarly, if you function best with a high degree of structure in groups, while your co-leader believes that any structuring should come from the members, this difference of opinion might have a detrimental effect on the group.

For these reasons, it is wise to select a co-leader who has a philosophy of leadership that is compatible with yours, though this does not mean that both of you need to have the same style of leading. You can have differences that complement each other; it is when these differences lead to fragmenting the group that problems occur.

Summary of Initial Stage

Stage characteristics.   The early phase of a group is a time for orientation and determining the structure of the group. Some of the distinguishing events of this stage are:

- Participants test the atmosphere and get acquainted.
- Members learn the norms and what is expected, learn how the group functions, and learn how to participate in a group.
- Members display socially acceptable behavior; risk taking is relatively low, and exploration is tentative.
- Group cohesion and trust are gradually established if members are willing to express what they are thinking and feeling.
- Members are concerned with whether they are included or excluded, and they are beginning to define their place in the group.
- Negative feelings may initially surface as a testing to determine if all feelings are acceptable.
- A central issue is trust versus mistrust.
- There are periods of silence and awkwardness; members may look for direction and wonder what the group is about.
- Members are deciding whom they can trust, how much they will disclose, how safe the group is, whom they like and dislike, and how much to get involved.
- Members are learning the basic attitudes of respect, empathy, acceptance, caring, and responding—all attitudes that facilitate trust building.

Member functions and possible problems.   Early in the course of the group, some specific member roles and tasks are critical to the shaping of the group. Some of these functions are:

- taking active steps to create a trusting climate
- learning to express one's feelings and thoughts, especially as they pertain to in-group interactions
- being willing to express fears, hopes, concerns, reservations, and expectations concerning the group
- being willing to make oneself known to others in the group
- being involved in the creation of group norms
- establishing personal and specific goals that will govern group participation
- learning the basics of group process, especially how to be involved in group interactions

Some possible problems that can arise are:

- Members may wait passively for "something to happen."
- Members may keep to themselves feelings of distrust or fears pertaining to the group and thus entrench their own resistance.
- Members may keep themselves vague and unknown, making meaningful interaction difficult.
- Members may slip into a problem-solving and advice-giving stance with other members.

Leader functions.* The major tasks of group leaders during the orientation and exploration phase of a group are:

- teaching participants some general guidelines and ways to participate actively that will increase their chances of having a productive group
- developing ground rules and setting norms
- teaching the basics of group process
- assisting members in expressing their fears and expectations, and working toward the development of trust
- modeling the facilitative dimensions of therapeutic behavior
- being open with the members and being psychologically present for them
- clarifying the division of responsibility
- helping members establish concrete personal goals
- dealing openly with members' concerns and questions
- providing a degree of structuring that will neither increase member dependence nor promote excessive floundering
- assisting members to share what they are thinking and feeling about what is occurring within the group
- teaching members basic interpersonal skills such as active listening and responding
- assessing the needs of the group and facilitating in such a way that these needs are met
- sharing your expectations and hopes for the group
- showing members that they have a responsibility for the direction and outcome of the group
- making sure that all the members participate in the group's interaction, so that nobody feels excluded
- working toward decreasing the members' dependency on the leader

---

STAGE 2: TRANSITION STAGE—DEALING WITH RESISTANCE

Characteristics of the Transition Stage

Anxiety. The transition stage is generally characterized by increased anxiety and defensiveness. These feelings normally give way to genuine openness

---

*Exercises and activities designed to help students develop specific skills for each of these stages are found in the student's manual accompanying this book, *Manual for Theory and Practice of Group Counseling*, second edition.

and trust in the stages that follow. Often the participants articulate their anxieties in the form of statements or questions to themselves or to the group, such as:

- I wonder whether these people really understand me and whether they care.
- What good will it do to open myself up in here? Even if it works, what will it be like when I attempt to do the same outside of this group? What if I lose control?
- I see myself standing before a door but unwilling to open it for fear of what I'll find behind it. I'm afraid to open the door into myself, because, once I open it a crack, I'm not sure I'll be able to shut it again. I don't know whether I'll like what I see or how you'll respond if I show you what is locked within me.
- How close can I get to others in here? How much can I trust these people with my inner feelings?

Anxiety grows out of the fear of letting others see oneself on a level beyond the public image. Anxiety also results from the fear of being judged and misunderstood, from the need for more structure, and from a lack of clarity about goals, norms, and expected behavior in the group situation. As the participants come to trust more fully the other members and the leader, they become increasingly able to share of themselves, and this openness lessens their anxiety about letting others see them as they are. Gazda (1978) observes that the participants' self-disclosure at a level deeper than mere "historical" matters signals the beginning of the transition stage. Mahler (1969) sees the leader's central task at this phase as helping the members recognize and deal with their resistances and defenses against anxiety.

Conflict and struggle for control.   Many writers point out the central role that conflict plays during the transition stage of a group. Yalom (1975) sees this stage as characterized by conflict as well as by dominance and rebellion. Negative comments and criticism occur more frequently, and people may be quite judgmental of others and yet unwilling to open up to the perceptions that others have of them. In Yalom's eyes, the transition stage is a time of struggling for power—among the members and with the leader—and establishing a social pecking order. The struggle for control is an integral part of every group: "It is always present, sometimes quiescent, sometimes smoldering, sometimes in full conflagration" (Yalom, 1975, p. 306).

Schutz (1973a), too, sees control as the central issue in the second stage of a group. Characteristic group behaviors include competition, rivalry, a jockeying for position, a struggle for leadership, and frequent discussions about the procedure for decision making and division of responsibility. Schutz (1973a) contends that at this point the primary anxieties of participants relate to having too much or too little responsibility and too much or too little influence. For Hansen et al. (1980), conflict arises out of the discrepancy between the members' real selves and the stereotyped images they project and is often expressed in challenge to the views that others have of them.

Before conflict can be dealt with and constructively worked through, it must be recognized. Too often both the members and the leader want to bypass conflict, out of the mistaken assumption that conflict is indicative of negative traits and of a poor relationship. If conflicts are ignored in a group, what originally produced the conflicts festers and destroys the chance for genuine contact. When conflict is recognized and dealt with in such a way that those who are involved in the conflict can retain their integrity, the foundations of trust between the parties are established. Recognizing that conflict is inevitable and that it can strengthen trust is likely to reduce the probability that members and leader will try to dodge the conflicts that are a natural part of a group's development.

Ignoring conflicts and negative feelings requires energy, and that energy can be better employed to develop an honest style of facing and working through inevitable conflicts. Rogers (1970) observes that the first expression of significant here-and-now feelings is frequently related to negative attitudes toward other group members or toward the leader. According to Rogers, expressing negative feelings is one way to test the freedom and trustworthiness of the group. Members are discovering whether the group is a safe place to disagree, to have and express negative feelings, and to experience interpersonal conflict. They are testing the degree to which they can be accepted when they are not "being nice." The way conflict is recognized, accepted, and worked with has critical effects on the progress of the group. If it is poorly handled, the group may retreat and never reach a productive working stage. If it is dealt with openly and with concern, the members discover that their relationships are strong enough to withstand an honest level of challenge.

Certain group behaviors tend to elicit negative feelings that reflect conflict:

- remaining aloof and hiding behind the stance of observer
- talking too much and actively interfering with the group process through questioning, giving abundant advice, or in other ways distracting people from their work
- dominating the group, using sarcasm, belittling the efforts that are being made, and demanding attention

When intermember conflict is the result of transference, it can be detected in statements such as:

- You seem so self-righteous. Every time you begin to talk, I want to leave the room. You remind me of my ex-husband.
- You bother me so because you look like a well-functioning computer. I don't sense any feeling from you. My father and you would have made a great team!
- Your attempts to take care of everyone in here really bother me. You rarely ask anything for yourself, but you are always ready to offer something. Just like my mother—I felt that I could never do anything for her, because she needed nothing.

Challenging the group leader. Often conflicts also involve the group leader. As a group leader, you may be challenged on professional as well as personal grounds. You may be criticized for "being too standoffish" and not revealing enough of yourself, or you may be criticized for "being one of the group" and revealing too much of your private life. Here are some of the comments you may hear from your group:

- You're judgmental, cold, and stern.
- No matter what I do, I have the feeling that it'll never be enough to please you. You expect too much from us.
- You really don't care about us personally. I sense that you are just doing a job and that we don't count.
- You don't give us enough freedom. You structure and control everything.
- You push people too much. I feel that you aren't willing to accept a no.

It is helpful to distinguish between a *challenge* and an *attack*. An attack can take the form of "dumping" or "hit-and-run" behavior. Members who attack group leaders with statements like "This is how you are" don't give the leaders much chance to respond, since the leaders have already been judged, categorized, and dismissed. It is quite another matter to openly confront leaders with how the members perceive and experience them. A member leaves room for dialogue when she says: "I'm aware that I'm not opening up in here. One reason is that, if I do, I feel that you will push me beyond where I want to go." This member openly states her fears but leaves enough room for the leader to respond and to explore the issue further. This is a challenge, not an attack.

Challenging the leader is often a participant's significant first step toward autonomy. Most members experience the struggle of dependence versus independence. If the group is to become free of the leader dependency that is characteristic of the initial group stage, the leader must allow and deal directly with these revealing challenges to his or her authority. Fried (1972) indicates that groups are initially focused on the leader and held together partly by identification with the leader. But, if the group is led appropriately, the members become more autonomous and eventually achieve a peer feeling with one another and with the leader. Fried says:

> After considerable anxieties have been understood and shed, and after conflicts between submission and angry protest have been settled, a good feeling arises; the group members become cooperative with one another and feel fond of the leader, though they become familiar with his shortcomings [1972, p. 67].

The way in which you accept and deal with challenges to you personally and to your leadership style greatly determines your effectiveness in leading the group into more advanced levels of development. Because I value the opportunities that challenges from group members offer, I attempt to deal with these challenges directly and honestly, to share how I am affected by the confrontation, to ask members to check out their assumptions, and to tell them how I see myself in regard to their criticism. I believe in keeping the lines of communication open, and I consistently try to avoid slipping into a "leader role" that entails diluting the challenge as a means of self-defense. I agree with Levine (1979), who stresses the value of dealing directly with challenges as a way of fostering the autonomy of the group and who sees in the leader's response to challenge a clear message:

If the therapist ignores, discounts, or fights the challenge, the message to the group will be clear: the therapist does not want to allow this kind of autonomy to the group. . . . The members will either accept the counter-challenge and fight for their autonomy or be frightened into reverting back to a parallel mode of behavior, leaving the therapist clearly in command of the group [pp. 124–125].

Resistance

Resistance is behavior that keeps oneself or others from exploring personal issues or painful feelings in depth. Resistance is an inevitable phenomenon in groups, and, unless it is recognized and explored, it can seriously interfere with the group process. Resistance, however, is not merely something to be overcome. Since resistance is an integral part of one's typical defensive approach to life, it must be recognized as a way of protecting oneself from the anxieties mentioned in the last section. For group leaders not to respect the members' resistances is akin to their not respecting the members themselves. An effective way of dealing with resistances is to treat them as an inevitable aspect of the group process; that is, the leader acknowledges that resistance is a member's natural response to getting personally involved in a risk-taking course. An open atmosphere that encourages people to acknowledge and work through what-ever hesitations and anxieties they may be experiencing is essential. The par-ticipants must be willing to recognize their resistance and to talk about what might be keeping them from full participation.

In the following pages we'll explore in depth the most common forms of resistive behaviors in groups. But, before we proceed with our discussion, two points need to be made. One is that the members' unwillingness to cooperate is not always a form of resistance in the proper sense of the term. There are times when member "resistance" is the result of factors such as unqualified leaders, conflict between co-leaders, dogmatic or authoritarian leadership style, failure on the part of the leader to prepare the participants for the group experience, and lack of trust engendered by the leader. In other words, group members may be unwilling to share their feelings because they don't trust the group leader or because the group is simply not a safe place in which to open up. It is imperative that those who lead groups look honestly at the sources of resistance, keeping in mind that not all resistance stems from the members' lack of willingness to face unconscious and threatening sides of themselves.

The other point is a warning against the danger of categorizing people and reducing them to labels such as "the monopolist," "the intellectualizer," "the dependent one," or "the quiet seducer." Most textbooks on group counseling devote several pages to "problem group members" and to various ways of categorizing them (see, for example, Dinkmeyer & Muro, 1979; Hansen et al., 1980; Ohlsen, 1977; Trotzer, 1977; Yalom, 1975). Although it is understandable that prospective leaders will be interested in learning how to handle "problem members" and the disruption of the group they can cause, the emphasis should be on actual *behaviors* rather than on labels. Regardless of the type of behavior a member exhibits as a characteristic style, he or she is more than that partic-ular behavior. If you see and treat a person just as a "monopolizer" or an "advice giver" or a "help-rejecting complainer," you contribute to cementing that particular behavior instead of helping the person work on the problems behind the behavior.

For example, if Maria is treated as a "monopolizer" and is not encouraged to explore the impact she has on the group, she will continue to see herself as others see her and respond to her. You can help Maria, as well as the entire group, by investigating the reasons for her need to keep the spotlight on herself and the effects of her behavior on the group. People need to become aware of the defenses that may prevent them from getting involved in the group and of the effects of these defenses on the other members. However, they should be confronted with care and in such a way that they are challenged to recognize their defensive behaviors and invited to go beyond them.

Another limitation of identifying "problem members" rather than problem behaviors is that most of those who participate in groups exhibit, at one time or another, some form of resistance. Occasional advice giving, questioning, or intellectualizing is not in itself a problem behavior. As a matter of fact, the group leader needs to be aware of the danger of letting participants become overly self-conscious of how they behave in the group. If clients become too concerned about being identified as "problem group members," they won't be able to behave spontaneously and openly. With these cautions in mind, let's now examine the behaviors that hinder group functioning.

Intellectualizing.   A common way of manifesting resistance is by analyzing and dissecting what occurs in the group and thus avoiding the experience of intense feelings. Most people use this defense occasionally, and for some—too frightened to allow themselves to experience intense feelings—this type of defense may even be necessary. The problem arises when intellectualizing becomes a characteristic of a person's style of operating in group. The following questions—to oneself or to others—are indicative of intellectualizing:

- Why does this person feel this way?
- What stage of group development are we in now?
- Why did I feel touched when Sally was talking about her children? I mean, what are the real reasons for my feelings? What exactly made me respond the way I did?

The problem with intellectualizing is that it becomes a substitute for feeling, and thinking about an experience becomes devoid of emotional qualities. Thinking is a valuable part of group process, but it needs to be integrated into the person's emotional life and behavior. Conceptualizing about what has happened in a group is useful as long as it is not a way of avoiding full experiencing.

Questioning.   Questions that are aimed at gathering data can interfere with the group process. "Why" questions typically have the effect of distracting people from what they are experiencing emotionally. If a member is feeling deep sadness and another member asks a series of "why" questions, the person is sure to lose contact with the sadness. Some participants develop a habit of questioning others, and in so doing they intervene at inappropriate times. Questioners need to recognize that they are keeping themselves safe and unknown through their questions while expecting openness on the part of the person being questioned.

One useful way of dealing with questioning behavior is to ask the participants to attempt to refrain from asking closed questions of a probing nature and to make statements instead. The reason is that most questions are basically statements in disguise. For example, if Herb wants to know why Jan has trouble with her instructors, instead of asking why, he could tell her that he too is afraid of dealing assertively with his instructors and that he is interested in her struggle. By declaring that he too has trouble relating to authority figures, Herb gives something of himself and risks some personal investment with Jan. As a leader, you can help the members of your group make statements rather than ask questions by instructing them to share what was going on with them at the moment they wanted to ask a question.

Advice giving.   Perhaps one of the most common errors made by both group members and leaders is to consider group counseling as synonymous with advice giving. The desire for quick solutions is common to all of us and is understandable. But, when we offer someone a "ready-made" answer to a problem the person is struggling with, we deprive that person of the opportunity to find his or her own answer at the appropriate time. Those who give advice too freely are often uncomfortable with the struggles and uncertainties others are going through; for these people, advice becomes a way of dealing with their own anxieties. Frequently, the very issues that the advice givers address are the ones that they may not have really looked at or resolved in their own life. Also, a pattern of advice giving conveys feelings of superiority, because those who give advice assume that they have an answer for everything and that they know what is best for others.

Those who give advice freely are saying quite a bit about themselves, their own values, and their own unresolved needs. For example, Elsie talks about the guilt she feels about leaving her parents and striking out on her own. Donna quickly intervenes and gives Elsie all the reasons why she *should* leave now and why she *shouldn't* feel guilty. If the group members were to focus on Donna, they might find out that she has unresolved dependency problems of her own. Thus, Donna may be indirectly attempting to deal with her dependency conflicts by trying to straighten Elsie out.

Band-Aiding.   Related to advice giving is "Band-Aiding," or the constant attempt to lessen pains, soothe wounds, and alleviate feelings of sadness, loneliness, or loss. Band-Aiding is a misuse of support, because the therapeutic process involves the full emotional experiencing of events that may trigger pain. If these situations are to be worked through, clients must be encouraged to express whatever emotion they feel. The healing of psychological wounds involves the ventilation and release of feelings that may be intensely painful. Most people who experience this process report a sense of peace accompanied by real relief when the process is over.

It takes considerable energy to keep a lid on intense emotions, and the attempt to do so may cause more tension than the actual experience and expression of the emotions. When other members are quick to rush in to offer support or to minimize the pain, they help the person keep the lid on emotions that are demanding expression. Band-Aiding may be done in the name of compassion for others, yet it is invariably an attempt to handle one's own discomfort. Like the advice giver, the person who "Band-Aids" finds it difficult to observe the struggles and pains of others, and thus he or she tries to distract the person who is experiencing the pain. Band-Aiding can be a form of resistance when those who demonstrate this behavior avoid acknowledging their own emotional vulnerability. Thus, their attempt to comfort others is actually an attempt to avoid dealing with potentially painful issues in their own lives. Genuine expressions of care, concern, and support are quite different from Band-Aiding, because real caring focuses primarily on the interests of the other person.

Avoidance. Avoidance behaviors are very common manifestations of resistance. Avoidance keeps the person from participating fully in the therapeutic experience and interferes with the establishment of a cohesive and productive group. Here are some common forms of avoidance behaviors:

- failing to show up for group sessions or always being late
- using humor to cover one's own feelings or to dissipate the intense feelings of others
- becoming an "assistant leader" by typically focusing on others—offering interpretations, making suggestions, and asking questions—while leaving oneself out as a participant
- trying to change the subject every time the group work becomes serious and intensive
- remaining vague and unclear
- telling oneself that others in the group have real problems and that, by comparison, one's own concerns are quite insignificant
- finding "good reasons" to avoid voicing feelings and thoughts

The effective group leader deals with avoidance by gently challenging people to become aware of their avoidance behaviors. Learning to recognize when and how one is avoiding can be a significant step toward deciding to face anxiety-arousing situations.

Nonparticipation. Silence and withdrawal are behaviors that tend to puzzle group leaders and members alike. Group participation does entail verbal involvement that reveals to a greater or lesser degree the member's reactions to what is happening in the group. People who typically say "I don't have much to say" or "I can learn a lot by just listening to others without talking all the time" have a negative impact on the group by their silence. According to Egan (1976), silence is at least unconsciously manipulative and counterproductive. Even though silent participants may be learning something from the group, Egan says, they are not contributing their share and are therefore violating the group contract.

Yalom (1975) sees a silent person as a "problem patient" who rarely benefits from the group. He suggests that, the greater the verbal participation, the greater the sense of involvement and the value the person has for others and himself or herself. Yalom also notes that silent behavior is never silent. He suggests that silence, like any other behavior, is indicative of a person's interpersonal style outside of group. The counselor's task is to help silent members understand the meaning of their silence.

There are many reasons for nonparticipating behavior, and these should be explored within the group. Some of these reasons are:

- fear of being accepted or of being rejected
- fear of looking foolish, inappropriate, or stupid
- unwillingness to face oneself
- the feeling that one doesn't have anything worthwhile to say and that, even if one did, others would say it better
- fear of certain members or of the leader
- fear of risking self-revelation
- uncertainty about how groups function
- fear that confidentiality will not be maintained
- resistance, particularly if the person doesn't really want to be in the group

What can you do about nonparticipatory behavior in the group you lead? You can begin by telling how the silence affects you. You can invite members to explore what their silence means to them and how they are affected by it. You can involve other group members by asking them to react to nonparticipatory behavior. But, in doing this, you need to be careful to avoid calling consistently on the silent person and to assume the full responsibility for drawing the person out, thus relieving the person of the responsibility of initiating interactions.

Shyness should not be confused with nonparticipation. Some group members may be basically shy and still be actively involved in the group, participating in their own way. To label a shy person a "problem member" is to do this person an injustice. Shy people may have a need to be more outgoing, but this value should not be pushed on them. Such people can get much from a group, yet in order for this to happen their shyness must be respected. At the same time, they can be encouraged to participate verbally by sharing their reactions as they pertain to the group. It is also good to reinforce verbal behavior on their part.

Monopolizing. At the opposite end of the participation spectrum are those who exhibit an inordinate need for attention by monopolizing the activities of the group. These individuals' high degree of self-centeredness is manifested by talking too much, by dwelling on storytelling, and by continually "identifying with others"—that is, by taking others' statements as opportunities to take the focus away from them and put it on themselves. Monopolizing is generally a way of dealing with anxiety; when the attention is not directed toward them, monopolizers become anxious and attempt to regain control of the group through some form of manipulation.

At the beginning, members may welcome someone who is willing to talk a lot, but soon they get tired of seeing the same person dominate the group's time. As the group progresses, other members typically become increasingly intolerant of the person who monopolizes. If these feelings of annoyance are not dealt with openly in the group, they tend to get stored up and then released explosively. As a consequence, the person who has been dominating the group becomes even more resistant and monopolistic. For this reason, it is essential that the person who is monopolizing be gently challenged to look at the effects that this behavior has on the group and what is avoided through the monopolizing behavior.

Storytelling.   Storytelling refers to any form of talk about oneself, others, and out-of-group life with the intent of avoiding the risk of disclosing oneself. People who engage in long-winded and detailed recitations of outside events— especially when these recitations are devoid of feelings—are likely to bore others and to lose contact with them. Although the rest of the group may tolerate the situation for a while and be willing to pay the price of being bored, eventually storytellers need to be told how they are being experienced by others. Appropriate feedback from the group can help these individuals become aware that they are not establishing effective contact. With the group's help, those who tell stories can learn to speak in personal terms and focus on feelings, thoughts, and reactions.

It is very important to understand the difference between storytelling and self-disclosure. Storytelling provides data about the person but no disclosure of what the person is feeling and thinking in the moment. Self-disclosure, as we saw earlier, expresses present concerns and is a means to the end of fuller self-understanding. Since self-disclosure is an essential aspect of group work, the importance of not confusing it with storytelling cannot be emphasized enough.

Dependency.   Dependency is manifested in a variety of behaviors. Dependent people may present themselves as helpless and incapable of providing answers for themselves, or they may clearly indicate that they expect others to protect them and take care of them.

Dependency often takes the form of a "Yes, but" style of interaction. The person asks for help, and the group gives feedback, perhaps indicating alternatives that the person had not considered. Without even pausing to let the feedback sink in, the person quickly responds with a "Yes, but" type of rebuttal. Yalom (1975) describes this person as a "help-rejecting complainer"—one who seems to take pride in the insolubility of his or her problems. The other group members become bored and irritated at first and then frustrated and confused.

It is essential to realize that dependent persons do not benefit from being allowed to manipulate others into futile attempts to help them. Being unwilling to listen to feedback—no matter what is suggested—they will always find reasons to prove that it won't work. A good place to begin helping dependent people rely on their own resources is to refuse to satisfy their dependency needs. By not reinforcing their helpless attitude and by pointing out to them the various ways in which they keep themselves dependent on others, the group will offer these participants the opportunity to begin to examine the needs that underlie their dependent behaviors.

Hostility and aggression. Hostile-aggressive behavior is difficult to deal with in a group because most of the time it is manifested indirectly. People often express hostility in subtle ways—nonverbally through frowns, detached and bored expressions, disruptive gestures, and slouched postures; verbally, through caustic remarks, sarcasm, jokes, and other hit-and-run maneuvers. Extremely hostile-aggressive people are not good candidates for group work. Because of their defensiveness, they rarely acknowledge their fears, and they use their hostile-aggressive behavior to keep themselves distant from others. Also, extreme hostility can have a very negative impact on the group climate, since the other participants will not open up and make themselves vulnerable if they feel that they will be "put down" or ridiculed.

Hostility is often directed toward the leader rather than toward other group members. For example, Karen keeps questioning the group leader's motives over and over again. She challenges his authority, expresses doubts about his leadership style, and behaves competitively with him in group. Assuming that the leader is capable, Karen's behavior may be indicative of resistance. Her confrontations with the leader may cover up her fear of becoming overdependent on him or on the group and her reluctance to discuss her feelings with the other participants.

Group collusion is a particular form of hostility—of group hostility, to be precise. Several members get together and form a clique that operates outside the group and in which they vent their hostility toward the leader and other members. Yet, during the group itself, these individuals refuse to bring out the negative feelings they so freely discuss when the group is over. This form of resistance makes group process impossible, because it keeps the clique members from becoming involved in the group.

As a leader, you need to be aware of your own reactions to hostility and be willing to express them without "dumping" on the hostile person or persons. Others in the group need to do the same. Like any other behavior, hostility and aggressiveness are indicative of underlying feelings—for example, feelings of inadequacy or the fear of getting close to people. If these underlying emotions can be dealt with openly, hostility is likely to give way to direct and constructive behavior.

Other Problem Behaviors

The scope of this book does not allow a detailed description of all the problem behaviors that occur in groups. The following is a brief overview of other common forms of behaviors that interfere with group process.

Acting superior. Members who act superior may send condescending messages indicating—in subtle and not-so-subtle ways—that they can't receive anything of value from others in the group or that now their lives leave nothing to be desired. Needless to say, comments such as "I can identify with you because at one time I was where you are now" are likely to raise anger on the part of others and lead to alienation.

Moralizing. Moralizing is expressed by telling others how they should feel or what they should or should not do, and by judging them as a whole rather than considering individual characteristics. People who moralize try to impose their beliefs on others, and they show no respect for others' opinions. For Yalom (1975), the central characteristic of the "self-righteous moralist" is the need to be right and to demonstrate that others are wrong. When confronted with moralizing behavior, group participants may become unwilling to expose their weaknesses for fear that their self-disclosures will be used against them.

Seductive behavior. This type of behavior is an attempt to manipulate others in order to avoid genuine contact. It can take many forms, one of which is to withdraw and expect others to take the initiative. The person in effect says "If they really care about me, they will come and draw me out." Playing helpless and pretending to be fragile are other ways of attempting to manipulate people. A danger of seductive behavior is that the other members or the leader can get caught in counterseductive games.

Scapegoating. Scapegoating occurs when a participant or participants become victims and are blamed for what is wrong in the group. By directing blame to others, those who are doing the scapegoating divert attention from themselves. Ganging up on one individual by pelting that person with negative reactions is one form of scapegoating. Trotzer (1977) says that, when this occurs, it is the leader's task to intervene to protect the person being singled out and to make sure that the other members face up to their own responsibility. According to Trotzer, seeing that participants don't use people outside the group as scapegoats for their lack of willingness to take action is another vital task that needs to be performed by the leader.

Dealing with Your Own Reactions to Problem Behaviors

As a group leader, you must learn to recognize and deal with the various manifestations of resistance in group members. This need doesn't mean, however, that you should focus only on the resistant behavior of the client to the exclusion of your own dynamics. When group members exhibit disruptive behavior, you are likely to respond with strong feelings. You may be threatened by those members who dominate and attempt to control the group; you may be angered over uncooperative behavior; and you may blame certain individuals or the group as a whole for the slow pace or lack of productivity of the group. Thus, in dealing with problem behaviors, you need to take into account your own feelings and behavior.

I am not suggesting that a leader should not think of ways to deal actively with members who exhibit defensive behavior. (As a matter of fact, I encourage you to ask fellow students, colleagues, and supervisors for suggestions on how to handle resistance.) What I'm saying is that you also need to be willing to focus on your own defensive reactions to members' behaviors that you perceive as interfering with productive group process. If you ignore your own reactions, you are in essence leaving yourself out of the interactions that occur in the group. Your own responses—be they feelings, thoughts, or observations—can be the most powerful resource at your disposal in effectively handling the resisting behaviors you'll encounter. If you ignore your own dynamics and refuse to bring your own reactions into the group process, you deprive the members of the possibility of having an honest, direct, and constructive exchange with you as a person and as a leader. Because of this, I discuss transference and countertransference in some detail. It is during the transition stage that your personal reactions to members who pose problems for you and the group are most likely to bog you down. Group leaders often begin to feel incompetent when the group is marked by conflict, when members display a variety of resistances, and when their own unfinished business comes to the surface. Leaders may overidentify with some of the problems the members are wrestling with, and their objectivity and therapeutic effectiveness then becomes limited.

Transference refers to the unconscious process whereby clients project onto the counselor past feelings or attitudes toward significant people in their lives. Although transference as a concept stems from psychoanalysis, the phenomenon is not restricted to the psychoanalytic approach. *Countertransference* refers to the feelings aroused in the counselor by clients; these feelings have more to do with unrecognized or unresolved issues in the counselor's past relationships than with any feature of the therapeutic relationship.

Transference.   I believe that, regardless of your theoretical orientation, you need to be aware of the feelings and expectations that you, as a leader, elicit in the members of your group. Unless these feelings are recognized and explored in the group, meaningful work may never occur. Participants sometimes develop unrealistic expectations of the group leader by casting him or her into a fixed role that meets their own needs. Corey and Corey (1982) describe five such roles.

1. *The expert.* Some people enter a group with the expectation that the leader will know what is best for them, do the work for them, and perhaps even offer a recipe for happiness. Thus, they wait, respectfully and hopefully, to be shown the way. If they don't get what they hope for, they soon begin resenting the leader for not doing his or her job properly.

2. *The authority figure.* During the initial phases of a group the participants tend to be dependent on, and often inhibited by, the leader, whom they see as an authority figure. Members often remark that they feel judged, that they see themselves as insignificant when they are with the leader, and that they doubt that they will ever be able to measure up to the leader's expectations. This attitude may indicate that the members are turning the leader into a substitute parent and that, in doing so, they expect him or her to confirm them as worthwhile persons. By elevating the counselor to a superior place, these clients inevitably put themselves in an inferior position and discount their own value. The result of this process is eventual resentment toward the leader— resentment that tends to make a relationship based on genuine respect and liking impossible.

3. *The superperson.* Clients often need to view the group leader as a person who has "arrived." If the leader is "fully together as a person," they reason, there is hope that they too will eventually be self-actualized and perfectly adjusted. When these members discover that the leader is far from perfect, they may become disappointed and even resentful. On their part, leaders need to avoid the trap of deluding themselves into believing that they are superpersons.

4. *The friend.* The dynamics of making a friend out of the group leader are similar to the dynamics of making a parent out of the leader. Some members hope that, by developing a friendship, they will receive special attention from the leader. They want to be approved of and accepted at a more intimate level than on a client basis. If the leader allows these members to achieve what they want, he or she may do a disservice to them. By relying too heavily on their relationship with the counselor, the members may fail to develop friendships on the outside.

5. *The lover.* Some group members seek to turn the therapeutic relationship into a romantic one. They may think that, if they are able to attract the leader, they will occupy a special place in the group. Chances are that they will be disappointed, for they are usually searching for the love that is missing in their lives now or that they didn't get from significant people when they were children or adolescents. Their needs are too great and their expectations too high to have a realistic chance to be met. Leaders must be aware of the fact that seductive behavior on the part of a member tends to generate countertransference. Unless leaders recognize their own motivations and unresolved conflicts, their ability to lead might be negatively affected.

Countertransference.   Countertransference occurs when the leader's own needs become entangled in the therapeutic relationship to the extent that these needs obstruct or even destroy the leader's objectivity. Corey, Corey, and Callanan (1984) describe five ways in which countertransference is commonly manifested.

1. *The need for constant reinforcement and approval* can be a source of countertransference. Group leaders may have an inordinate need for reassurance concerning their effectiveness, in much the same way that members may develop an excessive need to please the leader in order to feel appreciated. If this need for reassurance is strong enough, much of what leaders do in the group may be designed to get the approval they seek so desperately. For example, leaders may avoid challenging the members for fear of being disliked.

2. Leaders may *see themselves in their clients.* Whereas it is necessary for leaders to have empathy, some beginning leaders identify with members' struggles to the extent that they lose their objectivity and become unable to help the members work on their problems. These leaders become so lost in the members' worlds that they cannot separate their own feelings from those of the members.

3. Occasionally *sexual and romantic feelings* develop between leaders and clients. Seductive behavior on the part of a group member can easily lead to seductive behavior on the part of the counselor. It should be noted, however, that the mere existence of sexual feelings in the leader toward a member is

not always a sign of countertransference and an impediment to effective counseling. The problem arises when leaders don't recognize their own dynamics,
or when their own needs have priority over those of the clients, or when the
sexual element becomes the focus of the therapeutic relationship. Feelings of
attraction can be recognized and even acknowledged frankly without becoming
central to the interaction or acted out.

4. *Compulsive advice giving* is another common manifestation of countertransference. The leader's need to dispense advice may be a direct outcome of
the leader's own unresolved conflicts and a manifestation of the need for immediate solutions to problems. The leader's tendency to give advice can easily be
encouraged by clients who are prone themselves to seek immediate answers
to their questions and struggles. The opportunity to give advice places leaders
in a superior position—one that they may come to enjoy—and they may end
up believing that they have all the answers for all the members. Here, too,
leaders need to be aware of their own dynamics and make sure that the clients'
needs take priority over their own.

5. *A desire to develop social relationships with group members* may stem from
countertransference. Occasionally, participants indicate that they would like
to develop a more personal relationship with the leader than is possible in the
group situation. Even experienced therapists sometimes must deal with the
question of whether a therapeutic relationship can coexist with a social one.
When this question arises, leaders need to explore their own feelings and
needs. They may find, for example, that their position in the group makes them
more attractive than they would be if they were not the leader. Thus, they may
want to establish social contacts with group members because such relationships may be difficult to come by when they are not in their leader role. Or
they may discover that they are looking for the intimacy that is missing in their
lives. This kind of self-awareness will make it possible to deal effectively with
the ultimate question of whether social relationships with clients interfere with
the therapeutic relationship and even defeat the purpose of therapy. Another
point the leader needs to keep in mind is that jealousy is likely to occur when
other members discover that they don't have the "favored relationship" with
the leader that some members have.

In dealing with countertransference, supervision is most helpful. As a trainee
you have the opportunity to explore with your supervisor and fellow group
leaders your feelings of attraction or dislike toward certain members and learn
a lot about yourself in the process. If you are leading a group alone and no
longer have supervision, it is important that you be willing to consult with a
qualified professional so that you can work through unresolved problems that
may lie behind your feelings of countertransference. One of the advantages of
working with a co-leader is that the partner can offer valuable feedback from
an objective point of view and thus help you see things that may be blocked
from your awareness.

On the matter of handling transference and countertransference constructively, it may be of value to consider these four points:

1. Don't accept uncritically what group members tell you about yourself. For
example, if some participants tell you that you come across as distant, judg-

mental, and aloof, first think about this feedback to determine whether it is accurate. Then you may wish to check with other group members. If you keep getting the same feedback, it is likely that you do present yourself to others as an aloof and distant expert and that transference has little to do with the feedback. Be especially careful when people tell you how wise, perceptive, lovable, attractive, powerful, dynamic, and caring you are, and keep in mind that some members may have an unrealistic view of you.

2. Critical evaluation of feedback doesn't mean discounting all positive comments. Obviously, the feelings that members have toward you as a group leader are not necessarily manifestations of transference. Members can feel genuine affection and respect for you, and this may be a function of the person you are rather than a transference reaction. The same holds true with negative feelings, which may be generated not by transference but by your behavior in the group. In sum, not all feelings that members direct toward you need to be "analyzed" as transferences and "worked through" for the client's good. If you keep receiving consistent feedback, pay attention to it, check its validity, and, if it is valid, act on it.

3. Similarly, not all your positive and negative feelings toward the members of your group can be classified as countertransference. It is natural for you to be attracted to some and put off by some. Your reactions may be a function of the person's behavior in the group and not a sign that you have unresolved conflicts and blocked areas. It is a mistake to assume that you will care for all members equally or that you should always remain objective. Countertransference is indicated by exaggerated and inappropriate responses to certain members or by persistent feelings that tend to recur with certain people in various groups. The fact that you are sexually attracted to some members or bored with others does not indicate that you have a problem that needs to be solved. The essential thing is that you recognize your feelings for what they are and that you don't get yourself into emotional entanglements that can be extremely counterproductive.

4. When transference or countertransference is in operation, the unresolved conflicts are often acted out rather than verbalized. When group leaders verbalize their feelings rather than defensively acting out, they are presenting a model of awareness for the members, who may previously have only known acting out as a way to handle anxieties and transference.

Co-Leader Issues at the Transition Stage

As you can see, the transition stage is a critical period in the history of the group, for, depending on how conflict and resistance are handled, the group can take a turn for better or for worse. If you are working with a co-leader, there are a few particular problems that can easily develop at this time. You can efficiently use the time you have for meeting before and after sessions to focus on your own reactions to what is occurring in the group.

1. *Negative reactions toward one leader.* If members direct a challenge or express negative feelings toward your co-leader, it is as important to avoid taking sides with your co-leader in attacking members as it is to side with the

members in ganging up against the co-leader. What is called for in such an instance is for you to nondefensively (and as objectively as possible) continue your leadership by facilitating a constructive exploration of the situation.

2. *Challenge to both co-leaders.* Assume that several members direct negative feelings to both you and your co-leader, saying: "You leaders expect us to be personal in here, yet we don't know anything about you that is personal. You should be willing to talk about your problems if that is what you expect us to do!" In such a case, difficulties can develop if one of you responds defensively while the other is willing to deal with this confrontation from the members. Ideally, both co-leaders would be willing to talk about the confrontation objectively; if not, this would surely be a vital topic to discuss in the co-leaders' meeting outside of group or during a supervision session. I don't want to convey the impression that all difficulties should be reserved for a private discussion between the co-leaders. As much as possible, matters that pertain to what is happening during sessions should be discussed with the entire group. The failure to do this can easily lead to a *you* versus *them* split within the group.

3. *Dealing with problem behaviors.* I discussed a variety of difficult members that you and your co-leader might have to confront. I want to caution against the tendency of co-leaders to chronically discuss what such members are doing or not doing and never explore how such behavior affects them as leaders. It is a mistake to dwell almost exclusively upon strategies for curing problem members while ignoring the leaders' personal reactions to such problematic behaviors.

4. *Dealing with countertransference.* It is not realistic to expect a leader to work equally effectively with every member. At times, this is due to countertransference reactions on the part of one of the leaders. For example, a male leader could have strong and irrational negative reactions to one of the women in the group. It may be that he is seeing his ex-wife in this member and responding to her in cutting ways because of his own unresolved issues over the divorce. When this occurs, the co-leader can be therapeutic for both the member and the leader who is being nontherapeutic. The co-leader can intervene during the session itself as well as explore these inappropriate reactions with the other leader outside the session. Co-leaders who are willing to be objective and honest with each other can have a positive impact through this process of mutual confrontation.

Summary of Transition Stage

Stage characteristics. The transitional phase of a group's development is marked by feelings of anxiety and defenses in the form of various resistances. At this time members are:

- concerned about what they will think of themselves if they increase their self-awareness, and concerned about others' acceptance or rejection of them
- testing the leader and other members to determine how safe the environment is

- struggling with wanting to play it safe versus wanting to risk getting involved
- experiencing some struggle for control and power and some conflict with other members or the leaders
- challenged with learning how to work through conflict and confrontation
- reluctant to get fully involved in working on their personal concerns because they are not sure others in the group will care about them
- observing the leader to determine if he or she is trustworthy, and learning from this person how to resolve conflict
- learning how to express themselves so that others will listen to them

Member functions and possible problems.   A central role of members at this time is to recognize and deal with the many forms of resistance. Tasks include:

- recognizing and expressing any negative feelings
- respecting one's own resistances but working with them
- moving from dependence to independence
- learning how to confront others in a constructive manner
- recognizing the unresolved feelings from the past as they are being acted out in relation to the group leader
- being willing to face and deal with reactions toward what is occurring in the group
- being willing to work through conflicts, rather than avoiding them

Some possible problems can arise with members at this time.

- Members can be categorized according to some kind of "problem type," or they can limit themselves with some self-imposed label.
- Members may refuse to express persistent negative feelings, thus contributing to the climate of distrust.
- If confrontations are poorly handled, members may retreat into defensive postures, and issues will remain hidden.
- Members may collude with one another by forming subgroups and cliques, expressing negative reactions in these cliques outside of the group but remaining silent in the group.

Leader's key tasks.   Perhaps the central challenge that leaders face during the transition phase is the need to intervene in the group in a sensitive manner and at the right time. The basic task is to provide both the encouragement and the challenge necessary for the members to face and resolve the conflicts that exist within the group and their own resistances and defenses against anxiety (Mahler, 1969). Hansen et al. (1980) emphasize the necessity for the leader to help the participants work through this stage of conflict and confrontation, so that the group can move away from superficial interaction to an effective level of interpersonal functioning. As I indicated earlier, the genuine cohesion that allows for productive work to develop demands that this difficult phase of defensiveness and conflict be experienced and dealt with successfully.

The following are some of the major tasks that you need to perform to successfully meet the basic challenge you face as a group leader during this critical period in a group's development:

- teaching group members the importance of recognizing and expressing their anxieties
- helping participants recognize the ways in which they react defensively and creating a climate in which they can deal with their resistances openly
- noticing signs of resistance and communicating to the participants that some of these resistances are both natural and healthy
- teaching the members the value of recognizing and dealing openly with the conflicts that occur in the group
- pointing out behavior that is a manifestation of the struggle for control and teaching the members how to accept their share of responsibility for the direction of the group
- providing a model for the members by dealing directly and honestly with any challenges to the leader as a person or as a professional
- assisting the group members in dealing with any matters that will influence their ability to become autonomous and independent group members

Leaders need to be especially active during the first and second stages of a group. During the transition stage, active intervention and structuring are important, because generally the participants have not yet learned to work effectively on their own (Mahler, 1969). For example, if a conflict arises, some members may attempt to move on to more pleasant topics or in some other way ignore the conflict. Group leaders need to teach members the value of expressing their feelings, no matter how negative.

Mahler (1969) argues that, if this phase of conflict is not worked through and appropriate norms for self-expression are not established, only a superficial level of group cohesion will develop. Mahler, too, emphasizes that the leader's role is to promote the members' self-direction. He also says that the group has moved into a working stage when the members demonstrate the willingness and ability to provide leadership for themselves and to assume increasing self-direction as a group; instead of relying primarily on the leader, the participants begin to trust the resources that exist within their peers. Mahler notes that the completion of the transition stage is indicated by the participants' clear commitment to use the group for their own self-discovery and fulfillment of personal goals.

CONCLUDING COMMENTS

This chapter has addressed various issues of group membership and group process that are central to your effectiveness as a group leader. We have focused on key concerns as the group is being formed, at its initial phase, and at the transitional period in a group's history. Emphasis has been given to the central characteristics of the group at each phase, the member functions and possible problems, group process concepts, and the leader's key tasks. Attention has also been given to co-leader issues during each period of development. It has been mentioned several times that your approach to leadership functions and skills hinges on your understanding of the roles members play at the various stages in the group. Only if you are clear in your own mind about the various aspects of productive and unproductive member behaviors can you help group participants acquire the skills necessary for a successful group experience and correct behaviors that hinder self-exploration and involvement in the group. The next chapter continues this story of the unfolding of a group.

5

LATER STAGES IN THE DEVELOPMENT OF A GROUP

INTRODUCTION

Continuing the discussion of the evolutionary process of a group in action, this chapter focuses on the working stage, the final stage, and the postgroup issues of follow-up and evaluation. We will look at the major characteristics of the group at each phase, the member functions and possible problems that are likely to occur, and the group leader's key functions.

STAGE 3: WORKING STAGE—COHESION AND PRODUCTIVITY

The working stage is characterized by exploration of significant problems and by effective action to bring about the desired behavioral changes. This is the time when participants need to realize that *they* are the ones who are responsible for their lives. Thus, they must be encouraged to decide for themselves the issues they want to explore in the group; they need to learn how to become an integral part of the group and yet retain their individuality; and they must filter the feedback they receive and make their own decisions concerning what they will do about it. Consequently, it is very important that at this stage neither the group leader nor the other members attempt to decide on a course of action or make prescriptions for the individual.

Development of Group Cohesion

Group cohesion refers to the attractiveness of the group for the participants and to a sense of belonging, inclusion, and solidarity. Although group cohesion may begin to develop in the early stages of a group, it is at this stage that it becomes a key element of the group process. If trust has been established and if conflict and negative feelings have been expressed and worked through, the group becomes a cohesive unit. It is, in a sense, as if the group had gone through a testing period and the members had said to themselves "If it's OK to express negative feelings and conflict, then maybe it's OK to get close."

In my experience, I have found that cohesion occurs when people open up and take risks. The honest sharing of deeply significant personal experiences and struggles binds the group together, because the process of sharing allows members to identify with others by seeing themselves in them. Since group cohesion provides the group with the impetus to move forward, it is a prerequisite for the group's success. Without a sense of "groupness" the group remains fragmented, the members become frozen behind their defenses, and the work that is done is of necessity superficial. Groups do not become cohesive automatically. Cohesion is the result of the commitment of the participants and the leader to take the steps that lead to a group-as-a-whole feeling.

Although group cohesion is not in itself a sufficient condition for effective group work, in a sense all the characteristics of a well-functioning group are contingent on it. Cohesion fosters action-oriented behaviors such as self-disclosure, immediacy, mutuality, confrontation, risk taking, and translation of insight into action. Also, without group cohesion the participants don't feel secure enough to maintain a high level of self-disclosure.

What does the research say about the role of cohesion in the successful outcome of a group? In a summary of experiential group research, Bednar and Kaul (1978) note that it is assumed that group cohesion is a prime therapeutic factor in groups and that successes and failures are frequently attributed to it. But, they state, there is relatively little clear and systematic research on the specific factors that are thought to affect cohesion. Bednar and Kaul add: "The research that has been published has led to less consistency of results and interpretation than one would wish. In short, there is little cohesion in the cohesion research" (p. 800).

The study of process and outcomes of encounter groups by Lieberman, Yalom, and Miles (1973) does give an indication that attraction to the group is a determinant of outcome. Those individuals in the study who didn't feel a sense of belonging or attraction to the group showed a high likelihood of experiencing negative outcomes. Also, groups with a higher level of cohesiveness were more likely to have a positive outcome than groups characterized by low cohesiveness.

Although cohesiveness is necessary for effective group work, it can also actually hinder the group's development. When cohesiveness is not accompanied by a challenge to move forward by both the members and the leader, the group can reach a plateau. The group enjoys the comfort and security of the unity it has earned, but no progress is made. As Hansen et al. (1980) point out, the achievement of cohesiveness and some degree of stability should signal the beginning of a lengthy working process.

In many of the adult groups that I lead there are common human themes that most of the members can relate to personally, regardless of their age, sociocultural background, and occupation. Whereas members are likely to be aware in the earlier stages of the group of the differences that they feel separate them, it is quite common as the group reaches a level of cohesion for members to comment on how they are alike in the feelings that connect them. Some of these responses are as follows:

- I'm not alone in my pain and with my problems.
- I'm more lovable than I thought I was.
- I used to think that I was too old to change and that I'd just have to settle for what I have in life. Now I see that what I feel is no different from what the younger people in here feel.
- I'm hopeful about my future, even though I know that I have a long way to go and that the road will be rough.
- There are a lot of people in here I feel close to, and I see that we earned this closeness by letting others know who we are.
- Intimacy is frightening, but it's also rewarding.
- People can be beautiful once they shed their masks.
- I learned that the loneliness I felt was shared by most people in this group.

As a group becomes cohesive, it is not uncommon for a woman in her early 20s to discover that she is very much like a man in his late 50s. Both of them may still be searching for parental approval, and they may both be learning how futile it is to look outside of themselves for confirmation of their worth as persons. A man learns that his struggles with masculinity are not too different from a woman's struggles with her femininity. A woman learns that she is not alone when she discovers that she feels resentment over the many demands her family makes upon her. An older man sees in a younger male member "his son" and allows himself to feel tenderness and compassion that he did not let himself experience earlier.

There are other common themes evolving in this stage that lead to an increase of cohesion: remembering painful experiences of childhood and adolescence; becoming aware of the need for and fear of love; becoming able to express feelings that have been repressed; discovering that one's worst enemy lives within oneself; struggling to find a meaning in life; feeling guilt over what one has done or failed to do; longing for meaningful connections with significant people; and beginning a process of finding one's identity. The leader can foster the development of cohesion by pointing out the common themes that link members of the group.

Characteristics of an Effective Working Group

Stage 3 is characterized by productiveness. Now that the group has truly become a group and the members have developed leadership skills that allow them a greater degree of autonomy, the group is less dependent on the leader. During this stage, mutuality and self-exploration increase, and the group is focused on producing lasting results. Although the specific characteristics of a cohesive and productive group do vary somewhat with the type of group, there are some general trends that identify a group in its working stage:

• There is a here-and-now focus. People have learned to talk directly about what they are feeling and doing in the group sessions. They are generally willing to have meaningful interactions with one another.

• Members more readily identify their goals and concerns, and they have learned to take responsibility for them. They are less confused about what the group and the leaders expect of them.

• Most of the members feel included in the group. Those who are not active know they are invited to participate, and their lack of participation does not discourage others from doing meaningful work.

• In many ways, the group has almost become an orchestra in that individuals listen to one another and do productive work together. Although the participants may still look to the leader for direction, in a way that individual musicians look to the conductor for cues, they also tend to initiate a direction toward which they want to move.

• Members are willing to work and practice outside the group to achieve behavioral changes. They are willing to try to integrate feelings, thinking, and behaving in their everyday situations. They are becoming able to catch themselves when they think and act in old patterns, and they are likely to challenge themselves to think and behave in more constructive ways.

• Members continually assess their level of satisfaction with the group, and they take active steps to change matters if they see that the sessions need changing.

Therapeutic Factors of a Group

This section presents an overview of the major therapeutic factors that contribute to the successful accomplishment of the two main tasks of this stage: developing insight and using it to achieve constructive behavior change. The purpose of the following brief overview is simply to offer a summary of the specific factors that ensure that a group will move beyond the security of cohesiveness into productive work. However, two major factors of the working stage—self-disclosure and confrontation—will be addressed in some detail.

Trust and acceptance.   Group members at the working stage trust one another and the leader or at least openly express their lack of trust. Trust is manifested in the participants' willingness to take risks by sharing meaningful here-and-now reactions and in their attitude of acceptance. Feeling that they are accepted, the members come to recognize that in the group they can be who they are without risking rejection. For example, they dare to assert themselves, because they are aware that they don't have to please everybody. Acceptance involves affirming a person's right to have certain feelings and to express them. Acceptance promotes group identification and a sense of belonging, which are instrumental to the healing process. The group works against alienation—the very opposite of belonging—by providing a unique place where people can become truly involved with one another (Dinkmeyer & Muro, 1979).

Empathy and caring.   Empathy involves a deep and subjective understanding of another's struggles: it is the capacity to recall, relive, and tap one's feelings through the intense experiences of others. In groups, cohesion develops when the participants realize that they are not alone in their struggles and that they share a gamut of similar emotions. By understanding the feelings of others— such as need for love and acceptance, hurt about past experiences, and lone- liness, as well as joy and enthusiasm—members come to see themselves more clearly. Empathy means caring, and, in a group, caring is expressed by genuine and active involvement with the other members. It is also expressed by com- passion, support, tenderness, and even confrontation. As people open them- selves to others by showing their pain, struggles, joy, excitement, and fears, they make it possible for others to care for them.

Hope. If change is to occur, members must believe that change is possible, that they need not remain trapped in their past, and that they can take active steps to make their lives richer. Hope is therapeutic in itself, for it gives mem- bers the confidence to commit themselves to the demanding work that a group requires and motivates them to explore alternatives.

Commitment to change. I said earlier that, for change to occur, a person must believe that change is possible. But hope alone is not enough. Construc- tive change requires a firm resolve to actually do whatever is necessary in order to change. This means deciding *what* to change as well as *how* to change it. Participants need to formulate a plan of action, commit themselves to it, and use the tools offered by the group process to explore ways of implementing it. The support offered by the group is invaluable in encouraging the members to stick with their commitments even when they experience temporary setbacks.

Intimacy. As Schutz (1973a) has pointed out, the issue of intimacy becomes very relevant in the third stage of a group. The questions of being liked or disliked and of not being close enough or being too intimate are often a source of great anxiety. According to Schutz, after problems of control are resolved, affection becomes a predominant issue. Therefore, expression of positive and negative feelings and heightened emotionality between pairs of people are quite com- mon at this stage.

Genuine intimacy develops in a group after people have revealed enough of themselves for others to identify with them. I've found that intimacy increases as people work through their struggles together. As work proceeds, members see that, regardless of their differences, they all share certain needs, wants, anxieties, and problems. When members learn that others have similar prob- lems, they no longer feel isolated; identification with others eventually brings about closeness, which allows the members of the group to help one another work through fears related to intimacy. The ultimate goal is to understand how one has avoided intimacy outside of the group and how one can accept inti- macy in life without fear.

Personal power. A major agent of change is the power that individuals experience when they are able to tap the reserves of their spontaneity, creativ- ity, courage, and inner strength. This may be the first time that the person knows what this power means—not control over others but the capacity to use inner resources to take charge of one's life.

Catharsis. The expression of pent-up feelings can be therapeutic, because it releases energy that has been tied up in withholding certain threatening feelings. This emotional release, which often occurs in an explosive way, leaves the person feeling freer. Also, keeping a lid on anger, pain, frustration, hatred, and fear means keeping spontaneous feelings such as joy, affection, delight, and enthusiasm from emerging.

My experience has taught me that catharsis *may* be a vital part of a person's work in a group, especially if the person has a reservoir of unrecognized and unexpressed feelings. But I have also learned that it is a mistake to assume that no real work occurs without a strong ventilation of feelings, since many people appear to gain benefit from their group experience in the absence of catharsis. After catharsis has occurred, it is extremely important to work through the feelings that emerged, to gain some understanding of the *meaning* of the experience, and to make new decisions based on such understanding.

Cognitive restructuring. Although catharsis may bring release to the individual and stimulate the group process, cathartic experiences alone, with no real effort to understand them or to apply what one has learned from them, are of limited usefulness. A central part of the work done in a group consists of challenging and exploring beliefs about situations. Data from the Lieberman et al. (1973) study of encounter groups support this view. In this study, emotionality was related to successful outcomes when it was accompanied by some form of cognitive learning. In other words, understanding the *meaning* of intense emotional experiences is necessary to further self-exploration. This cognitive component includes explaining, clarifying, interpreting, providing the cognitive framework needed for change, formulating ideas, and making new decisions. In summary, catharsis can be a very useful tool for change, if the person attempts to conceptualize and put into words the emotional experience.

Freedom to experiment. Experimentation with different modes of behavior is a significant aspect of the working stage. The group is a safe place in which to experiment and try out novel behavior. After trying new behavior, members can decide how much they want to change their current behavior. In everyday transactions, people often behave in rigid and unimaginative ways, for they don't dare to deviate from familiar and predictable ways of behaving. With group support, participants can practice more functional ways of being and behaving. Role playing is often an effective way to practice new skills in interpersonal situations; then these skills can be applied to out-of-group situations.

Benefiting from feedback. Feedback from other members of the group can be of great help to the person who is exploring a problem, attempting to resolve a difficult situation, or trying different ways of behaving. When observations and reactions are expressed honestly and with care, the individual who receives them can judge the impact that he or she has on others. Then it is up to the person to decide how to utilize this information. Members of an effective working group help one another through the process of mutual sharing of real struggles and by having the courage to engage in personal work in the sessions.

Self-disclosure.   Since self-disclosure is the principal vehicle of group interaction, it is critical that group participants have a clear understanding of what self-disclosure *is* and *is not*. In essence, self-disclosure means revealing oneself to others. In the group situation, one level of self-disclosure implies sharing one's persistent reactions to what is happening in the group. The willingness to reveal ongoing thoughts and feelings is one of the most effective forms of self-disclosure in groups. Another level of self-disclosure entails revealing current struggles, unresolved personal issues, goals and aspirations, pain, joy, strengths and weaknesses, and the meaning of certain personal experiences. If people are unwilling to share of themselves, they make it very hard for others to care for them.

On the other hand, self-disclosure does *not* mean revealing one's innermost secrets and digging into one's past. Nor does it mean "letting everything hang out" or expressing every fleeting reaction toward others. Self-disclosure should not be confused with telling stories about oneself or with letting group pressure dictate the limits of one's privacy.

The willingness to make oneself known to others is a basic requirement at every stage of a group. During the working stage, most members are willing to risk disclosing threatening material. Disclosure is not an end in itself; it is the means by which open communication can occur within a group. If disclosure is limited to safe topics or if it is mistaken for exposing secrets, the group cannot move beyond a superficial level. There are many barriers within us that keep us from self-disclosure—for example, fear of the intimacy that accompanies self-revelation, avoidance of responsibility and change, feelings of guilt and shame, fear of rejection, and cultural obstacles to disclosure.

Egan (1976) suggests that self-disclosure should be related to the here and now; that is, when members talk about something that occurred outside of the group or in the past, they need to relate this material to what is happening in the group at the moment. By focusing on the here and now, participants make direct contact with one another and generally express quite accurately what they are experiencing in the present. The interactions become increasingly honest and spontaneous, because members are more and more willing to risk revealing their reactions to one another.

It is also essential to teach group members how to give appropriate feedback to those members who engage in self-disclosure. I think of self-disclosure as a way of inviting reactions from others, but these reactions must be given effectively. For instance, assume that a member expresses and works through some painful events in her life. She may have experienced ambivalent feelings about sharing pain that she had kept locked up within her for many years. What is most helpful is for members to share with her how she affected them personally. What did this pain touch in others in the group? It would be inappropriate feedback if members gave her pat reassurance, bombarded her with advice (or worse yet with pity), or told her how she should feel. Others in the group can help this woman accept some painful experiences in her life if they are able to demonstrate that they can hear, understand, and identify with some part of her struggle.

Confrontation.   Like self-disclosure, confrontation is a basic ingredient of the working stage; if it is absent, stagnation results. Constructive confrontation is an invitation to examine discrepancies between what one says and what one does, to become aware of unused potential, and to carry insights into action. When confrontation takes place in the supportive environment of a group, it can be a true act of caring.

In a successful group, confrontation occurs in such a way that the confronters share their reactions to (not judgments of) the person being confronted. A negative style of confrontation—that is, confrontation done in a hostile, indirect, or attacking way—is avoided, because misuse of confrontation may leave people feeling judged and rejected. Done with care and sensitivity, confrontation by others ultimately helps members develop the capacity for the self-confrontation necessary to work through the problems they need to resolve.

Confrontation is an issue that group members, as well as group leaders, frequently misunderstand; it is often feared, misused, and seen as a negative act to be avoided at all costs. In my opinion, although support and empathy are certainly essential to group process, they can become counterproductive if carried to an excess. In other words, a group can cease to be effective if its members have colluded to interact only on a supportive level and agreed to focus almost exclusively on strengths and positive feedback. Unwillingness to challenge the others to take a deeper look at themselves results in overly polite and supportive exchanges that bear little resemblance to everyday interactions and that provide no incentive to extend oneself.

Group leaders can productively devote time to helping the participants clear up their misconceptions regarding confrontation and learn *what* to confront and *how* to confront in a constructive way. One of the most powerful ways of teaching constructive and caring confrontation is for leaders to model this behavior in their interactions in the group. By being direct, honest, sensitive, respectful, and timely in their confrontations, leaders provide the members with valuable opportunities to learn these skills through observing the leader's behavior.

Egan (1977) sees confrontation as an invitation to examine some aspect of one's interpersonal style. Challenging others to look at themselves with greater depth and awareness can motivate them to take action to make changes in their lives. The absence of this challenge can lead to complacency and to unwillingness to make full contact with others.

Here are some practical guidelines for effective confrontation. The first five are offered by Egan (1977, pp. 218–221).

- Confront in a spirit of accurate understanding.
- Be tentative, as opposed to dogmatic, but avoid being apologetic.
- Be concrete by describing specific behavior; avoid judging and categorizing the person.

- Confront only those people you care for and with whom you want to reach deeper closeness.
- Confront only when you have earned the right to do so.

In addition to Egan's guidelines, I typically emphasize the following points about effective confrontation:

- Be sensitive with regard to how the confrontation is being received; it may help to imagine receiving the confrontation you are directing toward another person.
- If the person being confronted becomes increasingly defensive and closes up, stop and discuss this attitude with the person.
- Accept the possibility that the other person may not be ready for your confrontation.
- Don't make the person responsible for what *you* are feeling, but do let the person know how you feel about him or her.
- Avoid imposing your decisions and your time frame on others; allow them time to reflectively consider your feedback to them, and don't expect an immediate decision.
- Apply to yourself what you say to others, in order to determine whether you are willing to do yourself what you are challenging others to do.

Commentary. As my colleagues and I have written elsewhere (Corey, Corey, Callanan, & Russell, 1982b), not all groups reach the working stage that is being described here. This does not necessarily mean that the leader is ineffective. Changing membership in a group can block its progress. Some populations simply may not be ready for the level of intensity that is often part of a working phase. If the tasks of the initial and transition stages were never mastered, then the group can be expected to be stuck. For instance, some groups don't get beyond the hidden agendas and unspoken conflicts that were typical of earlier sessions. Or the members may simply not be willing to give much of themselves beyond safe and superficial encounters. They may have made a decision to stop at a safe level characterized by mutual support, rather than also challenging one another to move into unknown territory. Early interchanges between members and the leader or among members may have been abrasive, thus creating a climate of hesitancy and unwillingness to trust others. The group may be oriented toward solving problems or patching up differences and problems. This orientation can discourage self-exploration, for as soon as a member raises a problem, some members may rush in with advice on how to remedy the situation. For reasons such as these and others, some groups never progress beyond the initial stage or the transition stage.

Corey et al. (1982b) have also observed that, when a group does get to the working stage, it doesn't necessarily progress as tidily as the above characterization may suggest. Earlier themes of trust, unconstructive conflict, and the reluctance to participate surface time and again in a group's history. As one member put it, "There is no trust heaven in groups!" Trust is not a matter that is dealt with once and for all during the early stages of development. As the group faces new challenges, deeper levels of trust have to be earned. Also, considerable conflict may be resolved during the initial stage or transition stage, but new conflicts emerge in the advanced phases and must be faced and worked through. As is true with any intimate relationship, the relationships in the group are not static. Utopia is never reached, for the smooth waters may well turn into stormy seas for a time. Commitment to function as a group is necessary to do the difficult yet rewarding work of progressing.

Co-Leader Issues at the Working Stage

I cannot overemphasize the importance of meeting with one's co-leader throughout the duration of the group. Many of the issues I have suggested earlier for discussion at these co-leader meetings also apply to the working stage. I will briefly consider a few other issues that are particularly relevant to this stage.

Ongoing evaluation of the group.   Co-leaders can make it a practice to devote some time to appraising the direction the group is taking and its level of productivity. If the group is a closed one with a predetermined termination date (say, 20 weeks), co-leaders would do well to evaluate the group's progress around the tenth week. This evaluation can be a topic of discussion privately *and* in the group itself. For example, if both co-leaders agree that the group seems to be bogging down and that members are appearing to lose interest in the sessions, they should surely bring these perceptions into the group so that members have the opportunity to look at their degree of satisfaction with their direction and progress.

Discussion of techniques.   It is useful to discuss techniques and leadership styles with a co-leader. One of the leaders might be hesitant to try any technique because of fearing to make a mistake, because of not knowing where to go next, or because of passively waiting for permission from the co-leader to introduce techniques. Such issues, along with any stylistic differences between leaders, are topics for exploration.

Theoretical orientations.   It is not essential that co-leaders share the same theory of group work, for sometimes differing theoretical preferences can blend nicely. You can learn a lot from discussing theory as it applies to practice. Therefore, I encourage leaders to read, attend workshops and special seminars, and then discuss what they are learning with their co-leaders. Doing so can result in bringing to the group sessions some new and interesting variations.

Self-disclosure issues.   This topic was discussed earlier in this chapter, but I want to add here the value of co-leaders' exploring their sense of appropriate and therapeutic leader self-disclosure. For example, if you are willing to share with members your reactions that pertain to group issues yet are reserved in disclosing personal outside issues, while your co-leader freely and fully talks about his or her marital situation in the group, then members may perceive you as holding back. This is another issue you might want to discuss both in the group and privately with your co-leader.

Confrontation issues. What has been said above about self-disclosure also applies to confrontation. You can imagine the problems that could ensue from one leader's practice of harsh and unrelenting confrontations to get members to open up, if the other leader believes in providing support to the exclusion of any confrontation. One leader can easily be labeled as the "good guy," while the confronting one is seen as the "bad guy." If such differences in style exist, they surely need to be talked about at length between the co-leaders if the group is not to suffer.

Summary of Working Stage

Stage characteristics. When a group reaches the working stage, some of the central characteristics include the following:

- The level of trust and cohesion is high.
- Communication within the group is open and involves an accurate expression of what is being experienced.
- Leadership functions are likely to be shared by the group, in that members interact with one another freely and directly.
- There is a willingness to risk threatening material and to make oneself known to others; members bring to the group personal topics they want to discuss and understand better.
- Conflict among members is recognized and dealt with directly and effectively.
- Feedback is given freely and accepted and considered nondefensively.
- Confrontation occurs in a way in which those doing the challenging avoid slapping judgmental labels on others.
- Members are willing to work outside the group to achieve behavioral changes.
- Participants feel supported in their attempts to change and are willing to risk new behavior.
- Members feel hopeful that they can change if they are willing to take action; they do not feel helpless.

Member functions and possible problems. The working stage is characterized by the exploration of personally meaningful material. To reach this stage, members have certain tasks and roles, which include:

- bringing into group sessions issues they are willing to discuss
- being willing to give others feedback and being open to considering feedback from others in the group
- assuming some leadership functions, especially by sharing their personal reactions of how they are affected by others' presence and work in the group
- being willing to practice new skills and behaviors in daily life and to bring the results to the sessions
- offering both challenge and support to others and engaging in self-confrontation
- continually assessing their level of satisfaction with the group and actively taking steps to change their level of involvement in the sessions if necessary

Some problems that may arise with members at this time are:

- Members may form a collusion to relax and enjoy the comfort of familiar relationships and avoid challenging one another.
- Members may gain insights in the sessions but not see the necessity of action outside of group to bring about change.
- Members may withdraw because of anxiety over others' intensity.

Leader functions.   Some of the central leadership functions at this stage are:

- providing systematic reinforcement of desired group behaviors that foster cohesion and productive work
- looking for common themes that provide for some universality and linking one or more members' work with that of others in the group
- continuing to model appropriate behavior, especially caring confrontation; sharing personal reactions; and disclosing ongoing reactions to the group
- supporting the members' willingness to take risks and assisting them in carrying this behavior into their daily living
- interpreting the meaning of behavior patterns at appropriate times so that members will be able to engage in a deeper level of self-exploration and consider alternative behaviors
- being aware of the therapeutic factors that operate to produce change and intervening in such a way as to help members make desired changes in feelings, thoughts, and actions
- focusing on the importance of translating insight into action; encouraging members to practice new skills
- encouraging members to keep in mind what they want from the group and to ask for what they want

---

STAGE 4: FINAL STAGE—CONSOLIDATION AND TERMINATION

Of all the group-leadership skills perhaps none is more important than the capacity to assist members in transferring what they have learned in the group to their outside environments. It is during the termination phase that consolidation of learning occurs; this is a time for summarizing, pulling together loose ends, and integrating and interpreting the group experience.

I see the initial and final stages of a group as the most decisive times in the group's life history. If the initial phase is effective, the participants get to know one another and are able to establish their own identity in the group, an atmosphere of trust develops, and the groundwork is being laid for later intensive work. The final stage of a group's development is critical because it is at this time that members engage in the cognitive work necessary to make decisions regarding what they have learned about themselves in the group situation. If this phase is poorly handled by the group leader, the chances that the members will be able to use what they have learned are greatly reduced. Worse yet, members can be left with unresolved issues and without any direction on how to bring these issues to closure.

It is essential that termination issues be brought up early in the course of a group's history. In every beginning the end is always a reality, and members need periodic reminders from the leader that their group will eventually end. Unless leaders recognize their own feelings about termination and are able to deal with them constructively, however, they are in no position to help members deal with separation issues. Some group leaders find endings difficult, for a variety of reasons, and they tend to ignore feelings of sadness or grief that some will experience as a group comes to an end.

I agree with Shapiro's (1978) view that termination is often the phase of group work that is handled most ineptly by group leaders. He gives as reasons the leader's own needs for reassurance and resistance to terminating the group, as well as his or her lack of training for this especially difficult stage. There is a danger that, as group members become aware that the end of the group is nearing, they will isolate themselves so that they will not have to deal with the anxiety that accompanies separation. Work generally tapers off, and new issues are rarely raised. If members are allowed to distance themselves too much from the group experience, they will fail to examine the possible effects of their in-group experience on their out-of-group behavior. Thus, it is crucial that group leaders help the participants put into meaningful perspective what has occurred in the group.

Effective Ways of Terminating a Group

This section deals with ways of terminating the group experience by exploring questions such as these: How can members best complete any unfinished business? How can members be taught, as they leave the group, to carry what they have learned with them and to use it to deal more effectively with the demands of their daily existence? What are the relevant issues and activities in the closing phases of a group? Because of space limitations, most of my discussion focuses on the termination of a *closed group*—that is, a group that consists of the same members throughout its life and whose termination date has been decided in advance.

Dealing with feelings.   During the final stages of the group, it is a good practice for the leader to remind people that there are only a few sessions remaining, so that members can prepare themselves for the termination of the group and achieve successful closure of the group experience. Members need help in facing the reality that their group will soon end. Feelings about separation, which often take the form of avoidance or denial, need to be fully brought out and explored. It is the leader's job to facilitate an open discussion of the feelings of loss and sadness that accompany the eventual termination of an intense and highly meaningful experience. As Yalom (1975) says, the counselor has the responsibility to keep group members focused on the reality and meaning of the ending of their group. The members can be helped to face separation by the leader's disclosure of his or her own feelings about terminating the group.

During the initial phase, members are often asked to express their fears of *entering* fully into the group. Now, they should be encouraged to share their fears or concerns about *leaving* the group and having to face day-to-day realities without the group's support. It is not uncommon for members to say that they have developed genuine bonds of intimacy and found a trusting and safe place where they could be themselves without fear of rejection and that they dread the prospect of being deprived of this intimacy and support. Also common are concerns of not being able to be as trusting and open with people outside the group. The leader's task is to remind the participants that, if their group has been special—close, caring, and supportive—it did not occur by accident; the members made the choice and the commitment to work together to accomplish what they eventually accomplished. Therefore, they can make similar choices and commitments, and be equally successful, in their relationships outside the group. This "boost of confidence" is not intended to deny the sense of loss and the sadness that may accompany the ending of a group. On the contrary, mourning the separation can be an enriching experience if the members of the group are encouraged to fully express their grief and anxiety.

Preparing for the outside world. During the consolidation stage, group leaders need to prepare the participants to deal with those with whom they live and work. Role playing can be extremely helpful for practicing different ways of responding to the people who are significant in one's life. By trying out new ways of dealing with significant others in a symbolic way through role playing, members can get valuable feedback from others and consider new alternatives.

As Libo (1977) remarks, participants who are leaving a group tend to focus on how they can change others. The focus should instead be on changing oneself. Libo believes that when *you* change, others in your life are likely to change as well. Thus, if you want more affection, you need to be more affectionate. The feedback from the group can help members to concentrate on changing themselves rather than making plans to change others.

Examining the effects of the group on oneself. Toward the end of the group it is useful to give all members an opportunity to put into words what they have learned from the entire group experience and how they intend to apply their increased self-understanding. To be fruitful, this examination must be concrete and specific. Statements such as "This group has been great. I really grew a lot, and I learned a lot about people as well as myself" are so general that the person who made the comments will soon forget *what* specifically was meaningful about the group experience. When someone makes this kind of sweeping statement, the leader can help the person express his or her thoughts and feelings more concretely by asking questions: How has the group been good for you? In what sense have you grown a lot? What do you mean by "great"? What are some of the things you actually learned about others and yourself? I believe that focusing on the specific, conceptualizing, and sharing feelings and impressions increase the chances that members will retain and use what they have learned.

Giving and receiving feedback. The giving and receiving of feedback is one of the crucial processes during the final phases. Although in an effective group people have been sharing their perceptions and feelings at each session, the opportunity to give and receive summary feedback has a value of its own. To help participants take advantage of this opportunity, during one of the last few sessions I generally ask the members to give a brief summary of how they have perceived themselves in the group, what conflicts have become clearer, what were the turning points, what they expect to do with what they have learned, and any other comments that will give others a picture of what the group has meant to them. Then the others in the group give feedback concerning how they have perceived and how they have felt about that person. I have found that concise and concrete feedback that also relates to the hopes and fears that the person has expressed is most valuable. Vague comments such as "I think you're a neat person" are of scarce long-term value. I've found that it is useful to ask members to write down specific feedback in their journals. If they do not record some of the things that people say to them, they tend to forget quickly. If they make a record, they can look at what others told them months later to determine if they are progressing toward their goals.

Completing unfinished business.   Some time needs to be allotted to working through any unfinished business relating to transactions between members or to group process and goals. Even if some issues are not resolved, members should be encouraged to talk about them. For example, a member who has been silent throughout most of the group may state that she never felt safe enough to talk about her real concerns. Although it may be too late to work through this issue to everyone's satisfaction, it is still important to look at it and not leave it dangling.

Carrying the learning further.   I routinely discuss the various ways in which participants can go further with what they've learned in the group. These ways may include participation in other groups, individual counseling, or some other kind of growth experience. Mahler (1969) calls the ending stage of the group a "commencement," for now members can apply what they've learned to future problems and thus give their lives new directions. Also, participation in a successful group generally results in awareness of a number of specific issues. Members are not always able to work through these issues thoroughly; thus, they need to continue the process of exploration by finding other avenues of personal growth.

Co-Leader Issues at the Final Stage

It is critical that co-leaders agree on termination. They need to be in tune with each other about not bringing up new material that can't be dealt with adequately before the end of the group. At times, certain members may have saved up some topics until the very end, almost hoping that there would be no time to explore them; it could be tempting for one of the co-leaders to initiate new work with such a member while the other co-leader is set upon bringing the group to an end.

There are some other specific areas that you and your co-leader can talk about during the final stage to ensure that you are working together to effectively wrap up the group experience. These topics for discussion include:

- Are there any members that either of you is concerned about and any things you might want to say to certain members?
- Are there perceptions and reactions either of you has about the group that would be useful to share with the members before the final session?
- Are both of you able to deal with your own feelings of separation and ending? If not, you may collude with the members by avoiding talking about feelings pertaining to the termination of the group.
- Have both of you given thought to how you can best help members review what they've learned from the group and translate this learning to everyday situations?

Summary of Final Stage

Stage characteristics.   During the final phase of a group, the following characteristics are typically evident:

- There may be some sadness and anxiety over the reality of separation.
- Members are likely to pull back and participate in less intense ways, in anticipation of the ending of the group.
- Members are deciding what courses of action they are likely to take.
- There may be some fears of separation as well as fears about being able to implement in daily life some of what was experienced in the group.
- There is likely to be some feedback: members may express their fears, hopes, and concerns for one another and tell one another how they were experienced.
- Group sessions may be devoted partly to preparing members to meet significant others in everyday life. Role playing and behavioral rehearsal for relating to others more effectively are common.
- Members may be involved in evaluation of the group experience.
- There may be some talk about follow-up meetings or some plan for accountability so that members will be encouraged to carry out their plans for change.

Member functions and possible problems.   The major task facing members during the final stage of a group is consolidating their learnings and transferring what they have learned in the group to their outside environments. This is the time for them to review and put into some cognitive framework the meaning of the group experience. Some tasks for members at this time are:

- to deal with their feelings about separation and termination
- to prepare for generalizing their learnings to everyday life situations
- to give feedback that will give others a better picture of how they are perceived
- to complete any unfinished business, either issues they have brought into the group or issues that pertain to people in the group
- to evaluate the impact of the group
- to make decisions and plans concerning what changes they want to make and how they will go about making them

Some possible problems that can occur at this time are:

- Members may avoid reviewing their experience and fail to put it into some cognitive framework, thus limiting the generalization of their learnings.
- Due to separation anxiety, members may distance themselves.
- Members may consider the group an end in itself and not use it as a way of continuing to grow.

Leader functions. The group leader's central tasks in the consolidation phase are to provide a structure that allows participants to clarify the meaning of their experiences in the group and to assist members in generalizing their learnings from the group to everyday life situations. Group leader tasks at this period include:

- assisting members in dealing with any feelings they might have about termination
- providing members an opportunity to express and deal with any unfinished business within the group
- Reinforcing changes that members have made and ensuring that members have information about resources to enable them to make desired changes
- assisting members in determining how they will apply specific skills in a variety of situations in daily life
- working with members to develop specific contracts and homework assignments as practical ways of making changes
- assisting participants to develop a conceptual framework that will help them understand, integrate, consolidate, and remember what they have learned in the group
- providing opportunities for members to give each other constructive feedback
- reemphasizing the importance of maintaining confidentiality after the group is over

---

POSTGROUP ISSUES: FOLLOW-UP AND EVALUATION

I have stressed the importance of the formation of a group and repeatedly emphasized that the quality of the preparatory activities greatly affects the group's progress through the various stages. Just as important is the work that confronts the leader once the group has come to an end. Two issues are dynamically related to the successful completion of a group's development: follow-up and evaluation. The questions that need to be raised are: What kind of follow-up should be provided after the termination of a group? What is the group leader's responsibility in evaluating the outcomes of a group? How can the leader assist members to evaluate the effectiveness of their group experience?

The Follow-Up Session

It is wise at the final session of a group to decide on a time for a follow-up session to discuss the group experience and put it in perspective. I routinely schedule a follow-up meeting three months after the conclusion of a short-term intensive group. I think that a follow-up session is also of great value for groups that meet over a period of time on a weekly basis. These sessions are valuable not only because they offer the group leader an opportunity to assess the outcomes of the group but also because they give the members the chance to gain a more realistic picture of the impact that the group has had on them and their peers.

At the follow-up session, members can discuss the efforts they have made since the termination of the group to implement their learning in the real world. They can report on the difficulties they have encountered, share the joys and successes they have experienced in life, and recall some of the things that occurred in the group. A follow-up session also provides people with the opportunity to express and work through any afterthoughts or feelings connected with the group experience. At this time the mutual giving of feedback and support is extremely valuable.

I believe that the element of accountability that a follow-up session encourages maximizes the chances of long-lasting benefits from the group experience. Many people have reported that simply knowing that they would be coming together as a group one, two, or three months after the group's termination and that they would be giving a self-report provided the stimulus they needed to stick with their commitments. Finally, the follow-up session offers leaders another opportunity to remind participants that they are responsible for what they become and that, if they hope to change their situation, they must take active steps to do so.

A criticism that Gazda (1978) formulates about short-term time-limited groups is their failure to provide for follow-up. I think that his suggested guidelines for follow-up apply equally well to groups that have met on a weekly basis and to weekend encounter groups. According to Gazda, group leaders are responsible for these follow-up services:

- planning a follow-up session
- becoming acquainted with professionals to whom they can refer group participants when the leaders themselves cannot continue a professional involvement
- informing participants of other sources of assistance

After the termination of a group, some of the participants may seek other avenues to further the process of growth begun in their group. Having been away from the group for some time, the former members may be more amenable to the idea of joining another group or seeking individual counseling to work through certain areas that they believe need further exploration. Thus, the follow-up session is an ideal place to discuss other avenues for continued growth.

Individual Follow-Up Sessions

Besides the whole-group follow-up, I endorse the idea of group leaders' arranging for a one-to-one follow-up session with each member. These postgroup individual interviews, which may last only 20 minutes, help the leader determine the degree to which members have accomplished their goals, because in the individual session members may reveal reactions that they would not share with the entire group. Also, this one-to-one contact tells the participants that the leader is concerned and does care. The individual interview provides ideal opportunities to discuss referral sources and the possible need for further professional involvement—matters that are probably best handled individually. Furthermore, the combination of individual postgroup interviews and a group follow-up session gives leaders much valuable information about the level of effectiveness of the group and provides the opportunity to discuss how future groups could be improved.

Although it is ideal to conduct individual follow-up sessions, I realize that this may not be practical in some settings. In a community mental-health clinic, for example, it might be difficult to arrange for this kind of follow-up. One option is a telephone call.

Evaluating Results

I have referred several times to the need for the leader to evaluate the results of a group. Personally, I find it difficult to objectively assess outcomes by using empirical procedures. I have made attempts at objective assessment by administering a variety of tests and inventories both before and after a group experience to determine the nature and degree of change in participants. But in my experience none of these measures is adequate to detect subtle changes in attitudes, beliefs, feelings, and behavior. Consequently, I have come to rely on subjective measures that include a variety of self-reports.

Rogers' (1970) perspective on research of groups substantiates my view. According to Rogers, a naturalistic study that concentrates on the personal and subjective views of the participants provides the deepest insights into the meaning of the group experience. These self-reports give a picture of both the process and the outcomes from the points of view of the participants. Rogers maintains that this phenomenological type of study "may well be the most fruitful way of advancing our knowledge in these subtle and unknown fields" (1970, p. 133). Some of the subjective procedures I typically rely on to evaluate a group and decide ways to improve future groups involve the use of "reaction papers," individual postgroup interviews, group follow-up meetings, and questionnaires that I mail to participants.

Generally I ask people *before* they enter a group to put down in writing what their current concerns are and what they expect from the group. During the course of the group I strongly encourage members to keep an ongoing journal of their experiences in the group and in their everyday lives between sessions. I'm convinced that this writing process helps participants focus on relevant trends and on the key things they are discovering about themselves and others through group interaction. After the group ends, I ask members to write a couple of reaction papers before our follow-up group meeting. These postgroup papers give participants a chance to recall significant occurrences in the group and provide them with an opportunity to discuss what specifically they liked most and least about the group. Now that the group has ended, participants can evaluate the impact of the group differently. Many people have told me that these postgroup reaction papers are very useful, because they provide the impetus necessary to continue on one's own the work initiated in the group situation. The writing process is a useful tool for self-evaluation and is in itself therapeutic.

Finally, I often give a brief questionnaire that members fill out at the time we come together for the postgroup meeting. The questionnaire relates to members' evaluation of the techniques used, their perceptions of the group leader, the impact of the group on them, and the degree to which they think they have changed because of their participation in the group. The following questions are designed to get information on key matters:

- Did the group have any negative effects on you?
- How has the group influenced you in relation to others?
- Have your changes been lasting so far?

The questionnaire is a good way to get members focused right before the exchange of reactions that occurs in the follow-up session. It, too, provides useful data for evaluating the group.

Postgroup Issues for Co-Leaders

Once the group finally ends, I encourage co-leaders to discuss their experience in leading with each other and attempt to put the entire history of the group into perspective. What follows are some ideas that you might want to explore with your co-leader as a way to integrate your experiences and learnings.

- Discuss the balance of responsibility between the co-leaders. Did one co-leader assume primary responsibility for directing, while the other followed? Did one leader overshadow the other?
- Was one co-leader overly supportive and the other overly confrontive?
- How did your styles of leadership blend, and what effect did this have on the group?
- Did you agree on basic matters such as evaluation of the group's direction and what was needed to keep the group progressing?
- You can talk about what each liked and did not like about leading with the other. You can benefit by a frank discussion of what each of you learned from the other personally and professionally, including weaknesses and strengths, skills, and styles of leading.
- It would be helpful to evaluate each other in addition to evaluating yourselves. Comparing your self-evaluation as a leader with your co-leader's evaluation of you can be of great value. What is especially useful is to be aware of certain areas needing further work; in this way, each of you can grow in your capacity to lead effectively.*
- You both can learn much from talking about and reviewing the turning points in the group. How did the group begin? How did it end? What happened in the group to account for its success or failure? This type of global assessment helps in understanding group process, which can be essential information in leading future groups.

*Group leader evaluation forms and self-evaluation scales are given in the student manual that accompanies this text: *Manual for Theory and Practice of Group Counseling* (second edition), Monterey, California: Brooks/Cole Publishing Company, 1985.

Summary of Postgroup Issues

Member functions and possible problems. After their group is terminated, the members' main functions are applying in-group learnings to an
action program in their daily lives, evaluating the group, and attending some
type of follow-up session (if appropriate). Some key postgroup tasks for members are:

- finding ways of reinforcing themselves so that they will continue with what
  they learned in group
- keeping some record of their changes, including progress and problems,
  so that they can determine the long-term effects of their group experience
- finding ways of continuing with new behaviors through some kind of self-
  directed program for change
- attending an individual session, if it is scheduled, to discuss how well their
  goals were met, or attending a follow-up group session to share with fellow
  members what they have done with their group experience after termination

Some possible problems that can occur at this time are:

- If members have difficulty applying what they learned in the group to
  everyday situations, they might become discouraged and discount the value
  of the group.
- Members may have problems in continuing with new behaviors without
  the supportive environment of the group.
- Members may forget that change demands time, effort, and practice, and
  thus they may not use what they've learned.

Leader functions. The last session of the group is not a signal that the
leader's job is finished, for there are important considerations after termination.
Follow-up and evaluation procedures should be implemented. Leaders have
the following tasks after a group ends:

- offering private consultations if any member should need this service, at
  least on a limited basis to discuss a member's reactions to the group
  experience
- if applicable, providing for a follow-up group session or individual interviews to assess the impact of the group
- finding out about specific referral resources for members who want or need
  further consultation
- encouraging members to find some avenues of continued support and
  challenge so that the ending of the group can mark the beginning of a
  search for self-understanding
- developing an organized approach for evaluating the results of the group
- assisting members to develop contracts that will enable them to make use
  of support systems among the group members and outside the group
- if applicable, meeting with the co-leader to assess the overall effectiveness
  of the group

CONCLUDING COMMENTS

I have mentioned more than once that the stages in the life of a group do not generally flow neatly and predictably in the order described in the last two chapters. In actuality there is considerable overlap between stages, and, once a group moves to an advanced stage of development, there may be temporary regressions to earlier developmental stages.

These chapters have been designed to give you a general idea of the life of a group and of your main functions as a leader at each of the various stages. Knowledge of the major tasks that confront participants and leader during the different phases of the group's evolution allows you to intervene at the right time and with a clear purpose. Knowledge of the group's critical turning points enables you to assist the members in mobilizing their resources, so that they can successfully meet the demands facing them as their group progresses. Knowledge of the typical pattern of groups gives you an overall perspective that enables you to determine which interventions are useful and which ones are not. Also, this perspective allows you to predict certain crises in the life of the group and find ways of resolving these crises successfully.

REFERENCES AND SUGGESTED READINGS FOR PART ONE

American Association for Counseling and Development. *Ethical standards.* Falls Church, Va.: Author, 1981.

American Association for Marriage and Family Therapy. *Code of professional ethics.* Claremont, Calif.: Author, 1975.

American Group Psychotherapy Association. *Guidelines for the training of group psychotherapists.* New York: Author, 1978.

American Mental Health Counselors Association. *Code of ethics for certified clinical mental health counselors.* Falls Church, Va.: Author, 1980.

American Psychiatric Association. *Task force report 1: Encounter groups and psychiatry.* Washington, D.C.: Author, 1970.

American Psychological Association. Guidelines for psychologists conducting growth groups. *American Psychologist*, 1973, 28(10), 933.

American Psychological Association. Ethical principles of psychologists. *American Psychologist*, 1981, 36(6), 633–651.

Arbuckle, D. *Counseling and psychotherapy: An existential-humanistic view.* Boston: Allyn & Bacon, 1975.

Association for Specialists in Group Work. *Ethical guidelines for group leaders.* Falls Church, Va.: Author, 1980.

Association for Specialists in Group Work. *Professional standards for training of group counselors.* Alexandria, Va.: Author, 1983.

Atkinson, D. R., Morten, G., & Sue, D. W. *Counseling American minorities.* Dubuque, Iowa: William C. Brown, 1979.

Bass, S., & Dole, A. Ethical leader practices in sensitivity training for prospective professional psychologists. *Journal Supplement Abstract Series*, 1977, 7(2), 47–66.

Bednar, R. L., & Kaul, T. J. Experiential group research: Current perspectives. In S. L. Garfield & A. E. Bergin (Eds.), *Handbook of psychotherapy and behavior change* (2nd ed.). New York: Wiley, 1978.

Bindrim, P. A report on a nude marathon: The effect of physical nudity upon the practice of interaction in the marathon group. *Psychotherapy: Theory, Research and Practice*, 1968, 5(3), 180–188.

Blustein, D. L. Using informal groups in cross-cultural counseling. *Journal for Specialists in Group Work*, 1982, 7(4), 260–265.

Brodsky, A. M., & Hare-Mustin, R. T. (Eds.). *Women and psychotherapy: An assessment of research and practice.* New York: Guilford Press, 1960.

Bugental, J. F. T. *The search for authenticity: An existential approach to psychotherapy.* New York: Holt, Rinehart & Winston, 1965.

Carkhuff, R. R. *Helping and human relations.* Vol. 1: *Selection and training.* New York: Holt, Rinehart & Winston, 1969. (a)

Carkhuff, R. R. *Helping and human relations.* Vol. 2: *Practice and research.* New York: Holt, Rinehart & Winston, 1969. (b)

Carkhuff, R. R., & Berenson, B. G. *Beyond counseling and therapy* (2nd ed.). New York: Holt, Rinehart & Winston, 1977.

Cole, S. A. Self-help groups. In H. I. Kaplan and B. J. Sadock (Eds.), *Comprehensive group psychotherapy* (2nd ed.). Baltimore: Williams and Wilkins, 1983.

Corey, G. Description of a practicum course in group leadership. *Journal for Specialists in Group Work*, 1981, 6(2), 100–108.

Corey, G. *Case approach to counseling and psychotherapy.* Monterey, Calif.: Brooks/Cole, 1982. (a)

Corey, G. *Theory and practice of counseling and psychotherapy* (2nd ed.). Monterey, Calif.: Brooks/Cole, 1982. (b)

Corey, G. *Manual for theory and practice of counseling and psychotherapy* (2nd ed.). Monterey, Calif.: Brooks/Cole, 1982. (c)

Corey, G. Practical strategies for planning therapy groups. In P. Keller (Ed.), *Innovations in clinical practice: A sourcebook.* Sarasota, Fla.: Professional Resource Exchange, 1982. (d)

Corey, G. Group counseling. In J. A. Brown & R. H. Pate (Eds.), *Being a counselor: Directions and challenges.* Monterey, Calif.: Brooks/Cole, 1983.

Corey, G., & Corey, M. *Groups: Process and practice* (2nd ed.). Monterey, Calif.: Brooks/Cole, 1982.

Corey, G., with Corey, M. *I never knew I had a choice* (2nd ed.). Monterey, Calif.: Brooks/Cole, 1983.

Corey, G., Corey, M., & Callanan, P. In-service training for group leaders in a prison hospital: Problems and prospects. *Journal for Specialists in Group Work,* 1981, 6(3), 130–135.

Corey, G., Corey, M., & Callanan, P. *A casebook of ethical guidelines for group leaders.* Monterey, Calif.: Brooks/Cole, 1982.

Corey, G., Corey, M., & Callanan, P. *Issues and ethics in the helping professions* (2nd ed.). Monterey, Calif.: Brooks/Cole, 1984.

Corey, G., Corey, M., Callanan, P., & Russell, J. M. A residential workshop for personal growth. *Journal for Specialists in Group Work,* 1980, 5(4), 205–215.

Corey, G., Corey, M., Callanan, P., & Russell, J. M. Ethical considerations in using group techniques. *Journal for Specialists in Group Work,* 1982, 7(3), 140–148. (a)

Corey, G., Corey, M., Callanan, P., & Russell, J. M. *Group techniques.* Monterey, Calif.: Brooks/Cole, 1982. (b)

Corlis, R., & Rabe, P. *Psychotherapy from the center: A humanistic view of change and of growth.* Scranton, Pa.: International Textbook, 1969.

Davis, K. L., & Meara, N. M. So you think it is a secret. *Journal for Specialists in Group Work,* 1982, 7(3), 149–153.

Diedrich, R. C., & Dye, H. A. (Eds.). *Group procedures: Purposes, processes, and outcomes.* Boston: Houghton Mifflin, 1972.

Dies, R. R. Current practice in the training of group psychotherapists. *International Journal of Group Psychotherapy,* 1980, 30(2), 169–185.

Dies, R. R., & MacKenzie, K. R. (Eds.). *Advances in group psychotherapy: Integrating research and practice.* New York: International Universities Press, 1983.

Dinkmeyer, D. C., & Muro, J. J. *Group counseling: Theory and practice* (2nd ed.). Itasca, Ill.: Peacock, 1979.

Dinkmeyer, D. C., Pew, W. L., & Dinkmeyer, D. C., Jr. *Adlerian counseling and psychotherapy.* Monterey, Calif.: Brooks/Cole, 1979.

Dyer, W., & Vriend, J. *Counseling techniques that work.* New York: Funk & Wagnalls, 1977.

Egan, G. *Face to face: The small-group experience and interpersonal growth.* Monterey, Calif.: Brooks/Cole, 1973.

Egan, G. *Interpersonal living: A skills/contract approach to human-relations training in groups.* Monterey, Calif.: Brooks/Cole, 1976.

Egan, G. *You and me: The skills of communicating and relating to others.* Monterey, Calif.: Brooks/Cole, 1977.

Egan, G. *The skilled helper* (2nd ed.). Monterey, Calif.: Brooks/Cole, 1982.

Ellis, A. A weekend of rational encounter. In A. Burton (Ed.), *Encounter: The theory and practice of encounter groups.* San Francisco: Jossey-Bass, 1969.

Fried, E. Individuation through group psychotherapy. In C. J. Sage & H. S. Kaplan (Eds.), *Progress in group and family therapy.* New York: Brunner/Mazel, 1972.

Gartner, A., & Riessman, F. *Self-help in the human services.* San Francisco: Jossey-Bass, 1977.

Gazda, G. M. *Group counseling: A developmental approach* (2nd ed.). Boston: Allyn & Bacon, 1978.

Gazda, G. M. (Ed.). *Basic approaches to group psychotherapy and group counseling* (3rd ed.). Springfield, Ill.: Charles C Thomas, 1982.

Gazda, G. M., Asbury, F., Balzer, F., Childers, W., & Walters, R. *Human relations development: A manual for educators* (2nd ed.). Boston: Allyn & Bacon, 1977.

Golembiewski, R. T., & Blumberg, A. (Eds.). *Sensitivity training and the laboratory approach* (3rd ed.). Itasca, Ill.: Peacock, 1977.

Hansen, J. C., Warner, R. W., & Smith, E. M. *Group counseling: Theory and process* (2nd ed.). Chicago: Rand McNally, 1980.

Ivey, A., & Authier, J. *Microcounseling: Innovations in interviewing, counseling, psychotherapy, and psychoeducation* (2nd ed.). Springfield, Ill.: Charles C Thomas, 1978.

Johnson, D. W. *Reaching out: Interpersonal effectiveness and self-actualization* (2nd ed.). Englewood Cliffs, N.J.: Prentice-Hall, 1981.

Johnson, D. W., & Johnson, F. P. *Joining together: Group theory and group skills* (2nd ed.). Englewood Cliffs, N.J.: Prentice-Hall, 1982.

Jourard, S. *Disclosing man to himself.* New York: Van Nostrand Reinhold, 1968.

Jourard, S. *The transparent self* (Rev. ed.). New York: Van Nostrand Reinhold, 1971.

Kopp, S. *If you meet the Buddha on the road, kill him!* New York: Bantam, 1976.

Kottler, J. A. The development of guidelines for training group leaders: A synergistic model. *Journal of Specialists in Group Work,* 1981, 6(3), 125–129.

Kottler, J. A. *Pragmatic group leadership.* Monterey, Calif.: Brooks/Cole, 1983.

Lakin, M. *Interpersonal encounter: Theory and practice in sensitivity training.* New York: McGraw-Hill, 1972.

Levine, B. *Group psychotherapy: Practice and development.* Englewood Cliffs, N.J.: Prentice-Hall, 1979.

Lewis, J. *To be a therapist: The teaching and the learning.* New York: Brunner/Mazel, 1978.

Libo, L. *Is there a life after group?* New York: Anchor Books, 1977.

Lieberman, M. A. Group methods. In F. H. Kanfer & A. P. Goldstein (Eds.), *Helping people change* (2nd ed.). New York: Pergamon Press, 1980.

Lieberman, M. A., & Borman, L. D. *Self-help groups for coping with crisis.* San Francisco: Jossey-Bass, 1979.

Lieberman, M., Yalom, I., & Miles, M. *Encounter groups: First facts.* New York: Basic Books, 1973.

Lowen, A. *Betrayal of the body.* New York: Macmillan, 1967.

Mahler, C. A. *Group counseling in the schools.* Boston: Houghton Mifflin, 1969.

May, R. (Ed.). *Existential psychology.* New York: Random House, 1961.

Merritt, R. E., & Walley, D. D. *The group leader's handbook: Resources, techniques and survival skills.* Champaign, Ill.: Research Press, 1977.

Mintz, E. E. *Marathon groups: Reality and symbol.* New York: Avon, 1972.

Mullan, H., & Rosenbaum, M. *Group psychotherapy: Theory and practice* (2nd ed.). New York: Free Press, 1978.

Napier, R. W., & Gershenfeld, M. K. *Groups: Theory and experience* (2nd ed.). Boston: Houghton Mifflin, 1981.

National Association of Social Workers. *Code of ethics.* Washington, D.C.: Author, 1979.

National Training Laboratory Institute. *Standards for the use of laboratory methods.* Washington, D.C.: Author, 1969.

Nolan, E. Leadership interventions for promoting personal mastery. *Journal for Specialists in Group Work,* 1978, 3(3), 132–138.

Ohlsen, M. M. *Group counseling.* New York: Holt, Rinehart & Winston, 1977.

Pedersen, P., Draguns, J., Lonner, W., & Trimble, J. (Eds.). *Counseling across cultures* (Rev. ed.). Honolulu: University Press of Hawaii, 1981.

Plotkin, R. Confidentiality in group counseling. *APA Monitor,* March 1978, p. 14.

Rogers, C. R. *Client-centered therapy.* Boston: Houghton Mifflin, 1951.

Rogers, C. R. *On becoming a person.* Boston: Houghton Mifflin, 1961.

Rogers, C. R. *Freedom to learn.* Columbus, Ohio: Merrill, 1969.

Rogers, C. R. *Carl Rogers on encounter groups.* New York: Harper & Row, 1970.

Rogers, C. R. *A way of being.* Boston: Houghton Mifflin, 1980.

Rose, S. D. *Group therapy: A behavioral approach.* Englewood Cliffs, N.J.: Prentice-Hall, 1977.

Rosenbaum, M. The responsibility of the group psychotherapy practitioner for a therapeutic rationale. In R. C. Diedrich & H. A. Dye (Eds.), *Group procedures: Purposes, processes, and outcomes.* Boston: Houghton Mifflin, 1972.

Rosenbaum, M. Ethical problems of group psychotherapy. In M. Rosenbaum (Ed.), *Ethics and values in psychotherapy: A guidebook.* New York: Free Press, 1982.

Rosenbaum, M., & Snadowsky, A. *The intensive group experience: A guide.* New York: Collier Macmillan, 1976.

Rudestam, K. E. *Experiential groups in theory and practice.* Monterey, Calif.: Brooks/Cole, 1982.

Schutz, B. M. *Legal liability in psychotherapy.* San Francisco: Jossey-Bass, 1982.

Schutz, W. *Joy: Expanding human awareness.* New York: Grove, 1967.

Schutz, W. *Here comes everybody: Bodymind and encounter culture.* New York: Harper & Row, 1971.

Schutz, W. *Elements of encounter.* Big Sur, Calif.: Joy Press, 1973. (a)

Schutz, W. Encounter. In R. Corsini (Ed.), *Current psychotherapies.* Itasca, Ill.: Peacock, 1973. (b)

Shaffer, J. B., & Galinsky, M. D. *Models of group therapy and sensitivity training.* Englewood Cliffs, N.J.: Prentice-Hall, 1974.

Shapiro, J. L. *Methods of group psychotherapy and encounter: A tradition of innovation.* Itasca, Ill.: Peacock, 1978.

Soloman, L. N., & Berzon, B. (Eds.). *New perspectives on encounter groups.* San Francisco: Jossey-Bass, 1972.

Stevens, J. O. *Awareness: Exploring, experimenting, experiencing.* Moab, Utah: Real People Press, 1971.

Sue, D. W., Bernier, J. E., Durran, A., Feinberg, L., Pedersen, P., Smith, E. J., & Nuttall, E. V. Position paper: Cross-cultural counseling competencies. *The Counseling Psychologist,* 1982, *10*(2), 45–52.

Trotzer, J. *The counselor and the group: Integrating theory, training, and practice.* Monterey, Calif.: Brooks/Cole, 1977.

Truax, C. B., & Carkhuff, R. R. *Toward effective counseling and psychotherapy: Training and practice.* Chicago: Aldine, 1967.

Van Hoose, W., & Kottler, J. *Ethical and legal issues in counseling and psychotherapy.* San Francisco: Jossey-Bass, 1977.

Yalom, I. D. *The theory and practice of group psychotherapy* (2nd ed.). New York: Basic Books, 1975.

Yalom, I. D. *Inpatient group psychotherapy.* New York: Basic Books, 1983.

Zimpfer, D. G. Professional issues. In D. G. Zimpfer (Ed.), *Group work in the helping professions: A bibliography.* Washington, D.C.: Association for Specialists in Group Work, 1976.

PART TWO

Theoretical Approaches to Group Counseling

Leading a group without an explicit theoretical rationale is somewhat like attempting to fly a plane without a map and without instruments. Techniques and procedures must be based on a theoretical model, although group leaders need to formulate their own conception of the group process and develop a personal approach to group work. Some students think of a theoretical model as a rigid structure that prescribes step by step what to do in specific situations. That's not my understanding of theory. I see theory as a set of general guidelines that the group leader can use in his or her practice. A theory is a map that provides direction and guidance in examining one's basic assumptions about human beings, in determining one's goals for the group, in clarifying one's role and functions as a leader, in explaining the group interactions, and in evaluating the outcomes of the group.

Developing a theoretical stance involves more than merely accepting the tenets of any one theory. It is an ongoing process in which group leaders keep questioning the what, how, and why of their practice. I encourage my students to take a critical look at the key concepts of the various theories and to also consider the theorists behind them, since a theory is generally a personal expression of the theorist who developed it. I further encourage my students not to blindly follow any theory in totality, so that they will remain open and seriously consider the unique contributions as well as the limitations of the different approaches. If someone swallows a theory whole, the theory never gets properly digested and integrated. The personal theoretical stance that each therapist needs to develop must be closely related to the therapist's values, beliefs, and personal characteristics. Thus, the first step in developing one's own approach is to come to an increased awareness of self.

I also warn my students of the danger of discarding a theory in its entirety because of one's objections to some aspects of that theory. For example, some students initially see little practical relevance in the psychoanalytic approach. They object to the lengthy period of time required by analysis, they consider the analysis of unconscious material as being beyond their scope of competence, and they typically don't appreciate the anonymous role of the therapist. I encourage these students to examine the model to see what concepts they *can* incorporate. Being critical of certain dimensions doesn't imply closing oneself off prematurely from potentially valuable ideas that a theory has to offer.

When practitioners don't recognize the limitations of any one theory, they are likely to misuse it and to assume that a theory is an axiom as well as a set of proven facts rather than a tool for inquiry. If your theoretical perspective causes you to ignore all others, you may force your clients to fit the confines of your theory instead of using the theory to understand your clients. The problem with adopting a theory in full and buying all of its elements is that one becomes a "true believer." And the problem with true believers is that they severely limit their vision by screening out anything that doesn't fit their preconceived structures. Also, since they assume that their approach contains the whole truth, they are likely to try to impose it on others and to expect the same complete acceptance from them.

In Part One we looked at the various elements that are required for the effective practice of group leadership. In the chapters of Part Two we'll explore ten theoretical approaches to group counseling and examine how these positions influence a leader's actual practice.

6

THE PSYCHOANALYTIC APPROACH

INTRODUCTION

Most of the models of group work that are presented in this textbook have been influenced by psychoanalytic theory. Some of these approaches are basically extensions of the analytic model, others are modifications of analytic concepts and procedures, and some have emerged as a reaction against psychoanalysis. It is fair to say that most theories of group counseling have borrowed some principles and therapeutic techniques from psychoanalysis.

Although many of you, as group counselors, will have neither the training nor the motivation to conduct analytic groups, you can still rely on psychoanalytic concepts as a dimension of your perspective. You may not have the therapeutic skills required for use of those techniques that are designed to uncover unconscious material and that aim at personality reconstruction, yet the basic psychoanalytic concepts *can* become an integral part of your own theoretical approach. For this reason I have included a fairly detailed overview of the psychoanalytic and psychosocial perspectives in this book.

This chapter gives attention to the stages of development in both the individual's life and in the evolution of the life of the analytic group. Although Sigmund Freud made significant contributions to our understanding of the *psychosexual development* of the individual during early childhood, he wrote little about the *psychosocial* influences of human development beyond childhood. Because of this gap, I have given special emphasis to Erik Erikson's (1963, 1982) psychosocial perspective, which provides a comprehensive framework for understanding the individual's basic concerns at each stage of life from infancy through old age. Erikson can be considered a psychoanalyst as well as an ego psychologist who built upon Freudian concepts by continuing the story of human development where Freud left off. As you will see, there are important implications for the practice of group work that grow out of Erikson's psychosocial theory.

Historical Background

In discussing the key concepts and basic techniques that characterize a psychoanalytic group, I draw in this chapter on some of the major themes elaborated by Freud. However, Freud did not translate his basic concepts into the practice of group therapy. He focused on individual psychodynamics and on treatment in the dyadic relationship between a patient and an analyst. As you will see, Freud's ideas and contributions do have implications for the practice of analytic-group therapy.

The first person credited with applying psychoanalytic principles and techniques to groups is Alexander Wolf, a psychiatrist and psychoanalyst. He began working with groups in 1938 because he did not want to turn away patients who needed but could not afford intensive individual therapy. His experiences increased his interest in this approach, and he made it his primary mode of therapy. Wolf stresses psychoanalysis *in* groups (as opposed to psychoanalysis *of* groups), since he has consistently maintained that he does not treat a group. Rather, his focus is on each individual in interaction with other individuals. His approach is aimed at a controlled and systematic regression of the personality in the service of strengthening the ego.

Wolf developed group applications of basic psychoanalytic techniques such as working with transference, free association, dreams, and the historical determinants of present behavior. He stresses the re-creation of the original family, so that members can work through their unresolved problems. Their reactions to fellow members and to the leader are assumed to reveal symbolic clues to the dynamics of their relationships with significant figures from their family of origin. Although these reactions are taken from the *here and now*, there is a constant focus on tracing them back to the early history of the members.

Goal of the Analytic Group

The goal of the analytic process is the restructuring of the client's character and personality system. This goal is achieved by making unconscious conflicts conscious and by examining and exploring this intrapsychic material. Specifically, psychoanalytic groups reenact the family of origin in a symbolic way via the group, so that the historical past of each group member is repeated in the group's presence. Mullan and Rosenbaum (1978) speak of this process as the *regressive-reconstructive* approach to psychoanalytic group therapy. This term refers to the regression into each member's past in order to achieve the therapeutic goal of a reconstructed personality that is characterized by social awareness and the ability to be creatively involved in life. Mullan and Rosenbaum view the group as a "slice of life" that in many respects duplicates the original family. Indeed, the group itself is seen as an evolving family in that the group leader applies understanding to the familylike connections that arise among the members and between the members and the therapist. In this regressive-reconstructive therapy there is a minimum of structure imposed by the leader, and the group is heterogeneous, representing various segments of everyday life. This heterogeneity increases the chances of the group's being a microcosm of society, which will allow for a reexperiencing of conflicts that originated in the family context.

The thrust of analytic groups, according to Kutash and Wolf (1983), rests with the creative growth of the individual ego. They see the term *group therapy* as a misnomer, for the focus is on the individual, not the group. These writers stress that psychoanalysis in groups is a treatment of ailing individuals in a group setting, rather than a treatment of ailing groups. Further, Wolf (1983) asserts that a group's preoccupation with group dynamics, with here-and-now interactions, and with cohesion can distract from the central core of analytic work. He believes that the exploration of intrapsychic processes enables the members to develop a detailed self-understanding of the nature of their submission to the significant people in their nuclear family and to the other members in their current group. Wolf states that the psychoanalytic group sponsors the clients' individuation and nonconformity and the recovery of their lost self.

The Therapeutic Process

The therapeutic process focuses on re-creating, analyzing, discussing, and interpreting past experiences and on working through defenses and resistances that operate at the unconscious level. (*Working-through* is a psychoanalytic concept that refers to repetition of interpretations and overcoming of resistance, thus allowing the client to resolve dysfunctional patterns that originated in childhood and to make choices based on new insights.) Insight and intellectual understanding are important, but the feelings and memories associated with self-understanding are crucial. Because clients need to relive and reconstruct their past and work through repressed conflicts in order to understand how the unconscious affects them in the present, psychoanalytic group therapy is usually a long-term and intensive process.

Most practitioners with a traditional analytic orientation value the anonymous role of the leader, because they believe that such a role encourages members to project toward the leader the feelings they had for significant people in their lives. Many analytically oriented group therapists, however, place less value on the nondisclosing role of the leader and tend to share their personal reactions with the group's members. All analytic and analytically oriented therapists consider the process of analyzing and interpreting transference feelings as the core of the therapeutic process, since it is aimed at achieving insight and personality change.

Advantages of psychodynamic groups. A group format that utilizes psychoanalytic concepts and techniques has some specific advantages over individual analysis:

• Members are able to establish relationships that are similar to those that existed in their own families; this time, however, the relationships occur in a group setting that is safe and conducive to favorable outcomes.

• Group participants have many opportunities to experience transference feelings toward other members and the leader; they can work through these feelings and thus increase their self-understanding.

• Participants can gain more dramatic insight into the ways their defenses and resistances work.

• Dependency on the authority of the therapist is not as great as in individual therapy, for group members also get feedback from other members.

• Group members learn that it is acceptable to have and express intense feelings—feelings that they may have kept out of awareness.

• In the group setting, members have many opportunities to learn about themselves and others, in fact and in fantasy, through interactions with peers as well as with the leader. The material for analysis is available not only in terms of historical recollection but also on the basis of interaction with fellow members.

• The group setting encourages members to examine their projections. It is difficult for them to cling to some of their resistances and distortions when others in the group confront them on the ways that they are misrepresenting reality. Furthermore, observing similar conflicts in others can help ease defensiveness and show them they are not alone. Resistance melts away in the atmosphere of mutual revelation and exploration in a group to a greater extent than is typically true of one-to-one therapy.

• Analysis in groups immediately confronts the idealistic expectation of having an exclusive relationship with the therapist. It fosters a common effort by members to join together to recreate their past so they can become liberated from neurotic and restricting influences from their early childhood. The experience of supporting others and the discovery of universal struggles encourage a fuller range of responses than does individual therapy.

KEY CONCEPTS

Influence of the Past

Psychoanalytic work focuses on the influence of the past as a determinant of current personality functioning. Experiences during the first six years of life are seen as the roots of one's conflicts in the present. Thus, analytic-group work attends to the historical basis of current behavior for the purpose of resolving its persistence in the present.

When I consider the most typical problems and conflicts that one observes in group work, the following come to mind: inability to freely give and accept love; difficulty in recognizing and dealing with feelings such as anger, resentment, rage, hatred, and aggression; the inability to direct one's own life and resolve dependence/independence conflicts; difficulties in accepting one's own sexual identity; and guilt over sexual feelings. According to the Freudian view, these problems of adult living have their origin in early development. Early learning is not irreversible; but, to change its effects, one must become aware of how certain early experiences have contributed to one's present personality structure.

Although practitioners with a psychoanalytic orientation focus on the historical antecedents of current behavior, it is a mistake to assume that they dwell on the past to the exclusion of present concerns. A misconception about psychoanalytic work on the part of many students is that it resembles an archeological venture whose participants are involved almost exclusively in digging out relics from the past. As Locke (1961) points out, psychoanalytic-group work consists of "weaving back and forth between past and present, between present and past" (p. 30). "It is essential that the therapist move back and forth in time, trying always to recapture the past or to see the repetition in the present and to become aware of the early traumatic event which made for the neurotic pattern of the individual today" (p. 31).

Thus, it is essential that participants understand and use historical data in their group work. At the same time, they also need to be aware of the pitfalls of getting lost in their past by recounting endless and irrelevant details of their early experiences. In Wolf's (1963) view, the recital of yesterday's events can be uselessly time consuming and inhibitory of progress. Wolf sees this use of history as essentially a form of resistance, and he suggests that talking about events in one's childhood is not as useful as dealing with the past in relation to here-and-now interactions within the group. He says:

> History has the greatest significance when evoked and recalled by the discovery and analysis of resistance and transference in the moment of their occurrence—that is, when history has a bearing on the present which is meaningful to both the patient and the therapist. The present neurotic behavior is envisioned as a photograph of the *significant* past. Careful scrutiny of the immediate moment will recall pertinent traumatic events [1963, pp. 296–297].*

So present events are the focus, and they are connected with the past by describing the present feeling or thought and relating it to past feelings or thoughts.

The Unconscious

The concept of the unconscious is one of Freud's most significant contributions and is the key to understanding his view of behavior and the problems of personality. From the Freudian perspective, most of human behavior is motivated by forces that are outside the conscious experience. What we do in everyday life is frequently determined by unconscious motives and needs. Painful experiences during early childhood and the feelings associated with them are sealed off from consciousness and buried in the unconscious. The early traumas are such that conscious awareness would cause intolerable anxiety to the child. The child's repression of them does not automatically lift with time, and the client reacts to threats to the repression as if the anxiety associated with the early events would still be intolerable if these were recalled. Thus, the "shadow of the past" haunts the present. But the trauma was intol-

*From "The Psychoanalysis of Groups," by A. Wolf. In M. Rosenbaum and M. Berger (Eds.), *Group Psychotherapy and Group Function*. Copyright © 1963, 1975 by Basic Books, Inc. This and all other quotations from this source are reprinted by permission.

erable only to the *child;* with an adult perspective on the world, the client can handle the memory with relative ease. Therefore, the therapist helps make the unconscious conscious, and the anxiety is *not* intolerable; hence, the client is helped to be free of the tyranny of the past repressions.

Unconscious experiences have a powerful impact on our daily functioning. Indeed, Freud's theory holds that most of our "choices" are not freely made; rather, they are determined by forces within us of which we are not aware. Thus, we select mates to meet certain needs that may have never been satisfied; we select a job because of some unconscious motive; and we continually experience personal and interpersonal conflicts whose roots lie in unfinished experiences that are outside the realm of our awareness.

According to the psychoanalytic theory, consciousness is only a small part of the human experience. Like the greater part of the iceberg that lies below the surface of the water, the larger part of human experience exists below the surface of awareness. The unconscious stores up all of the repressed material. The aim of psychoanalysis is to make the unconscious material conscious, for it is only when we become conscious of the motivations underlying our behavior that we can choose and become autonomous, freeing ourselves from past fears. The unconscious can be made more accessible to awareness by working with dreams, by using free-association methods, by learning about transference, by understanding the meaning of resistances, and by employing the process of interpretation. Analytic therapists move back and forth between reality and fantasy, conscious and unconscious, rational and nonlogical, thought and feeling.

The concept of the unconscious has deep significance for analytic group therapy. The focus on unconscious motives deemphasizes the here and now and interpersonal interactions per se. The emphasis is instead on intrapsychic processes—that is, on dealing with one's own dynamics. This includes focusing on the historical determinants of current behavior, exploring the meaning of dreams and fantasies, dealing with resistances, and working through transference distortions. In the psychoanalytic view, a group that ignores the role of the unconscious and focuses *exclusively* on conscious here-and-now interactions among participants is more an encounter group than a therapy group. Also, denial of the manifestations of the unconscious as it operates in a group makes in-depth work with individual members almost impossible.

Although it is true that exhaustive work with the unconscious determinants of behavior and personality reconstruction is beyond the scope of group counseling as it is generally practiced, I believe that group counselors need to have an understanding of how unconscious processes operate. This understanding provides the counselor with a conceptual framework that helps him or her make sense of the group interactions, even if the unconscious is not directly dealt with by the members.

Anxiety

In order to appreciate the psychoanalytic model, one must understand the dynamics of anxiety. Anxiety is a feeling of dread and impending doom that results from repressed feelings, memories, desires, and experiences bubbling to the surface of awareness. We experience anxiety when we sense that we are dealing with feelings that threaten to be out of our control. Often anxiety is "free-floating"; that is, it is vague and general, not yet having crystallized into specific form.

Wolf (1983) points out that anxiety emerges when defenses or resistances are attacked. He writes that many members experience anxiety over the idea of joining an analytic group. During the course of the group, anxiety is revealed in many ways in the members' interactions. Mullan and Rosenbaum (1978) view anxiety as a necessary part of regressive-reconstructive group therapy. As the defenses of the members are dissolved, the result is the experiencing of anxiety. This anxiety is seen as a necessary by-product of taking risks in the group, a process that eventually leads to constructive changes.

Transference

Transference is a basic concept of the psychoanalytic approach. As you may remember from our earlier discussion, transference refers to the unconscious shifting to the therapist by the client of feelings, attitudes, and fantasies (both positive and negative) that stem from reactions to significant persons from the client's past. The key issue of transference is the distortion imposed on the therapeutic relationship by prior relationships, usually childhood ones. Analytic technique is designed to foster the client's transference. But the therapeutic setting, unlike the original situation, does not punish the person for experiencing or expressing these feelings. If a client perceives the therapist as a stern and rejecting father, he or she does not receive from the therapist the expected negative responses. Instead, the therapist accepts the client's feelings and helps the client understand them.

By reliving their past through the transference process, clients gain insight into the ways in which the past is obstructing present functioning. Insight is achieved by working through unresolved conflicts that keep the person fixated and that make full emotional growth impossible. Basically, the negative effects of painful early experiences are counteracted by working through similar conflicts in the therapeutic setting.

Since transference also manifests itself in groups through the members' attempts to win the approval of the leader, these attempts can be explored to find out whether they reflect the client's need for universal approval and how such a need governs the person's life. Remember that groups can provide a dynamic understanding of how people function in out-of-group situations.

If the transference relationship is poorly handled by the therapist, the client may become resistive to the point that therapeutic progress is arrested. There are therapists who encourage client dependency in order to derive a feeling of power from the extreme need that clients develop for them. The result is often regression to a childlike situation in which the therapist is cast in a parental role. One of the advantages of group therapy is that, because of the presence of other group members, this kind of dependency and concomitant regression are not as likely to occur as in individual therapy.

Multiple transferences.   Group therapy also offers the possibility of multiple transferences. In individual therapy the client's projections are directed toward the therapist alone; in group therapy they are also directed toward other members. The group constellation provides rich possibilities for reenacting past unfinished events, especially when other members stimulate such intense feelings in an individual that he or she "sees" in them a father, mother, spouse, ex-lover, boss, and so on.

The element of rivalry that often exists in a group can also be valuable therapeutic material to explore. Group participants tend to compete for the attention of the leader—a situation reminiscent of earlier times, when they had to vie for their parents' attention with their brothers and sisters. Thus, sibling rivalry can be explored in group as a way of gaining increased awareness of how the participants dealt with competition as children and how their past success or lack of it affects their present interactions with others.

The opportunity that psychoanalytic groups offer for multiple transferences is stressed by several authors. The group is a conducive milieu in which to relive significant past events because "the group of today becomes the family of yesterday" says Locke (1961, p. 102). Wolf (1963) and Wolf and Schwartz (1962) observe that the group members serve as transference figures for other members and that the main work of the analytic group consists of identifying, analyzing, and resolving these projections onto family surrogates in the group. The leader has the task of helping members discover the degree to which they respond to others in the group as if they were their parents or siblings. By interpreting and working through their transferences, participants become increasingly aware of their fixations and deprivations and of the ways in which past events interfere with their ability to appraise and deal with reality.

Mullan and Rosenbaum (1978) call the focusing on and using of transference reactions the "hallmarks of psychoanalysis." These authors also discuss the value of using a male and a female as co-therapists. This arrangement replicates faithfully the original nuclear family and it enables members to reenact early expectations of their father and mother.

Kutash and Wolf (1983) contend that the recognition and resolution of transferences constitute the core of psychoanalysis in groups. They write: "The multiplicity of ways in which a patient dresses up the other members accurately reanimates the old family, disclosing in the action both his history and the richly divergent facets of his personality" (p. 134). In a similar vein, Kolb (1983) states: "The familylike atmosphere of a group setting may provide multiple transferences, as well as a transference to the group as a whole" (p. 41).

Countertransference

I discussed countertransference in Chapter 4 and pointed out that from time to time the therapist's own feelings and needs become entangled in the therapeutic relationship, obstructing or even destroying objectivity. According to psychoanalytic theory, countertransference consists of a therapist's unconscious emotional responses to a client. Its essence lies in the distortion of the therapist's perception of a client's behavior. Thus, group leaders need to be alert to signs of unresolved conflicts within themselves that could interfere with the effective functioning of a group and create a situation in which members are used to satisfy the unfulfilled needs of the leader. If, for example, a group leader has an extreme need to be respected, valued, and confirmed, he or she can become overdependent on the members' approval and reinforcement. The result is that much of what he or she does is designed to please the group members in order to ensure their continued support. Other manifestations of countertransference include:

- seeing oneself in certain clients—overidentifying and overempathizing with them to the point of becoming unable to work effectively with them
- projecting onto clients some traits that one despises in oneself; turning the client into a scapegoat—a person who is not amenable to treatment or someone with whom one simply cannot work
- engaging in seductive behavior and taking advantage of the leader's role to win the special affection of certain group members
- becoming overprotective by being a substitute benign parent

Wolf (1983) makes it clear that no analytic leader is totally free of transference or countertransference involvement. To the degree that countertransference is present, the leader experiences a struggle in objectively understanding a member. Kutash and Wolf (1983) contend that countertransference interferes with group therapy because these reactions deny reality. They describe countertransference as the leader's "unconscious, involuntary, inappropriate, and temporarily gratifying response to the patient's transference demands" (p. 135).

The therapist's unresolved conflicts and repressed needs can seriously interfere with the group process and induce the therapist to abuse his or her position of leadership. Therefore, the analytic approach requires that therapists undergo psychoanalysis to become conscious of their own dynamics and of how these dynamics can get in the way of their therapeutic tasks.

Resistance

In psychoanalytic therapy, *resistance* is defined as the individual's reluctance to bring into conscious awareness threatening unconscious material that has been previously repressed or denied. It can also be viewed as anything that prevents members from dealing with unconscious material, thus keeping the group from making progress. Resistance is the unconscious attempt to defend the self against the high degree of anxiety that the client fears would result if the material in the unconscious were uncovered. As Locke (1961) put it, group members need to protect themselves against the "flooding of the conscious by the forbidden feeling, fantasy, or memory" (p. 72). Resistance is the "fight to maintain the defense"; thus, it is "the defense of the defense."

One method of therapeutically dealing with resistance is through free association; this includes an uncensored and uninhibited flow of ideas produced by the client that offers clues about the person's unconscious conflicts. According to Wolf (1983) and Wolf and Schwartz (1962), resistances emerge with clarity as members continue to free-associate with one another, as they reveal more of themselves, and as old feelings recur in the present. When these defenses surface, they are observed, analyzed, and interpreted. Support offered by the group helps the person break through his or her defenses. Durkin (1964) stresses that resistance is a basic part of the analytic group, and she warns group leaders not to be surprised by or impatient with it. She also warns leaders not to interpret resistance, which is a natural phenomenon of all groups, as a sign of their own ineptness, because such an interpretation would seriously interfere with their task of helping the members break through the resistance so that therapeutic progress can continue.

There are many kinds of resistances, some relating to apprehension about joining a group, some to participation in the group process, and some to the desire to leave the group (Locke, 1961). One common resistance stems from the belief that one cannot benefit from the group situation, because help cannot come from people who are themselves in trouble. Wolf (1963) lists other sources of resistance in group members: fear that one's privacy will be invaded; need to "own" the therapist exclusively; fear of "meeting" again one's original family in the group—namely, recognizing one's parents or siblings in some of the participants—and having to deal with the anxiety produced by these encounters; unconscious fear of giving up neurotic trends; and anxiety about the freedom that a group offers—including the freedom to discuss anxiety.

Wolf (1963) also explores other forms of resistance, which surface during the advanced stages of group analysis. Members may "go blank" when they are asked to free-associate about other group members, or they may escape personal exploration by simply watching others and refusing to participate. Some members hide behind the analysis of other members, and some engage in lengthy recitations of their life histories, thus avoiding the challenge of facing the present. Additional manifestations of resistance include:

- always arriving late or not showing up at all
- maintaining an attitude of complacency or indifference
- hiding behind a wall of silence or talking incessantly
- intellectualizing
- exhibiting an exaggerated need to help others in the group
- showing distrust
- behaving uncooperatively
- acting out
- using the group for mere socializing

These are by no means the only manifestations of resistive behavior; what they all have in common is the fear of recognizing and dealing with that part of oneself that is locked in the unconscious. Avoidance behavior, whatever form it may take, represents the individual's defense against this fear and the anxiety it produces.

How do group analysts deal with resistance? Durkin (1964) maintains that, in order to penetrate and work through resistances, the therapist needs to enlist the cooperation of members. Therefore, he or she must start with the client's immediate problems as they are manifested through resistive behaviors. Durkin stresses the importance of dealing with disappointments and resentments, because members will otherwise become increasingly angry, less desirous of opening up, and more resistant. Thus, resistances are not just something to be overcome. Because they are valuable indications of the client's defenses against anxiety, they should be acknowledged and worked through by therapist and client together, with the clear understanding that they are both working toward the same ends. Generally, it is best to call attention to those manifestations of resistance that are most readily observable and to work with these behaviors first. In doing so, care should be taken not to label or censure group members, because unacceptable criticism will only increase resistive behaviors. It can also be useful to bring other group members into the analysis of individual members' resistances.

BASIC TECHNIQUES

Free Association

The basic tool for uncovering repressed or unconscious material is free association—communicating whatever comes to mind, regardless of how painful, illogical, or irrelevant it may seem. In the group context, members are expected to report feelings immediately, without trying to exercise censorship, and the group discussion is left open to whatever the participants may bring up, instead of revolving around a preestablished theme. Foulkes (1965) refers to this process as "free-floating discussion" or "free group association."

Wolf (1963) describes one adaptation of free association to groups—the so-called "go-around technique," which uses free association to stimulate member interaction. After a good rapport has developed in the conducive atmosphere fostered by sharing dreams and fantasies, members are encouraged to free-associate about each person in the group. Each participant goes around to each of the other members and says the first thing that comes to mind about that person. According to Wolf, the go-around method of free association makes all the members adjunct therapists; that is, instead of remaining passive recipients of the leader's insights, the participants actively contribute to the interpretation of key meanings. Wolf (1963) contends that, if a client "will say whatever comes into his head about another, he will intuitively penetrate a resistive facade and identify underlying attitudes" (p. 289). As a result, inner feelings are revealed, the participants become less guarded, and they often develop the ability to see underlying psychic conflicts. Also, all group members have an opportunity to know how they are viewed by the other participants.

In summary, the purpose of free association in a group is to encourage members to become more spontaneous and to uncover unconscious processes, so that they can achieve keener insights into their psychodynamics. This procedure also promotes a feeling of unity in the group, fosters interaction, and promotes active participation in the group process.

Interpretation

Interpretation is a therapeutic technique used in the analysis of free associations, dreams, resistances, and transference feelings. In making interpretations, the group therapist points out and explains the underlying meaning of behavior as it is manifested by dreams and resistances, as well as by other forms of behavior. Interpretations are designed to accelerate the therapeutic process of uncovering unconscious material. The assumption is that well-timed and accurate interpretations can be used by the client to integrate new data that will lead to new insights. Interpretation is a powerful medicine, and it is a procedure that requires considerable skill on the part of the therapist. If therapists force their interpretations on clients in a dogmatic fashion, clients are likely to close off and become increasingly defensive. If clients are presented with an accurate interpretation at an inappropriate time, they may fight the therapeutic process and resist other therapeutic interventions.

In his discussion of the process of interpretation, Wolf (1983) states that the group leader is alert for ways to help the members translate their behavior into an exploration of hidden material. The leader guides the members in recognizing and exploring their unconscious motivations, and this is done largely by making timely interpretations. Through these leader interpretations, the historical roots of current behavior are brought into consciousness and into the group, where they can be dealt with and explored.

In making interpretations, a few general rules are useful.

• Interpretations that are presented as hypotheses and not as facts are more likely to be considered by clients. For example, Sam keeps making inappropriate interventions when other members express intense feelings and thus causes the others to lose contact with their feelings. The leader finally intervenes and says: "Sam, you seem to want to reassure Julie by trying to convince her that everything will work out for her. I have a hunch that you become uncomfortable when you see a person in pain; so you rush in, trying to take that person's pain away. Could it be that you're trying to avoid painful experiences yourself?" This comment alerts Sam to a possible reason for his in-group behavior. If Sam thinks about the leader's interpretation, he may discover other meanings that he is not now conscious of. Whether he will respond nondefensively has a lot to do with the manner in which the interpretation is made. In this case, the leader's tentative approach doesn't pose a threat and doesn't push Sam into accepting something that he may not be ready to accept.

• Interpretation should deal with material that is close to the client's awareness. In other words, the therapist needs to interpret material that clients have not yet seen for themselves but that they are ready and able to incorporate.

• Interpretation should begin from the surface and go as deep as the client can emotionally tolerate.

• It is best to point out a form of defense or resistance before interpreting the feeling or conflict that lies underneath the defense or resistance.

Interpretations can be directed to the group as a whole as well as to individual participants. For example, group members may be operating under the unspoken agreement that they will be polite and supportive and that they will not challenge one another. By observing the group process and sharing his or her observations with the group, the therapist can be instrumental in helping the members see their hidden motives and reach a deeper level of interaction. Here, too, *how* the leader presents the observations is crucial, and the general guidelines I've outlined for individual interpretations also apply to group interpretations.

Bion's method of interpretation of group process.   The interpretation of the group as a whole was developed by W. R. Bion (1959), a British psychiatrist. Bion provided the group with no direction or structure. As a result of this style of leadership (or lack of it), group members typically grew confused and angry and displayed many other reactions. Bion became more interested in the group's dynamics than in the individual's dynamics; thus, he formulated interpretations of the group as a whole rather than of individual members' reactions.

As he continued to work with groups, Bion observed three basic assumptions that groups develop on their way to becoming a "work group": *dependency, fight-flight,* and *pairing.* The dependency-oriented group attempts to coax the professional leader to do for it what it feels it cannot do for itself. The fight-flight group resists structure by the leader or another member by rebelling against or ignoring the person. Members of the pairing group form dyads and hope that these pairings will do the work that they need to do as individuals. It was Bion's goal to help the participants achieve the ability to function effectively in work groups. Toward this goal, all of his interpretations were group interpretations. He would confront the group members with their behaviors that reflected one of the three basic assumptions. His hope was that, as the members became aware of their unrealistic demands on the group leader and on one another, they would develop more realistic and effective methods of functioning as individuals within the group.

Yalom (1975) gives Bion credit for his contributions to viewing the group as a whole, for his focus on the here-and-now interactions and events within the group, and for his attempt to understand unconscious forces that influence the activity within the group. Although Yalom acknowledges the innovative aspects of Bion's group psychology of the unconscious, he takes a critical view of what he considers to be a highly restricted role of the group leader. In his opinion, there is limited therapeutic effectiveness in groups in which the leader remains impersonal, hidden, and passive and restricts his or her behavior to impersonal group interpretation. Yalom says that a powerful body of research demonstrates the critical role of the relationship in the therapeutic process. Surely this relationship variable was lacking in Bion's approach. Although Yalom does not quarrel with the importance of the group-as-a-whole phenomenon and group-process interpretation, he does contend that the curative factors operating in a group are mediated by other leader activities, including norm-shaping activities. He writes: "What I do strenuously disagree with is a restriction of the therapist role. Interpretation, as I have indicated, does play an important role in therapy, but it is by no means the only ingredient in successful therapy" (p. 188).

Sharing of insights by members.   One of the advantages of the psychoanalytic method in groups is that members are encouraged to share their insights about other participants. This process can be very supportive and can accelerate progress. Even though the members do not systematically make interpretations, leaving that function to the therapist, they can have a deep effect on other members by being direct, unrehearsed, and confrontive. As members become more familiar with one another, they become increasingly able to recognize defensive strategies and offer very perceptive observations. Fellow members' reactions may elicit more consideration and thought than those coming from an expert, but they may also be resisted with more tenacity. Some group therapists are concerned that a member may make inappropriate comments—that is, insights that the person in question is not ready to handle. This concern is somewhat lessened by what typically happens when someone is presented with an insight that is timed poorly or inaccurately: generally the person rejects the insight or in some way discounts it on the ground that it comes from a peer rather than from an expert.

Wolf, Schwartz, McCarty, and Goldberg (1972) observe that the therapist's interpretation of dreams, fantasies, transference, resistance, defensiveness, slips of tongue, and free associations allows the group members to become aware of these phenomena both in themselves and in others. Here too, as in free association, the group members are adjunct therapists as well as patients, for they interpret the manifestations of the unconscious in themselves and in others in the group. Elsewhere Wolf (1963) writes that successful analysts learn to value the useful contribution of the group to mutual insight. The group can greatly benefit from the sharing of interpretations, because "patients sometimes show themselves to be closer to the unconscious truth than their physician" (p. 313).

Dream Analysis

Dream analysis is an essential procedure for uncovering unconscious material. Freud saw dreams as "the royal road to the unconscious," because they express unconscious needs, conflicts, wishes, fears, and repressed experiences. When a dream is shared in a group setting and worked through, the participant gains new insight into the motivations and unresolved problems behind the dream. Some motivations are so unacceptable to the person that they can be expressed only in disguised or symbolic form. Thus, an advantage of working with dreams in a group is that it allows members to deal in a concrete way with feelings and motivations that otherwise they couldn't face. After exploring the various facets and possible meanings of a dream in a supportive group, members may be more willing to accept themselves and explore other unresolved problems that elicit feelings of guilt and shame.

It should be noted that dreams have both a *manifest* (or conscious) content and a *latent* (or hidden) content. The manifest content is the dream as it appears to the dreamer; the latent content consists of the disguised, unconscious motives that represent the hidden meaning of the dream. A psychoanalytic group works at both levels. Since dreams are viewed as the key that unlocks what is buried in the unconscious, the goal is to search for the latent beneath the manifest and to gradually uncover repressed conflicts.

In her article "The Dream in Psychoanalytic Group Therapy," Kolb (1983) takes the position that dreams can be viewed from both an intrapersonal and an interpersonal perspective. She contends that the dream experience itself, often without interpretation, taps unconscious mental activity in a manner unequaled by most other clinical experiences. She adds: "The contributions of the group members provide additional material not only to understand the dream and the dreamer but also to work on and to work out the dynamics of the other contributors from their own associations" (p. 51).

In the first session, group members are told that the sharing of their dreams, fantasies, and free associations is essential to the analysis and understanding of the dynamics behind confused thinking, feeling, and behaving. Even though the therapist may have a great deal of insight into someone's dream, he or she generally gives little analysis during the early stages of a group. Instead, the members are encouraged to offer their own analyses as far as they wish and are able (Mullan & Rosenbaum, 1978).

According to Wolf (1963), the interpretation of dreams is an essential aspect of the analytic process and should continue throughout the various stages of a group. It is an essential technique because the unconscious material that dreams reveal has a liberating effect on the participants. Members are encouraged to interpret and free-associate with one another's dreams in order to reach the deepest levels of interaction. Wolf reports that the entire group becomes "engrossed in dream analysis with its attendant associations, catharsis, sense of liberation and mutuality, all of which contribute toward the group unity which is so important in the first stages of treatment" (p. 287). Wolf stresses the importance of a nonjudgmental attitude on the part of the leader toward the emerging unconscious material. The leader's tolerant approach encourages a similar attitude in the members, and the group soon becomes a new compassionate and supportive family.

Besides their value for unblocking unconscious material from the client's past, according to Locke (1961), dreams also contain a wealth of meaningful material concerning what is going on in the group, since the members' dreams reveal their reactions to the therapist and to the other members and point to multiple transferences. The procedure that Locke uses to analyze dreams in groups consists of having the dreamer report the dream and tell the group what meanings and associations the dream has for him or her. Then the group as a whole responds; other group members give their reactions to the dream and suggest cross-associations. The result is interstimulation within the group.

The exploring of dreams in a group has another valuable aspect. As members analyze the dreams of others and offer their own associations, they also project significant dimensions of themselves. In other words, the group members are both interpreting *and* projecting—a process that often leads to extremely valuable insights. Wishes, fears, and attitudes are revealed as members associate with one another's dreams. One person's dream becomes the dream of the whole group—a process that is the "true essence of dream work in group psychoanalysis" (Locke, 1961, p. 133). Readers interested in a more detailed discussion of dream work in an analytic group are referred to Wolf and Schwartz (1962, pp. 135–161) and to Kolb (1983).

Insight and Working-Through

Insight means awareness of the causes of one's present difficulties. In the psychoanalytic model, insight is also an awareness, intellectual as well as emotional, of the relationship between past experiences and present problems. As clients develop keener insight, they become increasingly able to recognize the many ways in which these core conflicts are manifested, both in the group and in their daily lives. New connections are formed, and dominant themes begin to emerge. For example, if in the course of group work some members discover that they need to please everyone at all costs, they come to see the effects of their need for approval on their lives and the ways in which they seek approval.

But the analytic process doesn't stop at the insight level; working through core problems and conflicts is an essential aspect of analytically oriented group and individual therapy. Thus, if group members hope to change some aspect of their personality, they must work through resistances and old patterns—typically a long and difficult process. Working-through is one of the most complex aspects of analysis, and it requires deep commitment. It is a process that applies to unresolved conflicts, attitudes and needs, resistances, transference feelings toward the leader and other members, and other unfinished business from the past.

The working-through process represents the final phase of the analytic group and results in increased consciousness and integration of self. According to Wolf and Schwartz (1962), the leader, after discovering the dynamics of an individual's problems and symptoms, carefully maps a course of action to deal with them. These authors maintain that participants make progress and change as a result of a cooperative effort between group leader and client within the context of a thoughtful and flexible treatment plan.

It should be mentioned that early conflicts are rarely *completely* worked through. Most individuals may, from time to time, have to deal again with these deeply rooted issues. Thus, it is a mistake to think of working-through as a technique that frees the individual from any vestige of old patterns.

ROLE AND FUNCTIONS OF THE GROUP LEADER

A primary function of analytic-group leaders is to help participants gradually uncover the unconscious determinants of their present behavior. The means by which this function is performed are paying attention to unconscious conflicts, using free-association methods, analyzing the hidden meanings of dreams, interpreting resistance and transference, and assisting members to identify and work through unfinished business that leads to present conflicts. When skillfully handled, this leader role provides a useful model for the members to emulate when responding to one another. Thus, members are expected to share their insights concerning behavior in the group, suggest interpretations, deal confrontively with the resistances they observe, encourage silent members to speak, deal assertively with acting-out behavior, and offer support as others are working through difficult material. In sum, members learn to play a therapeutic role for one another.

In spite of the great variations one finds among psychoanalytically oriented group therapists, most of them have a leadership style that is characterized by objectivity, warm detachment, and relative anonymity. The goal is to foster transference. Some leaders believe that the more anonymous therapists remain, the more do members project onto them their own images of what they expect leaders to be—images that are seen as expressions of the members' unconscious needs. A central task of the leader is to work out and work through these transference distortions—toward the leader as well as other members— as they become manifested in group. As the group interaction increases, the leader has the function of pursuing unconscious motivations in participants and of investigating the historical roots of these motivations through analysis and interpretation. Other functions of the leader include:

- creating a climate that encourages members to express themselves freely
- setting limits to in-group and out-of-group behavior
- giving support when support is therapeutic and the group is not providing it
- helping members to face and deal with resistances within themselves and in the group as a whole
- fostering the members' independence by gradually relinquishing some leadership functions and by encouraging interaction
- attracting the members' attention to the subtle aspects of behavior and, through questions, helping them explore themselves in greater depth

According to Wolf (1983), the most significant function of the group therapist is to promote members' interpersonal relationships beyond the one with the therapist. Wolf suggests that an exclusive involvement with the therapist can insulate the client and lead to a symbiotic relationship. The promoting of interaction with others in the group expands the member's choices and fosters growth.

Other functions and tasks of the leader are identified by Wolf (1963) and Wolf and Schwartz (1962):

- making efforts to acknowledge errors and being secure enough to be willing to transfer some leadership functions to the group when to do so can be therapeutic
- avoiding a dictatorial attitude or a style of leadership aimed at converting members to the leader's point of view
- welcoming manifestations of transference in the group as opportunities for fruitful work
- guiding members toward full awareness and social integration
- seeing the group as a potentially powerful catalytic agent
- recognizing the participants' potential ability to assist in the interpretation and integration of material produced by other members and their capacity to be close to the unconscious truth of one another
- being alert to the individual differences within the group
- employing the skills necessary to resolve intragroup conflict
- maintaining an optimistic attitude when the group falters
- modeling simplicity, honesty, and directness
- setting the tone of emotional freedom by being open about one's own feelings
- watching for destructive alliances within the group

To be able to effectively carry out these many functions, group leaders have the paramount obligation to understand their own dynamics throughout the therapeutic process. To do so, they may need consultation and occasional supervision. Their own personal therapy can be most valuable in helping them recognize signs of countertransference and ways in which their own needs and motivations influence their group work.

As noted earlier, psychoanalytic-group therapists tend to maintain a stance characterized by objectivity, warm detachment, and relative anonymity. Foulkes (1965) refers to the therapist as a "conductor," a participant member who is nondirective yet active. The leader's main function, Foulkes says, "is that of analyst, catalyst, and interpreter" (p. 79). In a similar vein Mullan and Rosenbaum (1978) state that the group leader "maintains an anonymity and privacy about himself and his extra-group life" (p. 129), without, however, hiding his affective and human side. Leaders do not use the group for their own therapy.

Wolf et al. (1972) are representative of those psychoanalytic group practitioners who do focus on the therapist/client relationship and on the importance of the group leader's personal characteristics. After working within the framework of analytic group therapy for many years, Wolf and his associates have come to the conclusion that success depends not only on the theoretical and technical constructs of psychoanalysis but also on the therapist as a person. They assert that the focus of psychoanalysis has gradually shifted from the patient's psychodynamics to the *relationship* between therapist and client:

> We are, rather, committed to the idea that the psychoanalyst as a person enters into the analytic relationship. This does not mean that he gives up his objectivity, his commitment to listening and exploring the patient or making the patient's needs central to the therapeutic experience. What it does mean is that the personality of the psychoanalyst enters globally into the relationship and that there are trans-therapeutic experiences that the patient has in the interaction with the person of the analyst, his philosophy of life, his system of values [1972, p. 52].

FREUD'S AND ERIKSON'S VIEW OF DEVELOPMENTAL STAGES AND ITS IMPLICATIONS FOR GROUP WORK

Introduction

This section of the chapter describes a developmental model that has many important implications for group work. This model is based on Erikson's eight stages of human development and on the Freudian stages of psychosexual development. Note that Erikson did not write for the group practitioner. However, I think that his concept of the developmental crises at each of the life stages has great relevance for group therapy.

Earlier I mentioned the central role that early development plays in psychoanalytic thought. In this section I'll briefly describe the stages of the individual's psychosexual and psychosocial development from birth through late adulthood and the implications of these stages for the practice of group work. In my opinion, a combination of the Freudian *and* psychosocial views of development provides the group leader with the conceptual framework required for understanding trends in development, major developmental tasks at each stage of life, critical needs and their satisfaction or frustration, choice potentials at each stage of life, critical turning points or developmental crises, and the origins of faulty personality development that lead to later personality conflicts.

Freud developed a model for understanding early development, especially its psychosexual aspects. Erikson (1963, 1982) built on and extended Freud's ideas by stressing the psychosocial aspects of development and by carrying his own developmental theory beyond childhood. Although Erikson was intellectually indebted to Freud, he did not accept all of Freud's views. He viewed human development in a more positive light than Freud did and emphasized growth and the rational side of human nature, whereas Freud emphasized the abnormal aspects of development.

Erikson's theory of development holds that *psychosexual* and *psychosocial* growth occur together and that at each stage of life we face the task of establishing an equilibrium between ourselves and our social world. Erikson described development in terms of the entire life span, which he divided into eight stages, each of which is characterized by a specific crisis to be resolved. According to Erikson, each *crisis* represents a *turning point* in life. At these turning points we can either achieve successful resolution of our conflicts and move forward or fail to resolve the conflicts and regress. To a large extent, our lives are the result of the choices we make at each stage.

Implications for group work.   Why describe in detail Erikson's developmental stages? Because I believe that group counselors need to understand the major developmental tasks for various age periods if they are to deal effectively with the concerns of group members. The focus of my presentation is on the influence each of these stages has on the person's current functioning. Therefore, I emphasize how the needs and potential crisis points of the pre-adult stages are often manifested in the problems that adults bring with them to groups.

This conceptual framework is useful for all group leaders, regardless of their theoretical orientation. Irrespective of the model underlying one's group practice, the following questions need to be raised as group work proceeds:

- What are some of the themes that give continuity to this person's life?
- What are his or her ongoing concerns and unresolved conflicts?
- What is the relationship between this individual's current problems and significant events in earlier years?
- What influential factors have shaped the person's character?
- What were the major turning points and crises in the person's life?
- What choices did the individual make at these critical periods, and how did he or she deal with these various crises?
- In what direction does the person seem to be moving now?

Stage 1: Infancy—Trust versus Mistrust

According to Erikson (1963), an infant's basic task is to develop a sense of trust in self, others, and the world. Infancy is a time when the individual needs to count on others and to feel wanted and secure. By being held, caressed, and cared for, the baby learns basic trust.

Freud labeled this period the *oral stage:* sucking the mother's breast satisfies the infant's need for food and pleasure. According to the Freudian psychoanalytic view, the events of this period are extremely important for later development. Infants who don't get enough love and food may later develop greediness and acquisitiveness, because material things become substitutes for what the child really wanted and didn't get—food and love and attention from significant others. Later personality problems that stem from the oral stage include a mistrustful view of the world, a tendency to reject love, fear of loving and trusting, and the inability to establish intimate relationships.

Erikson sees the first year of life in terms of *trust* versus *mistrust.* If the significant others (especially the mother) in an infant's life provide the necessary love and satisfy its physical needs, the infant develops a sense of trust. If, on the other hand, the mother is not responsive to the baby's needs, the infant develops an attitude of mistrust toward the world, especially toward interpersonal relationships. Clearly, infants who feel accepted are in a more favorable position to successfully meet future developmental crises than are those who don't receive adequate nurturing. Children who receive love generally have little difficulty in accepting themselves, whereas children who feel unwanted and unloved tend to experience difficulties in accepting themselves.

Implications for group work. The connection between these ideas and the practice of group psychotherapy seems quite clear. One of the most common problems that people bring to a group is the feeling of being unloved and uncared for and the concomitant acute need for someone who will deeply care and love. Time after time, group members recall early feelings of abandonment, fear, and rejection, and many of them have become fixated on the goal of finding a symbolic "parent" who will accept them. Thus, much of their energy is directed to seeking approval and acceptance; generally, they don't find what they are looking for, because their needs are insatiable. The problem is compounded by the fact that, being unable to trust themselves and others, these individuals are afraid of loving and of forming close relationships.

Group leaders can assist these clients to express the pain they feel and to work through some of the barriers that prevent them from trusting others and fully accepting themselves. Erikson (1968) observed that these clients tend to express their basic mistrust by withdrawing into themselves every time they are at odds with themselves, others, or the world. This withdrawal is most apparent in psychotic individuals, who withdraw to the point that they stop eating and become oblivious to their surroundings. According to Erikson (1968), trust is the way to make contact with such persons:

> What is most radically missing in them can be seen from the fact that, as we attempt to assist them with psychotherapy, we must try to "reach" them with the specific intent of convincing them that they can trust us to trust them and that they can trust themselves [p. 97].

The ultimate goal of therapy is to free oneself of the need of searching for an *ideal* parent "out there" and find what one is seeking inside oneself—becoming one's own parent, so to speak. This goal implies acceptance of the past and the understanding that, no matter how little love one has received from others, love is available in oneself.

Stage 2: Early Childhood—Autonomy versus Shame and Doubt

Freud called the next two years of life the *anal stage*, because the anal zone comes to be of major significance in the formation of personality. The main tasks children must master during this stage include learning independence, accepting personal power, and learning how to express negative feelings such as jealousy, rage, aggression, and destructiveness. Thus, it is at this stage that children begin their journey toward autonomy. They play an increasingly active role in taking care of their own needs and begin to communicate what they want from others. This is also the time when children continually encounter parental demands; they are restricted from fully exploring their environment, and toilet training is being imposed on them. The Freudian view is that parental feelings and attitudes during this stage have significant consequences for later personality development. Compulsive orderliness or extreme messiness have their roots in the ways parents rear children during this time.

From Erikson's viewpoint, the years between 1 and 3 are a time for developing a sense of *autonomy*. Children who don't master the task of gaining some measure of self-control and the ability to cope with the world develop a sense of *shame* and *doubt* about themselves and their adequacy. At this age, children need to explore the world, they need to experiment and test their limits, and they need to be allowed to make mistakes and learn from these mistakes. If parents do too much for their children and try to keep them dependent, they are likely to inhibit the children's autonomy and hamper their capacity to deal with the world successfully.

During the anal stage, children experience feelings of hostility, rage, and aggression. If they are taught, directly or indirectly, that they are bad for merely having these feelings, children soon learn to bottle up these emotions. Having learned that parental love is conditional and that, if they express "negative" feelings, love is going to be withheld, children repress anger and hostility. Thus the process of disowning feelings is set in motion, and it often leads to the inability later in life to accept many of one's own real feelings.

Implications for group work. By understanding the dynamics of this stage of life, the group leader can gain access to a wealth of useful material for group practice. Many of those who seek help in a group have not learned to accept their anger and hatred toward those they love and need to get in touch with the disowned parts of themselves that are at the bottom of these conflicting feelings. In order to do this, they may need to relive and reexperience situations in their distant past in which they began to repress intense feelings. In the safe environment of the group, these individuals can gradually learn ways of expressing their locked-up feelings, and they can work through the guilt associated with some of these emotions. Groups offer many opportunities for catharsis (expressing pent-up feelings) and for relearning.

Another implication of this stage for group work relates to participants who have a limited degree of autonomy and are full of self-doubts. Fearing that they cannot stand alone, these individuals have developed a life-style characterized by leaning on others. These people join a group to reacquire their potential for power and to develop the ability to define who they are and what they are capable of doing—in brief, to gain psychological control of their lives. Here, too, the group situation offers the opportunity to investigate how one's emotionally dependent style originally developed and to learn concrete ways of becoming more self-reliant.

Stage 3: The Preschool Age—Initiative versus Guilt

Freud called the years from 3 to about 6 the *phallic stage*, because during this period sexual activity becomes more intense, the focus of attention is on the genitals, and sexual identity takes form. Preschool children become curious about their bodies; they explore them and experience pleasure from genital stimulation; they show increased interest in the differences between the sexes and ask questions about reproduction. The way in which parents respond, verbally and nonverbally, to their children's emerging sexuality and sexual interest is truly crucial in determining the kinds of attitudes, sexual and otherwise, that their children develop.

Since this is a time of conscience formation, one critical danger is the parental indoctrination of rigid and unrealistic moral attitudes, which can lead to warped conscience development. Also, if the parents manifest a negative attitude toward their children's increased sexual awareness, children learn that their sexual feelings are evil, that their bodies and sexual pleasure are "dirty," and that their curiosity about sexual matters is unacceptable. As a consequence, they become guilty about their natural impulses, afraid of asking questions and thinking for themselves, and prone to blindly accept parental teachings. Sexual feelings and interest in sexual matters become anxiety provoking and are thus repressed. The denial of one's sexuality established at this age is then carried over into adult life and provokes severe conflicts, guilt, remorse, and self-condemnation.

Erikson places more stress on social development than on sexual issues and contends that the basic task of the preschool years is to establish a sense of *competence* and *initiative*. This is the time for becoming psychologically ready to pursue activities of one's own choosing. If children are allowed the freedom to select meaningful activities, they tend to develop a positive outlook characterized by the ability to initiate and follow through. But, if they are not allowed to make at least some of their own decisions or if their choices are ridiculed, they are likely to develop a sense of *guilt* over taking initiative. Typically, they will refrain from taking an active stance and will increasingly let others make decisions for them.

This is a time when adequate role models are extremely important, for children at this age learn much through imitation and identification. If these models are poor ones, the child is kept from learning skills and attitudes necessary for successfully meeting the developmental tasks at future stages of development.

Implications for group work.   Group leaders need to have an understanding of the critical tasks of this period and of the problems that can originate at this age and continue into adulthood. In most therapy and counseling groups, participants struggle with issues related to sex-role identity. Many men and women have incorporated stereotypic notions of what it means to be a man or a woman, and they have consequently repressed many of their feelings that don't fit these stereotypes. A group can be the place where these women and men challenge such restricting views and become more whole.

Because concerns about sexual feelings, attitudes, values, and behavior are often kept private, people feel very much alone with their sexual concerns. Groups offer the chance to openly express these concerns, to correct faulty learning, to work through repressed feelings and events, and to begin to formulate a different view of oneself as a female or male sexual being. Perhaps the most important function of a group is that it gives permission to have feelings and to talk honestly about them.

Stage 4: The School Age—Industry versus Inferiority

Freudians call middle childhood the *latency stage*. After the torrent of sexual impulses of the preceding years, this period is relatively quiescent. There is a relative decline in sexual interests, which are replaced by interests in school, playmates, sports, and a whole range of new activities. Around 6, children begin to reach out for new relationships with others in the environment.

Erikson stresses the active, rather than the latent, aspect of this stage (ages 6–12) and the unique psychosocial tasks that must be met at this time if healthy development is to take place. Children need to expand their understanding of the physical and social worlds and continue to develop appropriate sex-role identities. They must also form a sense of personal values, engage in social tasks, learn to accept people who are different from them, and acquire the basic skills needed for schooling. According to Erikson, the central task of middle childhood is the achievement of a sense of *industry*, and failure to do this results in a sense of *inadequacy* and *inferiority*. Industry refers to setting and achieving goals that are personally meaningful. If children fail at this task, they are unlikely to experience a sense of adequacy as adults, and the subsequent developmental stages will be negatively influenced.

Implications for group work.   The following are some of the problems originating at this stage that group leaders may expect to encounter in their group work:

- a negative self-concept
- feelings of inadequacy relating to learning
- feelings of inferiority in establishing social relationships
- conflicts about values
- confused sex-role identity
- unwillingness to face new challenges
- dependency and lack of initiative

To see how the leader's knowledge of the problems and promises of this period of life can help the therapeutic process, let's look at a participant who suffers from feelings of inferiority. Michelle fears failure so much that she shies away from college because she is convinced that she could never make it. In a group, Michelle can be helped to see possible connections between her current inadequacy feelings and some events that occurred when she was in elementary school. Perhaps she had a series of negative learning experiences, such as being told, openly or not, by her teachers that she was stupid and couldn't learn. Or perhaps she was severely reprimanded for any attempts she made to learn something new. Before Michelle can overcome her inadequacy feelings with regard to the demands of college, she may have to go back to the traumatic events of her childhood, relive them, and express the pain she felt then. Through the support of the group she can experience again many of her buried feelings and begin to put the events of her past in a different perspective. Eventually, she may also come to realize that she doesn't have to wreck her academic career now because of something that happened in grade school.

Stage 5: Adolescence—Identity versus Role Confusion

Adolescence is the stage of transition between childhood and adulthood. It is a time for continually testing limits, for rejecting ties of dependency, and for establishing a new identity. It is most of all a time of conflict, especially the conflict between the desire to break away from parental control and the fear of making independent decisions and living with the consequences.

In Freudian theory, the final psychosexual stage of development, called the *genital stage,* is the longest and extends far beyond adolescence; it begins at the time of puberty and lasts until senility sets in, at which time the individual tends to regress to earlier stages. Although Freud didn't deny the existence of conflict during adolescence, he didn't emphasize it. He maintained that, in spite of societal restrictions and taboos, adolescents can find ways of dealing with their sexual energy by investing it in a variety of socially acceptable activities such as forming friendships, engaging in the arts or in sports, and preparing for a career.

As was mentioned earlier, Freud emphasized the crucial significance of the first five years of life in determining an individual's adult personality. In essence, he saw the developmental period from birth to age 5 as the foundation on which later personality development is built. Thus, he focused on that period and didn't devote much attention to the events of later childhood or to those of adulthood. Erikson picked up where Freud left off and devoted a great deal of attention to the later stages, especially adolescence (ages 12–18), and saw the crisis that characterizes adolescence—the identity crisis—as the most important of all the life crises.

What does Erikson mean by *identity crisis*? He means that most conflicts of the adolescent years are related to the development of a personal identity. Adolescents struggle to define who they are, where they are going, and how they will get there. Because all kinds of changes—physical as well as social— are taking place and because society puts many and diverse pressures on them, many adolescents have difficulty finding a stable identity. They experience pressure from school, from their parents, from their peer group, from members of the other sex, and from society at large, and these demands are often conflicting. In the midst of this turmoil, the adolescent has the task of ultimately deciding where he or she stands in the face of these varying expectations. If the adolescent fails, *role confusion* results, and the person will lack purpose and direction in later years.

Clarifying and integrating one's values into an organic system that is personally meaningful is another difficult and anxiety-filled task of adolescence. In order to develop a personal philosophy of life, adolescents must make key decisions in a broad spectrum of areas—ethics and sexual morals, religious beliefs, life expectations, values in intimate relationships, education, and career, to name just a few. In meeting the challenges of adolescence, young people need adequate models, for most values are learned not by direct instruction but by contact with people who provide inspiration through the example of their lives. And often the models are inadequate or even nonexistent. Adolescents are especially aware of duplicity in adults, and they have a low tolerance for phoniness. They are influenced more by what they observe than by what they are told they *ought* to be.

Implications for group work.   The unresolved problems of adolescence are manifest in many of the problems that adults bring to a group. In most of the groups I've led, one of the most persistent themes is the search for identity: Who am I? How did I get this way? What do I really stand for? Where am I going, and how will I get there? If I get there, what will it ultimately mean? Adults continue to wrestle with identity issues and with the need to clarify these issues. If they failed to achieve a sense of personal identity when they were adolescents, they have difficulties in most areas of their adult lives. Until they recognize the unfinished business that lingers from those early years, they cannot effectively meet the challenges presented by the other stages of life.

Every time I lead a group, I observe how much time needs to be devoted to the resolution of dependence/independence conflicts that are so prevalent in adolescence. In many ways it is as though some of the participants relived their adolescence in the group, and they often go through experiences that they sealed off during that time. For example, they may have allowed others to make all the major decisions for them; now in the group they become conscious of how they have let themselves give up self-direction for the comfort of direction from others. Through a relearning process, they take active steps that gradually lead to taking charge of their own lives.

Group counseling is especially suited for adolescents. It provides a forum in which they can express and explore conflicting feelings and discover that they are not alone in these conflicts. A group context allows open questioning of and/or modification of values and an opportunity to practice communication skills with peers and adults. In a group setting, adolescents can safely experiment with reality, test their limits, express themselves, and be heard. Corey and Corey (1982) offer guidelines for starting an adolescent group and suggestions for maintaining it.

Stage 6: Young Adulthood—Intimacy versus Isolation

In Erikson's view, we enter adulthood after we have mastered the conflicts of adolescence and established a firm personal identity. During the sixth stage— young adulthood (ages 18–35)—our sense of identity is tested again by the challenge of *intimacy* versus *isolation.*

An essential characteristic of the psychologically mature person is the ability to form intimate relationships. In order to achieve true intimacy with others, we need to have confidence in our own identities, because intimacy involves commitment and the ability to share and to give from our own centeredness. The failure to achieve intimacy leads to alienation and isolation. Young adulthood is also a time for focusing on one's interests, for becoming established in an occupation, and for carving out a satisfying life-style. It is a time for dreams and life plans but also a time for productivity.

Implications for group work. For the group counselor, the main issue of this life period that needs to be dealt with relates to creating and maintaining meaningful and nourishing interpersonal relationships. Typically, young adults bring to a group the problems related to adjusting to living with another person and the concerns related to establishing a family. The central struggle of this period is the intimacy crisis—a struggle between the need to maintain a sense of one's own separateness and the need to establish close relationships. The successful resolution of the intimacy crisis involves achieving a balance between taking care of oneself and actively caring for others. Those who fail to strike this balance either focus exclusively on the needs of others, thus neglecting themselves and their own needs, or are so self-centered that they have little room for concern about the welfare of others.

In the groups for adults that I've led, considerable time is typically devoted to exploring the members' priorities. Participants struggle with the many implications of interpersonal intimacy; they talk about their unfulfilled dreams; they question the meaningfulness of their work; they wonder about the future; and they reevaluate the patterns of their lives to determine what changes they need to make. Perhaps the greatest value of a group for people engaged in these struggles is the opportunity to take another look at their dreams and life plans and determine the degree to which their lives reflect these aspirations. If the gap is great, the participants are encouraged to find ways of changing the situation.

Stage 7: Middle Age—Generativity versus Stagnation

The seventh stage (ages 35–60) is characterized by a need to go beyond ourselves and our immediate families and be actually involved with helping and guiding the next generation. The mature years can be one of the most productive periods of our lives, but they can also entail the painful experience of facing the discrepancy between what we set out to accomplish in young adulthood and what we have actually accomplished.

Erikson sees the stimulus for continued growth during this stage in the conflict between *generativity* and *stagnation*. Generativity is a broad concept that is manifested in the ability to love well, work well, and play well. If people fail to achieve a sense of productivity, they begin to stagnate and to die psychologically. When we reach middle age, we become more sharply aware of the inevitability of our own eventual death. This awareness of mortality is one of the central features of the midlife crisis and colors our evaluations of what we are doing with our lives. For the first time, we must deal with the fact that we will not achieve what we believed we were going to achieve—that we have not lived up to our earlier expectations.

Implications for group work. The changes that occur during this life stage and the crises and conflicts that accompany them represent valuable opportunities for group work. Participants are often challenged to make new assessments, new adjustments, and new choices in order to open up new possibilities and reach new levels of meaning. For example, most parents have to adjust to the departure of their children from their lives. If they focused much of their efforts on their children, they now need to look elsewhere for a sense of purpose and self-fulfillment. In groups, participants can explore ways of finding new productive pursuits. Knowledge of adult development allows the group leader to watch for signs of the hopelessness that so many people experience during middle age and to help the person go beyond the destructive view that "that's all there is to life." It takes caring and skilled leadership to inspire people to look for new meanings and to "invent themselves" in novel ways.

Stage 8: Later Life—Integrity versus Despair

The eighth, and last, stage of life confronts the individual with some crucial developmental tasks, such as adjusting to the death of his or her spouse and/ or friends, maintaining outside interests, adjusting to retirement, and accepting losses in physical and sensory capacities. But the central task of the final stage is reviewing the past and drawing conclusions.

According to Erikson, the successful resolution of the core crisis of this stage—the conflict between *integrity* and *despair*—depends on how the person looks back on the past. *Ego integrity* is achieved by those who feel few regrets; they see themselves as having lived productive and worthwhile lives, and they feel that they have coped with their failures as well as their successes. They are not obsessed with what might have been and are able to derive satisfaction from what has been. They see death as a part of the life process and can still find meaning and satisfaction in the time left.

Failure to achieve ego integrity leads to feelings of despair, hopelessness, guilt, resentment, and self-rejection. People with this perspective are constantly aware of unfinished business; they yearn for another chance at life that they know they will never have and cannot accept the thought of dying, because they have wasted their lives. Thus, they are desperate.

Implications for group work. Groups for the elderly are becoming increasingly popular, as Burnside's (1978) excellent book *Working with the Elderly: Group Processes and Techniques* indicates. She describes four common types of groups for the elderly:

- *reality-oriented groups*, which are designed for regressed older persons who have been diagnosed as suffering from chronic brain syndrome
- *remotivation-therapy groups*, which focus on simple matters of daily living and emphasize discussion of specific issues of interest to the participants
- *reminiscing groups*, which are designed to remember and reconstruct the past
- *psychotherapy groups*, which are intended to explore the problems that are common among older people, provide a supportive milieu, enhance a sense of belonging, and offer opportunities for reality testing

Corey and Corey (1982) point out that, to work successfully with the elderly in a group situation, the leader must take into account the basic limitations in their resources for change without adopting a fatalistic attitude that would only reinforce their sense of hopelessness. Those who lead groups for the elderly need to be realistic about what they can expect. Although dramatic personality changes are quite unlikely, change—no matter how small and subtle—does occur and has a meaningful and beneficial impact on the participants.

Burnside (1978) notes that group work with the elderly is characterized by a need for more structure and direction than work with other age groups. Because of the elderly's special physical and psychological problems, group leaders are challenged to devise methods that provide support, encouragement, and empathy. One of the most important elements of group work with the elderly is, in Burnside's opinion, careful and effective communication between leader and members. (For those of you who want to do further reading on the topic of group work with older persons, I recommend Burnside, 1978, and Corey and Corey, 1982.)

The salient issues of this stage of life have implications not only for group leaders who work with older adults but also for those who work with young or middle-aged adults. Often these younger people express the fear of getting older. As they begin to see the years slip by, they feel the increasing pressure of making something of their lives. Some worry about being all alone when they are old, and some are afraid of financial or physical dependency on others. Group leaders can help these people realize that perhaps the only way to deal constructively with these fears is to prepare now for a satisfying life as they grow old. Asking the question "What would you like to be able to say about your life when you reach old age?" is a good way to start. What the members say in answer to this question (to themselves and in group) can dictate the decisions they need to make now and the specific steps they must take in order to achieve a sense of integrity at a later age.

STAGES IN THE DEVELOPMENT OF ANALYTIC GROUPS

The following brief overview of the stages in the progression of analytic groups is based largely on Wolf (1963, 1983), who has identified and described the six stages under discussion. Other sources for this summary include Durkin (1964), Erikson (1963), Foulkes (1965), Glatzer (1978), Kaplan (1967), Kolb (1983), Kutash and Wolf (1983), Mullan and Rosenbaum (1978), Saravay (1978), Whitaker and Lieberman (1964), and Yalom (1975). It should be mentioned that the six stages, which refer to levels of individual as well as group development, blend together; in other words, not every group proceeds along a straight line of development or achieves the highest possible level of differentiation, nor are there any sharp lines of demarcation between the stages (Saravay, 1978; Wolf, 1963).

Stage 1: Preliminary Individual Analysis

Typically, analytic groups consist of eight to ten persons, with a balance of women and men. A heterogeneous group—in terms of different personality structures and disorders, ethnic and sociocultural backgrounds, ages, and educational levels—is usually preferred, because it represents a microcosm of society and offers more opportunities for reproducing the members' original families. However, Wolf (1963) excludes psychopaths, alcoholics, the mentally retarded, and hallucinating psychotics.

Rosenbaum (see Mullan & Rosenbaum, 1978, pp. 64–67) talks about the importance of a person's *suitability* for participation in psychoanalytic-group therapy. The following are deemed to be characteristics that a candidate for analytic group therapy should possess: reality contact, ability to relate interpersonally, flexibility, and the potential to serve as a catalyst for the group.

The psychosocial perspective on individuals also has implications for the developmental stages of a group. Kaplan (1967) proposed that analogues of Erikson's model of human development characterize the evolution of all types of groups. The period of group formation relates to the stage of infancy, in which trust versus mistrust is the central developmental crisis. In this stage, group leaders should be aware that many clients who initially seek out a group are looking for an ideal parent to take care of them and to love them unconditionally. It is hoped that by the termination of the group these members will no longer have the infantile need for such an ideal parent "out there" to protect them because they will have made significant changes in order to become their own ideal parent. Another implication of this stage is the development of trust in the group therapist and the other members. If a climate is created during these early sessions in which members can trust one another, then the demanding work that faces them in later stages is much more likely to be successfully accomplished. If trust as a group does not develop, the group is likely to get bogged down, and productive work will not take place.

Stage 2: Rapport through Interpretation of Dreams and Fantasies

The interpretation of dreams begins during the group's early sessions and continues throughout the history of the group. But it is at this second stage that dream work and free association in connection with dreams are instrumental in developing a climate of trust in the group.

The analytic-group leader also encourages the group to present fantasies and daydreams. Members are asked to avoid censorship of their associations to other members' productions. Through this process, the dreamer's psychodynamics are analyzed as well as the dynamics of those who associate to another's dreams and fantasies (Kutash & Wolf, 1983). Wolf (1983) sees the successful conclusion of this stage as an open sharing of dreams, fantasies, and critical problems.

Stage 3: Interaction through Interpersonal Free Association

The third stage is characterized by intense use of free association—the uncensored communication of thoughts and feelings as they occur. Free association, as I said earlier, is the basic tool for translating repressed and unconscious material. In groups the purpose of the free-association process is to assist members in uncovering their unconscious psychodynamics and to promote unity and positive feelings in the group.

According to Wolf (1983), interaction among members followed by free association typically leads to the recollection of significant early childhood material. The interaction within the group often spontaneously leads to the free association. Through this process, the members' history becomes apparent in the group. The leader may take the lead in helping members free-associate to early derivatives of their past, making clear the ways in which the past is being repeated in the present. However, it is not the leader alone who facilitates interpersonal free association. As Glatzer (1978) observes, fellow members play a significant role in the process during this stage of a group's development. She writes that other members may verbalize for a person when he or she is having difficulty finding words. They may free-associate, introspect, and help inhibited members in various ways to regress to fantasy material. They can also challenge a member to examine and analyze certain behavior when the member is stuck or is repeating the same neurotic pattern. The members look for signs of change in one another, and they may well put pressure on certain members to use the insights they are acquiring to change their behavior. Members often accept interpretations from other members that they might reject if they came from the leader (Kolb, 1983).

From the psychosocial perspective of Erikson (1963), this period of group development is somewhat like the stage of early childhood, in which the individual is struggling to develop a sense of *autonomy*. Just as children need to learn how to recognize and express feelings of hostility, rage, and aggression, so do group members need to learn how certain neurotic patterns that were established at that time are being repeated in the group. Further, the group as a whole must learn how to deal with feelings of hostility and the ambivalence between wanting autonomy and wanting to be taken care of and protected.

Of course, when anger and hostility are overtly expressed by a member at this early stage, anxiety rises in the group. Some members will try to rescue the group leader. Again, what is going on in the group does provide rich material for understanding one's history and how this is connected with present behavior.

Stage 4: Analysis of Resistance

Resistance must be recognized and dealt with if a group is to move forward. It is at this stage that resistances emerge clearly as members continue to work on their dreams and free-associate about the other members. When the defenses have surfaced, they are worked through by analyzing and interpreting the material that reveals their existence.

Kolb (1983) takes the position that the group is a valuable medium for people who wear a heavy character armor. The combined reality testing of the group appears to be more powerful than the individual resistance of any particular member. Wolf (1983) notes that members directly challenge one another's resistive maneuvers and demand an end to them. However, it is also possible for group members to resist by being comfortable with one another and failing to challenge one another's defenses. This can be done by avoiding conflict-laden topics. Members may unconsciously collude to avoid stressful but potentially growth-inducing material (Kutash & Wolf, 1983).

Saravay (1978) describes this time in a group as one of rebellion against the leader. The members achieve a cohesive sense of identity as a group and are internalizing group norms and values. It is during this phase that members may demonstrate resistance in passive/aggressive ways. An exaggerated passivity may settle over the group. The members may withhold material and become overly polite. They may defend themselves with isolation, intellectualization, and displacement by becoming preoccupied with unimportant details about the rules of behavior. This is a critical time in the life of a group, and it takes considerable skill on the leader's part to promote understanding of these forms of resistance. For the group to move ahead, the resistance of individuals and of the group as a whole must be brought out and analyzed.

Stage 5: Analysis of Transference

According to Mullan and Rosenbaum (1978), the recognition, analysis, and interpretation of transference *and* countertransference are perhaps the most distinctive features of analytic groups. Successful group therapy depends to a great extent on dealing effectively with transference and countertransference. It is at the fifth stage that these features become most prominent in the life of a group. Mullan and Rosenbaum contend that it is critical to recognize a member's fear of change as well as the history of trauma that blocked him or her from growth. They suggest that listening in a nonjudgmental way is essential, for doing so promotes a *positive transference.*

At this period in a group, a "working alliance" is ideally being established— that is, a healthy and realistic collaboration between the members and the leader and among the members. Glatzer (1978) contends that the group process stimulates the unfolding of the working alliance in all members. Once the group reaches a high level of cohesion, the members can tolerate amazing amounts of criticism both from other members and the leader. Thus, it appears to be a fruitful time to work through repetitive, primitive patterns (Kolb, 1983).

Saravay (1978) says that at this time members are freer to express affection, and this openness and warmth begin to affect their relationship to the leader. Members are often attracted to the leader's private life. When the leader frustrates their curiosity, this action symbolizes earlier exclusion in the family.

From a psychosocial view, this stage of a group's development could parallel later childhood through the adolescent period. Thus, the task of a group is to develop a sense of initiative, competence, and identity. Not only do the individual members become clearer about their ego boundaries and move forward in the separation/individuation process, but the group as an entity can also assume an identity. At this stage in the evolution of the group, the members have been together for a considerable period of time, and a sense of cohesiveness and shared identity result from the mutual disclosures and explorations that have occurred in the group.

Stage 6: Conscious Personal Action and Social Integration

At the sixth, and final, stage, members can more readily identify their own transferences and contribute to the interpretation of the transferences of others.

In Wolf's (1963) view, when members can analyze and resolve their own transference involvements and can avoid getting caught in other members' countertransferences, they have completed their group work and are ready to leave. A similar point is made by Mullan and Rosenbaum (1978), who say that members are not ready to terminate until there is a sufficient reduction in their transferences toward both the group leader and the other members, even if the process takes several years.

Saravay (1978) states that this terminal phase is characterized by the dissolution of powerful transference distortions operating within the group. At this stage there is a pattern of shared leadership, and a realistic separation/individuation of role has taken place. The group's transference distortions of the leader have been worked through, and the members now view the leader more realistically.

There are some parallels between this stage of group development and Erikson's stages of later adolescence through adulthood. You will recall that the adolescent years are times of struggling for identity and that various levels of adulthood are characterized by finding appropriate roles, developing intimacy, and finding ways of growing and engaging in meaningful life tasks. A group also must discover its identity and begin to branch out.

This final stage of a group's development entails a deepening of genuine cohesion, which, according to Kutash and Wolf (1983), comes about only after the liberation of the suppressed ego in each group member. For this to occur, it is necessary for the individual resistances and transferences to have been worked through.

Wolf et al. (1972) stress two goals for this stage: to help members find more effective ways of relating to other people and to promote the members' personal growth so that they can think independently and stand by themselves. The technique of the *alternate session* has proven quite successful in the pursuit of both these goals. The alternate session takes place, without the group leader, at the home of one of the members. Supposedly these leaderless sessions contribute to an intimate atmosphere that stimulates uninhibited participation. Attitudes and feelings toward the therapist are ventilated and then brought into the regular sessions.

In enumerating the many advantages of the alternate session, Mullan and Rosenbaum (1978) mention development of true cohesion in the group, increase of the creative potential of each member, opportunity to test one's need to act out as well as one's control, enhancement of the group's therapeutic function, and heightened group centeredness. Mullan and Rosenbaum see the leader's absence as requiring a shift of responsibility, a search for new goals and values, different relationship patterns, and mutual efforts to cope with problems—all factors that contribute to greater autonomy in the members. The alternate session also provides ways of testing this newly acquired autonomy, since the participants' ability to function without the leader may be an indication of their readiness to separate from the therapist. Finally, the alternate session can enhance the regular sessions because it attests to the leader's faith in the members' ability to use their own resources within the group to work toward personal action and social integration.

APPLICATIONS OF PSYCHOANALYTIC CONCEPTS TO FAMILY THERAPY

A theme that runs through the writings of many contemporary family theorists is that we tend to bring into our present family the pathological patterns that we acquired in our family of origin. It is helpful for those who are working with family groups to keep a psychoanalytic perspective in the background as a way of understanding the intrapsychic patterns that unfold during family-therapy sessions. For example, a father may keep his own father "alive within him" by treating his children in the same way that he was treated by his father. In many ways he may "become his father" by incorporating his father's dynamics and ways of responding to the world. Further, it may be helpful to be alert for some of the reasons that the family couple were attracted to each other and married to begin with. To what degree did she marry a man to fill the shoes of her father? Did she marry a man who was much like her father, or one who was almost the opposite of her father? What was he looking for in his marriage to her? Is there any sense in which he married his mother? Was he, or is he now, expecting his wife to meet the needs that were frustrated by his mother? In what ways are the mother and father parenting in the same style in which they were reared? Although I want to caution about the dangers of forming hasty impressions and then jumping to conclusions and presenting clients with ill-timed interpretations, at the same time I'd like to suggest the importance of being on the lookout for dynamics that date back to childhood.

This chapter has discussed the dynamics of projection and transference as they operate in groups. Such factors are even more apparent in working with an intact family group. The mother who is extremely harsh with her teenage daughter and who constantly berates her for flaunting her sexuality may be projecting her own unconscious impulses onto her daughter. The therapist could ask himself or herself the questions "Is the mother attributing to her daughter her own secret fantasies and wishes?" "Is the mother still sexually restricted and suffering from guilt that stems from her own childhood experiences in her family?" Again, I do not suggest that, if you're working with such a mother, you make interpretations that are not grounded in clinical evidence. It is helpful, however, to think about what you see going on in a family from a psychodynamic perspective.

Consider the father who adopts an aloof stance with his maturing daughter. At one time she enjoyed physical closeness with him, but as she became more of a woman, she was puzzled and hurt by what appeared to be his rejecting tone. She now misses physical affection with her father and wonders if she did something wrong. Could it be that the father does not know how to express the feelings of tenderness that he has toward her? Is he afraid that his love may be tinged by sexual feelings? Can he recognize any sexual attraction that he might have for his daughter, or does he find some way to deny his feelings? In a related situation, consider the mother who develops hostility toward her sensual and vital daughter, who may be getting most of the father's attention. Is the mother able to handle her own feelings of jealousy? Is she competing with her daughter for the love of her husband? Does seeing her daughter emerging into a vital young woman remind her of what she missed in her own adolescent years? Or does it confront her with her own aging and the loss of certain opportunities that her daughter enjoys?

Therapists of any orientation could well ask themselves to what degree dysfunctional family patterns are the result of the unresolved personal issues of the mother and the father. In family therapy these unfinished situations show up in a repetition of the old patterns within the current family. A major part of the family therapist's challenge is to help all the members eventually become aware of and take responsibility for their projections and see that their family problems may remain as long as they are saddled with psychological vulnerabilities from the past. This approach indicates that one powerful avenue of improving the family as a system is to make some fundamental changes within the personality structure of the parents. As they become aware of unconscious needs and motivations, as they experience old psychic wounds, and as they begin to understand the dynamic connection between their experiences as children and their role as parents, then new possibilities open up for them to initiate some basic changes in their present family situation.

Due to limitations of space, it has been possible to point out only a few of the ideas that can be gleaned from the psychodynamic approach in working with families. If you have an interest in pursuing this topic in more detail, I recommend Meissner's (1978) chapter "The Conceptualization of Marriage and Family Dynamics from a Psychoanalytic Perspective" and Nadelson's (1978) chapter "Marital Therapy from a Psychoanalytic Perspective." Paulino's (1981) excellent book *Psychoanalytic Psychotherapy: Theory, Technique, Therapeutic Relationship and Treatability* is another good resource.

EVALUATION OF THE PSYCHOANALYTIC MODEL

I find the practical application of some of the psychoanalytic methods rather limited, at least in terms of the groups I lead. Probably the factor I find most limiting is the prolonged period of time usually required for effective therapy. But, since I don't have to embrace the theory in totality, there is much in it that I consider of great value. First of all, the analytic model provides me with a conceptual framework that contributes to my understanding of certain factors within the individual that are of crucial importance for a group leader. I need, for example, to consider the individual's past in order to fully understand the origins and functions of his or her present behavior. Many of the conflicts brought to a group are rooted in early childhood experiences. While I'm not advocating that one should become preoccupied with the past—digging it up and then dwelling on it—I think that ignoring the influence of the past leads to superficial group work. I believe that leader and participants need to have an emotional and intellectual understanding of how one's past continues to influence one's present and that such an understanding gives people more control over the influence that the past has on their present life.

Another psychoanalytic concept I use in my group practice is resistance. Even when members are in a group by their own choice, I observe stubborn resistances, especially during the early development of a group. As I indicated earlier, these resistances are manifestations of various fears; unless they are dealt with, they are not going to go away. Therefore, I find it necessary to face the resistances that surface within a group by talking about them and exploring them fully. In fact, I typically ask members to share with the group the ways in which they expect their own resistances to interfere with their group work. Some members seem to know quite well that they will sabotage themselves and resist change by intellectualizing, or by being overly nurturing to fellow members, or by convincing themselves that their problems are really not very pressing. If members recognize their resisting behaviors when they occur, they have a chance to do something about them.

An approach that integrates Freud's psychosexual stages of development with Erikson's psychosocial stages is in my view most useful for understanding key themes in the development of personality. Unless group practitioners have a good grasp of the major tasks and crises of each stage of development, they have little basis for determining whether developmental patterns are normal or abnormal. Also, a synthesis of Freud's and Erikson's theories offers a general framework for recognizing conflicts that participants often explore in groups.

The concepts of transference and countertransference have deep implications for group work. Although not all feelings between members and leader are the result of transference or countertransference, it is necessary for a leader to be able to understand the value and role of these processes. I find the use of the analytic concept of projection quite useful in exploring certain feelings within the group, because projections toward the leader and toward other members are valuable cues to unresolved conflicts within the person that can be fruitfully worked through in the group.

The group can also be used to re-create past life situations that continue to have an impact on the person. In most groups there are individuals who elicit feelings of attraction, anger, competition, avoidance, aggression, and so forth. These feelings may be similar to those the members experienced toward significant people in the past. Thus, members will most likely find symbolic mothers, fathers, siblings, and lovers in their group. These transferences within the group and the intense feelings that often characterize them are fruitful avenues to explore in the context of the group.

Interpretation is an analytic technique that I use with individual clients as well as groups. As I mentioned before, the manner in which interpretations are made and their timing determine their effectiveness as a therapeutic tool. I avoid giving interpretations as dogmatic decrees from "the expert." Instead, I present them in tentative ways, as hunches about an individual's behavior or an event in the group. For example, I don't *tell* Charles that the reason for his hostility toward women is an unresolved Oedipus complex. I don't even tell him—less dogmatically—that there may well be some unfinished situation involving his relationship with his mother or other significant woman. Instead, I ask Charles to consider the possibility that his present attitudes and behavior may be in some way related to some feelings that he had toward a significant woman in his past. Thus, he can consider my hypothesis and determine for himself whether my hunch is correct.

Similarly, there are times when I find it useful to share my observations and hunches about something related to group process—for example, the group's proclivity to deal only with safe topics, with very little risk taking on the part of most members. I'll say something like "Lately I've noticed that people have backed away from the intensity we've had in this group for a while. I wonder whether you've noticed the same thing. If you have, how do you account for it?" This approach allows for the possibility that the participants may not share my impression. But, if they concur with me, they are encouraged to find the reason for themselves. For example, they may discover that they are frightened of the group interaction's intensity and feel a need to become less involved for a while. If they have no suggestions, I am likely to offer my own interpretation, with the understanding that it is only a hunch. Most likely, the participants will react to it and, more often than not, suggest other factors that in their views account for the problem.

Dealing with anxiety, another psychoanalytic concept, and the defenses against anxiety provides a useful framework for intense group work. Typically, patterns of defenses and defensive styles can be observed in any group. Thus, members have the opportunity to challenge some of their defensive strategies, and, in the process of learning how to communicate in nondefensive ways, they can also learn much about themselves. The group thus provides a place where defenses can be experienced and recognized and where one can learn new ways of responding.

Through participation at conventions and analytically oriented workshops, I have learned that many practitioners trained in classical psychoanalysis modify analytic concepts and techniques to fit group situations. I've encountered a number of therapists who think in psychoanalytic terms but draw on other therapeutic models to work with analytic concepts such as the unconscious, defenses, resistances, transference and countertransference, and the significance of the past. They also borrow techniques from other approaches, effectively integrating these techniques into their psychoanalytic perspective.

For those of you who are interested in attending workshops in psychoanalytic groups for training purposes, perhaps the best contact is the American Group Psychotherapy Association, Inc., 1995 Broadway, 14th Floor, New York, NY 10023. Each February it sponsors a conference that entails two-day workshops in psychodynamic groups (and other group orientations as well), and full-day and half-day workshops, many of which are directed toward issues of interest to psychodynamic practitioners. The AGPA does have a student-member category.

QUESTIONS FOR REFLECTION AND DISCUSSION

1. To what extent do you think that psychoanalytic groups are designed for and appropriate for all sociocultural and socioeconomic groups? For what populations do you think such groups are best suited? In what cases do you think these groups are not suitable?
2. Compare and contrast psychoanalysis in groups with one-to-one therapy. What are some advantages of group analysis over the dyadic situation? What are some limitations and disadvantages?

3. What are your thoughts about alternate sessions as a supplement to regular sessions with the leader? What is the rationale for a group meeting without the leader? What values do you see in this method? What are some possible problems involved in alternate sessions?

4. In general, psychoanalytic groups focus on the intrapsychic dynamics of the individual, and there is emphasis on relating everything that occurs in the group to historical determinants. What do you think of this focus on the individual's dynamics? What are some advantages and disadvantages of such a focus?

5. The psychoanalytic group in some ways replicates the original family of the members. Emphasis is put on recognizing and exploring multiple transferences in a group as a way of dealing with early familial issues. What are the possibilities of such a focus? How can a group demonstrate ways in which an individual reacted to significant figures in his or her family as a child? To what degree do you think doing this can be an emotionally corrective experience?

6. Review the psychosexual and psychosocial stages of human development, which consist of an integration of Freud's and Erikson's ideas. How do these stages apply to you? Are there any critical turning points in your life that have an impact on who you are today? What applications of this developmental framework do you see for group counseling?

7. What do you imagine it would be like for you to be a member of a psychoanalytic group? Knowing what you do of yourself, what resistances might you experience? How would you manifest your resistance? How do you think that you'd deal in a group with your resistance?

8. What concepts and techniques from the psychoanalytic approach would you be most interested in incorporating into your style of group leadership?

9. From an analytic perspective, therapists are not totally free of countertransference reactions. As a group leader, are such reactions likely to interfere with your objectivity in understanding certain members and in dealing with them therapeutically? What kind of members do you think you'd have the greatest difficulty in working with therapeutically? What specific behaviors of members are most likely to trigger irrational responses in you and thus distort your ability to function effectively as an objective leader? How do you see your reactions to certain types of members as related to your own unresolved personal issues?

10. Psychoanalytic-group leaders tend to maintain a stance characterized by objectivity, warm detachment, and relative anonymity. What do you think of this style and role of a group leader? What are your reactions to Kolb's (1983) statement pertaining to self-disclosure by group leaders? "My personal opinion is that self-disclosure is appropriate inasfar as it fills the gap in the patient's presenting problem. However, self-disclosure without therapeutic reflection seems to me to be the other side of the coin—a narcissistic, omnipotent leadership attitude" (p. 48). To what degree do you agree or disagree with this view of leader self-disclosure? How comfortable are you with the stance and role of analytic leaders, and to what degree would you want to assume such a stance?

RECOMMENDED SUPPLEMENTARY READINGS

Psychoanalysis in groups (Wolf & Schwartz, 1962) offers an excellent overview of the stages of development of an analytic group, the role of the group analyst, and the practical aspects of the analytic group process. This book also discusses the alternate session, acting out, dreams, working-through, and the misuse of the group.

Beyond the couch: Dialogues in teaching and learning psychoanalysis in groups (Wolf, Schwartz, McCarty, & Goldberg, 1970) presents basic psychoanalytic concepts that apply to the theory and technique of analytic groups. Specific issues such as the training experience, the alternate session, extragroup socialization, transferences in the group, the nature of supervision, transference theory, and termination are explored.

Group psychotherapy: Theory and practice (Mullan & Rosenbaum, 1978) is written mainly from a psychoanalytic perspective. Part II deals with the psychoanalytic method and innovations. Stages of group development, the alternate session, conceptual foundations of the analytic group, transference and countertransference, and the group organization are a few of the topics covered. I highly recommend this book for both beginning and advanced group practitioners.

The International Journal of Group Psychotherapy is the official publication of the American Group Psychotherapy Association, Inc. It is published quarterly by International Universities Press, Inc., 315 Fifth Avenue, New York, NY 10016. Membership in the American Group Psychotherapy Association includes a subscription to this journal. Write to the American Group Psychotherapy Association, 1995 Broadway, 14th Floor, New York, NY 10023 for a membership application. This is an excellent journal, which emphasizes articles dealing with the theory and practice of psychoanalytic groups. The AGPA has a student-member category.

REFERENCES AND SUGGESTED READINGS*

Ackerman, N. W. Psychoanalysis and group psychotherapy. In M. Rosenbaum & M. Berger (Eds.), *Group psychotherapy and group function.* New York: Basic Books, 1963.

Arlow, J. A. Psychoanalysis. In R. J. Corsini (Ed.), *Current psychotherapies* (2nd ed.). Itasca, Ill.: Peacock, 1979.

Baruch, D. *One little boy.* New York: Dell (Delta), 1964.

Battegay, R. The value of analytic self-experience groups in the training of psychotherapists. *International Journal of Group Psychotherapy,* 1983, *33*(2), 199–213.

Bion, W. R. *Experience in groups and other papers.* New York: Basic Books, 1959.

Blum, G. *Psychoanalytic theories of personality.* New York: McGraw-Hill, 1953.

*Brenner, C. *An elementary textbook of psychoanalysis* (Rev. ed.). Garden City, N.Y.: Anchor Press, 1974.

Burnside, I. M. (Ed.). *Working with the elderly: Group processes and techniques.* North Scituate, Mass.: Duxbury, 1978.

Corey, G. *I never knew I had a choice* (2nd ed.). Monterey, Calif.: Brooks/Cole, 1983.

Corey, G., & Corey, M. S. *Groups: Process and practice* (2nd ed.). Monterey, Calif.: Brooks/Cole, 1982.

*Durkin, H. *The group in depth.* New York: International Universities Press, 1964.

*Erikson, E. *Childhood and society* (2nd ed.). New York: Norton, 1963.

*Erikson, E. H. *Insight and responsibility: Lectures on the ethical implications of psychoanalytic insight.* New York: Norton, 1964.

Erikson, E. H. *Identity: Youth and crisis.* New York: Norton, 1968.

Erikson, E. H. *The life cycle completed.* New York: Norton, 1982.

Foulkes, S. H. *Therapeutic group analysis.* New York: International Universities Press, 1965.

*Books and articles marked with an asterisk are suggested for further study.

Foulkes, S. H., & Anthony, E. J. *Group psychotherapy: The psychoanalytic approach* (2nd ed.). London: Penguin Books, 1965.

Freud, S. *Group psychology and the analysis of the ego.* London: Hogarth, 1948.

Freud, S. *An outline of psychoanalysis.* New York: Norton, 1949.

Freud, S. *The interpretation of dreams.* New York: Basic Books, 1955.

Freud, S. *The sexual enlightenment of children.* New York: Collier, 1963.

Glatzer, H. T. The working alliance in analytic group psychotherapy. *International Journal of Group Psychotherapy*, 1978, *28*(2), 147–161.

Goldman, G. D., & Milman, D. S. *Psychoanalytic psychotherapy.* Reading, Mass.: Addison-Wesley, 1978.

*Hall, C. S. *A primer of Freudian psychology.* New York: New American Library, 1954.

Hedges, L. E. *Listening perspectives in psychotherapy.* New York: Jason Aronson, 1983.

Johnson, J. A. *Group therapy: A practical approach.* New York: McGraw-Hill, 1963.

Kaplan, S. R. Therapy groups and training groups: Similarities and differences. *International Journal of Group Psychotherapy*, 1967, *17*, 473–504.

*Kolb, G. E. The dream in psychoanalytic group therapy. *International Journal of Group Psychotherapy*, 1983, *33*(1), 41–52.

*Kutash, I. L., & Wolf, A. Recent advances in psychoanalysis in groups. In H. I. Kaplan & B. J. Sadock (Eds.), *Comprehensive group psychotherapy* (2nd ed.). Baltimore: Williams and Wilkins, 1983.

Langs, R. L. *The techniques of psychoanalytic psychotherapy* (Vol. 1). New York: Jason Aronson, 1973.

Locke, N. *Group psychoanalysis: Theory and technique.* New York: New York University Press, 1961.

*Malcolm, J. *Psychoanalysis: The impossible profession.* New York: Random House (Vintage Books), 1981.

Meissner, W. W. The conceptualization of marriage and family dynamics from a psychoanalytic perspective. In T. J. Paulino & B. S. McCrady (Eds.), *Marriage and marital therapy: Psychoanalytic, behavioral and systems theory perspectives.* New York: Brunner/Mazel, 1978.

*Mullan, H., & Rosenbaum, M. *Group psychotherapy: Theory and practice* (2nd ed.). New York: Free Press, 1978.

Nadelson, C. C. Marital therapy from a psychoanalytic perspective. In T. J. Paulino & B. S. McCrady (Eds.), *Marriage and marital therapy: Psychoanalytic, behavioral and systems theory perspectives.* New York: Brunner/Mazel, 1978.

*Paulino, T. J. *Psychoanalytic psychotherapy: Theory, technique, therapeutic relationship and treatability.* New York: Brunner/Mazel, 1981.

*Pines, M. Psychoanalysis and group analysis. *International Journal of Group Psychotherapy*, 1983, *33*(2), 155–170.

Rosenbaum, M. Group psychotherapy. In M. Rosenbaum & A. Snadowsky (Eds.), *The intensive group experience.* New York: Free Press, 1976.

*Saravay, S. M. A psychoanalytic theory of group development. *International Journal of Group Psychotherapy*, 1978, *28*(4), 481–507.

Slavson, S. R. Freud's contributions to group psychotherapy. In H. M. Ruitenbeek (Ed.), *Group therapy today: Styles, methods, and techniques.* New York: Atherton, 1969.

Whitaker, D. S., & Lieberman, M. A. *Psychotherapy through the group process.* New York: Atherton, 1964.

*Wolf, A. The psychoanalysis of groups. In M. Rosenbaum & M. Berger (Eds.), *Group psychotherapy and group function.* New York: Basic Books, 1963.

Wolf, A. Psychoanalysis in groups. In G. M. Gazda (Ed.), *Basic approaches to group psychotherapy and group counseling* (2nd ed.). Springfield, Ill.: Charles C Thomas, 1975.

*Wolf, A. Psychoanalysis in groups. In H. I. Kaplan & B. J. Sadock (Eds.), *Comprehensive group psychotherapy* (2nd ed.). Baltimore: Williams and Wilkins, 1983.

*Wolf, A., & Schwartz, E. K. *Psychoanalysis in groups.* New York: Grune & Stratton, 1962.

*Wolf, A., Schwartz, E. K., McCarty, G. J., & Goldberg, I. A. *Beyond the couch: Dialogues in teaching and learning psychoanalysis in groups.* New York: Science House, 1970.

*Wolf, A., Schwartz, E. K., McCarty, G. J., & Goldberg, I. A. Psychoanalysis in groups: Contrasts with other group therapies. In C. J. Sager & H. S. Kaplan (Eds.), *Progress in group and family therapy.* New York: Brunner/Mazel, 1972.

*Wong, N. Fundamental psychoanalytic concepts: Past and present understanding of their applicability to group psychotherapy. *International Journal of Group Psychotherapy,* 1983, *33*(2), 171–191.

Yalom, I. D. *The theory and practice of group psychotherapy* (2nd ed.). New York: Basic Books, 1975.

*Yalom, I. D. *Inpatient group psychotherapy.* New York: Basic Books, 1983.

7

ADLERIAN GROUP COUNSELING

INTRODUCTION

While Sigmund Freud was developing his system of psychoanalysis, a number of other psychiatrists also interested in the psychoanalytic approach were studying the human personality independently. Two of these were Alfred Adler and Carl Jung. These three thinkers attempted to collaborate, but it became evident that Freud's basic concepts of sexuality and biological determinism were unacceptable to Adler and Jung. After eight to ten years of collaboration the three parted company, with Freud taking the position that the others had deserted him.

Later, a number of psychoanalysts deviated from Freud's position. Some of them, notably Karen Horney, Harry Stack Sullivan, and Erich Fromm, essentially became Adlerians in that their system, like Adler's, was strongly social in nature in contrast to Freud's biological (instinctual) emphasis. Even though the positions of Sullivan, Horney, and Fromm are usually called neo-analytic, it would be more logical, as Heinz Ansbacher has suggested, to call them neo-Adlerian, since they moved away from Freud's deterministic point of view and toward Adler's antideterministic view of human nature.

Another major difference between Freud and Adler involves the populations with which they worked. Freud focused on the individual psychodynamics of a neurotic population, and Freudian psychoanalysis was largely confined to more affluent people in individual psychotherapy. By contrast, Adler was a politically and socially oriented psychiatrist who showed a great deal of concern for the common person; part of his mission was to bring psychotherapy to the working class and to translate psychological concepts into practical methods for helping a varied population meet the challenges of life.

Because of Adler's basic assumption of the all-important *social* nature of human beings, he was interested in working with clients in a group context. Dinkmeyer (1975) provides a good summary of the major thrust of the Adlerian group model:

> The Adlerian approach places emphasis upon winning the patient's cooperation and helping him anticipate success. The psychological investigation which occurs in the group involves exploration of the family atmosphere, family constellation, and subjective interpretation of the approach to the life tasks. Concern is given to the individual's complaints, problems, and feelings; interpretations are made primarily about his motives, intentions, and goals. Reorientation occurs most effectively as the client is confronted with the mirror technique wherein he sees his goals and techniques and becomes aware of his power to make decisions [p. 226].

Adler's contributions to counseling, especially group counseling, are discussed in this separate chapter because of the far-reaching implications of his work and because of the renewed interest in Adlerian theory and practice. Allen (1971a) writes that Adler's system

> is attracting great attention, and the number of practitioners operating according to its tenets is growing rapidly. From a mere handful of adherents in this country a few decades ago, the number of its followers has grown into the thousands with some observers claiming as many as 20,000 laymen and professionals employing Adlerian techniques [p. 3].

The resurgence of interest in Adler's work is attested to by the increasing number of national and international institutes and societies that offer training in Adlerian techniques, including Adlerian group counseling. According to Manaster and Corsini (1982), as of 1977 there were Adlerian organizations in Austria, Denmark, France, Germany, Great Britain, Greece, Israel, Italy, the Netherlands, Switzerland, and the United States. In North America, there are the North American Society of Adlerian Psychology and about a dozen state or regional associations. Dinkmeyer, Pew, and Dinkmeyer (1979) give the addresses of 65 training institutes, societies, and family-education organizations, all in the United States. These authors also discuss the applications of Adlerian principles to group work with a wide population—very young children, older children, adolescents, college students, and adults. They also describe the application of the Adlerian approach to group counseling for teachers, to parent- and family-education groups, to family-therapy groups, and to marriage counseling.

KEY CONCEPTS

Overview of the Adlerian View of the Person

Adler's system emphasizes the social determinants, rather than the biological aspects, of behavior, its goal directedness, and its purposeful nature. This "socio-teleological" approach implies that people are primarily social beings motivated by social forces and striving to achieve certain goals. Paramount is the striving for significance, "a movement toward the fulfillment of the goal to achieve unique identity and to belong" (Dinkmeyer et al., 1979, p. 14). The search for significance is related to our basic feelings of inferiority with regard to others, which motivate us to strive for mastery, superiority, power, and— ultimately—perfection. Feelings of inferiority can thus be the wellspring of creativity; perfection, not pleasure, is the goal of life.

Freud's historical-causal approach saw behavior as governed by forces within us that are outside our control. Adler's system, instead, stresses self-determination and consciousness (rather than the unconscious) as the center of personality. We are not the victims of fate but creative, active, choice-making beings whose every action has purpose and meaning. Behavior can be understood only if one takes a holistic approach and looks at all actions from the perspective of the individual's chosen style of life. Each of us has a unique life-style, which develops in our early childhood to compensate for and overcome some perceived inferiority and which influences our experience of life and our interactions with others. Our life-styles consist of our views about ourselves and the world and of the distinctive behaviors in which we engage to pursue our goals.

Because of its stress on responsibility, on the striving for superiority, and on the search for value and meaning in life, Adler's approach is basically a growth model. Adlerians reject the idea that some individuals are psychologically "sick" and in need of a "cure." Instead, they view their work as teaching people better ways to meet the challenges of life tasks, providing direction, and offering encouragement to those who are discouraged.

Holism

The Adlerian approach, also known as *individual psychology*, is based on a holistic view of the person. The word *individual* does not imply a focus on the individual as opposed to persons in groups. Rather, it means that the person is viewed as a unity, or an indivisible whole. Since humans are not divided into discrete parts, personality is unified and can be understood only when regarded as a whole. One implication of this view is that the client is seen as an integral part of a social system. There tends to be more focus on interpersonal factors than on intrapersonal ones. The therapist is oriented toward understanding the client's social situation and the attitudes he or she has about it. Viewing people in relationship to social systems is basic to group and family therapy.

Creativity and Choice

From the Adlerian perspective, humans are not merely determined by heredity and environment. Instead, they have the capacity to influence and create events. Adler believed that *what* we are born with is not crucial, but rather the *use* we make of our natural endowment. Adlerians do recognize the fact that there are biological and environmental conditions that limit our capacity to choose and to create. Although they reject the deterministic stance of Freud, they do not go to the other extreme by maintaining that individuals can become whatever they want. The Adlerian position is that within the framework of limitations we have a wide range of choices open to us. Manaster and Corsini (1982) write that we are self-made and therefore must take credit for our personality:

> Life is simply not determined by heredity and environment: the individual has choice, has freedom of will. We are not simply pawns in a complicated calculus of factors beyond ourselves. We are thinking units who, although caught in the web of influences of biology and society, nevertheless can extricate ourselves and move around freely and self-directed. We have a unique capacity among living creatures to determine our destiny to a considerable extent [p. 12].

It is clear that from the Adlerian viewpoint healthy people strive to become the master of their fate. Adlerians practice on the assumption that self-determination leaves no room for clients to take refuge in the role of a passive victim. As an illustration of the implications of this view, consider the confrontive quality of Rudolph Dreikurs' typical remark to a man who complained about his wife's behavior and who tried to play a helpless role. Dreikurs (1967) confronted him with the question "And what did you do?" Dreikurs, a friend and collaborator of Adler's and the main person to bring Adler's ideas to the United States, developed a style of challenging clients to become aware of the ways in which they were active participants in situations they perceived as problematic. His therapy was aimed at showing clients that, although they could not directly change the behavior of others, they did have power to change their own reactions and attitudes toward others.

Phenomenology

Adler's psychology was perhaps the first major theory that stressed a phenomenological orientation toward therapy. It is phenomenological in that it pays attention to the subjective fashion through which people perceive their world. This "subjective reality" includes the individual's views, beliefs, perceptions, and conclusions. In Adlerian group counseling, the behavior of the members is understood from the vantage point of their unique striving in life and from a view of the world through their eyes.

As you will see in chapters that follow, many contemporary theories have incorporated this notion of the client's subjective perception of reality, or personal world view, as a basic factor explaining behavior. Some of the group approaches that have a phenomenological perspective are psychodrama, existential therapy, person-centered therapy, Gestalt therapy, the cognitive therapies (especially Albert Ellis' rational-emotive therapy), and Glasser's reality therapy.

Teleology

According to Adler, all forms of life are characterized by a trend toward growth and expansion. Adler replaced deterministic explanations by a teleological (purposive, goal-oriented) explanation. Humans live by goals and purposes as well as by causes.

Individual psychology contends that we can be understood best by looking at where we are going and what we are striving toward. Thus, in contrast to the Freudian psychoanalytic emphasis upon the past, Adlerians are interested in the future, without downplaying the importance of how one's past influences one's strivings in the present or toward the future. The three aspects of time are dynamically interrelated. Our decisions are based on what we have experienced in the past, on our present situation, and on what we are moving toward in our lives. In short, Adlerians look for a continuity in a client's life.

Social Interest

According to Manaster and Corsini (1982), *social interest*, known as *Gemeinschaftsgefühl*, is possibly the single most distinctive and valuable concept in individual psychology. The term *social interest* refers to an individual's attitudes in dealing with the social world, and it includes striving for a better future for humans. Adler equated social interest with a sense of identification and empathy with others. He said that social interest means "to see with the eyes of another, to hear with the ears of another, to feel with the heart of another" (Adler, 1956, p. 135).

Individual psychology rests on a central belief that our happiness and success are largely related to a social connectedness. As social beings, we have a need to be of use to others and to establish meaningful relationships in a community. Since we are embedded in a society, we cannot be understood in isolation from the social context. Adler believed that we have strong needs to feel united with others and that only when this is the case will we be able to act with courage in facing and dealing with life's problems. Adlerians contend that there are three main tasks that are essential for us to successfully master: our relationships with friends, our work, and our family relations (including love).

This key concept of social interest has significant implications for group counseling; the general goals of the group are to increase self-esteem and to develop social interest. The group focuses on discovering the mistaken assumptions that members have made that keep them from feeling adequate and from being interested in others. Dinkmeyer (1975) uses a procedure for group members to introduce themselves that entails having them address themselves to the three life tasks. The members present how they function:

1. socially with friends and acquaintances—how they get along with others and what sense of belonging and acceptance they experience
2. in work, including their degree of involvement, the meaning they derive from work, and what they are able to do for others through their work
3. with their family and others they love. Are they able to receive love and give it to others? How comfortable are they with their sexual identification? What is the quality of intimacy in their lives?

From what has been said about social interest, it is clear that humans have a strong need to belong and to find a significant place in society. Manaster and Corsini (1982) contend that the absence of this feeling of belonging and of being wanted is one of the most devastating of all emotions. They write: "Individual Psychology asserts that humans not only need other humans, but they also need to be needed, to have a feeling of belonging" (p. 47). They continue by showing that social interest is the goal of therapy: "Adlerians generally equate social interest and mental health. Persons without social interest cannot be healthy, whereas persons with social interest may be healthy" (p. 50).

This concept is applied to group counseling by structuring the group so that members can meet some of their needs for affiliation with others. Alienation, which is the opposite of social interest, is seen as a major problem of contemporary society. It is hoped that one of the outcomes of a group experience will be that members grow to increasingly accept themselves, even though they are imperfect. Out of their greater ability to accept themselves, they will be more capable of establishing meaningful relations with others and of being productive members of society.

Inferiority/Superiority

In his earlier writings Adler spoke about feelings of inferiority, which are typically associated with early recognition of our dependent position vis-à-vis adults and nature. He did not view this inferiority as a negative force. On the contrary, out of our basic inferiority comes the motivation to master our environment. We attempt to compensate for feelings of inferiority by finding ways that we can control the forces in our lives, as opposed to being controlled by them.

Our goal striving involves moving from a feeling of inferiority to one of superiority. According to Ansbacher (1974), inferiority feelings and compensation lost their primary importance for Adler over the years. In his later writings, Adler spoke more of the goal of success and the urge toward perfection, or becoming what we are able to become. This urge implies a tendency to seek a level of competence that we think is necessary for moving closer to self-conquest and self-mastery.

Life-Style

Adler saw us as actor, creator, and artist of our life. In striving for goals that are meaningful to us, we each develop a unique style of life (Ansbacher, 1974). This concept helps to explain how all our behavior fits together so that there is some consistency to our actions. Everything we do is related to the final goal of our life.

None of us has developed exactly the same style as anyone else. In striving for the goal of superiority, some people develop their intellect, others develop their physical being, and so on. Our style of life helps to explain our distinctive behaviors. It is learned from early interactions in the family, especially during the first five years of life. Adler believed, along with Freud, that the earliest impressions lay the foundation of our life-style. But he stressed that the childhood experiences in themselves were not crucial; rather, it is our *attitude* toward these events that is significant. Adler emphasized that the early influences may lead to the developing of a faulty life-style. However, we are not doomed to remain the victims of unfortunate experiences from our past. We can use childhood experiences to *consciously* create our own life-style.

Behavioral Disorders

Adler saw emotional disorders as "failures in life." He wrote: "All failures—neurotics, psychotics, criminals, drunkards, problem children, suicides, perverts, and prostitutes—are failures because they are lacking in social interest" (1956, p. 156). Psychological and behavioral disorders can be considered as erroneous ways of living, or mistaken assumptions. This can include a faulty life-style, a mistaken goal of success, and underdeveloped social interest. Since Adlerians maintain that clients do not suffer from a disease but from a "failure" to solve life problems and the tasks set by life, therapy is based on an educational model, not a medical model. Applied to group counseling, this emphasis means that much of what goes on in a group is a process of teaching clients a better approach so that they can succeed.

APPLICATION OF ADLERIAN PRINCIPLES TO GROUP WORK

Rationale for Group Counseling

Adler and his co-workers used a group approach in their child-guidance centers in Vienna as early as 1921 (Dreikurs, 1969). Rudolf Dreikurs, a colleague, extended and popularized Adler's work, especially with regard to group applications, and used group psychotherapy in his private practice for over 40 years. Dreikurs' rationale for groups is the following: "Since man's problems and conflicts are recognized in their social nature, the group is ideally suited not only to highlight and reveal the nature of a person's conflicts and maladjustments but to offer corrective influences" (1969, p. 43). Inferiority feelings can be challenged and counteracted effectively in groups, and the mistaken concepts and values that are at the root of social-emotional problems can be deeply influenced by the group, since the group is a value-forming agent.

The group provides the social context in which members can develop a sense of belonging and a sense of community. Dinkmeyer (1975) writes that group participants come to see that many of their problems are interpersonal in nature, that their behavior has social meaning, and that their goals can best be understood in the framework of social purposes. Some of the specific therapeutic factors that Dinkmeyer describes operating in Adlerian groups are:

- The group provides a mirror of the person's behavior.
- Members benefit from feedback from other members and the leaders.
- Members both receive help from others and give help.
- The group provides opportunities for testing reality and for trying new behavior.
- The group context encourages members to make a commitment to take action to change their life.
- Transactions in the group help members understand how they function at work and at home and also reveal how members seek to find their place in society.
- The group is structured in such a way that members can meet their need for belonging.

Goals of Adlerian Counseling

According to Dinkmeyer et al. (1979), Adlerian counseling has four major objectives, which correspond to four phases of the therapeutic process. These goals, which apply to both individual and group counseling, are:

1. establishing and maintaining an empathic relationship between client and counselor that is based on mutual trust and respect and in which the client feels understood and accepted by the counselor
2. providing a therapeutic climate in which clients can come to understand their basic beliefs and feelings about themselves and discover why these beliefs are faulty
3. helping clients develop insight into their mistaken goals and self-defeating behaviors through a process of confrontation and interpretation
4. assisting clients in discovering alternatives and encouraging them to make choices—that is, put insights into action

---

PHASES OF THE ADLERIAN GROUP

Like the psychoanalytic approach to groups, Adlerian group counseling involves the investigation and interpretation of one's early past. However, as the following discussion indicates, there are some fundamental differences between Adlerians and Freudians.

In writing about the characteristics of the Adlerian approach to group work, Dreikurs (1969) outlines four phases of group counseling, which correspond to the four goals of counseling just listed and which overlap to some extent:

1. establishing and maintaining the proper therapeutic relationship
2. exploring the dynamics operating in the individual (analysis)
3. communicating to the individual an understanding of self (insight)
4. seeing new alternatives and making new choices (reorientation)

Phase 1: Establishing and Maintaining the Relationship

In the initial phase, the emphasis is on establishing a good therapeutic relationship based on cooperation and mutual respect. Group participants are encouraged to be active in the process, for they are responsible for their own participation in the group. It is not always easy to create an active atmosphere, because even those clients who are most eager to make progress may be unwilling to do the work required for effective group participation and may be determined to prove that they are helpless (Dreikurs, 1969). Dreikurs saw the group as conducive to a good relationship between client and counselor. In the group situation there is ample opportunity to work on trust issues and to strengthen the relationship between member and leader. Also, by witnessing positive changes in peers, participants can observe the ongoing value of group work.

The Adlerian therapeutic relationship is a relationship between equals. Therapist and client work together toward mutually agreed-upon goals. A contract may be a part of this shared therapeutic venture. In groups, the contract indicates what clients want and expect from the group and specifies the responsibilities of leader and participants. Adlerians believe that counseling, individual or in groups, progresses only when the therapeutic process focuses on what *clients* see as personally significant and on areas *they* want to explore and change. This is what Dreikurs (1967) says of the collaborative nature of the Adlerian therapeutic relationship and of the necessity for the alignment of the client's and the therapist's goals:

> Therapeutic cooperation requires an alignment of goals. When the goals and interests of the patient and therapist clash, no satisfactory relationship can be established. Winning the patient's cooperation for the common task is a prerequisite for any therapy; maintaining it requires constant vigilance. What appears as "resistance" constitutes a discrepancy between the goals of the therapist and those of the patient [p. 65].

Phase 2: Analysis and Assessment—Exploring the Individual's Dynamics

The aim of the second phase is twofold: understanding one's life-style and seeing how the life-style affects one's current functioning in all the tasks of life (Mosak, 1979). The leader may begin by exploring how the participants function currently at work and in social situations and how they feel about themselves and their sex-role identities. Dinkmeyer et al. (1979) write that this initial assessment can be accomplished by pinpointing the clients' priorities, perhaps by asking questions such as "What are your main goals in life? Success? Power? Security? Pleasing others by meeting their expectations?" The goal is to lead people away from the absurdity of the "only if" position—for example, "Only if I succeed in pleasing others at all times do I avoid feeling like a failure."

According to Dreikurs (1969), the individual's goals and current life-style become much more obvious in interactions with others in the group. Also, individuals may respond differently when they are confronted by fellow participants than when they are confronted by the counselor alone.

Analysis and assessment rely heavily on the exploration of the client's *family constellation*, which includes evaluating the conditions that prevailed in the family when the person was a young child in the process of forming life-style convictions and basic assumptions. Dinkmeyer et al. (1979) describe a family-constellation questionnaire that provides insight into the client's self-perception, sibling relationships, significant forces in his or her life, and key decisions the client has made.

Another assessment procedure is asking clients to report their *early recollections*—specific incidents recalled from early childhood, with the feelings and thoughts that accompanied their occurrence. These early recollections are more than a report; they reveal beliefs, "basic mistakes," self-defeating perceptions, and unique laws of psychological movement (Dinkmeyer et al., 1979, p. 88). Adlerians contend that people remember only those past events that are consistent with their current views of themselves (Adler, 1958). Dreikurs (1969) adds that, once people develop such views, they perceive only that which fits their views. This self-perception strengthens the person's "private logic," which in turn helps the individual maintain his or her basic convictions. Early recollections provide a basic understanding of how we view and feel about ourselves, how we see the world, what our life goals are, what motivates us, what we believe in, and what we value.

The life-style investigation, which includes exploration of family background and one's life story, reveals a pattern of *basic mistakes*. Mosak (1979) writes that the life-style can be conceived of as a personal mythology. People behave as if the myths were true, because, for them, they are true. Mosak lists five basic mistakes: (1) overgeneralizations, (2) impossible goals, (3) misperceptions of life and its demands, (4) denial of one's basic worth, and (5) faulty values.

During the assessment phase the counselor's main task is to integrate and summarize data from the life-style investigation and to interpret how the mistaken notions and personal mythology influence the client now. This is done in a clear and concise way so that clients can recognize their own dynamics and pinpoint their assets. The analysis of the life-style is an ongoing process and helps client and counselor develop a plan for counseling.

According to Dreikurs (1969), analysis of the life-style and of its psychodynamic forces can be carried out in both individual and group settings, but the group format offers certain definite advantages:

> The patient's goals and movements become much more obvious in the interaction with his fellow group members than in the limited interaction between him and the therapist. Furthermore, the therapist no longer depends entirely on the verbal reports by the patient about his interaction with others outside of the therapeutic session; he sees him in action during the session. Not infrequently, the patient appears in a quite different light when confronted by other members of the group, than when he is alone with the therapist. Certain facades of his personality may become more pronounced, or visible [pp. 44–45].

Dinkmeyer et al. (1979) describe various techniques that the counselor can use to assess and analyze a problem. Some of these techniques are:

• *Paraphrasing.* The leader checks out the group members to make sure that he or she clearly understands what they are saying. Then the leader encourages the participants to clarify their views, beliefs, attitudes, and behaviors through group interaction.

• *Confrontation.* Done with care, sensitivity, and perceptivity, confrontation is the process by which the leader helps clients become aware of discrepancies—for example, discrepancies between their insights and their actions or between their behaviors and their intentions. It is a challenge and/or a question designed to help participants think about the purpose of their behavior and engage in deeper self-exploration.

• *"The question."* This is a technique Adler used as a way of determining whether a problem was due to functional or to organic causes. The counselor asks "What would be different if . . . ?"

• *Tentative hypotheses.* To minimize resistance and to open communication channels, the leader's suggestions about the purpose of a member's behavior in the group situation are presented tentatively as hypotheses or hunches.

Phase 3: Insight

Whereas the classical analytic position is that personality cannot change unless there is insight, the Adlerian view is that insight is only a step toward change and not a necessary prerequisite for it (Dreikurs, 1969). People can make abrupt and significant changes without much insight. Mosak (1979) defines insight as "understanding translated into constructive action." He contends that the Freudian notion that insight must precede behavioral change frequently results in extended treatment and encourages clients to postpone taking action to change. Mere intellectual insight can lead to the endless "Yes, but" game of "I know I should stop, but . . ."

In a group context the insight phase is concerned with helping participants understand *why* they function as they do. Members learn about themselves by exploring their own goals, personal mythology, and life-style. Dreikurs (1969) contends that it is during this and the next phase that clients receive the greatest benefit from a group. The group facilitates the process of gaining insight, because, as members experience resistance in themselves, they can also observe resistance in other group members. There is enough similarity in basic mistaken attitudes and faulty motivations among all participants to allow the members to observe themselves in others and to help one another (Dreikurs, 1969).

Interpretation is a technique that facilitates the process of gaining insight into one's life-style. Interpretation deals with the reasons why members behave the way they do in the here and now. By offering an outside frame of reference, the counselor helps participants see their behaviors from a different perspective and thus gain access to a wider range of alternatives (Dinkmeyer et al., 1979). Interpretations are never forced on the client; they are presented tentatively in the form of hypotheses: "Could it be . . . ?" "I have a hunch that I'd like to share with you . . ." "It seems to me that . . ." Therefore, interpretations are open-ended sharings that can be explored in group sessions. The ultimate goal of this process is that clients will come to understand their own role in creating a problem, the ways in which they maintain the problem, and what *they* can do to improve the situation.

Phase 4: Reorientation

The reorientation phase deals with considering alternative attitudes, beliefs, goals, and behaviors. One of the aims is to teach participants how to become more effective in dealing with the tasks of life. Another aim is to challenge and encourage clients to take risks and make changes. *Encouragement* is a basic aspect of this phase. Through encouragement, clients begin to experience their own inner resources and the power to choose for themselves and to direct their own lives.

Dreikurs (1969) believes that groups are especially useful during the reorientation phase, because they stimulate action and new orientations. In groups people can recognize in themselves the mistaken attitudes of the other members and thus become aware of their own self-defeating beliefs and behaviors. In a group they can also more easily recognize that their basic premises are incorrect and unjustified. Encouragement, so necessary at this stage, is found in the support of the group and in its equalitarian nature, which removes social distance and reduces the risk of self-disclosure. In Dreikurs' words, "It is this social atmosphere of equality which characterizes a therapy group and which exerts one of the most effective therapeutic influences on each one of its members" (1969, p. 47).

Reorientation is the action phase of a group, when new decisions are made and goals are modified. To challenge self-limiting assumptions, members are encouraged to act *as if* they were the persons they wanted to be. Members are asked to "catch themselves" in the process of repeating old patterns that lead to ineffective behavior. Commitment is an essential ingredient of the reorientation phase; if clients hope to change, they must be willing to set tasks for themselves and do something specific about their problems. Commitment is also needed to translate new insights into concrete action.

ROLE AND FUNCTIONS OF THE ADLERIAN COUNSELOR

The concept of the anonymous counselor is not part of the Adlerian view. An anonymous counselor would increase the distance from the client and interfere with the equalitarian, person-to-person relationship basic to the Adlerian approach. As Mosak (1979) writes, the Adlerian counselor has feelings and opinions and is free to express them.

Other Adlerian writers stress the active role of the counselor as a participant in a collaborative therapeutic effort. "We bring this active dimension to the counseling process by being concerned with the purpose of behavior and the unique laws of psychological movement of each individual" (Dinkmeyer et al., 1979, p. 72). Another evidence of the Adlerian counselor's active role is the commitment to active procedures such as confrontation, self-disclosure, interpretation, and analysis of prevailing patterns. The counselor challenges the clients' beliefs and goals and helps them translate what they have learned in the group process into new beliefs and behaviors. Dinkmeyer et al. (1979) point out that counselors serve as models for their clients, who often learn more from what counselors do, in group as well as in their personal lives, than from what they say. This implies that counselors need to have a clear sense of their own identity, beliefs, and feelings. They must also be aware of the basic conditions that are essential for the growth of clients—empathy, respect, care, genuineness, openness, positive regard, understanding of the dynamics of behavior, and the ability to use action-oriented techniques that stimulate changes in clients.

ADLERIAN FAMILY COUNSELING

Adlerians have a long history of working with families and studying family dynamics. Adler presented demonstrations with family groups in the child-guidance clinics of Vienna. The Adlerian approach is unique in giving special attention to the relationships between siblings and the position a person occupied in his or her family. Additionally, because Adlerians view most human problems as social in nature, they may give greater importance to the relationships between people than they do to the psychodynamics of the individual, as is usually the case in family counseling.

Goals of Adlerian Family Counseling

The basic goal of this approach is to facilitate the improvement of parent/child relationships and to enhance the relationships within a family. Teaching family members how to better deal with one another and how to live together as social equals is part of this goal. Dinkmeyer et al. (1979) state: "This aim is accomplished by sharing with the family group the principles of democratic conflict resolution, by reorienting the family members away from destructive modes of communication, and, most importantly, by teaching all members of the family to be agents of encouragement" (p. 221).

Responsibility of Family Members in the Counseling Process

One assumption is that family counseling is undertaken voluntarily. Family members are expected to attend a series of sessions and also to become involved in seriously carrying out homework assignments. Parents may be asked to join a parent study group, in which they are given information that they can apply to improving their family life. In this process the family counselor functions as a facilitator of learning for all who attend the sessions. Counselors assume the role of helping parents better understand the factors that contribute to the difficulties at home, and they suggest ways to deal with these problems. Ultimately, it is hoped, family members will learn effective strategies for resolving their own conflicts and the problems in their family by relying on the principles of showing respect for one another. Family members learn how to focus on issues that are dividing the family and how to reach new agreements or make compromises, and they actively participate in responsible decision making.

Techniques of Family Counseling

Many of the techniques used in family counseling were pioneered by Adler, although some of them have been discovered independently of his influence. A brief summary of these basic techniques, as described by Lowe (1982), follows.

The *initial interview* begins the process of counseling family groups. The purpose of the interview is to help the counselor diagnose children's goals, evaluate the parents' methods of child rearing, understand the climate in the home, and be able to make specific recommendations for change in the family situation. This process focuses on encouragement and on the strengths of all members of the family. It is essential that rapport be established so that productive work can be done. The family constellation is given special attention in this initial interview. Family members may be asked how they spend a typical day. A certain view of life begins to emerge based on the pattern of interaction between siblings and the children's position in the family. The parents are also asked how they view their family situation. For example, they are asked to talk about what concerns them about their children. The family counselor also makes an appraisal, but a more objective one, which includes hypotheses related to the goals of the children, the family atmosphere, methods of training, and assessing the strengths of the family members. The interview ends with a series of recommendations that involve homework for the parents and significant others.

Role playing and other action-oriented methods are often a part of the sessions. Interpretation is a basic part of Adlerian counseling and continues during all of the sessions. Its purpose is to provide some insight for family members, but more important than having them merely see and understand what they are doing is encouraging them to translate what they are learning into behavioral terms. In other words, insights that do not result in an action program and behavioral changes are of little real value.

EVALUATION OF THE ADLERIAN APPROACH TO GROUPS

My group practice has been influenced by several Adlerian concepts, some of which I've incorporated in my work. Emphasis on the social forces that motivate behavior and the search for mastery, superiority, and power are two of them. Another is the interest in patterns that people develop, often as a consequence of early childhood experiences, and that reflect the influence of their relationships with their parents and siblings. Also, the notion that we develop a unique life-style as a response to our perceived inferiority is to me quite intriguing.

The Adlerian approach deviates in many ways from the psychoanalytic model. Most Adlerians consider themselves as very separate from the Freudians and maintain that much of Adler's work was done independently of Freud. There are, however, some important commonalities between the two approaches, including a focus on critical periods of development, an interest in early recollections, and an emphasis on interpretation. As we have seen, there are also a number of areas in which the two approaches differ.

In my opinion, one of the strengths of the Adlerian approach is its eclectic nature. It is a holistic approach that encompasses the full spectrum of human experience, and practitioners have a great deal of freedom in working with clients in ways that are uniquely suited to their own therapeutic style. Even though Adlerians accept the same theoretical concepts, they do not have a monolithic view of the therapeutic process. Manaster and Corsini (1982) mention that Adlerians are much less rigid and dogmatic than are many therapists who adhere to other systems. Some Adlerians are very directive, and others are more nondirective. Some are willing to engage in personal self-disclosure, and others rarely make personal disclosures to their clients. Adlerians who were trained by Adler tend to ask for one early recollection, whereas those who were trained by Dreikurs might routinely ask for as many as ten recollections as a part of the life-style interview. Adlerian practitioners are not bound to follow a specific procedure, nor are they limited to using certain techniques. They are eclectic in that they can use their judgment in applying a wide range of techniques that they think will work best for a particular client. The basic criterion is that therapeutic techniques fit the theory and the client. Thus, therapists are encouraged to grow both personally and professionally by being inventive.

It is difficult to overestimate the contributions of Adler to contemporary therapeutic practice. As mentioned earlier, the emphasis of the Adlerian approach on social factors of personality lends itself exceptionally well to working with individuals in groups, including parent-education groups, teacher groups, and families. Adler's influence went beyond group counseling, however, extending into the community mental health movement. According to Ansbacher (1974), the trend toward community mental health, including the use of paraprofessionals, is in line with Adler's early efforts. Abraham Maslow, Viktor Frankl, and Rollo May have acknowledged their debt to Adler. Both Frankl and May see Adler as an existential thinker and a forerunner of the existential movement because of his position that human beings are free to choose and are entirely responsible for what they make of themselves. This view makes Adler also a forerunner of the subjective approach to psychology, which focuses on the internal determinants of behavior—values, beliefs, attitudes, goals, interests, personal meanings, subjective perceptions of reality, and striving toward self-realization.

In my opinion, one of Adler's most important contributions is his influence on other systems; some of his concepts can be recognized in most of the theories discussed in this book. From several points of view the Adlerian model is a forerunner of most other approaches to counseling and therapy. The following brief overview of the areas in which Adler's views are recognizable in other models illustrates this point.

- *Psychodrama:* focus on the here and now, on the universality of human struggles, and on early experiences and family relationships; use of ventilation and spectator therapy
- *Existential approach:* emphasis on the need to face the realities of life, on the importance of finding meaning and purpose in one's existence, on accepting personal responsibility, on seeing alternatives and making new choices, and on striving for mastery and self-actualization; use of confrontation
- *Person-centered approach:* holistic view of behavior, focus on growth, subjective perspective, and view that humans are always in the process of becoming and striving toward goals; stress on the importance of empathy and support, active listening, and acceptance
- *Gestalt:* focus on the here and now, on nonverbal communication, on learning to take risks to live fully, and on dealing with impasses
- *Transactional analysis:* attention to the individual's life plan, focus on re-evaluating old decisions and making new and more appropriate ones, equalitarian relationship between client and therapist, and goal alignment; use of therapeutic contracts as a way of providing direction for sessions
- *Behavior therapy:* emphasis on encouragement and positive reinforcement and on concreteness, problem solving, and decision making; use of contracts, analysis, and assessment
- *Rational-emotive therapy:* attention to mistaken attitudes and faulty beliefs and to the need to learn new orientations; clients' confrontation of self-defeating internalized sentences; use of analysis and action methods
- *Reality therapy:* focus on commitment as a prerequisite for change, on responsibility and strengths; use of reorientation and reality testing; similarity between the concept of success and failure identity in reality therapy and the concept of encouragement and discouragement in the Adlerian model

As you proceed with your study of the other therapeutic models, I encourage you to continue to pay attention to the similarities and differences among these approaches. Such a comparative perspective will deepen your understanding of the group process, help you formulate your own approach to group work, and increase the number of practical applications that these systems offer to your work as a group leader.

If you find that your thinking is allied with the Adlerian approach, you might consider seeking training in Individual Psychology or becoming a member of the North American Society of Adlerian Psychology. There is a student-member category (currently $30 a year), which also includes the bimonthly *Newsletter* and the quarterly journal, *Individual Psychology: The Journal of Adlerian Theory, Research, and Practice.* For further information on membership or training workshops, write the North American Society of Adlerian Psychology, 159 North Dearborn, Chicago, IL 60601.

QUESTIONS FOR DISCUSSION AND REFLECTION

1. What are your thoughts about Adler's idea that inferiority can actually be the basis for success? Can you relate the striving for superiority to your own life?
2. Adler talks about the family constellation and birth order as important factors in shaping one's personality. What implications do these concepts have for group counseling? How can a group replicate a family? How do these ideas relate to your own life?
3. Social interest is a key Adlerian concept. How can a group increase social interest, and how is the group an appropriate form of intervention in the light of Adlerian principles?
4. What major contrasts do you see between Freud and Adler? Do you see a basis for integrating some psychoanalytic concepts with Adlerian ones?
5. How might you work with the concept of style of life in a group setting?
6. What is your evaluation of Adler's view that we can be understood only by looking at our goals and our future strivings? Again, how might you integrate this idea into actual practice in a group?
7. Adlerians see group counseling as a form of teaching and learning, and because of this they make use of advice and information. What possible advantages and disadvantages do you see in this focus?
8. What are some key Adlerian principles that you could use to understand your own life better?
9. What are your reactions to the four phases of the Adlerian group? How could they apply to groups you might want to lead?
10. For what kind of clients do you think Adlerian groups would be best suited? Do you think they would be appropriate for all populations? Explain.

RECOMMENDED SUPPLEMENTARY READINGS

Individual Psychology (Manaster & Corsini, 1982) is a very readable overview of Adlerian psychology. The authors trace the approach's history, describe its current status, present a clear summary of key Adlerian concepts, including the dynamics of personality, and discuss the application of these concepts to the practice of both individual and group counseling. Several excellent chapters are devoted to the theory and practice of counseling, including descriptions of Adlerian techniques that can be applied to working with individuals, groups, and families. This is an accurate and up-to-date presentation of the Adlerian approach.

The Individual Psychology of Alfred Adler (Ansbacher & Ansbacher, 1964) is a comprehensive collection of Adler's writings that shows the development and refinement of his thinking. This is one of the definitive sources of the Adlerian approach.

Superiority and social interest: A collection of later writings (Adler, 1973), edited by H. L. Ansbacher and R. R. Ansbacher, contains various writings by Adler on topics such as his basic assumptions, his theory of the neuroses, case studies, and his views of religion and mental health. It also has a biographical essay on Adler and a chapter on the increasing recognition of Adler's influence on current practice.

Adlerian counseling and psychotherapy (Dinkmeyer, Pew, & Dinkmeyer, 1979) gives a good basic presentation of the theoretical foundations of Adlerian counseling and applies basic concepts to the practice of group counseling and group psychotherapy. Other chapters deal with topics such as the development of personality, psychopathology, counseling theory, the phases of the counseling process, counseling with various populations, Adlerian group methods, and counseling techniques applied to working with marital and family counseling. This is an interesting, informative, and readable source.

Theories of personality (Schultz, 1981) presents excellent summaries of the Freudian and neo-Freudian models. Freud, Adler, Horney, Fromm, Sullivan, Jung, and Erikson are discussed. A biographical sketch of each theorist adds interest and provides a good frame of reference for understanding the theory.

Individual Psychology: The Journal of Adlerian Theory, Research, and Practice is one of the best resources for staying current in the applications of Adlerian psychology. Information for this journal and a bimonthly *Newsletter* can be obtained by writing to the North American Society of Adlerian Psychology, 159 North Dearborn, Chicago, IL 60601.

Adlerian family counseling, a film featuring Dr. Oscar Christensen of the University of Arizona, is a valuable resource. Information can be obtained from the Educational Media Corporation, Box 21311, Minneapolis, MN 55421.

REFERENCES AND SUGGESTED READINGS*

Adler, A. The Individual Psychology of Alfred Adler. In H. L. Ansbacher & R. R. Ansbacher (Eds.), *The Individual Psychology of Alfred Adler.* New York: Harper & Row, 1956.

Adler, A. *What life should mean to you.* New York: Capricorn, 1958.

Adler, A. *Social interest: A challenge to mankind.* New York: Capricorn, 1964.

*Adler, A. *The practice and theory of Individual Psychology.* Paterson, N.J.: Littlefield, Adams, 1969.

*Adler, A. *Superiority and social interest: A collection of later writings* (3rd rev. ed.) (H. L. Ansbacher & R. R. Ansbacher, Eds.). New York: Viking Press, 1973.

Allen, T. W. The Individual Psychology of Alfred Adler: An item of history and a promise of revolution. *The Counseling Psychologist,* 1971, 3(1), 3–24. (a)

Allen, T. W. A life style. *The Counseling Psychologist,* 1971, 3(1), 25–29. (b)

Allen, T. W. Adlerian interview strategies for behavior change. *The Counseling Psychologist,* 1971, 3(1), 40–48. (c)

*Ansbacher, H. L. The increasing recognition of Adler. In H. L. Ansbacher & R. R. Ansbacher (Eds), *Alfred Adler: Superiority and social interest* (3rd rev. ed.). New York: Viking Press, 1973.

Ansbacher, H. L. Goal-oriented Individual Psychology: Alfred Adler's theory. In A. Burton (Ed.), *Operational theories of personality.* New York: Brunner/Mazel, 1974.

*Ansbacher, H. L., & Ansbacher, R. R. (Eds.). *The Individual Psychology of Alfred Adler.* New York: Harper & Row (Torchbooks), 1964.

Dinkmeyer, D. Adlerian group psychotherapy. *International Journal of Group Psychotherapy,* 1975, 25(2), 219–226.

Dinkmeyer, D. C., & Muro, J. J. *Group counseling: Theory and practice* (2nd ed.). Itasca, Ill.: Peacock, 1979.

*Books and articles marked with an asterisk are suggested for further study.

*Dinkmeyer, D. C., Pew, W. L., & Dinkmeyer, D. C., Jr. *Adlerian counseling and psychotherapy.* Monterey, Calif.: Brooks/Cole, 1979.

Dreikurs, R. *Psychology in the classroom: A manual for teachers.* New York: Harper & Brothers, 1957.

Dreikurs, R. Basic principles in dealing with children. In R. Dreikurs, R. Corsini, R. Lowe, & M. Sonstegard (Eds.), *Adlerian family counseling.* Eugene: University of Oregon Press, 1959.

Dreikurs, R. *Group psychotherapy and group approaches: The collected papers of Rudolf Dreikurs.* Chicago: Alfred Adler Institute, 1960.

Dreikurs, R. *Psychodynamics, psychotherapy, and counseling: Collected papers.* Chicago: Alfred Adler Institute, 1967.

Dreikurs, R. Group psychotherapy from the point of view of Adlerian psychology. In H. M. Ruitenbeek (Ed.), *Group therapy today: Styles, methods, and techniques.* New York: Aldine-Atherton, 1969.

Dreikurs, R., Corsini, R., Lowe, R. N., & Sonstegard, M. (Eds.). *Adlerian family counseling.* Eugene: University of Oregon Press, 1959.

Dreikurs, R., & Mosak, H. H. The tasks of life. I. Adler's three tasks. *The Individual Psychologist,* 1966, 4, 18–22.

Dreikurs, R., & Mosak, H. H. The tasks of life. II. The fourth task. *The Individual Psychologist,* 1967, 4, 51–55.

Dreikurs, R., & Soltz, V. *Children: The challenge.* New York: Meridith Press, 1964.

Ellenberger, H. *The discovery of the unconscious.* New York: Basic Books, 1970.

Erickson, R. C. Viewing the therapeutic community through Adlerian spectacles. *International Journal of Group Psychotherapy,* 1982, 32(2), 201–216.

Gushurst, R. S. The technique, utility, and validity of life style analysis. *The Counseling Psychologist,* 1971, 3(1), 31–40.

Hansen, J. C., Warner, R. W., & Smith, E. J. *Group counseling: Theory and process* (2nd ed.). Chicago: Rand McNally, 1980.

Losoncy, L. Encouragement therapy. In R. J. Corsini (Ed.), *Handbook of innovative psychotherapies.* New York: Wiley, 1981.

*Lowe, R. N. Adlerian/Dreikursian family counseling. In A. M. Horne & M. M. Ohlsen (Eds.), *Family counseling and therapy.* Itasca, Ill.: Peacock, 1982.

*Manaster, G. J., & Corsini, R. J. *Individual Psychology: Theory and practice.* Itasca, Ill.: Peacock, 1982.

Mosak, H. Adlerian psychotherapy. In R. J. Corsini (Ed.), *Current psychotherapies* (2nd ed.). Itasca, Ill.: Peacock, 1979.

Mosak, H., & Mosak, B. *A bibliography of Adlerian psychology.* Washington, D.C.: Hemisphere, 1975.

Prochaska, J. O. *Systems of psychotherapy: A transtheoretical analysis.* Homewood, Ill.: Dorsey Press, 1979.

Ruitenbeek, H. M. (Ed.). *Group therapy today: Styles, methods, and techniques* (2nd ed.). Chicago: Aldine-Atherton, 1969.

Ryckman, R. M. *Theories of personality.* New York: Van Nostrand, 1978.

Schultz, D. *Theories of personality* (2nd ed.). Monterey, Calif.: Brooks/Cole, 1981.

Sonstegard, M., Dreikurs, R., & Bitter, J. The teleoanalytic group counseling approach. In G. M. Gazda (Ed.), *Basic approaches to group psychotherapy and counseling* (3rd ed.). Springfield, Ill.: Charles C Thomas, 1982.

8

PSYCHODRAMA

INTRODUCTION

Psychodrama, created and developed by J. L. Moreno, is a group-therapy approach in which the client acts out or dramatizes past, present, or anticipated life situations and roles in an attempt to gain deeper understanding and achieve catharsis. Significant events are acted or reenacted to help the client get in contact with unrecognized and unexpressed feelings, provide a channel for the full expression of these feelings, and encourage new behavior.

Psychodrama had its origins in the Theater of Spontaneity, which Moreno started in Vienna in 1921. People who participated in the Theater were not professional actors, and they didn't have any scripts. Instead, they played out in a spontaneous manner events from the daily newspaper or topics suggested by the audience. After the act, people in the audience were invited to discuss their experiences as they observed the performance. Moreno found that the personal problems, and thus the reactions, of the people in the audience influenced not only the choice of the topic but also the way in which the participants played their parts. Moreno also found that both the persons who were involved in the play and the people in the audience experienced a psychological release of pent-up feelings (catharsis). The Theater of Spontaneity led Moreno to the development of the group methods and specialized therapeutic techniques that were later incorporated into psychodrama.

Psychodrama was designed to facilitate the expression of feelings in a spontaneous and dramatic way through the use of role playing. One of the values of psychodrama in group work is that it is frequently interpersonally oriented, allowing a maximum number of people to play various roles and receive feedback about the impact of these roles (Orcutt, 1977). The techniques of psychodrama lend themselves very well to producing lively group interaction, exploring interpersonal problems, experimenting with novel ways of approaching significant others in one's life, and reducing one's feelings of isolation. (Although psychodramatic therapy is interpersonally oriented, *intrapersonal* aspects of group members' lives are explored.) Zerka Moreno (1983) writes that "psychodrama represents a major turning point away from the treatment of the individual in isolation and toward the treatment of the individual in groups, from treatment by verbal methods toward treatment by action methods" (p. 158).

In many ways, psychodrama was the precursor of many other group approaches, including Gestalt, encounter, and some applications of behavior-therapy groups. Many of these orientations use techniques that were originally developed by J. L. Moreno, and many of the role-playing and action-oriented methods used in these groups are adaptations of the specialized techniques pioneered by Moreno. Schutz (1971) writes that virtually all the encounter techniques that he had prided himself on inventing had actually been used by Moreno as much as 40 years before he (Schutz) used them. Schutz credits Moreno with establishing the groundwork for Gestalt therapy and encounter-group methods, and he maintains that Moreno's contributions are probably not sufficiently acknowledged in this country.

Other authors acknowledge Moreno's influence and pioneering work. Blatner (1973) writes that many of the techniques that were originally developed by Moreno have been adapted for use in guided fantasy, improvisatory dramatics, psychosynthesis, Gestalt therapy, bioenergetics, sensory awakening, and other encounter techniques. Yablonsky (1974, pp. 219–222) cites evidence for his claim that Moreno's concepts and techniques influenced Fritz Perls' development of Gestalt therapy. He also notes that, although we often think of marathon groups as a recent innovation, Moreno was conducting nonstop weekend workshops in psychodrama in the early 1940s.

KEY CONCEPTS

View of Human Nature

Moreno stressed that individuals are fully responsible for their actions and for the persons they are and will be. Thus, we see in Moreno a precursor of existentialists such as Camus and Sartre. This view of Moreno's approach is shared by Greenberg (1974), who writes that, in his "here-and-now" philosophy, Moreno is comfortably at home with the modern existentialists. Moreno rejected Freud's position that only through a lengthy process of psychoanalysis can humans become free of the irrational forces that rule them. For Moreno, freedom from the bondage of irrational forces can be achieved through intervention with psychodramatic methods, because in psychodrama therapeutic breakthroughs often occur suddenly and spontaneously. However, it is to be noted that these breakthroughs do not necessarily free the client from the bondage of ruling unconscious forces. The working-through and integration aspects of the therapeutic process still take time.

Action

Moreno's action-oriented methods represent an extension of the psychoanalytic approach, which he saw as passive. Moreno considered the psychoanalytic method as constricting, rather than freeing, the individual. He was convinced of the therapeutic value of acting out one's problems rather than merely talking about them. In contrast to psychoanalysis, the psychodramatic method emphasizes personal interaction and encounter, focus on here and now, spontaneity and creativity, full expression of feelings, and reality testing.

Although Moreno repudiated psychoanalytic therapy, his methods are grounded in psychoanalytic concepts. Psychodrama and psychoanalysis differ substantially in technique, but not in the goals of psychotherapy. A special characteristic of the psychodramatic method is that it is applicable to almost any theoretical framework.

Encounter and Tele

The *encounter* is defined by Greenberg (1974) as that which occurs when individuals immediately and meaningfully confront themselves or significant others on the psychodramatic stage. The encounter always occurs in the context of the here and now, regardless of whether the enactment relates to a past event or to an anticipated one.

Effective psychodrama consists of taking a moment or a particular situation in one's life and expanding it in various dimensions. Through this process, individuals have the opportunity to reexperience the event or to experience it in a novel way and thus gain insight into themselves.

Encounter and therapeutic interaction are illustrated as follows by Moreno (1914, p. 3):

> A meeting of two:
> Eye to eye
> Face to face
> And when you are near
> I will tear out your eyes
> And place them instead of mine
> And you will tear out my eyes
> And place them instead of yours
> Then I will look at you
> With your eyes
> And you will look at me
> With mine.

Encountering is at the very core of psychodrama, for through this process persons not only meet but also understand one another on a deep and significant level. By their very nature, encounters entail an element of surprise, because they are not rehearsed or forced. The encounter entails dimensions of both transference and empathy, yet it goes beyond transference and empathy. The process of encountering fosters a sense of community in a group, which builds the trust that is necessary for productive work.

Related to encounter is the concept Moreno termed *tele*, the two-way flow of feelings between persons in a psychodramatic group. Tele consists of both positive and negative feelings, and it is the quality that binds a group together. Through tele there is a strengthening of bonds, a promotion of continuity and stability, and a sense of group cohesion. Tele is the sum total of the feeling aspects of empathy, transference, and countertransference; it is the factor responsible for the increased interaction among participants of a group. In this sense, tele is a therapeutic factor related to change. Healing of individuals occurs through an interpersonal-reciprocal-empathic feeling.

Spontaneity and Creativity

Moreno considered spontaneity and creativity to be characteristics of the self-realized person. According to Greenberg (1974), the amount of spontaneity displayed by a person in various situations is a reliable index of that individual's mental health, social competence, and level of interpersonal involvement. Most of us can be highly creative if we allow ourselves to be spontaneous. Moreno observed that children, in contrast to adults, are able to enter into role-playing and fantasy situations without any difficulty and to freely express their feelings. As we grow older, we become less and less spontaneous. To remedy this tendency, Moreno and his associates developed spontaneity-training methods aimed at freeing people from limiting scripts and rigid and stereotyped responses. They adopted techniques that encouraged the uninhibited participation of the audience, and they stressed the need to get in touch with one's fantasies and feelings by acting out situations that trigger certain emotions. Moreno assigned so much importance to spontaneity that he considered spontaneity training as the way of enabling people to take dramatic steps in the future and to meet new situations from a fresh perspective.

Dealing with the Present

In psychodrama the emphasis is on acting out conflicts or crisis situations in the present, as opposed to merely verbalizing about them in a detached way. The theory is that reliving and reexperiencing a scene from the past gives the participants the opportunity to examine how that event affected them at the time it occurred and a chance to deal differently with the event *now*. In essence, this is designed to be a corrective emotional experience, in that, through the enactment and the subsequent catharsis, insight often occurs. Anticipated events are also enacted in the here and now to give participants increased awareness of the available options.

Psychodrama places importance on the past, present, *and* future; the past can come to life when it is brought into the here and now, as can the future. Z. T. Moreno (1983) contends that the future has typically been a neglected dimension in therapeutic practice. Because we live with some concern for the future, Moreno thinks, it is useful to develop techniques for helping people act out situations that they expect to happen, so that they can be better prepared for them. In this sense, psychodrama can be considered a rehearsal for life.

Catharsis and Insight

Catharsis occurs when stored-up feelings are finally expressed. In psychodrama, catharsis is brought about by verbally and physically acting out an emotion-laden situation. This release of pent-up feelings is more meaningful when participants deal with real-life situations and when they get actively involved in a spontaneous expression of what they are feeling. Anger, sadness, hatred, rage, and despair, as well as joy and ecstasy, are tapped and released. Both the participants in a psychodrama and members of the audience can experience catharsis and thus achieve insight—a new and increased understanding of a conflict situation.

Reality Testing

The psychodramatic group provides the members with an opportunity to test reality, because the group consists of real people and real-life situations. The assumptions and fantasies of an individual can be checked out for validation with other members. Also, others in the group can suggest alternatives for action, many of which may have not been considered by the individual.

Consider the following example of how a psychodramatic group offers members ways to test reality. A young woman may be in great emotional pain over what she sees as her father's indifference to her and the ways that he has passed up opportunities to demonstrate whatever love he had for his daughter. After concluding a psychodramatic enactment in which the young woman tells her father of her feelings of missing this love with a father, she may still be angry with him and expect him to make the first move to change matters. During the discussion phase, others in the group can point out that she is making the assumption that *he* must be the person to initiate a closer relationship. In reality, the father may well be fearful of showing her affection and attention, thinking that she is not interested in such a relationship with him. The group can be instrumental in helping her see that, if she wants to change her relationship with her father, she may have to make the initial move.

Role Playing

Role playing entails acting a part in an impromptu production. The acting out of a role does not have to be some kind of artificial performance. It can be an expression of what a person genuinely feels, fears, or would like to become. In a sense, we play multiple roles in everyday life; some of them are an extension of our unique identity, and others are stultifying and restrict our identity. In psychodrama, members are given the freedom to try out a diversity of roles, thereby getting a sharper focus on parts of themselves that they would like to present to others. Playing roles also enables participants to get in contact with parts of themselves that they were not aware of. Psychodrama offers members many opportunities to challenge stereotyped ways of responding to people and to break out of behaving within a rigid pattern. It allows them to continue to create new dimensions of themselves. Even if they fail in a new role, they know that they will have many opportunities to try again until they learn new behavioral approaches to the situations that bring them anxiety.

Although role playing is part of the essence of psychodrama, it can be used by therapists of various theoretical orientations. It has been employed by psychoanalysts, by Adlerians, by Rogerians, and by eclectic therapists (Corsini, 1966). As you will see, different forms of role playing are often used in Gestalt groups, in transactional analysis, in rational-emotive therapy, and in behavioral groups. In psychodrama, role playing is typically characterized by a high degree of emotional intensity and often leads to a catharsis and some degree of insight. Also, in a psychodrama group, the various members are used to play various characters and parts so that scenes from an individual's life can be replayed in a group session. In Gestalt groups, the focus is also on getting into contact with and expressing feelings, but the one particular member working assumes all the roles in a given scene and interchangeably acts out the multiple characters; Gestalt groups do not encourage other members to play roles for the person doing a piece of work in a session. In behavioral groups, as you will see later, role playing is a central procedure in helping members unlearn old and ineffective behavior patterns and acquire new and effective ways of behaving. In contrast to the psychodrama group, however, the behavioral group is not concerned with ventilation of feelings so much as with practicing specific skills and rehearsing concrete behaviors for given situations that are problematic for members. So, although role playing is a basic part of many therapeutic approaches to group work, it is practiced in different ways with a different purpose in various types of group.

As it is used in psychodramatic groups, role playing can serve three primary functions, as Corsini (1966) has noted. It can be used as a method of *diagnosis*. As members role-play various situations, the group leader has ample opportunities to learn more about how they think and feel (as well as what they do). Role playing can also be used as a means of *instruction*. Through a modeling process, members learn more effective interpersonal skills by observing a variety of ways to deal with problems. Finally, it can be used as a method of *training*, for by getting involved in the active process of playing roles, members often develop new insights and new coping skills.

BASIC COMPONENTS OF THE PSYCHODRAMATIC METHOD

The psychodramatic method consists of the following components: a stage, a director, a protagonist (the person who is the focus of the psychodrama), auxiliary egos (representatives of persons not present), and an audience (the group) (Haskell, 1973).

The Stage

The stage represents an extension of the life space of the protagonist, and as such it should be large enough to allow for movement of the protagonist, the auxiliary egos, and the director. The stage area should simulate, at least symbolically, each scene that the protagonist recalls. If a stage is not available, a section of the room can be designated as the action area, and all the action takes place in that area as if it were a stage. Props can be used and placed in the action area, and, when a protagonist emerges from the group, he or she moves to this area to create the psychodrama.

The Director

A second component of a psychodrama is the director, who is the chief therapist. According to J. L. Moreno (1953, 1964), the director has the role of producer, catalyst/facilitator, and observer/analyzer. Directors help in the selection of the protagonist, and then they decide which of the special psychodramatic techniques are best suited for the exploration of the person's problem. They organize the psychodrama, play a key role in warming up the group, and pay careful attention to what emerges in the psychodrama. Directors function as therapists (catalysts/facilitators) in that they assist the protagonist in developing a scene, facilitate the free expression of feelings, and at times make therapeutic interpretations to help the protagonist gain a new understanding of a problem. Haskell (1973) describes specific functions of psychodrama directors, which include the following:

- planning the session so that various group members have an opportunity to be the protagonist and so that the problems presented are relevant to the needs and interests of the group
- providing an accepting and tolerant atmosphere that lends itself to spontaneous expressions of feelings associated with meaningful events
- warming up the group so that the participants will be psychologically ready to freely and fully explore personal issues and identify their goals
- providing support and direction for the protagonist; this includes providing the protagonist and the group with appropriate techniques designed to enhance the enactments or reenactments
- encouraging spontaneity and catharsis and helping the protagonist interpret what he or she experiences during the psychodrama
- offering suggestions with regard to relationships that might be explored, scenes that might be enacted, and experiments that might be tried
- whenever necessary, stopping the action for clarification and making sure that the roles are being properly enacted
- paying careful attention to the reactions of the group members and, if it seems appropriate, trying to bring other participants into the psychodrama; also, assisting other members in deriving therapeutic benefits from the experience
- protecting the protagonist from being verbally attacked by other members of the group or from being subjected to simplistic directives and advice on what should be done to resolve his or her problem
- leading a group discussion after the action is over—a function that entails trying to draw in as many members as possible to share what they experienced during the psychodrama, what they learned from it, and what experiences and feelings they think they have in common with the protagonist, and giving the protagonist feedback
- summarizing the experience on the basis of the feedback obtained in the discussion and the enactments, thus providing a good closure for one experience and a direct lead into another area of exploration

Corsini (1966) concludes that effective directors possess three essential characteristics: creativity, courage, and charisma. Asserting that directing role playing involves technical skills and *creativity*, Corsini makes it clear how many variables the director must attend to. Directors must not only depend on their own resources for being inventive but also find ways of tapping the creativity within the group. They must make decisions about what aspects of a psychodrama to focus on, and they must quickly arrange for reenactment of certain scenes. Also, they must be able to function as a guide by using their clinical expertise and technical knowledge to help individuals bring to the surface, explore, and work through their personal concerns. Directors must also be able to stop the action at an appropriate time and find ways of involving as many members as possible in the protagonist's work. Effective directors are able to invent techniques that will highlight a member's struggles. They must be able to improvise, yet at the same time their improvisations must have structure and meaning.

Directors must also have *courage*, for many of the techniques they use involve some degree of risk and of the unknown. Although they are not impulsive, good psychodrama leaders trust their clinical hunches enough to allow themselves to try out techniques that can have a powerful effect on the members.

Finally, directors have *charisma*, with a high degree of enthusiasm and spontaneity. Using their charisma, they are able to encourage members to give up control and take risks in trying new behaviors.

In addition to the characteristics of courage, charisma, and creativity, qualities such as self-confidence, self-knowledge, and clinical expertise are essential. According to Fine (1979), "The challenge to the therapist is to use his own personhood, including his theoretical and therapeutic models, to attend to the immediate personal and interpersonal happenings within the group" (p. 444).

It is well for group leaders who are interested in incorporating psychodrama into their style of leadership to realize that they do not have to be perfect in their first attempts to apply its methods. I have found that some beginning leaders become needlessly intimidated when they think about the personal qualities and skills needed for effectively using psychodrama. With supervised practice, experience as a member of a psychodramatic group, and specialized training, they *can* acquire competence in this powerful approach.

The Protagonist

The protagonist is the person selected by the group and the director to enact or reenact an important event from the past or present or to act out an anticipated situation. It is the protagonist who selects the event to be explored. The protagonist is asked to reenact the substance of the event, without attempting to recall the exact transaction or words. Spontaneity is encouraged. Verbal communication may be permitted for a short time, but as soon as possible the director encourages the protagonist to move into action rather than merely talk about the event.

Even when a scene from the past is being reenacted, the focus is still on the here and now. Protagonists are asked to deal with the significant people in their past as though these symbolic figures were present. This here-and-now focus intensifies the feelings that are experienced and provides a new understanding of the relationships between protagonists and significant people in their past.

Fine (1979) describes the protagonist as the composer of an opera. It is the protagonist who writes the score and the lyrics. The director, like the conductor of the opera, follows the script and facilitates the interpretation of the drama. Others in the group do become personally involved with the protagonist, yet when they function as auxiliaries they are much like musicians following scores. According to Fine, auxiliaries function as extensions of the protagonist by assuming the frame of reference of the protagonist. In the enactment of the psychodrama the protagonist's fears and fantasies come to life and enable the protagonist to modify his or her own intrapsychic and interpersonal processes.

The protagonist generally selects the group members who will serve as auxiliary egos. These choices are made for both conscious and unconscious reasons. Some choices are made on the basis of characteristics of group members that are similar to those of the actual significant others. When a choice is made on this basis, the interaction between the protagonist and auxiliary egos is likely to be more spontaneous, real, and thus effective. Directors may take exception to this rule if they want a group member to assume a role with particular therapeutic potential.

It is the protagonist's job to teach the auxiliary egos how to play their roles. This sometime entails giving an auxiliary ego some background on the person he or she is to play and a feeling for the style of that person. Protagonists teach an auxiliary ego the behavioral style of a significant other by acting out that part.

It is important that, as protagonists act out a situation, they have the freedom to explore any aspect of the situation (and related relationships) that seems significant to them. It is the protagonists, not the director, who examine and explore, and it is crucial that their decisions be respected. Although the director may encourage the protagonists to reenact a situation or deal with an anticipated event, the protagonists decide whether they are willing to follow the director's suggestions. Also, the director may employ a particular technique, but protagonists always have the right to say that they don't want to move in that direction. Effective psychodrama requires sensitivity, on the part of both the director and the group members, to what the protagonist is ready and willing to explore. Protagonists should never be coerced or pressured; the auxiliary egos and the director are there to serve them.

At the end of a scene the protagonist or the director may suggest that the protagonist assume a different role in the same scene to determine whether he or she can respond more effectively. Another suggestion is that the protagonist fantasize about the future by acting out how things might be one year hence, thus sharing private thoughts with the audience.

A basic Morenean concept is that the protagonist is viewed as an instrument of the group. When the protagonist is selected by the group, he or she is the person in whom the group's problems are most clearly crystallized. Psychodrama thus becomes more a group process, rather than individual therapy within a group.

The Auxiliary Egos

The term *auxiliary ego* refers to anyone in the group who assists the director and protagonist in the psychodramatic production. Auxiliary egos may assume two functions. First, they may portray the roles of significant others in the life of the protagonist. These persons may be living or dead, real or imagined. Auxiliaries may also play the roles of inanimate objects, pets, or any emotionally charged object or being that is relevant to the protagonist's psychodrama.

Second, auxiliary egos serve as therapeutic agents. They may, for example, be a *double* for the protagonist. In this case, they verbalize certain feelings that they imagine the protagonist is experiencing but not expressing.

In summarizing the functions of auxiliary egos, Blatner (1973) comments on how these members encourage the protagonist to become more deeply involved in the here and now of the drama. Through effective use of the auxiliary egos, a psychodrama can assume greater power and intensity.

Auxiliary egos use information about significant others given to them by the protagonist through role reversal, both at the beginning of the enactment and throughout the drama. It is the director's responsibility to assess whether the role expansion is working more for the protagonist's benefit or for the auxiliary's. In the case of the latter, the auxiliary may be redirected by the director. The director should be sure to discuss this development during the sharing phase of the group, because it usually has significant therapeutic implications for the auxiliary. It should be underscored that psychodrama is a *group process* and that auxiliary work has great therapeutic potential for group members. Auxiliaries should be permitted freedom of expression in their role portrayals. Playing someone else's role often serves as a vehicle for getting in touch with parts of the self not uncovered while playing one's own role. Again, the leader's task is to make sure that the spontaneity of total group involvement is tempered with some degree of purpose and structure if a psychodrama is to avoid turning into a forum for mere dramatics.

The Audience

Even when people in the group are not protagonists or auxiliary egos in a psychodrama, they can still benefit in vicarious ways. They can identify with the protagonist, they can experience a release of their own feelings through their empathy, and they can gain insight into some of their own interpersonal conflicts.

The other group members (the audience) provide valuable support and feedback to the protagonist. An action scene is generally followed by a discussion that involves the entire group. At this time other members are asked to share some experiences of their own that are related to the scene they just observed, and they provide the person with feedback concerning alternative ways of dealing with the situation. Spontaneous reactions and personal sharing are encouraged; members are typically asked to refrain from analyzing the protagonist, offering pat solutions, criticizing, and offering impersonal interpretations. Because of the variety in group membership, the audience's reactions can help the protagonist understand the impact he or she has on others. In this way, reality testing is made possible.

PHASES OF THE PSYCHODRAMATIC PROCESS

Psychodrama consists of three phases: (1) the *warm-up* (or *preaction*) phase, (2) the *action* phase, and (3) the *discussion*, or *sharing*, phase.

The Warm-Up Phase

Moreno emphasizes the necessity of a warm-up period designed to get the participants ready for the experience. Such readiness involves being motivated enough to formulate one's goals and feeling secure enough to trust the others in the group. There are many ways to conduct a productive warm-up phase. For example:

- The director gives a brief talk about the nature and purpose of psychodrama, and participants are invited to ask questions.
- Each member is briefly interviewed by the director in the group setting. A lead question might be "Is there a present or past relationship that you'd like to understand better?" If each person in the group responds to this question, a basis for group cohesion is being established.
- Members can form several sets of dyads and spend a few minutes sharing a conflict that they are experiencing and that they'd like to explore in the session.

In addition to structured techniques aimed at warming up a group for action, there are unstructured warm-ups, including the process by which a protagonist emerges from the spontaneous interaction at the beginning of a group session. It is critical that the leader pay close attention to verbal and nonverbal cues as the protagonist describes the issue to be explored. For example, a member may describe himself as reserved and distant from others. He may use some metaphoric or symbolic language that has rich implications. In talking about letting others get close to him, he may allude to guard shields that he has carefully built to protect himself from the pain of rejection. Early in the course of a psychodrama, the director guides the protagonist in establishing the scene in which some significant event took place. In doing this, the leader can draw upon important cues the protagonist gave in presenting his situation, including facial expressions, figures of speech, and body posture. The process of warming up occurs as the protagonist is establishing the scene.

Whatever techniques are used in this getting-acquainted process, it is essential that members know that they will not be coerced to work on issues they choose not to explore. During the warm-up phase, members need to be assured that the working environment is a safe one, that they are the ones to decide *what* they will reveal and *when* they will reveal it, and that they can stop whenever they feel that they want to stop. If participants have the impression that they will be pressured to "perform" and badgered to go further than they feel ready or willing to, the morale of the group will suffer and the members will resist participation. The techniques are less important than the spirit and purpose of the warm-up: anything that facilitates the cohesion of the group and the establishing of trust is a useful tool for this phase.

According to Blatner (1973), the most important issue in the warm-up phase is creating an atmosphere that fosters *spontaneity*. In his view, the necessary conditions for spontaneous behavior to occur include:

- a sense of trust and a climate of psychological safety
- group norms that allow for the expression of emotions and for the inclusion of intuitive dimensions

- an element of playfulness
- a willingness to explore and engage in novel behavior

Blatner emphasizes the importance of the director's own warm-up as a key factor in creating a climate that encourages spontaneous behavior on the part of the group. It is during the warm-up period that directors are developing their own spontaneity. By communicating a sense of authenticity and warmth, directors foster a sense of confidence and trust in the group. Similarly, modeling risk taking, self-disclosure, humor, spontaneity, creativity, empathy, and the acceptability of expressing emotions and acting them out contributes to the group's cohesion. A theme may begin to emerge, and a protagonist may be selected and move onto the stage for action.

The Action Phase

The action phase includes the acting out and working through of a past or present situation or of an anticipated event. With the assistance of the director and other group members, protagonists act out their problems and relationships on the stage for their own benefit and for that of others who share in the learning experience. A single action phase may consist of one to several scenes. Scenes are constructed and enacted or reenacted as they relate to the protagonist's issues. They may be interpersonal or intrapersonal in nature and usually progress from peripheral issues (presenting problems) to more central issues (the real or deeper problems). The duration of the action phase varies, depending on the director's evaluation of the protagonist's involvement and on the level of involvement of the group.

Haskell (1973) offers some guidelines for directors during the action phase of psychodrama. Here are some of them:

- The protagonist should be encouraged as soon as possible to enact scenes involving conflicts in relationships.
- All the action should be geared to the here and now. Thus, if a person is dealing with a past situation and says "Then I told him," the director intervenes and says "You are telling him *now*."
- The protagonist needs the freedom to select the event, time, place, and people involved in the situation.
- Generally it is wise to deal first with less significant events and leave the reenacting of more traumatic experiences for later on.
- Protagonists should be asked to reconstruct a situation as faithfully as possible, without, however, being overly concerned with recalling the exact words exchanged, so that the flow of action is not inhibited. Instead, they need to know that the essence of an interaction, *as they recall it,* is what's important.
- Protagonists should be encouraged to express themselves as fully as possible, both verbally and nonverbally. However, the director needs to exert caution so that rage is expressed symbolically—for example, by hitting a pillow—and people are not injured.
- Protagonists can be given the opportunity to play the role of each person in their scene (role reversal); this can help them develop an understanding of how others perceived and felt about an event.

The Sharing and Discussion Phase

The third phase of psychodrama is the sharing, or discussion, phase. The participants are asked to share with the protagonist their observations of and reactions to the psychodrama in a constructive and supportive way. The director's task is to initiate and lead a discussion that includes as many participants as possible, so that feedback can be maximized. The director needs to watch for attempts by members to analyze the protagonist or confront the person harshly at a time when, having just finished revealing some intimate life experiences, he or she is most vulnerable. It is essential that protagonists be given an opportunity for closure of the experience. If protagonists have opened themselves up and expressed deep feelings, they need to be able to count on the support of the group in order to be able to integrate psychologically what they have just experienced. If no such opportunity is available through discussion and sharing, the protagonists may leave the session feeling rejected and lost instead of feeling freer and with a greater sense of direction.

Blatner (1973) sees this final stage as a time for working through the protagonist's concerns expressed in the psychodrama. This is accomplished by behavioral practice and audience input and by bringing closure and integration to the psychodrama. Also, after the action portion of the psychodrama, the protagonist needs to restore equilibrium. Blatner describes three ways in which the protagonist achieves this balance:

- by developing mastery over a particular conflict or problem
- by receiving group support and feedback
- by engaging in behavioral practice

The function of behavioral practice is to create a climate that allows for experimentation with a variety of new behaviors. Then the person can implement some of these new behaviors with significant others outside the group and cope with situations more effectively. To get behavioral practice, the protagonist presents the situation as it was originally presented in the action phase. Various techniques, such as role reversal, future projection, mirroring, and feedback, are often used to help the protagonist get a clearer idea of the impact of his or her new behavior. (These techniques are described later in the chapter.)

The *sharing period* is a critical aspect of the final stage of a psychodrama. Blatner (1973) comments that, after an intense enactment, the protagonist is typically vulnerable to the judgment of others in the group. For this reason, it is crucial that the sharing from the audience be of a personal, rather than analytical or interpretive, nature. The director must reinforce the kind of sharing that entails self-disclosure, support, and emotional involvement on the part of the members. If participants attempt to analyze or to provide solutions, the director needs to intervene, for example by asking questions such as:

- How has Jane's (the protagonist) drama affected you?
- What feelings were stirred up in you as you were participating in Jane's drama?
- What experiences in your life relate to Jane's situation?
- Are there any feelings you had toward Jane that you'd like to share with her?

Some form of *closure* is essential. A period of discussion can be useful for "winding down" the emotional pitch to a more cognitive level and for helping protagonist and audience integrate key aspects of the session. Although the emotional aspects of an enactment are of great therapeutic value, a degree of cognitive integration will maximize the value of the emotional components. Protagonists can be asked to express what they have learned from the particular enactment and the insights they have acquired. It is also a good practice to encourage the protagonist to talk about the personal meaning of reliving a situation. Protagonists can be stimulated to think of a possible course of action that will permit them to cope with repressed feelings and of practical ways of dealing more effectively with similar problem situations in the future.

A word of caution concerning closure is in order. Both Leveton (1977) and Blatner (1973) discuss the importance of dealing with unfinished business during the final phases of a psychodrama. Blatner proposes that, before closing a session, the director allow members to verbalize any unspoken feelings that have developed during the psychodrama. He says that, although it is not always necessary to work things out, it is important that the existence of unfinished business (unspoken feelings) be mentioned before the session closes. Leveton, too, acknowledges that it is not always possible or even desirable to resolve unfinished business. Realistically, although some problems will be opened up and fruitfully explored, the protagonist may be far from having resolved the issue. Leveton (1977) suggests that the director announce to the group that an incomplete situation does not indicate failure. Protagonists can gain a good deal of insight and take some significant steps in coping with difficult personal conflicts, and yet their business may still be unfinished. Further exploration and work are generally necessary, and members need to be warned of the danger of attempting premature and forced closure of an issue.

Leveton also discusses the unrealistic expectations of those practitioners who attempt to "cure the whole group." She points out that some practitioners have gargantuan egos and that they expect perfection. Unless everything is settled, these leaders feel that they have failed; in order to avoid such feelings, they may try to force closure in situations where participants are better off if they are encouraged to continue thinking about what has occurred. One of the most challenging tasks for any psychodrama director is learning to bring closure to a session without keeping members from further self-exploration, which is necessary for an in-depth resolution of their problems.

TECHNIQUES

Psychodrama uses a number of specific techniques designed to intensify feelings, lead to catharsis, and bring about increased self-understanding; this understanding of self comes about by a process of working through and integrating material that has surfaced in a psychodrama. These techniques are instrumental to the success of the psychodramatic process. However, a technique is not an end in itself but a means to the spontaneous expression of feelings by the participants. Thus J. L. Moreno (1953) warns about the misuse of techniques simply to stir up a dramatic performance.

Directors have latitude to invent their own techniques or modify standard ones. Blatner (1973) stresses the fact that psychodrama can be very powerful; practitioners need to bring humility and commitment to the practice of their technical skills, and they need to know when to apply these techniques. Effective psychodrama consists of far more than the mere use of certain techniques, no matter how skillful; practitioners must learn to know, and work with, the members' psychological worlds in an educated, trained, sensitive, caring, and creative manner.

I suggest that you keep these cautions in mind as you read the following overview of some standard psychodramatic techniques. These techniques are described in detail in the following sources: Blatner (1973), Corsini (1966), Greenberg (1968, 1974), Haskell (1973), Leveton (1977), J. L. Moreno (1958, 1964), Z. T. Moreno (1959, 1965, 1983), and Starr (1977).

Self-presentation. The protagonist gives a self-portrayal in order to introduce the actor. Let's assume that Jack, the protagonist, wants to explore his relationship with his daughter, Laura. He may do so by demonstrating how he typically approaches her. Jack's self-presentation gives the audience a sense of how he experiences himself in the father/daughter relationship. In the course of the self-presentation, Jack may state the problem as he sees it and may say something about his daughter.

Presentation of the other. In addition to presenting himself or herself, a protagonist may present another significant person (such as mother, father, sibling, lover, close friend, teacher, or relative). The protagonist presents a completely subjective perspective of this significant person. Z. T. Moreno (1983) makes the point that protagonists must act out the truth as they feel it and from their own subjective stance, regardless of how distorted their presentation may appear to the other members or the leader.

For example, Jack, the protagonist, presents his daughter. Preferably, he plays the role of Laura and demonstrates how she typically responds. As a variation, the director can interview Jack as he plays the role of his daughter. This technique will give the director and the group a clearer picture of how Jack perceives his daughter and how he thinks Laura perceives him.

Role reversal. The protagonist switches roles with another person on the stage. Typically, the director suggests a role reversal when it appears that the protagonist would benefit by attempting to "walk in the shoes" of the person with whom he or she is experiencing conflict. In the case of Jack, he could "become his daughter" while another member assumes his role as a father. By playing the role of Laura as he experiences her, Jack may begin to come to a clearer understanding of how *she* feels.

Stating that role reversal is at the heart of role-playing theory as demonstrated in psychodramatic groups, Z. T. Moreno (1983) maintains that this technique encourages maximal expression in conflict situations. Through the process of protagonists' enacting the roles of other persons with whom they are in conflict, their distortions of these relationships can be brought to the surface, explored, and corrected in action. By reversing roles, protagonists can reintegrate, redigest, and grow beyond situations that keep them unfree. Role reversal allows members to fully express their perceptions of reality, to get feedback from others in the group about their subjective views, and to make modifications of their perceptions to the extent that they discover distortions. Role reversal is probably the most important action technique in the psychodramatic approach. It can be used throughout the drama to correct or modify the principal auxiliary's role portrayal and to present additional information to the auxiliary. More importantly, it is used throughout the action phase to increase the protagonist's depth of perception of the significant other.

Soliloquy.   Basically, the soliloquy is a monologue in which the protagonist speaks directly to the audience by expressing some uncensored feelings and thoughts. For example, Jack may be asked to verbalize his thoughts during the course of a role reversal. This soliloquy gives Jack the chance to get a sense of what he believes his daughter is thinking and feeling but perhaps not expressing directly. Jack could also be asked to soliloquize after he has portrayed himself. He would do this by summarizing his thoughts, expressing his feelings, and examining them more closely.

Double technique.   An auxiliary ego stands behind the protagonist and acts with or even speaks *for* him. The double serves to mirror the inner thoughts and feelings of the protagonist, often expressing material beneath the consciousness of the protagonist. The double may serve an integrative function and also intensify the interaction between the protagonist and the auxiliary ego. In Jack's case, the double technique might be used if he felt stuck or felt overwhelmed by his daughter. The double would then help Jack stay in contact with and express his feelings. Effective doubling often results in the escalation of an interaction, and it is likely to provide the protagonist with the needed catalyst to say things that until now have remained unexpressed.

Multiple double technique.   The multiple double technique can be used effectively when the protagonist has ambivalent feelings. Two or more doubles participate in the drama, representing different facets of the protagonist. With Jack, one double may represent the side of him that misses his daughter and wants to express love, and the other double can be the "cold father" who really wants to have nothing to do with her. The doubles may speak at the same time, or they may take turns. If the doubles are effective, the father's ambivalent feelings toward his daughter can be successfully portrayed on the stage, and Jack may come to see which side within him is stronger. Also, he may get a clearer picture of the feelings and attitudes he'd like to express to his daughter.

Mirror technique.   An auxiliary ego assumes the role of the protagonist by mirroring the protagonist's postures, gestures, and words as they appeared in the enactment. During the auxiliary ego's mirroring, the protagonist is not on the stage, so that, by observing his own behavior as reflected by another person, he can see himself as others do. This process may help the protagonist develop a more accurate and objective picture of himself. For example, if Jack is mirrored as demanding, critical, aloof, and cold, he is likely to wonder whether that's the way his daughter perceives him. This technique might be particularly useful if others in the group saw Jack differently from the way he saw himself or if he had difficulty presenting himself verbally or in action.

The magic shop. The magic shop is often used as a warm-up technique before the action phase. It may also be elaborated upon throughout the action phase. This technique is frequently used with protagonists who are unclear about what they value, who are confused about their goals, or who have difficulty assigning priorities to their values. An auxiliary ego or the director is the storekeeper in a magic shop filled with imaginary qualities. These qualities are not for sale, but they can be bartered for. Thus, clients exchange qualities they possess for desired qualities. Jack, for example, may want to exchange his competitive style for the ability to open up to his daughter in a loving way. This technique can help Jack assess his priorities and see what is keeping him from getting what he wants from his relationship with Laura.

Future projection. The technique of future projection is designed to help group members express and clarify concerns they have about the future. These concerns could include wishes and hopes, dreaded fears of tomorrow, and goals that provide some direction to life. For example, members who have anxiety over an upcoming interview are asked to act out a future scene so that they can deal with their fears. Not only can they come into contact with their feelings, but they can also gain insight into behaviors that are likely to impede an effective interview. They can get feedback on the way they present themselves in the interview, and they can practice various behavioral styles to prepare themselves psychologically for what they might see as a stressful experience. It is important to repeat that the future concerns are not merely discussed and talked about; the anticipated event is brought into the present moment and acted out. Members may act out either a version of the way they hope the interview will ideally proceed or their version of the most horrible outcome.

Dream work. A unique feature of psychodrama is its experiential approach to dream work (as opposed to the psychoanalytic methods of analysis and interpretation), which calls for the protagonist to reenact the dream. For example, if a member of the group wanted to work on a dream in a psychodrama, she would assume a position in bed, reconstruct the dream, leave the bed, and act out the dream in the here and now. Auxiliary egos would be used to enact the roles of the dream characters. Through this process, the protagonist could change various elements of her dream, thus gaining insights into certain personality patterns by acting out the new elements of her dream.

Didactic psychodrama. Zerka Moreno (1983) has pointed out that psychodrama can be a valuable teaching method for students and professionals in the mental-health field. For example, instead of merely talking about their "difficult clients" in a supervision group, students or therapists can assume the roles of these clients. This approach is rich with potential for unearthing countertransference feelings, which can then be fully explored in a supervision group. Other members can present alternative ways of dealing with the difficult clients, as well as feedback to help separate client problems from therapist projections.

ROLE AND FUNCTIONS OF THE DIRECTOR AND ETHICAL ISSUES

We have already discussed many of the functions that the director of a psychodramatic group must perform. There are other, more general observations that need to be made with regard to these functions. Since psychodrama is a powerful method, it is essential that the director have theoretical, technical, and practical knowledge of psychodramatic technique. In order to fully appreciate the potential values and risks inherent in these techniques, he or she needs to have experienced them as a participant. Inept leadership—manifested, for instance, in forcing people into situations with which they are not ready to deal—can have serious negative consequences for the participants.

For example, although there is definite value in using members as auxiliary egos, there is also the ever-present risk that they will bring their own distortions to the roles they play, further complicating the protagonist's life. The same situation occurs when members project their own conflicts onto the protagonist and offer quick interpretations and solutions to thorny issues. Another key problem that requires skillful handling by the director is that, unless there is an adequate debriefing process, participants may be left hanging with some very unproductive unfinished business. For all these reasons, the sensitivity and expertise of the psychodrama-group director are crucial if the experience is to be a therapeutic one.

Blatner (1973) emphasizes that psychodrama is not a panacea. He cautions practitioners against the danger of romanticizing a single approach, thus becoming blind to the limits of that approach and to the values of other methods. Blatner encourages his readers to obtain some supervised training in the use of psychodrama before attempting to apply any but the most basic psychodramatic techniques. Recognizing that psychodrama is a powerful form of therapeutic intervention, he underscores the importance of the practitioner's knowledge and ability to deal therapeutically with what surfaces in a psychodrama.

Leveton (1977) issues a warning about the irresponsible use of psychodramatic procedures. Skilled directors, Leveton says, are willing to devote the necessary time to developing their skills and have undergone a training program under the supervision of an experienced clinician. Leveton describes some of the "new students" she has encountered whose "cups may run over with techniques" and who have no fear of using these techniques, no matter what the circumstances.

In agreement with Blatner and Leveton are J. L. Moreno and Elefthery (1982), who caution that psychodrama is a potent method and that the potential for harming clients is great when it is practiced by untrained persons. They emphasize how essential it is for leaders to have a thorough knowledge of group dynamics and to know their own limitations as well as the limitations of the method for certain client populations. They write that psychodrama should be used very carefully, if at all, with acting-out individuals, with a seriously disturbed population, or with a sociopathic population. It is especially important that leaders have the experience and knowledge to deal with underlying psychopathology. Also, they must have considerable sensitivity so that they do not push disturbed clients past a point that is therapeutic. It is also critical that leaders exercise good judgment in structuring situations so that members are not likely to open up old wounds without getting some closure to them. Moreno and Elefthery suggest that, in addition to training and supervision in psychodramatic methods, a leader who wants to practice this approach should play the role of a protagonist a number of times. If leaders have experienced techniques personally, they have a much better framework for knowing when particular methods are called for and for anticipating their effects.

Both Blatner (1973) and Moreno and Elefthery (1982) discuss the danger of leaders' being attracted to psychodrama to fill their egotistical needs. It is critical that they be aware of how their own personal problems and needs might interfere with their functioning in a therapeutic way. In this regard, countertransference issues must be worked through before the leader can hope to have a therapeutic impact on the group. Blatner (1973) asserts "If the director is not aware of his counter-transference reactions, he may fall into the major error of pushing and coercing his clients, or allowing other group members to act out his own needs" (p. 92). If group leaders are not secure in their professional competence, they may easily become impatient with what they perceive as the "slow progress" of their clients. Out of their desire to speed up the pace of their clients and to see more immediate results, they may resort to a variety of manipulations designed to stir up emotions for the sake of drama. Although spontaneity is one of the basic concepts of psychodrama, it can be misused. On this issue, Blatner (1973) again makes an excellent point when he writes: "Exhibiting any and all impulses is not the purpose of developing spontaneity. When grossly misused, this kind of expressiveness could be called *pathological spontaneity*" (p. 91). Therefore, it is imperative that a group leader's spontaneity, inventiveness, and courage to try new techniques be tempered with a measure of caution, respect for the members, concern for their welfare, and a sense of the possible outcomes of the techniques suggested.

I believe that, in addition to having been a protagonist in a group many times, a director must have had a substantial period of personal psychotherapy. Psychodrama can be a very directive technique and thus lends itself to abuse through countertransference. The dangers of this abuse can be greatly lessened, if not avoided, with the personal awareness gleaned from individual psychotherapy.

APPLICATIONS OF PSYCHODRAMA TO FAMILY THERAPY

Psychodrama can be a dynamic approach to working with family groups. Many of the psychodramatic techniques that have been described in this chapter can be utilized in family therapy to help members of a family express and work out basic conflicts. Rather than having family members simply tell their stories and engage in lengthy reports of situations, the leader can direct them to reenact the particular situation in question. Role-playing techniques are especially powerful in bringing to the surface how each member perceives what is going on in that family.

Consider the Miller family, which comes for therapy because its members do not seem to be able to coexist peacefully. Besides Mr. and Mrs. Miller, there are a teenage son and a teenage daughter. An initial assessment of the family makes it clear that Mrs. Miller is constantly criticizing the daughter, Ann, and comparing her unfavorably with her older brother, Sam. It does not seem that Ann can do anything to please her mother, so Ann has developed negativistic ways of acting. Sam seems somewhat independent and keeps himself busy with a part-time job, school activities, and seeing friends. Both parents see Sam as the successful one and say they are baffled over the way Ann has turned out. Mrs. Miller complains that her husband does not take any interest in family matters, that he buries himself in his work, and that he blames her for most of the family's problems because of her constant nagging at both Ann and him. He says he feels deficient as a husband because he can never seem to do what his wife expects, so he stays away from home as much as possible. The family sought counseling because of Mrs. Miller's insistence and her conviction that she simply could not continue living as they were. What are some possibilities for exploring and resolving the Miller family's problems by drawing upon psychodramatic procedures?

One approach would be for the family to reenact a recent problem situation as though it were happening in the present. A family argument that resulted in people's slamming doors and leaving could be replayed as each family member experienced that scene. After each member has reacted to the situation, the therapist, as arbitrator, could point out what he or she sees going on in the family. The therapist might then ask the members of the family to exchange identities for a time through role reversals. The scene might look like this: Ann becomes her mother, Mrs. Miller becomes Ann, and Sam and Mr. Miller reverse roles. Later Mrs. Miller might reverse roles with Mr. Miller, and Ann and Sam could assume each other's identity. If such a procedure is related to a particular conflict situation that involved the entire family, the possibilities for therapeutic breakthroughs are immense. Each person is likely to gain some appreciation for the others' position in the family. Of course, it would take some skillful intervention on the therapist's part to assure that each person brought out his or her feelings and perceptions. Some timely and appropriate interpretations could illuminate the dynamics within the family. The members might also be given tasks to do outside of the session. For example, for a week Mr. and Mrs. Miller might try exchanging roles as an experiment to determine what might happen and what could be learned.

Once it could be ascertained what each member wanted, especially as it pertained to living in the family, the therapist could set the stage for a future projection. He or she might ask: "Imagine that you could find a way to live cooperatively and that you were able to work out the conflicts that you say keep you divided as a family. What would you hope your family would be like?

What would you want to be able to say to one another? What do you want from one another?"

Even though this section is brief, I hope that you can see some lively possibilities of utilizing many of the psychodramatic techniques I've described, even if you do use them in combination with some other theoretical orientation. These techniques could be used productively with any of the theories in this book. The basic idea consists of having the family reenact past concerns in the here and now in the office. The focus is upon the subjective perceptions and reactions of each family member, along with therapist interventions to prevent the participants from slipping into a blaming stance. By using such procedures, family members are often able to alter certain misperceptions, inaccurate estimates of the situation, and biases. This approach prevents endless discussions about problem topics and encourages clients to experience and live out their problems in front of their own eyes with the therapist as an objective, yet involved, consultant. Not only can family members pinpoint issues, but they can also experiment with different ways of feeling, thinking, acting, and responding.

EVALUATION OF PSYCHODRAMA

I value psychodrama's action-oriented methods and role playing mainly because they lead the participants to the direct experience of real conflicts. I confess that I have little patience with endless talk about problems, since it has been my experience that members profit very little from talking about themselves in a detached, storytelling manner. But, for the participants to learn about themselves, role playing must be designed to fit a specific situation, and certain role-playing techniques must be used to provide further understanding of actual conflicts in the members' lives. If a psychodrama is set up just to give the members an idea of what it's like, I question the outcomes.

In my own practice, I tend to use psychodramatic methods whenever a member is undergoing a conflict situation that can be acted out. I see these methods as useful not only for the person who is the focus of the action but for other participants as well. Most of the times that I've used psychodrama, the result has been participation by other members. Also, it is a method that binds people together because it offers opportunities to become aware that one's own struggles are also the struggles of others.

There is another reason why I value psychodrama. Often people simply don't see other ways of behaving with the significant persons in their lives. In psychodrama other group members can demonstrate alternative ways of responding and thus provide the person with different frames of reference. For example, in a role-playing situation, Nora approaches her husband, Ralph, with a litany of all his shortcomings—that he's selfish, that he doesn't care, that he doesn't show his feelings or truly share his life with her. Another member can show Nora a different way of relating to her husband, one that is not accusatory and that won't cause him to close up and ignore her complaints. As a result, Nora may want to try new approaches, which she may not even have considered before.

It is not necessary for a group practitioner who wants to develop a psycho-drama workshop to adhere to the action-oriented methods that have been described in this chapter. These methods can be integrated into the framework of other group approaches. Despite the value of psychodrama, I have found that some of the psychodrama workshops I have attended as a participant are needlessly restrictive. These techniques are often quite useful and appropriate; yet I am not in favor of converting every interaction into dramatic form. Inte-grated into other systems, such as some of the cognitive styles of behavior therapy, psychodrama can provide the exploration of emotions that these other systems often downplay. But I think that the psychodramatic group can be enhanced by more emphasis on the cognitive aspects of the process and by deeper investigation of the meaning of the cathartic experience.

Although I have seen the value of catharsis—the release of pent-up rage, hurt, guilt, sorrow, anger, and other repressed feelings, which often come out in indirect ways—my experience with groups has taught me time and again how essential it is to provide a context in which members can come to an understanding of what these bottled-up emotions have done to them, to others, and to their relationships. Yet emotional release and self-understanding alone do not seem sufficient for lasting changes in one's way of thinking/feeling/behaving. I am convinced that such deep changes will come about only if members are taught how to transfer what they have learned in their sessions to everyday situations. It is also critical to teach them ways of maintaining these positive emotional and behavioral changes. This can be done by helping people plan ways of coping effectively when they meet with frustration in the world and when they experience regression by seeming to forget the lessons they have learned in their group. An excellent time for this cognitive work and plan formulation is during the sharing sessions after each psychodrama has been brought to a close. Simply encouraging people to "get in touch with their feelings" does not seem potent enough to goad them into *doing* something different when they meet with future difficulties. Thus, rehearsals for future encounters, coupled with constructive and specific feedback, can be of real value to those members who want to develop alternative means of relating to significant people in their lives.

In terms of the major limitations and cautions in the use of psychodramatic methods, I've discussed in a previous section matters such as the need for training and supervised experience, coupled with therapist self-awareness. In short, it is true that psychodrama is both a powerful and risky approach to group work, yet most of the concerns I have in this area can be offset by an honest and ongoing self-evaluation on the part of a practitioner who is trained in the use of these techniques with the particular population in question.

One of the criticisms of psychodrama is that research has been inadequate. Although there are reports in the literature on case studies, on innovations in psychodramatic methods, on applications of the procedures to diverse pop-ulations, and on process-and-outcome research studies, it is difficult to eval-uate this literature due to the differences in therapeutic styles and behaviors of practitioners (Rudestam, 1982).

In closing, I'd like to recognize the profound impact of J. L. Moreno on the field of group therapy. The more I learn about the techniques that he pioneered, the more aware I become of his genius as a practitioner. It is an understatement to merely say that he was a man far ahead of his time. With his visionary perspective he created methods for integrating feelings, fantasies, and actions. As you read about other group therapeutic approaches, you will see how many of the basic concepts and techniques of psychodrama appear in what are sometimes referred to as "innovative therapies." As I mentioned earlier in this chapter, many of the experiential therapies borrow heavily from psychodrama, and even cognitive, behavior-oriented therapies make frequent use of role-playing procedures. Thus, learning about psychodrama is of value because of the many ways it can be integrated with the therapies that you will study in the remainder of this book.

If you are interested in learning more about the practical values and applications of psychodrama, I urge you not to limit yourself to reading about the approach in journals and books. Instead, I encourage you to seek out some advanced training and supervision and some reputable workshops where you can experience psychodrama as a group member. You will not only learn how this therapy approach works in a group but will also be able to work on some personal concerns and find new ways of dealing with them.

The best source of information about training and programs leading to certification in psychodrama is the American Board of Examiners in Psychodrama, Sociometry and Group Psychotherapy, P.O. Box 844, Cooper Station, New York, NY 10276. The board was founded in 1975 to establish national professional standards in psychodrama, sociometry, and group psychotherapy and to certify qualified professionals on the basis of these standards. This organization has a booklet listing trainers, educators, and practitioners in psychodrama.

QUESTIONS FOR REFLECTION AND DISCUSSION

1. What are some of the most striking differences, in terms of basic concepts and therapeutic techniques, between psychodramatic and psychoanalytic groups? Do you see some ways of thinking in psychoanalytic terms while working with group members in a psychodramatic format?
2. For what populations do you think psychodramatic techniques would be most appropriate? Can you think of any clients whom you would not recommend for psychodrama?
3. What are your reactions to dealing with both the past and the future as though these events were happening in the present? What are some advantages you can see in this present-centered focus? Do you see any problems with bringing all experiences into the "now" and asking clients to reenact a past event or act out some expected future event?
4. How might you respond to a group member who refused to get involved in any type of role playing on the ground that doing so was artificial? If the person were to say to you "Why do you want me to go back and relive a painful period in my life? I have tried to forget about those difficult times.

What good will it do me to open up that can of worms?" how might you respond?

5. What are some specific psychodramatic techniques that you'd like to include in the groups you are leading or might someday lead? How can you incorporate some basic concepts and practices of psychodrama into the model of group counseling that you favor?

6. If you were to employ role-playing procedures in a group you were leading, or if you wanted to create a psychodrama as a way to work with a member's problem, what steps would you take to prepare the members for these techniques? What are some ways you can think of to "warm up" your group so that the members are trusting enough to get involved in the process?

7. In the section of this chapter on the role of the director and ethical issues, a number of the risks involved in practicing psychodrama were mentioned. What are your reactions to these cautions and concerns as they apply to you?

8. What kind of training and experience would you deem essential before you felt confident in employing some of the techniques you have read about in this chapter?

9. How might you go about preparing an agency you worked for to allow you to organize and lead a psychodramatic group? What concerns or objections might you expect to hear from the administrators of such an agency?

10. If you were a member of a psychodramatic group, how do you imagine that you'd respond to getting involved in the techniques that you've just read about? What kind of member would you be?

RECOMMENDED SUPPLEMENTARY READINGS

Acting-in: Practical applications of psychodramatic methods (Blatner, 1973) is a guide for practitioners interested in using psychodramatic techniques in a group setting. This brief book is written very clearly and contains excellent discussions of the basic elements of psychodrama, its methods, stages, principles, and applications, as well as some of its pitfalls. Beginners who want a good overview of psychodrama will find this book extremely valuable.

The psychodramatic method (Haskell, 1973) and *Socioanalysis: Self-direction via sociometry and psychodrama* (Haskell, 1975) are two short books that supply beginning group practitioners with a basic grasp of concepts and techniques of psychodrama, sociodrama, and role playing.

Psychodrama for the timid clinician (Leveton, 1977) offers an excellent and eclectic view of psychodrama. The writing is clear, vivid, and very interesting. A number of psychodramatic techniques are described and illustrated through case examples that attest to the author's skills and creativity in applying these techniques. Group leaders can greatly benefit from reading the book and following the author's encouragement to use experiential techniques in group work.

Psychodrama: Rehearsal for living (Starr, 1977) contains good material on role playing and role training, on setting the stage, and on warm-up and training techniques. Particularly good is the section on the applications of psychodrama. Other chapters deal with applications of psychodramatic methods to marital therapy, children's groups, work with alcoholics and drug abusers, and psychotics' and outpatient groups.

Psychodrama: Theory and therapy (Greenberg, 1974) is a reader that covers the theory of psychodrama, its history and development, specialized techniques and treatment, and evaluation of the method. This interesting collection of articles gives the reader a good grasp of the various aspects of psychodrama.

For those of you who are interested in an in-depth study of the history and evolution of psychodrama, as well as its applications to many different problems and populations, I suggest that you consult the annotated bibliography prepared by Samuel Cardone in Corsini's (1966) book *Roleplaying in psychotherapy*. This bibliography is the result of a review of the periodical literature up to 1965; these articles deal with both the theoretical and practical dimensions of psychodrama, and the 133 abstracts attempt to capture the language style of the authors of each of these articles. Another source is the official publication of the American Society of Group Psychotherapy and Psychodrama, which is entitled *Group Psychotherapy, Psychodrama, and Sociometry*.

REFERENCES AND SUGGESTED READINGS*

Blatner, H. A. *Psychodrama, role-playing, and action methods*. Thetford, U.K.: Blatner, 1970.

* Blatner, H. A. *Acting-in: Practical applications of psychodramatic methods*. New York: Springer, 1973.

Corsini, R. J. *Methods of group psychotherapy*. New York: McGraw-Hill, 1957.

* Corsini, R. J. *Roleplaying in psychotherapy*. Chicago: Aldine, 1966.

Fine, F. J. Psychodrama. In R. J. Corsini (Ed.), *Current psychotherapies* (2nd ed.). Itasca, Ill.: Peacock, 1979.

Greenberg, I. A. *Psychodrama and audience attitude change*. Beverly Hills, Calif.: Behavioral Studies Press, 1968.

Greenberg, I. A. (Ed.). *Psychodrama: Theory and therapy*. New York: Behavioral Publications, 1974.

Greenberg, I. A. (Ed.). *Group hypnotherapy and hypnodrama*. Chicago: Nelson-Hall, 1977.

Greenwald, H. (Ed.). *Active psychotherapy*. New York: Atherton, 1967.

Haskell, M. R. *An introduction to socioanalysis* (2nd ed.). Long Beach, Calif.: California Institute of Socioanalysis, 1972.

Haskell, M. R. *The psychodramatic method* (4th ed.). Long Beach: California Institute of Socioanalysis, 1973.

Haskell, M. R. *Socioanalysis: Self-direction via sociometry and psychodrama*. Long Beach: Role Training Associates of California, 1975.

* Leveton, E. *Psychodrama for the timid clinician*. New York: Springer, 1977.

Moreno, J. L. *Einladung zu einer Begegnung*. Vienna: Anzengeuber, 1914.

Moreno, J. L. *Psychodrama* (Vol. 1). Beacon, N.Y.: Beacon House, 1946.

Moreno, J. L. *Who shall survive?* Beacon, N.Y.: Beacon House, 1953.

Moreno, J. L. *Psychodrama* (Vol. 2). Beacon, N.Y.: Beacon House, 1958.

Moreno, J. L. *Psychodrama* (Vol. 1, Rev. ed.). Beacon, N.Y.: Beacon House, 1964.

Moreno, J. L., & Elefthery, D. G. An introduction to group psychodrama. In G. M. Gazda (Ed.), *Basic approaches to group psychotherapy and group counseling* (3rd ed.). Springfield, Ill.: Charles C Thomas, 1982.

Moreno, Z. T. A survey of psychodramatic techniques. *Group Psychotherapy*, 1959, *12*, 5–14.

* Moreno, Z. T. Psychodrama rules, techniques, and adjunctive methods. *Group Psychotherapy*, 1965, *18*(1–2), 73–86.

* Moreno, Z. T. Psychodrama. In H. I. Kaplan & B. J. Sadock (Eds.), *Comprehensive group* (2nd ed.). Baltimore: Williams and Wilkins, 1983.

Orcutt, T. L. Roles and rules: The kinship and territoriality of psychodrama and Gestalt therapy. *Group Psychotherapy, Psychodrama, and Sociometry*, 1977, *30*.

Rudestam, K. E. *Experiential groups in theory and practice*. Monterey, Calif.: Brooks/Cole, 1982.

*Books and articles marked with an asterisk are suggested for further study.

Schutz, W. C. *Here comes everybody: Bodymind and encounter culture.* New York: Harper & Row, 1971.

Siroka, R. W., Siroka, E. K., & Schloss, G. A. (Eds.). *Sensitivity training and group encounter.* New York: Grosset & Dunlap, 1971.

Starr, A. *Psychodrama: Rehearsal for living.* Chicago: Nelson-Hall, 1977.

Yablonsky, L. A brief view of Moreno. In I. A. Greenberg (Ed.), *Psychodrama: Theory and therapy.* New York: Behavioral Publications, 1974.

Yablonsky, L. *Psychodrama.* New York: Basic Books, 1976.

9

THE EXISTENTIAL APPROACH

INTRODUCTION

The major approaches to psychotherapy can be grouped into three broad classifications: (1) the psychodynamic approach, which emphasizes insight, unconscious motivation, and personality reconstruction; (2) the various forms of behavior modification and the rational-cognitive styles of behavior-oriented therapies, such as transactional analysis, rational-emotive therapy, and reality therapy; and (3) those models that are often referred to as the "third force" and that I find convenient to lump together under the heading "existential-humanistic therapies"—existential therapy, person-centered therapy, and Gestalt therapy, to name just a few. These approaches are largely experiential and relationship oriented, and they differ from the other two groups of models on philosophical grounds and in terms of their belief about the nature of the therapist/client relationship.

In the past the connection between philosophical issues and psychotherapy was rather tenuous. In recent years, especially because of the prominence achieved by the existential approach, the connection has become much more substantial, and the issues of freedom, responsibility, choice, and the meaning of being fully human have become the focus of much concern.

In contrast to the empirical approach that dominated psychology for many years, existentially oriented psychologists argue that human behavior cannot be understood by relying only on objective methods—that is, by approaching human beings as objects to be understood from an external point of view. These psychologists stress the need to take into consideration the individual's

219

internal frame of reference and subjective experience. The writers who call for this personalistic approach include Arbuckle (1975), Bugental (1965, 1976, 1978), Frankl (1963, 1965), Jourard (1968a, 1971), Kemp (1971), Maslow (1968, 1970), May (1961, 1967; May, Angel, & Ellenberger, 1958), and Yalom (1980).

Existential therapy can best be considered as an *approach*, or *philosophy*, by which a therapist operates. As such, it is not a separate school or a neatly defined, systematic model with specific therapeutic techniques. Mullan (1979) refers to the method of existentialism as a nonsystem when it is compared with most other group approaches. The group leader cannot assume that he or she alone knows the purpose of the group; rather, it is up to each participant to discover this purpose. I will focus in this chapter on the basic themes, or universal human concerns, of this approach, which have significant implications for the existentially oriented group leader.

It is important to remember that the existential approach developed as a reaction to two other major models—psychoanalysis and behaviorism. Specifically, it rejects the psychoanalytic and behavioristic positions' deterministic, reductionistic, and mechanistic view of humans. The psychoanalytic view sees freedom as restricted by unconscious forces, irrational drives, and past events. The behavioristic position sees freedom as restricted by sociocultural conditioning. Existential psychotherapy, in contrast, is a dynamic approach that focuses on four ultimate concerns that are rooted in human existence—death, freedom, isolation, and meaninglessness (Yalom, 1980). It is grounded on the assumption that we are free and therefore entirely responsible for our choices and actions. We are the author of our life, and we draw up the blueprints for its design. A basic existential premise is that we are not the victim of circumstances, because, to a large extent, we are what we choose to be or not to be. Thus, one of the goals of the therapeutic process is to challenge clients to discover alternatives and choose among them. For many clients, the recognition of the ways that they have kept themselves in a victimlike stance marks the beginning of change. We can recognize that we do not have to remain the passive victim of our circumstances, and by accepting this, we can consciously become the architect of our life.

The Relationship between Humanistic Psychology and Existential Therapy

In my earlier writings I attempted to blend some key concepts of humanistic psychology with existential therapy, only to find that students had a difficult time separating these two approaches. Indeed, some writers with an existential orientation to therapy speak about an existential-humanistic approach (see Bugental, 1978; Burton, 1967). In this revised edition I have decided to focus on existential therapy as it applies to groups. But I hope a brief discussion will clarify the distinction between the humanistic approach and the existential approach.

The focus of humanistic psychology.   Synthesizing their theories from many divergent fields and approaches, humanistic psychologists contended that people could not be studied and understood in segmented fashion. Rather, humans must be studied in complete relation to how they interact with others and with the world. Some key figures in the development of humanistic psychology included Carl Rogers, Rollo May, Abraham Maslow, and James Bugental. From its earliest days, the humanistic movement was characterized by certain central themes that focus on the capacities unique to humans—namely, love, choice, creativity, purpose, relatedness, meaning, values, self-actualization, autonomy, responsibility, ego transcendence, humor, and spontaneity. According to humanistic psychologists, any therapy that aims at growth must take these human capacities into account. To a large extent, the encounter-group movement in the 1960s and 1970s grew out of the humanistic force.

Unfortunately, as with many movements, humanistic psychology became associated with antiintellectualism, living impulsively without consideration for future goals or for others, and a self-orientation that fostered a "doing-your-own-thing" approach to life. According to Yalom (1980), some of the key leaders of humanistic psychology became disenchanted with the irrational trends in the movement. Yalom does mention that a hazy relationship links humanistic psychology with existential psychotherapy, since they share many basic tenets and assumptions. Also, many humanistic psychologists have an existential orientation—Maslow, Rogers, May, Fritz Perls, and Bugental.

The focus of existential psychotherapy. Existentialism is a branch of philosophical thought that began in Europe. The key existential writers did not address themselves to psychotherapeutic concerns directly. Existentialism ranges from the negative (Jean-Paul Sartre) to the positive (Martin Buber). The existential tradition emphasized limitations and the tragic dimensions of human existence. The focus was on being in the world alone, facing the anxiety of this isolation and of nonbeing.

Perhaps one of the key figures responsible for bringing existentialism from Europe and translating key concepts into psychotherapeutic practice is May. His writings have had significant impact on existentially oriented practitioners. According to May, becoming a person is not an automatic process, yet people do have a desire to fulfill their potential. It takes courage to be, and our choices determine the kind of person we become. There is a constant struggle within us. Although we want to grow toward maturity and independence, we realize that expansion is often a painful process. Hence, the struggle is between the security of dependence and the delights and pains of growth. Along with May, another significant recent source of contemporary existential therapy is Yalom's (1980) work.

The Focus of This Chapter

In this chapter we'll examine some key concepts of the existential approach and their implications for group practice. These key concepts are self-awareness, self-determination and responsibility, existential anxiety, death and nonbeing, the search for meaning, the search for authenticity, and aloneness and relatedness. Rather than focusing on group techniques, this chapter stresses understanding how these key concepts can be applied in a group with an existential orientation.

In keeping with this spirit, I have written this chapter from the perspective of my own interpretation of the existential approach. I have focused on concepts that receive attention by most existential writers and practitioners, and I have summarized and integrated some of the major themes running through various humanistic writings as these themes apply to group practice.

KEY CONCEPTS

Therapeutic Goals

The existential group represents a microcosm of the world in which the participants live and function. Its members meet for the purpose of discovering themselves as they are by sharing their existential concerns and by making themselves known to others.

In writing about the goals of an existential group, Mullan (1979) makes it clear that each group member must go through a painful process to discover his or her own goals in the group. At the beginning, a group experience is painful because rules and routines are lacking and because members are searching for, but cannot find, roles to play. They find that their pregroup behavior does not work for them in the therapy group. Members often question the role of the leader, as well as the value of the group for themselves. Mullan contends that, in their journey to become more authentic, members typically experience suffering and despair as they face their human condition. Eventually, this depression gives way to periods of calm and joy, but the road is a rough one.

Watson (1977) identifies the therapeutic goal as increasing the clients' awareness of options and potentials, helping them to make choices, and promoting an attitude of commitment:

> The aim of therapy is not to alleviate a symptom or to help the patient "adjust" to society, but rather to have the patient discover her own being. If therapy is successful, the patients experience their existence as real and become fully aware of this existence so that options and potentials become evident and change is therefore seen as possible [p. 168].

The members of an existential group are confronted over and over with the fact that they cannot escape from freedom and that they are responsible for their existence. Accepting this freedom and this responsibility generates anxiety, and so do the risk and uncertainty associated with making choices. Another goal of the existential group is to help participants face and deal with these anxieties.

An existential group might be described as people making a commitment to begin and to continue a lifelong journey of self-exploration. The group provides the encouragement for members to begin listening to themselves and paying attention to their subjective experience. This process of inner searching gives emphasis to what members discover within their own stream of awareness when this stream is not directed by the therapist. By being willing to openly share and explore universal personal concerns, members develop a sense of mutuality. The close ties that they feel with one another give them many opportunities for using the group culture differently from other aspects of their culture. Ofman (1983) illustrates what he sees as the essence of the existential group: "We are a conversation. We need each other. The actualization of this need and the creation of an authentic environment for its satisfaction are what the existential group is all about" (p. 113). In short, an existential group is a place where people can be together in deeply meaningful ways without the superficiality characteristic of so many meetings.

Self-Awareness

The capacity for self-awareness separates us from other animals and enables us to think and make choices. The greater our awareness, the greater our possibilities for freedom. Even though we are subject to the deterministic forces of sociocultural conditioning and to the limitations imposed by our genetic endowment, we are still able to make choices based on our awareness of these limiting factors. As May (1961) stated, "No matter how great the forces victimizing the human being, man has the capacity to know that he is being victimized and thus to influence in some way how he will relate to his fate" (pp. 41–42). Furthermore, because of our self-awareness, we come to recognize the responsibility associated with the freedom to choose and to act.

Implications for group work. As we saw earlier, the basic goal of existential therapy is to expand self-awareness and thus increase choice potential. In groups this goal is pursued by helping members discover their unique "being-in-the-world" through the ways they are in the group. By trying to answer some key questions, participants seek to define themselves and become aware of the central dimensions of their existence: To what degree am I aware of who I am and of who I am becoming? How do I experience my world? What meanings do I attach to the events I experience? How can I increase my self-awareness? In what concrete ways does expanded consciousness increase my choice potential and my range of alternatives?

In the group situation, participants have the opportunity to express their own unique feelings and their subjective views of the world. They do this largely by the way they present themselves and act in the group. The focus is on the present—on observing and experiencing how oneself and others are in the here and now—so that members can become increasingly aware of the unknown dimensions of their own beings.

In the group, participants are explicitly confronted and learn to deal with the anxiety that arises from having to choose who they are right there and then and from being experienced by others when they are stripped of the securities of their everyday roles. As we shall discuss in detail later in the chapter, existentialists view anxiety in positive terms. Anxiety "individuates" us, it awakens us to the "inauthenticity" of merely being who others want us to be, and reflects the understanding that we are unique and have the potential for moving toward our own unique possibilities.

But anxiety is uncomfortable. The desire to avoid the anxiety associated with increased self-awareness can lead participants to use their freedom to actually decrease their self-awareness and thus withdraw from life. Kemp (1971) indicates that, in order to escape anxiety, clients can relinquish their identity (often unconsciously) by submerging themselves in the group, by meeting life situations without struggle, and by attempting to live by fulfilling the expectations of others. The result is that they also relinquish contact with themselves and give up their individuality.

Thus, I believe that group leaders need to alert the members of their groups to the price they must pay for seeking greater self-awareness. As people become more aware of their existences, they find it increasingly difficult to "go back home again." If living in ignorance of the quality of one's existence can lead to staleness, it can also bring a certain degree of contentment or, at least, security. As we open doors that were previously closed, we can expect to encounter more struggle as well as the potential for enhancing the quality of our living. The experience can be exciting and joyful but also frightening and at times depressing. This is an issue that at least should be mentioned and explored during the early phases of a group, so that members are aware of the need to consider whether they are willing to pay the price that increased self-awareness entails.

What are the options that a higher degree of self-awareness permits us to recognize? Here are some of them:

- We can choose to expand our awareness, or we can choose to limit our vision of ourselves.
- We can determine the direction of our own lives, or we can allow other people and environmental forces to determine it for us.
- We can use our potential for action, or we can choose not to act.
- We can choose to establish meaningful ties with others, or we can choose to isolate ourselves.
- We can search for our own uniqueness, or we can allow our identity to be lost in conformity.
- We can create and find meaning in our life, or we can lead an empty and meaningless existence.
- We can engage in certain risks and experience the anxieties that accompany deciding for ourselves, or we can choose the security of dependence.
- We can make the most of the present by accepting the inevitability of our eventual death, or we can hide from this reality because of the anxiety it generates.
- We can commit ourselves to striving to utilize our full potential, or we can settle for functioning with only a small fraction of our capacity.

Example.   The following example is meant to illustrate how participants in a group can gradually achieve a higher level of awareness. This and the examples that illustrate the other key concepts in this chapter were drawn from my experience with the groups I have led. To protect the identity of the clients, I have changed the names and the specific circumstances, and I have chosen examples that have a universal quality—that is, examples that are illustrations of experiences that occur frequently in a group.

When Crystal first entered the group, she could see no value in expressing intense emotions and insisted that she *had* to be rational no matter what. She tried very hard to keep her feelings harnessed at all times, because she was afraid that she'd "go crazy" if she allowed herself to feel intensely. This need to tightly control her feelings manifested itself in several ways. For example, when other group members relived painful emotional events, Crystal panicked and tried to leave the room, and she often attempted to defuse the expression of intense emotions by others in the group. However, during one session another person's work triggered some very painful memories in Crystal, which she felt fully because, for some reason, she allowed herself to relive a scene from her childhood related to her parents' divorce. Suddenly Crystal became that frightened child again, pleading with her parents to stay together and letting herself "go emotionally out of control."

This unexpected experience made Crystal aware that she had been keeping a lid on her strong feelings and that her defenses against "hurting too much" had resulted in her difficulty in getting close to others, in expressing anger, and in manifesting the love she claimed she felt for her family now. She also learned that she wouldn't "go crazy" by permitting herself to experience the depth of her feelings. After that experience Crystal chose to open herself to feelings and not to run out of the room when she was afraid she couldn't take the intense emotions of other members.

Self-Determination and Personal Responsibility

Another existential theme is that we are self-determining beings—namely, that we are free to choose among alternatives and that we are responsible for directing our lives and shaping our destinies. The existentialists' view is that, although we are thrust into the world, how we live and what we become are the results of our choices. As Sartre (1971) put it, our existence is a given, but we do not have, and cannot have, a fixed, settled "nature" or "essence." We are constantly faced with having to choose the kind of person we want to become, and, as long as we live, we must continue to choose. Sartre (1971) remarked: "Man being condemned to be free carries the weight of the whole world on his shoulders; he is responsible for the world and for himself as a way of being" (p. 553). For Sartre, we are free in that we are nothing but what we *do*, and what we do is not the result of our past.

Russell (1978a) notes that, in Sartre's view, we can never find anything in the world that has a meaning independent of us and that we are responsible for the world as a significant place. Russell adds: "Each time we act we thereby choose and create ourselves as we want to be, and this is never finished—what we are is never settled—but is created in each of the deeds that constitute us" (p. 262). According to Russell, we are responsible for the consequences of our actions and for our failure to act: "I author the meaningfulness of my world in giving significance to my situation. . . . It is when I see myself as the *author* of my actions and (relatedly) of the significance I give my world that I get an enlarged sense of my responsibility for this" (p. 261).

Viktor Frankl, an existential psychiatrist, stresses the relationship between freedom and responsibility and insists that freedom can never be taken from us, because we can at least choose our attitude toward any given set of circumstances. To support this statement, Frankl draws from his own experiences in a German concentration camp, where the prisoners were stripped of every semblance of freedom. He contends that, even in a situation of such extreme powerlessness, people can ultimately be their own master, because the attitude they assume toward their suffering is of their own choosing: "Life ultimately means taking responsibility to find the right answer to its problems and to fulfill the tasks which it constantly sets for each individual" (Frankl, 1963, p. 122). In Frankl's brand of existential therapy, *logotherapy*, this means that clients create their problems and the distress they experience. They are responsible for (but not to blame for) the symptoms that restrict their ability to live freely and fully. It is not mere chance or the actions of others that are causing them to be miserable, since they are creating their situation. It is essential that clients recognize and accept their part in creating their distress, for until then, they will not change. If they wait around for others to change or for the environment to change, they may well increase their own misery and hopelessness instead of taking action to make something happen differently.

Implications for group work. The main task of the group leader with regard to the issue of self-determination is to confront members with the reality of their freedom. Very often group participants present themselves as victims, talk about their feelings of helplessness and powerlessness, and place the blame for their miseries on others and on external circumstances. In short, clients often are not aware that they *do* have choices or that they are severely restricting the range of available alternatives. As long as they continue to live as though they were prisoners, they can never hope to experience their personal power.

A good place to start on the road to greater self-determination is to become aware of how one is restricting one's freedom and of the roles one has been programmed to play. When people come to *believe* that they can direct their destiny, they ultimately assume control of their life.

Yalom (1980) contends that the group provides the optimal conditions for therapeutic work on personal responsibility. If the group has a here-and-now focus, the members can be encouraged to observe how they create victimlike stances for themselves. In Yalom's view, members are responsible for the interpersonal position they assume in the group setting, which also gives a glimpse of how they behave in life situations. Members can challenge other members who describe themselves as being victimized by external conditions. Through the process of ongoing feedback, members learn to see themselves through others' eyes, and they learn the ways that their behavior affects others. Further, they learn how the group situation represents situations in their everyday life. Building on these discoveries, the members also see how their behavior influences their self-perceptions and self-evaluations and can take responsibility for changing them.

From Yalom's (1980) perspective, the existential group leader encourages the members to assume responsibility for their functioning as a group. By doing so, individual members are learning ways to take greater responsibility for their life:

> The interactional therapy group enhances responsibility assumption not only by making members aware of their personal contribution to their unsatisfying life situ-

ations but also by accentuating each member's role in the conduct of the group. The underlying principle is that if members assume responsibility for the functioning of the group, then they become aware that they have the ability (and obligation) to assume responsibility in all spheres of life [p. 240].

Examples. Edward had reluctantly joined one of my groups. I say "reluctantly" because he had serious misgivings about the value of participating in a group. At 52, Edward had settled into a dull, predictable, but comfortable and safe life-style as a successful business executive. When he joined, he presented himself with this statement: "I don't know if this group will do me any good or not. Frankly, I think that I'm too old to change and that what I have is the most I can hope to get from life. I believe that things will probably stay as they are." In spite of his own statement and in spite of the fact that his life was orderly and safe, he felt that he was "drying up" and that life had lost zest. He was ready for a change, even though he was not sure whether change was possible.

Through his involvement in the group, Edward began to realize that he did have options—many more than he ever thought possible. All along, Edward had blamed his wife, his three sons, and his daughter for the fact that he couldn't change jobs and live the kind of life he wanted for himself. He was, of course, avoiding the responsibility for his own problems by focusing on what his family expected, often without ever verifying whether they did expect what he thought they did.

The other members and I challenged Edward to begin thinking for himself about how *he* wanted his life to be different. I asked him questions such as "If you were to continue living for the rest of your life as you are now, with no basic changes, how would you feel about it?" "Assume that your family would be willing to make the changes in life-style that you want to make. How would your life be different one year from now? And five years from now?" "What steps can you take today that will help you make some of the changes you want? What is preventing you from taking these steps?"

By the time Edward left the group, he at least saw that he didn't have to live a "life without any seasoning." Although he had not made any major commitments to change, he did feel that, if he wanted to change, he could and that, if he was willing to take risks, his life would be richer. In my eyes, this recognition that he *did* indeed have choices was more important than the specific choices he was going to make. My task as a group leader was *not* to push him to make choices that I thought were desirable but simply to use the forces within the group to help him recognize that he was both free and responsible for the direction of his own life. I believe that the central function of the group leader is to help people accept the fundamental challenge of taking a stand concerning their lives.

In another of my groups, one of the participants refused to take responsibility for her lack of freedom by blaming her parents. When confronted with her dependency, Violet would defend herself by saying: "If I'm afraid of life, it's because *they* didn't care enough when I was a child. I fear men now because my father was a cold fish who never made me feel lovable and worthwhile. If only my mother had pushed me to do more things on my own, instead of doing everything for me, today I would have the confidence of standing on my own two feet." And so it went with Violet. She kept investing her energies in finding reasons for her fear of living and in blaming her parents for her problems rather than in trying to find out what *she* could actually *do now* to take charge of her life.

Basically, my work with Violet in the group consisted of confronting her with the fact that, as long as she continued to cling to her past to justify her unwillingness to make decisions for herself, she would remain helpless. Violet was challenged to decide whether she wanted to remain the "victim" or whether she wanted to begin to exercise her freedom to design her life so that she could live effectively. Some time after the group terminated, Violet reported:

> Sometimes I wonder what it would be like if I had never been in the group and learned what I did about myself. I felt safer then, because I was faced with fewer choices than I am now. Before, the world was a bleak place—one in which I knew no joy—yet it was safer. There were fewer challenges. Even if I could return to that time of safety and dependency, I know that I would not. I've come too far to go back. There are times, though, when I question if it has been worth it.

Existential Anxiety

From the existential viewpoint, anxiety is a basic characteristic of being human; thus, it is not necessarily pathological. On the contrary, anxiety can be a strong motivational force toward growth. As we saw earlier, anxiety results from having to make choices without clear guidelines and without knowing what the outcome will be and from being aware that we are ultimately responsible for the consequences of our actions. In Kierkegaard's words, existential anxiety is "the dizziness of freedom." At some level we know that, for new dimensions of ourselves to emerge, old parts of ourselves must die. The knowledge that, in order to grow, we must exchange familiar and secure ways for new and unknown ones is in itself a source of anxiety. Although we may not welcome this anxiety, it is the price we must pay for engaging in the process of becoming what we are capable of becoming.

Anxiety acts as a catalyst for growth by encouraging us to take action for change. It serves as a signal that our activities are growing stale and unexciting and that we are ready for movement and change. Sidney Jourard (1968a) writes that it is at those times when we find our existence dull and boring that we can transcend our limitations by daring to attempt new ways of being. We know that we are ready to make changes when we experience staleness, depression, anxiety, guilt, or even despair. Jourard indicates that we have a choice with regard to how we respond to the anxiety produced by living in ways that are no longer fulfilling. We can allow ourselves to fully experience the emotions that tell us that "all is not well" and thus become aware of the need to change. Or we can repress them and ignore the signals, so that we can continue to live in the security of our stale lives and avoid change. Jourard (1968b) says: "If you help me give up old projects which are no longer satisfying, delightful, or fulfilling and encourage me to dare new ones, you are helping me to grow" (p. 12). When we blunt existential anxiety, we constrict our lives and limit our choices. Thus, the price we pay is steep indeed.

Implications for group work.   In a line of thought that is similar to Jourard's, Bugental (1978) describes therapeutic work with existential anxiety as a stripping away of defenses, much like the peeling of an onion. At the core of therapy, clients eventually come to terms with the underlying conditions of being human that are related to the anxiety they experience. These sources of existential anxiety must be faced and worked through in therapy; they involve recognition of our separateness and our need to be with others, of our guilt over not living authentically, of the emptiness in the universe and lack of meaning, of the burden of responsibility associated with choosing for ourselves, and of our fear of death and nonbeing. As therapy progresses and the resistances are peeled away, clients often painfully recognize how much energy they have put into maintaining an idealized image of themselves that is impossible to achieve. They also see that they must let go of old images of themselves that lead to a restricted existence. As clients give up their phony roles, they are able to bring a renewed quality to their living. A death of their old self occurs, which allows room for some kind of breakthrough experience. Yet such a process is typically anxiety provoking, for clients are giving up rigid ways of being that are familiar. As Bugental (1978) says: "In a very real sense, the client must go out of control for at least a brief period because the ways on which control has previously depended have been bound up with old patterns of being. Until they are truly let go of, they cannot be replaced" (p. 79).

Because anxiety is uncomfortable, we sometimes attempt to allay it or escape it altogether. But, even if we manage to escape anxiety, the conditions that are producing it do not disappear as if by magic. Therefore, one of the leader's tasks is to encourage participants to accept anxiety as growth-producing and to help them find the courage to face and to fully experience their anxieties. The next step is to encourage members to make a commitment to action. Through the support of the leader and of other participants in the group, the individual can be inspired to explore unknown paths and to investigate new dimensions of self. This search can lead to even greater anxiety, but, if the person is in the process of growth, he or she knows that anxiety doesn't have to be devastating and that it is the price one must pay for breaking out of constricting modes of existence.

In my groups I make sure that participants understand the crucial difference between existential and neurotic anxiety. Whereas existential anxiety can be a strong motivational force toward growth, neurotic anxiety "results whenever a person evades existential anxiety by failing to confront it directly and make active choices in spite of it" (Shaffer, 1978, p. 29). Thus, neurotic anxiety, far from being a liberating agent, further constricts the person's life.

Example.   For much of her life, Ann had allowed others to make decisions for her—among them, and perhaps the most important, the decision that religious faith is necessary if one is to find order and purpose in life. She had accepted her parents' religious values and had become very dependent on her church to make moral decisions for her. Through her work in a group, Ann came to see more and more clearly that, if she wanted to grow, she needed to take full responsibility for her choices and stop letting the church make key decisions for her. Thus, she decided to look within herself for strength and direction. This decision brought Ann a great deal of anxiety. She continued to ask herself "Am I doing the right thing?" and "What if the ethical decisions I'm making now on my own are wrong? Worse, what if they are irresponsible and selfish?"

It took Ann some time to begin to trust herself—even longer to let go of the need to lean on some kind of authority for her answers and for instant comfort and security. A little at a time, however, she began to experience a new sense of power—the exhilarating feeling that *she* was directing her life—even though she kept struggling all along with conflicts and doubts. Surely Ann would have been more comfortable had she continued to rely on external guidance. Yet, when she realized that she was using religion to keep herself from becoming independent, she chose to think for herself, even though she had no guarantee that such a choice was a wise one.

Death and Nonbeing

The existentialist considers the concept of death instrumental to the discovery of meaning and purpose in life. The realization of our finitude—nonbeing— gives meaning to existence because it makes every act count. Life has meaning precisely because it must end. The present is precious because it is all we really have. It is our temporal nature that makes us feel the urgency to do something with our life—to make a choice between affirming life by trying to become the person we are capable of becoming and allowing life to slip by us and eventually realizing that we've never been truly alive. Yalom (1980) summarizes this notion as follows:

> Death and life are interdependent: though the physicality of death destroys us, the *idea* of death saves us. Recognition of death contributes a sense of poignancy to life, provides a radical shift of life perspective, and can transport one from a mode of living characterized by diversions, tranquilization, and petty anxieties to a more authentic mode [p. 40].

Mullan (1979) makes the point that death is an element to be dealt with and accepted in the existential group, since it is always present. For members to face this issue and work with the anxiety it brings, the leader cannot ignore it. According to Mullan:

> The death motif is awakening and challenging and not, as some claim, morbid and nihilistic. Through its use patients are bombarded with the insignificance of their ordinary pursuits. Their usual customs, routines, conventions, and habits all come under fire. Once they have faced the certainty of their death, many persons cease to be victims of the past in which their parents' irrational authority was so pronounced. Suddenly they find that they must act now and with greater intensity than before [p. 173].

Because many of us are afraid of facing the reality of our own death and the anxiety that goes with it, we might attempt to escape the awareness of this reality. But the price for trying to flee from the confrontation with nonbeing is awesome. In May's (1961) words, "The price for denying death is undefined anxiety, self-alienation. To completely understand himself, man must confront death, become aware of personal death" (p. 65). Frankl (1963) concurs and adds that it is not *how long* we live but *how* we live that determines the quality and meaningfulness of our life.

Implications for group work. Awareness of death and the anxiety it generates has significant implications for the practice of group work. The concern with living life fully, rather than merely existing, is a recurrent theme in most groups I have led. Generally I tackle this theme by encouraging group members to honestly ask themselves how they experience the quality of their lives. Then I ask them to answer this same question as if they knew that they were about to die. How do the two answers differ? Are there decisions they made that they have not followed through or opportunities for change that they have ignored? By reflecting on the unfinished business in their lives, participants may come to realize that they are not living the kind of life they'd like to live, and they may be able to identify the reasons for their unsatisfactory existence.

In my own practice, I find it valuable to expand the concept of physical death to other kinds of death. Even though we are physically alive, we may be dead or dying in important areas of life. Perhaps we are numb to our feelings or caught up in deadening roles. Perhaps we have lost our intellectual curiosity and wonderment about life. Perhaps our relationships with the significant people in our lives are characterized by routinized and devitalizing acts. Perhaps what we do has lost meaning. A group can be a good place to recognize the areas in which we have gone stale and to confront ourselves with what we are willing to do in order to change and flourish again.

The process of change, as I pointed out earlier, always entails allowing parts of us to die in order to make room for new growth. And growth often demands that we be willing to let go of familiar ways of being. We may need to experience a period of mourning over our losses before we can move forward and establish new patterns. Groups offer a safe place to express this sadness, to explore the ambivalence that generally accompanies change, and to experiment with new ways of being.

Example. In an earlier book, *I Never Knew I Had a Choice* (Corey, 1983), I discussed the concept of *freedom in dying*—the notion that even in dying we still have choices concerning how we face and deal with what is happening to us. As I was writing that section of the book, a friend and former group member, Jim Morelock, was dying. He permitted me to use his real name and to share some of the significant moments in his dying.

Jim was 25 years old. He was full of life and seemed to have a bright future when he discovered that he had a rare form of cancer. In the group Jim talked about his fears of dying and expressed his anger about the reality that he wouldn't be able to put to use much of what he had learned about himself, because his time was so limited. As he put it, "I finally learned that I have a lot to offer and that I'm lovable. I'd sure like to hang around and enjoy all those people that love me!"

His own gifts and active interest in life, as well as his counseling and group experience, enabled Jim to face death with courage and to infuse it with meaning. Even after he learned that his illness was terminal, he continued to take a course at the university, because he liked the contact with people there. He decided not to remain in a hospital and not to undergo chemotherapy, primarily because he didn't want to prolong his life if he couldn't live it fully. Jim made a choice to accept God into his life, which gave him peace and serenity. He did many of the things he most wanted to do, maintaining an active interest in life and in the world around him. More than anyone I know, Jim took care of unfinished business. He said everything he wanted to say to his family and close friends and made all the arrangements for his own funeral, including asking my wife, Marianne, to deliver the eulogy.

Jim showed me that his style of dying was no different from his style of living, and through him I have learned much about dying and about living. Shortly before his death, Jim told me that he didn't have regrets about the way he had lived his life, because in those short 25 years he had lived more fully than many older people. He also commented that, although we may not have a choice concerning our losses in dying, we can still choose our attitude toward death. Through his own way of dying, Jim gave very special meaning to his words, because "I don't know of anyone who shows better than Jim how we remain free to choose our attitude toward life and toward life's ending" (Corey, 1983, p. 344).

The Search for Meaning

The struggle for a sense of significance and purpose in life is a distinctively human characteristic. We search for meaning and personal identity, and we raise existential questions—Who am I? Where am I going and why? Why am I here? What gives my life purpose and meaning? For the existentialists, life does not have positive meaning in itself; it is up to us to create meaning. As we struggle in a world that often appears meaningless and even absurd, we challenge values we never challenged before, we discover new facets of ourselves, we try to reconcile conflicts and discrepancies, and, in so doing, we create our meaning in the world.

Frankl has devoted his career to developing an existential approach to therapy that is grounded on the role of meaning in life. According to him, the central human concern is to discover meaning that will give one's life direction. On the basis of his clinical work and study, Frankl has concluded that a lack of meaning is the major source of existential stress and anxiety in modern times. He views existential neurosis as the experience of meaninglessness. Many people come to therapy because of an *existential vacuum*, or a feeling of inner void that results from not pursuing meaning. Therefore, according to Frankl, therapy should be designed to help clients find meaning in their life.

Frankl (1963) says that there are many ways of finding meaning—through work, through loving, through suffering, and through doing for others. According to Frankl, the therapist's function is not to tell clients what their particular meaning in life should be but to encourage them to discover meaning for themselves. He believes that even suffering can be a source of growth and that, if we have the courage to experience our suffering, we can find meaning in it. Suffering can be turned into achievement by the stand we take in the face of it. By confronting pain, despair, and death and by trying to understand their meaning for us, we turn the negative sides of life into triumph.

Implications for group work. Both the issue of finding meaning and the related question of challenging and perhaps discarding values that are no longer meaningful are commonly explored in groups. Discarding old values without finding new and more suitable ones to replace them is a concern that many participants share. Some people live by a value system that they have never challenged and that was handed down to them and merely incorporated. Others have lost their own identity by submitting to group pressure, thus denying their inner reality in order to conform to social mores.

One of the tasks of the therapeutic process is to confront clients with evidence of the fact that they are living by unexamined values that no longer contribute to a meaningful existence. We may not be responsible for having acquired values that don't help our quest for meaning, but we are certainly responsible for clinging to them and for failing to find new ones. Some useful questions that can be explored in a group setting are:

- Do you like the direction of your life? If not, what are you doing about it?
- What are the aspects of your life that satisfy you most?
- What is preventing you from doing what you really want to do?

With the support of the group, participants can find the strength to question and discard certain values and to create an internally derived value system that is consistent with their way of being. This process is likely to generate anxiety, at least for a time, and they will flounder in the absence of clear-cut values. The leader's job is to remind these people that learning to develop the self-trust necessary to look within, discover one's own values, and live by them is a long and difficult process that requires determination and patience.

Examples. The following examples illustrate the challenges group members face when they attempt to redefine their lives and develop a value system that is their own.

Priscilla was reared with extremely conventional values, and she had never really examined them. She felt compelled to be a "proper lady" at all times, as if her parents were watching over her shoulder. Whenever she was doing something that she thought her parents wouldn't approve of, Priscilla seemed to "hear mother and father speaking," telling her what she *should* do and what she *ought* to feel. In various group exercises, Priscilla "became her parents" and spoke for them by lecturing each of us about how we ought to change our ways.

At one point I urged her to act as if she had no choice but to remain forever the nice and proper lady her parents expected her to be and asked her to exaggerate this ladylike behavior in the group for several sessions. Afterward she reported that doing so "made her sick" and that she would change, no matter how difficult the task was going to be. Although Priscilla still respected some of the core values she had learned at home, she wanted the freedom to retain some of those values and discard others without feeling guilty. Her work in the group and outside of it gave her new freedom to develop her own set of values—values that were meaningful to her and that allowed her to live by her own expectations and not by those of others.

When Herman joined the group, he complained that he felt empty and worthless and that he saw himself as a rock—devoid of life and impossible to penetrate. Since Herman was questioning the meaning of his life—he kept referring to himself as lifeless, empty, and dead—my co-leader and I invited him to give in to what we saw as a death wish. We said: "Since you say that you feel dead and empty most of the time, let yourself die here now. Lie down over there and imagine that you *are* dead. We'll cover you with a sheet, and we'll all talk about you as if you were dead—how we saw you and how we felt about you. We'll even give you a eulogy. Stay underneath the sheet and allow yourself to feel fully the deadness you so often refer to. When you decide that you want to throw off your sheet and begin to live, do so."

Herman stayed there for most of the session, and, when he finally "came to life," he related his experience to the group with deep emotion. As a result, he began to see *how* he was cutting himself off from people and how he was contributing to his own numbness. He was then able to explore and identify new ways of relating to others, making contact, and overcoming his psychological and emotional deadness.

I want to emphasize that the technique we used with Herman is very powerful and that it can elicit intense emotions. It is important that the leader possess the therapeutic skills necessary to work sensitively and effectively with whatever may result from the technique. It is also essential that a high level of trust exist between the member and the leader before such a technique is implemented, since it can be seen as hurtful by the client.

The Search for Authenticity

The theologian Paul Tillich (1952) used the phrase "the courage to be" to convey the essence of the courage it takes to affirm ourselves and to live from the inside. Discovering, creating, and maintaining the core deep within our being is a difficult and never-ending struggle.

Being authentic means doing whatever is necessary to define and affirm ourselves. Shaffer (1978, p. 29) writes: "In an authentic existence a person confronts directly the ever-emergent possibility of nonbeing, makes decisions in the face of uncertainty, and takes responsibility for them." Keen (1970) says that the "authentic being is born of anxiety"—the anxiety of never knowing if we are making the "right choices" and yet demonstrating the courage to act. Keen continues: "To choose this or that course, to opt for one value or another under conditions of cognitive ambiguity, is to have control over oneself, to be an agent and to establish oneself as valid" (p. 65).

When we lead an authentic existence, we are constantly becoming the person we are capable of becoming. Living authentically also entails knowing and accepting our limits. The "Alcoholic's Prayer" offers a good example of this knowledge and acceptance: "God grant me the serenity to accept the things I cannot change, courage to change the things I can, and wisdom to know the difference."

A quote with a different twist, one that Frankl is fond of using, is Goethe's admonition: "If we take man as he is, we make him worse; but if we take him as he should be, we help him become what he can be." Frankl sees it as the therapist's task to challenge clients to become their full and authentic selves by getting engaged in life and making commitments. His logotherapy, since it is concerned with people's spiritual dimensions and higher aspirations, provides inspiration to continually seek the meaning that is necessary to live authentically.

We can lead inauthentic lives by giving up the quest for self-definition, by submerging our identity in a group, and by allowing others to determine who and what we will become. Rather than trusting ourselves to search and find the answers within, we sell out by becoming what others expect us to be, and in the process we become strangers to ourselves. Alienation and estrangement are a predicament faced by many people in society. Josephson and Josephson (1962) described the alienated person as follows: "The alienated man is every-man and no man, drifting in a world that has little meaning for him and over which he exercises no power, a stranger to himself and a stranger to others" (p. 11). For Moustakas (1975), alienation is "the developing of a life outlined and determined by others, rather than a life based on one's own inner experience" (p. 31).

Riesman (1950) speaks of people who, by becoming "other-oriented," have lost contact with themselves and live in inauthentic ways. Ignoring their inner prompting, they take all their cues from others. They are finely tuned to what others expect of them, and, in their perennial quest for conformity, they lose themselves in the values and standards of others. As May (1953) observes, these people are able to *respond* but not to actively *choose*. One of May's clients said "I'm just a collection of mirrors, reflecting what everyone expects of me" (p. 15). Indeed, one of the most common fears expressed by people in groups is the fear that, if they take an honest look at themselves, they will discover that they are just empty shells with no core and no substance. Therefore, they are afraid of shedding masks and pretenses, because, once those are gone, nothing will be left.

A concept related to inauthenticity is guilt. *Existential guilt* grows from a sense of incompleteness and from the realization that we are not utilizing our full potentials—in sum, from leading an inauthentic existence. According to the existentialists, this neglect of potentiality leads to a narrowing of our lives; although it may help us cope with the unknown, it does hamper our development. Ultimately, the loss of the sense of being becomes psychological sickness, or neurosis. To the extent that we fail to fulfill our potentials, we become sick. Neurosis, then, is the result of the failure to become what we could become. Jourard (1968a, 1968b) sees the "neurotic" person as someone who chooses a rigid, encapsulated existence—safe, yet suffocating.

At the other end of the spectrum is what Maslow (1968, 1970, 1971) called the *self-actualizing person*. For Maslow and the other humanistic psychologists, human beings strive for self-actualization, which is the tendency to become all that we are able to become. Although all people have a natural tendency toward developing their uniqueness and fulfilling their potentials, the process is not an automatic one. Because growth entails a struggle between our desire for security and dependence and our desire for self-actualization, we must decide which side of the struggle we want to commit ourselves to.

The characteristics of self-actualizing people, according to Maslow, include inner direction and resistance to being defined by others, the capacity to tolerate and even welcome uncertainty, acceptance of others and of oneself, a fresh perception of the world, spontaneity and naturalness, autonomy, a need for privacy and solitude, deep caring for others and the capacity to form intimate relationships, a sense of humor, and the absence of artificial dichotomies within oneself (such as weakness/strength, love/hate, and work/play).

Implications for group work. The struggle for authenticity has deep implications for group work. A group provides a powerful context in which to look at oneself, decide whether one is a fully functioning person or the reflection of what others expect, and consider what choices might be more authentically one's own. In a group setting, members can openly share their fears related to living in unfulfilling ways and come to see how they have compromised their integrity.

Examples. The case of Martha, a 45-year-old woman who had devoted a major portion of her life to her family, represents a situation characteristic of many women who have been members of my groups and personal-growth workshops. For most of her life Martha had depended almost totally on her roles as wife, mother, and homemaker as sources of identity. As her daughters and sons entered high school and then college and finally left home, Martha kept asking herself more and more frequently "Is there more to life than what I've done so far? Who am I besides all the roles I've responsibly filled? What do *I* want to do with the rest of my life?"

Martha returned to the university and obtained a degree in human services and psychology—a critical turning point in her life because of the many new doors that her degree opened for her. She engaged in a number of projects that enriched her life, including specialized work with the elderly. Through her program of studies, Martha joined several intensive personal-growth workshops, which gave her the opportunity to pose and debate questions such as: Do I have the courage to find out if I can create a new identity for myself? Will I be able to withstand pressures from my family to remain the way they want me to be? Can I give to others and at the same time give to myself? These questions indicate Martha's growing awareness that she needed to be a person in her own right and that she wanted to live an authentic existence. Her self-questioning also shows that she knew that making choices entails doubts and struggles that one must resolve for oneself.

In one of our workshops Sid loudly exclaimed that he was sick and tired of being a "pleasant phony." He was painfully aware of his need to please everyone and to win approval at all costs, and he was very afraid of losing his own identity by trying to fulfill whatever expectations others had of him. Our work in the group proceeded along these lines:

Jerry (group leader): Sid, I'd like you to take your best shot at pleasing each of us. Since you rehearse internally this pleasing bit much of the time, it shouldn't be too difficult to do out loud. Are you willing to try this experiment?

Sid: Sure, but I hate to try to please everyone in here. I want to get away from that!

Jerry: OK. But maybe this will be a beginning. Stand up and go around to each of us and tell us *exactly* what you imagine you'd have to say to please us and get our approval. Start with me.

Sid: Well, Jerry, you'd be pleased with me if I were a self-revealing, risk-taking client who decided what he wanted for himself and went after that!

Jerry: Good. Now keep going around.

Sid: And, Sue, you'd approve of me if I'd be helpless and let you mother me. Fred, I know you'd like me better if I told you what a great guy I thought you were. And you, Marie, would like me if I came out and said directly what I felt instead of trying to figure out what it was that you might want.

After Sid revealed what he imagined would please each of us, he was given an opportunity to share with us what it was like for him to go through this experiment. He got some valuable feedback from others, which, he said, gave him a clearer picture of how he was losing himself by trying so desperately to win universal approval. I asked Sid to actually *practice* in the group being as pleasing as he could, and I encouraged him to go up to members during breaks and say "Right now, I want you to approve of me, and I think I can get this by . . ." The goal of all of this was to exaggerate Sid's style of seeking others' approval to the point that he would eventually be able to seek approval within himself rather than from others.

Aloneness and Relatedness

The existentialists believe that ultimately we are alone—that we alone can give a sense of meaning to our lives, that we alone must decide how we will live, that we alone must find our own answers, and that we alone must decide whether we will be or not be. Because awareness of our ultimate aloneness can be very frightening, some of us try to avoid it by throwing ourselves into casual relationships and frantic activities, trusting that they will numb our fear and anguish.

We also have the choice of experiencing our aloneness and trying to find a center of meaning and direction within ourselves. Only if we make this choice and succeed at establishing our own identity as an individual can we relate genuinely and meaningfully to others. We must stand alone before we can truly stand beside another.

There is a paradox in the proposition that we are existentially both alone and related. Yet, it is this very paradox that describes the human condition. We are social beings, and we depend on interpersonal relationships for our humanness. We have a desire for intimacy, a hope to be significant in another's world, and a desire to feel that another's presence is important in our world. But, unless we can stand alone and find our own strength within ourselves, we cannot have nourishing relationships with others, based on fulfillment and not on deprivation.

   Implications for group work.   In groups, participants have the opportunity to relate to others in meaningful ways, learn to be themselves in the company of other people, and find reward and nourishment in the relationships they establish. They also learn that it is not in others that they can find the answers to questions about significance and purpose in life. If their struggle for self-awareness is successful, they come to realize that, no matter how valuable the relationships, they are ultimately on their own.

   The friendships that participants establish within the group are valuable also because they teach people how to relate to others outside of the group. In a group, people recognize their own struggles in others, and this often results in a bond. Even though they may accept that ultimately they are existentially alone, they also come to realize that they are not alone in their struggles and that others, too, are courageously looking at themselves and trying to establish their own identities.

   Example.   The case of Zeke shows that a person can be with others and at the same time be very much alone. During a group session Zeke said that he felt cut off from everyone in the group and described himself as a "spectator who seemed out of place." I asked him if he would be willing to experiment with *really* separating himself from the group and observing us from a distance. He agreed to leave the room, sit outside on the balcony, and observe what was going on through the window. I asked him to be aware of what he was thinking and feeling as he sat out there observing. Zeke was told to return to the group when he was ready to talk about what he had experienced sitting on the outside.

   When he returned, he said that for the first time he realized how safe it was for him to keep himself in a spectator role, that he was beginning to hate this role, and that he was ready to do something different. I asked Zeke if he would go around to each person in the group and complete these two sentences: "One way I have kept you at a distance is by . . ."; "One way I could be closer to you is by . . ." After he had "made the rounds," he described the circumstances in which he typically felt alone, even when surrounded by many people. Zeke spoke of his desire to achieve intimacy and of his fears of approaching people. His work in the group had intensified his attempts to keep himself separate but finally resulted in a desire to change.

ROLE AND FUNCTIONS OF THE GROUP LEADER

Unlike many other group approaches, the existential model puts more emphasis on experiencing the client in the present moment than on using a particular set of techniques. Thus, technique follows understanding. This means that the primary concern of the therapist is to *be with* the client and to understand his or her subjective world. There are no "right" techniques for this approach, because the task is accomplished through the therapeutic encounter between client and therapist.

In the existential view, therapy is a partnership and a shared venture between the therapist and the client. To develop this partnership, the therapist focuses on the human side of the person-to-person relationship and brings himself or herself as a person to it. Therapy is seen as an "invitation to change" and an "invitation to re-invent one's being," to use Jourard's (1971) expressions. Change comes from the relationship itself. In the group context, change is brought about not only by the relationship with the leader but also by the relationships with other members. Thus, a primary role of the existential group leader is to foster meaningful relationships among participants. This can be done by having the members focus on key existential concerns and providing a climate in which these concerns can be fully explored. A therapeutic community is thus established, based on the commonality of shared struggles. The members make a commitment to confront one another about their unused potentials and inauthentic behaviors and to support one another in the common endeavor to open the door to oneself.

The existential-group leader sets the tone for the group, not by introducing techniques and by *doing something*, but rather by *being* and *becoming somebody*. Mullan (1979) describes the leader's role in this way:

> The existential group leader questions his existence and expresses an unremitting search for the meaning of life and death. More obvious to the members, he brings to the group a dedication to face therapy's (life's) paradoxes, to unravel the group's (life's) problems, and to identify the immediate meaning of the group's being together. Change occurs in the patient when he, too, faces life's paradoxes and searches for meaning [pp. 165–166].

Bugental (1978) contends that it is essential for therapists to have a commitment to continue facing their own existential concerns and to becoming the person they are capable of becoming:

> The ideal therapist recognizes that the emotions, conflicts, biases, and anxieties of the therapist's own life inevitably have their effects on the client's life, and this is not an idle recognition. Thus the ideal therapist accepts the responsibility for continuing self-monitoring to reduce the untoward impact of the therapist's distress on the client [p. 34].

Mullan (1978) describes how challenges by the group leader bring about personality changes in members (including changes in thinking, feeling, and behaving). The group sessions tend to shake up the conventional ways in which members view the world. When their status quo is jarred, they have a better chance of facing themselves and of changing. Mullan sums up the matter thus: "This, then, is what the existential group therapist is about. He establishes the conditions for the enhancement of each member's consciousness, directing him to face his *human condition*" (p. 379).

Williams and Fabry (1982) emphasize the leader's function in challenging members to move from where they are to where they want to be, to see the opportunities for learning from failure, to detect the growing edge of a crisis, to be aware of their styles of avoidance and escape from personal responsibility, and to reach out beyond their present limited vision toward a vision that is yet to be realized. Although the leader is a vital force in the group, he or she also encourages each member to accept responsibility for group life. Members are encouraged to participate and initiate and not to wait for the group leader to manage conflicts within the group. The leader conveys to the members the value of personal sharing as opposed to diagnostic probing and interpreting. Members learn that the best way to help others is by offering illustrations of how they themselves have dealt with and are continuing to deal with conflicts and existential concerns.

APPLICATION OF THE EXISTENTIAL APPROACH TO FAMILY THERAPY

Although I am not aware of any books that deal with existential family therapy, other approaches have incorporated some existential themes in their framework. For instance, Walter Kempler's (1981) work *Experiential Psychotherapy within Families* is primarily a Gestalt approach to family therapy. Even though Kempler considers himself a Gestalt therapist, it is clear that he is closely aligned with an existential-phenomenological approach. In his description of the theory and practice of family experiential psychotherapy, Kempler emphasizes paying attention to the encounters, or interpersonal interactions, in the here-and-now therapeutic situation. Further, he maintains that the therapist promotes the goals of therapy by participating fully as a person. As you will see in the descriptions of many of the therapies that follow, existential concepts such as making choices, accepting the responsibility that goes along with freedom, creative uses of anxiety, and the search for meaning and values are a basic part of many therapeutic approaches to family therapy. It is very possible to be grounded in existential principles and work with families by using cognitive, behavioral, and action-oriented methods.

In what follows, let me describe a few selected existential concepts that make sense to me in working with family groups. I would approach a family with the basic assumption that the members are shaping their destiny by the choices being made. People are not merely victims who are passively molded by outside forces, and this includes the family situation. I assume that, if family members are unhappy about the way they exist with one another, then they are capable of doing something to bring about change. Surely they can change the way they allow themselves to be affected by others in their family, even if they are not always able to change the structure of their family life. If family members come to therapy because they are stuck in destructive patterns, or stagnant in the ways they are living together, or are facing conflicts that they have been unable to work out, then I see hope. Drawing upon an existential framework, something like the following could be said to this family:

> You are here because you realize that so far you have not been able to effectively resolve some issues that are dividing you as a family. A hopeful sign is that you care enough about improving your situation that you have not given up and have come here for some direction. A place that we might begin is to have each of you describe how it feels for you to be in your family. I hope that, as each of you talks, the others

can *really* listen and get a sense of what the person is saying, rather than thinking of how you will defend or justify your position. Each of you might want to add something about the ways you'd like your family to be different. What would you like to see less of? What would you most want in your family that you see as missing now?

Remarks in this spirit during the early phase of family therapy are directing each member to give full expression to his or her personal world. My guess is that what freezes many families in unproductive patterns is their lack of willingness to experience the world from another's point of view. Being caught up in proving that one is "right" and attempting to blame others for the problems in the family are bound to result in most of the members' feeling not understood or cared about. But showing a willingness to see the world through another's eyes is in itself therapeutic and could get the family moving in a positive direction. Once members of a family are able to hear and listen to one another, I might make some of the following statements as the sessions progress:

- "What are some of the ways that you see yourself as contributing to the problems your family is facing? What do you see yourself as able to do to bring about change? What steps are you willing to take to bring these changes about?"
- "What choices are open to you that you have not yet made? What is stopping you from making some of these choices?"
- "If your family structure were to remain as it is now, how do you imagine life would be for you a few years from now?"
- "I hear you saying that you feel isolated and lonely in your family. What is it that you are not saying to someone in here that you have wanted to say? Are you willing to take the risk of asking for what you want from this person now?"
- "You say that you feel impotent in being able to change the way you interact as a family. Could you let yourself imagine that you did have the power to bring some unity into your family?"

The direction I'd like to pursue is having all the members decide if their family means enough to them to invest in the work that it will take to change the structure of the family. To the degree that it is possible, I'd want them to consider what they could do to work toward the vision they expressed.

EVALUATION OF THE EXISTENTIAL APPROACH

From a conceptual standpoint there are many features of the existential approach that I value and that I have incorporated into my practice. I work on the basic assumption that people have the capacity to become increasingly self-aware and that expansion of awareness results in greater freedom to choose one's own direction in life. I share the existentialists' view that we are not bundles of instincts or the products of conditioning. Thus, I base my group work on the premises that people are not victims of their past or of the external world and that they have the power to decide for themselves and take action, so that their life is their own and not a reflection of the expectations of others.

I value this approach because it has brought back the person into central focus and because it addresses itself to the central question of what it means to be human. It portrays humans as continually actualizing and fulfilling their potential.

Another great contribution of the existential approach is its emphasis on the person-to-person quality of the therapeutic relationship—an emphasis that humanizes psychotherapy and reduces the chances of its becoming a mechanical process in the hands of technicians. From the standpoint of my practice, this approach encourages and challenges me to tap and bring to my work my own experiences and my very humanness. It leaves my own modes of existence open to challenge, because I couldn't be genuine with others or help them face their existential concerns without doing the same in my own life. My willingness to remain open to my own struggles determines the degree to which I can be a significant and positive influence for others in a group.

The existential view stresses that techniques follow understanding. I appreciate this view because it lessens the danger of abusing techniques. Too often leaders use techniques merely to "get things going" in a group. When the focus is on understanding the world of the participant, the leader's first concern is with genuinely grasping the core struggles of others and *then* drawing on certain techniques to help the participants explore these struggles more fully in the group. In my own work, I've found that an existential view does provide the framework for understanding universal human concerns. These concerns, which come up over and over again in groups, include wrestling with the problem of personal freedom, dealing with self-alienation and estrangement from others, facing the fear of death and nonbeing, finding the courage to live from within one's center, searching for a meaningful life, discovering a personal set of values, being able to deal constructively with anxiety and guilt, and making self-actualizing choices.

On the other hand, I recognize that the existential approach has its own limitations. Many of the existentialist concepts are quite abstract and difficult to apply in practice. Existential theorists such as Sartre, Kierkegaard, Nietzsche, and Heidegger were not writing for group counselors and therapists! As I mentioned at the beginning of this chapter, existentialism began as a formal philosophical movement and, although eventually it led to existential approaches within both psychology and psychiatry, its philosophical nature still dominates the model. Beginning as well as advanced group practitioners who are not of a philosophical turn of mind tend to find many of the existential concepts lofty, abstract, and elusive. Even those group counselors who are sympathetic toward the core ideas of this perspective are often at a loss when they try to apply these concepts to group practice, since very few authors have spelled out existential applications to group work.

For those of you who want to experience existential groups, I'd suggest attending the conferences sponsored by the Association for Humanistic Psychology. At its annual meetings, members can participate in a variety of workshops that are based on existential and humanistic concepts. For information about joining, write to the Association for Humanistic Psychology, 325 Ninth Street, San Francisco, CA 94103. Membership dues include the quarterly *Journal of Humanistic Psychology*, the *AHP Resource Directory*, a *Newsletter*, priority for attendance at special events, and professional networking services.

QUESTIONS FOR REFLECTION AND DISCUSSION

1. What are some of the major contrasts between the psychoanalytic approach and the existential approach? Do you see any basis for integrating psychoanalytic and existential concepts as they apply to the practice of group counseling?

2. What are some key concepts of the existential approach that you find personally meaningful? Which of these basic ideas, if any, would you most want to include in your framework in approaching a group?

3. In this chapter, the statement is made that anxiety results from having to make choices without clear guidelines and without knowing what the outcome will be. What implications are there for you as a group leader if you accept this view of anxiety? What are your thoughts on the role anxiety plays in a group?

4. Mullan (1979) makes this statement: "Death as an element to be dealt with, faced, and accepted is always present in the existential group if it is not ignored by the therapist" (p. 173). To what degree do you think that you have faced your own finite nature? Do you have a tendency to avoid reflecting on your own death? How do you think that your answers here will have an influence on your ability to deal with the theme of death as it emerges in your groups?

5. An existential theme is that we are free to choose among alternatives and that we are responsible for directing our life and shaping our destiny. To what extent do you think that you have taken an active stance in shaping the person that you are? What are some critical choices that you have made, and how do these choices affect you now? How do you see your answers to these questions as relevant to how you might deal with the struggles over choices of the members in your groups?

6. According to Frankl, it is not the therapist's job to tell clients what their particular meaning in life should be but rather to encourage them to discover meaning for themselves. Can you think of some ways that you might challenge members to find meaning in their life? How might you deal with the member who continued to look to you for answers and direction?

7. Some existential therapists assume that the driving force behind many interpersonal relationships is existential isolation. If you accept this notion that humans are ultimately alone in the world, what are the implications for group counseling? To what degree might groups contribute to members' avoidance of their aloneness? How might a group help a person feel less isolated and less alienated?

8. In the existential group it is assumed that intensity is achieved only when the therapist abandons rigid practices for selecting members, fixed rules, routines, and techniques (Mullan, 1979). How comfortable do you feel as a group leader with this orientation? Do you think that groups will become cohesive and engage in productive work without the use of techniques? Do you think you can employ group techniques and still retain an existential outlook on group work? Explain.

9. According to Yalom (1980), there are four ultimate concerns that make up the core of existential therapy—death, freedom, isolation, and meaning-

lessness. From your vantage point, what meaning do these existential themes have for you personally? How are these human concerns related to your life and your struggles? Based on your experiences in life, what would you hope to be able to teach the people who were in your groups? What meaning do these existential concerns have for the focus you might want to bring to a group you were leading?

10. How might you deal with those group members who spent a great deal of time trying to convince you that they were not responsible for their lives? If they attempted to hold others in their life responsible for their current problems, what might you be inclined to say or do in the group?

RECOMMENDED SUPPLEMENTARY READINGS

There are no books that I am aware of that deal explicitly and exclusively with the application of the existential approach to group counseling. Some of the following sources contain related material that group leaders can use to apply this model to their work with groups.

Existential psychotherapy (Yalom, 1980) is a superb treatment of ultimate human concerns of death, freedom, isolation, and meaninglessness as these issues relate to therapy. This book has depth and clarity, and it is rich with clinical examples that illustrate existential themes. If you were to select just one book on existential therapy, this would be my recommendation as a comprehensive and interesting discussion of the topic.

Existential-phenomenological alternatives for psychology (Valle & King, 1978) contains several excellent chapters on the implications of the existential tradition for psychotherapy. The most relevant are Chapters 13, 14, and 15.

Humanistic psychology (Shaffer, 1978) offers a clear and concise description of the evolution of humanistic psychology and of the central concepts of this approach. Chapter 6 deals with encounter groups.

The transparent self (Jourard, 1971) is a significant work based on the thesis that our lack of openness results in sickness, maladjustment, and alienation. The chapters on psychotherapy, groups, and the "disclosing therapist" are especially relevant to our discussion. I recommend that you read Chapters 15–19.

Managing anxiety: The power of knowing who you are (Koestenbaum, 1974) is a self-help book with exercises and activities. It deals with pain, consciousness, meaninglessness, death, guilt, and other existential themes.

Man's search for himself (May, 1953) is a classic. It deals with key existential themes such as loneliness, anxiety, the experience of becoming a person, the struggle to be, freedom, choice, responsibility, and religion.

Existential psychology (May, 1961) is a reader that examines and evaluates the role of existential psychology. Maslow, May, Rogers, and Allport are among those who have contributed essays.

I never knew I had a choice (Corey, 1983) is a self-help book written from a humanistic perspective. It contains many exercises and activities that leaders can use for their group work and that they can suggest as "homework assignments" between sessions. The topics covered include our struggle to achieve autonomy; the roles that work, love, sexuality, intimacy, and solitude play in our lives; the meaning of loneliness, death, and loss; and the ways in which we choose our values and philosophies of life. Each chapter is followed by numerous annotated suggestions for further reading.

Psychotherapy and process: The fundamentals of an existential-humanistic approach (Bugental, 1978) is a concise and comprehensive overview. It is highly readable, and the clinical examples provide a sense of realness to the discussion of concepts. An excellent source.

REFERENCES AND SUGGESTED READINGS*

Arbuckle, D. Reaction to Kemp. *The Counseling Psychologist*, 1971, 2(3), 32–36.

* Arbuckle, D. *Counseling and psychotherapy: An existential-humanistic view.* Boston: Allyn & Bacon, 1975.

Brammer, L. Existential views: Counseling supplement or substitute? *The Counseling Psychologist*, 1971, 2(3), 37–41.

Buber, M. *I and thou.* New York: Scribner's, 1958.

Bugental, J. F. T. *The search for authenticity: An existential-analytic approach to psychotherapy.* New York: Holt, Rinehart & Winston, 1965.

Bugental, J. F. T. *The search for existential identity: Patient-therapist dialogues in humanistic psychotherapy.* San Francisco: Jossey-Bass, 1976.

* Bugental, J. F. T. *Psychotherapy and process: The fundamentals of an existential-humanistic approach.* Reading, Mass.: Addison-Wesley, 1978.

Burton, A. *Modern humanistic psychotherapy.* San Francisco: Jossey-Bass, 1967.

* Corey, G. *I never knew I had a choice* (2nd ed.). Monterey, Calif.: Brooks/Cole, 1983.

Curry, A. E. Group psychotherapy: Some phenomenological considerations. *Review of Existential Psychology and Psychiatry*, 1966, 6(1, Winter).

* Frankl, V. *Man's search for meaning.* New York: Washington Square Press, 1963.

Frankl, V. *The doctor and the soul.* New York: Bantam, 1965.

Greening, T. *Existential-humanistic psychology.* Monterey, Calif.: Brooks/Cole, 1971.

Heidegger, M. *Being and time.* New York: Harper & Row, 1962.

Hora, T. Existential psychiatry and group psychotherapy. In G. M. Gazda (Ed.), *Basic approaches to group psychotherapy and group counseling* (2nd ed.). Springfield, Ill.: Charles C Thomas, 1975.

Josephson, E., & Josephson, M. (Eds.). *Man alone: Alienation in modern society.* New York: Dell, 1962.

* Jourard, S. *Disclosing man to himself.* New York: Van Nostrand Reinhold, 1968. (a)

Jourard, S. Growing awareness and the awareness of growth. In H. Otto and J. Mann (Eds.), *Ways of growth: Approaches to expanding awareness.* New York: Viking, 1968. (b)

* Jourard, S. *The transparent self* (Rev. ed.). New York: Van Nostrand Reinhold, 1971.

* Keen, E. *Three faces of being: Toward an existential clinical psychology.* New York: Appleton-Century-Crofts, 1970.

Kemp, C. G. Existential counseling. *The Counseling Psychologist*, 1971, 2(3), 2–30.

Kempler, W. *Experiential psychotherapy within families.* New York: Brunner/Mazel, 1981.

Kierkegaard, S. *Concluding unscientific postscript.* Princeton, N.J.: Princeton University Press, 1941.

Kierkegaard, S. *The concept of dread.* Princeton, N.J.: Princeton University Press, 1944.

Koestenbaum, P. *Managing anxiety: The power of knowing who you are.* Englewood Cliffs, N.J.: Prentice-Hall, 1974.

Koestenbaum, P. *Is there an answer to death?* Englewood Cliffs, N.J.: Prentice-Hall, 1976.

Kopp, S. *If you meet the Buddha on the road, kill him!* New York: Bantam, 1976.

Maslow, A. *Toward a psychology of being* (2nd ed.). New York: Van Nostrand Reinhold, 1968.

Maslow, A. *Motivation and personality* (2nd ed.). New York: Harper & Row, 1970.

* Maslow, A. *The farther reaches of human nature.* New York: Viking, 1971.

* May, R. *Man's search for himself.* New York: Norton, 1953.

* May, R. (Ed.). *Existential psychology.* New York: Random House, 1961.

May, R. *Psychology and the human dilemma.* New York: Van Nostrand Reinhold, 1967.

May, R., Angel, E., & Ellenberger, H. F. (Eds.). *Existence: A new dimension in psychiatry and psychology.* New York: Basic Books, 1958.

Moustakas, C. *Individuality and encounter.* Cambridge, Mass.: Doyle, 1968.

Moustakas, C. *Loneliness and love.* Englewood Cliffs, N.J.: Prentice-Hall, 1972.

*Books and articles marked with an asterisk are suggested for further study.

Moustakas, C. *The touch of loneliness.* Englewood Cliffs, N.J.: Prentice-Hall, 1975.

Mullan, H. Existential group psychotherapy. In H. Mullan & M. Rosenbaum (Eds.), *Group psychotherapy: Theory and practice* (2nd ed.). New York: Free Press, 1978.

*Mullan, H. An existential group psychotherapy. *International Journal of Group Psychotherapy,* 1979, *29*(2), 163–174.

Ofman, W. V. Existential group psychotherapy. In H. I. Kaplan & B. J. Sadock (Eds.), *Comprehensive group psychotherapy* (2nd ed.). Baltimore: Williams and Wilkins, 1983.

Perls, F. *Gestalt therapy verbatim.* Lafayette, Calif.: Real People Press, 1969.

Riesman, D. *The lonely crowd.* New Haven, Conn.: Yale University Press, 1950.

Rogers, C. *On becoming a person.* Boston: Houghton Mifflin, 1961.

Russell, J. M. Sartre, therapy, and expanding the concept of responsibility. *The American Journal of Psychoanalysis,* 1978, *38*, 259–269. (a)

Russell, J. M. Saying, feeling, and self-deception. *Behaviorism,* 1978, *6*(1), 27–43. (b)

Russell, J. M. Sartre's theory of sexuality. *Journal of Humanistic Psychology,* 1979, *19*(2), 35–45.

Sartre, J.-P. *Being and nothingness.* New York: Bantam, 1971.

Severin, F. *Discovering man in psychology: A humanistic approach.* New York: McGraw-Hill, 1973.

Shaffer, J. B. *Humanistic psychology.* Englewood Cliffs, N.J.: Prentice-Hall, 1978.

Stevens, J. O. *Awareness: Exploring, experimenting, experiencing.* Moab, Utah: Real People Press, 1971.

Tillich, P. *The courage to be.* New Haven, Conn.: Yale University Press, 1952.

*Valle, R. S., & King, M. (Eds.). *Existential-phenomenological alternatives for psychology.* New York: Oxford University Press, 1978.

Watson, R. An introduction to humanistic psychotherapy. In S. Morse & R. Watson (Eds.), *Psychotherapies: A comparative casebook.* New York: Holt, Rinehart & Winston, 1977.

Williams, D. A., & Fabry, J. The existential approach: Logotherapy. In G. M. Gazda (Ed.), *Basic approaches to group psychotherapy and group counseling* (3rd ed.). Springfield, Ill.: Charles C Thomas, 1982.

*Yalom, I. D. *Existential psychotherapy.* New York: Basic Books, 1980.

10

THE PERSON-CENTERED APPROACH

INTRODUCTION

The person-centered approach to group counseling (which was originally known as *client-centered* therapy) was developed by Carl Rogers. It is grounded on the assumption that human beings tend to move toward wholeness and self-actualization and that individual members, as well as the group as a whole, can find their own direction with a minimal degree of help from the group leader, or "facilitator." The person-centered approach emphasizes the personal qualities of the group leader rather than techniques of leading, because the primary function of the group facilitator is to do what is necessary to create a fertile and healing climate in the group. Such a climate is established between group members and facilitator by creating a relationship based on certain attitudes such as accurate empathic understanding, acceptance, positive regard, warmth, caring, respect, genuineness, immediacy, and self-disclosure. As the facilitator projects such attitudes and as an accepting and caring climate emerges, it is presumed that members will drop their defenses and work toward personally meaningful goals—a process that eventually will lead to appropriate and useful behavioral change.

The contemporary person-centered approach to group counseling is best considered as the result of an evolutionary process that continues to remain open to change and refinement. Certain trends go back more than 40 years. In the early 1940s Rogers developed what was known as *nondirective counseling* as a reaction against traditional individual therapy. He caused a great furor

247

when he challenged the basic assumption that the counselor is the expert and the client should be in a passive role. He also challenged the validity of such widely used therapeutic procedures as suggestion, giving of advice, counselor direction, teaching, diagnosis, and interpretation. A common theme originating in Rogers' early writings and continuing to permeate all of his works is a basic sense of trust in the client's ability to move forward in a positive and constructive manner if the appropriate conditions fostering growth are present. According to Rogers, there is a *formative tendency* in nature, or a central source of energy that seeks fulfillment and actualization, involving both the maintenance and the enhancement of the organism. Although person-centered therapy has changed over the years, this perspective of trust has remained at the foundation of the approach. Another common theme is the therapist's desire to facilitate the client's struggle for liberation and willingness to be changed by the therapeutic relationship (Wood, 1982).

In the early 1950s Rogers developed a systematic theory of personality and applied this self theory to the practice of counseling individuals, which led him to rename his approach *client-centered therapy* (Rogers, 1951). At this time his professional interests were mainly devoted to individual therapy. During the next decade he and his associates continued to test the underlying hypotheses of the client-centered approach by conducting studies of the process and the outcomes of therapy.

In the early 1960s Rogers and his associates began applying this approach to small groups. In addition, the basic philosophy of the approach was applied to education in what was called student-centered teaching/learning (Rogers, 1969). Groups were also developed for various populations, including those in positions of leadership. In the 1960s and 1970s Rogers did a great deal to spearhead the development of basic encounter groups and personal-growth groups (1970). As the fields of application grew in number and variety, the term *person-centered* won favor over *client-centered* in the 1970s. It was during this period that interest shifted from individual to group therapy, and there was also a change from the use of reflection as the basic procedure to a stress on experiencing and encountering. Emphasis was placed not just on the therapist's ability to reflect accurately what clients were expressing but also on therapist congruence and the willingness of the therapist to become increasingly involved in the therapy. The basic encounter groups made it difficult to distinguish between "therapy" and "growth," and these small groups (which generally consisted of not more than 12 persons and a facilitator) did much to revolutionize the practice of therapy.

In 1973 Rogers and some of his colleagues initiated a new form of person-centered group known as the *community for learning.* These were large groups with more than 100 people (and even groups up to 2,000 for brief periods) who worked and lived together for two weeks. Rogers used many types of groups for various populations in many places in the world. His influence spread to working with couples and families (Rogers, 1972); his ideas were also applied to administration, minority groups, community relations, interracial and intercultural groups, and international relationships (Rogers, 1977). More recently,

Rogers has been interested in learning in large groups, and the implications of such a process for the future (1980).

The person-centered approach is akin to the existential approach in that they share fundamental principles. As you recall from the previous chapter, Rogers was one of the key figures in the development of humanistic psychology in the 1950s. Other writers have contributed to the approach by developing systematic skills for the training of counselors, based partly on the work of Rogers. Thus, some of the extensions of Rogers' ideas will be briefly alluded to in this chapter through the works of Carkhuff (1966, 1969), Egan (1976, 1977, 1982), Ivey (1983), and Ivey and Authier (1978). These writers have focused on specific leader behaviors rather than the attitudes of the leader.

KEY CONCEPTS

Central Hypothesis of the Person-Centered Approach

The basic tenet that underlies the person-centered approach to group work is stated briefly by Rogers (1980): "Individuals have within themselves vast resources for self-understanding and for altering their self-concepts, basic attitudes, and self-directed behavior; these resources can be tapped if a definable climate of facilitative psychological attitudes can be provided" (p. 115). According to Rogers (1959, 1980), the necessary climate that releases our formative, or actualizing, tendency is characterized by three attitudes of the therapist—genuineness, "unconditional positive regard," and empathy.

The first element is the genuineness, realness, or *congruence* of the therapist (or facilitator of the group). In short, the greater the extent to which facilitators become involved in the group as a person, putting up no professional front, the greater is the likelihood that the members will change and grow in a constructive manner. Good facilitators are aware of the feelings and attitudes they are experiencing in a group and are willing to share what they are experiencing when it is appropriate and facilitative in the group. This means that facilitators express their persistent feelings even if doing so is risky. It also implies that the process of a group is influenced by the *person* of the facilitator as much as by the individuality of the group participants.

The second element is the attitude called *unconditional positive regard*, which is an acceptance of and caring for the members. As we will discuss later, this caring on the facilitator's part is nonpossessive in that the members are prized in a total way rather than a conditional way.

The third facilitative aspect is an *empathic understanding* of the members' internal and subjective frame of reference. Facilitators show this empathy when they are able to sense accurately the feelings and personal meanings that the members are experiencing. It is also important for facilitators to be able to communicate this understanding to the members. The greater the degree to which these three attitudes and conditions are actually experienced and demonstrated by facilitators in a group situation, the greater will be the movement of the members in a constructive and growth-oriented direction. Rogers makes it clear that the theory, practice, and research of the person-centered approach rest on the directional process in life and on a basic trust in human beings. "We can say that there is in every organism, at whatever level, an underlying flow of movement toward constructive fulfillment of its inherent possibilities" (1980, p. 117).

Trust in the Group Process

Rogers (1970) expresses a deep sense of trust in the ability of the group to develop its own potential and that of its members. This trust in the group process leads Rogers to shy away from specific goals for a particular group. As he puts it, "The group will *move*—of this I am confident—but it would be presumptuous to think that I can or should *direct* that movement toward a *specific* goal" (p. 45).*

The condition for group movement, as seen by Rogers, is the development of an accepting and trusting atmosphere in which the members can show aspects of themselves that they usually conceal and move into new behaviors. Examples of such movement within a group include members' moving

- from playing roles to expressing themselves more directly
- from being relatively closed to experience and uncertainty to becoming more open to outside reality and tolerant of ambiguity
- from being out of contact with internal and subjective experience to becoming aware of it
- from looking for answers outside of themselves to a willingness to direct their own lives from within
- from lacking trust and being somewhat closed and fearful in interpersonal relationships to being more open and expressive with others

Active Listening

Active and sensitive listening is what Rogers *does* when he facilitates a group. "I listen as carefully, accurately, and sensitively as I am able, to each individual who expresses himself. Whether the utterance is superficial or significant, I *listen*" (1970, p. 47). It is apparent that Rogers listens to more than the words; he also hears the *meaning* behind the verbal and nonverbal content. In this regard, he is concerned with facilitating the truest expression of the person's subjective experience.

My experience in training and supervising group leaders has made it clear that, although counselors will intellectually acknowledge the importance of listening, many lack basic skills in listening and responding to clients. One way of developing such skills is by becoming aware of the barriers to listening and responding. Some common barriers that I observe are:

- focusing too much on answers or solutions to problems before clients have the chance to explore their feelings about their problems

---

*From pp. 45–48, 56 and based on pp. 15–37, 126 in *Carl Rogers on Encounter Groups*, by Carl R. Rogers. Copyright © 1970 by Carl R. Rogers. This and all other quotations from this source are reprinted by permission of Harper & Row, Publishers, Inc. Published in the British Commonwealth by Penguin Books Ltd.

- giving advice too readily and thereby discouraging clients from struggling
- asking too many closed questions or developing a style that leads to superficial questions and answers
- being overly directive instead of offering group members an open invitation to talk and express themselves fully and freely
- categorizing group members and then listening to them selectively to confirm these biases
- paying too much attention to words and failing to observe other behaviors that signal the meanings behind the words

Effective listening and responding skills are prerequisites for the existence of genuine empathy and understanding between group leaders and participants. My approach is to focus on the barriers that get in the way of effective attending noted above. I have found that, by working with practical examples of these barriers, the blocks can be removed.

Empathy

A central concept in the person-centered group approach is that of accurate empathy, which is basically the ability to enter the subjective world of others and the ability to communicate this understanding. Rogers (1961) defined empathy as the capacity to see the world of another by assuming the internal frame of reference of that person. As he put it, "To sense the client's private world as if it were your own but without ever losing the 'as if' quality—this is empathy, and it seems essential to therapy" (p. 284). But sensing, even understanding, the client's private world is not enough. The counselor must also be able to effectively communicate this understanding to the client.

Rogers (1975) considers empathy as "an unappreciated way of being" for many group practitioners. He makes a case for regarding empathy as one of the most potent factors in bringing about learning and self-directed change, thus locating power in the person and not in the expert. Rogers summarizes some general research findings concerning empathy as follows:

1. Therapists of many different orientations agree that attempting to sensitively and accurately understand others from the others' viewpoint is a critical factor in being an effective therapist.

2. One of the main functions of empathy is that of facilitating exploration of self. Where a high degree of empathy exists, there is a corresponding high degree of client self-exploration. Clients come to a deeper self-understanding through a relationship in which they *feel* that they are being understood by others. Research has demonstrated that clients who feel understood by their therapists are encouraged to share more of themselves.

3. Empathy dissolves alienation, for the person who receives empathy feels connected with others. Furthermore, those who receive empathy learn that they are valued, cared for, and accepted as they are. Rogers (1975) makes this point as follows: "Empathy gives that needed confirmation that one does exist as a separate, valued person with an identity" (p. 7).

4. The ability to exhibit empathy depends on the person development of the therapist. Rogers (1975) has come to the conclusion that "the more psycholog-

ically mature and integrated the therapist is as a person, the more helpful is the relationship he provides" (p. 5).

5. Being a skilled diagnostician and making interpretations is not related to empathy, which, at its best, is accepting and nonjudgmental. In fact, for Rogers "true empathy is always free of any evaluative or diagnostic quality" (1975, p. 7).

Levels of empathy. The practice of empathy is sometimes distorted into simply assuming and mirroring back the client's subjective view of the world. Other writers such as Egan (1982) and Carkhuff (1969) maintain that counselors who merely function as a mirror and don't share themselves are not being as effective as they might be. The contention of these authors is that, although the basic level of empathy is essential, it is not enough. Thus, Carkhuff writing about "additive dimensions" and Egan writing about "advanced accurate empathy" suggest a further step wherein counselors become actively involved in the therapeutic relationship by disclosing their own reactions as they relate to the here-and-now client/counselor relationship. By sharing themselves appropriately, counselors facilitate deeper self-exploration than is possible by merely reflecting back what the client expresses.

Therapist self-disclosure is thus a central part of higher levels of empathy. This disclosure *may* involve the group leader's expressing personal concerns, especially if these concerns affect his or her ability to be present for the group. If therapists are preoccupied with personal matters, Rogers (1970) argues, they don't listen as fully as they could, and, if they keep their concerns private, the group is apt to perceive the therapist's lack of presence as somehow *their* (the members') fault—two conditions that impede group process.

Implications for group leaders. As suggested earlier, empathic understanding is essential to developing the climate of acceptance and trust necessary for the success of the group. The ability to effectively express empathy rests on an attitude of genuine caring and on the sincere desire to understand the world of another. Presupposing the correct attitude, empathy is a skill that can be developed—and it is a skill that an effective group leader needs to develop. As Carkhuff (1966) has shown, a therapeutic relationship can be "for better or for worse": therapists have the potential to affect their clients either positively or negatively, and empathic understanding is preeminently a skill that influences the degree to which clients become functional in their world.

In working with group counselors, I have found that many mistakenly assume that, unless they themselves have directly experienced the same problems voiced by group members, they can't be empathic. Such an assumption can severely limit the leader's potential sphere of influence. Clearly, one need not experience incest to empathize with a group member's anguish over reliving painful sexual experiences. One need not have been abandoned by a parent to feel and experience the sadness of abandonment. It is not necessary to have been divorced to share a client's anger, hurt, and sadness of separation. Such experiences come in many forms and, at one level or another, are common to us all. It is not the specific experience that is essential. What is essential is a willingness on the part of the group leader to face his or her own unique life problems. There are situations in every life that trigger feelings of isolation, rage, resentment, guilt, sadness, loss, or rejection—to name a few of the *feelings* that will be expressed in groups. By remaining open to one's own emotions, by allowing oneself to be touched by the emotions of others, and by reexperiencing certain difficult events, any group leader's capacity to be psychologically present for others will increase.

A note of warning: the fact that one has worked through a problem doesn't mean that the problem has been solved once and for all. Even if the group leader has worked through a problem identical to that posed by a participant, the leader's solution may not be a viable one for that person. Further, a counselor who has managed the feat of "arriving" at a solution to a problem often is in danger of losing his or her capacity to share experientially with struggling group members who are still trying to "arrive."

Unconditional Positive Regard and Warmth

As we have seen, the goal of person-centered groups is to create a climate in which the basic actualizing tendency can freely express itself in each participant and in the group as a whole. For this growth force to be released within individuals and within a group, unconditional positive regard is another necessary factor.

According to this viewpoint, positive regard involves communicating a caring that is unconditional and that is not contaminated by evaluation or judgment of the client's feelings and thoughts. In other words, group leaders value and accept members without placing stipulations and expectations on this acceptance; they tell the client "I accept you as you are," not "I'll accept you when ...." Acceptance, however, is not to be confused with approval; therapists can accept and value their clients as separate persons, with a right to their separateness, without necessarily approving of some of their behavior.

Associated with this attitude of positive regard is an attitude of nonpossessive caring and warmth—namely, an attitude that is not dependent on the therapist's own need for approval and appreciation and that can be expressed in subtle ways such as gestures, eye contact, tone of voice, and facial expression. A genuine expression of caring can be sensed by the client and will promote his or her development. Artificial warmth can be as readily perceived and is likely to inhibit the client's change and growth. Obviously, once a client senses that the therapist's expression of warmth is more a technique than a genuine feeling, it becomes difficult for that client to trust the genuineness of other reactions of the therapist.

Related to the concept of accepting the individual group member with unconditional positive regard, caring, and warmth is the idea of developing an attitude of acceptance of the group as a whole. Just as Rogers (1970) believes in the capacity of the individual to find his or her own direction, so does he believe in accepting a group where it is, without attempting to impose a direction on it. He says: "From my experience I know that if I attempt to push a group to a deeper level, it is not, in the long run, going to work" (p. 48).

Elsewhere it is evident that Rogers has faith in the capacity of a group to move on its own initiative, although he does note that anxiety and irritation may result from the lack of externally imposed structure. Rogers (1970) gives his groups permission to determine for themselves how they will spend their time, and he may open a session with the statement "We can make this group experience whatever we want it to be." Rogers relates an experience with a group of high-level educational administrators who talked continually about trivial matters in an intellectual and superficial manner. In keeping with his philosophy and despite his feelings of annoyance and boredom, Rogers upheld the participants' right to engage in social chatter and his right not to endure it—he left the group and went to bed.

Certainly Rogers' solution was consonant with his philosophy. However, one may value the person-centered approach to group work without having to tolerate what one might consider to be excessive and nonproductive floundering. Thus, if you were facilitating the group described by Rogers, you might wish to confront it with your feelings as a participant/leader. Such a confrontation could take any one of the following forms:

- I'd like for each of you to say something regarding what you feel about being in this group so far.
- I'm aware that I've been impatient and bored for some time. It seems that we're staying on a very superficial level, unwilling to say much that is personal about ourselves.
- I'm wondering how most of you might feel if the group were to end now. I have the uncomfortable feeling that we are avoiding any productive work.

Being a group leader entails encouraging group members to focus on what they are doing and not doing; being a sincere group leader often entails expressing one's reactions to what is occurring. Ultimately, group members have the power to move or not to move to a deeper level, yet the leader can encourage them to look at their behavior and decide what they might do differently. It seems to me that a group leader can be a catalyst for change within a group without violating the principles and the spirit of the person-centered approach.

Implications for group leaders.   It has been my experience that group leaders in training often struggle with what they feel is the monumental task of being able to *feel* accepting or being able to demonstrate positive regard. Some tend to burden themselves with the unrealistic expectation that they must *always* be accepting and that they must consistently respond with warmth in all situations. Thus, it is also my experience that group leaders need to develop an accepting attitude toward themselves as well—an acceptance of the fact that at times they won't feel warmth or unconditional positive regard. It is not necessary to feel a high level of warmth and positive regard all the time in order to be an effective group leader. Like empathy, these attitudes are not an either/or condition; rather, they occur on a continuum of gradations. Being an effective group leader starts with accepting oneself and continues by bearing in mind that the greater the degree of valuing, caring, and accepting of a client, the greater the opportunity to facilitate change in the client.

Other leaders in training have a need to be active and directive and thus have real difficulty in dealing with Rogers' idea of accepting a group where it is. I think it is important that leaders accept their personal limits and preferences and that they see that it is possible to be *for* one's clients and still be directive and intervene in ways not strictly consistent with the person-centered approach.

Genuineness and Self-Disclosure

According to Rogers, a characteristic of the therapeutic relationship that is more important than any discussed so far is *congruence*—a term that implies that the therapist is real, or genuine. Genuineness means that what the therapist expresses externally is congruent with his or her inner experience, at least during the time of therapy. In other words, genuineness means that therapists don't pretend to be interested when they are not, that they don't fake attention or understanding, that they don't say what they don't mean, and that they don't adopt behaviors designed to win approval. They can perform their professional functions without hiding behind their professional roles. Genuine therapists are basically true to themselves in their various interactions, yet they can discriminate between being appropriately and inappropriately themselves.

In practice this means that, although leaders are essentially honest in their encounters in the group, they are not indiscriminately open, and they know the boundaries of appropriate self-revelation. Moreover, genuine leaders realize the importance of taking responsibility for any feelings they express in the group and the importance of exploring with clients persistent feelings that may block their ability to be fully present. Through their own authenticity, congruent group leaders offer a model that helps their clients work toward greater realness.

Some group leaders have difficulty with "being themselves." Often that difficulty stems from the misapprehension that genuineness entails expressing *every* immediate thought or feeling or being spontaneous without any restraint or consideration of the appropriateness and timeliness of one's reactions. Another difficulty is seen when leaders, in the name of being "authentic," make themselves the focal point of the group by discussing their personal problems in great detail. Clearly, and as indicated above, even the expression of genuineness must be handled with discretion. Leaders need to examine honestly their motivations for discussing their personal issues and ask themselves whether the disclosure serves the client's needs or their own. Clearly, if the leader has had an experience similar to that of a client, the sharing of feelings about the experience can be therapeutic for the client. But it is important that the focus remains on the client and that it does not shift away to the counselor. Leaders who frequently make themselves the focal point of group discussion may be using the group as a platform to air their personal problems.

Egan (1982) summarizes general guidelines for appropriate counselor disclosure as follows:

> Sharing yourself is *appropriate* if it helps clients achieve the treatment goals outlined in this helping process—that is, if it helps them talk about themselves, if it helps them talk about problem situations more concretely, if it helps them develop new perspectives and frames of reference, and if it helps them set realistic goals for themselves. Helper self-disclosure that is exhibitionistic or engaged in for "effect" is obviously inappropriate [p. 199].

Egan (1982) also talks about the values of counselor self-disclosure, a few of which are modeling self-disclosing behavior to members, being a positive social influence, decreasing role distances, increasing the counselor's ability to *work with* clients, and creating an authentic relationship. In the early stages of therapy, counselor self-disclosure can encourage the clients to explore themselves. As the therapeutic process advances, such disclosure can promote deeper self-understanding on the clients' part. Furthermore, the quality and the timing of disclosure are critical. On this issue, there is evidence that premature sharing of personal material by the facilitator may be disruptive, whereas more timely disclosures could be constructive (Dies, 1973).

Respect

Egan (1982) modified Rogers' facilitative conditions by adding the notion of respect. Respect can be described as an attitude of valuing others for who they are. A respecting attitude communicates the message "You share in the power of this relationship. You are a separate and unique person, with the right to see things from your vantage point." Like warmth, respect is often communicated through subtle, nonverbal behavior by the therapist; like lack of genuine warmth, lack of respect is generally readily perceived by the client. Some leader behaviors that communicate an active stance of respect are discussed by Egan (1982):

- being "for" the client
- demonstrating a willingness to work with the client
- regarding and treating the client as unique
- supporting the client's desire for self-determination
- assuming good will on the client's part
- attending fully to the client by actively listening and striving to understand
- suspending critical judgment
- taking the time and making the effort to develop accurate empathy
- reinforcing constructive action on the client's part
- being real and genuine with the client

An attitude that indicates respect on the part of the group leader can be a significant factor in helping group members to learn self-respect. Such an attitude also offers a model for group participants in dealing with one another. Often people in counseling lack self-respect and don't value their power as an individual. When they perceive respect emanating from the leader, they may begin to value the power within themselves.

The following are statements that illustrate how a group leader can project respect or disrespect toward clients. Note that, even if these statements are not openly made, they can be subtly conveyed.

Statements that show respect:
- My hope is that we can work together in this group and make it a place where you will all feel free to express your feelings.
- Assuming that you believe that this group can help you, I also assume that each of you wants to make constructive changes in life-style.

- I find it difficult to agree with some of your values; yet I firmly support your right to think differently from the way I do.

Statements that show disrespect:
- You guys are all alike. You're all out for a free ride, and you'll take advantage of anyone you can.
- I'm not much interested in what you feel. I just want to know when you'll change your behavior.
- I think that many of you are pretty hopeless; I don't believe that you want to change or, for that matter, that you are capable of it.

Immediacy

As I said earlier, some group leaders and therapists have difficulty in being "genuine." To overcome this difficulty, they adopt the dubious practice of bringing their personal problems to group sessions, convinced that to air personal difficulties is a sure sign of genuineness. Often these therapists work so hard at being real through indiscriminate display of personal difficulties that they end up being quite inauthentic.

These leaders could spare themselves a good deal of anxiety and unnecessary, fruitless work by discriminating between disclosure of what they think and feel in the therapeutic relationship and disclosure of what they think and feel in their personal lives. What is important is that leaders learn when and how to express those reactions that relate to their person-to-person encounters in the group situation. This form of relating is called *immediacy* and has been defined as being genuine in one's relationships.

Egan (1982) refers to immediacy as "you-me talk," and he sees the need for therapists (whom he calls "helpers") to learn the skills of being able to openly and directly explore what is happening in the here and now of the interpersonal relationship. According to Egan, direct, mutual talk is called for when therapists become aware that either they or their clients have *unverbalized* thoughts and feelings about what is happening in a session, particularly if these unverbalized thoughts and feelings are interfering with the session in any way. Examples of situations in groups that call for this kind of talk include trust issues (when a leader senses a lack of trust in a group or in a certain member), directionless sessions (where people seem unclear about what to do and where little investment is evident), and boredom in the group.

Concreteness

Although concreteness is not a factor that Rogers discusses, Carkhuff (1969), Egan (1976, 1982), and Ivey and Authier (1978)—all writers who have based their work on many of the concepts of the person-centered orientation—stress the importance of concreteness in the counseling process. Concreteness means specificity in discussing one's concerns, feelings, thoughts, and actions. It is a factor that is extremely important during the early stages of a group, when the members are defining what they want to attain from their participation in the group. Without concreteness, counseling loses intensity. If group sessions lack vitality and members are bored, it could be useful to pose the questions "Are we being specific and concrete about what we want? Are we not, instead, being overly vague and general in discussing our wants or needs?" If clients talk in generalities, there is no focus, and, if the group lacks focus, little movement can be expected during the sessions.

The group leader needs to recognize lack of concreteness, to help members become aware of the vagueness of their statements, and to assist them in becoming more specific. Following are two illustrations of vague statements, with responses that can help restore concreteness and promote focus:

- *Statement:* I want to get in touch with my feelings.
  Response: What feelings? What does "in touch" mean?
- *Statement:* I'm generally feeling sort of weird.
  Response: In what ways do you feel weird?

Confrontation

A common mistake made by some counselors who employ a person-centered approach is overemphasizing support, almost to the exclusion of being challenging. Being a genuine group counselor involves a willingness to confront in a therapeutic manner. Confrontation is not, as sometimes erroneously held, an attack or aggressive behavior on the leader's part. Ivey and Authier (1978) define confrontation as "the pointing out of discrepancies between or among attitudes, thoughts, or behaviors" (p. 145). Egan (1982) views confrontation as an *invitation* for people to examine their behaviors more honestly and indicates that confrontation should be done in the spirit of accurate empathy, in a tentative manner, and with care. Confrontation can be seen as an extension of caring and can be done in such a manner as to encourage those confronted to look at certain incongruities and to become aware of ways in which they may be blocking some of their strengths.

Furthermore, confrontation need not address weaknesses but can be aimed at the client's untapped strengths. In speaking about confrontation in groups, Rogers (1970) does not endorse the type of confrontation that is judgmental and attacks another's defenses.

In my own training of group leaders I offer the following guidelines regarding the use of confrontation by counselors:

- Remember that confrontation must be based on respect for others and that it is aimed at challenging others to look at unrecognized and unexplored aspects of themselves.
- Use confrontation only if you want to get closer to a client and only if you are willing to stay with the person after the confrontation.
- Learn to discriminate between what may be a judgmental attack and a caring challenge. For example, instead of saying "All you do is take from the group; you never give anything of yourself," you may say "I'm aware that you rarely speak in the group, and I miss hearing from you. I'm wondering whether your silence is OK with you or whether you'd like to be more verbally active. Are you aware of anything that is preventing you from expressing your feelings and thoughts?"
- When you confront a person, address his or her specific behaviors that affect others in the group and explain exactly what the effect is.

• Take responsibility for your behaviors instead of making others responsible for how you respond. Thus, instead of saying "You *make* me angry when you go off on your tangents," say "I get impatient and angry when you digress." Instead of saying "You're boring," say "I'm aware that I have a hard time staying with you when you speak, and I find that I'm becoming bored."

In sum, confrontation should be done in such a manner as to preserve the dignity of the one confronted, without prejudice to the person, and with the purpose of helping the person identify and see the consequences of his or her behavior. Most importantly, confrontation should open up the channels of communication and not close them.

Barriers to Effective Therapeutic Conditions

As I have mentioned, my associates and I conduct in-service training workshops for group leaders. Typically, these workshops in group process involve some didactic presentation and the teaching of group-leadership skills. The majority of the workshops are devoted to experiential learning, and the participants actually lead groups and then receive feedback from the members and ourselves. In the course of these workshops, many of our students express feelings of inadequacy as group leaders and a sense of frustration and hopelessness; they see little change occurring in the members of their groups, and they perceive that their clients are resistant and don't enjoy coming to groups. In many instances the problems besetting these students can be traced back to the fact that the conditions of active listening, empathy, positive regard, warmth, and acceptance are in some measure lacking in their groups. What follows is a list of specific problems that militate against the development of these therapeutic conditions.

1. *Lack of attending.* Often these prospective group leaders show that they don't really listen; they are preoccupied with a message that *they* want to impart to their groups and use the group as a vehicle for indoctrination. Or they ask many closed questions and are preoccupied with problem solving rather than with problem understanding. In short, many of our students talk too much and listen too little.

2. *Lack of empathy.* At times we observe that leaders are highly judgmental and critical and that they create a dichotomy between "we," the treatment staff, and "they," the clients. Instead of forming an alliance with their clients, they sometimes see the group members as enemies. These counselors often fail to see any of themselves in those they work with.

3. *Absence of counselor self-disclosure.* Some agencies and institutions foster, even require, an aloof and undisclosing leader role. Group counselors are given the messages "Avoid being personal," "Don't get involved," "Avoid sharing anything about yourself, even if it affects the relationship." Leaders are expected to change the behavior of members, yet they are expected to keep themselves out of their interactions with group members—clearly an unreasonable and self-defeating expectation.

4. *Lack of positive regard.* There are some group counselors who are intolerant of the people they are supposedly helping and who cling to assumptions that keep their clientele in stereotyped categories. Such prejudice on the part

of group leaders makes client change difficult, if not impossible. Admittedly, it may be difficult to maintain positive regard, warmth, and acceptance toward people who are in a treatment program for acts such as wife beating, child abuse or neglect, child molesting, or murder. It is not necessary to condone such actions, and it may not even be possible to avoid feeling negative toward those who have committed such acts. But it is important to try to set aside one's reactions at least during the course of the group. And it *is* possible to allow oneself not to see these people only as "child abusers," "antisocial personalities," "criminals," and so on.

5. *Lack of warmth and acceptance.* Related to lack of positive regard are some attitudes that we have seen counselors demonstrate—impatience, coldness, abruptness, put-downs, sarcasm, and hostility toward those they are attempting to help. Unless counselors recognize these attitudes, there is little chance that they will modify them and a large chance that they will continue to lead unsuccessful groups.

6. *Lack of belief in the therapeutic process.* Underlying the concepts of positive regard and acceptance is the belief that people *can* change and improve their personal condition. Ivey and Authier (1978) state: "If one is to be a helper, one must believe that people can be helped" (p. 133). In our in-service group-process workshops we have frequently met practitioners who lead groups only because they are required to do so and who do not believe in the effectiveness of group techniques. In a climate in which leader enthusiasm, motivation, and faith in groups are absent, is it surprising that leaders find that their groups are somewhat less than successful? After all, how can group members be expected to have faith in a process that the group leader does not believe in? No wonder that little change occurs and that the members are resistant and don't enjoy coming to the group.

ROLE AND FUNCTIONS OF THE GROUP LEADER

As I mentioned earlier, the person-centered approach stresses the attitudes of the group leader far more than the mastering of techniques. In fact, Rogers (1970) takes a dim view of the use of techniques to get a group moving. If and when techniques are used, Rogers believes, the group needs to be made a party to them. He states:

> I try to avoid using any procedure that is planned; I have a real "Thing" about artificiality. If any planned procedure is tried, the group members should be as fully in on it as the facilitator, and should make the choice themselves as to whether they want to use that approach [p. 56].

Rogers also cautions against the facilitator's making interpretive comments. Such comments, he feels, are apt to make the group self-conscious and slow the process down. Thus, Rogers believes that, if there are to be group-process observations, they should come from members—a view that is consistent with his philosophy of placing the responsibility for the direction of the group on the members. The term *facilitator* reflects the importance of interactions between group members. The role of the facilitator is to do what is necessary to create a climate in a group under which the actualizing tendency will be released.

The person-centered group encourages the members to explore the incongruities between their beliefs and behaviors and the urgings of their inner feelings and subjective experiencing. As the members become more aware of these incongruities within themselves, their view of themselves expands. Changes occur in the members' willingness to listen to themselves, to trust their inner promptings, and to rely on them as a basis for their behavior (Meador, 1975).

The person-centered approach assumes that members need the group setting and the time to express what they are ordinarily afraid to express on their own. Given the unstructured approach, along with a facilitator who refuses to do the traditional "leaderly" things, the group members, who are accustomed to following authorities, must eventually rely upon themselves to formulate a purpose and a direction. Although the group members tend to flounder in their attempt to please others, eventually they will express their boredom and frustration, because the facilitator does not do anything to rectify the situation (Coulson, 1970). Thus, members are helped to begin listening to themselves and other members by a facilitator who will not act as an expert who will save them. They are challenged to struggle and to express themselves, and out of this struggle they have a basis for learning how to trust themselves. Coulson (1970) summarizes this role of the facilitator and its impact on the group:

> The leader of an encounter group errs if he tries to *make* the group happen. He errs in missing the opportunity to find out what people *really* are like when they are not being manipulated. He errs in taking away from the members the rare opportunity to be what *they* want to be, without performance expectations. He errs also because *it simply isn't necessary* to manufacture the events of encounter. I am quite convinced that there is something in each of us which longs to be personal, even if ordinarily we don't dare it. If this is what we *want*, then it will come out in time if there is a sufficiently uncluttered occasion with other people [p. 10].

In his discussion of the role of the facilitator in the person-centered group, Bozarth (1981) identifies the following major characteristics:

- Facilitators are willing to participate as a member of the group.
- They demonstrate a willingness to attempt to understand and to accept each member of the group.
- They are willing to share their struggles when such personal issues exist, if doing so is appropriate and timely.
- Facilitators are willing to give up the power of control and the image of the expert; instead, they seek ways of having personal influence.
- They trust in the ability of the members to move in positive and healthy directions without their advice.

To help delineate the differences between the person-centered approach and other therapeutic models, I have listed some procedures that are not generally considered as part of the facilitator's repertoire:

- advice giving
- catalysts and techniques to initiate action
- diagnosis and evaluation

- structure and directive intervention
- tasks given to members to do outside of the session

The person-centered approach emphasizes instead certain attitudes and skills as a necessary part of the facilitator's style:

- listening in an active and sensitive way
- reflecting
- clarifying
- summarizing
- linking
- sharing of personal experiences
- encountering and engaging others in the group
- demonstrating an attitude of nonevaluative caring for the members and showing respect for them
- supporting and challenging the members
- going with the flow of the group rather than trying to direct the way the group is going
- affirming a client's capacity for self-determination

It might be mentioned that effective person-centered facilitators are not bound by rigid rules, and *at times* they do many of the things that I listed as not being a standard part of the facilitator's repertoire. On this point, Gendlin (1974) advises facilitators to do whatever they want as long as they "stay in touch at all times with the person's directly felt concrete experiential datum—and help the person also to stay in touch with that, and get into it" (p. 220). If facilitators follow this guideline, then they will continually discover what the members are experiencing.

What is basic to this approach to group work is the focus on the members as being the center of the group, not the leader. Members of the person-centered group are often as facilitative as or more so than the leader. On this point Lieberman, Yalom, and Miles (1973) make the following statement in their famous group study: "Change does not revolve around the solitary sun of the leader; the evidence is strong that psychosocial relations in the group play an exceedingly important role in the process of change" (p. 428). In a similar line of thinking, Wood (1982) captures the essence of the facilitator's role when he writes: "Success is not marked by how well the facilitator shines in presenting the cardinal attitudes but in how well the group's creative, growthful wisdom is released and the benefits of growth afforded its members. If the group can create a facilitative climate, the formative tendency will do the rest" (p. 257).

Rogers (1970) sees climate setting as the primary function of the group facilitator. This climate that Rogers wishes to have his leaders establish is one that promotes psychological safety for the participants (and by "safety" he does *not* imply that members will be spared the pain of new insights). Rogers captures the essence of what it means to establish a psychologically safe climate and to "be there for another" with the following words:

> I would like the individual to feel that whatever happens *to* him or *within* him, I will be psychologically very much *with* him in moments of pain or joy, or the combination

of the two, which is such a frequent mark of growth. I think I can usually sense when a participant is frightened or hurting, and it is at those moments that I give him some sign, verbal or nonverbal, that I perceive this and I am a companion to him as he lives in that hurt or fear [1970, p. 48].

In summary, person-centered group leaders use themselves as instruments of change in a group. Their "role" is to be without a role; their central function is to establish a therapeutic climate in which group members will interact in honest and meaningful ways. Clearly, it is the leader's attitudes and behavior that are the powerful determinants of the accepting group atmosphere conducive to real communication—not the techniques that he or she employs.

THE PERSON-CENTERED GROUP PROCESS

Characteristics of the Group

The typical size of the person-centered group is 8 to 12 members. The group might meet on a weekly basis for about three hours for an unspecified duration. However, a more common format is for these groups to meet for a weekend or longer in an intensive format. The residential aspect of small personal-growth groups and encounter groups affords members opportunities to work on personal issues that are troubling them and to become a community as a group. Although these groups often meet from Friday until Sunday, with time out for meals and sleep, they might also meet for a period of ten days to two weeks.

In their discussion of the mechanics of organizing and conducting a person-centered group, both Meador (1975) and Wood (1982) state that there are no rules for the selection of group members. Because of the personal nature of this approach, each facilitator admits a person if the two can agree that the person could probably benefit from the experience and contribute to the group. There are no stated ground rules that members must abide by. When people meet in a group, they formulate together the rules for their own meetings. Wood (1982) notes that groups generally adopt their own rules prohibiting physical violence, setting meeting times, governing the admittance of new members, and adopting a procedure for terminating the group. Also, groups may expect that each member attend each complete meeting of the group.

Stages of the Group

On the basis of his experience with numerous groups, Rogers (1970) has delineated some process patterns that occur in any type of group employing the person-centered approach when most of the conditions that were discussed in this chapter are present. It needs to be emphasized that the following process patterns, or trends, don't occur in a clear-cut sequence and that they may vary considerably from group to group.

1. *Milling around.* The lack of leader direction inevitably results in some initial confusion, frustration, and "milling around"—either actually or verbally. Questions such as "Who is responsible here?" "What are we here for?" or "What are we supposed to be doing?" are characteristic and reflect the concern felt at this stage.

2. *Resistance to personal expression or exploration.* Members initially present a public self—one they think will be acceptable to the group. They are fearful and resistant to revealing their private selves.

3. *Description of past feelings.* Despite doubts about the trustworthiness of the group and the risk of exposing oneself, disclosure of personal feelings does begin—however hesitantly and ambivalently. Generally, this disclosure deals with events outside of the group; members tend to *describe* feelings in a there-and-then fashion.

4. *Expression of negative feelings.* As the group progresses, there is a movement toward the expression of here-and-now feelings. Often these expressions take the form of an attack on the group leader, usually for not providing the needed direction. In general, expression of negative feelings toward the group leader or others precedes the expression of positive feelings. (A possible reason for this may be that members are testing the group to see whether it is a safe place to express *all* feelings.)

5. *Expression and exploration of personally meaningful material.* If the expression of negative feelings is seen by the members as acceptable to the group, a climate of trust emerges. Because of this feeling of trust, members decide to take the risks involved in disclosing personal material. At this point the participants begin to realize that the group is what they make it, and they begin to experience freedom. Such perceptions make members willing to let others know deeper facets of themselves.

6. *Expression of immediate interpersonal feelings in the group.* Members tend to express both positive and negative feelings toward one another. Usually these feelings are explored at this stage.

7. *Development of a healing capacity in the group.* Next, members begin to spontaneously reach out to one another, expressing care, support, understanding, and concern. In other words, members become therapeutic for one another by relating in facilitating ways. At this stage, helping relationships are often formed within the group that offer members aid in leading more constructive lives outside of the group.

8. *Self-acceptance and the beginning of change.* Self-acceptance marks the beginning of change in group members. At this stage, participants begin to accept aspects of themselves that they formerly denied or distorted; they get closer to their feelings and consequently become less rigid and more open to change. As members accept their strengths and weaknesses, they drop their defenses and welcome change—a process that promotes further change.

9. *Cracking of facades.* Here individual members begin to respond to the group demand that masks and pretenses be dropped. This revealing of deeper selves by some members validates the theory that meaningful encounters can occur when people take the risk of getting beneath surface interaction. At this stage, the group strives toward deeper communication—a process that occurs as individual members increasingly reveal their immediate feelings to the group.

10. *Feedback.* In the process of receiving both positive and negative feedback, members acquire a lot of data concerning how others experience them and about the impact they have on others. This information often leads to new insights that help members decide on aspects of themselves that they want to change.

11. *Confrontation.* Here members confront one another in what is usually an intensely emotional process involving positive and negative feedback. Confrontation can be seen as a stepping up of the interactions described in earlier stages.

12. *The helping relationship outside the group sessions.* By this stage, members have begun making contacts outside the group. Here we see an extension of the process described above, under number 7.

13. *The basic encounter.* Because in the group the members come into closer and more direct contact with one another than is generally the case in everyday life, genuine person-to-person relationships occur. At this point, members begin to experience how meaningful relationships can be when there is a commitment to work toward a common goal and a sense of community.

14. *Expression of positive feelings and closeness.* As the sessions progress, an increasing warmth and closeness develops within the group—a process that is due to the realness of the participants' expression of feelings about themselves and toward others. This therapeutic feeling of closeness leads to the last and most important process.

15. *Behavior changes in the group.* As members experience increased ease in expressing their feelings, their behaviors, mannerisms, and even their appearance begin to change. They tend to act in an open manner; they express deeper feelings toward others; they achieve an increased understanding of themselves; they develop new insights into their problems; and they work out more effective ways of being with others. If the changes are effective, the members will carry their new behaviors into their everyday lives.

As noted above, the stages of a person-centered encounter group, as adapted from Rogers (1970), don't necessarily occur in a neat and predictable order. What is important to keep in mind is that each stage describes a *process* and that each process tends to produce the sought-after change within a group and its individual members.

PERSON-CENTERED APPROACH TO FAMILY THERAPY

Rogers (1961) writes about the implications of client-centered therapy for family life in his book *On Becoming a Person.* He stresses the point that relationships in a family can be lived on a real basis, as opposed to living by pretenses. This means allowing family members to express thoughts and feelings openly, learning two-way communication, accepting and respecting one another, and being willing to allow others to be separate individuals. Just as Rogers emphasizes that clients in individual therapy or members of a group will come to trust themselves, he asserts that family members can become more trusting of themselves if the proper conditions exist. These basic conditions are realness, openness, caring, understanding, acceptance, positive regard, and active listening.

Family members often struggle with the question of trusting other members with their genuine feelings and responses. Some families that come to therapy are highly defensive, and real expression is absent. The climate of the family sessions is therefore geared to giving each member the freedom to be real, both in the sessions and at home. The following questions can be asked: What do family members do with feelings of resentment, guilt, shame, love, and jealousy? Do they think that they have to keep certain feelings hidden because such expression is not permitted?

Another major problem is that some members of a family might feel that they are not being seen and treated as a separate person with a unique identity. Sometimes there are stipulations to love and acceptance. For example, a mother may imply that her children must excel in everything they do or must live up to her expectations of who and what they should be if they are to gain her approval and affection. This situation would be brought to the surface during the sessions so that it could be explored in some depth.

Part of the therapist's function is to facilitate open and direct lines of communication when there has been a breakdown of communication patterns within the family. The core conditions of the therapeutic relationship that were described earlier in this chapter have direct applicability to person-centered family therapy. A basic assumption is that the attitudes of the therapist will to a large extent determine how open family members will be with one another in their sessions. The therapist does not approach the family as the expert who will prescribe a treatment plan; rather, he or she attempts to mobilize the resources that exist within the family. As is true of individual and group therapy, the formative tendency will operate if each family is viewed as a group of unique individuals possessing the potential for their own growth as well as that of the family. Thayer (1982) describes the ability of family members to move toward actualization and find the resources to effectively deal with their problems as individuals and as a family: "They are capable of shaping their own growth both as individuals and as a family group. In essence, the family members are their own architects. The therapist shows a tremendous respect for the family's potential to be self-determining" (p. 192). He describes the process of family therapy as a weaving together of individual and interpersonal growth.

EVALUATION OF THE PERSON-CENTERED APPROACH

Because the person-centered approach is very much a phenomenological one, based on the subjective world view of the client, I consider it an excellent basis for the initial stages of any group, regardless of the group's particular approach. In this approach, the stress is on truly listening to, and deeply understanding, the client's world from his or her internal and subjective frame of reference. Critical evaluation, analysis, and judgment are suspended, and the focus is on grasping the feelings and thoughts being expressed by the other. I see this form of listening and hearing as a prerequisite to any group approach, particularly during the early stages, when it is essential that members feel free to explore their concerns openly. Unless the participants feel that they are understood, surely any technique or intervention plans are bound to fail.

Many of the problems I've found among group leaders in training (which I discussed earlier in this chapter) stem, I suspect, from the failure to reach an understanding of the members' subjective world—an understanding that can be achieved only by very careful listening and by restraining the tendency to dive in too quickly to solve group members' problems.

As stated earlier, the person-centered approach is based on the premise that the attitudes of the leader and the relationship between leader and members are far more important than any techniques that the leader may employ. Again, I see this as an approach that can be used by any group model. In essence, many of the attitudes that Rogers sees as essential are or should be common to all therapeutic models. For example, respect and caring for clients are necessary for any therapeutic movement to occur; without them, the group is bound to reach an impasse. I doubt that any approach would question the value of the basic therapeutic conditions stressed by Rogers, although different therapies might and do place different values on the importance of specific conditions.

The emphasis placed by the person-centered approach on the person of the group leader is something that has much meaning for me. In training and supervising group leaders, I've found an eagerness on their part to acquire techniques they can use when certain problems arise in a group and a relative lack of interest in learning how the kind of person they are influences the process of the group. This is not to suggest that technique-related questions such as the following are not germane, useful, or even critical:

- What do I *do* if nobody wants to work in the group?
- How do I handle an aggressive member? a silent member? one who monopolizes? one who won't open up?
- What can I do to motivate people who don't want to be in the group?
- What do I do when things get too intense in the group?

What I'm suggesting is that group leaders would do well to show more interest in questions related to themselves and their attitudes—questions such as:

- Am I genuinely interested in people?
- What personal needs are met by my being a group leader?
- Am I authentically myself in a group, or do I hide behind the role of "leader"?
- Am I able to accept people, or do I have a need to direct their lives?
- Am I willing to take time to understand others, or do I force them to follow my agenda?
- Do I offer a proper model for what I hope and expect the members in my group to become?
- What kind of model am I?

Some people think that in order to practice within the spirit of the person-centered approach one must tolerate excessive floundering and a totally loose structure. I myself am not patient with such situations. I've found that I'm most effective, and the group seems to be most productive, when there is a structure that offers some direction yet grants freedom to the members. Thus, I typically provide the most structure at the beginning and ending stages of a group. Generally, I use techniques to enhance and to highlight the existing material in the group, rather than using them to get things moving. Although I don't like to use techniques to induce emotions, I do use them to help members experience certain emotions and to explore their feelings or problems.

Because initiating and directing are part of a leadership style that appears suited to my personality, I find that I am **unduly limited by a strict adherence** to a model that stresses listening, understanding, reflecting, and clarifying—practices that I see as useful but insufficient. The point that I wish to make here is that whatever techniques one employs or avoids, whatever style one adopts or refrains from, the leader's approach should be adapted to the needs of the group and its members and should, at the same time, fit the personality and style of the leader. Every approach has something of value to offer; the trick is to be aware of those aspects of each model that work for us and of those aspects that may work against us.

A problem that I have observed among beginning group leaders concerns the *way* in which some apply the person-centered approach; by remaining passive listeners, they also remain hidden as persons. Some of this nonassertive behavior seems to stem from a fear of making mistakes. But, whatever the reason, the excessive use of a passive approach results in submerging the uniqueness of the leader under a timid stance. Certainly it is true that the possibility for harming a person is smaller in less directive approaches than in more directive ones. But a question naturally arises: how much good can leaders do if they become so focused on the group members that they ignore themselves as powerful agents of change in a group? Also, I should add, this misapplication of the person-centered approach runs contrary to Rogers' emphasis on leader authenticity.

My central criticism of the person-centered approach—an approach I see as a good place to begin, but not as a good place to end—is not what it contains but, rather, what it omits. Personally, I don't subscribe to the notion that technical skills and knowledge are unimportant. I believe in the value of action, of therapeutic direction—at least at times—of timely interpretations, and of more directive skills than are found in the person-centered approach.

Meador and Rogers (1979) state that the person-centered approach rests on three attitudes, which are considered both *necessary and sufficient* to effect client change: therapist congruence, accurate empathic understanding, and unpossessive caring. Although I agree that these conditions are necessary for therapy to occur, I don't agree that they are sufficient. For me they are the necessary foundation on which group leaders must then build the *skills* of therapeutic intervention.

Ethical Issues

Several ethical issues arise out of the person-centered approach to group work. Some of them pertain to the lack of professional qualifications required of the group facilitator, the screening and selection procedures, the absence of any orientation and preparation of members for a group experience (especially in preparing people for possible life changes that might come out of group participation), the absence of ground rules and policies, and the possible psychological risks associated with encounter and personal-growth groups.

Some person-centered groups are facilitated by professionally qualified individuals who have academic training, knowledge of group process, and supervised experience. However, such professional qualifications are not seen as necessary in order to function as a facilitator. Indeed, in many cases the most effective facilitator of a group might be one of the members with no previous background in group work, either as a member or as a leader. Wood (1982) asserts that the best facilitator is not necessarily the person with the most training or the appropriate credentials. In apparent agreement with Wood is Corsini (1970), who writes: "I have trained some two hundred people to be group therapists, and I have found, in my judgment, a slight negative correlation between training and ability in group work" (p. 29). And Bozarth (1981) writes that critics have questioned the ethics of facilitators who do not have certification or academic credentials.

The screening and selection procedures are another issue that causes some practitioners (including myself) to be concerned about the person-centered group. As we have seen, the matter of systematic or uniform screening of people for a group is not seen as essential. The basic criterion is whether a person wants to join a group and has realistic expectations as determined by the person and the convenor. Both Meador (1975) and Wood (1982) state that there are no rules for selection of members. Although they are not held for the purpose of psychotherapy, weekend encounter groups and personal-growth workshops of two weeks' duration are often open to the public. In essence, participants are self-selected. Wood (1982) justifies this practice for nontherapy groups on the ground that experiences at the La Jolla Program demonstrate that these practices work: "Upwards of 5,000 persons have participated in the training program and thousands more in the weekend experiences. After 14 years of the program's existence there have been no incidents that persuade the directors to be selective in accepting members for groups" (p. 251).

Questions can still be raised: Can people be trusted to know enough to responsibly engage in self-screening? What are the ethical considerations regarding seriously disturbed individuals who are seeking therapy in a group that is led by a facilitator without academic training and professional experience in group leading? Is it ethical to allow anyone who wants to become part of a workshop to do so, regardless of the size of the group?

Another ethical consideration relates to the matter of orientation and preparation of group members. As we discussed, there is a minimum of preparation in advance of a typical person-centered group. The task for planning sessions— deciding how time will be spent and what will occur in the group—is in the hands of the group participants. The question can be raised whether it would not be wise for leaders to prepare members if they are to get the most from a group experience.

Research Efforts

To his credit, Rogers has consistently demonstrated a willingness to state his formulations as testable hypotheses and to submit his hypotheses to research efforts. This has been especially true of individual therapy and to some extent of the applications of the person-centered approach to groups. His theories of therapy and personality change have had tremendous heuristic effect, and, though much controversy surrounds this approach, even Rogers' critics give him credit for conducting extensive research on the process and outcomes of psychotherapy. Wood (1982) has pointed out that studies on person-centered groups have been hampered by the slow development of appropriate methods to examine groups in naturalistic settings. Wood contends, however, that the available research to date supports the theory and practice of the person-centered approach to group therapy. In his view, what is needed is research into the formative tendency. He would also like to see more research into the nature of the large group, with emphasis on the range of possible benefits and dangers, the role of composition, and possible implications.

Rogers and his associates have conducted research to determine the efficacy of the basic encounter groups described in this chapter. Rogers (1970) describes a systematic follow-up study that he conducted to assess the outcomes of small groups led by himself and his associates. The follow-up questionnaire—essentially a self-reporting instrument that identified reactions to group participation as well as the value of applying what was learned in the group to everyday life situations—was sent to 500 group participants. The study was conducted three to six months after the group experience. The following were some of the general findings of Rogers' study: two individuals felt that the experience had been mostly damaging and had changed their behavior in negative ways; a "moderate number" viewed their group experience as neutral and saw very little behavior change after the group; another "moderate number" felt that the group had only temporarily changed their behavior; most of the participants viewed the experience as deeply meaningful and positive—one that had made a significant and continuing impact and that had produced positive results in their behavior. (The study also contained open-ended questions that were designed to give a sample of the subjective perceptions of the group experience.)

It should be noted that psychologists who favor the empirical approach in evaluating the effects of individual and group counseling criticize the self-report style of Rogers' research as being too subjective. It should also be noted, however, that the self-report approach is consistent with the basic assumption of person-centered theory that only the individual can determine the meaning of a therapeutic experience. For readers interested in further details and in Rogers' able defense of his method of conducting outcome studies of encounter groups, I suggest consulting Rogers (1970, pp. 126–134).

Perhaps one of the best ways to evaluate a person-centered group is by participating in one. If you have an interest in finding out more about the sort of workshops described in this chapter, you can write to Center for Studies of the Person, 1125 Torrey Pines Road, La Jolla, CA 92037.

QUESTIONS FOR REFLECTION AND DISCUSSION

1. What are the advantages of leader-directed groups? the disadvantages? What are the tasks best suited for groups with leaders? for leaderless groups? Under what conditions do individuals perform better alone? in a group?
2. From what you know of yourself, how comfortable do you think you'd be in an unstructured group situation as a leader? How might you function as a leader if there were no plans in advance, no agenda, and no precon-

ceived structure and you refrained from using any techniques to get things moving?

3. What implications do you see in using a person-centered approach in working with a family group? Can you think of ways to apply the key concepts of this approach to counseling families?

4. What are your thoughts on the matter of selecting members to participate in a group? Can you think of both advantages and disadvantages to the absence of screening and selection procedures?

5. What are the advantages of having group facilitators who are not professional psychotherapists? the disadvantages? What are the qualities you would want in a group facilitator whom your loved one would be working with?

6. What are some key concepts and basic attitudes of the person-centered approach that you think could be effectively integrated into any other theory of groups?

7. Do you think that you can adopt a person-centered philosophy and still incorporate techniques from some of the directive therapies into your group leading? Can you view people from a person-centered perspective, yet assume a more active and central role in leadership? Explain.

8. What are your thoughts about the role of the person-centered facilitator of groups? Would you feel comfortable in being a member in a group you were leading or facilitating? In what sense might you be a member, and how might you function differently from the other members?

9. Review the basic attitudes of the person-centered group leader (genuineness, unconditional positive regard, empathy, respect, and so forth). Which of these attitudes do you think you'd have the greatest difficulty in living by and in translating from a belief you hold into concrete actions?

10. With what populations, and with what types of group, do you think the person-centered approach would be the most effective? In what cases, if any, do you think this approach would be inappropriate and ineffective?

RECOMMENDED SUPPLEMENTARY READINGS

Carl Rogers on encounter groups (Rogers, 1970) is an excellent introduction to encounter groups. It is a readable account of the process and outcomes of encounter groups, change as a result of these groups, and glimpses of the subjective struggles and experiences of those who participate in such groups.

On becoming a person (Rogers, 1961) is an important work addressing the characteristics of the helping relationship, the philosophy of the person-centered approach, and practical issues related to therapy. I especially recommend reading Chapters 2–9, 16, and 17.

Carl Rogers on personal power: Inner strength and its revolutionary impact (Rogers, 1977) describes the effectiveness of the person-centered approach in dealing with problems encountered in professions, marriage and family life, education, and even politics. A chapter is devoted to the description of a two-week workshop from the planning stages to its outcome.

A way of being (Rogers, 1980) contains a series of updated writings on Rogers' personal experiences and perspectives, as well as chapters on the foundations and applications of a person-centered approach. Especially useful are the chapters on person-centered communities, large groups, and perspectives on the world and person of tomorrow.

REFERENCES AND SUGGESTED READINGS*

American Psychological Association. Carl Rogers on empathy. *The Counseling Psychologist*, 1975, *5*(2, Whole Issue).

Bergin, A. E., & Strupp, H. H. *Changing frontiers in the science of psychotherapy.* Chicago: Aldine-Atherton, 1972.

*Bowen, M., Miller, M., Rogers, C. R., & Wood, J. K. Learnings in large groups: Their implications for the future. *Education*, 1979, *100*(2), 108–116.

* Bozarth, J. D. The person-centered approach in the large community group. In G. Gazda (Ed.), *Innovations to group psychotherapy* (2nd ed.). Springfield, Ill.: Charles C Thomas, 1981.

Carkhuff, R. R. Toward explaining success or failure in interpersonal learning experiences. *Personnel and Guidance Journal*, 1966, *44.*

Carkhuff, R. R. *Helping and human relations* (2 vols.). New York: Holt, Rinehart & Winston, 1969.

Combs, A., Avila, D., & Purkey, W. *Helping relationships: Basic concepts for the helping professionals* (2nd ed.). Boston: Allyn & Bacon, 1978.

Corsini, R. J. Issues in encounter groups: Comments on Coulson's article. *The Counseling Psychologist*, 1970, 2(2), 28–34.

* Coulson, W. R. Major contribution: Inside a basic encounter group. *The Counseling Psychologist*, 1970, 2(2), 1–27.

Coulson, W. R. *Groups, gimmicks, and instant gurus.* New York: Harper & Row, 1972.

Dies, R. R. Group therapist self-disclosure: An evaluation by clients. *Journal of Counseling Psychology*, 1973, *20*, 344–348.

Egan, G. *Interpersonal living.* Monterey, Calif.: Brooks/Cole, 1976.

Egan, G. *You and me.* Monterey, Calif.: Brooks/Cole, 1977.

Egan, G. *The skilled helper* (2nd ed.). Monterey, Calif.: Brooks/Cole, 1982.

Evans, R. *Carl Rogers: The man and his ideas.* New York: Dutton, 1975.

Gendlin, E. T. Client-centered and experiential psychotherapy. In D. A. Wexler & L. N. Rice (Eds.), *Innovations in client-centered therapy.* New York: Wiley, 1974.

Ivey, A. E. *Intentional interviewing and counseling.* Monterey, Calif.: Brooks/Cole, 1983.

Ivey, A. E., & Authier, J. *Microcounseling: Innovations in interviewing, counseling, psychotherapy, and psychoeducation* (2nd ed.). Springfield, Ill.: Charles C Thomas, 1978.

Lieberman, M. A., Yalom, I. D., & Miles, B. B. *Encounter groups: First facts.* New York: Basic Books, 1973.

Meador, B. D. Client-centered group therapy. In G. Gazda (Ed.), *Basic approaches to group psychotherapy and group counseling* (2nd ed.). Springfield, Ill.: Charles C Thomas, 1975.

Meador, B. D., & Rogers, C. R. Person-centered therapy. In R. J. Corsini (Ed.), *Current psychotherapies* (2nd ed.). Itasca, Ill.: Peacock, 1979.

Rogers, C. *Client-centered therapy.* Boston: Houghton Mifflin, 1951.

Rogers, C. The necessary and sufficient conditions of therapeutic personality change. *Journal of Consulting Psychology*, 1957, *21*, 95–103.

Rogers, C. A theory of therapy, personality, and interpersonal relationships, as developed in the client-centered framework. In S. Koch (Ed.), *Psychology: A study of science.* New York: McGraw-Hill, 1959.

* Rogers, C. *On becoming a person.* Boston: Houghton Mifflin, 1961.

Rogers, C. *Freedom to learn.* Columbus, Ohio: Merrill, 1969.

* Rogers, C. *Carl Rogers on encounter groups.* New York: Harper & Row, 1970.

Rogers, C. *Becoming partners: Marriage and its alternatives.* New York: Delacorte, 1972.

Rogers, C. Empathic: An unappreciated way of being. *The Counseling Psychologist*, 1975, *5*(2), 2–9.

Rogers, C. *Carl Rogers on personal power: Inner strength and its revolutionary impact.* New York: Delacorte Press, 1977.

*Books and articles marked with an asterisk are suggested for further study.

* Rogers, C. *A way of being*. Boston: Houghton Mifflin, 1980.

Rogers, C., & Wood, J. K. Client-centered theory. In A. Burton (Ed.), *Operational theories of personality*. New York: Brunner/Mazel, 1974.

Thayer, L. A person-centered approach to family therapy. In A. M. Horne & M. M. Ohlsen (Eds.), *Family counseling and therapy*. Itasca, Ill.: Peacock, 1982.

* Wood, J. K. Person-centered group therapy. In G. Gazda (Ed.), *Basic approaches to group psychotherapy and group counseling* (3rd ed.). Springfield, Ill.: Charles C Thomas, 1982.

11

GESTALT THERAPY

INTRODUCTION

Gestalt therapy, a form of existential therapy developed by Fritz Perls, is based on the premise that individuals must find their own way in life and accept personal responsibility. The focus is on what the client experiences in the present moment and on the blocks that the person must overcome to achieve full awareness of the here and now.

The basic goal of a Gestalt group is to challenge the participants to become aware of how they are avoiding responsibility for their awareness and to encourage them to look for internal, rather than external, support. Moment-to-moment awareness of one's experiencing, together with the almost immediate awareness of one's blocks to such experiencing, is seen as therapeutic in and of itself.

As clients acquire present-centered awareness and a clearer perception of their blocks and conflicts, significant unfinished business emerges. It is assumed that the way to become an autonomous person is to identify and deal with unfinished business from the past that interferes with current functioning. By reexperiencing past conflicts as if they were occurring in the present, clients expand their level of awareness, sometimes gradually and sometimes explosively, and are able to face, recognize, and integrate denied and fragmented parts of themselves, thus becoming unified and whole.

The Gestalt view is that we are essentially responsible for our own conflicts and that we have the capacity to deal with our life problems. Therefore, the approach of the Gestalt group is basically noninterpretive. Group members make their own interpretations and statements and discover the meaning of their experiences. Leaders avoid interfering with the clients' interpretations and focus instead on whatever the person seems to be experiencing at the moment. Gestalt leaders tend to be active and use a wide range of action-oriented techniques designed to intensify the members' feelings and experiences.

Gestalt therapy has been described as the integration of phenomenology and behaviorism (Zinker, 1977). On the one hand, it deals with the *subjective* world of the client's perceptions, or here-and-now experiencing. Gestalt therapists attempt to capture the person's way of being in the world, and from this subjective vantage point they try to help the client stretch the boundaries of his or her world. On the other hand, Gestalt therapy is also a behavioral approach, in that the basic methodological tool is the *experiment.* Group members are constantly being urged to try on a new style of behavior, to give expression to certain dimensions of their personality that are dormant, and to test out alternative modes of behavior so as to widen their ability to respond in the world. According to Zinker, Gestalt experiments are anchored in the experiential life of the members as they present themselves in the situation. Prefabricated exercises that are imposed on the group without having experiential roots are not within the province of phenomenology and Gestalt therapy, since they do not grow out of a living context for the group.

KEY CONCEPTS

Therapeutic Goals

Gestalt therapy has several important aims. One is to challenge clients to move from "environmental support" to "self-support." According to Perls (1969a), the aim of therapy is "to make the patient *not* dependent upon others, but to make the patient discover from the very first moment that he can do many things, *much* more than he thinks he can do" (p. 29).

Gestalt therapy does not attempt to help the individual adjust to society; rather, it strives to help the client find his or her own center within. Perls (1969a) said: "If you are centered in yourself, then you don't adjust any more— then, whatever happens becomes a passing parade and you assimilate, you understand, and you are related to whatever happens" (p. 30).

The basic aim of Gestalt therapy, which underlies all others, is the attaining of awareness. Awareness, by and of itself, is seen as curative. Without awareness, clients don't possess the tools for personality change. With awareness, they have the capacity to recognize the impasses and blockages that they create and find within themselves the resources necessary to solve their problems and discover the conditions that will make change possible. It is awareness that allows clients to recognize, face, and reintegrate parts of themselves that they have disowned and thus become unified and whole. As Latner (1973) says, once we have achieved enough integration, we can carry on the process of our own development by ourselves.

The question of therapeutic goals can be considered from the point of view of personal goals for each member and of group-process goals for the group as a whole. Zinker (1980) describes the following individual goals:

- integrating polarities within oneself
- achieving contact with self and others
- learning to provide self-support instead of looking to others for this support
- becoming aware of what one is sensing, feeling, thinking, fantasizing, and doing in the present
- defining one's boundaries with clarity
- translating insights into action
- being willing to learn about oneself by engaging in creative experiments

There are also goals for the members to achieve on the group level, some of which are:

- learning how to ask clearly and directly for what they want or need
- learning how to deal with one another in the face of conflict
- learning how to give support and energy to one another
- being able to challenge one another to push beyond the boundaries of safety and what is known
- creating a community that is based on trust, which allows for a level of deep and meaningful work
- learning how to make use of the resources within the group rather than relying upon the group leader as the director

The Here and Now

One of Perls' most significant contributions is his emphasis on learning to appreciate and experience fully the present: the present is the only significant tense, for the past is gone and the future has not yet arrived. He notes, however, that for most people the power of the present is lost because, instead of being in the present, they ruminate about the past or engage in endless plans and resolutions for the future. As they direct their energies toward what might have been or to what might be, their capacity to seize the power of the moment diminishes dramatically.

Perls (1973) made it clear that Gestalt is an *experiential* therapy, not a verbal or interpretive one, and that it is aimed at helping clients make direct contact with their experience in the immediacy of the moment. In the Gestalt view, if we think and talk about an experience, we interrupt the flow of present-centered experiencing and become detached from ourselves.

This focus on the present doesn't indicate a lack of interest in the past. The past *is* important but only insofar as it is related to our present functioning. In Gestalt groups, participants bring past problem situations into the present by reenacting the situation as if it were occurring now. For example, if a group member begins to talk about the difficulty she had when she was younger and attempted to live with her father, the therapist would typically intervene with a request that she "be here now" with her father and speak directly to him. The therapist might say "Bring your father into this room now, and let yourself go back to the time when you were a child. Tell him now, as though he were here and you were that child, what you most want to say."

It is not uncommon for group members to question a leader about the purpose and value of bringing a past event into the present by reenacting it. The member might well ask: "I feel foolish talking to my father in that empty chair just like the time when I was 10 years old. Why can't I tell the group what I remember about that time?" (In Gestalt terms this is known as "aboutism" instead of direct experiencing.) Although it is probably unwise for the group leader to engage in a lengthy theoretical explanation of the rationale behind present-centered techniques, the leader should surely have a clear understanding of the reasons for this focus. In some brief way, the leader can offer a simple explanation for the technique or can invite the member to discuss more fully her feeling foolish in the group and how this feeling might prevent her from engaging in what could be a powerful experiment.

For group leaders, it is useful to know that many problems that members bring up relate to unfinished situations with significant people in their life. In this example, the group member may harbor feelings of resentment and mistrust toward men, based on her convictions that men will simply not be there for her in time of need. She might connect this present feeling to old feelings associated with her alcoholic father, who continually let her down and brought much pain into her life. Based on her early decision not to trust men, she may be projecting her negative feelings toward all men now. Concluding that, if her own father could not be counted on for love and protection, then surely other men will not be more trustworthy, she now looks for evidence to support her hypothesis. The Gestalt group leader would invite her to in some way deal with her father symbolically in the here and now. She might have a dialogue with him, becoming both her father and herself. She could now say all the things that she wanted to say to her father as a child but, because of her fear, kept deep inside herself. She might tell her father what she most wanted from him then, and what she still wants with him now.

Of course, there are many creative possibilities within the group. She could look at the men in the group, expressing to each some of her resentments. In making contact with each man in the group, she could share her fantasies of all the ways that they would let her down or of what she would like from them now yet is afraid to ask for. The theoretical rationale for this technique is rooted in the assumption that the emotions that were overwhelming to her as a child were dealt with by some form of distortion or denial. The Gestalt leader encourages her to reexperience these past events by reliving them in the here and now so that the emotions that were repressed can come to the surface. With the support of the leader and the group members, she can allow herself to experience feelings that she has sealed off from awareness, and she can now work through some of these feelings that are keeping her stuck. By challenging her assumptions of how men are, she is able to establish a new basis for relating to men.

The technique of making a situation a present one can be applied to future events. If the above group member is afraid of a future confrontation with her father, she'll be asked to live her expectations in the here and now by speaking directly to her father in the group and by expressing her fears and hopes. Thus, she may say to her father: "I want to tell you how much I'd like to be close to you, but I'm afraid that, if I do so, you won't care. I'm afraid of saying the wrong things and pushing you even further away from me."

Perls (1969a) maintains that we tend to cling to our past in order to justify our unwillingness to assume responsibility for the present direction of our life. By staying in the past, we can play endless games of blaming others for the way we are, and we never really face our own capacity to move in a different direction. We get caught up in the process of making resolutions and rationalizing about our lifeless state. We would rather do anything than become conscious of how we keep ourselves from being fully alive.

Since Gestalt therapy focuses on the power of the present, most Gestalt techniques are designed to put clients into closer contact with their ongoing experiencing and increase their awareness of what they are feeling from moment to moment. Polster and Polster (1973) say: "A most difficult truth to teach is that only the present exists now and that to stray from it distracts from the living quality of reality" (p. 7).*

Awareness and Responsibility

Awareness is the process of recognizing what we are thinking about and what we are feeling, sensing, and doing. Awareness should not be confused with introspection or insight; rather, "at its best, awareness is a continuous means for keeping up to date with one's self. . . . It is always there, like an underground stream, ready to be tapped into when needed, a refreshing and revitalizing experience" (Polster & Polster, 1973, pp. 211–212).

The task of the member of a Gestalt group is to pay attention to the structure of his or her experience and to become aware of the *what* and *how* of such experiencing. Whereas the psychoanalytic approach is interested in *why* we do what we do and not in how we do it, the Gestaltist asks "what" and "how" questions but rarely "why" questions. Perls (1969a) says that *why* is a dirty word in Gestalt therapy, because it leads to rationalizations and, at best, to clever explanations but never to understanding. By contrast, Perls adds, focusing on what people experience in the immediate situation and on how they experience it does lead to increased awareness of the present. By attending to the continuum of awareness—that is, by staying with the moment-to-moment flow of experiencing—clients discover how they are functioning in the world.

According to Perls' colorful description, the two legs on which Gestalt therapy walks are the *now* and the *how*. The essence of Gestalt theory hinges on these two words: *now* covers all that exists, and it is the basis of awareness; *how* covers behavior and what is involved in an ongoing process. Perls contends that all else is irrelevant. To help clients get focused on the present and experience more intensely their immediate feelings, the Gestaltist asks questions that lead to present-centeredness:

---

*From *Gestalt Therapy Integrated: Contours of Theory and Practice*, by I. Polster and M. Polster. Copyright 1973 by Brunner/Mazel, Inc. This and all other quotations from this source are reprinted by permission.

- What are you experiencing now?
- What is going on inside you as you are speaking?
- How are you experiencing your anxiety in your body?
- How are you attempting to withdraw at this moment, and how are you avoiding contact with unpleasant feelings?
- What is your feeling at this moment—as you sit there and attempt to talk?
- What is happening to your voice as you talk to your father now?

In order to attain present-centered here-and-now awareness of our existence, Gestalt therapy focuses on the obvious—on the surface of behavior—by concentrating on the client's movements, postures, language patterns, voice, gestures, and interactions with others. Since many people fail to see what is obvious (Perls, 1969a), the Gestalt therapist challenges clients to learn how to use their senses fully, to become aware of how they avoid the obvious, and to become open to what is here now. Polster and Polster (1973), too, point to the value of focusing on the surface of behavior and stress the need to provide a climate in which clients can become more clearly focused on their changing awareness from moment to moment. Polster and Polster write:

> Life *is* as plain as the nose on your face when you are willing to stay with that which is presently clear, moving from one moment of actual experience to the next, discovering something new in each, something which moves forward, developing the theme of its own movement and culminating in illuminations which were inaccessible in the beginning [p. 46].

As I said earlier, through awareness we can become whole again by recognizing, accepting, and integrating denied parts of ourselves and by reconciling our polarities and dichotomies. And, as we become aware, we are able to assume responsibility for our actions and our experiences. We become aware that what we are thinking, feeling, valuing, sensing, and doing are all parts of us—we are this person who is experiencing right now (Latner, 1973), and we assume responsibility for being that person.

The core of Gestalt therapy relates to helping members assume responsibility for whatever they are experiencing and doing, rather than placing blame on others for who and what they are now. For Perls, personal responsibility is *not* the same as meeting obligations. In his view, mature individuals do not try to meet the expectations of others and live by obligations to others; rather, they are concerned with living by their own expectations and being true to themselves.

Briefly then, the crux of assuming responsibility is becoming aware of moment-by-moment experiencing and seeing how we are providing meaning to this experience. It means that we avoid manipulating others by fixing upon them the blame for whatever we are feeling and doing. Nobody is *making* us feel any way or take any particular course of action. It also means that we do not keep ourselves helpless by expecting others to support us in a variety of ways when we are able to provide this support to ourselves. One way we can promote an increasing sense of personal responsibility is by becoming aware of the ways in which we give away our power by making others responsible for us. Another way is to separate our own expectations from what we think others expect of us and then to make a conscious decision to live by our own expectations.

Unfinished Business and Avoidance

Unfinished business relates to unexpressed feelings, such as resentment, hate, rage, pain, hurt, anxiety, guilt, and grief, and to events and memories that linger on in the background and clamor for completion. Unless these unfinished situations and unexpressed emotions are recognized and dealt with in the now, they keep interfering with present-centered awareness and with our effective functioning. In writing about the effects of unfinished business, Polster and Polster (1973) say: "These incomplete directions *do seek* completion and when they get powerful enough, the individual is beset with preoccupation, compulsive behavior, wariness, oppressive energy and much self-defeating behavior" (p. 36).

Foulds (1975) describes ways of dealing with unfinished business in an experiential Gestalt group. He says that, if group members stay with their continuum of awareness for a time, significant unfinished situations emerge and can then be dealt with. Foulds maintains that group members, by becoming aware of what they are experiencing and of what they are avoiding, can resolve uncompleted situations that impinge on their present life and can thus free their energies and mobilize their resources.

A concept related to unfinished business is avoidance, which refers to the means people use to keep themselves from facing unfinished business and from experiencing the uncomfortable emotions associated with unfinished situations. Perls (1969a) says that most people would rather avoid experiencing painful emotions than do what is necessary to change. Therefore, they become stuck and are unable to get through the impasse, blocking their possibilities of growth.

Because we have a tendency to avoid confronting and fully experiencing our anxiety, grief, guilt, and other uncomfortable emotions, the emotions become a nagging undercurrent that prevents us from being fully alive. Perls speaks of the catastrophic expectations that we conjure up and that keep us psychologically stuck: "If I express my pain fully, people will be embarrassed, and they won't have anything to do with me"; "If I were to express my anger to the significant people in my life, they would abandon me"; "If I ever allowed myself to mourn over my losses, I might sink so deep into depression that I'd never get out of that hole."

Perls maintains that these fantasies keep us from living, because we use them to avoid taking the necessary risks that growth demands. Thus, the Gestalt therapist encourages expressing in the now of the therapeutic session intense feelings never directly expressed before. If a client says to the group that she is afraid of getting in touch with her feelings of hatred and spite, she may be encouraged by the therapist to become her hateful and spiteful side and express these negative feelings to each group member. By experiencing the side of herself that she works so hard at disowning, this participant begins a process of integration and allows herself to get beyond the impasse that keeps her from growing.

During a group session, a member says that he feels empty and powerless. The therapist is likely to encourage him to stay with these uncomfortable feelings, even to exaggerate them—to "be empty," to "be powerless." The theory is that, if this person can endure and truly experience the depth of his feelings, he most likely will discover that whatever catastrophic expectations he has with regard to those feelings are more of a fantasy than a reality and that his helplessness and void will not destroy him. Experiencing dreaded emotions leads to integration and growth.

This is what Latner (1973) says about making and enduring contact with unpleasant emotions:

> It is also the risky aspect of therapy, for while we are experiencing emotions that we have tried to avoid in the past, only the safety of the therapeutic context serves to assure us that we will survive this encounter with our pain. To succeed in therapy, we must be willing to take these risks and make what is unpleasant part of our life [p. 191].

By going beyond our avoidances, we make it possible to dispose of unfinished business that interferes with our present life, and we move toward health and integration.

Layers of Neurosis and Modes of Defense

Perls (1970) has likened the unfolding of adult personality to the peeling of an onion. In order for individuals to achieve psychological maturity, they must strip off five layers of neurosis. These superimposed growth disorders are (1) the phony, (2) the phobic, (3) the impasse, (4) the implosive, and (5) the explosive. The first layer we encounter, the *phony layer*, consists of reacting to others in stereotypical and inauthentic ways. This is the level where we play games and get lost in roles. By behaving *as if* we are a person that we are not, we are trying to live up to a fantasy that we or others have created. Once we become aware of the phoniness of game playing and become more honest, then we experience unpleasantness and pain.

The next layer we encounter is the *phobic layer*. At this level we attempt to avoid the emotional pain that is associated with seeing aspects of ourselves that we would prefer to deny. At this point our resistances to accepting ourselves the way we actually are pop up. We have catastrophic fears that, if we recognize who we really are and present that side of ourselves to others, they will surely reject us.

Beneath the phobic layer is the *impasse*, or the point where we are stuck in our own maturation. This is the point at which we are sure that we will not be able to survive, for we convince ourselves that we do not have the resources within ourselves to move beyond the stuck point without environmental support. Typically, this is the time when we attempt to manipulate the environment to do our seeing, hearing, feeling, thinking, and deciding for us. At the impasse we often feel a sense of deadness and feel that we are nothing. If we hope to feel alive, it is essential that we get through the impasse.

If we allow ourselves to fully experience our deadness, rather than denying it or running away, then the *implosive level* comes into being. Perls (1970) says that it is necessary to go through this implosive layer in order to get to the authentic self. By getting into contact with this layer, or our deadness and inauthentic ways, we expose our defenses and begin to make contact with our genuine self.

Perls contends that peeling back the implosive layer creates an explosive state. When we contact the *explosive layer*, we let go of phony roles and pretenses, and we release a tremendous amount of energy that we have been holding in by pretending to be who we are not. To become alive and authentic, it is necessary to achieve this explosion, which can be an explosion into pain and into joy.

A concept related to these layers of personality is that of resistance and ego defense mechanisms. From a Gestalt perspective, resistance refers to defenses we develop that prevent us from experiencing the present in a full and real way. The five layers of neurosis represent a person's style of keeping energy pent up in the service of maintaining pretenses. There are also ego defense mechanisms that prevent people from being authentic. Three major channels of resistance that are challenged in Gestalt therapy are *introjection, projection,* and *retroflection.*

Introjection involves the tendency to uncritically accept others' beliefs and standards, without assimilating them to make them congruent with who we are. These introjects become alien to us, because we have not analyzed and restructured them. When we introject, we passively incorporate what the environment provides, spending little time on getting clear what we want or need.

Projection is the reverse of introjection. In projection we disown certain aspects of ourselves by ascribing them to the environment. When we are projecting, we have trouble in distinguishing between the inside world and the outside world. Those attributes of our personality that are inconsistent with our self-image are disowned and put onto other people. By seeing in others the very qualities that we refuse to acknowledge in ourselves, we avoid taking responsibility for our own feelings and the person that we are.

Retroflection consists of turning back to ourselves what we would like to do to someone else. For example, if we lash out and injure ourselves, we are often directing aggression inward that we are fearful of directing toward others. Typically, these maladaptive styles of functioning are done out of our awareness; part of the process of Gestalt therapy is to help us discover a self-regulatory system so that we can deal realistically with the world.

Energy and Blocks to Energy

Because members need energy to work in group sessions, Gestalt leaders pay special attention to where energy is located, to how it is used, and to how it can be blocked. Blocked energy can be thought of as *resistance,* and there are a number of ways in which it can show up in the body. One member will experience tension in his neck and shoulders, and another member will experience shortness of breath. Another person will typically speak with a restricted voice, by holding back power. A few other ways that these blocks to energy will manifest themselves are keeping one's mouth shut tightly (as though one were afraid what might slip out); slouching; looking at the ground or in the air as a way of avoiding contact with others' eyes; keeping one's body tight and closed; talking in a fast and staccato fashion; being emotionally flat; and experiencing body sensations such as a lump in the throat, a quivering of the mouth, a hot and flushed feeling, shaking movements of the hands and legs, or dizziness.

In commenting on the value of focusing on the client's energy in therapeutic work, Zinker (1977) says that clients may not be aware of their energy or where it is located, and they may experience it in a negative way. From his perspective, therapy at its best is "a lively process of stoking the client's inner fires of awareness and contact" (p. 24). This process involves a therapeutic relationship that awakens and nourishes the client in such a way that the therapist does not become sapped of his or her own energy. Zinker maintains that it is the therapist's job to help clients locate the ways in which they are blocking energy and to help them transform this blocked energy into more adaptive behaviors. This process is best accomplished when resistance is not viewed as a client's refusal to cooperate and as something simply to be gotten around. Instead, therapists can learn to welcome resistance and use it as a way of deepening therapeutic work. Members can be encouraged to recognize how their resistance is being expressed in their body, and, rather than trying to rid themselves of certain bodily symptoms, they can actually delve fully into tension states. By allowing themselves to exaggerate their tight mouth and shaking legs, they are able to discover for themselves how they are diverting energy and keeping themselves powerless.

Methods of working with the body can be fruitfully combined with other techniques in a Gestalt group. Reichian body-work concepts and techniques are particularly useful in working with energy and blocks to energy. Wilhelm Reich's (1949, 1967, 1969) central idea was that emotions are an expression of the movement of body energy and that chronic tensions block this flow of energy and thus block emotions. He associated forms of resistance with specific patterns of "muscular armoring." He emphasized the value of loosening and dissolving this muscular armor, along with dealing with psychological issues in an analytic way. Reich demonstrated that relaxing these patterns of muscular armoring could release bottled-up emotions. In his therapy work he paid attention to nonverbal behaviors such as the client's general appearance, facial expressions, tensions in various parts of the body, and gestures. As a way of helping his clients increase their awareness of their body and character traits, he asked them to exaggerate certain habitual behaviors that were thought to be a part of character armor. Reichian body work included emphasis on breathing in a spontaneous and relaxed way. Methods that deepened the client's breathing led to an opening of the feelings. His approach focused on working with muscular tensions, such as a tight jaw, neck, or mouth, frowns, and so forth. Reichian work is based largely on a reading of the body and proceeds in a systematic way, beginning with the eyes and ending with the pelvis. Reich's therapeutic work increasingly dealt with freeing intense emotions such as pleasure, rage, fear, pain, and anxiety through working with the body. He found that after repressed emotion was expressed, chronic muscular and psychological tension could also be released.

It is interesting to note that Perls was a patient and a student of Reich's, and in his writings Perls credits Reich with having had a significant influence on the concepts and techniques of Gestalt therapy. It is good to add the caution that, before group leaders even consider incorporating some of the Reichian body techniques in a Gestalt group, they should have extensive training and supervision in these techniques. Even though Gestalt leaders might not have had such training, however, they can still make use of some of these concepts by learning how to pay attention to the energy flow and blockage as evidenced by looking at the bodies of the group members. Also, members can be taught how to pay attention to what they are experiencing within their own body, so that they can learn from the messages that their body is sending them.

ROLE AND FUNCTIONS OF THE GROUP LEADER

Perhaps the best way to describe the functions of the Gestalt therapist or group leader is to review how Gestalt therapy proceeds. (Note that the following discussion applies to group as well as individual therapy.) According to Perls (1969a), the goal of therapy is the client's maturation and the removal of "blocks that prevent a person from standing on his own feet." In order to achieve this goal, the therapist helps the client make the transition from external to internal support by locating the *impasse.* Perls described the impasse as the place where people get stuck—the point at which they avoid experiencing threatening feelings and attempt to manipulate others by playing the game of being helpless, lost, confused, and stupid. These games permit clients to remain stuck and thus avoid doing what they need to do in order to resolve pressing unfinished business.

One of the therapist's functions is to challenge clients to get through the impasse so that growth is possible. It is a difficult function indeed, because at the point of impasse clients think that they have no chance of survival; they simply don't believe that they can find inside themselves the means for going on. So they give up their own eyes and ears and desperately try to manipulate others into doing their seeing and hearing for them. If therapists are not careful, they can easily get caught up in the manipulations of their clients. If they try to be "helpful," they may foster dependency and helplessness and reinforce the client's belief that he or she doesn't have the ability to cope with life. Then clients can give in to their catastrophic expectations and avoid challenging their fears that keep them stuck.

The therapist must confront clients so that they will face what they are doing and decide whether they will develop their potential. This confrontation consists of challenging clients to fully experience whatever blockages and barriers are within them and to make contact with the frustration resulting from the feeling of being stuck. Perls saw frustration as essential for growth: "We apply enough skillful frustration so that the patient is forced to find his own way, discover that *what he expects from the therapist, he can do just as well himself*" (1969a, p. 37). This is how Perls summed up the role of the therapist: "My function as a therapist is to help you to the awareness of the here and now, and to frustrate you in any attempt to break out of this. This is my existence as a therapist, in the therapy role" (1969a, p. 74).

It is clear, then, that much of the Gestalt group leader's work consists of frustrating the members. It takes a good deal of strength on the leader's part to avoid getting trapped by the members' manipulations into taking responsibility for their well-being. Group leaders who try to be too helpful by doing too much of the clients' work actually contribute to the members' feelings of incompetence. Although Gestalt leaders insist that the members assume responsibility for raising their own level of consciousness, they nevertheless can take an active role in creating experiments designed to help the members tap their resources. As Zinker (1977) points out, the therapist, functioning much like an artist, invents experiments with clients to augment their range of behaviors.

> The therapist lends a structure, a form, a disciplined process to the formulations constantly generated by the relationship between himself and his client. The therapist creates an ambiance, a laboratory, a testing ground for the client's active exploration of himself as a living organism. This is the therapist's primary responsibility to his client [p. 5].

Zinker goes on to say that the group leader is not always the person who invents the experiments. Rather, the leader's function is to create an atmosphere and structure in which the group's own creativity and inventiveness can emerge. For example, a theme of loneliness may come up in a group. Here a central task of the leader is to orchestrate this theme by connecting members with one another and finding ways to involve the group as a whole in exploring loneliness.

Gestaltists employ a wide range of techniques to help clients gain awareness and experience their conflicts fully. It should be made clear, however, that, although the skillful and appropriate use of techniques is an important function of the therapist, Gestalt is much more than a collection of techniques. Techniques cannot be separated from the personality of the therapist who uses them, and overuse of techniques may keep the therapist hidden and lead to "phony therapy that *prevents* growth" (Perls, 1969a, p. 1).

Polster and Polster (1973) see the therapist as nothing less than an artist involved in creating new life. Yet, in Gestalt, as in most other approaches, the danger exists that the therapist will lose sight of the true meaning of the therapeutic process and become a mere technician. Therapists should use their own experience as an essential ingredient in the therapy process and never forget that they are far more than mere responders, givers of feedback, or catalysts that don't change themselves (Polster & Polster, 1973). Since the client/ therapist relationship is the core of the therapeutic process, the use of techniques should never be allowed to interfere with the authenticity of the relationship. Techniques need to be individually tailored to each client, and they need to be the outgrowth of the therapeutic encounter—an encounter grounded in the mutual experiencing of client and therapist.

In essence, therapists need to invent their own techniques, which are basically an extension of their personality: "Techniques emerge out of the unique needs of each situation. The therapist must be as unique as each moment. If he copies another therapist, or continually falls back on gambits that have worked well in the past, he becomes mechanical, inauthentic, irresponsible" (Latner, 1973, p. 204). To achieve that uniqueness, therapists must be in tune not just with the persons before them but also, and most importantly, with themselves. If clients are to become authentic, they need contact with an authentic therapist on a genuine I/Thou basis. As Simkin (1982) writes:

> Gestalt therapists aim for transparency of self rather than cloaking themselves in the mantle of therapist and encouraging transference reactions. This is not to say that

transference does not occur in Gestalt therapy. Rather, an attempt is made to minimize rather than maximize transference reactions by dealing with what is ongoing at the moment in the therapist-patient interactive process" [p. 359].

For Zinker (1977), creative therapists possess a rich personal background, having opened themselves to a range of life experiences and become able to celebrate life fully. In short, they are able to use themselves as a person as they function as a therapist. In addition to being a mature and integrated person, creative therapists also possess certain capacities, abilities, and technical skills. Out of their experimental attitude, they use themselves, other group members, and objects and events in the group environment in the service of inventing novel visions of the members. Some of the specific skills that Zinker mentions as being related to the functioning of creative therapists are the following:

- the capacity to identify energy within the members and to move with this energy
- a sensitivity to introducing experiments in a timely and appropriate fashion
- the ability to be flexible by letting go of some things and moving to other areas that are more lively
- the willingness to push and confront members so that they will get their work done, along with the ability to know when to back off
- the ability to help members express their feelings and summarize what they are learning after they complete an experiment
- the wisdom to know when to let members stay confused so that they can learn to find clarity in their own way

From this discussion of the role and functions of the Gestalt group leader, it should be apparent that skilled leadership entails a great deal more than merely grabbing one technique after another from a Gestalt bag. Who the leader is as a person and how he or she functions in the group, creatively drawing upon technical expertise, are the critical factors that determine the potency of leadership.

APPLICATIONS AND TECHNIQUES

As was mentioned earlier, Gestalt therapy employs a rich variety of action-oriented techniques designed to intensify what group members are experiencing in the present moment. Gestalt therapy encourages "becoming a conflict" or "being what we are feeling" as opposed to merely talking about conflicts, problems, and feelings. It cannot be overemphasized that these techniques need to be tailored to the individuals within the group and to the unique context of a particular group interaction. Applied mechanically, or inappropriately, the techniques become mere gimmicks that can result in increased defensiveness by the members and in even less authentic living on their part. Simkin (1982) discourages the use of stereotyped exercises of any kind and prefers to reinforce natural, creative expressions in his Gestalt groups. However, he acknowledges that some Gestalt therapists use structured exercises. For example, at the beginning of a session, leaders may ask for a go-around in which each participant makes a brief here-and-now statement of what he or she is aware of. Members may be asked to declare if they have any personal issues they are willing to explore or what they want from the session. In this way, session time can be maximized by focusing on common themes.

It is useful to differentiate between a group *exercise* and a group *experiment.* With group exercises, leaders prepare some kind of structured technique before the group meets. Members might be asked to pair up and talk, or a catalyst might be introduced into the group to provide a specific focus for work during a session. In contrast, the group *experiment* is a creative happening that grows out of the group experience; as such it cannot be predetermined, and its outcome cannot be predicted (Zinker, 1977). Therefore, it is essential to keep in mind that the techniques described in this chapter are not arbitrarily imposed upon a group to *make* something happen. Rather than being used as catalysts for stirring up action in a group, these techniques are best conceived of as experiments that grow out of the ongoing interplay among the members.

To increase the chances that members will benefit from Gestalt techniques, group leaders need to communicate the general purpose of these techniques and to create an experimental climate. "Let's try something on for size and see how it fits" conveys this experimental attitude on the part of the leader. The message also says that the leader is not trying to prove a point and that the members are free to try something new and determine for themselves whether it's going to work. In discussing the need for a brief explanation of the purpose of the technique, Passons (1975) observes that clients may be puzzled by certain Gestalt exercises—for example, by being asked to talk to an empty chair, or to "be their sadness," or to become aware of what they are "saying" with their bodies—and that a brief explanation can dispel this perplexity and lead to greater willingness to experiment. Occasional explanations also foster trust in the leader by making clear that the exercise has a therapeutic purpose and is not an attempt to "trick" someone.

Polster and Polster (1973) see the experiment in Gestalt therapy as an attempt to "restore the connection between aboutism and action." They say:

> The experiment in Gestalt therapy is an attempt to counter the aboutist deadlock by bringing the individual's action system right into the room. Through experiment the individual is mobilized to confront the emergencies of his life by playing out his aborted feelings and actions in relative safety. A safe emergency is thus created where venturesome exploration can be supported [pp. 234–235].

Like the Polsters, Zinker (1977) views the experiment as a way of modifying a member's behavior in the group context. Zinker asserts, as we have seen, that Gestalt therapy is a combination of phenomenology and behavior modification. He sees therapeutic work as rooted in the subjective perspective of the members; at the same time, experiments are introduced in such a manner that behavior is modified in a timely way. As the cornerstone of experiential learning, the experiment transforms talking about a situation into actual doing and rejects stale theorizing in favor of trying on novel behaviors with a sense of excitement and imagination. Zinker emphasizes that each aspect of an experiment is presented at a point of developmental readiness for the client. In this way, experiments can be considered graded activities aimed at specific modifications of behavior. Zinker compares an experiment to a symphony:

An elegant experiment or, more accurately, series of experiments, is like a symphony. There is a beginning movement in which information is introduced and a general theme emerges. The second movement has a searching quality in which many details are filled in and the person's understanding of the theme is enriched. The third movement may uncover an important developmental dynamics of the larger theme, and the fourth ends in a sense of resolution and integration, as well as celebration of the self [pp. 154–155].

It is clear that the emphasis is upon *inviting* (not commanding) members to examine their behaviors, attitudes, and thoughts. Leaders can encourage members to look at certain incongruities, especially gaps between their verbal and nonverbal expression. Thus, the Gestalt group is characterized by challenge and positive confrontation. This confrontation is aimed at helping the members pay attention to what they are doing and experiencing in the here and now, not in a harsh or critical insistence that they be different than they are. Also, confrontation does not necessarily have to be aimed at weaknesses or negative traits; members can be challenged to recognize the ways that they block their strengths and ways that they are not living as fully as they might. In this sense, confrontation can be a genuine expression of caring that results in positive changes in a member, not a brutal assault on a defenseless member. Of course, it cannot be overstressed that members must be prepared for taking part in experiments. They need to know that they can choose to go along, and that they can also decide to stop when they want. Rather than pushing them into experimenting, the spirit is always one of inviting them to discover something new about themselves.

Keep in mind these introductory comments as you read the following pages, which describe several Gestalt techniques, their rationales, and their applications to group situations. As with all other techniques, here, too, it is up to the individual practitioner to integrate the exercises into his or her own therapeutic style, so that the techniques become expressions of the personality of the leader. My discussion is based on a variety of sources—among them, Brown (1971), Foulds (1975), Levitsky and Perls (1970), Passons (1975), Perls (1969a), Perls, Hefferline, and Goodman (1951), Polster and Polster (1973), Stevens (1971), and Zinker (1977). Note that I have modified some of the techniques to fit the needs of the group situation.

Language Exercises

Gestalt emphasizes the relationship between language patterns and personality. It suggests that our speech patterns are often expressions of our feelings, thoughts, and attitudes and that, by focusing on our overt speaking habits, we can increase our self-awareness (Passons, 1975). Words can bring us to ourselves, or they can take us away from ourselves. The following Gestalt interventions, by making us more aware of some of our speech patterns, can enhance our self-awareness and bring us closer to ourselves.

It should be noted that the following language exercises require a great deal of skill on the part of the leader. Unless, through the leader's help, the members are able to see the value of paying attention to the impact of their language style, they will come to feel that everything they say and do is subject to unnecessary scrutiny.

It. "It" talk is a way of depersonalizing language. By using *it* instead of *I*, we keep distant from our experience. When group members say "It's frightening to come to this group," they can be asked to change the sentence to "I'm frightened to come to this group." Substituting personal pronouns for impersonal ones is a way of assuming responsibility for what we say.

You. Often group participants say something like "You feel hurt when someone rejects you." By using "you" talk, people detach themselves from whatever they may be feeling. Therefore, members are asked to pay attention to the differences between the above statement and "I feel hurt when someone rebuffs me." By changing a "you" statement to an "I" statement, we reveal ourselves, and *we* take responsibility for what we are saying. Beginning a sentence with the word *you* tends to put others on the defensive and makes us disown our own experience.

Questions. In a Gestalt group, members are discouraged from asking questions. Questions direct attention to other people and can easily put others on the defensive. Also, questions often demand that those being questioned reveal themselves, while those who ask them keep themselves safe behind their interrogation. Group members who tend to ask too many questions are asked to experiment with any of the following:

- Instead of asking a question, make a direct statement to the person, and share your own motivation for your question.
- Avoid "why" questions, because they lead to a chain of "why/because" exchanges. Try instead "how" and "what" questions.
- Practice making "I" statements. By doing so, you take responsibility for your position, your opinions, and your preferences.

Qualifiers and disclaimers. By paying attention to the qualifiers they attach to their statements, group members can increase their awareness of how they diminish the power of their messages. A common example is the use of *but:* "I like you, but your mannerisms drive me up the wall"; "I often feel depressed, but I don't know what to do to change the situation"; "I think that this group is helping me, but people outside are so different from those in here." In each of these cases the word *but* essentially discounts the statement that precedes it. Without making group members excessively self-conscious, the leader can encourage them to pay attention to the impact of the use of qualifiers and disclaimers. Also, participants can be asked to substitute the word *and* for the word *but* and experiment with omitting qualifiers such as *maybe, sort of, possibly, I guess,* and *I suppose,* thus changing ambivalent messages into clear and direct statements.

"Can't" statements. Group members often say "I can't" when they really mean "I won't." Sally says "I simply can't talk to my father and tell him what I feel; he'd never understand me." It would be more precise and more honest for Sally to say that she *won't* make the attempt to talk with her father. Essentially, Sally is unwilling to (won't) take the risk or sees it as not being worth the effort. If a group leader consistently and gently insists that members substitute *won't* for *can't*, he or she assists them in owning and accepting their power by taking responsibility for their decisions.

"Shoulds" and "oughts."   Some group members seem to be ruled by "shoulds" and "oughts": "I should be interested in what others say in this group"; "I ought to care for everyone, and, if I don't, I feel terrible"; "I should express only positive feelings"; and so on. The list of "shouldisms," both in daily life and in a group situation, is endless. Members can at least become aware of the frequency of their "should" and "ought" remarks and of the feelings of powerlessness that accompany their use.

One way of increasing one's awareness of the limitations imposed by a "should" standard is to experiment with changing phrases such as "I have to" or "I should" to "I choose to." For example, if Fred says "I hate to stay in school, but I *have to* because my parents expect this of me," he could say instead "I don't like school, and I *choose to* stay in school because I don't want to have a hassle with my parents."

Nonverbal Language

Perls maintains that, when we block an aspect of our personality, the denied side finds ways of expressing itself—for example, in our movements, gestures, posture, and voice. Therefore, skilled therapists listen not just to the verbal level of communication but also, and even more keenly, to the message behind the words, which is often conveyed in the voice tone, pitch, and volume, in the speed of delivery, and so forth. Perls puts it quite bluntly:

> The sound tells you everything. Everything a person wants to express is all there— not in words. What we say is either mostly lies or bullshit. But, the voice is there, the gesture, the posture, the facial expression, the psychosomatic language. It's all there if you learn to more or less let the content of the sentences play the second violin only [1969a, p. 54].

The group setting offers many opportunities to explore the meaning of non-verbal messages. Such explorations are especially useful when participants exhibit nonverbal cues that are incongruent with what they are saying verbally. For example, Frank tells the group leader that he is angry at him for passing him over, and, as he utters his angry words, he is smiling. The leader is likely to call to Frank's attention the discrepancy between his angry words and his smile. Frank may then be asked to carry on a dialogue between his words and his smile, or he may be asked to "become his smile" and give this smile a voice: "What is your smile saying?" This procedure gives Frank the opportunity to discover for himself the meaning of the discrepancy. In fact he may be saying "I want to let you know that I'm upset that you passed me by, yet I don't want to risk your disapproval by letting you know how angry I am."

The following are other examples of how the exploration of nonverbal expressions can increase members' awareness of what they are really experiencing in the moment.

• Dan typically carries himself in a slouched posture. The leader says: "Become aware of your posture, go around the group, and tell what your posture says about yourself to each member of the group. Complete the sentence 'I am my posture, and what I am telling you about me is . . .' "

• Marilyn tends to speak in a soft voice and with a very tight mouth. The leader invites her to give a speech to the group and consciously exaggerate these mannerisms. She could "become her tight mouth" and say something like "I'm holding my words and myself back from you. I'm not going to be open, and, if you want something from me, you'll have to pry me open."

• John comes across as though he were always delivering a lecture to an audience. Group members have told him that his voice and his style of speaking create a barrier between him and the others. He could be asked to stand before the group and give a lecture, perhaps on the value of lecturing people.

Examples of how one deals with nonverbal cues are endless. Creative group leaders can invent a wide variety of spontaneous techniques designed to help participants become increasingly aware of what they are communicating through their eye contact, mannerisms, subtle gestures, tone of voice, and hand movements, as well as through their whole bodies. Group leaders would do well to avoid making bold interpretations—for example, that keeping one's arms crossed means that one is closed—and instead encourage members to merely pay attention to the nonverbal cues they emit. Passons' (1975) caution is worth considering: "Generalizations are tempting, as there are certain patterns of meanings in nonverbal behaviors. However, these are risky and are best offered as hunches, since incorrect interpretations can lead a counselee away from the flow of his experience" (p. 104).

Techniques Related to Assuming Responsibility

The Gestalt approach emphasizes taking full responsibility for ourselves—that is, being aware of our thoughts, feelings, and actions and avoiding making others responsible for what we are experiencing. Assuming responsibility also means recognizing our projections, reidentifying with them, and becoming what we project (Perls, 1969a).

Frequently group members dodge responsibility for their feelings by assigning the blame to others. Thus, they will say that the *group* is boring them or that someone in the group is *making* them angry. A Gestalt exercise designed to help individuals recognize and own their feelings instead of projecting them onto others is known as "I take responsibility for . . ." Pauline says that she feels that the group is excluding her and making her feel like an outsider. The leader can suggest to Pauline that she make direct statements to several members such as "I feel left out of the group, and I take responsibility for feeling excluded" or "I feel like an outsider, and I take responsibility for this feeling."

Unwillingness to assume responsibility is a common problem—in and outside groups. As long as, when we are scared, angry, critical, or confused, we say "*You* are making me feel this way," we delegate control to others and refuse to take charge of our own lives. Since one of the goals of Gestalt groups is to get members to assume responsibility for themselves, the leader keeps confronting participants with their unwillingness to take responsibility, so that they can come to recognize and accept their feelings instead of projecting them onto others.

Experiments with Dialogues

Because a goal of Gestalt therapy is to effect integrated functioning and the acceptance of aspects of one's personality that have been disowned and denied, Gestalt therapists pay close attention to splits and polarities in personality function. Fantasy dialogues, a uniquely Gestaltian technique, are meant to promote awareness of internal splits and eventual personality integration. These dialogues can take many forms—for example, dialogues between opposing sides or polarities within oneself (like tender/tough, masculine/feminine, loving/hateful, aggressive/passive) and dialogues with a parent or other significant person, fantasized others, or inanimate objects.

Understanding how polarities are related to inner conflicts is central to Gestalt therapy. A variety of experiments with dialogues can help members increase their awareness of the dichotomies within themselves and help them come to terms with dimensions of their personality that seem to oppose each other. Our self-concept often excludes painful awareness of the polarities within us. We would rather think of ourselves as bright than as dull, as kind than as cruel, as loving than as unloving, and as sensitive than as indifferent. Typically, we may resist "seeing" in ourselves those parts that we don't want to accept as being *part* of who we are. Although we can recognize the altruistic side of ourselves, we might have trouble coming to terms with our self-centered nature. Ideally, as we move closer to becoming psychologically mature and healthy, we are aware of most of the polarities within ourselves, including those thoughts and feelings that society does not sanction. As we become more tolerant of the complexities and seeming contradictions within us, there is less of a tendency to expend energy on fighting to disown those parts of our nature that we don't want to accept.

Zinker (1977) calls this movement toward self-acceptance the "stretching of the self-concept." He makes the critical point that, if we do not allow ourselves to be unkind, we will not be genuinely kind; if we are able to contact the unkindness that is a part of us, then our boundaries of the self stretch so that real kindness can emerge with greater richness. For Zinker, when one side of the polarity gets stretched, it is almost automatic that at some point the other side also stretches:

> In order to grow as a person and have more productive conflict experiences with others, I have to stretch my self-concept. I have to teach myself to invade that part of me which I do not approve of. There are various techniques involved in this process. First, I must uncover that part of myself which is disowned. Second, I need to come into contact with the disowned part of myself. This is the preliminary step—getting in touch with how I keep secrets from myself" [pp. 202–203].

Dialogue experiments are a powerful method of contacting parts of our nature that we work hard at keeping secret from both ourselves and others. Learning how to carry on a conversation between our feminine and masculine sides, for instance, is one way of bringing to the surface inner conflicts we might have with these polarities. Alternatively, becoming each side as fully as we can is a way to *experience* both of these facets of our personality.

Dialogue experiments are typically used to heighten awareness of introjections and projections. *Introjection*, as was mentioned earlier, is the process by which we uncritically take in aspects of other people, especially parents, and incorporate them into our personality. The danger of uncritical and wholesale acceptance of another's values as one's own is that it can prevent personality integration. Gestalt techniques are aimed at getting these introjections out in the open, so that we can take a good look at what we have been swallowing whole without digesting it.

For example, by experimenting with dialogues, Hal becomes aware of some of the messages that he has bought without question: one must be practical; one ought to cling to security and never launch on a new path unless one has carefully assessed all the odds; only irresponsible people seek fun for the sake of fun—in other words, a long list of "dos," "don'ts," "shoulds," and "shouldn'ts" that keep him from enjoying life. At last, Hal begins to realize that he has listened to these directives from others and given others the power to direct his life. He also becomes aware that he wants to reclaim this power for himself. Some of the fantasy dialogues that help Hal to see his introjections more clearly are dialogues with the different facets of himself.

The dialogues can be carried out with the empty-chair technique or with the two-chair technique. Sitting on one chair, Hal becomes one of his introjects—say, the side of him that doesn't have any fun. Speaking in the present tense, Hal "becomes the serious side" and says: "You can't let yourself go; you may go off the deep end and never accomplish anything. Be serious; be practical; get rid of foolish notions." Then Hal switches chairs and "becomes the fun side." He says to the serious side: "You are dull and demanding. If I listen to you, I'll never feel like I've done enough to earn the right to play. Let me show you how to loosen up and have fun." The dialogue proceeds back and forth, all for the purpose of giving Hal an increased awareness of which side is dominant and of how it feels to be in either role. The goal is not to get rid of either side but to integrate the polarities. If he reaches this goal, Hal will recognize that he can be *both* serious and light, and that *he* is the one who can make this happen through awareness.

Projection is the attribution of one's ideas, feelings, or attitudes to others—especially those very ideas, feelings, or attitudes one does not want to see and accept in oneself. In working with projections, participants are asked to identify with and become a particular characteristic that they attribute to others. For example, if Cindy says that she cannot trust the group—she feels that, if she opened up, no one would care or even know what she was talking about—she is asked to play the role of the untrustworthy person. By becoming the other, she may be able to discover the degree to which the distrust is due to an inner conflict between the side that wants to trust and the side that cannot trust. In what is known as "playing the projection," Cindy is asked to go to other members in the group and play the role of the untrustworthy person by completing the sentence "You don't trust me because, if you do, I'll . . ." The exercise may enable Cindy to experience the inner conflict more intensely and see more clearly the two sides of herself.

Making the Rounds

In this exercise a person goes around to each of the group members and says something that he or she usually does not communicate verbally. For example, assume that Larry sees himself as a self-made man who needs nothing from others. Although Larry may not *say* this about himself, the theme of "I can do it by myself" runs through much of his life. For the purpose of seeing how this theme actually determines what Larry does, he could be asked to stand before each member in the group and tell that person something about himself, and then add ". . . and (or but) I can do everything by myself." Thus, Larry goes to Sue and says "I never ask for emotional support from others, and at times I feel lonely . . . but I can do everything by myself." He then goes to Marie and says "I make all the decisions in my business . . . and I can do everything by myself." The aim of this experiment is to have Larry feel fully what it's like for him to do everything by himself. Ultimately, he may decide to continue to do things for himself, but with the awareness of the price he pays for doing so. Or he may come to see that he doesn't have to be totally self-reliant and that he can be independent while letting others do things for him from time to time.

The following are a few more examples of the use of making the rounds:

- Paul says that he is afraid of women. He could make the rounds and say to each woman "I'm afraid of you because . . ."; or "If I were to get close to you, . . ."
- Susan worries about boring people in the group. She might be asked to make the rounds and, for each person, complete the sentence "One way I could bore you is by . . ." or "You would be bored if I . . ."
- Pam says that she feels distant from the rest of the group, even though she would like to have a sense of identification. Pam could make the rounds and experiment with completing the sentence "One way I feel distant from you is . . ." or "The way we are different from each other is . . ."

I tend to suggest a go-around when I sense avoidance and fear. Typically, I ask the members whether they would like to try this technique in order to deal with their fears. If they say yes and make the rounds, they may be able to confront their fears and try a different behavior, which may snap them out of their frozen position. And, as a result, they may discover that their fears were quite unfounded.

Fantasy Approaches

Experimenting with a diversity of fantasy situations in a group can lead to significant growth. Fantasy can promote personal awareness in a number of ways, as the following brief list suggests.

- Fantasy can be used when members are too threatened to deal with a problem in concrete terms. For example, members who are afraid to be assertive can imagine themselves in situations in which they *are* assertive. Thus, they can compare what they feel when they are passive with what they feel when they are able to ask for what they want.

• Fantasy approaches are useful in dealing with catastrophic expectations, which often result in a sense of paralysis. Members who are afraid to express what they think and feel to someone they love can be guided through a fantasy situation in which they say everything they want to say but are afraid to express. Essentially the person speaks in the here and now to the loved one (as if he or she were present) in front of the group. The leader may say: "Your mother (or some other significant person) is in this empty chair. Come up to the chair and say what you *most* want her to hear and that you never told her. What are you feeling now? Are you willing to tell how you feel? Tell her now all the terrible things you imagined would happen if you told her what you kept from her." There is a possible psychological value in working through these feelings in the safety of the fantasy approach, because the person may be able to release submerged feelings that have become split off. Note that it is *not* necessary that the person express these feelings in real life; as a matter of fact, to do so could be unwise.

• Fantasy can be used to express and explore feelings of shame and guilt. In the technique known as "I have a secret," the leader asks members to fantasize about a well-guarded secret. They are not asked to reveal the secret in the group but only to imagine themselves disclosing the secret to the others. The leader may ask "What are people thinking about you?" "How do you feel about letting others know your secret?"

• Fantasy is a useful and safe way to explore the members' fears about getting involved in the group. For example, I often ask members to imagine the thing they most fear occurring in the group. If, for example, some members are afraid of being rejected by the group, they can be directed to imagine that everyone is systematically rejecting them and then work with the feelings associated with this fantasy.

There are constructive uses of fantasy that, after having been tried in the group, can be carried outside of it. At times I invite members to picture themselves as they wish they were in interpersonal situations. They might share their fantasies aloud in the group as they experience themselves in powerful, alive, creative, and dynamic ways. Then they can be asked to try acting in the group *as if* they were the person they imagined themselves to be. If the experiment is successful, members may feel encouraged enough to try the new behavior in real-life situations.

Rehearsal

For Perls much of our thinking is rehearsing. We rehearse for roles we think we are expected to play, and we worry that we may not say the "right" thing and perform "properly." Internal rehearsing consumes much energy and frequently inhibits spontaneity. The rehearsal technique invites members to say *out loud* what they are thinking silently. I value rehearsal experiments especially when it is obvious that members are doing a lot of blocking and censoring and when what they say seems carefully measured out for a certain effect. For example, during the initial stages of one of my groups, Joan was quite silent and appeared to be developing an observer's stance. When I asked her if she was indeed saying everything she wanted to say, she shook her head in denial. So I asked her to express aloud some of the random thoughts she had as she was sitting there in silence.

Rehearsal can also be fruitful when a member is anticipating some future confrontation. Assume that Sam wants to tell his boss that he doesn't feel appreciated and that he wants to be recognized for his accomplishments. Sam can, in fantasy, picture himself standing before his boss, ready to tell him what he wants to say. Sam's out-loud rehearsal could go something like: "I'm standing here like a fool. What if I mess up? He won't listen to me, and I don't really have anything to say. How can I let him know what I'm thinking? Right now I feel like running away and apologizing."

In a Gestalt group the participants share their rehearsals with one another in order to become more aware of the many preparations they go through in performing their social roles. By doing so, they become more aware of how they strive to please others, of the degree to which they want to be accepted and approved, and of the extent of their efforts to avoid alienating others. And then they can decide whether this role playing is worth the effort.

Reversal Techniques

Certain symptoms and behaviors often represent reversals of underlying or latent impulses. The reversal technique asks participants to become a side of themselves that they rarely or never express, because they don't want to see it and accept it. The theory underlying the use of this technique is that integration is possible when people allow themselves to plunge into the very thing that produces anxiety and make contact with those parts of themselves that have been submerged and denied. Groups provide plenty of timely opportunities for using reversal techniques.

I remember the case of a young man who was excessively nice, overly polite, and constantly trying to "do things" for other people. I suggest that he experiment with asking other people in the group to do something for him. He had great difficulty carrying out my suggestion, but eventually he succeeded. The exercise made him aware of how uncomfortable he was with accepting something from others. Also, it gave him an increased awareness of the denied side of himself and a chance to integrate it.

Other examples of the reversal method are requesting someone who says almost nothing to take on the role of monopolizer and deliberately interrupt the group; inviting someone with inferiority feelings to play the role of being superior; and suggesting to someone who pays compliments to everybody to say something negative to each person in the group. Time and time again, I've found that this and similar techniques truly help people become aware of and reconcile polarities within themselves.

Just as the empty-chair experiment gives members an opportunity to take ownership of opposing forces within themselves, so does experimenting with giving expression to a dimension that is kept hidden often result in a creative integration of polarities. For example, the member who habitually presents a tough exterior may well be afraid of contacting a sensitive side of himself. If he is invited to experiment with being the side that he works so hard at denying, he is likely to find joy in broadening his emotional and behavioral range, and if he does not like the results of the experiment, he can always go back to the "tough-guy" role.

The Exaggeration Exercise

This experiment involves becoming more aware of the subtle signals and cues we send through body language. Movements, postures, and gestures are exaggerated, so that the meanings they communicate become clearer. By exaggerating the movement or gesture repeatedly, the person experiences more intensely the feelings associated with the behavior and becomes more aware of its inner meaning.

For example, if the leader notices that Sandy consistently nods her head in an approving way when people speak, he or she could ask Sandy to go before each group member and really give in to her head nodding while, at the same time, putting words into this action. Other examples of behavior that lends itself to the exaggeration technique are habitually smiling while expressing painful or negative emotions, trembling, clenching one's fists, tapping one's foot, crossing one's arms tightly, and pointing a finger at someone.

For example, a member I'll call Jill stated "I feel burdened by listening to everyone's problems in here!" At an earlier session, Jill had been confronted by Fred for intervening so quickly and trying to make him feel better when he was working on conflicts he was having with his family. Jill then revealed that during her childhood years she typically assumed the role of family arbitrator, always doing her best to smooth over the battles in her family. Jill eventually says that she is sick and tired of carrying everyone's burdens, for it weighs her down and gives her a heavy feeling.

A technique for working with the material that Jill is providing involves asking her to pick up some heavy objects and hold them as she looks at each person in the group. Jill can be invited to allow herself to get into the experience of the heaviness and being burdened. For example, while holding the heavy objects she might make the rounds and complete the sentence "Looking at you I am burdened by . . ." Or she might say something to each member like "Here, let me take on all your burdens; I really enjoy carrying everyone's problems and I just wouldn't know what to do if I didn't have all these burdens weighing me down!" Even though Jill says that she is sick and tired of carrying around everyone's burdens, we encourage her to allow herself to give in to the part of herself that feels burdened and experiment with telling others all the benefits of being this way. The rationale here is that, if Jill can fully experience being burdened, then there is a good chance that she can allow herself to experience shedding these burdens and being light, at least for a few moments. Again, this experiment is related to the reversal experiment and the empty-chair experiment in that the member is asked to play with polarities. Often the best way to discover the aspect of ourselves that we say we'd like to experience more of is to allow ourselves to stay with that part of us that we want to avoid.

Dream Work

Consistent with its noninterpretive spirit, the Gestalt approach does not interpret and analyze dreams. Instead, the intent is to bring the dream back to life, to recreate it, and to relive it as if it were happening now. For those readers who are interested in a detailed presentation of the Gestalt approach to dream work, good sources are Downing and Marmorstein (1973), Perls (1969a), Rainwater (1979), and Zinker (1977). A brief description of this approach follows.

Group members don't report their dreams in the past tense: they relive them and act them out in the present, transform key elements of the dream into a dialogue, and become a part of the dream. Perls assumes that each part of a dream is a projection of oneself and that all the different parts are expressions of one's own contradictory and inconsistent sides. Therefore dreams contain existential messages. They represent our conflicts, our wishes, and key themes in our lives. By making a list of all the details in a dream—remembering each person, event, and mood—and then acting out ("becoming") each of these parts as fully as possible, one becomes increasingly aware of one's opposing sides and of the range of one's feelings. Eventually the person comes to appreciate and accept his or her inner differences and integrate the conflicting forces— each piece of work on a dream leading to further assimilation and integration. By avoiding analyzing and interpreting the dream and focusing instead on becoming and experiencing it in all its aspects, the client gets closer to the existential message of the dream. Freud called the dream "the royal road to the unconscious"; Perls (1969a) called it "the royal road to integration" (p. 66).

Rainwater (1979) offers some helpful suggestions to dreamers for exploring their dreams:

- Be the landscape or the environment.
- Become all the people in the dream. Are any of them significant people?
- Be any objects that link and join, such as telephone lines and highways.
- Identify with any mysterious object, such as an unopened letter or an unread book.
- Assume the identity of any powerful force, such as a tidal wave.
- Become any two contrasting objects, such as a younger person and an older person.
- Be anything that is missing in the dream. If you don't remember your dreams, then speak to your missing dreams.
- Be alert for any numbers that appear in the dream, become these numbers, and explore associations with them.

Rainwater (1979) suggests that in working with a dream you notice how you feel when you wake up. Is your feeling state one of fear, joy, sadness, frustration, surprise, anger? Identifying the feeling tone may be the key to finding the meaning of the dream. In working with dreams in Gestalt style, she suggests, dreamers can focus on questions such as the following:

- What are you doing in the dream?
- What are you feeling?
- What do you want in the dream?

- What are your relationships with other objects and people in the dream?
- What kind of action can I take now? What is my dream telling me?

Group experiments can emerge out of the dream work of individuals in a group. Zinker (1977) has developed an approach he calls *dream work as theater*, which goes beyond working with an individual's dream. After a dream is reported and worked through by a participant, a group experiment is created that allows other members to benefit therapeutically from the original imagery of the dreamer. Based on his assumption that all the members share certain archetypal themes, Zinker suggests that various images within a dream can be used to enhance self-understanding. Each plays out a part of the dream. This offers the group participants many opportunities for enacting certain dimensions of the dream that relate both to the dreamer and to their own life.

For example, assume that one of the members, Joan, has had a dream that contains a broken-down car, a man shooting at people in the car, and a woman trying to save the passengers in the car. One member may choose to take on the identity of the person doing the shooting, another can take on the role of one of the people in the car being shot at, and still another can be the car that doesn't function. Each of the members can play out his or her part, and the dreamer can help them understand the characters or objects in the dream. The group leader can facilitate the production of the dream as a dramatic and therapeutic experience for the entire group. There are many advantages to this approach in terms of increasing group cohesion and linking one member's work with others.

The dreams of group participants might have some implications for how they feel in their group (Polster & Polster, 1973). In the example given above, Joan might discover that she feels frightened in the group and would like to escape. She might feel attacked (shot at) by one or more members, with a woman coming to her rescue. In this case, Joan can act out her dream in the group by selecting the person that she feels most seriously attacked by and talking to that person directly. She can then become the broken-down car— her powerless vehicle of escape—and see what associations this association brings. Joan can also pick out the woman in the group whom she feels most supported by and have a dialogue with her. She might reverse roles, becoming the person doing the shooting. Working with the dream in this way has rich potential for dealing with unfinished business with others in the group.

I make frequent use of Gestalt techniques in working with dreams in the groups I lead, as I find these techniques lively. Let me describe the dream work I did with Sue in the course of one of my training groups. After Sue agreed to share and explore her dream, even though she felt apprehensive about it, I asked her to report the dream as if she were dreaming it now.

"We are at your house for a group, Jerry," she began. "There are many people around. I feel that I'm just one of them—not special at all. It's lunch time, and you're serving each of us three ladles of—of slop. Exactly the same amount to each person. Now it's my turn; you dish up three ladles of this slop—just like all the others. I'm thinking that I'm no different from the rest. This stuff looks awful, but at least it's *nourishing* slop.

"This is another scene," Sue continued. "There is fog, thick fog. The group is coming to an end. You send us home, out in the fog. I step out into the fog, and I'm scared because I can't see where I'm going."

After Sue had finished reporting her dream, I asked her to "become the nourishing slop" and speak for the slop. If the slop could speak, what would it say? Then I asked her to "become Jerry who's dishing up this nourishing slop." What is he thinking, feeling, saying? Finally I asked Sue to "become the fog" and give voice to it. Next I told her to be herself in her dream and create a dialogue with the slop, with Jerry, and with the fog.

When she finished acting out the various parts of her dream, I asked Sue what she had learned from the experience and what *she* thought the dream was telling her. The essence of her dream, she thought, was that in my eyes she was just one of the many members of the group—nobody special—and that she was given the same old slop that everybody else was getting; but at least it was a safe and nutritious diet—no matter how dull. The fog represented her leaving the group and going into an uncertain world, a world in which she wasn't sure she could find her way. We explored in depth Sue's conflict between wanting to remain in a safe but dull world and stepping into a new but uncertain one.

STYLES OF GESTALT GROUPS AND WORKSHOPS

Gestalt therapy can be practiced in a variety of ways, whether it is in an individual or a group setting. In groups, it can be applied in the puristic form that Perls developed, which is characterized by focus on a single member at a time. Basically, this style is individual therapy done in a group setting, in which a member and the leader work together while other members observe the process. When the interaction between leader and member is over, the leader typically asks members to give feedback and to relate their own reactions to what occurred. In this form of Gestalt practice, direct and spontaneous interaction within the group is discouraged. A volunteer takes the "hot seat" and focuses as much as possible on the here and now, while the leader applies the Gestalt techniques described earlier to intensify the person's present-centered awareness.

Gestalt-oriented groups can also function in a less puristic fashion. These groups are characterized by more freedom of spontaneous interaction. Latner (1973) points out that there are regional styles of Gestalt practice. Gestalt therapists on the West Coast, who have been greatly influenced by Fritz Perls, tend to pay attention to the issues of self-awareness, centering, and responsibility. On the East Coast, Gestaltists tend toward a more interactive model, longer-term groups, more attention to the cognitive side of the therapeutic process, and a greater variety of personal styles.

Polster and Polster (1973) describe the "floating hot seat," a technique that encourages other members to get involved in a member's work in a spontaneous way. With this approach, there is an understanding that whatever takes place within the group has relevance and potential for interaction among the members. In this way, members avoid sitting by passively observing one member's work and waiting for their turn. An interactional focus is promoted whereby members can be touched by one another's work and can use this work as a way of getting into an exploration of their own personal issues.

In the kind of group process advocated by the Gestalt Institute of Cleveland, attention is given to the intrapersonal, interpersonal, and group levels of functioning. In Zinker's (1977) view, purist Gestalt à la Fritz Perls does not encourage the building of a community in a group. Although he agrees that people learn vicariously by observing a leader work with one member in the "hot seat," he contends that they have little feeling of kinship and interaction with one another. It becomes a matter of doing individual therapy with an audience observing the process. One of the disadvantages of this traditional style, from Zinker's perspective, is that the therapist does all of the work and does not allow the group members to take charge of the unfolding situation. By contrast, the Cleveland style of Gestalt group process operates on several key principles: the primacy of the present group experience, the process of emerging group awareness, the value of active contact between participants, and interactional experiments that are suggested by an actively involved leader. Regardless of what the members are doing, they are encouraged to be aware of themselves as a member of society and to be aware of their role in the group as it changes from moment to moment.

The Gestalt techniques and experiments described in this chapter can also be fruitfully incorporated by group leaders who are not primarily Gestalt oriented. As an example, although Elizabeth Mintz is not classified as a "Gestalt therapist," it is obvious that her style of group leadership is largely Gestalt oriented. As a clinical psychologist who was trained in the psychoanalytic tradition, she found that traditional psychoanalytic concepts were limiting. Mintz was not willing to adopt the purely experiential and feeling-oriented approach characteristic of the encounter-group movement. In my opinion the Mintz group model combines effectively the affective and cognitive dimensions of human experience.

Mintz describes many experiential and Gestalt techniques that she uses in her marathon groups to facilitate more intensive here-and-now experiencing and awareness of feelings than is usually possible in a psychoanalytic group that stresses verbal interaction and insight. However, unlike some Gestalt practitioners who stop at the experiential level and put little stock in the cognitive dimension of therapy, Mintz integrates the cognitive and interpretive aspects of therapy to help group members discover the *meaning* of what they experience. This approach facilitates the integration of experience that allows participants to apply what they have learned to their interactions in the group and to their daily lives.

Mintz (1972) sees the power of a marathon group in the successful integration of two dimensions: the reality experience and the symbolic experience. Participants are together for a sustained period of time—a situation that promotes intensity. The honest expression of feelings in the here and now is encouraged; social pretenses are set aside in favor of genuine interaction in a climate of tolerance and experimentation. If a marathon is successful, an immense range of emotions is expressed and explored with more authenticity than is typical in most social settings.

A marathon group is seen as a microcosm of reality in which participants can come to a fuller awareness of themselves and of the impact they have on others and where they can learn skills and attitudes needed for enhancing the quality of their interpersonal living. In addition to this *reality* dimension, the marathon has a *symbolic* dimension. Largely through fantasy methods, the participants can reenact past conflicts and arrive at a new emotional and intellectual understanding of how the past affects them now; in turn, such awareness can result in greater self-acceptance.

The marathon group is aimed not at treating sick people but at helping adequately functioning people reach their maximum potential. To those who suffer from a sense of alienation, existential emptiness, and meaninglessness, the group offers a potent medium for exploring their current levels of functioning and for investigating the changes they want to make.

The Mintz model of a marathon group has many Gestalt characteristics and uses a variety of Gestalt techniques. The following are some of these characteristics and techniques:

- Feedback and free exchange of feelings among members are encouraged.
- Direct member-to-member communication is encouraged, and gossiping (talking *about* a member) is discouraged.
- Attention is given to nonverbal communication, and a variety of nonverbal experiments are used to heighten feelings and stimulate interpersonal relating.
- The focus is on the here and now. Talk about the past or matters external to the group is brought to the present in the group. Participants often use fantasy exercises to bring significant people in their lives into the room in a symbolic way.
- Regression to childhood experiences in the safe and accepting atmosphere of the group, followed by reintegration of the childhood trauma on a more mature level, is believed to promote personal integration. The prolonged duration of the marathon makes such integration possible.
- Mintz's marathon groups use the following Gestalt techniques: making the rounds, asking members to exaggerate a trait, reversals, fantasy trips within the body, conflict games, dialogue games, nonverbal relating, role playing, resistance games, symbolic encounters, reliving past traumatic situations in the present through fantasy, body-awareness techniques, and reexperiencing unfinished business, this time with a different ending.

GESTALT FAMILY THERAPY

Kempler (1982) defines Gestalt family therapy as a model that focuses on the present moment and on experiencing what the family is doing in the therapy session. Gestalt family therapists pay attention to what people say, how they say it, what happens when they say it, how their words correspond to their actions, and what they are attempting to accomplish. "The conversational anchor point is the current conflict of the day and what can be done to resolve it in place of a more analytical or understanding (seeking why) orientation" (Kempler, 1982, p. 141).

Elsewhere, Kempler (1981a) describes his Gestalt/experiential approach to family therapy thus:

> The term experiential is used to describe this approach wherein the working session itself is used as a laboratory in which we have new experiences. It is not a "talking about" therapy but rather an action therapy. By working within the framework of the current family, by examining the nature of new encounters during the therapy session, and with full participation of the therapist as a person within the group, we shape the essential forces for attaining the goal [p. 8].

Kempler's basic objective is to use family sessions to get the participants to engage themselves fully as "vitally concerned combatants," as opposed to passive spectators or mere commentators about their family situation. He is mainly concerned with the *what* and the *how* of behavior as it is manifested in the current situation.

Although Kempler identifies himself as a Gestalt therapist, he does not employ many of the standard techniques. Instead, he emphasizes the therapist's personal involvement with the family. In Kempler's view, experiential family therapy is a personal matter for each therapist, and therapeutic techniques, or "tools of therapy," tend to distance the therapist from the family. "There are no tools or skills; there are only people" (Kempler, 1981a, p. 72). Rather than relying upon techniques, Kempler aims at making an impact on the family by making sure they hear him *emotionally* as well as verbally. He directs his attention to the behavior that arises in the encounter in the office, and he reacts as fully and richly as he can as a participant in this encounter. Kempler's style is direct and confrontive, and for him it appears to work effectively.

Consider the following scenario in which Kempler (1981b, pp. 178–179) confronts a husband who is whimpering about his wife in a session. The husband asks helplessly: "What can I do? She stops me at every turn." This set the stage for the following interchange:

Therapist (sarcastically to provoke him): You poor thing, overpowered by that terrible lady over there.

Husband (ducking): She means well.

Therapist: You're whimpering at me and I can't stand to see a grown man whimpering.

Husband (firmer): I tell you, I don't know what to do.

Therapist: Like hell you don't (offering and at the same time pushing). You know as well as I that if you want her off your back you just have to tell her to get the hell off your back and mean it. That's one thing you could do instead of that mealy-mouthed apology "She means well."

Husband (looks quizzical; obviously he is not sure if he wants to chance it with either of us but is reluctant to retreat to the whimpering child posture again): I'm not used to talking that way to people.

Therapist: Then you'd better get used to it. You're going to have to shape up this family into a group that's worth living with, instead of a menagerie where your job is to come in periodically and crack the whip on the little wild animals.

Husband: You sure paint a bad picture.

Therapist: If I'm wrong, be man enough to disagree with me and don't wait to get outside of here to whimper to your wife about how you didn't know what to say here.

Husband (visibly bristling and speaking more forcefully): I don't know that you're wrong about what you're saying.

Therapist: But how do you like what I'm saying?

Husband: I don't. Nor do I like the way you're going about it.

Therapist: I don't like the way you're going about things either.

Husband: There must be a more friendly way than this.

Therapist: Sure, you know, whimper.

Husband (with deliberate softness): You're really a pusher, aren't you?

Therapist: How do you like me?

Husband: I don't.

Therapist: You keep forgetting to say that part of your message. I can see it all over you but you never say it.

Husband (finally in anger): I'll say what I damn please. You're not going to tell me how to talk . . . and how do you like that? (He socks his hand.)

Therapist: I like it a helluva lot better than your whimpering. What is your hand saying?

Husband: I'd like to punch you in the nose, I suppose.

Therapist: You suppose?

Husband (firmly): Enough. Get off my back and stay off.

Therapist (delighted to see his assertion): Great. Now, about the rest of them (waving to his family). I'd like to see if there's anything you'd like to say to them.

Husband (looks at each one of them and then settles on his wife): He's right. I take an awful lot of nonsense from you and I hate it (still socking his hand). I don't intend to take any more. I'll settle with the kids my way. If you don't like it that's too bad.

After this encounter, Kempler asked others in the family what they thought about what they had just witnessed. The man's wife said nothing, and his children looked pleased. Kempler, who was also pleased with what he had seen, said to the man:

> I like you better when you are being the man I know you are. I had the fleeting thought that maybe you will become a tyrant, but I know you won't. I'm not afraid of your power. I saw you taste it here and use it very justly with us [1981b, pp. 179–180].

This vignette gives a flavor of Kempler's style of Gestalt/experiential family therapy. It shows that the therapist must be willing to bring his or her personality, reactions, and life experiences to the family encounter. The therapist's willingness to engage with others in the family group models for them ways that they can struggle for what they perceive as their identity. In Kempler's view, genuine therapy occurs when individuals put themselves on the line and vigorously clarify who they are to one another.

If you are interested in learning more about Gestalt family therapy, I highly recommend Kempler's (1981a) *Experiential Psychotherapy within Families* as exciting and provocative reading.

EVALUATION OF THE GESTALT APPROACH

I have incorporated several aspects of Gestalt therapy into my own style of group leadership, and I make frequent use of Gestalt techniques that I find valuable in facilitating the expression and exploration of intense feelings. In many ways my adaptation of the Gestalt approach resembles Mintz's adaptation, which I previously described.

In my view, one of Gestalt's limitations is its discounting of the cognitive side of therapy. Along with Mintz, I strongly believe that assisting participants to discover the meaning of their emotional experiences is a significant factor in producing personality changes that will extend beyond the group. To a great extent Perls adopted an antiintellectual position by derogating the cognitive factors of personality. His statement "Lose your mind and come to your senses" reflects his reaction against the cognitive therapy of the psychoanalytic approach and illustrates his focus on the role of feelings in therapy. Following this lead, many Gestalt group leaders have ignored the role of cognition and the value of conceptualizing in a group. With his preoccupation with experiencing feelings and the body, Perls went to the other end of the continuum from the traditional therapies of the time. However, the emphasis on feelings and the body at the expense of cognitive factors may not provide the optimum therapeutic balance (Rudestam, 1982).

A major concern I have about Gestalt therapy is the potential danger for abusing techniques. Typically, Gestalt therapists are highly active and directive, and if they do not have the characteristics mentioned by Zinker (1977)—sensitivity, timing, inventiveness, empathy, and respect for the client—the experiments can easily boomerang. Also, the members can grow accustomed to the leader's assuming the initiative in creating experiments for them, instead of coming up with some of their own experiments.

Related to the concern over creating dependency on the leader is the ethical issue raised by inept therapists who use powerful techniques to stir up feelings and open up problems that members have kept from full awareness, only to abandon the members once they have managed to have a dramatic catharsis. The failure to stay with members until they reach some level of closure on old business can prove very detrimental. I'm afraid that some therapists who are attracted to Gestalt procedures are more enthralled with their potential for dramatic impact than their potential for therapeutic change. I see a real danger in a leader who has a need for continual action and performance and thus employs one dramatic technique after another. This approach can be dangerous because of the therapist's power to manipulate the client with techniques. Some therapists have become so enthralled with Perls' dynamic personality and style that they mimic only his style, without fully understanding and incorporating the conceptual framework of Gestalt therapy. If these leaders are unaware of their own needs and motivations, they are likely to confront without caring and to manipulate members into doing what will bring excitement to them but no growth to the client.

In speaking of those therapists who attempt to mimic the style of Perls, Zinker (1977) points out that many of them do not have the courage to learn his sense of inventiveness and his way of creating dramatic learning. Simply copying the "master's" style is almost doomed to failure. The techniques will be lifeless, because they will not work creatively if they do not fit the existential situation. Toward the end of his life, Perls became acutely aware of the problems created by therapists who were trying to pattern their style after him. He became disturbed by disciples who wanted mainly to learn techniques instead of developing their own techniques as an expression of their uniqueness as a person.

It is easy to see that many of the Gestalt techniques offer a tempting place for group leaders to hide their personal responses and forget about the I/Thou relationship that Perls wrote about. It is possible for group leaders to keep themselves unknown and to mask their personal reactions to members in the group. Through the use of confrontive techniques, they can direct the pressure primarily toward the members. Group leaders who are power hungry can meet their own needs by gleefully putting members on the "hot seat" and thus avoid genuine contact with them. Apparently, even though Perls preached that the I/Thou relationship was crucial in Gestalt therapy, it was difficult for him to practice it, and he was often reluctant to share much of himself personally in his work. Kempler (1982) has criticized Perls for his use of power over clients. Kempler contends that Perls was manipulative and had a constant need to be the "top dog," while keeping his clients in an "under dog" position as they took the "hot seat." Perls was clearly in command of the situation as his audience observed and frequently admired his therapeutic prowess. Kempler (1982) is also critical of Perls' behavior on the ground that he was unwilling to reveal much of himself personally. Kempler calls Perls the puppeteer and the director. If anyone dared to challenge him to look at his behavior or his role in a relationship with a client, he retorted with a counter-challenge for them to examine their own motivations for confronting him.

I share Perls' own concern about Gestalt's becoming an "instant therapy." Some practitioners are so enamored of this approach that they are convinced that it can transform people almost magically in a very brief time. Perls (1969a) believed that he had developed a "better way," but he also made it clear that Gestalt is not a magic wand. He stressed that growth is a process that takes time: "You don't have to be on a couch or in a Zendo for twenty or thirty years, but you have to invest yourself, and it takes time to grow" (p. 2).

Some Gestalt practitioners tend to become enslaved by Gestalt injunctions such as "Always be in the present" or "Take responsibility for yourself." Guidelines are turned into rigid rules and applied dogmatically, with the result of interrupting rather than heightening the flow of experience. I can think of many situations in which stopping what members are doing and asking them to bring something into the here and now would be quite counterproductive. Gestalt leaders who have truly integrated their approach are sensitive enough to practice Gestalt therapy in a flexible way. They surely strive to help clients experience themselves as fully as possible in the present, yet they are not rigidly bound by dictates, nor do they routinely intervene with a directive whenever members stray from the present. Sensitively staying in contact with a member's flow of experiencing entails the ability to focus on the person and not on the mechanical use of techniques for a certain effect.

Another criticism that can be directed toward Gestalt therapy concerns the meager research that has been done to assess its effectiveness. On this matter, Simkin (1982) writes: "Most Gestalt therapists are busy practicing their art rather than evaluating it. Thus far there has been very little traditional research in the area of Gestalt therapy. This may change in the 1980's" (p. 376).

I agree with Rudestam (1982) that additional empirical research is needed to support the value of a popular and powerful therapeutic approach, one that has influenced the practice of many group leaders.

Even though there are some cautions about the practice of Gestalt therapy and some distinct limitations of the approach, I continue to value what it offers group practitioners on a practical level. It encourages genuine experimentation and allows for a great deal of creativity on the leader's and the members' part. As exciting and dynamic as Gestalt methods are, however, they are not for everyone. Simkin (1982) indicates when Gestalt therapy is an appropriate approach: "Gestalt therapy is the treatment of choice for people who are 'up in their head.' It is not for people who act out their impulses. It is most effective in the hands of competent well-trained clinicians" (p. 377).

With an approach that can have powerful effects on members—either constructive or destructive—ethical practice depends on the level of training and supervision of its therapists. For those of you who have become excited about including Gestalt techniques in your style of group leadership, I encourage you to attend a Gestalt workshop led by a competent professional. Just as I have real concerns about practitioners' employing psychodramatic techniques if they have not experienced them personally, I have the same concern over leaders who routinely use Gestalt techniques when their major source of learning about them has been through reading. Although reading is surely of value, I don't think that it is sufficient to produce skillful clinicians.

Some resources for training in Gestalt therapy are (1) Gestalt Institute of Cleveland, 1588 Hazel Drive, Cleveland, OH 44106 (Dr. Joseph Zinker is the director); (2) Gestalt Training Center, P.O. Box 2189, La Jolla, CA 92038, with Drs. Irv and Miriam Polster as co-directors; and (3) Gestalt Therapy Institute of Los Angeles, 620 Venice Boulevard, Venice, CA 90291.

QUESTIONS FOR REFLECTION AND DISCUSSION

1. Both Gestalt therapy and person-centered therapy share some features with the existential approach, yet they employ very different methods in a group. Although they have some common philosophical views of human nature, the former relies on therapist direction and techniques, whereas the latter deemphasizes techniques and therapist direction. Do you see any basis for the typically active/directive Gestalt leader to incorporate some person-centered concepts? Why or why not?

2. Do you see a possibility of thinking in psychoanalytic terms and using Gestalt techniques? What are some ways that you might integrate psychoanalytic concepts with Gestalt concepts and methods as a part of your leadership style?

3. What are some basic similarities and differences between psychodramatic groups and Gestalt groups? Again, do you see ways of blending some procedures from the two approaches in the groups you might lead?

4. Gestalt therapy focuses on what people are *experiencing* and *feeling* moment to moment. Do you think that this emphasis on feeling precludes thinking and conceptualization in therapy work? Explain.

5. What is your reaction to Perls' dictum "Lose your mind and come to your senses"?

6. What do you consider to be the major ethical considerations that need to be addressed in Gestalt group work? What are some safeguards that you can think of against the most common dangers associated with Gestalt groups?

7. What are some key Gestalt concepts and experiments that you can apply to the process of understanding yourself? How might you use some Gestalt techniques as a way of increasing your awareness and promoting personality change in yourself? What do you think it would be like for you to be in a Gestalt group?

8. If you were to include Gestalt techniques in your group, what are some of the ways you might prepare your members to increase their readiness to get involved in these techniques? What might you say to a member who asked what good it does to relive an event in the here and now, rather than merely telling a story about a problem in the past?

9. What are some ways that you might work with the body in therapy? What kind of training would you want before you introduced body-oriented techniques? What advantages, if any, do you see in incorporating body work, as opposed to limiting the group strictly to verbal methods? What risks, if any, do you see in working with the body?

10. What are your reactions to the Gestalt approach to working with dreams in a group setting?

RECOMMENDED SUPPLEMENTARY READINGS

Creative process in Gestalt therapy (Zinker, 1977) is a beautifully written book that is a delight to read. Zinker captures the essence of Gestalt therapy as a combination of phenomenology and behavior modification by showing how the therapist functions much like an artist in creating experiments that encourage clients to expand their boundaries. His concepts are fleshed out with rich clinical examples. The book shows how Gestalt can be practiced in a creative, eclectic, and integrative style.

Gestalt therapy verbatim (Perls, 1969a), which consists essentially of transcripts of lectures, workshops, seminars, and demonstrations given by the author, provides a graphic description of Perls' unique and dramatic therapeutic style. It is also an excellent source of information about "affective techniques" based on Gestalt-therapy exercises. The first part of the book deals primarily with the theory of Gestalt.

Gestalt therapy: Excitement and growth in the human personality (Perls, Hefferline, & Goodman, 1951) is one of the most important books in Gestalt therapy. The first half deals with applications of Gestalt principles to group situations. The rest of the book, rather difficult to read, discusses theoretical aspects of Gestalt therapy.

Gestalt therapy now (Fagan & Shepherd, 1970) is a collection of articles that gives a good indication of the diversity that exists among Gestalt-therapy practitioners. The articles deal with the theory, techniques, and applications of Gestalt therapy. I particularly recommend Chapters 7–11 and Chapter 18.

Gestalt approaches in counseling (Passons, 1975) is a clear, concise, and practical account of the application of Gestalt-therapy principles to group counseling. It contains some extremely useful material on group techniques related to present-centeredness, expanding awareness, verbal and nonverbal approaches, the use of fantasy, working with feelings, and dealing with the past and future. The book also offers an excellent, easy-to-read overview of the theoretical components of Gestalt therapy.

Gestalt therapy integrated: Contours of theory and practice (Polster & Polster, 1973) is a scholarly and penetrating treatment of some of the concepts underlying the practice of Gestalt therapy. Theory and practice are successfully integrated in the unique and personal style characteristic of the authors.

Beyond the hot seat: Gestalt approaches to group (Feder & Ronall, 1980) discusses the application of Gestalt theory to group practice. Separate chapters are devoted to Gestalt group process, Gestalt family therapy, training groups, intensive workshops, and other clinical applications.

REFERENCES AND SUGGESTED READINGS*

Brown, G. *Human teaching for human learning*. New York: Viking, 1971.

Daniels, V., & Horowitz, L. *Being and caring*. Palo Alto, Calif.: Mayfield, 1976.

Downing, J. (Ed.). *Gestalt awareness*. New York: Harper & Row, 1976.

Downing, J., & Marmorstein, R. (Eds.). *Dreams and nightmares: A book of Gestalt therapy sessions*. New York: Harper & Row, 1973.

Fagan, J., & Shepherd, I. (Eds.). *Gestalt therapy now*. New York: Harper Colophon, 1970.

* Feder, B. Safety and danger in the Gestalt group. In B. Feder & R. Ronall (Eds.), *Beyond the hot seat: Gestalt approaches to group*. New York: Brunner/Mazel, 1980.

* Feder, B., & Ronall, R. (Eds.). *Beyond the hot seat: Gestalt approaches to group*. New York: Brunner/Mazel, 1980.

Foulds, M. The experiential-Gestalt growth group experience. In R. Suinn & R. Weigel (Eds.), *The innovative-psychological therapies: Critical and creative contributions*. New York: Harper & Row, 1975.

Foulds, M., & Hannigan, P. Gestalt marathon group: Changes on a measure of personal and social functioning. *Journal of Humanistic Psychology*, 1978, *18*(1), 57–67.

James, M., & Jongeward, D. *Born to win: Transactional analysis with Gestalt experiments*. Reading, Mass.: Addison-Wesley, 1971.

* Kempler, W. *Experiential psychotherapy within families*. New York: Brunner/Mazel, 1981. (a)

Kempler, W. Experiential psychotherapy with families. In G. D. Erickson & T. P. Hogan (Eds.), *Family therapy: An introduction to theory and technique* (2nd ed.). Monterey, Calif.: Brooks/Cole, 1981. (b)

Kempler, W. Gestalt family therapy. In A. M. Horne & M. M. Ohlsen (Eds.), *Family counseling and therapy*. Itasca, Ill.: Peacock, 1982.

Kepner, E. Gestalt group process. In B. Feder & R. Ronall (Eds.), *Beyond the hot seat: Gestalt approaches to group*. New York: Brunner/Mazel, 1980.

Latner, J. *The Gestalt therapy book*. New York: Bantam, 1973.

* Levitsky, A., & Perls, F. The rules and games of Gestalt therapy. In J. Fagan & I. Shepherd (Eds.), *Gestalt therapy now*. New York: Harper Colophon, 1970.

Mintz, E. E. *Marathon groups: Reality and symbol*. New York: Avon, 1972.

---

*Books and articles marked with an asterisk are suggested for further study.

* Passons, W. R. *Gestalt approaches in counseling.* New York: Holt, Rinehart & Winston, 1975.
* Perls, F. *Gestalt therapy verbatim.* New York: Bantam, 1969. (a)
  Perls, F. *In and out of the garbage pail.* New York: Bantam, 1969. (b)
  Perls, F. Four lectures. In J. Fagan & I. L. Shepherd (Eds.), *Gestalt therapy now.* New York: Harper Colophon, 1970.
* Perls, F. *The Gestalt approach and eyewitness to therapy.* New York: Bantam, 1973.
  Perls, F., Hefferline, R., & Goodman, P. *Gestalt therapy: Excitement and growth in the human personality.* New York: Dell, 1951.
  Polster, I., & Polster, M. *Gestalt therapy integrated: Contours of theory and practice.* New York: Brunner/Mazel, 1973.
* Rainwater, J. *You're in charge! A guide to becoming your own therapist.* Los Angeles: Guild of Tutors Press, 1979.
  Reich, W. *Character analysis.* New York: Noonday Press, 1949.
  Reich, W. *The function of the orgasm.* New York: Bantam, 1967.
  Reich, W. *Selected writings.* New York: Noonday Press, 1969.
  Rudestam, K. E. *Experiential groups in theory and practice.* Monterey, Calif.: Brooks/Cole, 1982.
  Simkin, J. S. Gestalt therapy. In R. J. Corsini (Ed.), *Current psychotherapies* (2nd ed.). Itasca, Ill.: Peacock, 1979.
  Simkin, J. S. Gestalt therapy in groups. In G. M. Gazda (Ed.), *Basic approaches to group psychotherapy and group counseling* (2nd ed.). Springfield, Ill.: Charles C Thomas, 1982.
  Stevens, J. O. *Awareness: Exploring, experimenting, experiencing.* Moab, Utah: Real People Press, 1971.
  Stevens, J. O. *Gestalt is.* New York: Bantam, 1975.
  Synthesis. The farther reaches of Gestalt therapy: A conversation with George Brown. (Interview conducted by B. Carter & S. Vargiu.) Redwood City, Calif.: Synthesis Press, 1977.
  Van De Riet, V., Korb, M. P., & Gorrell, J. J. *Gestalt therapy: An introduction.* New York: Pergamon Press, 1980.
  Zinker, J. *Creative process in Gestalt therapy.* New York: Brunner/Mazel, 1977.
* Zinker, J. The developmental process of a Gestalt therapy group. In B. Feder & R. Ronall (Eds.), *Beyond the hot seat: Gestalt approaches to group.* New York: Brunner/Mazel, 1980.
  Zinker, J., & Nevis, S. *The Gestalt theory of couple and family interactions.* Cleveland: Gestalt Institute of Cleveland, 1981.

12

TRANSACTIONAL ANALYSIS

INTRODUCTION

Transactional analysis (TA) is an interactional therapy grounded on the assumption that we make current decisions based on past premises—premises that were at one time appropriate to our survival needs but that may no longer be valid. TA emphasizes the cognitive/rational/behavioral aspects of the therapeutic process. More specifically, it stresses the capacity of the person to change decisions and is oriented toward increasing awareness with the goal of enabling people to make new decisions (redecide) and thereby alter the course of their life. To achieve this goal, TA group participants learn how to recognize the three ego states (Parent, Adult, and Child) in which they function. They also learn how their current behavior is affected by the rules and regulations they received and incorporated as children and how they can identify the "life script" that determines their actions. Ultimately, they come to realize that they can now redecide and initiate a new direction in life, changing what is *not* working while retaining what serves them well.

As transactional analysis, which was originally developed by Eric Berne (1961), has evolved, its concepts and techniques have become particularly suited for group situations. TA provides an interactional and contractual approach to groups—interactional in that it places considerable emphasis on the dynamics of transactions between people; contractual in that group members are expected to develop clear statements of what they will change and how they will go about making these changes. These contracts establish the goals and direction of the group as well as a starting point for group process.

Historical Background

As is the case with many of the therapies described in this book, the founder of TA was trained as a Freudian psychiatrist. But Berne broke away from orthodox psychoanalysis because he believed that it was needlessly complex and that it did not result in effective treatment. Berne said he formulated most of the concepts of TA by paying attention to what his clients were saying. He began to see an ego image that related to the childhood experiences of his patients. He concluded that there was a Child ego state that was different from the "grown-up" ego state. Later, he postulated that there were two "grown-up" states: one, which seemed to be a copy of the person's parents, he called the Parent ego state; the other, which was the rational part of the person, he named the Adult ego state.

One of Berne's contributions was his perspective on how young children develop a personal plan for their life as a strategy for physical and psychological survival. He felt that people were shaped from their first few years by a script that they followed during the rest of their life.

As is true of many theories in this book, there is a parallel between the basic concepts of TA and the personal life of its founder. Claude Steiner (1974) has contended that Berne was himself under the influence of a life script that called for an early death of a broken heart. Apparently, Berne had strong injunctions against loving others and accepting the love that others had for him. His life could be characterized as work oriented, and his driving motivations were to write books on the development of a new theory (TA) and to cure people. In writing about Berne's life script, Steiner comments about his interest in people who had a history of heart disease. Berne died of a coronary occlusion when he was 60 years old, which was the age his mother had died of a coronary. Steiner believes that such a limited-life-expectancy script is by design and that in Berne's situation his heart gave way when he had completed the last two books he wanted to write.

Classical transactional analysis had been largely developed by the late 1960s. However, contemporary TA practitioners have moved in various directions and modified many of the basic concepts that Berne formulated. Because there are several models of TA, it is difficult to discuss practices that apply to all of them. This chapter will be primarily concerned with the basic concepts and therapeutic procedures developed by Berne, which were later built upon and expanded by Mary and Robert Goulding (1979), leaders of the *redecisional school* of TA. The Gouldings differ from the classical Bernian approach in a number of ways. They have combined TA with the principles and techniques of Gestalt therapy, family therapy, psychodrama, and behavior modification. The redecisional perspective emphasizes that we react to stresses, receive messages about how we should be in the world, and make early decisions about ourselves and others that become manifest in our current patterns of thinking, feeling, and behaving. People are seen as autonomous, responsible, and able to restructure their ways of thinking, feeling, and behaving through the process of making updated redecisions about themselves and the world. People are capable of transcending their early programming and choices by being able to understand their past decisions and by being able to make new choices in the present that will affect their future.

Basic Assumptions

Underlying the practice of TA group work is the premise that awareness is an important first step in the process of changing our ways of thinking/feeling/behaving. In the early stages of a group, techniques are aimed at increasing the participants' awareness of their problems and their options for making substantive changes in their life.

Another basic assumption of TA is that each of us is in charge of what we do, of the ways we think, and of how we feel. Robert Goulding (1982) contends that we are responsible for our behavior and for our thinking. He also asserts that others do not *make* us feel in a certain way; rather, we respond to situations largely by our choices. Goulding believes that the therapist's task is to confront clients on the ways they abdicate personal responsibility and insist that they assume responsibility along the way of therapy.

> Thus we believe that people are not victims, and that all of us are responsible for our own behavior, thinking, feeling, and body—and our psychotherapeutic work thus includes facilitating the patient's assuming his or her own autonomy, so that he or she gives up the victim position, and becomes a winner [1982, p. 321].

Rationale for a Group Approach

The practice of TA is ideally suited for groups. Berne believed that group therapy was quite useful in yielding information about one's personal plan for life that would take much more time to obtain through individual therapy. Redecisional therapy, as practiced by the Gouldings, is done in a group context in which members can experience their life script coming to life by reliving early memories and by interacting with others in the group. There are many avenues of self-understanding through analyzing transactions within the group. In the same way that Gestalt groups function in the here and now, TA groups bring past issues into the present. Because of the interaction within the group, TA group members are given many opportunities to review and challenge their past decisions and experiment with new ones.

In the TA group, which emphasizes teaching procedures (didactic methods), members are expected to master a basic vocabulary of TA concepts, such as *Parent, Adult, Child, strokes, decision, redecision, games,* and *scripts.* To become acquainted with the key concepts of TA and generally prepare for a TA group, members are urged to read certain works, including *Changing Lives through Redecision Therapy,* by Mary and Robert Goulding (1979); *The Power Is in the Patient,* by Robert and Mary Goulding (1978); *Scripts People Live,* by Steiner (1974); *Games People Play* and *What Do You Say After You Say Hello?* by Berne (1964, 1972); and *Born to Win,* by Muriel James and Dorothy Jongeward (1971). Group members are also encouraged to attend introductory TA courses, workshops, and conferences.

KEY CONCEPTS

The Ego States

TA identifies three ego states that encompass important facets of personality—Parent, Adult, and Child (P-A-C). According to TA, people are constantly shifting from one of these ego states to another, and their behavior at any one time is related to the ego state of the moment.

The Parent ego state is that part of personality that has been introjected from parents and parental substitutes. Harris (1967) describes the Parent as "a huge collection of recordings in the brain of unquestioned or imposed external events perceived by a person in his early years, a period which we have designated roughly as the first five years of life" (p. 40). When we are in the Parent ego state, we react to situations as we imagine our parents might have reacted, or we may act toward others the way our parents acted toward us. The Parent contains all the "shoulds" and "oughts" and other rules for living. When we are in that ego state, we may act in ways that are strikingly similar to those of our parents or other significant people in our early life. We may use some of their very words and phrases, and our posture, gestures, tone and quality of voice, and mannerisms may replicate those that we experienced in our parents. Such behavior occurs when the Parent in us is a positive ego state (a Nurturing Parent) or a negative one (a Critical Parent).

The Adult ego state is the objective and computerlike part of our personality that functions as a data processor: it computes possibilities and makes decisions on the basis of available data. This state is neither emotional nor judgmental but simply works with the facts and with external reality.

The Child ego state consists of feelings, impulses, and spontaneous actions. The Child can be either the Natural Child—that is, the spontaneous, impulsive, open, alive, expressive, often charming but untrained being within each of us— or the Adapted Child—the tamed version of the Natural Child and the part of us that learns to accommodate to the expectations of others in order to gain acceptance and approval. Berne describes the Adapted Child as "the one who modifies his behavior under Parental influence. He behaves as father (or mother) wanted him to behave: compliantly or precociously, for example. Or, he adapts himself by withdrawing or whining" (1964, p. 26). The modifications referred to by Berne result generally from traumatic experiences, demands, training, and decisions about how to get attention or other forms of "strokes."

In a TA group, members are first taught how to recognize which of the three ego states they are functioning in at any given time, with the aim of enabling them to consciously decide whether that state or another state is most appropriate or useful. For example, a member who typically responds to others in a Critical Parent style and who has contracted to become more tolerant toward others must recognize his or her habitual ego state before any steps can be taken to change.

Mary and Robert Goulding (1979) describe the value of ego-state awareness as follows:

> As patients learn to be more aware of the ego state they are in, they learn to better handle their feelings, to better recognize their position in their life script, to be more aware that they have been, or are, game playing. They become much more aware of their adaptive behavior, adaptive to their internal Parent and to the outside world. After becoming aware, they can knowingly choose to adapt or not to adapt [p. 26].*

*From *Changing Lives through Redecision Therapy,* by M. Goulding and R. Goulding. Copyright 1979 by Brunner/Mazel, Inc. This and all other quotations from this source are reprinted by permission.

The Need for Strokes

A basic premise of the TA approach is that humans need to receive both physical and psychological strokes in order to develop a sense of trust in the world and a basis for loving themselves. Steiner (1974) writes that "strokes are as necessary to human life as are other primary biological needs such as food, water, and shelter—needs which if not satisfied will lead to death" (p. 132). And, indeed, there is ample evidence that lack of physical contact can not only impair infant growth and development but can also in extreme cases lead to death. Psychological strokes—verbal and nonverbal signs of acceptance and recognition—are also necessary to people as confirmations of their worth.

Strokes can be either positive or negative. Positive strokes, which express warmth, affection, or appreciation either verbally or with a look or a smile, a touch or a gesture, are seen as necessary for the development of psychologically healthy people. Negative strokes, which are verbal and nonverbal messages that leave people feeling discounted and diminished as persons, are seen as impairing healthy psychological development. Interestingly, despite their ill effects, negative strokes are considered preferable to no strokes at all—that is, to being ignored. We are all familiar with cases of children who, feeling ignored and dismissed, act to elicit negative strokes from their parents because such responses are the only form of recognition they can get.

Positive strokes can be given either unconditionally or conditionally. Unconditional strokes—that is, strokes that are not predicated on the receiver's being or acting in a certain way—tend to elicit the feeling that one is significant just because one exists. Conditional positive strokes—strokes that entail a variety of stipulations that must be met before the strokes are given—typically tend to elicit the feeling that one is acceptable only *when* and *if* one meets certain expectations.

TA group members are taught how to recognize the strokes that motivate them and to become sensitive to the ways in which they discount themselves. Take, for example, a group member named Sara who continually puts herself down with self-deprecating remarks. She either doesn't hear or soon forgets the positive feedback she gets from others in her group. When paid a sincere compliment, Sara finds some way to play it down or make a joke of it. If she is the focus of positive attention or if she receives any display of tenderness, affection, or caring, she becomes extremely uncomfortable, yet she remembers and stores up any critical remarks and feels depressed. Sara, as Steiner (1974) would put it, collects the "cold pricklies" rather than the "warm fuzzies."

In her TA group Sara is confronted with the fact that she discounts her worth and doesn't allow others to give her positive strokes. She is also challenged to decide whether she wants to change this behavior. If Sara accepts the challenge to change, the group can help her learn how to ask for and accept positive strokes.

TA groups also teach members how to stroke themselves. Goulding and Goulding (1979) begin their marathon groups with a quiet time during which participants are asked to reflect on the question "What do you like about yourself?" The aim is to create a climate wherein clients can become aware of unrecognized strengths, which are deserving of self-generated positive strokes.

The Gouldings operate on the premise that clients will meet their therapeutic contracts to a greater extent through self-love than through self-hate.

Injunctions and Counterinjunctions

Another key concept of TA relates to injunctions, which Goulding and Goulding (1979) describe as parental messages stemming from the parents' Child ego state. Such messages, which are often expressions of parental disappointment, frustration, anxiety, and unhappiness, establish the "don'ts" by which children learn to live. Some of the basic injunctions that the Gouldings have identified are "Don't," "Don't be," "Don't be close," "Don't be important," "Don't be a child," "Don't grow," "Don't succeed," "Don't be you," "Don't be sane," "Don't be well," and "Don't belong."

The counterpart of injunctions are parental messages that come from the parents' Parent ego state, which are known as *counterinjunctions*. These messages convey the "shoulds," "oughts," and "dos" of parental expectations. Examples of counterinjunctions are "Be tough," "Be perfect," "Work up to your potential," "Do what I expect of you," "Hurry up," "Try hard," "Please me," "Be careful," and "Be polite." The problem with these counterinjunctions is that it is almost impossible to live up to them; thus, no matter how hard the person tries to be pleasing, he's bound to feel that he has not done or been enough.

In TA groups, members explore the "shoulds" and "shouldn'ts," the "dos" and "don'ts" that they have been trained to live by. The first step in freeing oneself from behaviors dictated by the often irrational and generally uncritically received parental messages is awareness of the specific injunctions and counterinjunctions that one has accepted as a child. Once group participants have identified and become aware of these internalized "shoulds," "oughts," "dos," "don'ts," and "musts," they are in a better position to critically examine them to determine whether they are willing to continue living by them.

Decisions and Redecisions

As indicated earlier, transactional analysis emphasizes cognitive/rational/ behavioral aspects, especially our ability to become aware of decisions that govern our behavior and of the capacity to make new decisions that will beneficially alter the course of our life. This section focuses on the decisions determined by parental injunctions and counterinjunctions and investigates how TA group members learn to relive these early decisions and make new ones.

Following is an example of decision making that has been dictated by parental injunctions. A TA group member, Bill, apparently received the parental injunction "Don't trust anybody." The decisions about the behavior resulting from this injunction are implicit in many of Bill's characteristic pronouncements: "If you don't let yourself care, you won't be hurt"; "If I keep to myself, I won't need anything from anyone"; "Whenever I've wanted something from another, I've been hurt. It's just not worth getting involved with, or even close to, others." Indeed, it became clear in group sessions that, by accepting his parents' injunction against trusting people, Bill consistently made decisions that caused him to avoid others. To support these decisions, Bill was able to find plenty of data—both in the group and in his everyday life—to maintain his view that trust will inevitably lead to hurt. Consequently he continued, often unwittingly, to abide by his parents' injunction.

In the TA group Bill not only had the opportunity to become aware of his decisions and of the injunction behind them but was also helped to investigate whether these decisions were still appropriate. At one time the decisions to avoid people might have been necessary for Bill's physical and psychological safety—a matter of sheer survival. In the group Bill was able to question whether such decisions currently served any purpose and determine whether they were instead thwarting his development. He made a new decision to trust people and to approach them as friends, not enemies.

Berne (1964, 1972) takes the position that, to a large degree, people are victims of their injunctions and of the decisions based on them. For Berne, how people are "scripted" by their parents in the long run *determines* their life plans. The Gouldings disagree with Berne's deterministic and victimlike stance and state that people are not passively "scripted," for "injunctions are not placed in people's heads like electrodes. . . . Each child makes decisions in response to real or imagined injunctions, and thereby 'scripts' her/himself" (Goulding & Goulding, 1976, p. 42).

Elsewhere Goulding and Goulding (1978, 1979) also point out that, even though injunctions and counterinjunctions carry the weight of parental authority, the child must *accept* these messages if they are to have an impact on his or her personality. The Gouldings add that many injunctions children live under are not issued by the parents but derive instead from the children's own fantasies and misinterpretations. It is important to note that, according to Goulding and Goulding, a single parental injunction may foster a variety of decisions on the part of the child, ranging from reasonable to pathological. For example, the injunction "Don't be stupid" may give rise to decisions ranging from "I'll never do *that* again" to "I'll let others make decisions" to "I *am* stupid, and I *always will be* stupid." Similarly, the injunction "Don't be you" may evoke decisions ranging from "I'll hide who I really am" to "I'll be someone else" to "I'll be a nobody" to "I'll kill myself, and then they will accept me and love me."

Whatever the injunctions people may have received and whatever the resulting life decisions may be, transactional analysis maintains that people can change by changing their decisions—by learning to redecide. In their groups the Gouldings develop an atmosphere in which members are challenged from the outset to make new decisions for themselves. Early in the course of a group, Robert Goulding (1975) asks: "What did you decide to do to screw up your life, and what are you going to decide now to unscrew it?" (p. 246).

The group work related to making new decisions frequently requires members to return to childhood scenes in which they eventually arrived at self-limiting decisions. For example, a member named Helga relives a scene with her parents when she was positively stroked for failing or another time when she was negatively stroked for succeeding. It was apparently at those times that Helga bought the injunction "Don't succeed." Helga is then challenged in the group to examine whether this decision, which may have been functional or even necessary in the past, is currently appropriate. Helga may redecide that "I will make it, and I am successful, even though it is not what you want from me."

Another group member, Gary, is able to see that he responded to his father's injunction "Don't grow" by deciding to remain helpless and immature. He recalls learning that, when he was independent, his dad shouted at him and, when he was helpless, he was given his father's attention. Because he wanted his father's approval, Gary decided "I'll remain a child forever." During a group session Gary goes back to a childhood scene in which he was stroked for his helplessness, and he talks to his father now in a way that he never did as a child. He says: "Dad, even though I still want your approval, I don't *need* it to exist. Your acceptance is not worth the price I'd have to pay. I'm capable of deciding for myself and of standing on my own two feet. I'll be the man that *I* want to be, not the boy that you want me to be."

In this redecision work, Helga and Gary enter the past and create fantasy scenes in which they can safely give up old and currently inappropriate early decisions, because both are armed with an understanding in the present that enables them to relive the scene in a new way. According to the Gouldings, it is possible to give a *new ending* to the scenes in which original decisions were made—a new ending that often results in a *new beginning* that allows clients to feel, think, and act in revitalized ways. Goulding and Goulding (1979) describe this aspect of redecision therapy:

> Again, *REDECISION* is a beginning. There is no magic. The person discovers his ability to be autonomous and experiences his new, free self with enthusiasm, excitement and energy. He goes out into his world to practice changing and the practice is a continuous process. He looks upon the world through a different pair of glasses, a different pair of eyes, not coloring the world muddy and tainted by his original decision, but seeing clearly, sharply, as if the rain had washed away the smog [p. 285].

Games

In his book *Games People Play*, Berne (1964) defined a game as "an ongoing series of complementary ulterior transactions progressing to a well-defined, predictable outcome" (p. 48) and described a variety of common games, including "Yes, but," "Kick me," "Harassed," "If it weren't for you," "Martyr," "Ain't it awful," "I'm only trying to help you," "Uproar," and "Look what you made me do!" Games always have some payoff (or else they wouldn't be perpetuated), and one common payoff is to support the decisions described in the preceding section. For example, people who have decided that they are helpless may play the "Yes, but" game; they may ask others for help and then greet any suggestions with a list of reasons why the suggestion won't work ("Yes, but . . .") and thereby feel free to cling to their helplessness. The "Kick me" game addicts are often people who have decided to be rejected; they set themselves up to be mistreated by others so that they can play the role of the victim whom nobody likes.

By engaging in game playing, people receive strokes and also maintain and defend their early decisions. They find evidence to support their view of the world, and they collect bad feelings. These unpleasant feelings that people experience after a game are known as *rackets.* They have much the same quality as feelings the people had as children. These rackets are maintained by actually choosing situations that will support them. Therefore, those who typically feel depressed, angry, or bored may be actively collecting these feelings and feeding them into long-standing feeling patterns that often lead to stereotypical ways of behaving. They also choose the games that they will play to maintain their rackets.

A group situation provides an ideal environment for the participants to become aware of the specific ways they choose game-playing strategies as a way of avoiding genuine contact and choose patterns of thinking/feeling/behaving that are ultimately self-defeating. Group members can learn about their own games and rackets by observing the behavior of others in the group, as well as by analyzing how their responses in the group are connected to their responses to life situations in early childhood. Members can begin by using the games they are currently playing in the group to understand that, although games often give the appearance of intimacy, their actual effect is to create distance between people. Later, as members become aware of the more subtle aspects of game playing, they begin to realize that games prevent close human inter-action and that it takes at least two to play a game. Consequently, if the mem-bers decide that they want to relate more closely to others, they also have to decide not to play games anymore.

Eventually members are taught to make connections between the games they played as children and the games they play now—for example, how they attempted to get attention in the past and how those past attempts relate to the games they play now in order to get stroked. The aim of this TA group process is to offer members the chance to drop certain games in favor of responding honestly—an opportunity that may lead them to discover ways of changing negative strokes and learn how to give and receive positive strokes.

Basic Psychological Life Positions and Life Scripts

Related to the concept of games is the concept of life positions and life scripts. Indeed, games—whether they elicit positive or negative strokes—are often used to support and maintain life positions and to play out life scripts. People seek security by maintaining that which is familiar, even though the familiar may be highly unpleasant. As we have seen earlier, games such as "Kick me" may be unpleasant, but they have the virtue of allowing the player to maintain a familiar, if negative, position in life (Meininger, 1973).

Transactional analysis identifies four basic life positions, all of which are based on decisions made as a result of childhood experiences and all of which determine how people feel about themselves and how they relate to others. The four basic positions are:

1. I'm OK—You're OK.
2. I'm OK—You're not OK.
3. I'm not OK—You're OK.
4. I'm not OK—You're not OK.

Generally, once a person has decided on a life position, there is a tendency for it to remain fixed unless there is some intervention, such as therapy, to change the underlying decisions.

The *I'm OK—You're OK* position is generally game free. It is characterized by an attitude of trust and openness, a willingness to give and take, and an acceptance of others as they are. In this position there are no losers, only winners.

I'm OK—You're not OK is the position of people who project their problems onto others and blame them, put them down, and criticize them. The games that reinforce this position involve a self-styled superior (the "I'm OK") who projects anger, disgust, and scorn onto a designated inferior, or scapegoat (the "You're not OK"). Briefly, this position is that of the person who needs an underdog to maintain his or her sense of OKness.

The *I'm not OK—You're OK* position is that of the depressed person, one who feels powerless in comparison with others. Typically such people serve others' needs instead of their own and generally feel victimized. Games supporting this position include "Kick me" and "Martyr"—games that support the power of others and deny one's own.

The *I'm not OK—You're not OK* position is the position held by those who have given up all hope, who have lost interest in life, and who see life as totally without promise. This self-destructive stance is characteristic of people who are unable to cope in the real world and may lead to extreme withdrawal, a return to infantile behavior, or to violent behavior resulting in injury or death of themselves or others.

Related to the concept of basic psychological positions is the life script, or plan for life. This script, as we have seen, is developed early in life as a result of parental teaching (such as injunctions and counterinjunctions) and the early decisions we make as children. Among these decisions is selecting the basic psychological position, or dramatic role, that we play in our life scripts. Indeed, life scripts are comparable to a dramatic stage production, with a cast of characters, a plot, scenes, dialogues, and endless rehearsals. In essence, the life script is a blueprint that tells people where they are going in life and what they will do when they arrive.

According to Berne (1972), through our early interactions with parents and others we receive a pattern of strokes that may be either supporting or disparaging. Based on this stroking pattern, we make a basic existential decision about ourselves; that is, we assume one of the four positions described above. This existential decision is then reinforced by continuing messages (both verbal and nonverbal) that we receive during our lifetime. It is also reinforced by the results of our games, rackets, and interpretations of events. During our childhood years we also make the decision whether people are OK and trustworthy (Berne, 1964; Harris, 1967). Our basic belief system is thus shaped through this process of deciding about ourselves and others. If we hope to change the life course that we are traveling, it helps to understand the components of this script, which to a large extent determines our patterns of thinking/feeling/behaving.

One function of the TA group is to help members, through a process known as *script analysis*, to become aware of how they acquire their life script and to see more clearly their life role (basic psychological life position). Script analysis helps members see the ways in which they feel compelled to play out their life script and offers them alternative life choices. Put in another way, this group process helps to relieve participants of the compulsion to play games that justify behavior called for in their life script. It should be mentioned here that Goulding and Goulding (1979) reject the rather passive concept of "scripting." They contend that we write our own script and that we can rewrite it. Consequently, the Gouldings do not deal much with scripts in their group therapy.

In addition to script analysis, the TA group offers opportunities to actually experience oneself in unfamiliar dominant life positions. For example, the members who have cast themselves in the "I'm not OK" role can become aware of how they relate to others in the group through games like "Kick me," whereby they elevate others and keep themselves feeling inferior and depressed. Once they have gained an awareness of how they keep themselves victims, they can use the group situation to experience an "I'm OK" role. Armed with an awareness of their habitual ineffective behavior and the newly acquired experience of functional behavior, participants are in a better position to effect a change in their experiences. Briefly, the aim of the TA group in this instance is to provide a vehicle for members to develop the life position "I'm OK—You're OK."

ROLE AND FUNCTIONS OF THE GROUP LEADER

Robert Goulding (1975) states that the primary function of TA-group therapists is to create a climate in which people can discover for themselves how they support a series of behaviors that render them ineffective. Specifically, they come to realize how the games they play support chronic bad feelings and how they hold on to these feelings to support their life script and early decisions. They also come to see how supporting the life script and early decisions enables them to continue living by injunctions that might at one time have served the need of physical or psychological survival but that are now obeyed simply because these injunctions are familiar and because people cannot conceive of being other than what they are. Another function of the TA therapist is challenging group members to discover and to experiment with more effective ways of being. In short, the function of the therapist is to help members acquire the tools necessary to effect change.

Goulding favors rapid and decisive therapy that is aimed at clients' autonomy; he objects to lengthy group therapy that fosters dependence and that strokes sickness. He encourages clients to rely on their own inner resources rather than continuing to look to the therapist for direction. Goulding sees himself as a guide and a mapmaker. It is the client who makes the journey.

Although TA is designed to develop both emotional and intellectual awareness, the focus is clearly on the cognitive/rational aspects. Thus, the role of the therapist is that of a teacher. Harris (1967) says that the therapist is a "teacher, trainer, and resource person with a heavy emphasis on involvement" (p. 239). As a teacher, the TA therapist explains concepts such as structural analysis, script analysis, and game analysis. As stated earlier, TA stresses the importance of equality in the relationship between leader and group members—an equality that is manifested through a contract between the group leader and the individual members that makes them partners in the therapeutic process. Consequently, the role of the therapist is to apply his or her knowledge to fulfilling the contract that the client initiates.

THERAPEUTIC PROCEDURES AND TECHNIQUES

This section discusses the implementation of the TA contract, the first step in the TA therapeutic process, and two approaches to other phases of TA group therapy. It should be noted that not all TA therapists conduct their groups according to the order and structuring described here.

Contracts: The Structure of the Therapeutic Relationship

Transactional analysis is largely based on the capacity and willingness of the group participants to understand and design a therapeutic contract that requires them to state their intentions and set personal goals. Gellert and Wilson (1978) define transactional analysis as a contract method of therapy and note that the therapeutic value of the contract depends on whether clients feel that they are successful in fulfilling it.

Contracts are specific and measurable and contain a concrete statement of the objectives that the group participant intends to attain and the criteria to determine how and when these goals are to be met. Contracts place the responsibility on members for clearly defining what, how, and when *they* want to change. Thus, from the very beginning, members learn that therapy is a shared responsibility and that they cannot passively wait for the group leader to assume the direction for working in a group. In short, the contract establishes the departure point for group activity—a point that is determined by the members for themselves.

Group members agree to work on specific issues within the group; the group leader contracts to direct the group along the lines that will lead to completing the contracts. Such contracts are specific and relate to how a member will behave in the group situation. For example, a woman who reacts to others in a highly critical way can design a contract that will lead to changing such behavior. Her contract describes *what* she will do to change her actions and experiences, *when* she will do it, and *how many* times. The contract can then be expanded to include situations outside the group.

Dusay (1983) asserts that a well-stated treatment contract makes it clear whether clients are obtaining what they want from therapy. He says that such a contract is an acceptable answer to the question "How will you know and how will I know when you get what you are coming to the group for?" Since everyone in the group knows the other participants' contracts, a productive focus can be developed in the group sessions. The process of TA treatment focuses primarily on change as defined by the contract, and there is an Adult to Adult agreement between the therapist and the client about what the process and the desired goal will be (Dusay & Dusay, 1979).

Meininger (1973) suggests some guidelines in making contracts. First, the members who seek change must decide *what* they *want* to change. Next, members need to formulate an honest, clear, specific, and reasonable statement of what they want or, alternatively, what they don't want. Vague contracts such as "I want to get in touch with my feelings" don't fulfill this requirement, because they don't offer a specific, measurable goal.

Following a statement of what is wanted, the next step requires members to determine what they are *willing* to do to obtain these wants. (Clearly, there is a significant difference between *wanting* changes and *willing* changes.) This step is extremely important, because TA insists that members be responsible for following through on their contracts and rejects any excuses such as "I tried," "I can't help it," and "I wish I could." Thus, members are encouraged to state clearly what they are willing to do and then to examine the factors that prevent them from doing what they say they want to do. To this end, clients are urged to ask themselves "How do *I* prevent *myself* from doing what I want to do? What is likely to interfere with my changing? What am I continuing to do that I no longer want to do?" Meininger (1973) states that it is important to look at the ways we prevent ourselves from keeping our contracts, but he also notes that failing to fulfill a contract may indicate that we contracted to change what we really don't want to change or that we were forced to agree to do what we really didn't want to do.

The final step in writing a contract, according to Meininger, involves answering the question "How will others know when I've successfully completed my contract?" In other words, the contract goals must be measurable, and they must state "how much" and "by when."

A final comment: Contracts are intended to be practical tools for helping people change themselves. As such, they cannot be rigid and should be open to revision. Long-term contracts can be limiting; thus, it is often useful to develop contracts in steps, subject to modification as members penetrate more deeply the areas that they seek to change. Furthermore, people sometimes make contracts that later prove unacceptable.

Unacceptable contracts—a topic addressed by Goulding and Goulding (1979)—include Parent contracts, contracts to change others, game contracts, forever contracts, and ulterior contracts. Parent contracts are generally based on what clients feel they *should* change rather than on what they themselves *want* to change. Contracts to change others are simply unworkable. We cannot change others; we can change only ourselves. In game contracts, clients seek therapist approval for actions that lead to the clients' feeling hurt or unhappy. Ulterior contracts (pacts between therapist and client to prevent the client from reaching his or her goals) are a denial of the client's power. Goulding and Goulding (1979) suggest that therapists pay attention to how their language patterns may convey a denial of autonomy. When therapists use words such as *try, can,* and *perhaps,* they reinforce the client's lack of autonomy.

The Classical Bernian Approach

Berne (1961) developed four techniques for conducting therapy groups, as ways of carrying out the contracts formulated between the leader and group participants: (1) structural analysis, (2) transactional analysis, (3) game analysis, and (4) life-script analysis.

Structural analysis.   Structural analysis is a tool by which group members become aware of the content and functioning of their ego states of Parent, Adult, and Child. The aim of structural analysis is to help members learn how to identify and analyze their own ego states, so that they can change behavioral patterns that they feel stuck with. The process allows participants to discover which ego state their behavior is based on. In turn, this awareness makes it possible for clients to discover what their options may be.

Berne (1961) discusses two types of problems related to the structure of personality that can be considered by structural analysis: (1) *exclusion* and (2) *contamination.*

1. *Exclusion* is manifested by a stereotyped attitude that is rigidly held to in threatening situations (Berne, 1961). Put in another way, exclusion consists of rigid ego-state boundaries that don't allow free movement; that is, one ego state "blocks out" another ego state. There are three forms of exclusion: the Constant Parent, the Constant Adult, and the Constant Child, in each of which the person relates primarily as Parent, as Adult, or as Child, respectively. The *Constant Parent*, which excludes the Adult and the Child, is typically found in duty-bound people, sometimes known as "workaholics." Such people are generally judgmental and demanding of others and have a difficult time playing. The *Constant Adult*, which excludes the Parent and the Child, is found in people who are highly objective—that is, who tend to be involved in, and concerned with, only facts. Such people often have the emotional appeal and spontaneity of a computer. The *Constant Child*, which excludes the Adult and the Parent, is typically found in people who refuse to grow up and face the demands of reality. Such people are reluctant to make their own decisions, preferring instead to remain dependent on others in order to avoid taking responsibility for their own behavior.

2. *Contamination* exists when the boundary of one ego state overlaps that of another one and the contents of the two states intermix. It is possible for either the Parent or the Child, or both, to contaminate the Adult. An example of the Adult's being contaminated by the Parent can be found in statements such as "Keep with your own kind, and never mix with people who are 'different' " or "Look out! People will take advantage of you." An example of the Adult's being contaminated by the Child is seen in statements like "Nobody ever likes me; everybody always picks on me" or "I deserve whatever I want—immediately."

Transactional analysis.   Transactional analysis, which is basically a description of what people do and say to one another, is best done in therapy groups, according to Berne (1961). When people, such as the members of a group, are interacting, they are in effect conducting transactions among their ego states.

Berne describes three types of transactions: (1) *complementary,* (2) *crossed,* and (3) *ulterior.*

1. *Complementary transactions* occur when a message sent from a specific ego state gets the predicted response from a specific ego state of another

person. For example, a complementary Child/Child transaction takes place when Fred's Child says "Let's dance" and Sharon's Child replies "Oh, yes! That's fun."

2. *Crossed transactions* occur when an unexpected response is made to a message that a person sends out—for example, when Sharon's Parent responds to Fred's invitation to dance (which comes from his Child) with "I'm not going to make a fool of myself on the dance floor!"

3. *Ulterior transactions* are more complex, because they involve more than two ego states and a disguised message. For example, Fred might say "Let's dance—that is, if you don't think we'll make fools of ourselves." Here there is a message from Fred's Child to Sharon's Child (see above) and a disguised message from Fred's Parent to Sharon's Child suggesting more decorous behavior.

Game analysis. Berne's (1964) *Games People Play* is an investigation of the defense strategies and "gimmicks" people use to prevent intimacy and manipulate others in order to get what they want. As indicated earlier, games have certain payoffs—generally a "bad" feeling that the player experiences and reinforcement of script decisions such as "Nobody loves me" or "No matter how hard I try, I can't make it." Berne (1964) stresses the importance of learning to observe and understand why games take place, what their payoffs are, and how they keep people apart.

The classical TA group devotes considerable time to helping members become aware of the games they initiate and participate in, so that they can come to develop intimate and nonmanipulative relationships. James and Jongeward (1971) write of the importance of clients' recognizing games and identifying their roles in these games. With regard to helping clients learn how to interrupt and avoid games, they state simply "The game may be foiled by a refusal to play or a refusal to give a pay-off" (p. 208).

Life-script analysis. Recall that life scripts are basically plans, decided on at an early age, for meeting our needs in the world as we see them from the viewpoint of our life position. Briefly, life-script analysis refers to that part of the TA therapeutic process devoted to identifying the life pattern of a person and involves both transactional and game analysis. As an example, Berne (1961) describes a common tragic script—the drama of a woman who marries one alcoholic after another. Generally this script calls for the heroine-wife to rescue, by means of a magical cure, the alcoholic husband, who, typically, is a victim of circumstances that he cannot control. It takes little imagination to see the endless possibilities for games and Parent, Adult, and Child transactions in such a drama and the collection of many feelings.

Script analysis helps demonstrate the process by which group members acquired a script and the strategies they employ to justify their actions based on it. The aim is to help members open up possibilities for making changes in their early programming. The participants are asked to recall their favorite stories as children, to determine how they fit into these stories or fables, and to see how these stories fit their current life experiences.

The analysis of the life script of a group member is based on the drama of his or her original family. Through the process of acting out portions of their life script in the group sessions, members learn about the injunctions they uncritically accepted as children, the decisions they made in response to these messages, and the games and rackets they now employ to keep these early decisions alive. The group leader can gather information about the family drama by taking a history of the childhood experiences of the members. Members can be asked the kind of drama that would probably result if their family were put on the stage. Other group members can be given a part to play in this family play.

These and other cognitive and emotive techniques often help the group participants recall early events and the feelings associated with them. The group setting provides a supportive place to explore the ways that these past situations are influencing the participants. By being a part of the process of the self-discovery of other members, each member increases the opportunities for coming to a deeper understanding of his or her own unfinished psychological business.

Didactic procedures such as the Karpman Drama Triangle (see Karpman, 1968) can be employed to help members identify scripts and games. The triangle has a "Persecutor," a "Rescuer," and a "Victim." Persecutors criticize others and invite others to assume the position of Victim. Rescuers depend upon helping or "saving" others in order to feel OK. If others do not play the role of Victim, then the Rescuers are not able to play their game of taking care of others. Victims assume a passive and helpless stance, maintaining that they have no power to change unless someone else changes first. It should be noted that the same individual might alternate between all three of these roles at different times in various situations. However, most group members have a favorite position in life, which may become evident in the way they behave in the group sessions. For example, Betty may quickly come to the rescue of any member who experiences sadness. Betty may do her best to provide such members with ready-made solutions for complex problems. In her life outside of the group, Betty may well depend on others to need her so that she can save them from pain. Another member, Jim, may assume a victimlike stance by continually complaining about how awful his life is and how he could change if only others would make certain changes first. The group situation allows members to analyze the positions they often take and the games they play, both in the group and in everyday life. As a result, group participants gain the capacity to take some initial steps to break out of self-defeating patterns. As the group members analyze their own life from a TA perspective, they can check the accuracy of their self-interpretations by asking for feedback from the leader and the other members.

Script analysis can be carried out by means of a script checklist. Steiner (1967) developed a life-script questionnaire that can be used as a catalyst in group situations to help members explore significant components of their life script—among them, life positions and games. In completing this script checklist, members provide basic information such as the general direction of their life, the models in their life, the nature of their injunctions, the payoffs they seek in life, and the tragic ending they expect from life.

The Gouldings' Redecisional Approach to Groups

The *redecision model*, developed by Goulding and Goulding (1979), is an approach that builds upon the foundation of transactional analysis as it was originally formulated by Berne, but it differs from the classical Bernian group model in a number of important respects. The following is a summary of the redecisional approach to TA groups, based on an adaptation of some of the chief works of the Gouldings (1976, 1978, 1979, 1982). It should be mentioned that the core of the work in this approach consists of helping clients make redecisions while they are in their Child ego state. This is done by having them reexperience an early scene as if the situation were occurring in the present. Merely talking about past events or understanding early feelings and decisions from the Adult ego state is not sufficient to push them beyond the places where they are stuck. The plan that helps members get into their Child ego state and make a new decision from that perspective can best be seen in the stages of redecision group therapy, which follow.

The initial stages of the group.   The first step in the group process consists of establishing good contact. To a large extent, the outcome for group members depends on the quality of the relationship that the group leader is able to establish with the members and the leader's competence. Even though the group leader makes good contact with the members and is competent, Robert Goulding (1982) has found, the members' most important symptom is typically not brought forward initially. He finds that group participants sometimes tell what they *think* is significant but avoid addressing more pertinent issues. Therefore, Goulding attempts to get at the chief complaint of the client. Obviously, the trust factor in the group has a lot to do with the willingness of clients to get to their chief complaint.

The next step in the process consists of making an inquiry into the actual contract for change. This contract puts a considerable degree of responsibility on the group member from the start to become an active agent in changing. A typical question is "What are you going to change about yourself today?" Notice that members are not asked to state what they hope to change or what the therapist will do to bring about change; nor are they asked what changes they want in the future. The emphasis is upon the client's *taking action now* to do something that will bring about change. Establishing a clear contract is essential, for this provides a concrete place to begin work in the group, and it gives a reference point from which to measure the success of the treatment.

The working stage of the group.   After contracts have been formulated, the Goulding group focuses on *rackets*—essentially collections of bad feelings that people experience when they play games and that they use to justify their life script and, ultimately, their decisions (Goulding & Goulding, 1979). The aim is to expose rackets of group members and have them take responsibility for them. For example, a person with an "anger racket"—one who is chronically angry—may be asked "What do you do to maintain your anger?" Beginning with recent events, the person is led back through his or her life in an attempt to remember early situations involving anger. As in Gestalt, members are asked to *be* in these situations—to recall them not as observers but as participants in the here and now. Members are asked to act out both their own responses and the responses of other significant people in the scene.

As I said earlier, Goulding asserts that people are responsible for their feelings and that they sometimes respond in a stereotyped and predictable way based on their rackets. Thus, from the initial sessions, participants are taught that they are autonomous and responsible for *both* their actions and their feelings (Goulding, 1975, p. 240).

During this stage of group work, the Gouldings also focus on games. Games are analyzed, mainly to see how they support and maintain rackets and how they fit with one's life script. In this connection, much work is devoted to looking for evidence of the participants' early decisions, to discovering the original injunction that lies at the base of these early decisions, and to determining the kinds of strokes that the person received to support the original injunction.

A major function of the TA group leader is to alert the members to take responsibility for their thinking/feeling/behaving. Members are challenged when they use "cop-out language," such as *can't, perhaps, if it weren't for, try,* and other words that keep members from claiming their own power. The leader also creates a group climate in which the members rapidly become aware of how they maintain their chronic bad feelings by their behavior and fantasy. It is the therapist's task to challenge them to discover alternate choices.

The Gouldings (1976) take the position that clients can change *rapidly,* without years of analysis. Consequently, the Gouldings stress the redecisional aspects of TA therapy on the assumption that, when clients perceive that they are responsible for their early decisions, they also have it in their power to change those decisions.

The Goulding approach to group therapy emphasizes helping participants reexperience early, highly emotional situations in order to generate the energy to break through the places where they are stuck. Goulding and Goulding (1979) state that their experience has taught them that "most good therapy is centered on assisting the patient to break through a series of impasses, which had their origins in childhood, and decisions he made about these messages" (p. 6).

Such breakthroughs, according to the Gouldings, usually require that participants remember and relive situations involving real parenting figures. Through the use of fantasy, in which group members reexperience how their parents sounded, acted, and looked, the therapist creates a psychological climate that allows members to feel the same emotional intensity they felt when, as children, they made their original decisions. The Gouldings stress that, if participants are to be successful in going beyond an impasse, they must be in the

Child ego state (actually reliving psychologically early scenes) rather than in their Adult ego state (merely thinking about new information and insights).

The final stages of the group. Once a redecision is made from the Child ego state, the changes in one's voice, body, and facial expressions are obvious to everyone in the group. However, Robert Goulding (1982) emphasizes the importance of reinforcement of this redecision by the client and by the others in the group. The group process provides support for members who begin to feel and behave in new ways. Group members are encouraged to tell a new story in the group to replace their old story, and they typically receive verbal and nonverbal stroking to support their new decision. Attention is also given to ways that members might devise other support systems outside the group. It is also important for members to plan specific ways that they will change their behavior, thinking, feeling, and body. The focus during the final phase of group work is challenging the members to transfer their changes from the therapy situation to their daily life and then supporting them in these changes. Before members set out on their own, it is important that they fantasize about how some of their changes are likely to lead to other changes. It is well for them to prepare themselves for the new situations they will face when they leave the group and to develop support systems that will help them creatively deal with new problem situations and new successes when they arise (for example, old anxiety arising from these successes).

THE TA APPROACH TO FAMILY THERAPY

Erskine (1982) points out that TA's procedures can be adapted to a wide variety of problem areas that typically arise in families. TA provides therapeutic options for working with family members cognitively, affectively, and behaviorally. Some clients prefer to have cognitive information before they attempt behavioral changes. Others need to express feelings that they have kept inside of themselves before they are open to making either cognitive or behavioral changes. Others want to see some specific changes in their behavior before they work on feelings and belief systems. TA therapists have methods to work with families that tap all three of these dimensions of human experience.

The basic goal of TA family therapy is to work within the structure of contracts that each person in the family makes with the therapist. In general, these contracts have the aim of a functional and interdependent family structure (Erskine, 1982).

As is true of any application of TA, the contractual model places the responsibility on the client for defining personal goals and for doing the work necessary to achieve these goals. According to Erskine (1982), in TA family-therapy sessions the members are asked to respond to one another directly with their thoughts and feelings and to be open to feedback from other members. They are expected to take the responsibility for their own behavior and how it affects the family as a unit. They are also responsible for deciding when they have completed their contract and then developing a new contract or ending the therapy.

Stages in TA Family Therapy

McClendon (1977) describes three stages in working with a family from a TA perspective. In the initial stage the focus is on the dynamics of the family as a system. The therapist invites each member of the family to talk about what brings him or her to therapy and what changes are being sought. At this early stage the techniques used are designed to increase awareness of how the family is functioning as a system, of the problems facing the family, and of the possibilities for change. Early in the sessions the members establish a contract with the therapist. At this time care is taken to avoid zeroing in on an "identified patient" who may be targeted as the "problem person" in the family. Instead, the focus is on gaining a clearer picture of the *family's* problems and of how the members are interacting. The therapist is likely to explain to the family how an individual's behavior appears to be affecting both the family as a unit and another member of the family. From the outset, members are taught to ask directly for what they want and to speak directly to another family member. Rather than talking indirectly about a person in the family, the therapist asks that they begin to look at one another and make direct statements.

McClendon's second stage consists of working therapeutically with each individual. Typically this work with an individual's dynamics is done in the context of the family sessions. The therapist might begin this work by selecting the person who has the most power in the family. For example, the focus might be on the mother, and the children and father would observe the therapist working with her intrapsychic dynamics. This could include working with the parental injunctions that the mother heard, her early decisions, and her life script. This type of work done openly in a family session can be of real value to the children as well as the mother, for they can become aware of some of the ways that parental messages are passed on from one generation to the next. The mother can see how she may be shaping her present family in light of what she learned in her family of origin. Working with each family member in this way typically illuminates the connection between the mother's and the father's experiences in their respective families and the way they respond to their children. It should be noted that in practice there is some going back and forth between the first and second stage. In the course of working with one family member certain changes will probably come about that may shed new light on the dynamics of the family; the focus may then return to working with the family as a unit.

In the third stage, the aim is reintegration of the entire family. After working with the family as a system to illuminate the nature of the members' transactions with one another, therapy has progressed to working with aspects such as the rackets, injunctions, decisions, and life script of individual family members. The final stage aims at developing a family structure in which each person will have his or her needs met and at the same time the family will provide the basis for harmony. At this stage the focus is on interdependence. It is hoped that each family member will be aware of the ways his or her behavior affects others in the family and that the members will have learned how to negotiate and work in a cooperative manner. The goal is for members to function both independently and interdependently, so they can be separate persons living in a healthy family.

EVALUATION OF TRANSACTIONAL ANALYSIS

Transactional analysis provides a cognitive basis for group process that is often missing in some experientially oriented groups. The insistence of this approach on having members get out of their victimlike positions and realize that they don't have to be chained to early decisions is, I believe, crucial to effective therapy. In my opinion, TA provides a useful conceptual framework for understanding *how* these early decisions are made, how they are related to present self-defeating life stances, how games perpetuate bad feelings, and how our lives are governed by old programs and scripts.

Indeed, I consider the emphasis on becoming aware of early decisions—decisions that might have been necessary for the psychological survival of the child but that may be outmoded, even detrimental, for the adult—to be one of the major contributions of TA. As I see it, many people are enslaved by their early decisions; they cling to parental messages, they live their lives by unexamined injunctions, and frequently they are not even aware of the fact that they are living in a psychological straitjacket. Conceptually, TA offers members tools they can use to become aware of how they keep themselves from being autonomous and a framework that allows them to search for ways to free themselves from an archaic life script and achieve a successful and meaningful life.

Personally, I favor integrating TA concepts and practices with Gestalt techniques. I find that the TA concepts of injunctions, early decisions, games, and the repetition of past transactions in present transactions provide a useful direction for group therapy. The same is true of TA's emphasis on taking personal responsibility for actions and feelings, on defining personal goals, and on committing oneself to a contract that specifies how these goals will be fulfilled. I find that Gestalt techniques are helpful in getting clients to experience, in the here and now, struggles that relate to these TA concepts. Thus, for me TA provides a general framework of concepts for group work, whereas Gestalt and other action-oriented techniques provide the tools for working with these concepts.

This blending of TA with Gestalt lessens, to some extent, certain objections that I have to both therapeutic approaches. As I see it, Gestalt does not sufficiently emphasize the cognitive factors, so that it tends to leave participants with many experiences that have little meaning attached to them, whereas TA overemphasizes cognitive factors, so that it can result in therapy that is intellectually stimulating but emotionally arid.

In all fairness, I should mention that some writers are opposed to combining transactional analysis with Gestalt therapy. Simkin (1979) has warned that the blending of TA theory with some Gestalt therapy techniques can result in ineffective therapy, unless this synthesis is carried out by a gifted clinician.

From Simkin's perspective, good therapeutic work encourages clients to integrate new behavior through awareness rather than by interrupting the experiential process to focus on cognitive explanations. He adds: "Mixing what is essentially a cognitive-rational approach (TA) with what is essentially an experiential-existential approach (Gestalt therapy) is like trying to amalgamate water and oil—they simply do not mix well unless you keep shaking them continuously. The moment you stop, they begin to separate" (p. 277).

There is some research that supports the idea of combining the cognitive features of transactional analysis with the experiential emphasis of Gestalt therapy. In an encounter-group study by Lieberman, Yalom, and Miles (1973), positive outcomes of a group experience were traced to a combination of *meaning attribution* (explaining, clarifying, providing a cognitive framework for change, interpreting, and assisting members to make sense of emotional experiences) and *emotional stimulation* (catharsis, confrontation, high self-disclosure, intense emotionality, and reexperiencing of emotional situations). These researchers found that, although emotional experiences may be related to learning, such experiences are not, in themselves, sufficient and that affective experiences need to be combined with some form of cognitive learning.

I particularly favor the Gouldings' approach to group therapy, which draws on the theory of personality development from the framework of transactional analysis. Working from a theoretical base provided by TA, the Gouldings use a combination of therapeutic methods, including psychodrama, fantasy and imagery, Gestalt techniques, behavior modification, desensitization, family-therapy procedures, and psychosynthesis. For example, the value the Gouldings place on cathartic emotional experiences is evidenced by their emphasis on having clients reexperience the early scenes in which they made decisions. At the same time, the Gouldings place considerable emphasis on helping group members reach a cognitive understanding of how outmoded patterns of thinking, feeling, and behaving are interrelated and how such patterns influence their current lives. The Gouldings (1979) note that pure Gestaltists may fail to give such cognitive feedback and that pure TA therapists seldom encourage the intense emotional work that leads to breaking through those impasses that prevent further growth. In summary, the Gouldings' approach to group therapy removes most of my criticism of the TA model.

Like most of the other approaches to therapeutic groups that have been discussed so far, TA can be criticized on the ground that its theory and procedures have not been adequately subjected to empirical validation. Indeed, many of the concepts formulated by Berne were stated in such a manner that it would be impossible to design a research study to test them. It appears that most of the claims that TA works currently rest on clinical observations and testimonials. Conducting well-designed research studies to evaluate the process and outcome of group therapy has surely not been one of the strengths of TA. This is not to say that there have been no attempts to study the outcomes of TA group therapy. Some well-designed research studies are described in various issues of the *Transactional Analysis Journal*. It appears that there is increasing interest in applying research to various groups that use TA principles. Some TA therapists contend that the use of specific contracts allows for built-in accountability. Measures can be taken to determine the extent to which members have fulfilled their contract and benefited from group therapy. In my opinion, TA could benefit by integrating the commitment to research that is characteristic of behavior therapy.

A final problem I have with transactional analysis relates to the way some TA practitioners use the structure and vocabulary of this system to avoid genuine contact with their clients or to keep from revealing their reactions. Although the structure of TA can provide a useful cognitive framework for understanding behavior, that same framework can be used by the therapist to avoid person-to-person interactions and to focus on labeling ego states, structuring contracts, and directing traffic between transactions.

Also, I have observed some TA group members who seem to be using TA jargon to deceive themselves into believing that they are becoming self-actualized when, in reality, they are only learning new terms to identify old processes. Some TA clients also tend to slip into the use of jargon as an intellectual front that they can safely hide behind. In fairness, I should emphasize that the dangers of becoming lost in the structure and vocabulary of TA can be lessened by a therapist who confronts members when they are misusing the model. I see much of value in the TA model, particularly for practitioners who are willing to combine TA theory with the concepts and therapeutic techniques of other models.

For those of you who want to learn more about TA group work, I encourage you to participate in a TA workshop or a group as a member. Experiencing TA as a member could benefit you personally by bringing many of the concepts in this chapter to life in a concrete way. Also, you may want to consider attending a teaching workshop where you can apply TA principles in a group setting. For further information, contact the International Transactional Analysis Association, 1772 Vallejo Street, San Francisco, CA 94123. This association provides guidelines for becoming a Certified Clinical Member. Before certification is granted, candidates must pass both a written and an oral examination, in which samples of their work are reviewed by a board of examiners to determine their level of clinical competence.

Another source of information about training workshops in TA is the Western Institute for Group and Family Therapy in Watsonville, California. The co-directors of this institute are Mary McClure Goulding and Robert Goulding.

QUESTIONS FOR REFLECTION AND DISCUSSION

1. To what degree do you think that children are "scripted" and then destined to live out their life in accord with this script? Do you think that children actually make decisions about the messages they receive, or do you think they accept the injunctions uncritically? How does your answer influence the manner in which you would work with a group?

2. What are some of the possibilities you can see in combining TA theory with Gestalt techniques? What are the advantages, if any, of such a merger of theories?

3. What are some of the major injunctions that you were exposed to, either verbally or nonverbally? What injunctions still have an influence on you?

4. What early decisions did you make about yourself and about others during your childhood years? To what extent are these decisions still an influential factor in your life? Are you aware of making any basic changes in your early decisions?

5. If you were to join a TA group, what kind of contract do you think you'd draw up? What are the advantages and disadvantages that you can think of in insisting that all group members formulate a therapeutic contract?

6. Consider the possibility that you might be a leader of a TA group. How do you think that your patterns of games, rackets, and early decisions would affect the way in which you worked with certain members in your group? Using what you know of yourself, are there any types of member that you think you might have particular difficulty working with?

7. TA is generally a didactic model of group therapy. Would you be comfortable in the role of teaching, along with the structuring that would be expected if you were to function within this model? What aspects of this educational model might you want to incorporate into your style of group leadership, even if you did not adhere to TA theory?

8. TA is direct. As a leader you would be talking with participants about the games they play and the ways they cling to chronic bad feelings. Do you think you would be able to be direct in working with members of your group to recognize their games and help them design contracts for what they would change?

9. Compare and contrast TA with psychoanalytic therapy with respect to the group leader's role and functions. Which role seems more compatible with your leadership style and view of group counseling? Why?

10. As you know, a contract is a basic part of a TA group. How do you think you'd proceed with one or more group members who refused to negotiate a contract with you? What might you do with a member who argued that making a contract seemed rigid?

RECOMMENDED SUPPLEMENTARY READINGS

Changing lives through redecision therapy (Goulding & Goulding, 1979) is the book I would recommend to a practitioner who had time to read only one book on the TA approach to group work. The authors describe their successful integration of Gestalt and behavior-modification techniques into their TA theoretical framework.

Born to win: Transactional analysis with Gestalt experiments (James & Jongeward, 1971) is a valuable source for both laypersons and group leaders. This easy-to-read book presents an overview of the principles of transactional analysis and a description of Gestalt experiments in such diverse areas as stroking, life scripts, parenting, childhood, personal and sexual identity, game playing, adulthood, and autonomy.

Scripts people live: Transactional analysis of life scripts (Steiner, 1974) is a comprehensive discussion of life scripts that can be applied to group work.

Principles of group treatment (Berne, 1966) provides a useful discussion of group structure and process from the TA perspective.

REFERENCES AND SUGGESTED READINGS*

Barnes, G. (Ed.). *Transactional analysis after Eric Berne.* New York: Harper College Press, 1977.

Berne, E. *Transactional analysis in psychotherapy.* New York: Grove Press, 1961.

Berne, E. *Games people play.* New York: Grove Press, 1964.

* Berne, E. *Principles of group treatment.* New York: Oxford University Press, 1966.

Berne, E. *Sex in human loving.* New York: Simon & Schuster, 1970.

Berne, E. *What do you say after you say hello?* New York: Grove Press, 1972.

Dusay, J. M. Transactional analysis in groups. In H. I. Kaplan & B. J. Sadock (Eds.), *Comprehensive group psychotherapy* (2nd ed.). Baltimore: Williams and Wilkins, 1983.

Dusay, J. M., & Dusay, K. M. Transactional analysis. In R. J. Corsini (Ed.), *Current psychotherapies* (2nd ed.). Itasca, Ill.: Peacock, 1979.

Erskine, R. G. Transactional analysis and family therapy. In A. M. Horne & M. M. Ohlsen (Eds.), *Family counseling and therapy.* Itasca, Ill.: Peacock, 1982.

Gellert, S. How to reach early scenes and decisions by dream work. *Transactional Analysis Journal,* 1975, 5(4).

Gellert, S. The psychotherapist as persecutor. *Transactional Analysis Journal,* 1977, 7(2).

Gellert, S., & Wilson, G. Contracts. *Transactional Analysis Journal,* 1978, 8(1).

Goulding, M., & Goulding, R. *Changing lives through redecision therapy.* New York: Brunner/Mazel, 1979.

Goulding, R. The formation and beginning process of transactional analysis groups. In G. Gazda (Ed.), *Basic approaches to group psychotherapy and group counseling* (2nd ed.). Springfield, Ill.: Charles C Thomas, 1975.

Goulding, R. Transactional analysis/Gestalt/redecision therapy. In G. Gazda (Ed.), *Basic approaches to group psychotherapy and group counseling* (3rd ed.). Springfield, Ill.: Charles C Thomas, 1982.

Goulding, R., & Goulding, M. Injunctions, decisions, and redecisions. *Transactional Analysis Journal,* 1976, 6(1), 41–48.

Goulding, R., & Goulding, M. *The power is in the patient.* San Francisco: TA Press, 1978.

Harper, R. *The new psychotherapies.* Englewood Cliffs, N.J.: Prentice-Hall, 1975.

Harris, T. *I'm OK—You're OK.* New York: Avon, 1967.

James, M., & Jongeward, D. *Born to win: Transactional analysis with Gestalt experiments.* Reading, Mass.: Addison-Wesley, 1971.

Jongeward, D., & James, M. *Winning with people: Group exercises in transactional analysis.* Reading, Mass.: Addison-Wesley, 1973.

Jongeward, D., & Scott, D. *Women as winners: Transactional analysis for personal growth.* Reading, Mass.: Addison-Wesley, 1976.

Karpman, S. Fairy tales and script drama analysis. *Transactional Analysis Bulletin,* 1968, 7(26), 39–43.

Lieberman, M. A., Yalom, I., & Miles, M. *Encounter groups: First facts.* New York: Basic Books, 1973.

McClendon, R. My mother drives a pickup truck. In G. Barnes (Ed.), *Transactional analysis after Eric Berne.* New York: Harper & Row, 1977.

McCormick, P. *Guide for use of a life-script questionnaire in transactional analysis.* San Francisco: Trans Pub, 1971.

Meininger, J. *Success through transactional analysis.* New York: Signet (New American Library), 1973.

Prochaska, J. O. *Systems of psychotherapy: A transtheoretical analysis.* Homewood, Ill.: Dorsey, 1979.

Rudestam, K. E. *Experiential groups in theory and practice.* Monterey, Calif.: Brooks/Cole, 1982.

*Books and articles marked with an asterisk are suggested for further study.

Simkin, J. S. Gestalt therapy. In R. J. Corsini (Ed.), *Current psychotherapies* (2nd ed.). Itasca, Ill.: Peacock, 1979.

Steiner, C. A script checklist. *Transactional Analysis Bulletin,* 1967, 6(22), 38–39.

Steiner, C. *Games alcoholics play: The analysis of life scripts.* New York: Grove Press, 1971.

Steiner, C. *Scripts people live: Transactional analysis of life scripts.* New York: Grove Press, 1974.

Weisman, G. *The winner's way: A transactional analysis guide for living, working, and learning.* Monterey, Calif.: Brooks/Cole, 1980.

Woollams, S., & Brown, M. *Transactional analysis.* Dexter, Mich.: Huron Valley Institute Press, 1978.

13

BEHAVIOR THERAPY

INTRODUCTION

Behavioral approaches are becoming increasingly popular in group work. One of the reasons for this popularity is the emphasis these approaches place on teaching clients self-management skills they can use to control their lives, deal effectively with present and future problems, and function well *without* continued therapy (Krumboltz & Thoresen, 1976; Mahoney & Thoresen, 1974; Thoresen & Mahoney, 1974). Writers with a behavioral orientation, such as Watson and Tharp (1981) and Williams and Long (1983), have devoted books to the subject of helping people work toward "self-directed behavior" and a "self-managed life-style." This goal is achieved through a wide variety of cognitive and behavioral action-oriented techniques. Most of these therapeutic techniques are procedures that clients can learn and practice on their own once they leave the group-counseling situation and employ them to solve interpersonal, emotional, and decision problems (Krumboltz & Thoresen, 1976).

The here-and-now focus of contemporary behavior therapy is stressed by Linehan, Bootzin, Cautela, London, Perloff, Stuart, and Risley (1978):

> Most behaviorally-oriented therapists believe that the current environment is most important in affecting the person's present behavior. Early life experiences, long time intrapsychic conflicts, or the individual's personality structure are considered to be of less importance than what is happening in the person's life at the present time. The procedures used in behavior therapy are generally intended to improve the individual's self-control by expanding the person's skills, abilities, and independence [p. 18].

The main defining features and the basic procedures of contemporary behavior therapy are discussed by Berkowitz (1982). This approach:

- focuses on selecting target behaviors to be changed and specifying the nature of the changes desired
- studies the observable events in the environment that are maintaining the behavior
- clearly specifies both the environmental changes and the intervention strategies that can modify behavior
- insists on data-based assessment and evaluation of treatment
- asks the question "Once a new behavior is established, how can it be maintained and generalized to new situations over a period of time?"

The term *behavior therapy* refers to the application of a diversity of techniques and procedures that are rooted in a variety of learning theories. Since no single theory undergirds the practice of contemporary behavior therapy, there is no single group model that, strictly speaking, can be called a "behavioral group." Rather, there are various types of groups that operate on behavioral and learning principles. On this matter, Goldfried and Davison (1976) contend that it is undesirable to restrict the label *behavior therapy* to a single "school" of therapy that is defined in terms of a particular set of concepts and procedures. They think that behavior therapy is best conceptualized as a general orientation to clinical practice that is based upon the experimental approach to the study of behavior.

A basic assumption of the behavioral perspective is that all problematic behaviors, cognitions, and emotions have been learned and that they can be modified by new learning. Rose (1980) contends that, although this modification process is often called "therapy," it is more properly an educational experience in which individuals are involved in a teaching/learning process. It is educational in that people are taught how to view their own learning process, develop a new perspective on ways of learning, and are encouraged to try out more effective ways of changing their behaviors, cognitions, and emotions. Many of the techniques employed by groups of different orientations (such as rational-emotive therapy, reality therapy, and transactional analysis) share this basic assumption of group therapy as an educational process, and they stress the teaching/learning values inherent in a group context.

Another assumption of the behavioral orientation is that the behaviors that clients express *are* the problem (not merely symptoms of the problem). Successful resolution of these problematic behaviors resolves the problem, and a new set of problems does not necessarily arise. This behavioral perspective is in contrast to the relationship-oriented and insight-oriented approaches, which place considerable emphasis on clients' achieving insight into their problems as a prerequisite for change. Whereas the insight-oriented approaches assume that, if clients understand the nature and causes of their symptoms, they will be better able to control their life, the behavioral approach assumes that change can take place without insight. Behavior therapists operate on the premise that changes in behavior can occur prior to understanding of oneself and that behavioral changes may well lead to an increased level of self-understanding.

Group leaders who operate from a behavioral perspective draw upon a wide variety of interventions that are derived from social-learning theory, such as reinforcement, modeling, shaping, cognitive restructuring, desensitization, relaxation training, coaching, behavioral rehearsal, stimulus control, and discrimination training. However, behavioral group leaders may develop other strategies from diverse theoretical viewpoints, provided their effectiveness in meeting therapeutic goals can be demonstrated. Therefore, these leaders follow the progress of group members through the ongoing collection of data before, during, and after all interventions. Such an approach provides both the group leader and members with continuous feedback about therapeutic progress. In this sense, the behavioral leader is both a clinician and a scientist who is concerned with testing the efficacy of his or her techniques.

Advantages of a group approach. Rose (1977) has pointed out that almost all the problems that are amenable to individual therapy can also be dealt with in a group context, because they have social and interpersonal dimensions. Many problems appear to be more amenable to group therapy, and groups offer some distinct advantages over individual treatment. What follows is a summary of some of these advantages of group methods, based upon the writings of Rose (1977, 1982, 1983) and Harris (1977).

• Since most of the problems of clients are interpersonal in nature, working with other clients offers a safe and therapeutic setting for acquiring and practicing social-interactional skills. The group provides members with an intermediate step between performing newly acquired behavior in therapy and transferring this performance to everyday life. In groups there are many opportunities to simulate the real world of most clients. Rose (1982) states that evidence indicates that the more the treatment situation represents the real world, the greater is the likelihood that generalization of learning will occur. Group members can serve as models for one another, resulting in more effective learning of appropriate behaviors and interpersonal skills. Through the process of helping other members, individual participants also learn to help themselves.

• The group setting offers powerful norms to control the behavior of individuals. Examples of some positive therapeutic norms are regular attendance, commitment to evaluating and working on one's problems, and encouragement by others to stick to a plan leading to behavioral and cognitive change.

• Group work provides a setting for more accurate assessment, because members can learn how their behavior affects others through the feedback they continually receive from both the other members and the leader. Further, groups provide a natural laboratory for learning the discussion skills that are the foundation of successful interpersonal relationships.

• As a microcosm of life, the group provides both the leader and the members with opportunities to evaluate the treatment process through observations of members (Harris, 1977).

• A group setting offers a control against therapist imposition of values. Group members appear to be less willing than clients in traditional dyadic therapy to accept arbitrary values of the therapist. The support of other members makes it easier for a person to disagree with the therapist. Thus, group therapists feel some pressure to make their values explicit (Rose, 1983).

KEY CONCEPTS

Behavior therapy has some unique characteristics that set it apart from most of the other group approaches discussed in this book. Thoresen and Coates (1978) summarize these characteristics by stating that behavior therapy relies on the principles and procedures of the scientific method. This implies that its concepts and procedures are stated explicitly, tested empirically, and revised continually. Assessment and treatment occur simultaneously. Research is considered essential to providing effective treatments and to advancing beyond current therapeutic practices; the laboratory extends to the consulting room and to the community at large. The specific unique characteristics of behavior therapy are (1) a focus on overt and specific behavior, (2) the precise spelling out of treatment goals, (3) a formulation of a specific treatment procedure appropriate to a particular problem, and (4) an objective evaluation of the outcomes of therapy.

Focus on Overt and Specific Behavior

As I said earlier, behavior therapy is not based on any one organic theory. It is an inductive approach that applies the experimental method to the therapeutic process. In brief, it is a model with many techniques but few concepts. Wolpe (1969) offers this definition: "Behavior therapy, or conditioning therapy, is the use of the experimentally established principles of learning for the purpose of changing unadaptive behavior" (p. vii).

In accordance with the spirit of the experimental method, the first concern is with isolating problem behaviors and specifically defining the desired changes. The group leader asks members to specify the behaviors they want to change and the new behaviors they want to acquire. Vague and general descriptions are considered useless and therefore unacceptable.

Precise Therapeutic Goals

In most behavior-therapy groups, the initial stages are devoted to formulating specific statements of the personal goals that members want to achieve—concrete problematic behaviors they want to change and new skills they want to learn. Behaviors that clients typically want to change include reducing anxiety in test-taking situations, eliminating phobias that interfere with effective functioning, losing excessive weight, and getting rid of addictions (to smoking, alcohol, or other drugs). New skills that clients typically want to acquire include:

- learning to ask clearly and directly for what one wants
- acquiring habits that lead to physical and psychological relaxation
- developing specific methods of self-control, such as exercising regularly, controlling eating patterns, and eliminating stress
- being able to say no without feeling guilty (Smith, 1975)
- learning to be assertive without becoming aggressive
- self-monitoring one's behavior or cognitions as a means to change
- learning to give and receive both positive and negative feedback
- being able to recognize and to challenge self-destructive thought patterns or irrational self-statements

- learning communication and social skills
- developing problem-solving strategies to cope with a variety of situations encountered in daily life

The task of the leader is to help the group members break down broad, general goals into specific, concrete, measurable goals that can be pursued in a systematic fashion. For example, if a group member says that he'd like to feel more adequate in social situations, the leader asks: "In what specific ways do you feel inadequate? What are the conditions under which you feel inadequate? Can you give me some concrete examples of the situations in which you feel inadequate? In what specific ways would you like to change your behavior?" The group can be used to help the members formulate answers to these difficult questions.

Formulation of a Treatment Plan and Application of Action-Oriented Methods

After members have specified their goals, a treatment plan to achieve these goals is formulated. In many types of behavioral groups, this is not an issue, because the group is designed for specific purposes—for example, groups tailored especially for behavior control, groups for dealing with reduction of test anxiety, and assertion-training groups. However, even when the group is designed to deal with a special problem area, there is still the matter of selecting appropriate behavioral methods and procedures that will enable participants to reach their therapeutic goals.

The most commonly used strategies are those that lend themselves to group interaction, such as modeling, behavioral rehearsal, coaching, homework, feedback, training, and information giving, which are defined later in this chapter. The interested reader can pursue the topic further by consulting the books suggested in "Recommended Supplementary Readings" at the end of this chapter.

Behavioral techniques are action oriented; therefore, members are expected to *do things*, not just reflect passively and engage in deep introspection. As Thoresen and Coates (1978) indicate, although cognitive and emotional insights are valued and active listening and empathic understanding are considered crucial skills, clients must be taught to take specific action if behavior change is to occur. Some of these action-oriented methods are described by Goldfried and Davison (1976), Kanfer and Goldstein (1980), Rose (1977), Rudestam (1980), Shelton and Ackerman (1974), and Wheelis (1973).

Objective Evaluation of Outcomes and Feedback

Because target behaviors are clearly identified, treatment goals specified, and therapeutic procedures delineated, it follows that the outcomes of therapy can be objectively assessed. Because behavioral groups emphasize the importance of evaluating the effectiveness of the techniques employed, assessment of progress toward goals is an ongoing process. For example, if a group is going to meet for 20 weeks for the purpose of learning how to relax and reduce stress, baseline data are likely to be taken at the initial session on stress levels. Then, every subsequent session may include an assessment of behavioral changes, so that members can determine how successfully their behavioral objectives are being met. Providing members with ongoing feedback is a vital part of the behavioral approach.

The decision to use certain techniques is based on their demonstrated effectiveness as ascertained through ongoing evaluation. The range of these techniques is quite wide, and many behaviorally oriented group counselors are very eclectic in their choices of treatment procedures. Lazarus (1971) says: "Technical eclecticism does not imply a random melange of techniques taken haphazardly out of the air. It is an approach which urges therapists to experiment with empirically useful methods" (p. 33).

Because of this eclecticism and because of the emphasis on demonstrating the effectiveness of the techniques with a variety of client populations, certain features of behavioral counseling can be incorporated into other therapeutic approaches. Regardless of their orientation, all therapists and group leaders can learn the value of accountability from an approach that stresses the systematic use of therapeutic procedures and the continual evaluation and reassessment of such procedures.

ROLE AND FUNCTIONS OF THE GROUP LEADER

Because behavioral group counseling is considered a type of education, group leaders perform teaching functions. They are expected to assume an active, directive role in the group and to apply their knowledge of behavioral principles and skills to the resolution of problems. Thus, they carefully observe behavior to determine the conditions that are related to certain problems and the conditions that will facilitate change.

In discussing the social learning that occurs in therapy through modeling and imitation, Bandura (1969, 1977) suggests that most of the learning that takes place through direct experience can also be acquired by observing the behavior of others. In Bandura's view, one of the fundamental processes by which clients learn new behavior is imitation of the social modeling provided by the therapist. Therefore, group leaders need to be aware of the impact of their values, attitudes, and behaviors on group members. If leaders are unaware of their power in actually influencing and shaping their clients' ways of behaving, they deny the central importance of their influence as human beings in the therapeutic process.

In addition to these broad functions, the behaviorally oriented group leader is also expected to perform a number of specific functions and tasks:

• Group leaders conduct intake interviews with prospective group members, during which the preliminary assessment and orientation to the group takes place.

• Teaching participants about group process and how to get the most from the group is another leader function. The leader explains the purpose of the group, orients members to the activities and structure of the sessions, reviews the expectations of the members, and gives them suggestions on how the group can be personally useful.

• Group leaders conduct an ongoing assessment of member problems. Through procedures such as the initial interview, selected tests and inventories, and group discussion, the leader helps each member to identify target behaviors that will give the group sessions some focus. This assessment includes a summary of the major strengths, interests, and achievements of each member, as well as a summary of those behaviors the member wants to change.

• A critical function of the leader is to help group members develop specific personal and group goals.

• Leaders draw upon a wide array of techniques designed to achieve the members' stated goals.

• The leader collects data to determine the effectiveness of treatment for each member.

• A major function of leaders is serving as a model of appropriate behaviors and values. Also, leaders prepare and coach members to model by role-playing for one another how an individual might respond in a particular situation.

• Leaders provide reinforcement to members for their newly developing behavior and skills by making sure that even small achievements are recognized.

• An essential aspect of the leader's role is teaching group members that they are responsible for becoming actively involved in the group and for implementing new behaviors outside therapy. The behavioral approach demands action and a plan for change. Leaders help members understand that verbalizations and insight are not enough to produce change. To broaden their repertoire of adaptive behaviors, members must take action, experiment in the group, and practice homework assignments in real-life situations.

• The leader helps members prepare for termination. Members are reminded well ahead of the group's ending date. Thus, they have adequate time to discuss their reactions, to consolidate what they have learned, and to practice new skills they hope to apply at home and work. Appropriate referrals are made when reasonable goals have not been achieved. Suggestions are given for social activities that can help members generalize their learning in the group.

To the functions listed above, Rose (1977, 1982, 1983) adds establishing group cohesion, teaching group members self-evaluation techniques, and modifying group attributes. Rose also emphasizes that group leaders must be sensitive to and deal with group problems as they arise. Data on group satisfaction, rate of assignment completion, participation, and attendance are often collected and used as a basis for determining problems. Once the problems are identified and acknowledged by the client, they are dealt with by means of systematic problem-solving procedures (Goldfried & D'Zurilla, 1969).

Other authors advocate that group leaders gradually, as the therapeutic process advances, make the group less structured. These authors suggest that members be given the opportunity to act as discussion leaders, therapeutic partners, and models for others in the group in order to enhance their self-management skills. Rose (1983) also emphasizes the importance of delegating many leadership responsibilities to the members as the group progresses.

Role of the Therapeutic Relationship in Group Process

There appears to be a tendency on the part of some critics to see the behavioral therapist as impersonal and mechanically manipulative. Most writers in this area, however—especially Wolpe (1958, 1969)—contend that a good personal relationship between therapist and client is an essential aspect of the thera-peutic process. However, although behavior therapists don't need to be cast in the cold and impersonal role that reduces them to programmed machines, it remains that most behaviorally oriented counselors and group leaders don't assign an all-important role to the therapeutic relationship. Most of them say that factors such as warmth, empathy, and genuineness are necessary but not sufficient conditions for behavior change to occur in the therapeutic process. Counselors and leaders need skills, they must know what techniques to employ, and they must be able to determine the effects of their therapeutic procedures. In short, they must be skilled technicians who also possess the human qualities that lead to the climate of trust and care necessary for the effective use of these therapeutic techniques. Goldfried and Davison (1976) contend that factors such as the therapist's persuasiveness, ability to create positive expectations toward therapy and toward behavior change, sensitivity and warmth, willingness to model appropriate behaviors and emotions, and willingness to engage in rel-evant self-disclosure are all likely to foster therapeutic progress. They see it as the therapist's function to prepare clients for behavior change. They challenge the notion that lack of progress is due simply to client resistance or the fact that some clients are "not ready for behavior therapy." It is clear that the effective practice of behavior therapy involves a lot more than merely applying techniques to solve specific problems.

According to Goldfried and Davison (1976), the personal influence of the therapist is important both in enlisting the client's active cooperation with the therapy sessions and also in encouraging the client to try out new ways of behaving in everyday life. Further, the client/therapist relationship can promote favorable client expectations for change and receptivity toward therapy. They add:

> While it is true that behavior therapy stresses the importance of the client-therapist relationship less than do other therapeutic approaches, instead attending more to specific therapeutic procedures, this in no way implies that behavior therapists need be cold and mechanical in their clinical dealings. One may be both tender-hearted and tough-minded at the same time when it comes to clinical behavior therapy [p. 55].

Although some group practitioners may be attracted to the behavioral model because they want to be directive and play the role of the expert, this should not be viewed as an inherent fault of the approach. I do think that there is a danger in underestimating the therapeutic power of the relationship the leader has with the members if he or she becomes overly preoccupied with merely implementing techniques. In my view, these techniques will have the greatest impact if they are used within the context of a trusting relationship.

STAGES OF A BEHAVIOR-THERAPY GROUP

The book *Group Therapy: A Behavioral Approach,* by Sheldon Rose (1977), con-tains an excellent description of the principles and procedures of behavior therapy in groups and of the stages of a behaviorally oriented group. This section is a summary of the key principles and procedures discussed by Rose (1977, 1980, 1982, 1983).

Initial Stage

Since prospective clients usually know very little about behavioral programs, before they join the group they are given all the pertinent information about group process. Pregroup individual interviews and the first group session are devoted to exploring the prospective members' expectations and to helping them decide whether they will join the group. Those who decide to join receive a treatment contract. This written contract spells out what the group leader expects from the member during the course of the group, as well as what the client can expect from the group leader. The contract, which is negotiated, serves to clarify mutual expectations.

During the early stages of the group the focus is on building cohesiveness, on becoming familiar with the structure of group therapy, and on identifying problematic behaviors that need to be corrected. Since the building of cohesion is the foundation for effective work during each stage of a group's development, the leader has a central role in the establishment of trust. According to Rose (1980), the leader must initially strive to make the group attractive to its members; create group situations that require social competence on the part of the members; create many functional roles that members can play in the group; delegate the leadership responsibility to the members in a gradual and appropriate manner; present situations in which the members function as therapeutic partners for each other; control excessive group conflict; and find ways of involving all members in the group interactions. Assessment is a vital component of these early sessions, because, before treatment can begin, problems must be stated in specific behavioral terms. Complex problems are not avoided but broken down into smaller components, so that they can be dealt with more adequately in the course of the group.

Rose (1977) indicates that the problems selected for treatment must be important enough for clients to make the commitment to work daily on them. Members must also be willing to talk about these problems in the group. To assist members in identifying and describing their problems, various methods of assessment are used, some of which are pretreatment questionnaires, behavioral checklists, interviews, diaries, feedback procedures, role playing, various exercises in group, and group discussions. Included in this assessment process is a discussion of the members' assets—their strengths, their competencies, and the aspects of themselves they like—to allow participants to build on their behavioral assets. This assessment process begins at the initial group session and is refined and expanded throughout the entire life of the group.

Once problematic behaviors have been specifically defined, they are systematically observed and measured by the client and others. This procedure provides what is known as *baseline data*, or information regarding current behavior before treatment, which can be used as a reference point to compare behavior before and after treatment. Like assessment, *monitoring* (the process of collecting data) continues throughout the group's history and concludes at the follow-up interview. Both group leader and members use these data to evaluate the effectiveness of the specific techniques, the group sessions, and the course of therapy in general.

When the baseline is established, the process of setting goals and developing a treatment plan begins. Participants are asked to formulate long-range as well as intermediate goals. Through their involvement in the selection of goals, group members become active and informed participants in the process of treatment planning.

After the goals have been identified, the group leader begins to select therapeutic strategies to meet these goals. Cormier and Cormier (1979) suggest that counselors obtain a commitment from the client to do the work necessary for goal attainment, preferably in the form of a written contract. This written contract makes the process more explicit, for it specifies the procedure followed to select goals and the strategy agreed upon, both in and out of the group, to achieve these goals.

There are several reasons for having a written contract. According to Gottman and Leiblum (1974), ethical practice suggests that, in any form of treatment, clients have a right to know in advance what they are committing themselves to. An unambiguous contract promotes trust and thus helps make the therapeutic alliance operational. Also, a contract sharpens the clients' awareness of their roles as active participants in the therapeutic process (Gottman & Leiblum, 1974). Finally, the contract serves to link specific therapeutic procedures to specific goals.

Working Stage: Treatment Plan and Application of Techniques

Treatment planning involves choosing the most appropriate set of procedures from among specific strategies that have been demonstrated to be effective in achieving behavioral change. It should be emphasized that the process of *assessment, monitoring,* and *evaluation* continues throughout the working stage of a group. Group leaders must go beyond the data they initially get at the pregroup interviews and initial group sessions. They must continually evaluate the degree of effectiveness of the sessions and how well treatment goals are being attained. To make this evaluation during the working stage, group leaders continue to collect data on matters such as participation, member satisfaction, attendance, and completion of agreed-upon assignments between sessions. These assessments also include gathering data to determine whether problems exist within the group and the degree to which group goals are being attained. Throughout the course of a group, individuals monitor their behaviors and the situations in which they occur. In this way, they can quickly determine those strategies that are effective or ineffective. By means of this continuing evaluation process, both the members and the leader have a basis for looking at alternative and more effective strategies. We now turn to a description of some of these strategies that are typically used during the working stage: reinforcement, contingency contracts, modeling, behavior rehearsal, coaching, cognitive restructuring, problem solving, stress inoculation, coping-skills techniques, and the buddy system.

Reinforcement. Reinforcement is a key intervention procedure in behavioral groups. In addition to the reinforcement provided by the group leader, other members reinforce one another through praise, approval, support, and attention. Booraem and Flowers (1978) stress the value of beginning each session with member reports of success rather than failure. This sets a tone of success in the group, provides reinforcement to those who did well in everyday life, and reminds the group that change is possible. Reports of success—no matter how modest the successful attempt was—are especially important when the members are doing better than they used to but are still falling short of their expectations and when their changing behavior is met with disapproval in their everyday environments. In these cases, the reinforcement and support of the group are critical if members are to maintain their gains.

If social reinforcement is a powerful method of shaping desired behaviors, so is self-reinforcement. Participants are taught how to reinforce themselves for their progress, in order to increase their self-control and become less dependent on the reinforcement of others.

Contingency contracts. Contingency contracts spell out the behaviors to be performed, changed, or discontinued; the rewards associated with the achievement of these goals; and the conditions under which rewards are to be received. Whenever possible, contracts also specify a time period for performing the desired behaviors. Contingency contracts, however, are used more with children than adults, since some adults find them patronizing. They are also used in family therapy.

Modeling. Role modeling is one of the most powerful teaching tools available to the group leader. One of the advantages of group counseling over individual counseling is that the group situation offers members a variety of social and role models they can imitate. The modeling function is performed by both leader and participants. Since people tend to imitate more rapidly and thoroughly those with whom they share common features, modeling by peers in the group facilitates observational learning on the part of other members.

What are the characteristics of effective models? Reviews of research (Bandura, 1969) indicate that a model who is similar to the observer in age, sex, race, and attitudes is more likely to be imitated than a model who is unlike the observer. Models who have a degree of prestige and status are more likely to be imitated than those who have a low level of prestige. If the client is too different from the model in many of these characteristics, the client tends to perceive the model's behavior as unrealistic. Also, models who are competent in their performance and who exhibit warmth tend to increase modeling effects. As much as possible, models should be reinforced in the presence of the observer, and observers should be reinforced for their imitation of the behavior that is modeled. Modeling of specific behavior is carried out in role plays during the sessions and *in vivo.* Modeling methods are used in groups for assertion training and in self-instructional training (teaching clients how to make more constructive self-statements and changing cognitive structures). The effect of modeling is enhanced by three other procedures: behavior rehearsal, coaching, and group feedback (Rose, 1982).

Behavior rehearsal. Most behavioral procedures involve some form of practice in which clients rehearse goal behaviors. The aim of behavior rehearsal is to prepare members to perform the desired behaviors outside the group, when modeling cues will not be available. New behaviors are practiced in a safe context that simulates the real world. Not only are members protected from adverse consequences while they are learning, but they can also benefit from positive reinforcement, which is likely to increase their willingness to experiment with the new behavior in their daily life (Rose, 1977). Cormier and Cormier (1979) point out that the actual practice of desirable behaviors should take place under conditions that are as similar as possible to the situations that occur in the client's environment, so that maximum generalization from the group to the real world will take place.

Behavior rehearsal, which can be thought of as a gradual shaping process, is a useful technique in teaching social skills. As Goldfried and Davison (1976) indicate, effective social interaction includes many behavioral components besides simply knowing *what* to say in a particular social situation. Specific factors such as vocal quality, rate of speech, gestures, body posture, eye contact, and other mannerisms are significant aspects. Goldfried and Davison suggest that it is wise to select only a few of these specific behaviors at a given time during a behavior rehearsal. They add that feedback is a useful mechanism of change during behavior rehearsals. This feedback can include the member's own subjective evaluation (which can be aided by either audio or videotaped replays of the rehearsal), the leader's commentary, and the reactions of other group members. As much as possible, Goldfried and Davison would like to see clients evaluate the adequacy of their own behavioral rehearsals, for this can help them learn to become more sensitive to their behavior and take corrective actions between sessions. Once members achieve successful performance in the group situation, they need to be made aware that application in real life is a basic part of behavior rehearsal. This can be accomplished by reminding members of the importance of completing homework assignments, by devoting some time in each session to deciding upon appropriate assignments, and by routinely beginning each group session by checking on the assignments of each member.

Coaching. In addition to the use of modeling and behavior rehearsal, group members sometimes require *coaching* (a technique that provides them with information about the appropriateness of their behavior). Coaching seems to work best when the coach sits behind the individual engaged in the behavior rehearsal. When a member is stuck and does not know how to proceed, another group member can serve as a coach by whispering suggestions. It is important when coaching is used, however, that it be reduced in subsequent role plays and that the member try out independent performances before trying out a new role in the real world.

Cognitive restructuring.   An individual's cognitive processes are likely to have implications for behavior change. Indeed, group members often reveal self-defeating thoughts and irrational self-talk when they find themselves in stressful situations. *Cognitive restructuring* is the process of identifying and evaluating one's cognitions, understanding the negative behavioral impact of certain thoughts, and learning to replace these cognitions with more realistic and appropriate thoughts. Ellis (1962) and Ellis and Harper (1975) have described in detail ways to identify self-defeating thinking, methods of sabotaging and undermining such irrational thinking, and methods of learning how to substitute rational thoughts in the place of irrational ones. Rose (1977) describes several forms of cognitive restructuring. Some clients suffer from acute anxiety because they lack correct information, because they have difficulty in controlling thoughts, because they cling to irrational and self-defeating beliefs, or because they have assigned self-deprecating labels to themselves. To manage such anxiety, clients can use certain strategies to change their cognitive processes. These procedures include providing corrective information, learning to control one's thoughts, dispelling irrational beliefs, and relabeling oneself.

Elsewhere, Rose (1983) describes the process of cognitive restructuring as applied to group work. Initially, members might be taught through group exercises how to differentiate between self-defeating and self-enhancing statements. Typically, group members provide one another with feedback and various models of a cognitive analysis. A further step is to encourage participants to devise self-enhancing statements that promote problem solving or effective actions. After clients decide on a set of realistic cognitive statements, then cognitive modeling is used, in which the members imagine themselves in stressful situations. They substitute self-enhancing statements for self-defeating remarks. In cognitive rehearsal, members go through similar steps as the model, and they get feedback from others in the group. After several trials in the group, members are given the assignment to practice a new set of statements at home before they try out a new style in the real world. In the final step of cognitive restructuring, homework is assigned at the end of each session and then monitored at the beginning of the following session. As members make progress, assignments can be developed at successive levels of difficulty.

Problem solving.   Problem solving is a cognitive-behavioral approach that enables individuals to develop a pattern of behavior to deal with various problems. The main goal of problem solving is to identify the most effective alternative to a particular problem situation and to provide systematic training in cognitive and behavioral skills that will help the client deal independently with problem situations in the real world. The stages in the problem-solving process are described by Goldfried and Davison (1976):

1. Training begins with a general orientation to the problem. At this time, clients are helped to understand why certain problem situations are likely to

occur and given the expectation that they can learn ways of effectively coping with these problems.

2. The next step consists of teaching clients to be specific in describing the *external* events leading to the problem situation as well as the *internal* events (thoughts and feelings). Clients define the problem situation, and then they formulate the problem by identifying their major goals and the aspects that make the situation problematic for them.

3. The suggestion of alternatives follows the formulation of the problem. Clients are instructed to brainstorm possible solutions and come up with diverse ways of coping with the situation.

4. After clients have identified most of the available responses, they are ready to make some decision about the best strategy to pursue. It is the client's task to predict which of the possible alternatives is the best to follow. In making this decision, it is often helpful for clients to consider the possible consequences of carrying out a particular course of action.

5. Following the decision-making phase, clients should be encouraged to take action on this decision and then to *verify* the degree of effectiveness of their course of action. This verification phase consists of having clients observe and evaluate the consequences of their actions in the real world.

Goldfried and Davison (1976) write that procedures such as modeling, coaching, and reinforcement are used during problem-solving training. Further, once clients have had an opportunity to observe the therapist (or other models) demonstrate effective problem-solving procedures, they should assume a more active role in problem solving. At this time, the therapist functions largely as a consultant who asks and answers questions, provides guidance, gives feedback, and encourages and evaluates real-life applications. Throughout this process, clients are taught self-control techniques, and they are encouraged to reinforce their own successful performance.

Stress inoculation.   Designed primarily by Meichenbaum (1977), stress inoculation has the purpose of providing members with a set of skills to effectively deal with future stressful situations. This procedure involves three phases: First is the educational phase, which is designed to provide clients with a conceptual framework for understanding the nature of their stressful reactions. In the second phase, clients practice specific cognitive and behavioral coping techniques and rehearse new skills. In the final phase, members are helped to apply the training and the new cognitive and behavioral skills they have acquired to varied stressful situations they encounter in everyday living. Stress-inoculation training typically includes a variety of therapy techniques. Some of these procedures are didactic training, discussion, cognitive and overt modeling, self-instructional and behavioral rehearsal, and reinforcement.

Coping-skills techniques.   A number of other, more general behavioral strategies have been found effective in coping with both specific and general stress situations. An example of a coping-skill strategy is relaxation training. Meichenbaum (1977) outlines a five-step treatment procedure that is used in teaching coping skills. First, clients are exposed to anxiety-provoking situations by means of imagery or by role playing. Then they evaluate their anxiety level. Clients also notice the anxiety-provoking cognitions they experience in the situation. The next step consists of a rational reevaluation of their cognitions or self-statements. Finally, clients note their level of anxiety after the rational reevaluation.

The buddy system.   Rose (1977) makes reference to the "buddy system" as a form of therapeutic alliance between members. Typically, a client is assigned or chooses another as a monitor and coach throughout the group-treatment process. Thus, the members monitor each other's behavior in the group, remind each other between meetings to stick to their commitments and practice their assignments, and play a supportive role both in and out of the group. This support system can be of value when members encounter setbacks or other difficulties in implementing their treatment program. Rose contends that the most important part of treatment occurs outside of the group with the practice of homework assignments in between sessions. Buddies can provide the needed support to actually carry out these assignments.

Final Stage

During the final stage of the behavioral group, the leader is primarily concerned with having members transfer the changes they have exhibited in the group to their everyday environment. Behaviorally oriented group leaders do not expect this generalization to occur by chance, so they structure the sessions in such a way that transfer of learning will be maximized and the newly acquired skills will be maintained after the group terminates.

Practice sessions involving simulations of the real world are used to promote transfer. Mischel (1971) observes that "generalization is enhanced to the degree that the stimulus conditions sampled in treatment are similar to those in the life situation in which the new behaviors will be used" (p. 468). Thus, in these practice situations, members rehearse what they want to say to significant people in their life, anticipate possible setbacks, prepare themselves for dealing with people who may be antagonistic toward their changed behavior, and practice alternative behaviors. Feedback from others in the group, along with coaching, can be of the utmost value at this final stage of group.

Training in leadership and independence is stressed by Rose (1977), who writes that "responsibility for each step of treatment gradually is delegated to the group as a whole and ultimately to the individual client" (p. 162). Although self-responsibility is emphasized throughout the life of the group, it is especially critical in planning for termination. Rose sums this up well when he writes: "The more practice the therapist can give in self-planning, the greater the likelihood that the client will be able to develop his or her own treatment plans as the inevitable new problem arises" (p. 162). Rose (1983) maintains that the leader's role changes from direct therapist to consultant in the final stage. Members are typically encouraged to join various social groups where they can practice and develop their newly acquired skills under less controlled conditions than the group. In addition, they are taught self-help cognitive skills such as self-reinforcement and problem solving as a way of preparing them for situations they have not encountered in the group. This move toward member independence from the group is essential if clients are to gain confidence in their ability to cope effectively with new problems. As the time of termination approaches, many of the initial assessment instruments are repeated as a way of evaluating the effectiveness of the group program.

Termination and follow-up are issues of special concern to behaviorally oriented group leaders. Gottman and Leiblum (1974) suggest that, if therapy continues too long, it may result in excessive dependency but that, if it ends too soon—before learning has transferred to extratherapy situations—it may have little lasting impact on the client. They add that, although therapy cannot and does not have to deal with all the actual and potential problems of clients, ideally, at the termination of their treatment, clients will have resolved some specific problems and learned more effective methods of coping with future ones.

The group leader is typically interested in what happens to clients after the termination of the group. Therefore, short- and long-term follow-up interviews are scheduled for a number of purposes: to compare the client's performance of the goal behavior before and after counseling, to determine the extent to which clients can use their newly acquired behaviors in their environment without relying on counseling, and to determine the extent to which clients have maintained desired behaviors and avoided undesired ones (Cormier & Cormier, 1979).

Gottman and Leiblum (1974) recommend arranging for a follow-up interview three, six, or twelve months after termination to assess how the client is performing. Rose (1977) claims that follow-up interviews and follow-up group sessions serve as "booster shots" for maintaining the changed behaviors and continuing to engage in self-directed change programs. In preparation for these postgroup meetings, Rose suggests giving assignments that clients can report on. Knowing that they will be accountable, clients feel some pressure to maintain and use the discipline they learned in the group. Members are encouraged to make use of their buddies and to discover alternative resources (which may include other groups or other forms of counseling) for continuing their progress.

APPLICATIONS AND TECHNIQUES

As was mentioned earlier, the behavior therapist uses a variety of specific techniques that can be systematically employed in a group setting and whose results can be objectively evaluated. Thus, through this process the techniques can be continually refined for therapeutic effectiveness. The use of techniques varies with the clients and/or problems the group deals with. There are behavioral groups for managing anxiety and stress; for dealing with depression; for controlling specific behaviors such as excessive drinking, eating, and smoking; for teaching people how to be more effective in interpersonal relating; and for treating specific fears—to mention a few. Behavior therapy in groups can be applied to a variety of settings, such as schools, mental hospitals, day-treatment centers, community clinics, and prisons. Entire volumes have been devoted to the principles and applications of behavior modification in various settings, with various populations, and for specific problems; the work of Craighead, Kazdin, and Mahoney (1976) is just one example.

In this section I'll describe some common behavioral techniques that are applicable to group work. For the purpose of this discussion, the techniques have been grouped under three general types of behavioral groups: (1) assertion-training groups, (2) groups for self-directed behavior change, and (3) the multimodal group therapy of Lazarus.

Assertion-Training Groups

A behavioral approach that has gained increasing popularity is assertion training—teaching people how to be assertive in a variety of social situations. For those who are interested in learning the specifics of planning, setting up, conducting, and evaluating assertion-training groups, a number of excellent sources are available, including Alberti and Emmons (1975, 1978), Cotler and Guerra (1976), Fensterheim and Baer (1975), Hall and Rose (1980), Lazarus and Fay (1975), and Smith (1975). An especially useful book is *Approaches to Assertion Training*, a collection of articles edited by Whiteley and Flowers (1978). It discusses the rationale and philosophy of assertion training and describes specific procedures and steps used in assertion-training groups. Also covered are applications to special problems and populations and approaches to evaluation and assessment.

Basic philosophy. The basic assumption underlying the practice of assertion training is that people have the right—mind you, not the obligation—to express their feelings, thoughts, beliefs, and attitudes. As Lange, Rimm, and Loxley (1978) have pointed out, "There is no law that says one *has* to be assertive," and clients shouldn't come to believe that they must be assertive in *all* social situations. Thus, the goal of assertion training is to increase the group members' behavioral repertoire so that they can make the *choice* of being assertive or not. Booraem and Flowers (1978) underscore the element of choice: "Many people cannot choose to be assertive because of anxiety, behavioral deficits, interfering cognitions, or any combination of these. The purpose of assertion training is to provide clients with the assertion alternative, which the client may then choose whether or not to exercise" (p. 17).

Another goal of assertion training is teaching people how to express themselves in a way that reflects sensitivity to the feelings and rights of others. The truly assertive individual does not rigidly stand up for his or her rights at all costs, riding roughshod over the feelings and opinions of others.

The purpose of assertion-training groups. Assertion training can be helpful for people who cannot ask others for what they want, who are unable to resist inappropriate demands, who have difficulty expressing feelings of love, gratitude, and approval as well as feelings of irritation, anger, and disagreement, and who feel that they don't have a right to have their own feelings and thoughts. Assertion training attempts to equip people with the skills and attitudes necessary to deal effectively with a wide range of interpersonal situations. The specific outcome goals of the training include:

- recognizing and changing self-defeating or irrational beliefs concerning one's right to be assertive
- developing an attitude that places value on one's right to express oneself *and* on the respect for the rights of others
- learning how to identify and discriminate among assertive, aggressive, and nonassertive behaviors
- increasing one's self-esteem to the point of becoming capable of taking the initiative
- being able to apply newly learned assertive skills to specific interpersonal situations

Conducting an assertion-training group.   Cotler (1976, 1978) provides some guidelines for setting up and conducting an assertion-training group. He suggests that the co-leader model (using a woman and a man) offers distinct advantages over the single-leader model because of the greater opportunities for modeling and coaching that the former provides. Cotler stresses the need, during the early stages of the group, to teach participants the general philosophy of assertion training. He gives several case examples to illustrate unassertive, aggressive, and assertive behavior and suggests ways of dealing with problem situations. Cotler also describes the goals of the group and the kinds of procedure used to help members reach their goals, such as role playing, coaching, behavior rehearsal, homework assignments, record keeping, and working in small steps.

Lange et al. (1978) describe in detail the format they use in their assertion-training groups. A group of eight to twelve participants meets once a week for two hours for about six to nine weeks. Like Cotler, Lange et al. use a co-leading model. In the first session they utilize structured exercises to create a trusting atmosphere and to encourage involvement on the part of the members. Also in the first session, they prepare the members for the cognitive and behavioral procedures that will be used.

The second session is devoted to developing a framework for valuing one's right to self-expression and for learning to identify and discriminate among assertive, unassertive, and aggressive responses. Structured exercises are employed, and members practice these responses after viewing films and/or listening to audio tapes.

The third session deals with cognitive-restructuring procedures. Typically, nonassertive individuals engage in irrational and self-defeating thoughts and self-verbalizations that contribute to their lack of assertiveness. Ellis (1962; Ellis & Harper, 1975) describes a method for dealing with and correcting these self-defeating attitudes and practices. This method attempts to make the participants aware of how their misconceptions and self-verbalizations can negatively influence their feelings and behavior. Exercises are used to help members see the connection between their beliefs and their feelings and behaviors. Awareness of such a connection is the first step toward actually replacing faulty beliefs and attitudes with more effective ones that recognize the value of assertiveness.

In the fourth session, members learn to initiate assertive behaviors instead of playing the role of passive responders. Exercises are employed to teach people how to initiate and maintain a conversation, how to deal with their fears in interpersonal situations, and how to make and refuse requests.

The remaining sessions are devoted to applying cognitive and behavioral techniques to specific real-life situations described to the group by the participants. Lange et al. (1978) use role-playing procedures to have the group members enact their typical behaviors in these situations, so that the behaviors can be evaluated by the group. Leader and participants offer feedback, stress the positive aspects they have observed, and make suggestions for change. The client then replays the situation trying to use new and more effective behaviors.

Booraem and Flowers (1978) describe a procedural model that uses a number of elements already described in this chapter—namely, behavior rehearsal, coaching, modeling, reinforcement, self-reinforcement, homework, and cognitive restructuring. They also use the techniques of formulating a hierarchy for practice and desensitization, as well as discrimination learning.

1. *Formulation of a hierarchy.* Group members formulate a list of situations requiring assertiveness, arranged in order of their performance anxiety. The members use this list to practice behavior rehearsals. Following the desensitization model, they begin with the items that generate the least discomfort and gradually proceed to situations that involve greater anxiety. They systematically rehearse situations in this hierarchy and proceed only when they feel satisfied with their performance—that is, when they are able to remain in a relaxed state while imagining the situation that used to produce anxiety. This model requires action on the part of the participants, for they practice, role-play, and rehearse actual situations. The model provides a graded approach that allows members to be successful by actually experiencing themselves becoming increasingly assertive.

2. *Discrimination learning.* Through the process of discrimination learning, participants become aware of the distinction among nonassertive, assertive, and aggressive responses. (For a detailed treatment of these differences see Alberti & Emmons, 1975, 1978.) Participants are taught to make these discriminations by observing the leader and other members model examples of each and by receiving direct teaching based on such examples of behavior styles. During the role-playing situations, members are given feedback concerning the degree to which they are perceived as assertive, aggressive, or nonassertive.

Another procedure for learning to determine the appropriateness of one's responses is keeping a record of one's assertive, unassertive, and aggressive behaviors outside the group. Participants are asked to keep a weekly diary of situations involving refusals, requests, and other transactions and to note especially those situations in which they would like to improve their assertive skills. Many of these situations are then role-played, coached, and discussed during the group sessions (Cotler & Guerra, 1976).

Target populations.   Assertion training can be applied to a variety of group populations. In a study of assertion-training programs in small groups, Rose (1977) concluded that this approach "now represents a well-defined and tested set of principles available to clinicians and clinical populations at nearly every level of sophistication" (p. 201). Assertion training is used to help people develop assertive behavior in work situations, marriage, sex, social situations, and family life (Fensterheim & Baer, 1975).

Alberti (1977) devotes a major section of his excellent book *Assertiveness: Innovations, Applications, Issues* to the applications of assertion training. Some of the client populations with which the approach has proved successful are children, adolescents, juvenile delinquents, married couples, divorced people, alcoholics, and people with phobias. The model has also been applied as an aid to weight control and as a way of helping people find jobs and overcome job dissatisfaction.

Whiteley and Flowers (1978) describe assertion-training programs for suicidal and depressed clients, sexual-assertiveness workshops for women, assertion training for the elderly, and assertion training as an adjunct to ongoing group therapy and as an entry strategy for consultation with school administrators. Generally speaking, the technique seems to offer unique benefits for those with social-skill deficits and for those who need to develop greater social-interactional skills. As indicated earlier, these programs draw on a variety of behavioral techniques to accomplish specific objectives in a group format.

Ethical principles.   As assertion training has gained in popularity in the last few years, responsible practitioners have expressed concern about the possible misuse of this counseling technique. Some of the areas of concern are unqualified trainers, illegitimate purposes, and application in inappropriate circumstances (Alberti, 1977). A statement of "principles for ethical practice of assertive-behavior training," developed by a group of nationally recognized assertion-training professionals, is presented in Alberti (1977). This document has important implications for those who lead assertion-training groups, especially with regard to the issue of client self-determination. Here are some of the specific guidelines contained in the above statement:

- Clients should be fully informed in advance of all procedures to be utilized.
- Clients should be given the freedom to participate or not to participate in certain activities.
- Clients should be provided with clear definitions of assertion training and assertiveness.
- Clients should be fully informed of the education, training, experience, and qualifications of the leader(s).
- Clients should be told what the goals and potential outcomes of assertion training are, including the risks involved and possible negative reactions from others.
- Clients should be made clearly aware of the respective responsibilities of leader(s) and client(s).
- Clients should be informed of the ethical guidelines concerning confidentiality in the specific training setting.

Groups for Self-Directed Behavior Change

There is a trend toward "giving psychology away"—that is, a tendency to teach people how to apply interpersonal skills to their everyday life. This trend implies that psychologists will share their knowledge with consumers so that people can lead increasingly *self*-directed lives and not be dependent on the experts for the effective management of the problems they encounter. Psychologists who share this perspective are concerned primarily with teaching people the skills they will need for self-direction.

Behaviorally oriented groups offer great promise for those who want to learn the skills necessary for a "self-managed life-style," to use Williams and Long's (1983) phrase. Areas in which one can learn to control behavior and bring about self-directed change are excessive eating, drinking, and smoking and inadequate self-discipline at work or in school. Some people cannot accomplish certain goals in their work because their efforts are hindered by lack of organization; they don't know where to begin with a project, how to sustain their efforts, and how to avoid the crippling discouragement they experience when they fail to attain their goals. It is in these and similar areas that behavioral groups for self-directed change can provide the guidelines and planning necessary to bring about change.

There are some excellent books on self-directed behavior and its implications for group work. One of the best is *Self-Directed Behavior: Self-Modification for Personal Adjustment,* by Watson and Tharp (1981). Other useful sources are Jeffery and Katz (1977), Mahoney and Thoresen (1974), Rudestam (1980), Thoresen and Mahoney (1974), and Williams and Long (1983).

Steps in self-directed change. Watson and Tharp (1981) describe a model designed for self-directed change. The steps they outline can be easily adapted to the needs of a group for behavior control. The steps are as follows:

1. *Selecting goals.* The initial stage is devoted to specifying the goals to be attained—that is, the specific changes that clients want to make. Goals should be established one at a time, and they should be measurable, attainable, positive, and significant for the person.

2. *Translating goals into target behaviors.* This step consists of defining the specific behaviors that will lead to the goals selected during the initial stage. Questions that need to be asked and answered are: What specific behaviors do I want to increase? What behaviors do I want to decrease? How can I reach my goals?

3. *Making observations about target behaviors.* This step requires focusing attention on behavior. It involves maintaining a record of behaviors, keeping track of certain behaviors and of the feelings associated with them, and assessing the behaviors.

4. *Developing a plan for change.* The next step leading to self-directed change involves formulating a plan for change. This entails negotiating a working contract and actually doing whatever is necessary to effect change. A successful plan cannot be vague and is characterized by these four features:

- *rules* that state the kinds of technique needed to bring about change in specific situations

- *goals and subgoals*, which should be stated precisely enough to be measured against performance
- *feedback*—namely, information concerning the level of performance based
  on self-observations and recording of behavior
- *checking of feedback against goals and subgoals*, in order to measure progress and determine whether the techniques being used are actually working

5. *Revising the plan.* Plans are revised to keep them functional as the person's
knowledge increases. They are always kept open because, as people learn how
to observe and evaluate their own behavior, they may devise a more effective
plan for change.

These systematic steps can be incorporated into the process of any group
whose members are working on goals they have formulated themselves. The
model can be usefully employed to eliminate undesirable behaviors and to
acquire new behavior patterns. The advantage of the group approach is that
members can reinforce and assist one another by making suggestions about
desirable changes, by offering constructive feedback, and by helping other
members set realistic goals. The buddy system is very supportive when members are experiencing problems as they try to apply to their everyday lives what
they are learning in the group. Also, members can profit from the plans that
others in the group devise and carry out; by observing others, they will be
stimulated to think creatively about changes they want to make for themselves
and about specific ways to make their plan work.

An example of a self-control group.   Kindy and Patterson (1980) designed
a group for clients who were 15 to 20 percent over their ideal weight. The main
purpose of the group was to teach members cognitive-behavioral self-control
skills that would enable them to change effectively those behaviors that had
contributed to their weight problem. Another goal was to train members in
autonomous problem-solving skills so that they could continue to control their
weight once they finished the program.

The group in the Kindy and Patterson (1980) study had six training sessions
with two follow-up sessions at three- and four-week intervals. Before the initial
group meeting, members were asked to complete a questionnaire and then
schedule a pregroup interview to review the information on the questionnaire
and discuss other pertinent matters. During the pregroup interview, members
completed a "weight-loss checklist" and were asked to monitor food intake
and various associated stimuli for four days before the initial group session.
This checklist and the pregroup monitoring provided baseline data for food
intake, identified appropriate and inappropriate eating patterns, and helped
orient members to the group treatment.

The group was designed to allow members to learn the verbal and behavioral
self-control skills in a relatively short time. The training sequence for new skills
in each session was set up to provide a cognitive framework for each skill by
teaching the principles involved in the skill, provide modeling of the application of the skill, and provide practice in the skill through procedures such as
written exercises and homework assignments.

Each of the group sessions had the following general structure:

- At the beginning of the session, each member was weighed, and his or her assignment was checked.
- The leaders gave out an agenda of behavioral goals, treatment procedures, and assignments. There was a review of key points from the previous session, and members had a chance to raise questions about the readings or their assignment.
- The leaders prompted a discussion among the members based on the results of the assignments. The approach of problem solving was typically used when a member identified a problem in keeping to the self-control program.
- The leaders gave a brief lecture on some salient concepts in the assigned readings or on new self-control skills.
- With the group's help, each member developed a specific plan designed to lead to behavioral change. These plans formed the basis of homework assignments for the week.
- At the end of each session, members were given their assignments and asked to evaluate the session.

A few points about this behavioral-cognitive program will be highlighted. Each member signed a weight-loss group contract that contained several specific expectations. Some of these were contacting one's buddy to monitor the weekly plan, coming to all of the sessions, and making specific plans for maintaining weight loss once the program had terminated. The members understood that this program involved a three-part plan of environmental control, reduction of caloric intake, and exercise. They also realized that they had to be active and to cooperate if the program were to be effective. It was up to each member to determine his or her own changes in life-style that would make it possible to lose weight. The members were expected to select their own goals, translate these goals into target behaviors, make observations about these behaviors, and develop a plan for change. The group process was particularly valuable in helping members develop realistic plans and revise them. Members learned not only from direct practice of new cognitive and behavioral skills but also from the modeling of their peers.

Multimodal Group Therapy

The previously described models of behavioral group therapy tend to be short term (6 to 12 sessions) and tend to deal with a homogeneous population. For example, assertion-training groups are short term, and the members are alike in wanting to learn ways of being assertive. Likewise, many of the self-directed groups are homogeneous in nature, and the treatment program is relatively brief. Members are taught skills they can apply in a program once they complete the group. The multimodal approach tends to be of longer duration and organizationally more like other forms of long-term group therapy. It also tends to be more heterogeneous, because time is available to permit greater individualization.

Lazarus has moved from a conceptualization of "broad spectrum behavior therapy" to "multimodal behavior therapy" (1971, 1981). Although most of the writing about multimodal therapy has been from the perspective of individual psychotherapy, Lazarus' formulation can be applied to group counseling and therapy (see Lazarus, 1982). A brief discussion of this approach is included in this chapter because of its potential to include all the major areas of personality functioning in group treatment. Multimodal group therapy takes into consideration the *whole person*.

The essence of Lazarus' multimodal approach is the premise that human beings are complex in that they move, feel, sense, imagine, think, and relate. According to Lazarus (1981), there are seven major areas of personality functioning: behavior, affective responses, sensations, images, cognitions, interpersonal relationships, and biological function. Although these modalities are interactive, they can be considered discrete functions and defended as useful divisions (Roberts, Jackson, & Phelps, 1980).

The multimodal therapist takes the view that a complete assessment and treatment program must account for each modality of the BASIC ID. Thus, the BASIC ID is the cognitive map that ensures that each aspect of personality receives explicit and systematic attention (Lazarus, 1981). Further, comprehensive therapy entails the correction of irrational beliefs, deviant behaviors, unpleasant feelings, bothersome images, stressful relationships, negative sensations, and possible biochemical imbalances. It is assumed that, since clients are troubled by a number of specific problems, it is best to employ a number of specific treatments. Multimodal therapists believe that, the more clients learn in therapy, the less likely it is that old problems will reoccur. Enduring change is seen as a function of combined techniques, strategies, and modalities.

There are some other basic assumptions underlying multimodal therapy. First, therapists must be effective as a person. Second, they need a range of skills and techniques to deal with the range of problems posed by their clients. Third, they must have "technical eclecticism"; that is, they should be able to employ any techniques that have been demonstrated to be effective in dealing with specific problems (Roberts et al., 1980). As Lazarus (1981, p. 13) says:

> The first letters of each of these modalities form the acronym BASIC IB. If we call the biological modality "D," for "Drugs," we have the more compelling acronym BASIC ID. (It is important to remember that "D" stands for much more than drugs, medication, or pharmacological intervention, but also includes nutrition, hygiene, exercise, and the panoply of medical diagnoses and interventions that affect personality.)

In multimodal group therapy, the process begins with a comprehensive assessment of all the modalities of human function. A modification of Lazarus' (1982) description of this first phase of group therapy is given below. Members are asked questions pertaining to the BASIC ID:

> *Behavior.* What are your chief strengths? What specific behaviors are keeping you from getting what you want? What would you like to change? What behaviors would you like to decrease or eliminate? What behaviors would you like to increase or acquire?
>
> *Affect.* What makes you laugh? What makes you sad? What are some emotions that are problematic for you?

Sensation. Do you suffer from unpleasant sensations, such as pains, aches, dizziness, and so forth? What do you particularly like or dislike in the way of seeing, smelling, hearing, touching, and tasting?

Imagery. How do you view your body? How do you see yourself now? How would you like to be able to see yourself in the future?

Cognition. What are the values that are most significant in your life? What are some ways that you meet your intellectual needs? What are the main "shoulds," "oughts," and "musts" in your life? Do they get in the way of effective living for you?

Interpersonal. What do you expect from the significant others in your life? What do they expect of you? What do you give to these people, and what do you get from them? Are there any relationships with others that you would hope to change? If so, what changes would you like to see?

Drugs. What is the state of your health? Do you take any prescribed drugs? What are your habits pertaining to diet and exercise?

It should not be thought that the above list is a complete representation of the BASIC ID, but a preliminary investigation into a client's BASIC ID brings out some central and significant themes that can be productively explored in a group. The preliminary questioning is followed by a detailed life-history questionnaire. Once the main profile of a person's BASIC ID has been established, the next step consists of an examination of the interactions among the different modalities. This second phase of work intensifies specific facets of the person's problem areas and permits the group therapist to understand the person more fully as well as devise effective coping and treatment strategies.

Lazarus (1982) believes that it is best to form groups that are relatively homogeneous with respect to problem areas and goals. Examples include people who are interested in learning to become more assertive, people who are concerned with weight loss, couples who are interested in improving the communication in their relationship, and individuals who want to quit smoking. Group therapy is seen as particularly appropriate (and the treatment of choice) when there is some reason to believe that other people will enhance the processes of learning, unlearning, and relearning. If the BASIC ID assessment reveals that the client has a negative self-image and feelings of inadequacy, then multimodal group therapy can be useful. Likewise, for clients whose assessment reveals interpersonal difficulties, group therapy would offer some distinct advantages over individual treatment.

It is Lazarus' (1982) position that a time-limited group (of approximately 20 sessions) appears to be the most effective format. When the group ends, members might become involved in individual therapy or become a member of another group. Lazarus has found that this format encourages the most active learning, unlearning, and relearning, the basis of multimodal methods. In terms of the methods that are used in the group sessions, Lazarus endorses an eclectic position. Thus, discussion, role playing, relaxation exercises, behavior rehearsal, cognitive restructuring, modeling, assertion-training exercises, and identifying feelings are but a few of the techniques employed. Lazarus emphasizes, however, that most substantial changes occur outside of the group; therefore, he relies heavily upon homework assignments and other performance-based methods, rather than relying exclusively on verbal and cognitive procedures. (For a more detailed discussion of these procedures, see Lazarus, 1981.)

The multimodal therapist tends to be very active during group sessions. Leaders function as trainers, educators, consultants, facilitators, and role models. They provide information, instruction, and feedback. Leaders also serve an important function by modeling assertive behaviors in the group, challenging self-defeating beliefs, offering constructive criticism and suggestions, offering positive reinforcements, and being appropriately self-disclosing. The multimodal approach to group work requires that the leader be flexible in using various methods and in conducting the group.

Brunell (1978) has discussed the multimodal treatment model as the basis for designing programs to meet specific problems in a mental hospital. According to Brunell, its major advantage in the hospital setting is that it provides a systematic framework for conceptualizing the presenting problems of the patients. The model encompasses specific goals, specifies treatment techniques to meet these goals, and provides a basis for systematic evaluation of the relative effectiveness of these therapeutic procedures. Another advantage of the multimodal approach is that the large pool of therapeutic resources available in a mental hospital can be used to meet the diverse needs of the population.

There are also applications of Lazarus' multimodal therapy model for an entire clinical service-delivery unit, as described by Roberts et al. (1980). The whole therapy program of a day-treatment program was subjected to a multimodal evaluation. Only those therapeutic interventions that passed muster with regard to multimodal analysis were kept in the program. The overall therapy program included group therapy, family therapy, a women's group, a communication group, couples therapy, dance therapy, assertion training, relaxation training, and other forms of traditional treatment. Roberts et al. found that, from an administrative and organizational perspective, the multimodal model was very useful in generating critical analysis and research as it applied to their service delivery system.

In summary, one of the values of the multimodal approach to group work is that it does provide a comprehensive view of assessment and treatment. It allows for the incorporation of diverse techniques. If a technique is proven effective for a given problem, it can become part of the multimodal therapist's approach. Thus, this model appears to foster an openness on the part of practitioners.

BEHAVIORAL APPLICATIONS TO FAMILY THERAPY

Behavior therapists have extended the principles of social-learning theory to the realm of family therapy. They contend that the relearning procedures that have proven useful in changing any behavior can be applied to changing problematic behavior within a family. Learning-oriented clinicians see an opportunity to induce significant behavioral changes in the family members by restructuring their interpersonal environments (Goldenberg & Goldenberg, 1980).

Liberman (1981) describes specific behavioral strategies in working with families. Essentially, how family members interact with one another can be translated into behavioral and learning terms by focusing on the consequences of behavior, or *contingencies of reinforcement*. This means that family members learn how to give one another recognition and approval for desired behavior, rather than rewarding maladaptive behavior with attention. Thus, the process of changing the contingencies by which people get recognition from the family is the basic principle of behavioral family therapy.

In his description of the tasks and techniques that characterize the main features of an application of behavior theory to family therapy, Liberman (1981) identifies three areas of technical concern for the therapist: (1) the creation of a positive therapeutic alliance, (2) making a functional analysis of the problems within the family, and (3) implementation of behavioral principles of reinforcement and modeling in the context of the interactions within a family.

Role of the therapeutic alliance.   Liberman emphasizes the role of a therapeutic alliance so that the therapist can function as a catalyst for promoting changes within the family system. As a behavior therapist with a humanistic and systems outlook, Liberman views the therapist as a teacher, as one who provides a model for change, initiates change by providing structure and guidance, and demonstrates genuine concern and understanding. Although the effective therapist must possess specific knowledge and skills, families are not helped by impersonal technicians. As Liberman (1981) puts it:

> The therapist using a behavioral model does not act like a teaching machine devoid of emotional expression. Just as therapists using other theoretical schemas, he is most effective in his role as an educator when he expresses himself with affect in a comfortable, human style developed during his clinical training and his life as a whole [p. 156].

The family assessment.   During the early phase of family therapy, along with establishing a warm and supporting climate, the therapist assesses the family's problems, making what is known as a *behavioral, or functional, analysis* of the problems. Behavior therapists are committed to a systematic analysis of precise and observable behaviors that need to be changed. In making this assessment, the therapist and the family collaborate to explore questions such as:

• What behavior is problematic? What are the behaviors that should be decreased or increased?
• What environmental and interpersonal contingencies currently support the maladaptive behavior? What is maintaining the undesirable behavior or lessening the chances for adaptive behavior?

As a part of this assessment process, which continues for the course of therapy, each member is asked: What changes would you like to see in others in your family? How would you like to be different from the way you now are? The therapist guides the family members in formulating specific behavioral goals.

Implementing behavioral strategies.   Once a behavioral analysis is made and specific goals are formulated, the third aspect of behavioral family therapy is to choose appropriate therapeutic techniques. According to Liberman, a valuable way to think about these strategies is as "behavioral change experiments," by which the family (with the therapist's guidance) reprograms the contingencies of reinforcement that operate in the family. The therapist helps the family devise the conditions by which social reinforcement (such as giving attention and approval) is made contingent on adaptive and desirable behavior. This strategy is designed to interrupt the patterns of reinforcing and maintaining undesirable behavior.

One example of a behavioral strategy designed to produce positive structural changes within a family is *contingency contracting*. Liberman developed this intervention strategy as a way of tapping the natural reinforcers in the family environment. Through this process, two or more family members exchange positively rewarding and desirable behaviors in each other. A contract is negotiated by which each participant specifies who is to do what, for whom, when, and under what conditions. Such contracts are clearly stated to the satisfaction of all involved in the process. Along with procedures such as modeling, shaping, behavioral rehearsal, and coaching, contingency contracting is directed toward helping family members open the lines of communication by making their wants known to one another in concrete terms. Such an approach that recognizes achievements can enhance the family as a system.

EVALUATION OF BEHAVIOR THERAPY

Criticisms of the Approach

Critics of behavior therapy often tend to focus on the deterministic position expounded by Skinner (1948, 1971). Although it is true that traditional behaviorism has rejected the notion of human freedom, it is clear that contemporary behavior therapy clearly emphasizes the role of cognitive factors and the self-control, or independence, of the client (Bandura, 1969; Goldfried & Davison, 1976; Kanfer & Goldstein, 1980; Lazarus, 1971, 1981; London, 1964; Mahoney & Thoresen, 1974; Meichenbaum, 1977; Rose, 1977, 1980, 1982, 1983; Thoresen & Mahoney, 1974). There is a trend toward broadening the scope of behavior therapy while retaining its essential features. For example, emphasis is being given to cognitive, emotional, and social elements in the learning process. In short, behavior therapists are reformulating their techniques in cognitive and social-learning terms instead of the traditional conditioning terms. There have been numerous examples in this chapter of groups designed primarily to increase the client's degree of control and freedom over specific aspects of his or her daily life. Krasner (1976) makes this point when he writes about the future trends in behavior therapy:

> A major point that derives from the social learning model is that the goal of helping individuals is to enable them to learn how to control, influence, or design their own environment. Implicit in this is a value judgment that individual freedom is a desirable goal and that the more an individual is able to affect his environment, the greater is his freedom [p. 646].

Other critics of the behavioral approach to group work argue that this model ignores the historical causes of present behavior and does not work with the past in the therapeutic process. There is some truth to this criticism. For example, consider this statement by Rose (1977): "By concentrating on specific behaviors as the targets of change, the behavior therapist de-emphasizes the relevance of early life histories. The therapist places less emphasis on subjective experience, insight, and general attitude than does the psychotherapist, and gives no attention to dreams" (p. 3). It seems clear that the behavior therapist opposes the traditional psychoanalytic Freudian approach, which assumes that early traumatic events are at the root of present dysfunction. As we have seen, the psychoanalytic theory holds that it is essential to discover the original causes, induce insight in the client, and work through past traumas. Behavior therapists may acknowledge that the deviant responses have historical origins, but they maintain that the responses are still in effect because they are still being maintained by reinforcing stimuli. They assume that past events are seldom still functional, in the sense of maintaining current problems. Therefore, behavioral practitioners place most of their emphasis on providing the client with *new* learning experiences (Goldfried & Davison, 1976). It is clear that the focus is on relearning new responses and changing environmental conditions as a necessary prerequisite for behavior change.

Although I think it is unfair to accuse behavior therapists of ignoring the past or considering it unimportant, I do believe that they fail to work with the past to the degree necessary. In my own work with groups I have found that most of the contemporary struggles of the participants appear to be firmly rooted in childhood experiences. Although I do not advocate getting bogged down in the past, I have found that it seems necessary for members to relive certain past experiences and resolve some basic conflicts that have lingered since childhood before new learning can proceed. In addition to giving more attention to the past than most behavior therapists, I also value focusing on subjective experiences (such as feelings and dreams) to a much greater extent than they do.

Dangers of the Approach

One of the dangers of the behavioral model is that, if too rigidly applied, it can lead the therapist to lose sight of the persons in the group by focusing exclusively on techniques and on the details of the members' specific problems. In my opinion, this focus on problems and symptoms can result in a failure to understand the meaning behind an individual's behavior. This is not to say that group therapy should focus on dealing with "underlying causes" of behavior. However, I prefer to deal with factors in one's *external* situation that may be eliciting behavioral problems *and* with one's *internal* reactions to these environmental variables. For example, in working with a male client who has great anxiety over relating to women, I would be interested in knowing what particular situations in his environment lead to this anxiety, *and* I would be concerned about his reactions to these situations. How does he feel when he is in the presence of women? What are some things he tells himself when he meets women? How does he perceive women in various situations? Therefore, my aim would not be to simply employ techniques to eliminate his anxiety; rather, I would want to explore with him the *meaning* of this anxiety. On this point Rose (1977) says: "The behavior therapist regards those behaviors about which the client expresses concern as *the* problem; they are not symptomatic *of* the problem. Successful resolution of the problematic behaviors resolves the problem; it does not, the therapist assumes, automatically lead to a new array of problems" (pp. 3–4).

Although I see this focus on problems and symptoms as a limiting factor of this approach, my concern is directed not to the model itself but to the way in which it is applied by some practitioners. I remember, for example, the case of an adolescent male client who was suffering from a variety of phobias. If I had dealt exclusively with his phobias, I would have ignored the basic problem behind the phobias—the fear of leaving home and taking the responsibility for supporting himself and making independent life decisions. Needless to say, my client's dependency problem was much deeper and more pervasive than any of his specific phobias.

Another client of mine came to me because she was overweight and didn't seem able to stick to any weight-loss plan. Although behavioral strategies would have been most useful in helping her lose weight, I realized immediately that she also needed to deal with the reasons behind her weight problem. Thus, I directed much effort toward exploring her feelings about being overweight, her reasons for overeating, the possible payoffs of her condition, and the issues she was avoiding by being overweight. In both of these cases my assumptions had to be based primarily on my clinical perceptions, and, of course, my assessment might have been wrong, which would have caused needless pain. This is the reason for the behavior therapist's insistence on the need for empirical referents to determine the adequacy of assessments. Ideally, the two approaches can be used together. The behavioral treatment and the insight-oriented treatment can complement each other.

Using Behavioral Methods with Other Approaches

I'd like to emphasize that a therapist need not subscribe totally to behavior therapy in order to derive practical benefits from the use of specific behavioral techniques. As a matter of fact, I believe that certain experiential and humanistic models can be enhanced by systematically incorporating some of the behavioral and cognitive techniques into their relationship-oriented frameworks. I am convinced that an understanding of the learning principles that operate within a group is critical for effective group leadership, regardless of one's orientation.

For example, behavioral principles operate behind such therapeutic procedures as modeling and reinforcement, which are used in almost any kind of group. Members are supported (reinforced) in their attempts to be honest, to take risks, to experiment with new behavior, to be active, to take the initiative, and to participate fully in the group. Also, the specificity of the approach helps group members translate fuzzy goals into concrete plans of action, and it helps the group leader keep these plans clearly in focus. Another contribution of the behavioral model is represented by the wide range of techniques that participants can use to specify their goals and to develop the skills needed to achieve these goals. Techniques such as role playing, coaching, guided practice, modeling, feedback, learning by successive approximations, and homework assignments can be included in any group leader's repertoire, regardless of his or her theoretical orientation.

Contributions of the Approach

More than any of the other therapies discussed in this book, behavior therapy is to be credited with conducting research to determine the efficacy of its techniques. Those approaches that do not work are eliminated, and new techniques are continually being improved. Rose (1983) sums this virtue up well: "Behavior therapy draws upon the best available empirical research to determine what kind of intervention is best suited to what kind of problem" (p. 102).

Two other contributions of behavioral group therapy are discussed by Rose (1983). First, treatment strategies are tailored to each group member, based on an assessment of the individual in the group setting. This makes the approach highly versatile and flexible. Second, a behavioral group is a concrete example of a humanistic approach in action. The individuals and the group contract for mutually determined goals. The members are involved in the selection of both goals and treatment strategies. In many groups, leaders help members move toward independence by delegating leadership functions to the members; the group leader assumes the role of an active consultant to the members to help them most efficiently attain their stated goals. Therapy then becomes a place where members learn how to learn and are encouraged to develop the skills necessary to deal effectively with solving any future problems they will face once they leave the group.

When many factors are taken into consideration, the behavioral approach stands up well in comparison with many other therapies, and it allows for the evolution of intervention methods. With the focus on research, these techniques can become more precise so that they can be implemented with specific types of client with a variety of specific problems. To a large degree I am in agreement with Goldfried and Davison's (1976) contention:

> We would suggest that behavior therapy has little to apologize for, particularly in the context of the history of other therapeutic enterprises. While there have indeed been follies committed in the name of behavior therapy, we would argue that it is behavior therapy that has most conscientiously and objectively pursued new knowledge, that we harbor precious few cherished myths about what we do, and that we are critical of our own endeavors [p. 278].

Regardless of which models influence our style of group leadership, the spirit of behavior therapy can encourage us to strive for accountability, rather than simply relying on faith and intuition that our practices are working.

In summary, the behavioral-cognitive model of group counseling and group therapy makes use of the combined methods of cognitive restructuring, problem solving, social-skills training, coping-skills training, modeling, behavior rehearsal, group feedback, reinforcement, and other tools for changing behavior. There is empirical support for each of these dimensions of group work, and preliminary data suggest that the cognitive-behavioral group model offers a promising set of treatment strategies with various types of clients (Rose, 1983). Those interested in a review of empirical research material on behavioral group therapy can consult the works of Upper and Ross (1979, 1980, 1981).

For those of you who have an interest in further training in behavior therapy, sources to contact are:

Behavior Therapy Unit
Temple University Medical School
Eastern Pennsylvania Psychiatric Institute
3300 Henry Avenue
Philadelphia, PA 19129

Dr. Sheldon D. Rose
School of Social Work
University of Wisconsin–Madison
Madison, WI 53706

Association for the Advancement of Behavior Therapy
420 Lexington Avenue
New York, NY 10017

The association has also published a *Directory of Graduate Study in Behavior Therapy*, which gives complete and up-to-date information on nearly 300 programs in clinical/counseling psychology, psychology internship, psychiatry residency, and social work.

QUESTIONS FOR REFLECTION AND DISCUSSION

1. What are some of the distinguishing features of a behavioral group that separate it from many of the other models covered in this book? To what extent do you think you could incorporate some behavioral concepts and techniques into the relationship-oriented and experiential therapies?

2. What role does assessment play in a behavioral group? Explain how assessment is an ongoing process and talk about the values of this process. Again, how could you include the focus on assessment in other therapeutic models?

3. What are some behavioral techniques that you would most want to include in your groups? How might you broaden the base of your style of leadership by including cognitive and behavioral methods?

4. What are some practical advantages of pregroup interviews and follow-up individual interviews and group sessions? In what ways might you build these into the design of a group?

5. Select a particular kind of group that you would be interested in organizing. Thinking from a behavioral perspective, what are some of the factors you would consider from the time you announced the group to the final group session? How would you design this group at each of its stages? Consider discussing your proposal with others in your class.

6. Mention some ethical considerations involved in behavioral group therapy. Which one issue do you consider to be the most significant?

7. What are your reactions to the focuses of behavior therapy—its emphasis on behavior rather than feelings and insight, interest in current problems rather than exploration of the past, concern with objective factors as opposed to subjective factors, and reliance on empirical validation of results rather than on clinical intuition?
8. Identify as many elements as you can from the behavioral perspective that will be operative in any group. For example, discuss the role of modeling, social reinforcement, and feedback in a group. How can systematically paying attention to some of these factors enhance a group?
9. What are the major shortcomings and limitations of the behavioral model? What is your major criticism of this theory as it is applied to group work?
10. What do you consider to be some of the most important contributions of the behavioral model?

RECOMMENDED SUPPLEMENTARY READINGS

Treating children in groups (Rose, 1972) and *Group therapy: A behavioral approach* (Rose, 1977) are two outstanding books on behavior therapy in groups. In the first one, Rose describes different types of therapy groups for children and some specific techniques for special populations. In the second one, Rose presents an exhaustive account of the principles and procedures of behaviorally oriented groups from their inception to their termination and follow-up stages. Special chapters are devoted to applications of behavioral strategies to a variety of groups.

Also by Rose (1980), *A casebook in group therapy: A behavioral-cognitive approach* is a reader containing contributions by 15 practicing group therapists. Among the topics covered are assertion training in groups, working with the elderly, prevention of obesity, working with elementary school children, communication and problem-solving skills training for couples, and group in-service training for paraprofessionals in group homes.

Cognitive behavior modification: An integrative approach (Meichenbaum, 1977) reflects a research orientation and is representative of the trend emphasizing the cognitive aspects of behavior therapy. Of particular value to the group practitioner are the chapters that deal with the cognitive factors in behavior-therapy theory and techniques.

Interviewing strategies for helpers: A guide to assessment, treatment, and evaluation (Cormier & Cormier, 1979) is a comprehensive and clearly written textbook dealing with training experiences and skill development. Its excellent documentation offers group practitioners a wealth of material on a variety of topics, such as assessment procedures, definition and selection of goals, development of appropriate treatment programs, and methods of evaluating outcomes.

The practice of multimodal therapy (Lazarus, 1981) is an excellent source of techniques and procedures that can be applied to behavioral group therapy. It represents an attempt to deal with the *whole person* by developing assessments and treatment interventions for all the modalities of human experience.

Clinical behavior therapy (Goldfried & Davison, 1976) is one of my favorite books on this perspective. It clearly and simply describes the essence of behavior therapy, the role of assessment, and the therapeutic relationship. It contains highly readable chapters on six major current behavior therapy techniques, and it is rich with clinical examples to illustrate concepts. Although it is not specifically written for group therapy, most of the material can be usefully applied to group work.

The newer therapies: A sourcebook (Abt & Stuart, 1982) contains a diverse overview of the cognitive therapies. In Part III, group approaches covered include family therapy, network therapies, a systems approach to group therapy, the strategic-systems therapies, and the use of poetry in groups.

Helping people change (Kanfer & Goldstein, 1980) is an excellent resource for a comprehensive overview of behavioral methods, including cognitive procedures, modeling, simulation and role playing, operant approaches, fear-reduction techniques, self-management strategies, cognitive-behavior modification, and group methods. Although this handbook is not specifically written for group practitioners, almost all of the chapters can be useful for group workers.

Assertion training is especially suited to groups. The sources I consider most useful for those interested in assertive-behavior training are *Approaches to assertion training*, by Whiteley and Flowers (1978); *Assertiveness: Innovations, applications, issues*, by Alberti (1977); and *Your perfect right: A guide to assertive behavior*, by Alberti and Emmons (1978).

There are also several excellent self-help instruction books that clearly describe a variety of techniques aimed at developing self-control and self-direction. These books can serve as useful supplements to any group counseling program, for members can use these procedures to practice new behaviors outside the group. The books I most recommend are: *Self-directed behavior: Self-modification for personal adjustment*, by Watson and Tharp (1981); *Toward a self-managed life style*, by Williams and Long (1983); *Self-control: Power to the person*, by Mahoney and Thoresen (1974); and *Behavioral self-control*, by Thoresen and Mahoney (1974).

The Behavior Therapist is a journal published by the Association for the Advancement of Behavior Therapy. Articles include reports on topical research and innovative treatment programs, commentaries that discuss controversial issues in behavior therapy, special features on important topics, reviews of the latest important books in the field, and news of the association. You can subscribe to the journal by writing to the AABT, 420 Lexington Avenue, New York, NY 10017.

The Cognitive Behaviorist is another valuable source for keeping current in this field. For information on getting this newsletter, contact Dr. E. Thomas Dowd, Counseling Psychology Program, 130 Bancroft Hall, University of Nebraska, Lincoln, NE 68588.

Behavior Group Therapy is the quarterly newsletter of the Group Therapy Special Interest Group of the AABT. It is published by the Interpersonal Skill Training and Research Project of the School of Social Work, University of Wisconsin-Madison, Madison, WI 53706. This newsletter is an excellent resource for keeping current in behavioral approaches to group work.

REFERENCES AND SUGGESTED READINGS*

Abt, L. E., & Stuart, I. R. (Eds.). *The newer therapies: A sourcebook.* New York: Van Nostrand Reinhold, 1982.

Alberti, R. E. (Ed.). *Assertiveness: Innovations, applications, issues.* San Luis Obispo, Calif.: Impact, 1977.

Alberti, R. E., & Emmons, M. L. *Stand up, speak out, talk back.* New York: Pocket Books, 1975.

* Alberti, R. E., & Emmons, M. L. *Your perfect right: A guide to assertive behavior* (3rd ed.). San Luis Obispo, Calif.: Impact, 1978.

American Psychological Association. Assertion training. *The Counseling Psychologist,* 1975, 5(4, Whole Issue).

American Psychological Association. The behavior therapies—Circa 1978. *The Counseling Psychologist,* 1978, 7(3, Whole Issue).

Azrin, N. H., Stuart, R. B., Risely, T. R., & Stolz, S. Ethical issues for human services (AABT ethical guidelines). *AABT Newsletter,* 1977, 4, 11.

Bandura, A. *Principles of behavior modification.* New York: Holt, Rinehart & Winston, 1969.

Bandura, A. *Social learning theory.* Englewood Cliffs, N.J.: Prentice-Hall, 1977.

* Beck, A. T. *Cognitive therapy and the emotional disorders.* New York: New American Library, 1976.

---

*Books and articles marked with an asterisk are suggested for further study.

Berkowitz, S. Behavior therapy. In L. E. Abt & I. R. Stuart (Eds.), *The newer therapies: A sourcebook*. New York: Van Nostrand Reinhold, 1982.

Binder, V. Behavior modification: Operant approaches to therapy. In V. Binder, A. Binder, & B. Rimland (Eds.), *Modern therapies*. Englewood Cliffs, N.J.: Prentice-Hall, 1976.

Booraem, C. D., & Flowers, J. V. A procedural model for the training of assertive behavior. In J. M. Whiteley & J. V. Flowers (Eds.), *Approaches to assertion training*. Monterey, Calif.: Brooks/Cole, 1978.

Brunell, L. F. A multimodal treatment model for a mental hospital: Designing specific treatments for specific populations. *Professional Psychology*, 1978, 9(4), 570–579.

Coates, T. J., & Thoresen, C. E. *How to sleep better*. Englewood Cliffs, N.J.: Prentice-Hall, 1977.

Cormier, W. H., & Cormier, L. S. *Interviewing strategies for helpers: A guide to assessment, treatment, and evaluation*. Monterey, Calif.: Brooks/Cole, 1979.

Cotler, S. B. Assertion training. In V. Binder, A. Binder, & B. Rimland (Eds.), *Modern therapies*. Englewood Cliffs, N.J.: Prentice-Hall, 1976.

Cotler, S. B. Assertion training: A road leading where? In J. M. Whiteley & J. V. Flowers (Eds.), *Approaches to assertion training*. Monterey, Calif.: Brooks/Cole, 1978.

Cotler, S. B., & Guerra, J. *Assertion training*. Champaign, Ill.: Research Press, 1976.

Craighead, W. E., Kazdin, A. E., & Mahoney, M. J. *Behavior modification: Principles, issues, and applications*. Boston: Houghton Mifflin, 1976.

Egan, G. *Interpersonal living: A skills/contract approach to human-relations training in groups*. Monterey, Calif.: Brooks/Cole, 1976.

Ellis, A. *Reason and emotion in psychotherapy*. New York: Lyle Stuart, 1962.

Ellis, A., & Harper, R. *A new guide to rational living*. Englewood Cliffs, N.J.: Prentice-Hall, 1975.

Fensterheim, H. Behavior therapy: Assertive training in groups. In C. J. Sager & H. Kaplan (Eds.), *Progress in group and family therapy*. New York: Brunner/Mazel, 1972.

Fensterheim, H., & Baer, J. *Don't say yes when you want to say no*. New York: Dell, 1975.

Flanagan, S. G., & Liberman, R. P. Ethical issues in the practice of behavior therapy. In M. Rosenbaum (Ed.), *Ethics and values in psychotherapy: A guidebook*. New York: Free Press, 1982.

*Flowers, J. V., & Booraem, C. D. Simulation and role playing methods. In F. H. Kanfer & A. P. Goldstein (Eds.), *Helping people change* (2nd ed.). New York: Pergamon Press, 1980.

Friedman, M., & Rosenman, R. A. *Type A behavior and your heart*. New York: Knopf, 1974.

Goldenberg, I., & Goldenberg, H. *Family therapy: An overview*. Monterey, Calif.: Brooks/Cole, 1980.

*Goldfried, M. R., & Davison, G. C. *Clinical behavior therapy*. New York: Holt, Rinehart & Winston, 1976.

Goldfried, M. R., & D'Zurilla, T. J. A behavioral-analytic model for assessing competence. In C. D. Spielberger (Ed.), *Current topics in clinical and community psychology* (Vol. 1). New York: Academic Press, 1969.

Goldstein, A. P. *Structured learning therapy: Toward a psychotherapy for the poor*. Elmsford, N.Y.: Pergamon Press, 1973.

Gottman, J. M., & Leiblum, S. *How to do psychotherapy and how to evaluate it*. New York: Holt, Rinehart & Winston, 1974.

*Hall, J. A., & Rose, S. D. Assertion training in a group. In S. D. Rose (Ed.), *A casebook in group therapy: A behavioral-cognitive approach*. Englewood Cliffs, N.J.: Prentice-Hall, 1980.

Harris, G. G. (Ed.). *The group treatment of human problems: A social learning approach*. New York: Grune & Stratton, 1977.

Houts, P., & Serber, M. (Eds.). *After the turn-on, what? Learning perspectives on humanistic groups*. Champaign, Ill.: Research Press, 1972.

Jeffery, D. B., & Katz, R. C. *Take it off and keep it off: A behavioral program for weight loss and exercise*. Englewood Cliffs, N.J.: Prentice-Hall, 1977.

* Kanfer, F. H. *Self-management methods.* In F. H. Kanfer & A. P. Goldstein (Eds.), *Helping people change* (2nd ed.). New York: Pergamon Press, 1980.

* Kanfer, F. H., & Goldstein, A. P. (Eds.). *Helping people change* (2nd ed.). New York: Pergamon Press, 1980.

Kelly, G. *The psychology of personal constructs.* New York: Norton, 1955.

Kindy, P., & Patterson, P. M. Behavioral-cognitive therapy in a group for the prevention of obesity. In S. D. Rose (Ed.), *A casebook in group therapy: A behavioral-cognitive approach.* Englewood Cliffs, N.J.: Prentice-Hall, 1980.

Krasner, L. The reinforcement machine. In B. Berenson & R. Carkhuff (Eds.), *Sources of gain in counseling and psychotherapy.* New York: Holt, Rinehart & Winston, 1967.

Krasner, L. Behavior modification: Ethical issues and future trends. In H. Leitenberg (Ed.), *Handbook of behavior modification and behavior therapy.* Englewood Cliffs, N.J.: Prentice-Hall, 1976.

Krumboltz, J. D., & Thoresen, C. E. *Behavioral counseling: Cases and techniques.* New York: Holt, Rinehart & Winston, 1969.

Krumboltz, J. D., & Thoresen, C. E. (Eds.). *Counseling methods.* New York: Holt, Rinehart & Winston, 1976.

* Lange, A., & Jakubowski, P. *Responsible assertive behavior: Cognitive-behavioral procedures for trainers.* Champaign, Ill.: Research Press, 1976.

Lange, A. J., Rimm, D. C., & Loxley, J. Cognitive-behavioral assertion training procedures. In J. M. Whiteley & J. V. Flowers (Eds.), *Approaches to assertion training.* Monterey, Calif.: Brooks/Cole, 1978.

Lazarus, A. A. Group therapy of phobic disorders by systematic desensitization. *Journal of Abnormal and Social Psychology,* 1961, 63, 504–510.

Lazarus, A. A. *Behavior therapy and beyond.* New York: McGraw-Hill, 1971.

Lazarus, A. A. Has behavior therapy outlived its usefulness? *American Psychologist,* 1977, 32(7), 550–554.

* Lazarus, A. A. *The practice of multimodal therapy.* New York: McGraw-Hill, 1981.

Lazarus, A. A. Multimodal group therapy. In G. M. Gazda (Ed.), *Basic approaches to group psychotherapy and group counseling* (3rd ed.). Springfield, Ill.: Charles C Thomas, 1982.

Lazarus, A. A., & Fay, A. *I can if I want to.* New York: Morrow, 1975.

Leitenberg, H. (Ed.). *Handbook of behavior modification and behavior therapy.* Englewood Cliffs, N.J.: Prentice-Hall, 1976.

Liberman, R. P. A behavioral approach to group dynamics. *Behavior Therapy,* 1970, *1,* 140–175.

Liberman, R. P. Reinforcement of cohesiveness in group therapy. *Archives of General Psychiatry,* 1971, *24,* 168–177.

* Liberman, R. P. Behavioral approaches to family and couple therapy. In G. D. Erickson & T. P. Hogan (Eds.), *Family therapy: An introduction to theory and technique* (2nd ed.). Monterey, Calif.: Brooks/Cole, 1981.

Liberman, R. P., King, L. W., DeRisi, W. J., & McCann, M. *Personal effectiveness: A manual for teaching social and emotional skills.* Champaign, Ill.: Research Press, 1975.

* Lieberman, M. A. Group methods. In F. H. Kanfer & A. P. Goldstein (Eds.), *Helping people change* (2nd ed.). New York: Pergamon Press, 1980.

Linehan, M., Bootzin, R., Cautela, J., London, P., Perloff, M., Stuart, R., & Risley, T. Guidelines for choosing a behavior therapist. *Behavior Therapist,* 1978, *1*(4), 18–20.

London, P. *The modes and morals of psychotherapy.* New York: Holt, Rinehart & Winston, 1964.

Mahoney, M. J., & Thoresen, C. E. *Self-control: Power to the person.* Monterey, Calif.: Brooks/Cole, 1974.

Meichenbaum, D. *Cognitive behavior modification: An integrative approach.* New York: Plenum, 1977.

Mikulas, W. *Behavior modification: An overview.* New York: Harper & Row, 1972.

Mischel, W. *Introduction to personality.* New York: Holt, Rinehart & Winston, 1971.

Moreno, J. L. *Psychodrama* (Rev. ed., Vol. 1). Beacon, N.Y.: Beacon House, 1964.

Murray, E. J., & Jacobson, L. I. Cognition and learning in traditional and behavioral therapy. In S. L. Garfield & A. E. Bergin (Eds.), *Handbook of psychotherapy and behavior change* (2nd ed.). New York: Wiley, 1978.

Paul, G. L. *Insight vs. desensitization in psychotherapy.* Stanford, Calif.: Stanford University Press, 1966.

Paul, G. L., & Shannon, D. T. Treatment of anxiety through systematic desensitization in therapy groups. *Journal of Abnormal Psychology*, 1966, *71*, 124–135.

Rathus, S. A. Assertive training: Rationales, procedures, and controversies. In J. M. Whiteley & J. V. Flowers (Eds.), *Approaches to assertion training.* Monterey, Calif.: Brooks/Cole, 1978.

Rimm, D. C., & Masters, J. C. *Behavior therapy: Techniques and empirical findings.* New York: Academic Press, 1974.

Roberts, T. K., Jackson, L. J., & Phelps, R. Lazarus' multimodal therapy model applied in an institutional setting. *Professional Psychology*, 1980, *11*(1), 150–156.

* Rose, S. D. *Treating children in groups.* San Francisco: Jossey-Bass, 1972.

* Rose, S. D. *Group therapy: A behavioral approach.* Englewood Cliffs, N.J.: Prentice-Hall, 1977.

* Rose, S. D. (Ed.). *A casebook in group therapy: A behavioral-cognitive approach.* Englewood Cliffs, N.J.: Prentice-Hall, 1980.

* Rose, S. D. Group counseling with children: A behavioral and cognitive approach. In G. M. Gazda (Ed.), *Basic approaches to group psychotherapy and group counseling* (3rd ed.). Springfield, Ill.: Charles C Thomas, 1982.

Rose, S. D. Behavior therapy in groups. In H. I. Kaplan & B. J. Sadock (Eds.), *Comprehensive group psychotherapy* (2nd ed.). Baltimore: Williams and Wilkins, 1983.

Rudestam, K. E. *Methods of self-change: An ABC primer.* Monterey, Calif.: Brooks/Cole, 1980.

Shelton, J., & Ackerman, M. *Homework in counseling and psychotherapy.* Springfield, Ill.: Charles C Thomas, 1974.

Sherman, A. R. *Behavior modification: Theory and practice.* Monterey, Calif.: Brooks/Cole, 1973.

Skinner, B. F. *Walden II.* New York: Macmillan, 1948.

Skinner, B. F. *Beyond freedom and dignity.* New York: Knopf, 1971.

Smith, M. *When I say no I feel guilty.* New York: Bantam, 1975.

Stolz, S. B., & Associates. *Ethical issues in behavior modification.* San Francisco: Jossey-Bass, 1978.

Storms, L. H. Implosive therapy: An alternative to systematic desensitization. In V. Binder, A. Binder, & B. Rimland (Eds.), *Modern therapies.* Englewood Cliffs, N.J.: Prentice-Hall, 1976.

Thoresen, C. E., & Coates, T. J. What does it mean to be a behavior therapist? *The Counseling Psychologist*, 1978, *7*(3), 3–21.

Thoresen, C. E., & Mahoney, M. J. *Behavioral self-control.* New York: Holt, Rinehart & Winston, 1974.

Upper, D., & Ross, S. M. (Eds.). *Behavioral group therapy 1979: An annual review.* Champaign, Ill.: Research Press, 1979.

Upper, D., & Ross, S. M. (Eds.). *Behavioral group therapy 1980: An annual review.* Champaign, Ill.: Research Press, 1980.

Upper, D., & Ross, S. M. (Eds.). *Behavioral group therapy 1981: An annual review.* Champaign, Ill.: Research Press, 1981.

Wanderer, Z., & Cabot, T. *Letting go.* New York: Putnam, 1978.

* Watson, D. L., & Tharp, R. G. *Self-directed behavior: Self-modification for personal adjustment* (3rd ed.). Monterey, Calif.: Brooks/Cole, 1981.

Wheelis, A. *How people change.* New York: Harper, 1973.

Whiteley, J. M., & Flowers, J. V. (Eds.). *Approaches to assertion training.* Monterey, Calif.: Brooks/Cole, 1978.

Williams, R., & Long, J. *Toward a self-managed life style* (3rd ed.). Boston: Houghton Mifflin, 1983.

Wolpe, J. *Psychotherapy by reciprocal inhibition.* Stanford, Calif.: Stanford University Press, 1958.

Wolpe, J. *The practice of behavior therapy.* New York: Pergamon Press, 1969.

Wolpe, J., & Lazarus, A. *Behavior therapy techniques.* New York: Pergamon Press, 1966.

Yates, A. J. *Behavior therapy.* New York: Wiley, 1970.

Yates, A. J. *Theory and practice in behavior therapy.* New York: Wiley, 1975.

14

RATIONAL-EMOTIVE GROUP THERAPY

INTRODUCTION

Albert Ellis, who founded rational-emotive therapy (RET) in the mid-1950s, is one of the pioneers in emphasizing the influential role of cognition in behavior. He is also a most energetic and productive individual. In his busy professional life, Ellis conducts about 80 individual and 8 group-therapy sessions weekly, along with about 200 talks and workshops for the public and psychological professionals yearly. He has published more than 40 books and 500 articles, mainly on the topic of RET. There is no doubt that he has played a central role in the recent interest in the cognitive-behavioral therapy movement.

Ellis (1979c) has described his emotional problems and consequent inhibited behavior during his youth. One of his problems was his fear of speaking in public. As a way of overcoming his anxieties, Ellis developed a cognitive-philosophical approach combined with an *in vivo* desensitization approach and homework assignments that involved speaking in public regardless of how uncomfortable he might initially be. With these cognitive-behavioral methods, Ellis states, he has virtually conquered some of his worst blocks.

As a part of his own psychoanalytic training, Ellis underwent three years of analysis. When he began his practice of psychotherapy, he routinely put his patients on the sofa and proceeded with them in a decidedly orthodox psychoanalytic way. Despite getting generally good results, he reports, he was dissatisfied with this approach. In accordance with classical technique, he would endure long and unhelpful silences and sit idly by with a limply held pencil (Ellis, 1962). He then began deviating from classical psychoanalysis and becoming more of a neo-Freudian therapist. Yet he was still not satisfied with what he observed. Therefore, he began to persuade and impel his clients to *do* the very things they were most afraid of doing, such as risking the rejection of significant others. Gradually Ellis became much more eclectic and more active and directive as a therapist. He acknowledges his debt to the ancient Greeks, especially to the Stoics. According to Ellis, one of the philosophical bases for RET is *phenomenological*. He quoted Epictetus as having said "It's never the things that happen to you that upset you; it's your view of them" (Weinrach, 1980). Thus, Ellis began to find the basis for his clients' emotional and behavioral difficulties in the way they subjectively responded to and interpreted reality, as opposed to the view that situations in the real world were causing their problems.

In his early formulations he stressed *rational* therapy, or the cognitive element in counseling, because this perspective was so radically different from other therapies in the mid-1950s. Later, RET was broadened to include both a cognitive and a behavioral dimension, as can be seen from his classic work, *Reason and Emotion in Psychotherapy* (Ellis, 1962). Recent modifications of RET include the addition of other behavioral techniques like relaxation, imagery methods, *in vivo* desensitization, flooding, and shame-attacking exercises (see Ellis & Grieger, 1977; Ellis & Harper, 1975; Ellis & Whiteley, 1979). Thus, RET can be viewed as a form of cognitively oriented behavioral model of therapy. It has evolved into a comprehensive and eclectic approach that emphasizes thinking, judging, deciding, and doing. But the approach still retains Ellis' highly didactic and directive quality, and RET is more concerned with the dimensions of thinking than with those of feeling.

RET is based on the assumption that we are born with a potential for both rational, straight thinking and irrational, crooked thinking. The irrational beliefs that are the cause of our emotional disturbance may have been originally incorporated from external sources, but we persist in these self-defeating beliefs by a process of self-indoctrination. In order to overcome the indoctrination that has resulted in irrational thinking, RET therapists employ active-directive techniques such as teaching, suggestion, persuasion, and homework assignments, and they challenge clients to substitute a rational belief system for an irrational one.

The rational-emotive approach does not consider the nature of the relationship between therapist and client as vitally important to the therapeutic process. What is given primary emphasis is the therapist's skill and willingness to challenge, confront, probe, and convince the client to practice activities (both in and outside of therapy) that will lead to constructive changes in the client's thinking and behaving. The approach stresses action—doing something about the insights one gains in therapy. Change, it is assumed, will come about mainly by a commitment to consistently practice new behaviors that challenge old and ineffective ones.

RET lends itself to group-oriented procedures, and frequently RET practitioners use group processes as a method of choice. The group is seen as offering the participants excellent opportunities for challenging self-destructive thinking and for practicing different behaviors.

KEY CONCEPTS

The A-B-C Theory

The so-called A-B-C theory of personality and emotional disturbance is central to RET theory and practice. According to Ellis (1979c), we "construct our emotions and behaviors in accordance with the premises and philosophies . . . that we have invented" (p. 35). These premises are shaped by our social environment, but, Ellis continues, "it is largely the way we react to the conditions around us, rather than the conditions themselves, that leads to our 'personality traits' and to our disturbances" (p. 35). The A-B-C theory maintains that, when people have an emotional reaction at point C (the so-called emotional Consequence), after some Activating event that occurred at point A, it is not the event itself (A) that causes the emotional state (C), although it may contribute to it. It is the Belief system (B), or the beliefs that people have about the event, that creates C. For example, if you feel rejected and hurt (C) over the event of not getting a promotion at work (A), it is not the fact that you weren't promoted that causes your hurt; it is your *belief* (B) about the event. By believing that not receiving a promotion means that you are a failure and that your efforts have not been appreciated and that they *should* be, you "construct" the emotional consequence of feeling rejected and hurt. Thus, human beings are largely responsible for creating their own emotional disturbances through the beliefs they associate with the events of their lives.

Ellis (1977b) maintains that people have the capacity to significantly change their cognitions, behaviors, and emotions. If they exert the choice they have as human beings to think and act differently, they can quickly change disturbance-creating patterns into constructive ways of living. According to Ellis, people can best accomplish this goal by avoiding preoccupying themselves with A and by acknowledging and yet resisting the temptation to dwell endlessly on emotional consequences at C. They can choose to examine, challenge, modify, and uproot B—the irrational beliefs they hold about the activating events at A. Ellis emphasizes that, because humans can think, they can also train themselves to change or eliminate their self-sabotaging beliefs by exercising self-discipline, by seeking the help of objective and rational-thinking people, by undergoing individual therapy or some form of workshop or group-therapy experience, and by reading RET books or listening to tapes.

Origins of Emotional Disturbance

Feelings of anxiety, depression, rejection, anger, guilt, and alienation are initiated and perpetuated by a self-defeating belief system based on irrational ideas that were uncritically embraced at an early age. These self-defeating beliefs are supported and maintained by negative, absolutistic, and illogical statements that people make to themselves over and over again: "I'm worthless"; "If I don't win everybody's love and approval, I'm a rotten person"; "I should be thoroughly competent in everything I do"; "I *must* have everything I want"; and so forth.

When people stay with rational, positive beliefs, they tend to feel happy, relaxed, or at least serene; when they harbor cynical, pessimistic, and hopeless ideas, they tend to feel sad, depressed, and hopeless. Therefore, effective therapy includes helping clients develop a realistic attitude toward the present and the future, dispute their irrational beliefs, and change their self-sabotaging statements to new, more rational, and empirically sound ones (Ellis, 1979b).

Confronting and Attacking Irrational Beliefs

As a cognitive type of therapy, RET teaches people to confront their disturbance-creating belief system. This goal is achieved by explaining how irrational ideas cause emotional disturbances, by attacking such ideas on scientific grounds, and by teaching clients how to challenge their thinking and how to substitute rational for irrational ideas.

This therapeutic process begins by teaching clients RET's A-B-C theory. When clients have come to see how their irrational beliefs and values are causally linked to their emotional and behavioral disturbances, they are ready to Dispute these beliefs and values at point D. D is the application of scientific principles to challenge self-defeating philosophies and dispose of unrealistic and unverifiable hypotheses. Ellis (1976, 1979a) says that most of our irrational ideas can be reduced to three main forms of what he calls *mus*turbation: (1) "I *must* be competent, and I *must* win the approval of all the significant people in my life"; (2) "Others *must* treat me fairly and considerately"; and (3) "My life *must* be easy and pleasant. I need and *must* have the things I really want." Ellis (1979a) says: "The rational-emotive therapist quickly and efficiently tries to show clients that they have one, two, or all three of these irrational Beliefs . . . and perhaps many of their corollaries and subheadings" (p. 4).

After D comes E, or the Effect of disputing—the relinquishing of self-destructive ideologies, the acquisition of a more rational and realistic philosophy of life, and a greater acceptance of oneself, of others, and of the inevitable frustrations of everyday life. This new philosophy of life has of course a practical side—a concrete E, if you wish. In the example I gave above, E would translate into a rational and empirically based conclusion: "Well, it's too bad that I didn't get that promotion. But it's not the end of the world. There may be other opportunities. Besides, not getting the promotion does *not* mean that I am a failure. So, I don't need to keep telling myself all that nonsense." Or a person might make a rational statement such as the following: "I'd like to have gotten the job, but I didn't. I regret that, but it's not awful, terrible, and horrible. It's bad enough that I lost it; I don't have to make myself miserable as well. I'm disappointed, but it's not awful unless I make it awful." And, according to RET theory, the ultimate result is the elimination of feelings of depression and rejection.

Self-Rating

According to Ellis (1979b), we have a strong tendency not only to rate our acts and behaviors as "good" or "bad" but also to rate *ourselves as a total person* as "good" or "bad" on the basis of our performance. Our self-ratings influence our feelings and actions, because this self-rating process constitutes one of the main sources of our emotional disturbances. Therefore, the RET therapist teaches clients how to separate the evaluation of their behaviors from the evaluation of their *self*—their *essence* and their *totality*—and how to accept themselves in spite of their imperfections. Some examples of self-rating are:

- The fact that I make mistakes means that I'm incompetent and worthless.
- I have committed "wrong" acts; thus, I am bad, evil, and shameful.
- If everyone doesn't accept me and approve of me, I am a terrible person.

Ellis (1979b) contends that this kind of self-rating inevitably leads to a lot of problems—among them, self-centeredness and self-consciousness; a tendency to damn oneself and others; the feeling that, no matter what one accomplishes, it is never enough; attempts to manipulate others; and the sabotaging of one's goals.

RATIONAL-EMOTIVE THERAPY IN GROUPS

RET as an Educational Model

As I said earlier, rational-emotive therapy emphasizes cognitive restructuring and relies heavily on the didactic side of the therapeutic process. Therapy is viewed largely as a matter of emotional and intellectual reeducation. Like most forms of teaching, RET is often done in a group setting, and many RET practitioners use group techniques as a method of choice. Rational-emotive group therapy avails itself of audiovisual presentations, bibliotherapy, films and television tapes, programmed instruction, and other teaching methods.

Ellis (1977b) expresses his view of RET in groups as follows: "I stoutly hypothesize that this kind of group intervention is more likely to lead to a quicker, deeper, and more elegant solution to the ubiquitous human condition of childish demandingness and perennial disturbability than any other contemporary form of psychotherapy" (p. 280).* To reach such a "solution," group members must learn to separate their rational beliefs from their irrational beliefs and to understand the origins of their emotional disturbances as well as those of other members. Participants are taught the many ways in which they can (1) free themselves of their irrational life philosophy so that they can function more effectively as an individual and as a relational being and (2) learn more appropriate ways of responding so that they won't needlessly feel upset about the realities of living. The group members help and support one another in these learning endeavors.

Goals

Ellis (1974a) sums up the main goals of rational-emotive therapy as a consistent attempt to induce the client "to *examine* fearlessly his fundamental philosophic premises, to *think* about them consciously and concertedly, to *understand* that they are based on illogical and inconsistent assumptions or deductions, and to *attack* them, by consistent verbal and motor activity, until they

*From *Handbook of Rational-Emotive Therapy*, by A. Ellis and R. Grieger. Copyright 1977 by Springer Publishing Company, New York. This and all other quotations from this source are reprinted by permission.

truly disappear or at least are reduced to minimal proportions" (p. 162). He adds: "This method of persuading, cajoling, and at times almost forcing the client to observe and to re-appraise his *own* conscious and unconscious philosophies of life is the essence of rational-emotive psychotherapy" (p. 162).

Ellis contends that rational-emotive group therapy can work well with large groups (of 50, 100, and more), utilizing a workshop format, or can be applied to small groups with 10 to 13 members. Small groups, Ellis (1982b) writes, have the following aims:

- Members are helped to understand the roots of their emotional and behavioral problems and to put these insights to use in overcoming their symptoms and learning more elegant ways of functioning both intrapersonally and interpersonally.
- Group participants develop an understanding of the problems of others, and they learn how to be of some therapeutic help to fellow group members.
- Members learn ways of minimizing life circumstances and their irrational reactions to them, so that they manage to disturb themselves less often than when they first joined the group.
- The participants learn to achieve both behavioral changes and basic cognitive changes, including learning how to cope with unpleasant realities; surrendering self-defeating thinking and replacing it with rational thinking; and stopping the practice of self-rating, instead learning to accept themselves as fallible humans.

Basically, group members are taught that *they* are responsible for their own emotional reactions, that they can change their emotional disturbances by paying attention to their self-verbalizations and by changing their beliefs and values, and that, *if* they acquire a new and more realistic philosophy of life, *then* they can cope effectively with most of the unfortunate events in their lives. Although the therapeutic goals of RET are essentially the same for both individual and group therapy, the two differ in some of the specific methods and techniques employed, as we shall see in the pages that follow.

Rationale

More than 20 years of experience in conducting and leading RET groups has confirmed Ellis' belief that a group is particularly effective in helping participants make constructive personality and behavior changes. Ellis (1977b) discusses many of the advantages of RET in groups, some of which are briefly summarized below:

1. Group members can remind one another of the desirability of accepting reality and work together to bring about positive changes.

2. Since RET emphasizes a vigorous attack on self-defeating thinking, other members can play a powerful role in challenging the individual's crooked thinking.

3. Group members can contribute suggestions, comments, and hypotheses and reinforce some of the points made by the leader.

4. The activity-oriented homework assignments that are a vital component

of RET are more effectively carried out in the group context than in one-to-one therapy.

5. The group offers an effective milieu for several active-directive procedures such as role playing, assertion training, behavior rehearsal, modeling, and risk-taking exercises.

6. The group serves as a laboratory in which behavior can be directly observed in action.

7. RET clients are often asked to complete homework report forms, which require going over the A-B-C's of upsetting situations and then learning how to correct faulty thinking and behaving. By hearing other members' reports and learning how they have dealt with the situations in question, participants can better deal with their own issues. Although these homework assignments can be done in individual sessions, a group format is more effective because the members can practice the behaviors they would like to increase or decrease in the real world. Thus, if a man is afraid to give his reactions to others, he can be encouraged to do so during the group sessions. The group serves as a laboratory where behavior can be directly observed, rather than merely be reported upon. It is therefore more difficult to hide or mask one's feelings.

8. In the group situation, members discover that, since their problems are far from unique, they don't need to condemn themselves for having these problems.

9. Through feedback from others in the group, participants begin to see themselves as others see them and notice quite clearly the behaviors that need to be changed. They also gain social skills during the sessions and in the socializing that takes place after the sessions.

10. When the statements members make indicate faulty thinking, the other members and the leader can immediately bring these mistakes to the person's attention so that the faulty thinking can be corrected.

11. By watching other members, participants are able to see that treatment can be effective, that people can change, that there are steps they can take to help themselves, and that successful therapy is the product of hard and persistent work.

12. In groups, clients have the opportunity to consider a wider range of alternatives to solving their problems than is possible in one-to-one therapy.

13. Disclosing intimate problems, some of which the person considers shameful, is therapeutic in itself. Self-disclosure enables participants to realize that taking risks pays off: their "revelations" generally don't have the dire consequences they feared so much, and, even if someone does criticize them, that is perhaps unfortunate but certainly not catastrophic.

14. Since RET is highly educational and didactic, it typically includes information giving and discussion of problem-solving strategies. Economically and practically, this is better done in a group than in an individual setting. The group also provides a format for teaching/learning/discussing/practicing, which encourages participants to become actively involved in their treatment.

15. The average duration of the RET group session (2¼ hours with the leader and another hour of postgroup work without the leader) provides enough time to effectively challenge rigidly held self-defeating beliefs.

16. Group procedures are especially useful for people who are rigidly bound by old patterns of dysfunctional behavior, because the group setting provides the challenge necessary to reevaluate these patterns and adopt healthier ones.

I'd like to note that, even though Ellis uses this long list of reasons to support his view that RET is especially suitable for group work, these same reasons can be adduced to support the group application of most of the therapeutic models covered in this book. Therefore, the points discussed by Ellis can be usefully considered by any group practitioner who is in the process of developing a rationale for a group counseling program, even if he or she has an orientation other than RET.

ROLE AND FUNCTIONS OF THE GROUP LEADER

The therapeutic activities of an RET group are carried out with one central purpose—helping the participants to rid themselves of illogical ideas and to replace them with logical ones. The ultimate aim is to enable group members to internalize a rational philosophy of life, just as they had internalized a set of dogmatic and false beliefs derived from their sociocultural environment.

In working toward this ultimate aim, the group leader has several specific functions and tasks. The first task is to show the group members *how* they have created their own misery. This is done by clarifying the connection between one's emotional/behavioral disturbances and one's values, beliefs, and attitudes. With the therapist's help, members come to see how they have uncritically accepted a series of "shoulds," "musts," and "oughts." The leader acts as a counterpropagandist who confronts members with the propaganda they originally accepted without questioning and demonstrates how they *now* continue to indoctrinate themselves with unexamined assumptions. The group leader persuades members to engage in activities that will act as counterpropaganda agents.

To help members move beyond the mere recognition that they originally incorporated irrational thoughts and that they now keep themselves emotionally upset by continuing to think illogically, the therapist strives to modify their thinking. RET assumes that people's illogical beliefs are so deeply ingrained that they will not change easily. Thus, it is the role of the leader to teach members how to challenge their assumptions and how to stop the vicious cycle of the self-rating and self-blaming process.

But getting rid of symptoms of disturbances is not enough. If only specific problems or symptoms are dealt with, other illogical fears are likely to appear. Thus, the final step in the therapeutic process is to teach members how to avoid becoming victims of future irrational beliefs. The therapist attacks the core of clients' irrational thinking and teaches them how to apply logical thinking when coping with future problems.

Because RET is an educative process, the leader's central role is to teach members ways of self-understanding and changing. RET practitioners employ a rapid-fire, highly directive set of techniques that emphasize cognitive aspects. The next section describes these techniques and discusses their implications for group practice.

THERAPEUTIC TECHNIQUES AND PROCEDURES

Ellis (1974a) stresses that RET lends itself to a wide range of behavioral and cognitive methods for behavior change. In keeping with RET's didactic nature, these methods are directive, confrontational, philosophic, and action oriented. RET is very skill oriented. It focuses on specific techniques for changing a client's specific thoughts in concrete situations in such a way that other group members can apply these skills to their own concerns. Thus, an RET group fosters the transfer to other members' personal issues better than many other approaches do. Even though one person may be working at a time, everyone else can be learning how to work on his or her own changes at the same time.

Active-Directive Therapy

Because people have a strong tendency to get emotionally upset and to behave dysfunctionally, because they think and feel in self-defeating ways, and because they keep harboring self-sabotaging thoughts even after some positive change has occurred, they will benefit more from a highly active and directive therapy than from a passive and nondirective therapeutic approach (Ellis, 1979b). These active-directive techniques include persuasion, homework assignments, self-control methods, education and teaching, suggestion, modeling and imitation, problem solving, role playing, behavior rehearsal, skill training, operant control of thinking and emoting, desensitization, and group feedback and support.

Disputing, Persuading, Teaching, and Informing

RET teaches clients to use the logico-empirical method to check and modify their values and attitudes about themselves and others. Unlike most therapies, RET deemphasizes the importance of a warm therapeutic relationship and the psychodynamic factors of the therapeutic process. Although RET employs many emotive-dramatic techniques, Ellis (1973b) indicates that all techniques had better be carried out in an active-directive manner, with the therapist playing the role of a teacher and not that of an intensely relating partner. Although the therapeutic relationship is not given primacy, it is also true that the RET therapist shows respect for the client. Clients learn that the therapist is not thinking disapprovingly and that they can trust that the therapist is actively working to help them. The therapist's behavior speaks for itself to prove these points.

In this didactic role, the therapist-teacher disputes the irrational, logically inconsistent, antiempirical, absolutistic, catastrophic, and rationalized ideas of clients and demonstrates how these ideas bring about unnecessary disturbances. The therapist persuades clients to change or surrender their irrational beliefs and the dysfunctional behaviors to which such beliefs contribute. This implies providing clients with information and instruction that will help them understand their own contribution to their emotional disturbances and the steps they can *now* take to make themselves less disturbed. Group members are taught to use thorough logical analysis, to vigorously undermine their faulty premises, and to empirically contradict the disturbance-creating thinking of other group members.

Homework Assignments

RET has consistently endorsed activity-oriented homework assignments to help people think, feel, and behave more rationally. These assignments, which are given by the leader as well as other group members, may be carried out in the group itself or outside of it, in which case the person is supposed to report the results to the group. Here are some examples of in-group homework assignments:

• A man who is very shy with women is required to approach female group members and systematically challenge his fears and expectations in graduated steps.

• A woman who tends to say very little in the group because she thinks that she has nothing to contribute is asked to make a contract to participate in the discussion at least once each session. She may also be advised to work on changing her irrational ideas about her inability to contribute something of value.

• Members who tend to view the group leader as a superbeing who should be believed without question are invited to challenge the leader in the group and to deal with their attitudes toward authority figures. This assignment allows clients to see how, by maintaining a helpless attitude in the presence of such figures, they keep themselves from growing up or being powerful.

Group members are encouraged to give themselves assignments to be carried out outside the group. For example, if a woman says that she feels socially inhibited, she can place herself in specific situations that enable her to challenge her inhibitions. By compelling herself to do the very things she fears doing, this woman begins to torpedo the underpinnings of her self-defeating and irrational ideas. If she is afraid to initiate contacts with others, she can examine her assumptions and catastrophic expectations about making these contacts. And, by actually taking the initiative, she may discover that she likes the outcome or that, even if she is not at all successful, there is nothing catastrophic about it.

Homework assignments are meant to do more than confront irrational beliefs; they are meant to give clients the necessary practice in *behaving* differently. Unlike some therapies that stop at the insight level, RET emphasizes the necessity of doing something about one's newly acquired insights. And homework is one good action-oriented way to practice new behaviors. In all his writings, Ellis stresses that cognitive, emotive, and behavioral changes will come about only through hard work and a commitment to sustained practice and action.

Role Playing and Modeling

The group setting is especially suited to many cognitive-behavior-modification methods such as assertion training, behavior rehearsal, and risk-taking procedures. Some members may hesitate to reveal themselves to the group for fear that, if they open up, everyone in the group will reject them. The group provides these members with an opportunity to risk self-disclosure and see what the consequences are. Other members may have trouble being direct with significant people in their life. In the group they can role-play being direct and assertive with significant others and use the group situation to try out and rehearse these new ways.

In an RET group, role playing also involves a cognitive evaluation of the feelings and beliefs experienced in the role-playing situation. Thus, if a member is trying to deal more effectively with a rejecting father who demands perfection, he can adopt a role quite different from his usual one—a role in which he no longer feels victimized by his father's lack of approval. Afterward, this person undertakes a cognitive analysis of the feelings experienced during the role enactment. To that effect, he may try to answer questions such as the following:

- Do I need my father's approval to survive?
- Will I ever be able to attain the level of perfection that my father demands?
- Can I accept myself although I shall never be perfect? Can I avoid destructive self-rating and self-blaming because of my imperfection?
- Do I *need* my father's approval, or do I simply *want* it?
- If I don't have his approval, is it awful, terrible, and horrible?
- Do I really have to be perfect before I can accept myself?

Ellis (1977b) strongly believes that role playing that entails a cognitive restructuring of the attitudes revealed by the experience is more effective than role playing without any kind of cognitive analysis and restructuring.

The learning that occurs through modeling and imitation is similar to that achieved through role playing. Bandura (1969) has pioneered the theory and practice of social modeling and imitative learning as it relates to behavioral change. By patterning our behavior after those people we perceive as models, we can bring about changes in our thinking, feeling, and behaving.

According to Ellis, effective therapy frequently includes imitating and modeling. In groups, both the leader and other members can serve as models. For instance, if a group member has found a way to identify and change self-destructive modes of thinking, feeling, and behaving, she can be an effective model for the other participants by demonstrating that constructive change *is* possible and by modeling the actual ways in which she has achieved these desirable changes.

In an RET group, modeling, too, involves a cognitive component. Ellis (1979b) says that, "when people explicitly perceive how they can use modeling, they can more easily and intensively help themselves than when they have little or no awareness of using imitation" (p. 131).

Operant Control of Thinking and Feeling

RET frequently makes use of Skinner's (1971) reinforcement principles to teach clients how to achieve self-directed behavioral change. Ellis (1976) points out that many of his clients learn to surrender irrational beliefs or change undesirable behaviors by reinforcing their performance of difficult tasks with something they truly enjoy. Therefore, RET practitioners show their clients how to use this technique (so-called operant conditioning) to accomplish something they consider very difficult or that they are afraid of doing.

Indeed, one of RET's goals is to teach clients better methods of self-management. Members' ultimate success depends on how effectively they can take charge of their life beyond the group sessions. Therefore, members are expected to apply rational principles to the new problems they encounter; in this sense they become their own therapists and continually teach themselves how to manage their life.

Skill Training

Related to self-management training is the training RET clients receive in specific skills (such as assertion, socializing, and studying) they would like to have. The assumption is that, by acquiring skills they formerly lacked, clients will feel more confident about themselves and will experience significant changes in the way they think, feel, and behave. Ellis (1979b) says: "These changes arise not merely from their increased skills but also from their perceptions of their abilities and their self-ratings about their newly acquired competencies" (p. 133). He concludes: "Just as skill training enables clients to change their perceptions of their abilities, so does helping them to perceive themselves differently enable them to acquire better skills" (p. 133). For example, if clients believe that they can make effective contact with others, there is a good chance that they actually will, or at least will be less negative if they don't succeed on a particular occasion.

Feedback

Feedback is very much a part of any group process, and RET groups are no exception. Members get feedback from the group with regard to their ineffective performances, irrational thinking, and self-sabotaging ideas, statements, and behaviors. Using this feedback, they can then practice new behaviors based on fresh or revised assumptions.

Although feedback can greatly contribute to the group process, it can also bog it down in numerous ways, as Ellis (1975b) observes:

> The best-intentioned group members can waste time in irrelevancies; lead the problem-presenter up the garden path; sidetrack and diffuse some of the therapist's main points; hold back because they inordinately look for the approval of other group members; bring out their own and others' minor instead of major difficulties; and otherwise get off on various non-therapeutic limbs. Group members can also bombard a presenter with so many and so powerful suggestions that he or she is overwhelmed and partly paralyzed [p. 311].

It is therefore the role of the therapist to keep the process on track.

A SPECIAL FORM OF RET GROUP: THE RET MARATHON

Ellis (1969b) has developed a special form of group therapy that he calls "A Weekend of Rational Encounter." Because this type of marathon utilizes the same cognitive-behavioral principles characteristic of other forms of RET, it has very little in common with the encounter marathons that emphasize here-and-now feelings and downplay thinking. The RET marathon is divided into two parts. The first part consists of 14 hours of continuous rational-encounter therapy followed by 8 hours of rest. The second part includes another 10 hours of therapy.

The initial stage consists of directed verbal and nonverbal activities designed to help participants get to know one another. During this early stage, members are expected to engage in risk-taking procedures and shame-attacking exercises, such as sharing their most shameful experiences with the group. At this stage, procedures designed to tap emotional expression are used, and no problem solving and decision making are attempted. As the marathon progresses, the same rational-cognitive and behavior-action methods used in the other forms of RET are employed.

During the later stages of the marathon, deep personal problems are explored within a highly cognitive framework. In the closing hours of the marathon, group members and the leader usually "smoke out anyone who has not as yet brought up any problem for detailed discussion" (Ellis, 1969b, p. 212). These participants are asked why they have said little about themselves, and they are encouraged to look for a major problem to bring out into the open.

Several questions are generally asked in the closing hours of the marathon. For example:

- What were the most significant experiences you had during this marathon?
- What did you learn about yourself?
- Are there some things that you did *not* say to the group or to some members of the group that you are willing to say now?

Before leaving the marathon, participants are given specific homework assignments. A postsession is held six to eight weeks later to check on the progress the participants have made with their assignments and to evaluate how well the members are functioning.

Ellis (1969b) writes enthusiastically about the value of the marathon format. He says that the marathon is "specifically designed to show group members what their fundamental self-defeating philosophies are and to indicate how they can work at changing these philosophies, in the here-and-now and thereafter" (pp. 126–127).

OTHER ADAPTATIONS AND APPLICATIONS OF RET IN GROUPS

Many of the cognitive-behavioral therapies owe a debt to Ellis, for they are essentially an offspring of RET and build on many of the basic principles that he has been teaching for more than two decades. For example, multimodal group therapy, developed by Arnold Lazarus and discussed in the previous chapter, shares many features with RET. According to Ellis (see Weinrach, 1980), multimodal therapy (BASIC ID) is largely another name for RET. Ellis contends that Lazarus has systematized some of the RET techniques, that the two approaches have only slightly different emphases, and that multimodal therapy overlaps about 80% with RET.

Arthur Lange (Lange & Jakubowski, 1976) is another practitioner who has drawn heavily from RET theory and techniques, in his case in developing a cognitive-behavioral model of assertion-training groups. Lange begins his groups by teaching clients the skills they need to function as an effective group member. He also teaches them basic cognitive principles, relying heavily upon RET for the key constructs. In his ten-week groups, Lange teaches the members the A-B-C model. Participants are taught how the ways people think about themselves influence them emotionally and behaviorally. They are taught about the "tyranny of the shoulds" and about the nature of catastrophic expectations, as well as being exposed to common rationalizations. Members learn how to identify irrational thinking and how to substitute preferences for demands. A large part of the group consists of teaching members ways to identify basic irrational ideas, which include ideas pertaining to rejection, competence, the standard that life should be fair, and the notion that people should be punished for being unfair. During these group sessions, members look for catastrophic and faulty thought patterns, learn to challenge absolutistic thinking, and listen to what they are telling themselves. The focus of the work in the sessions is on specific situations that give members difficulty. They start with an analysis of their self-talk, and then, after working on a cognitive level, they proceed to working on a behavioral level. In learning how to be assertive in a variety of situations, the group uses behavioral rehearsals. Members first tell what they think of their own performance in these role-playing situations, and then others provide feedback and other ways of dealing with the situation. This is one example of a creative blending of RET with behavioral procedures.

RATIONAL BEHAVIOR THERAPY IN GROUPS

An outgrowth and modification of RET group therapy is *rational behavior therapy* (RBT), as formulated by Maxie Maultsby, an associate of Ellis. Maultsby (1981) defines RBT as "a comprehensive, short-term behavioral approach to helping people learn to solve personal problems rationally in a nonthreatening, internally reinforcing group of people with similar interests in learning that skill" (p. 203). Like RET, RBT is comprehensive in that it deals with cognitive, emotive, and physical behaviors. Maultsby maintains that RBT is culture free and seems to be a useful approach for people from all social classes and races.

The basic goal of RBT in groups is to teach members how to counsel themselves rationally. Members are provided with tools so that, when the group is over, they will have a better ability to deal effectively with emotional problems.

According to Maultsby (1981), Ellis did not deal adequately with the question of how to get clients to accept emotionally what they know intellectually. Although many clients do know that certain ideas are silly or irrational, they still feel emotionally upset.

A short summary of how RBT works in groups follows. When people have experiences that they would like to deal with more effectively, they begin by writing a rational self-analysis. Basically, this consists of writing down the A-B-C's of their behavior. At A they write a simple description of the event they want to analyze and understand more fully. The B section contains all the thoughts and beliefs they had about the given event. At C they record the undesirable emotional reactions that they would like to replace with more desirable ones. This is basically the same structure as Ellis' RET formulation, except that Maultsby has developed a *written* self-analysis technique so that people can see clearly what they are doing. After they write down the A-B-C's, they ask certain questions to determine whether their thinking is rational:

- Are my thoughts based on facts? Where are the facts?
- Will my thinking protect me from harm?
- To what degree does my thinking help me achieve my goals?
- Will my thinking lead to desirable or undesirable interpersonal reactions?
- Will my thoughts result in the kind of feelings I would like to experience?

Maultsby is concerned with giving group members the tools they need to make a practical distinction between rational and irrational thinking, and he thinks that going through this written process of rational self-analysis is a helpful tool. To provide members with further guidelines for making this distinction, Maultsby added to RET what he calls the "four practical rules for rational thought and behavior":

1. What is rational corresponds to a description of objective reality.
2. A rational course of action is most likely to preserve one's life.
3. Rational behavior is instrumental in achieving one's short-term and long-term personal goals.
4. Rational thinking and behavior are least likely to result in negative emotions or conflict in one's environment.

Later, Maultsby built upon RET by adding the technique of *rational-emotive imagery*, through which undesirable habits are extinguished and are replaced with new and desirable habits. He also added other self-help techniques designed to get clients to think and behave rationally.

RBT is basically an emotional reeducational model, and thus didactic aids are a part of the sessions. Group members are given assigned readings, watch slide and videotape demonstrations of various self-help techniques used effectively, and present their problems to the group using the standard A-B-C format.

Typically, RBT in groups is under the direction of a single group leader who has three main functions:

1. to teach members the rational theory and techniques of emotional self-help
2. to monitor members in the process of their application of this theory and these techniques to their problems
3. to encourage equal participation of the members and to control the group process (Maultsby, 1981)

It can be seen that RBT in groups is essentially RET with a few adaptations, including written forms, certain structured questions to help members determine what is rational, and some emotive techniques to help them change on an emotional level what they say they know on a cognitive level. The RBT group leader assumes a directive role, based largely on a teaching model, with the aim of teaching people how to effectively solve their problems. According to Maultsby, ethical practice calls for such direction and structure:

RBT group leaders believe that it is unethical, if not inhumane, to encourage or to allow group members to ruminate blindly in emotional pain, hoping to discover accidentally or magically possible solutions to their problems. Instead, RBT group leaders believe it is their ethical duty to direct group members toward what seems to be the most efficient and the most effective way to solve their personal problems and to end their emotional pain without drugs [1981, p. 195].

Nevertheless, RBT group leaders also refuse to accept personal responsibility for the members' progress. It is the obligation of each group member to do what is necessary, both in the group and outside of it, to bring about therapeutic change.

RATIONAL-EMOTIVE FAMILY THERAPY

The goals of RET family therapy are basically the same as those of individual or group therapy. Members of a family are helped to see that they are responsible for disturbing themselves by taking the actions of other family members too seriously. They are encouraged to consider letting go of their demand that others in the family behave in ways they would like them to. Instead, RET teaches family members that they are primarily responsible for their own actions and for changing their own reactions to the family situation. Its stress is upon the reality that one family member has little power to directly change another. Members are shown, as a family, that they have the power to control their individual thinking and feeling patterns. Each person is in control of modifying his or her behavior, which might well have an indirect effect on the family as a unit.

Ellis (1982a) describes cognitive, emotive, and behavioral techniques that are appropriate in working with the family group. The *cognitive techniques* are geared to showing family members that they largely create their own emotional and behavioral disturbances. It is not a particular problem person within the family or a problem situation that causes disturbances; rather, it is the perception and interpretation of the situation that keep an individual upset. For example, assume that a family comes for therapy with the presenting problem of an acting-out daughter of 15 who seems to be disrupting the family. The girl is cutting her classes, using drugs, staying out all night, and in general engaging in negativistic and defiant behavior. The parents are greatly agitated and feel extremely frustrated in their attempts to control her. The RET family therapist would approach these parents with the challenge that they do not have the ability to directly change their daughter but that they can change their reactions to her disruptive behavior. They can modify their feelings, can challenge their belief that they are rotten parents who are to blame for her deviant behavior, and can behave differently toward her. In short, they have the power to do something about getting themselves out of emotional turmoil and perpetual conflict, *even if* their daughter is unwilling to change.

Emotive techniques are also used in working with family groups. These techniques are designed to show family members that their feelings are often the result of what they are thinking. Evocative and dramatic techniques are typically used to help people make basic philosophic changes. One example of such a technique is rational-emotive imagery, which is used to extinguish undesirable habits and replace them with new and desirable ones (Maultsby, 1981). In this technique, clients imagine their worst feelings (rage, horror, utter despair) and then change these to appropriate feelings. Role playing is most appropriate in working with a family as a way of giving members a chance to express pent-up feelings and ultimately change certain self-defeating behavior that is produced by negative feelings.

Behavioral techniques are a basic part of RET family therapy. Individual members are given homework assignments to be carried out in the actual situation rather than in the person's imagination. Instead of avoiding an unpleasant family scene, parents might be urged to face the situation and try a different way of behaving. The use of contracts, by which family members agree to do certain things, is appropriate as a means of modifying dysfunctional behavior.

EVALUATION OF RATIONAL-EMOTIVE THERAPY

What I Value in RET

There are several aspects of RET that I consider valuable enough to use in my own approach to group practice. Although I do believe that events and significant others in our past play a critical role in shaping our present beliefs about ourselves, I agree with Ellis that we are the ones who are responsible for maintaining self-destructive and irrational convictions about ourselves. True, we may have learned that, unless we were everything that others expected us to be, we could never hope to be loved and accepted. But the fact that at one time we uncritically accepted certain premises doesn't exempt us now from the responsibility of scrutinizing these and other irrational assumptions and replacing them with more rational ones, which will lead to different and more effective behavior.

I often ask group members to express the beliefs or assumptions that underlie the problems they are experiencing. One of the most common answers is that making mistakes is a terrible, unforgivable thing and that we should arrange our lives in such a way that we won't make mistakes. After probing to find out how the person came to accept such a belief, I generally pursue the issue with other questions—for example: Does this belief really make sense to you now? What would your life be like if you continued to live by these assumptions? Do you think that you'd be different if you could change some of these basic beliefs? If so, in what ways? What actions can you take now, in this group and in your everyday life, that will help you change some of the beliefs you hold?

In short, I value RET's emphasis on thinking and conceptualizing, and I am critical of some group approaches that denigrate the role of thinking as "detached analyzation" and "abstract head-tripping." In many sensitivity and encounter groups the focus is exclusively on "gut feelings," "here-and-now reactions," and emotional experiences; thinking, or any attempt to make sense of an emotional experience, is generally seen as an obstacle to "getting in touch with feelings." Although I do find considerable value in experiencing a catharsis and expressing pent-up feelings, I've found that, for an emotional experience to have significant and lasting effects, it is necessary to attempt to understand the meaning of the experience. And RET does indeed provide the framework for this vital cognitive dimension.

Like any action-oriented therapy approach, RET insists that newly acquired insights be put into action. Since I question the value of self-understanding unless clients begin to *act* on what they are learning about themselves, I couldn't agree more. The homework method is an excellent avenue for translating insights into concrete action programs. In my own groups, I often suggest assignments that can be carried out in group and that allow clients to practice new behaviors and experiment with a different style of being. I recall, for example, Stan, an older man who avoided women in his group because he was sure that they wouldn't want to waste their time talking with him. I asked Stan whether he wanted to change this pattern, and he said yes—that he wanted very much to initiate contact. So I suggested that during the afternoon he seek out the three women in our group he most wanted to talk with and to start a conversation with them. The behavior I suggested was experimental and new and was meant to allow Stan to see what would happen and to decide whether he wanted to continue with this different style of behavior. Note that these homework assignments don't have to be "given" by the leader; members can be encouraged to set tasks for themselves that will enable them to practice new assumptions and the resulting new behaviors.

Some Personal Concerns about RET

A major reservation I have with regard to RET concerns the dangers inherent in the therapist's confrontive and directive stance. Because the therapist has a large degree of power by virtue of persuasion and directiveness, brainwashing or other forms of psychological harm are more possible in RET than in other, less directive approaches. In RET groups there is a real possibility that, having decided that someone's beliefs are irrational, the group leader will work hard at converting that member to "sound thinking." Aside from the very relevant issue of what constitutes rational thinking and who is the judge of it, I question the value of getting rid of one system of irrational beliefs only to adopt a new set of questionable beliefs, particularly if these values are "pushed" by the group leader or, in some instances, by other group members. Because this approach is so directive and didactic, I see the potential for real abuse to clients. Therefore, it is essential that RET practitioners be highly aware of themselves and their own motivations and that they avoid imposing their value system on clients. This implies that the therapist's level of training, knowledge and skill, perceptiveness, and accuracy of judgment are particularly important in RET. Perhaps one ethical safeguard is for group leaders using RET procedures to openly discuss the issue of values and caution members to beware of pressure to change in a definite direction, one that might be alien to their value system.

Another danger I see in RET groups is the possibility of group pressure against members who resist certain changes. As I said earlier, feedback is potentially of great value, but ultimately it should be up to the person getting the feedback to decide what to do about it. If members cajole, push, demand, persuade, and attempt to do the thinking for other members, the results are at least questionable, since the very integrity of the individual members is at stake.

However, if RET is done in the manner prescribed by Ellis, these dangers are considerably lessened. Ellis rarely questions his clients' desires, preferences, values, or morality. What he does question is their "musts," "shoulds," and irrational demands. Thus, if someone says "I want romantic love" or "I prefer to be sexually abstinent," Ellis would rarely disagree. However, if the person said instead "I *must* be loved romantically" or "I *have* to be abstinent under all conditions," he would challenge such *must*urbatory views and encourage the client to change them to strong preferences. It is Ellis' belief that his brand of RET, by showing clients that even rationality is *desirable* but not *necessary*, minimizes bigotry, absolutism, and emotional disturbance—including the potential absolutism of members and leader.

The issue of RET's authoritarian and dogmatic approach has been addressed by other writers. Kleiner (1979), for example, asserts that the degree of authoritarianism of RET is determined by the degree of authoritarianism present in the RET therapist. Claiming that he has become a much less dogmatic and authoritarian therapist after becoming more aware of his own beliefs and prejudices, Kleiner says that therapists should encourage their clients to trust themselves and to question, challenge, and even reject the therapist's notions if they don't ring true. Kleiner also notes that the best safeguard against dogmatism and authoritarianism is an honest attempt on the part of the therapist to examine his or her own basic beliefs and values on an ongoing basis. I fully agree with Kleiner's view.

It is well to underscore that RET can be done by many people in a manner different from Albert Ellis' style. Since Ellis has so much visibility, it is worth distinguishing between the principles and techniques of RET and Ellis' very confrontational way of doing RET. A therapist can be soft-spoken and gentle and still use RET concepts and methods.

I'd like to note that RET has been subjected to extensive research studies. The book *Theoretical and Empirical Foundations of Rational-Emotive Therapy* (Ellis & Whiteley, 1979) brings together several interesting articles (some of which first appeared in *The Counseling Psychologist*) dealing with various and often controversial aspects of RET. A discussion of these issues would exceed the scope of this text. I am sure, however, that many of you will find the lively debate presented in the book very interesting and its wealth of research data and reference material quite valuable.

I encourage those of you who are interested in incorporating RET principles and techniques in your style of group leadership to consider taking an RET workshop. Training programs and brief workshops are offered by the Institute for Rational-Emotive Therapy in cities such as New York and Los Angeles. To be put on the mailing list for workshops, write to the Institute for Rational-Emotive Therapy, 45 East 65th Street, New York, NY 10021 or to the Institute for Rational-Emotive Therapy, 11333 Iowa Avenue, Los Angeles, CA 90025. Both branches offer certificate programs for eligible mental-health professionals, physicians, educators, clergy, counselors, and attorneys.

QUESTIONS FOR REFLECTION AND DISCUSSION

1. In your own experiences as a group member or a group leader, what are some of the common irrational beliefs that you have most frequently heard? How do you think a group offers an opportunity to challenge such ideas?

2. The goal of RET consists of urging clients to examine, to think about, and to understand and attack illogical assumptions about life. With the heavy emphasis given to thinking, do you think that feelings are given adequate emphasis in this therapy? Do you believe that people will make changes on an emotional and behavioral level if the focus is on attacking cognitive structures?

3. As an educational model, RET stresses teaching, learning, practicing new skills, logical thinking, carrying out homework assignments, and reading. As a group leader, to what degree would you be comfortable with such an educational focus? What aspects of RET would you want to include in your approach to groups, regardless of your theoretical orientation?

4. Compare and contrast RET with Gestalt therapy. What do you see as some of the major differences? Do you see any room to integrate the differing dimensions of these two therapies? If so, what factors might you combine in a group you were leading?

5. What criteria would you employ to determine whether a group member's ideas were rational? How would you determine if certain assumptions were self-defeating or constructive?

6. To what degree do you think the group leader's values become a central part of RET group therapy? How do you think the values held by the leader and by the members influence the group process?

7. Some might criticize RET group therapy on the ground that a participant is subjected to undue group pressure, both from the leader and the other members. This pressure could take the form of persuasion, giving advice, and expecting members to do certain outside assignments. Do you see any particular danger here? What are your reactions to this criticism?

8. RET calls for an active-directive group leader. Compare this role with that of the person-centered group leader, who gives as much leadership as possible to the members. Which leader role are you more comfortable with, and how do you think these contrasting leadership styles will change a group?

9. Like any action-oriented approach, RET insists that newly acquired insights be put into action, largely through homework assignments. This is a different perspective from those of psychoanalytic, person-centered, Gestalt, and some other experiential groups. What do you think of a model that is based on action outside of the sessions?

10. To what extent do you think that a personal and warm relationship between the members and the leader is a critical factor in RET group therapy?

RECOMMENDED SUPPLEMENTARY READINGS

Handbook of rational-emotive therapy (Ellis & Grieger, 1977) discusses both theoretical and applied aspects of RET and contains an excellent section on techniques. I especially recommend Chapter 1 (An Overview of the Clinical Theory of RET), Chapter 18 (RET in Groups), and Chapter 29 (The Present and Future of RET). If you want to read further on research data on RET, Chapters 2 and 3 are quite comprehensive.

Humanistic psychotherapy: The rational-emotive approach (Ellis, 1973b) is a clear and up-to-date presentation of the key concepts of RET, especially its humanistic and active-directive aspects. It is a very useful book that I recommend you read in its entirety.

A new guide to rational living (Ellis & Harper, 1975) is a self-help book that presents a straightforward approach to RET, based on homework assignments and self-questioning. It is easy reading, and many of the principles discussed can be applied to group work.

Theoretical and empirical foundations of rational-emotive therapy (Ellis & Whiteley, 1979) is the book I referred to at the end of my evaluation of RET. It represents a comprehensive treatment of the theoretical and practical aspects of RET and offers an interesting range of opinions by a number of professionals on a variety of issues, many of which were covered in this chapter. The book also contains several articles by Ellis.

The Institute for Rational-Emotive Therapy distributes books and other educational material from its headquarters in New York. A complete catalog of books, cassettes, pamphlets, and RET materials can be obtained by writing the institute at 45 East 65th Street, New York, NY 10021.

REFERENCES AND SUGGESTED READINGS*

Bandura, A. *Principles of behavior modification.* New York: Holt, Rinehart & Winston, 1969.

DiGiuseppe, R. A., Miller, N. J., & Trexler, L. D. A review of rational-emotive psychotherapy outcome studies. In A. Ellis & J. M. Whiteley (Eds.), *Theoretical and empirical foundations of rational-emotive therapy.* Monterey, Calif.: Brooks/Cole, 1979.

Dolliver, R. H. The relationship of rational-emotive therapy to other psychotherapies and personality theories. In A. Ellis & J. M. Whiteley (Eds.), *Theoretical and empirical foundations of rational-emotive therapy.* Monterey, Calif.: Brooks/Cole, 1979.

* Ellis, A. *Reason and emotion in psychotherapy.* New York: Lyle Stuart, 1962.

Ellis, A. Rational-emotive psychotherapy. In D. Arbuckle (Ed.), *Counseling and psychotherapy.* New York: McGraw-Hill, 1967.

Ellis, A. A cognitive approach to behavior therapy. *International Journal of Psychiatry,* 1969, *8,* 896–900. (a)

Ellis, A. A weekend of rational encounter. In A. Burton (Ed.), *Encounter: The theory and practice of encounter groups.* San Francisco: Jossey-Bass, 1969. (b)

Ellis, A. *Growth through reason: Verbatim cases in rational-emotive therapy.* Hollywood: Wilshire Books, 1973. (a)

* Ellis, A. *Humanistic psychotherapy: The rational-emotive approach.* New York: McGraw-Hill, 1973. (b)

Ellis, A. The group as agent in facilitating change toward rational thinking and appropriate emoting. In A. Jacobs & W. W. Spradlin (Eds.), *The group as agent of change.* New York: Behavioral Publications, 1974. (a)

Ellis, A. Rational-emotive theory: Albert Ellis. In A. Burton (Ed.), *Operational theories of personality.* New York: Brunner/Mazel, 1974. (b)

Ellis, A. *How to live with a "neurotic"* (Rev. ed.). New York: Crown, 1975. (a)

Ellis, A. Rational-emotive group therapy. In G. Gazda (Ed.), *Basic approaches to group psychotherapy and group counseling* (2nd ed.). Springfield, Ill.: Charles C Thomas, 1975. (b)

Ellis, A. Rational-emotive therapy. In V. Binder, A. Binder, & B. Rimland (Eds.), *Modern therapies.* Englewood Cliffs, N.J.: Prentice-Hall, 1976.

Ellis, A. The basic clinical theory of rational-emotive therapy. In A. Ellis & R. Grieger, *Handbook of rational-emotive therapy.* New York: Springer, 1977. (a)

---

*Books and articles marked with an asterisk are suggested for further study.

Ellis, A. Rational-emotive therapy in groups. In A. Ellis & R. Grieger, *Handbook of rational-emotive therapy.* New York: Springer, 1977. (b)

*Ellis, A. Rational-emotive therapy. In A. Ellis & J. M. Whiteley (Eds.), *Theoretical and empirical foundations of rational-emotive therapy.* Monterey, Calif.: Brooks/Cole, 1979. (a)

Ellis, A. Rational-emotive therapy: Research data that support the clinical and personality hypotheses of RET and other modes of cognitive-behavior therapy. In A. Ellis & J. M. Whiteley (Eds.), *Theoretical and empirical foundations of rational-emotive therapy.* Monterey, Calif.: Brooks/Cole, 1979. (b)

Ellis, A. The theory of rational-emotive therapy. In A. Ellis & J. M. Whiteley (Eds.), *Theoretical and empirical foundations of rational-emotive therapy.* Monterey, Calif.: Brooks/Cole, 1979. (c)

Ellis, A. Rejoinder: Elegant and inelegant RET. In A. Ellis & J. M. Whiteley (Eds), *Theoretical and empirical foundations of rational-emotive therapy.* Monterey, Calif.: Brooks/Cole, 1979. (d)

*Ellis, A. Rational-emotive family therapy. In A. M. Horne & M. M. Ohlsen (Eds.), *Family counseling and therapy.* Itasca, Ill.: Peacock, 1982. (a)

*Ellis, A. Rational-emotive group therapy. In G. Gazda (Ed.), *Basic approaches to group psychotherapy and group counseling* (3rd ed.). Springfield, Ill.: Charles C Thomas, 1982. (b)

*Ellis, A., & Grieger, R. *Handbook of rational-emotive therapy.* New York: Springer, 1977.

*Ellis, A., & Harper, R. A. *A new guide to rational living.* Englewood Cliffs, N.J.: Prentice-Hall, 1975.

*Ellis, A., & Whiteley, J. M. (Eds.). *Theoretical and empirical foundations of rational-emotive therapy.* Monterey, Calif.: Brooks/Cole, 1979.

Ewart, C. K., & Thoresen, C. E. The rational-emotive manifesto. *The Counseling Psychologist,* 1977, 7(1), 52–56.

Ewart, C. K., & Thoresen, C. E. The rational-emotive manifesto. In A. Ellis & J. M. Whiteley (Eds.), *Theoretical and empirical foundations of rational-emotive therapy.* Monterey, Calif.: Brooks/Cole, 1979.

Kleiner, F. B. Commentary on Albert Ellis' article. In A. Ellis & J. M. Whiteley (Eds.), *Theoretical and empirical foundations of rational-emotive therapy.* Monterey, Calif.: Brooks/Cole, 1979.

Lange, A., & Jakubowski, P. *Responsible assertive behavior: Cognitive-behavioral procedures for trainers.* Champaign, Ill.: Research Press, 1976.

Lazarus, A. A. Can RET become a cult? In A. Ellis & J. M. Whiteley (Eds.), *Theoretical and empirical foundations of rational-emotive therapy.* Monterey, Calif.: Brooks/Cole, 1979.

Lazarus, A. A. Multimodal group therapy. In G. Gazda (Ed.), *Basic approaches to group psychotherapy and group counseling* (3rd ed.). Springfield, Ill.: Charles C Thomas, 1982.

Mahoney, M. J. *Cognition and behavior modification.* Cambridge, Mass.: Ballinger, 1974.

Mahoney, M. J. A critical analysis of rational-emotive theory and therapy. *The Counseling Psychologist,* 1977, 7(1), 44–46.

Mahoney, M. J. A critical analysis of rational-emotive theory and therapy. In A. Ellis & J. M. Whiteley (Eds.), *Theoretical and empirical foundations of rational-emotive therapy.* Monterey, Calif.: Brooks/Cole, 1979.

Mahoney, M. J., & Arnkoff, D. B. Cognitive and self-control therapies. In S. L. Garfield & A. E. Bergin, *Handbook of psychotherapy and behavior change* (2nd ed.). New York: Wiley, 1978.

*Maultsby, M. C. Rational behavior therapy in groups. In G. Gazda (Ed.), *Innovations to group psychotherapy* (2nd ed.). Springfield, Ill.: Charles C Thomas, 1981.

Meichenbaum, D. Dr. Ellis, please stand up. In A. Ellis & J. M. Whiteley (Eds.), *Theoretical and empirical foundations of rational-emotive therapy.* Monterey, Calif.: Brooks/Cole, 1979.

Shelton, J. L., & Ackerman, J. M. *Homework in counseling and psychotherapy.* Springfield, Ill.: Charles C Thomas, 1974.

Skinner, B. F. *Beyond freedom and dignity.* New York: Knopf, 1971.

Smith, M. L., & Glass, G. V. Meta analysis of psychotherapy outcome studies. *American Psychologist,* 1977, *32,* 752–760.

Tosi, D. J. Personal reactions with some emphasis on new directions, application, and research. In A. Ellis & J. M. Whiteley (Eds.), *Theoretical and empirical foundations of rational-emotive therapy.* Monterey, Calif.: Brooks/Cole, 1979.

Walen, S., DiGiuseppe, R., & Wessler, R. L. *A practitioner's guide to rational-emotive therapy.* New York: Oxford University Press, 1980.

*Weinrach, S. G. Unconventional therapist: Albert Ellis. *Personnel and Guidance Journal,* 1980, *59*(3), 152–160.

Wessler, R. A., & Wessler, R. L. *The principles and practice of rational-emotive therapy.* San Francisco: Jossey-Bass, 1980.

15

REALITY THERAPY

INTRODUCTION

Like many of the other founders of therapeutic approaches described in this book, William Glasser was trained in classical psychoanalysis. He quickly became disenchanted, however, and began to experiment with innovative methods, which later came to be called reality therapy. His primary method of treatment was group therapy.

Glasser's early work focused on asking clients to recognize and take responsibility for what they were doing in the present, rather than dwelling upon feelings of what had happened to them in the past. As an example of this here-and-now focus, Glasser describes his work with a young woman who wanted to talk about her growing up without her parents (Evans, 1982). She attributed all of her present problems to the fact that her parents had not been in the picture and that she had been raised by her grandfather. Finally, Glasser told the woman that he was no longer interested in hearing stories about her grandfather and that, if they were to work together, he wanted her to talk about her plans for life, both now and in the future.

During the 1960s Glasser worked in public education as a consultant, and at this time he applied his basic concepts of reality therapy to the teaching/learning process. His interest was in how students and teachers interact with one another, how learning in schools can be connected to the lives of the students, and how schools can contribute to a sense of either success or failure in learners. In his book *Schools without Failure*, Glasser (1969) outlines practices in schools that can foster meaningful learning.

In 1976 Glasser published his *Positive Addiction*, which developed the theme that people can gain strength in their ability to manage their life if they are committed to some form of positive behavior, such as meditation, running, or yoga. Just as people who have negative addictions to drugs and alcohol become weaker, people who develop positive "addictions" grow stronger and gain confidence in themselves.

His most recent development of the principles of reality therapy is found in his book *Stations of the Mind* (1981), which describes the neurological and psychological basis for the clinical approach in his earlier works. The new direction for reality therapy is grounded in the assumption that we create an inner world. What is important is not the way the real world exists, but rather the way we perceive the world to exist. According to Glasser (1981), "Most of our lives are lived in a higher-order, unique personal world that we create in our head from our needs" (p. 116). In his updating of reality therapy, he explores the theme that behavior is the attempt to control our perceptions of the external world to fit our internal and personal world.

Reality therapy focuses on solving problems and on coping with the demands of reality in society. It stresses the individual's responsibility for changing his or her behavior. Thus, reality-therapy practitioners concentrate on what clients can practically do in their present situation to change their behavior and on the means for doing so. Clients are challenged to evaluate the quality of their behavior, formulate a plan for change, commit themselves to such a plan, and follow through with their commitment.

A basic assumption of Glasser's approach is that everyone has a "growth force," that this force impels one to develop a "success identity" (viewing oneself as worthy of love and as a significant person), and that any change in identity is contingent on behavioral change. Like behavior therapy, transactional analysis, and rational-emotive therapy, reality therapy is an active, directive, and didactic model; it stresses present behavior—not attitudes, insight, one's past, or unconscious motivations.

Over the past two decades, Glasser has been more interested in practice than in developing a theory. His work is aimed at putting a few basic concepts of reality therapy to work in a variety of settings, such as corrections institutions, schools, private practice, marital and family therapy, group work, and counseling in community clinics. As Glasser has mentioned, the principles of reality therapy need not be restricted to psychotherapists; rather, they can be used by parents, ministers, doctors, husbands, and wives in working on interpersonal relationships.

KEY CONCEPTS

Responsibility and Human Needs

The core of reality therapy is responsibility, which Glasser (1965) defines as the "ability to fulfill one's needs, and to do so in a way that does not deprive others of the ability to fulfill their needs" (p. 13).* The essential needs referred to here

---

*From *Reality Therapy: A New Approach to Psychiatry*, by William Glasser, M.D. Copyright © 1965 by William Glasser, Inc. Reprinted by permission of Harper & Row, Publishers, Inc.

are the need to love and to be loved, the need to feel a sense of worthiness, the need to have fun and enjoy life, the need to be free and in control of one's destiny. If we fail to fulfill the range of our basic needs, we often turn to negative forms of addictive behavior. A major goal of current reality therapy is to teach people better ways of fulfilling their needs and to help them effectively get what they want from life. In Glasser's words: "I want to teach people how the control system works and use the concepts of reality therapy not only to teach better behaviors but also to evaluate and improve their perceptions and their internal world" (1981, p. 267).

Responsibility, then, consists of learning how to realistically meet these basic psychological needs, and the essence of therapy consists of teaching people to accept that responsibility by showing them that they are not the victim of circumstances but the product of their own decisions and actions. In many ways, Glasser's approach is grounded on existential and phenomenological premises. He assumes that humans have a tendency to choose their own goals and direction in life. When people make choices that infringe on others' freedom, their behavior is irresponsible. It is essential that clients learn how to achieve their freedom so that others do not suffer in the process.

Success Identity

The goal of reality therapy is to help people achieve what is called a "success identity." Those who possess a success identity see themselves as being able to give and accept love, feel that they are significant to others, experience a sense of self-worth, become involved with others in a caring way, and meet their needs in ways that are not at the expense of others.

Those who seek therapy are often people who have a "failure identity": they see themselves as unloved, rejected, and unwanted, unable to become intimately involved with others, incompetent to make and stick with commitments, and generally helpless. Typically, individuals with a failure identity meet challenges with a despairing "I can't"—an often self-fulfilling prophecy that leads to further lack of success, which in turn supports a negative self-view and eventually makes these people see themselves as hopeless failures in life. Because reality therapy assumes that we are ultimately self-determining beings who become what we decide to become, the system is designed to teach people what they can practically do to change behavior that fosters a failure identity and to develop behavior that leads to a success identity.

Rejection of the Medical Model

Reality therapy rejects the conventional psychiatric concept of mental illness and the practice of psychological diagnosis. The practice of psychodiagnosis, whereby individuals are labeled as psychotics, sociopaths, or whatever, is dismissed as relatively useless—worse, as providing people the means by which they can deny responsibility for their own failures. As Glasser (1965) puts it, "Conventional psychiatry wastes too much time arguing over how many diagnoses can dance at the end of a case history, time better spent treating the ever-present problem of irresponsibility" (p. 49). In Glasser's (1981) current thinking, mental health is equated with the responsible fulfilling of one's needs or drives, and mental illness is what occurs when people are unable to control the world to satisfy their needs. Psychosis can be considered as "crazy activity"—which may be a person's best attempt to control his or her world. Psychotic persons who "hear voices" and who have many false beliefs are working toward organizing their inner world in such a way that they do not have to deal with the real world that they perceive as painful and that they think they cannot handle. Generally, psychotic individuals are so engrossed in their private world, characterized by distorted thoughts and perceptions, that they have little desire to deal with the real world.

Emphasis on the Present

Psychodynamic theories stress the influence of the past, especially early childhood experiences, on the client's current condition. Reality therapy stresses current behavior and is concerned with past events only insofar as they influence how the client *behaves* now. The focus on the present is characterized by the question so often asked by the reality therapist: *"What are you doing?"* As Glasser (1980) has noted, this emphasis on the present does not indicate that reality therapy rejects the notion that problems may be rooted in the past, since everything that people do is in some way related to their history. However, he adds:

> But since we can only correct for today and plan for a better tomorrow, we talk little about the past—we can't undo anything that has already occurred. Therefore, the reality therapist takes account of the past, believes in it, but deals with the present because dealing with the present respects the whole past [1980, p. 49].

It should be noted that the past may be discussed if doing so will help clients plan for a better tomorrow. When the past is explored, the emphasis is on past successes, not on misery. "What should be avoided is looking back for past failures. We have our hands full with dealing with present failure; we need not look in the past for more" (Glasser, 1980, p. 49).

Value Judgments

Unlike many conventional therapeutic approaches, reality therapy stresses the importance of getting clients to face the issue of right and wrong behavior— that is, the constructiveness or destructiveness of the behavior. It is the therapist's task to confront clients with the consequences of their behavior and to get *them* to judge the quality of their actions. According to Glasser (1965), if clients look honestly at their behavior and make a judgment about it, they can then see what *they* are doing to contribute to their failures. Indeed, unless clients eventually judge their own behavior, they will not change. In short, the therapist encourages clients to make value judgments about the quality of their behavior in order to determine what may be contributing to their failures and what changes may be undertaken to promote success.

Deemphasis on Transference

In contrast to the many psychodynamic theories that view the transference relationship as the core of the therapeutic process, reality therapy sees transference at best as unimportant. Glasser (1965) contends that people don't seek a replay of unsuccessful involvements in their past; rather, they seek satisfying interpersonal relationships *now*. The reality-therapy approach promotes such relationships between therapist and clients. Glasser (1965) says "We relate to patients as ourselves, not as transference figures" (p. 44). In addition, reality therapy maintains that transference can offer a way for the therapist to hide as a person and that it can prevent a genuine involvement between client and therapist. During the course of therapy, there may be a deep dependence upon the therapist for a time. However, clients are encouraged to become independent, and treatment ends once they are able to cope effectively with the demands of reality (Glasser, 1980).

Emphasis on Conscious Factors

Like the concept of transference, the role of the unconscious is given little attention in reality therapy and is seen as often detrimental to the therapeutic process. In Glasser's (1965) words: "Emphasis upon the unconscious sidetracks the main issue of the patient's irresponsibility and gives him another excuse to avoid facing reality" (p. 53). Elsewhere Glasser (1965) notes that, although insight into the unconscious may be interesting, it is not essential to behavior change. Since change in behavior *is* deemed essential to the therapeutic process, involvement in the unconscious is clearly considered an idle activity.

Existential/Phenomenological Orientation

Contemporary reality therapy is grounded in existential/phenomenological principles. It is based upon several assumptions that influence the group practitioner. One of these assumptions is that we are moved by inner forces. Although external forces have an influence on our decisions, our behavior is not *caused* by these environmental factors. As I have noted, Glasser maintains that we perceive the world in the context of our own needs and do *not* perceive the world as it really is. It is important that therapists understand that clients live both in the external world and also in their own internal world.

In addition to this focus on the subjective world, contemporary reality therapy continues to have a strong existential orientation. We are viewed as responsible for the kind of world we create for ourselves, we are not helpless victims, and we can create a better life. Glasser (1981) does not accept the notion that misery simply *happens* to us; rather, it is something that we often choose. He observes that clients are typically quick to complain that they are upset because people in their life do not behave as they would like them to. It is a powerful learning for us to recognize that we choose all of our behaviors, including feeling miserable and thinking that we are helpless victims. We choose misery in the attempt to reduce our perceptual errors. Thus, Glasser speaks of people *depressing* or *angrying* themselves, rather than being depressed or being angry. With this perspective, depression can be explained as an active choice that we make, rather than the result of being a passive and helpless victim. This process of "depressing" keeps anger in check, and it also allows us to ask for help. Glasser contends that, as long as we cling to the notion that we are victims of depression and that misery is something that happens to us, we will not change for the better. We can change only when we recognize and *act* upon the reality that what we are doing is the result of our choices.

The Essence of BCP Psychology

A recently developed key concept of reality therapy is BCP psychology, which is based on the premise that *behavior* is the *control* of our *perceptions*. Although we may not be able to control what actually *is* in the real world, we do attempt to control what we perceive. Behavior is best understood in the light of our attempt to control our perceptions to meet our own needs. In this process, we create our inner world. We are not locked into any one mode of behavior, although we must behave in some way. Our behavior has three components: doing, thinking, and feeling. Since it is often difficult to control what and how we are thinking and feeling, reality therapy focuses on what we are doing. It is typically easier to force ourselves to *do* something different than it is to feel or think something different. In order to grasp the key thrust of BCP concepts, the following short quotations are given below from Glasser's (1981) *Stations of the Mind:*

- "BCP teaches the difficult lesson that we both choose the world we want and choose the behavior that is our attempt to move the real world closer to the in-the-head world we want" (p. 238).
- "BCP teaches you to assume more responsibility for your internal world, and that is hard" (p. 246).
- "You must accept that all of your life, any behavior you choose, good or bad, is *your best choice at that particular time.* If you start searching for fault, you necessarily criticize yourself, increase your error and become more sick or disabled" (p. 246).

It is clear that adopting a self-critical and blaming stance will not help people change for the better. In group counseling, leaders can help members recognize that what they are doing is not working for them, help them accept themselves as a person, and guide them in making realistic plans to do better. Members can more easily choose better behavior if they come to realize that what they are doing, thinking, and feeling is not simply happening to them, but that they are indeed making choices.

ROLE AND FUNCTIONS OF THE GROUP LEADER

The central task of reality-therapy group practitioners is to become involved with the individual group members and then to help them face reality. This task requires the leader to perform several functions—among them:

- providing a model for responsible behavior and a model of a life based on a success identity
- establishing with each member a therapeutic relationship based on care and respect—one that encourages and demands responsible behavior
- actively promoting discussion of members' current behavior and actively discouraging excuses for irresponsible behavior
- introducing and fostering the process of self-evaluation of current behavior
- teaching members to formulate and implement plans to change their behaviors
- establishing a structure and limits for the sessions

- being open to challenge and exploring their own values with the group
- encouraging members to get involved with one another, to share common experiences, and to help one another deal with problems in a responsible manner
- assisting members in setting practical limits to the duration and scope of their therapy
- teaching members how to apply to everyday life what they have learned in the group

Reality-therapy group leaders assume a verbally active and directive role in the group. In carrying out their functions, they focus on the strengths and potential of the members rather than on their failures. Reality therapists assume that dwelling on limitations, problems, and failures tends to reinforce the client's basic failure identity. Therefore, they challenge members to look at their unused potential and to discover how to work toward creating a success identity.

APPLICATION OF REALITY THERAPY TO GROUP WORK

Glasser has developed eight principles, or concepts, that form the core of reality therapy. They are discussed in this section, which adapts and integrates material taken from various sources (Evans, 1982; Ford, 1982; Glasser, 1965, 1969, 1976b, 1980, 1981; Glasser & Zunin, 1979). These principles are:

1. personal involvement of the leader with the members
2. focus on current behavior
3. behavior evaluation
4. planning and action
5. commitment
6. refusal to accept excuses
7. no punishment
8. refusal to give up

Several points are important to keep in mind. First, although these concepts may seem clear and simple as they are presented in written form, they are difficult to translate into actual therapeutic practice, and it takes considerable skill and creativity to successfully apply them in group work. Although the principles will be the same when used by any certified reality therapist, the manner in which they are applied does vary depending on the therapist's style and personal characteristics. Finally, although the eight principles are applied in a progressive manner, with each step building on the previous one, they should not be thought of as discrete and rigid categories. There is a considerable degree of interdependence among these principles, and taken together they contribute to the total process that is reality therapy.

To provide an understanding of how these concepts actually operate in the group process, this section takes as an example a group of male adolescents who are in a detention facility for some type of criminal offense. Participation in the group constitutes one aspect of these youths' treatment program, and sessions are held several times a week for at least an hour. The evolution and development of this group, beginning with the involvement stage, will be summarized to demonstrate how reality-therapy principles actually work. For purposes of the example, assume that most of the youths in the group have a failure identity.

1. Personal Involvement with the Client

The first step in reality therapy is to "make friends" with the clients, which implies getting involved in their life and creating the rapport that will be the foundation of the therapeutic relationship. In a sense, this is the most important and demanding phase of therapy, for in the absence of personal involvement there can be no effective therapy. When reality therapy is ineffective, it is usually because genuine involvement has not been established. The genuine caring on the part of the therapist can go a long way toward building the bonds of trust that will be needed for clients to commit themselves to the challenges of making positive changes in their life.

For real involvement to take place, the leader must have certain personal qualities, including warmth, understanding, acceptance, concern, respect for the client, openness, and the willingness to be challenged by others. One of the best ways to develop this goodwill and therapeutic friendship is simply by listening to clients. Involvement is also promoted by talking about a wide range of topics that have relevance for group members—topics that relate to the members' current everyday behaviors and experiences and that play down misery and past failures. Once involvement has been established, the leader confronts the group members with the reality and consequences of their *current* behavior. This ongoing confrontation constitutes the essence of the group.

Because of the opportunity to form relationships with several other people besides the therapist, there is a definite advantage in practicing reality therapy in groups. The group milieu can do a lot to deepen caring and involvement. Not only does the group therapist care for the client, but others in the group also provide both support and an honest challenge to look at one's life. The nonpunishing atmosphere of the group can promote self-acceptance and the desire to make specific plans for better behavior (Glasser, 1976b). Group interaction is seen as especially important in helping individual members break the vicious circle of failure experiences, because, according to reality-therapy theory, people cannot gain a success identity by isolating themselves. Indeed, it is Glasser's (1976a) view that self-help implies being involved with others.

How does this principle of involvement apply to the case illustration described above? To begin with, we should note that many of the youths in the detention facility who are now being required to attend group-therapy sessions have never had any meaningful and positive involvements with others. Under such circumstances, how is it possible for a leader to establish a personal involvement with the youths and to facilitate involvement among the group members? First of all, the leader must establish his or her credibility by demonstrating a genuine concern and caring for the youths—seeing them not as they see themselves but as the successful and responsible persons they are capable of becoming. With that, the foundation for involvement is laid. Without this positive view of the participants' possibilities—or, even worse, by harboring the belief that the youths cannot change—the leader will foster the boys' sense of hopelessness and their inevitable resistance to seeing themselves in a more positive light.

It should be noted that one effective way to create a therapeutic climate for participants in involuntary or mandated groups is for the leader to explain to members some specific ways in which the group process can be of personal value to them. For example, if participants see the group as a place where they can learn to escape their particular pattern of repeated failures, they may take the first step toward involvement in the group. It should also be noted that involvement must be, and in fact is, controlled by the reality-therapy practitioner, who actively defines the nature and the purpose of the group as well as the limits of the group activities.

2. Focus on Current Behavior

Reality therapy concentrates on changing current behavior, not attitudes and feelings. That doesn't imply that attitudes are dismissed as unimportant; rather, the approach is that behavioral change is easier to effect than attitudinal change and of greater value in the therapeutic process. For that reason a client who expressed feelings of depression and helplessness would not be questioned about the reasons for the feelings or encouraged to explore them. Rather, the reality therapist would urge the person to identify those behaviors that were causing or supporting the feelings. The aim is to help clients understand *their* responsibilities for their own feelings. As a way of encouraging clients to look at what they are actually doing to contribute to their feelings, questions such as the following are likely to be asked:

- What are you doing now?
- What did you actually do this past week?
- What did you want to do differently this past week?
- What stopped you from doing what you say you want to do?
- What will you do tomorrow?

Listening to clients talk about feelings can be productive, but only if it is tied to what they are doing. According to Glasser (1980, 1981), what we are doing is easy to see and thus serves as the proper focus in therapy. So, feelings and thoughts are explored in reality therapy, but discussions centering on them, without strongly relating them to what people are doing, are counterproductive (Glasser, 1980).

Getting members to focus on what they are doing has the aim of teaching them that they can gain conscious control over their behavior, can control the choices they make, and can change their life. In this process, clients need to be helped to accept their part in contributing to their own problems. Although they may want to talk in detail about how others are not living up to their expectations and how, if only the world would change, they could be happy, such a tack will only solidify their victimlike position. Briefly, then, the focus of the reality-therapy group is on gaining awareness of current behavior, because this process, Glasser (1976b) maintains, is the only way in which a person can develop a positive self-image.

Relating this principle to the example of the group of juvenile offenders, one can see that the leader would discourage the youths from dwelling on their crimes and the reasons underlying their current feelings and attitudes about themselves and others. Rather, the leader would seek to encourage the youths to discuss the behavior that led to their sentence and would challenge them to trace and face the practical consequences of their behavior—in short, to evaluate their behavior and accept responsibility for it. According to Glasser, having traced the consequences of one's behavior to the present condition of failure, one is in a position to develop the capacity to make choices that can increase one's chances of success.

In connection with our example, it is of some interest to note how Glasser sees the behaviors that lead to criminal activity. Glasser (1976a) has described what he calls the behavior of the "weak"—a description that seems to relate to his earlier statements concerning irresponsibility (Glasser, 1965). He writes that the first choice of "weak" people faced with a painful situation is simply to give up. The second choice involves selecting from a variety of behaviors, including acting-out behavior (delinquency and sociopathic behavior), developing negative emotions (depression, dejection, and fears), choosing to become crazy (hallucinations, delusions, and other psychotic behavior), and developing psychosomatic symptoms (migraines, ulcers, and bodily aches). A third choice, which emerges as a consequence of being frustrated in the search for love, self-worth, and success, is described as a form of negative addition (drugs or alcohol). According to Glasser, if people come to understand that their present behavior is based on negative choices leading to increasing loss of self-worth and self-esteem, they are in a position to develop positive choices that can lead to a success identity.

3. Behavior Evaluation

Once group members can successfully identify and take responsibility for their current behavior, the reality therapist guides them to evaluate that behavior on the basis of what is good for them and for others (Glasser, 1976b) and, ultimately, to determine whether their behavior is leading to a success identity or a failure identity. Glasser (1980) notes that it is not the reality therapist's function to act as a moralist—decreeing what the client "should" be doing or imposing values. Indeed, the reality therapist is enjoined from offering any type of formula or advice or even directing clients to change. Glasser and Zunin (1979) put this matter as follows: "The therapist does not make value judgments for the patient for this would relieve him of the responsibility for his behavior. But the therapist guides the patient to an evaluation of his own behavior" (p. 320). Thus, the therapist's main effort focuses on assisting the client to determine the effects of his or her behavior and to accept the consequences.

It is important that therapists remain nonjudgmental about clients' behavior and do not adopt an attitude of criticism. Instead, they best serve clients when they challenge them to stop, look, and listen. If therapists can stimulate client self-questioning—"What am I doing now? Is it getting me where I want to go? Is my behavior working for me? Am I making constructive choices?"—the client will be more likely to begin to make changes. In writing about this nonjudgmental stance, Glasser (1980) observes:

> It is this stance that helps a client decide that he or she ought to try something else. When we judge people or criticize them, they are almost always forced to keep up their inadequate behavior to justify it.... Therefore, while we want our clients to judge their behavior (step three), we must again stress that it's they, not we, who make the judgments [p. 57].

Returning to the example of the youths in the detention facility, the group leader might ask them: "Does your behavior get you what you want? Where has your behavior led you? Does your behavior hurt you or others? Is your behavior fulfilling your needs?" More specifically, an adolescent who has been sentenced for robbing a liquor store to support a drug habit may be asked to evaluate the consequences of continuing his acts of robbery and to confront the probable consequences of being caught and jailed. Further, he may be directed to face the consequences of taking drugs. It is the task of the youth—with the therapist's help—to determine and evaluate the consequences of his actions and then decide whether he wants to change his behavior. It is not the task of the therapist to do his changing for him, nor can the therapist *make* him want to give up drugs and stealing and lead a more constructive life. In short, the therapist helps the client determine *what* needs to be changed, and the client determines *why* the change is needed.

Although Glasser (1976a) maintains that self-evaluation and self-correction are the foundation of reality therapy, he also warns that "how we criticize ourselves, however, is vitally important because we must learn to direct our criticism at those activities which it is possible to correct; otherwise we will be too hard on ourselves and may lock ourselves into failure" (p. 59). Glasser stresses that it is counterproductive for clients to fall into the self-critical trap of berating themselves for certain choices they have made. Instead of harshly criticizing themselves by finding fault, it is a good practice for a person to learn to say "I have an error, probably from a conflict, and I must figure out something better than what I am doing now" (Glasser, 1981, p. 246).

4. Planning and Action

Much of the work in reality therapy consists of helping members identify specific ways to change their failure behavior into success behavior. Once a client has made a value judgment on his or her behavior and decided to effect a positive change in that behavior, the therapist is charged with the task of assisting the client in developing a plan for behavioral changes. The art of such planning is to establish practical short-term goals that have a high probability of being successfully attained, because such successes will positively reinforce the client's efforts to achieve long-range goals.

Planning for responsible behavior is the core of the helping process. This is clearly a teaching phase of therapy. Therefore, therapy is best directed toward providing clients with new information and helping them discover more effective ways of getting what they want (Glasser, 1981). A large portion of the therapy time consists of making plans and then checking to determine how these plans are working. In a group context members learn how to plan realistically and responsibly through contact with both the other members and the leader. The members are encouraged to experiment with new behaviors, to try out different ways of obtaining their goals, and to carry out an action program. It is important that these plans not be too ambitious, for people need to experience success. The purpose of the plan is to arrange for successful experiences. Once a plan works, feelings of self-esteem will increase. It is clear that helpful plans are modest in the beginning and specify what is to be done, when it will be done, and how often. In short, plans are meant to encourage clients to translate their talk and intentions into actions.

How does this apply to the group we have used as an example? The members have failure identities stemming from an inability to relate to others effectively. Thus, they can use the group for the purpose of relearning interpersonal skills. The participants can be guided to make plans for change in the group and in the detention facility and assisted in implementing them. For example, a withdrawn and isolated youth who wants to come out of his shell can set the short-term goal of spending a few more minutes a day with others and speaking out within the group for the first time. Once he has succeeded in this behavior, he can expand his ability to relate to others within and without the group and eventually work toward his long-term goal—changing the behavior that led to his detention.

It is important to note that, in addition to being specific, concrete, and measurable, plans need to be flexible and open to modification as clients gain a deeper understanding of the specific behaviors that they want to change. In short, it is vital that clients run their plans, not vice versa.

Although the burden of responsibility for formulating and implementing plans for change rests with the group members, it is the task of the leader to create an accepting and nourishing atmosphere wherein such plans can be implemented. As Glasser (1976a) puts it:

> So while I believe in the importance of getting down to brass tacks and making plans, it has been my experience that you can make plans until hell freezes over but if you haven't the ability to produce a reasonably non-self-critical therapeutic milieu the client won't have the strength to carry the plans out [p. 151].

It should be emphasized that throughout this planning phase the group leader has the function of continually urging members to assume responsibility for their own choices and actions by reminding them that no one in the world will do things for them or live their life for them. Challenging members to make responsible plans calls for considerable skill and inventiveness. As Glasser (1980) writes:

> Nowhere is the need for ingenuity seen more clearly than in step four, the planning phase. Here the therapist, always moving toward figuring out a better way, suggests, urges, cajoles, draws out, drags out, and somehow or other gets a client to begin moving in a better direction to fulfill his or her needs. It takes a lot of strength to continually reject the person's excuses and keep saying that if we have a plan, we

have got to follow it through or make another one. It also takes some self-control to avoid becoming angry and retaliatory when a client tests, taunts, challenges, or berates you [p. 57].

The ultimate responsibility for making plans and following them through rests with the client. As active as the therapist is in the client/therapist relationship, therapy is merely a beginning. It is up to each client to determine ways of carrying these plans outside the restricted world of therapy and into the everyday world. But it should be remembered that effective therapy can be the catalyst that leads to this self-directed, responsible living.

5. Commitment

Typically, people with a failure identity have trouble making and keeping commitments, since part of their failure relates to breaking commitments. Clearly, formulating even the most reasonable and practical plan is a waste of time if the client lacks the willingness to implement it. Glasser and Zunin (1979) suggest that plans be put in writing in the form of a contract—a contract that will assist group members in holding themselves and others accountable for the carrying out of the plans.

Here one can readily see the value of a group, such as the one in our example. Once individual members make plans and announce them to the group, the group is in a position to help them evaluate and review these plans and to offer support and encouragement when needed. If individual members fall short of their commitments or in any way fail to implement their plans, that fact cannot be hidden from others and, more importantly, from themselves. If some members are able to follow through with their plans, they serve as models for the rest of the group. Others may realize that, if their peers can do what they have set out to do, so can they.

It is essential that members who are reluctant to make a commitment be helped to express and explore their fears of failing. Members may have many resistances and fear rejection. Therefore, the support of the group is especially critical during this phase. Members can be encouraged to begin each group session by reporting on the activities of the week, including the difficulties they encountered in sticking with their plans as well as the successes they had in trying out new behavior in the real world. Just as in behavioral groups, where the buddy system is used, reality therapy can encourage members to make contacts with each other during the week if they have trouble in sticking by their commitments.

Of course, there are always those who are unwilling to make *any* commitments. As was mentioned earlier, therapists cannot force change. But they can help such people look at what is stopping them from making a commitment to change. Sometimes people are convinced that they *cannot* change, that they cannot stick to any decision, and that they are destined to remain a failure. In such cases it is important that the client be helped to see clearly the consequences of not changing and then be guided to formulate very short-range, limited plans having goals that are easy to reach. Clients need to achieve some degree of success, and they need to believe that they do have the power to change. As far as this basic principle of reality therapy is concerned, the nature and scope of the plan are not as important as the commitment to *some* plan for change, however limited.

Commitment places the responsibility for changing directly on the clients. If members say over and over that they want to change and hope to change, they can be asked the question "Will you do it and when will you do it?" The danger, of course, is that the member's plan may not be carried out, which leads to an increase of frustrations and adds to the person's failures. Reality therapy tries to avoid this problem by not asking for any commitment that is not reasonable and possible (Glasser, 1981).

6. Refusal to Accept Excuses

No amount of careful formulation and conscientious commitment can guarantee that members will follow their plans. Such failures can and do occur, but Glasser (1965) warns therapists of the danger of excusing the person for failing to stick with a commitment or playing detective by asking fruitless questions about *why* the plan failed. Instead, he urges the therapist to teach members that excuses are a form of self-deception that may offer temporary relief but ultimately lead to failure and to the cementing of a failure identity. Glasser (1976b) puts it well when he says: "Excuses, rationalizations, and intellectualizations can become the death knell of any successful relationship; they have no place in reality therapy" (p. 61).

At the same time Glasser (1965) warns against deprecating those who fail to carry out their plans. He urges therapists to express genuine caring when they refuse to allow blaming and fault finding. The difficult and demanding task of the reality therapist is to care enough for his or her clients to insist that they face what is often a difficult truth: that it is *they* who are responsible for what they do.

Here again, we see the advantage of a group setting for reality therapy. If the group leader keeps asking members whether they *really* want to change, thus maintaining the focus on commitment to change, the group is likely to imitate the leader's style. When members don't carry out their plans, they can be asked several questions, such as: What happened? Was your plan realistic? Did you attempt too much too soon?

Also, people tend to be far less tolerant of others' excuses than they are of their own. Taking the example of the adolescent delinquents, it is likely that each one of them would lay the blame for his failures on the doorsteps of uncaring parents or an unfair society. It is less likely that others in the group would fail to see that the blame lies within the person—particularly if the group leader is adept at keeping the focus of discussion on individual responsibility.

7. No Punishment

Reality therapy holds that punishment is not a useful means of effecting behavioral change. Glasser (1965) maintains that punishment not only is inefficient in changing behavior but also reinforces the client's failure identity and damages the therapeutic relationship. Glasser sees even deprecating remarks as a form of punishment and warns the therapist to avoid them:

> In nonpunitive reality therapy the clients are never put down for not having done what they said they would do. If we don't put people down or punish in any way, we are justified in being firm about not accepting excuses, because without punishment or rejection there are no good reasons for excuses [1980, p. 55].

Therefore, instead of using punishment, the therapist challenges clients to see and to accept *reasonable consequences* that flow from their actions. Taking the example of the youths in the detention facility, the therapist would avoid deprecating a group member for, say, failing to attend a meeting. The therapist might, however, lead the boy to see that his failure to attend meetings could affect his chances for eventual release. By avoiding the use of critical statements, by not accepting any excuses, and by remaining nonjudgmental, therapists can ask clients if they *really* want to change. Clients can be asked to reevaluate to determine if they still want to stick by their commitments.

8. Refusal to Give Up

The final step of reality therapy is never to give up. Those with a failure identity expect others to give up on them. Therefore, no matter what clients say or do, it is therapeutically helpful for the therapist not to give up. It is not helpful for a therapist to assume that another person will never change or that a person is hopeless. The group leader must retain faith that the person has the capacity to change. This is a sign of real involvement. Glasser (1981) writes: "Some people take a great deal of time to develop more adequate behaviors, and if you give up while they still want you to help your giving up increases their error. A good therapist is stubborn and does not give up easily" (p. 278).

The concept of not giving up applies well to the example of the group of adolescent delinquents. A leading factor contributing to their delinquent behavior may well be the fact that many people in their life have given up on them and have showed little faith in their ability to succeed. The group leader who adopts a stance of refusing to give up and a commitment to keep trying to reach these adolescents challenges them to find ways of believing in themselves. Once the members believe that the leader and other members will not give up on them, the sense of belongingness is solidified, which allows for work to proceed. The members can then develop a sense of faith in themselves, for they know that they are no longer alone. Although it is up to them to make decisions about how they will live in the world, they also realize that they do have the capacity to resolve their problems and make some significant changes in what they are thinking, feeling, and doing.

REALITY THERAPY WITH THE FAMILY GROUP

The principles of reality therapy are well suited for counseling a family. The therapist's basic challenge is to apply in a creative way the eight steps just described. Ford (1982) discusses some principles and strategies in working with family groups. The therapist begins by discovering what each family member wants and assessing what each person is doing. The focus is on their past or present actions that may contribute to their strength and confidence. According to Ford, in counseling families it is essential to ascertain what the members have in common and develop some plan based on areas where they are in agreement.

The reality therapist assumes that all families have problems; what is essential is that they work on their relationships so that they can withstand the conflicts that are bound to arise. Family members are encouraged to learn rational and realistic ways of respectfully working out problems that sometimes divide the family. If children are brought to a session by the parents, Ford says, he pays particular attention to their strengths. He listens to the areas of belonging, love, self-worth, fun, and freedom. As a reality therapist, he is especially interested in helping children discover activities in which they can experience success and meet their need for self-worth. Again, here is where creativity is needed on the therapist's part to guide each family member in finding a route for his or her growth.

Elimination of criticism. According to Ford (1982), the major obstacle to rebuilding healthy relationships within the family is criticism. In the face of constant criticism, reconciliation is almost impossible. Therefore, parents are typically taught to devise alternate ways of relating with their children that do not involve constant criticism. Since parents might be at a loss to know what to do except criticize the actions of their children, Ford uses role playing and behavior rehearsal as ways to teach parents effective communications and relationship skills. As the therapist, he takes the part of the parent, and they play the roles of their children. In this situation he is teaching parents by coaching and modeling; they learn new skills and are expected to practice them during the sessions and at home. Once criticism is eliminated, there is room for dealing with children directly and respectfully by having them see the logical consequences of some of their actions and by dealing with problems in a reality-oriented manner.

As is true of both individual and group counseling, family therapy will not be effective unless those who are involved are willing to work at making changes. If one of the family members states that she is coming to the sessions only because her parents are making her attend, she can be asked if she is willing to work at changing certain relationships for a short period before deciding that therapy will not work. One of the therapist's jobs is to deal therapeutically with the resistance that one or more family members exhibit. The therapist can prompt an open discussion of resistive attitudes and behaviors in the sessions, and through this process the person may be willing to give the sessions a try. It is essential that all the members make some assessment of their family situation, and they must have a desire to make changes if the therapy is to be effective. Once the family members decide that they are willing to make an effort to change, a plan of action can be developed in much the same way as plans would be made in any group. The importance of commitment and following through with these plans applies to family therapy in the same way that it does to group therapy. With such a plan, the family members can then evaluate whether progress is being made toward the goals that they can agree upon.

EVALUATION OF REALITY THERAPY

Advantages of the Approach

A characteristic of reality therapy that I especially favor is the stress on accountability. For example, when a group participant indicates a desire to change certain behaviors, the leader confronts the member with a question about what is keeping the person from doing so. I appreciate the fact that it is the *members*, not the leader, who evaluate their behavior and decide whether they want to change.

Once the decision to effect a change of behavior has been made, reality therapy provides the structure for members to make specific plans, to formulate contracts for action, and to evaluate their level of success in changing behaviors. In most of my groups I have found it useful to employ these action-oriented procedures as a device to help members carry what they are learning in the group into their everyday life. I also ask that members state the terms of the contract clearly in the group and report to the group the outcome of their efforts to fulfill the contract. Other aspects of reality therapy that I endorse include the idea of not accepting excuses for failure to follow through with contracts and the avoidance of any form of punishment and blaming. As I see it, if people don't carry out a plan, it is important to discuss with them what got in their way; perhaps they set their goals unrealistically high; perhaps there is a discrepancy between what they *say* they want to change and what they actually want to change. (One can generally believe behavior; one cannot always believe words.)

I also like reality therapy's insistence that change will not come by insight alone; rather, members will have to begin *doing* something different once they determine that their behavior is not working for them. I have become increasingly skeptical about the value of catharsis as a therapeutic vehicle, unless the release of pent-up emotions is eventually followed up with some kind of action plan. My colleagues and I have worked in groups with people who seem to have immobilized themselves by dwelling excessively on their negative feelings and by being unwilling to take action to change themselves. Therefore, we continue to challenge such members to look at the futility of waiting for others to change. Increasingly, we have asked the members of our groups to assume that the significant people in their life might never change, which means that these members will have to take a more active stance in shaping their own destiny.

Group members must look inward and search for alternatives. Since other members and the group leader will not entertain rationalizations for their failing behavior, the members are forced to make the choice for themselves whether to change. Applied to the example used in this chapter of the adolescents in a detention facility, we can readily see that the leader will not allow these youths to endlessly complain about their parents' rejection, about the bad breaks in life they have experienced, and about their many encounters with failure. Whatever the reasons are for their being in an institution now, they will have to make a decision about where their behavior is leading them.

Reality therapy encourages clients to look at the range of freedom they do possess, along with the responsibilities of this freedom. In this sense, reality therapy is a form of existential therapy. I also like the emphasis on understanding the subjective, inner, and personal world of clients. This phenomenological view helps the therapist understand more fully how clients perceive their world, and such a perspective is an excellent means of establishing the rapport needed for creating an effective client/therapist working relationship. Understanding the personal world of the client does not mean that therapists have to adopt a "soft" approach; on the contrary, they can demonstrate their caring by refusing to give up on the client. A therapist who is willing to consistently maintain a sense of hope that clients can change can be the catalyst that instills a sense of optimism in these clients.

In my opinion, these emphases of reality therapy are well suited to brief interventions in crisis-counseling situations and to working with youths who are in institutions for criminal behavior. They also have value in work with clients who see themselves as the victims of the abusive actions of others. For example, family members who live with an alcoholic often feel that they are victims. Assume that you were working with a group of husbands who lived with alcoholic wives. These men might have a tendency to complain endlessly about all the ways they have tried to help their wife, they might feel helpless to change her, and they might see the source of most of their unhappiness in their wife's drinking behavior. In a reality-therapy group, these men would be challenged to look at their part in this situation. They could eventually realize that they could not directly change their wife, but they could change the effects they experienced in such situations. Instead of focusing so much on what their wife was doing and not doing, they could begin to focus more on their own options for changing themselves.

Reality therapy's advantages can also be seen in a group of parents with "incorrigible" children. These parents might have a common bond because of their feeling that their life is being destroyed by the acting-out behavior of their adolescent daughters and sons. A therapist can teach these parents how to consistently apply the principles of reality therapy in their dealings with their children. The parents can also be taught how to focus more on their options for changing their behavior, rather than on the problems they are having in trying to "straighten out" their children. Reality therapy, it seems, has much to offer groups of parents, groups composed of children and adolescents who are having behavioral problems and who continually get in trouble at school, groups of teachers who work with a variety of students, groups of people who recognize that their life-style is not working for them, and groups of people in institutions for criminal behavior. In many of these situations with these populations, it would be inappropriate to embark on long-term therapy that delves into unconscious dynamics and an intensive exploration of one's past.

Limitations of the Approach

Some critics object to reality therapy as being simplistic and superficial. I have to admit that I, too, have been critical of reality therapy on these grounds; however, I no longer think it is accurate to criticize reality therapy as being simplistic. As I've said, Glasser agrees that the eight steps of reality therapy are simple and clear cut to talk about but that actually putting them into practice is not a simple matter. A concern I have about this approach is the danger that group practitioners will resort to a simplistic way of applying the principles in their work. There is the danger of the group leader's assuming the role of a "preacher," of a moral expert, and of one who judges for the members how they should change. Clearly, if group members accept the leader's standards of behavior instead of questioning and struggling, they don't have to look within themselves to discover their own values. From my perspective, this is a very undesirable outcome. (Let me add here that Glasser would contend that, if therapists assume the role of moral experts and attempt to impose their values on clients, they are not practicing within the spirit of reality therapy.) Neither is it therapeutic for participants to mimic other members or the group leader in an unthinking manner. Certainly with the group's help, they may arrive at a useful standard to evaluate their own behavior, but ultimately it is up to each individual to make this assessment. Glasser (1980) puts this issue very clearly: "In the end everyone has to be responsible for his or her own life and for living in a world much larger than the limited world of therapy" (p. 53). Therefore, it is clearly a misconception when people are critical of reality therapists for assuming the role of judging the life-style and behavior of their clients. Glasser (1980, 1981) forcefully makes the point that clients must make their own value judgments and that it is not the place of therapists to be judgmental or to impose their version of reality on their clients.

In spite of the fact that I agree that an action program is essential for changes in behavior, my personal preference is to give more attention to the realm of expressing and exploring feelings than reality therapy calls for. Once involvement is attained in a group, my inclination is to give members many opportunities to express *feelings* that they may have kept buried for years. I think that therapeutic work is deepened by paying attention to the realm of feelings. Therefore, I draw heavily upon techniques from Gestalt therapy and psychodrama as a way of helping the members *experience* their feelings, rather than simply talking about their feelings or about situations. Further, I go along with transactional analysis, rational-emotive therapy, and the cognitive-behavior therapies in placing emphasis upon the role of *thinking* as a key determinant of behavior. I have found that many problems that show up behaviorally have a connection to the self-defeating statements that we often repeat to ourselves. So, in addition to encouraging members to come into full contact with the range of their feelings, I also try to get them to look at the thoughts and beliefs that contribute to their emotional and behavioral problems.

Another limitation I see is the tendency to carry valid points to an invalid extreme. For example, although it is true that focusing on the past can constitute avoidance of present responsibility, excluding the role of the past can easily lead to a superficial view and treatment of certain problems. Similarly, although there are advantages to focusing on conscious aspects of behavior, carried to an extreme this emphasis denies the powerful place of the unconscious in human experience. Again, there are potential advantages in downplaying transference in therapy, for it is true that therapists can keep themselves hidden as persons and rationalize most of the feelings of their clients toward them as neurotic manifestations of transference. However, eliminating transference as a part of a therapy approach doesn't eliminate unrealistic feelings that clients often transfer from significant others to their therapists. Indeed, by ignoring this dynamic process, one neglects much therapeutic material that could be fruitfully explored.

A criticism of reality therapy from a behavior therapist's perspective would be that empirical research is lacking to justify the claims that its procedures actually work. Glasser maintains: "Well, we do have a lot of research actually. We have a tremendous amount of research on school discipline showing that if the school puts in our program, discipline problems drop between 80 and 90 percent" (see Evans, 1982, p. 464). However, as Ford (1982) asserts, empirical evaluation and research have not been major activities in reality therapy to date. He explains this by observing that reality therapy is most popular with practitioners (especially in the fields of education, substance abuse, and corrections), not with research centers and universities. Thus, those who are looking for empirical data rather than advocacy data will probably be critical of reality therapy for its lack of attention to research.

In summary, although I think that there are some limitations in restricting the practice of group work to the reality perspective alone, I do see some unique values and contributions for group leaders. Even though Glasser is primarily interested in teaching and developing reality therapy, he does not discourage practitioners from learning techniques from other therapies (Evans, 1982). I accept the value of the principles and concepts of reality therapy, most of which can be fruitfully integrated into several of the other systems that have been discussed in this book. Furthermore, as I've indicated, reality therapy appears to work effectively for a variety of practitioners in a diversity of groups, and it has been successfully used in educational settings, in correctional institutions, in various mental-health agencies, and in private practice. Its principles can be used by parents, social-welfare workers, counselors, marriage and family therapists, school administrators, the clergy, and youth workers. As is true of all models, the practitioner must examine the principles and concepts of reality therapy to determine what elements can be effectively incorporated into his or her individual therapeutic style.

If you have interest in obtaining training in reality therapy, the best source to contact is the Institute for Reality Therapy, 7301 Medical Center Drive, Suite 202, Canoga Park, CA 91307.

QUESTIONS FOR REFLECTION AND DISCUSSION

1. Glasser asserts that people can make plans in the present and succeed at them even if they do not spend any time exploring past failures. Further, he suggests that dwelling on past failures may hamper present plans if

clients remain too aware of them and incorporate them in their plans. To what degree do you agree or disagree with this position?

2. Glasser contends that it is not necessary to explore feelings in order to correct them. What is your view on this issue?

3. In many respects, reality therapy is at the opposite end of the therapeutic spectrum from psychoanalytic therapy. What contrasts do you see between these two models? Do you agree or disagree with Glasser's objections to the psychoanalytic perspective?

4. What are some of the unique advantages of practicing reality therapy in groups as opposed to individual counseling? How can others in the group be helpful to a member in terms of making a behavioral evaluation, forming a realistic plan, and getting committed to an action program?

5. Compare and contrast reality therapy with the experiential therapies (such as person-centered therapy, Gestalt therapy, psychodrama, and the existential therapies). To what extent do you think reality therapy incorporates or fails to incorporate elements of these approaches into practice?

6. Some of the more cognitively oriented therapies (such as TA, rational-emotive therapy, and cognitive-behavior therapy) emphasize the role of one's thoughts, values, beliefs, and attitudes as crucial determinants of behavior. On the other hand, reality therapy focuses on behavior, not the cognitive realm. What are your thoughts on this matter?

7. What are your reactions to those who criticize reality therapy on the ground that it is simplistic? To what extent do you agree with Glasser's contention that, although the steps are simple to discuss, putting them into practice requires considerable therapeutic skill and creativity?

8. Reality therapy requires members to make an honest assessment of their current behavior to determine whether it is working for them. In considering some of the groups that you might want to organize, what problems might you anticipate with respect to actually getting the members to make such a value judgment?

9. With what you know about yourself, do you think you might be inclined to make value judgments *for* the members in your group? Might you be judgmental? To what degree do you think that your own values would affect the way you'd work with your group?

10. What are your reactions to Glasser's view that criticism and punishment are counterproductive in therapy? How might you deal with group members who were highly self-critical and blamed themselves for their problems?

RECOMMENDED SUPPLEMENTARY READINGS

Glasser has written little on group counseling; however, the principles and concepts discussed in the following books easily translate to group work.

Reality therapy: A new approach to psychiatry (Glasser, 1965) outlines the basic concepts of reality therapy and gives practical examples of how this theory works with delinquent girls and hospitalized psychotics, in private practice, and in the public schools.

Schools without failure (Glasser, 1969) is concerned mainly with the effects and problems of conventional education and suggests ways of implementing new approaches.

Those who are interested in group counseling at the elementary or secondary school level will find good material and some procedures applicable to group work.

Positive addiction (Glasser, 1976a) is an extension of Glasser's earlier writings. This self-help book describes a variety of what he calls "positive addictions," such as running and meditation, and shows how people can grow psychologically stronger through some form of positive addiction. Many of these ideas can be useful adjuncts to group work, especially with regard to suggestions about constructive use of time between group sessions.

Stations of the mind (Glasser, 1981) deals with new directions of reality therapy, and it is an expansion of Glasser's basic ideas. His contention is that we are driven by internal forces that push us beyond survival toward belonging, worthwhileness, and freedom. Humans construct a unique personal world, and what happens in the real world has little significance unless it relates to what is already inside one's personal world.

REFERENCES AND SUGGESTED READINGS*

* Evans, D. B. What are you doing? An interview with William Glasser. *Personnel and Guidance Journal*, 1982, 60(8), 460–465.
* Ford, E. E. Reality therapy in family therapy. In A. M. Horne & M. M. Ohlsen (Eds.), *Family counseling and therapy*. Itasca, Ill.: Peacock, 1982.
* Glasser, N. (Ed.). *What are you doing? How people are helped through reality therapy*. New York: Harper & Row, 1980.

Glasser, W. *Mental health or mental illness?* New York: Harper & Row, 1961.

Glasser, W. *Reality therapy: A new approach to psychiatry*. New York: Harper & Row, 1965.

Glasser, W. *Schools without failure*. New York: Harper & Row, 1969.

Glasser, W. *The identity society*. New York: Harper & Row, 1972.

Glasser, W. *Positive addiction*. New York: Harper & Row, 1976. (a)

Glasser, W. Reality therapy. In V. Binder, A. Binder, & B. Rimland (Eds.), *Modern therapies*. Englewood Cliffs, N.J.: Prentice-Hall, 1976. (b)

* Glasser, W. Reality therapy. An explanation of the steps of reality therapy. In N. Glasser (Ed.), *What are you doing? How people are helped through reality therapy*. New York: Harper & Row, 1980.
* Glasser, W. *Stations of the mind*. New York: Harper & Row, 1981.

Glasser, W., & Zunin, L. M. Reality therapy. In R. Corsini (Ed.), *Current psychotherapies* (2nd ed.). Itasca, Ill.: Peacock, 1979.

Kaltenbach, R. F. Reality therapy in groups. In G. M. Gazda (Ed.), *Basic approaches to group psychotherapy and group counseling* (3rd ed.). Springfield, Ill.: Charles C Thomas, 1982.

Powers, W. T. *Behavior: The control of perception*. Chicago: Aldine, 1973.

Zunin, L., & Zunin, N. *Contact: The first four minutes*. New York: Ballantine Books, 1973.

*Books and articles marked with an asterisk are suggested for further study.

PART THREE

Application
and
Integration

16

ILLUSTRATION OF A GROUP IN ACTION: VARIOUS PERSPECTIVES

INTRODUCTION

To give you a better picture of how the various approaches just discussed actually work in a group, this chapter describes a model group in action and the different ways in which practitioners of various orientations would deal with some specific issues and aspects of group work. My aim is to provide illustrative samples of group work and to give you some flavor of the differences and similarities among the various group approaches.

To adequately describe how all the orientations would apply to a group of ten people and two co-leaders could prove a cumbersome task. Thus, in order to simplify this project, I shall give a brief description of the group members and their problems and then demonstrate how several therapeutic approaches might be functional for each case. For this purpose, I have selected what I consider to be typical themes that emerge in many groups. I shall present each theme and then show how some of the group approaches might deal with it. It needs to be stressed that this chapter reflects my own biases and experiences with respect to the group themes I've selected, as well as my personal interpretation of how the various leaders would work with their groups. The actual implementation of any specific model, as well as the techniques and style of the group leader, would naturally vary from the theoretical models given below.

423

THE MODEL GROUP

Our model group is a closed and time-limited group with ten members (five women and five men) and two co-leaders. The setting is a community mental-health center, and our group is a part of the group-therapy program the center offers adults who have problems coping effectively with the demands of every-day living. These adults might be termed "normal neurotics"; although none of them is seriously disturbed, they all experience enough anxiety to seek therapy as a way of dealing more successfully with their personal problems.

All the group members have had some individual counseling, they are joining the group voluntarily, and they have agreed to come to all of the sessions, which take place once a week for two hours for the duration of the group. The group will meet for 20 weeks, during the course of which no new members will be admitted. Before making the decision to join the group and attend all its sessions, the members participated in a presession in which they met with the co-leaders to get acquainted and determine whether they wanted to have this type of group experience.

THE EMERGING THEMES

The themes I've selected from among the many that typically emerge during the life of a group are the following:

1. clarifying personal goals
2. creating and maintaining trust
3. dealing with fears and resistances
4. coping with loneliness and isolation
5. resolving dependence/independence conflicts
6. overcoming the fear of intimacy
7. dealing with depression
8. searching for meaning in life
9. challenging and clarifying values
10. dealing with the termination of the group

I'll approach these themes by describing how they apply in concrete ways to various members of our model group. For each theme, I'll present the *essence* of what these members explored at different sessions. Then, I'll show how the co-leaders of the group, using the various theoretical approaches, could deal with these themes, the individual members, and the group as a whole. I'll conclude by describing how I would use concepts and techniques from these various approaches to deal with some issues characteristic of the ending stages of a group.

THEME: CLARIFYING PERSONAL GOALS

As you know, in most groups the initial sessions are devoted to exploring group goals and clarifying the members' personal goals. Following is the essence of what each member of our model group hopes to get from his or her partici-pation in the group.

Emily (age 23, single, lives at home with her parents and attends college): I hope to get up enough courage to finally attempt to make it on my own. Though I don't like living with my parents because it limits me, I must admit that it's a comfortable arrangement.

Ed (age 60, an engineer, twice divorced and now living alone, has had drinking problems for years): I'm afraid of being isolated, but I'm also afraid that people will reject me. I want to learn to deal with these fears and with my depression and anxiety without having to resort to drinking.

Beth (age 55, a widow with two teenage sons living at home, has devoted most of her life to taking care of her sons and others): Maybe I could learn how to ask for something for myself without feeling so terribly guilty.

Robert (age 28, single, a social worker, has difficulty forming close interpersonal relationships, is afraid of women, and tends to "use" them): Sometimes I feel dead and numb, and I wonder if I'll ever change. I expect to work on my fears of getting close to women.

Joanne (age 35, three children and a miserable marriage, has recently returned to college): I've decided to stay with my husband until I finish college and get a good job and until my kids go to high school. I want to reexamine this decision and determine if the price is too high.

Sam (age 34, married, hates his work in maintenance and wants to change it but is not confident enough to do so): Besides making some vocational decisions, I hope to leave this group feeling better about myself and my possibilities.

Sharon (age 25, an executive secretary, lives with a man despite her parents' objections): I'm confused about what I really hope to get from this group. I know I feel guilty for letting my parents down, but I don't know if a group will help me or not.

Randy (age 47, a high school teacher, has been abandoned by his wife, who took the children with her): I can't concentrate. I keep thinking of her and our kids. I want to be able to deal with the anger and the pain I feel much of the time.

Judy (age 38, single, a university professor, is struggling to find new meaning for her life): I keep asking myself "Is this all there is to life?" I think I have a lot to be thankful for, yet I often feel empty. I want to take another look at my values and see if they still fit.

Boyd (age 22, a college student, lately has experienced moments of panic, anxiety, and some bouts of depression): There have been times that I wanted to commit suicide, and it scares me. I hope to understand some of my feelings. Also, I hope to find out that I'm not the only one who feels like this.

Some Therapeutic Approaches

Co-leaders with a *behavioral, TA,* or *reality-therapy* orientation will probably begin by having each member state his or her goals as clearly and concretely as possible. They will help the members formulate specific contracts for their own work—contracts that would provide a direction for the group. For example, in working with Robert, leaders with these orientations will have him clarify hat it is that he fears about women and how he sees himself as keeping ...tant. This effort may lead Robert to formulate a working contract as follows: "I agree to work with the women in this group by openly exploring my reactions to them. By dealing with the feelings I have toward women in the group, I may get a clearer understanding of the impact I have on women in general." As another example, Beth—the person who has trouble asking for what she wants— may be helped to develop a list of her specific wants and to formulate a contract to explore her feelings about trying to satisfy these wants.

From the *reality-therapy* perspective, the group leader may help members recognize that what they are doing is not working for them and encourage them to make a value judgment about the quality of their behavior. Members will be given hope that they are capable of making realistic plans for changing the aspects of their behavior that they decide to change. This goal of enabling members to choose better behavior is likely to come about if members realize that what they are doing, thinking, and feeling is not simply happening to them but that they are indeed making choices. Initially the members may be asked to think about the questions "What are you doing now? What do you want to do differently? Is what you are doing actually working for you? What do you want to get from this group?"

In an *Adlerian group* there will be emphasis on the alignment of the group members' goals and the leader's goals. Cooperation and focus on a common therapeutic task are essential if change is to occur. Attention will be devoted to the beliefs and mistaken perceptions that interfere with the members' progress in dealing with the challenges of life. The assumption of an Adlerian group is that the group process can be effective only if it deals with things that the members recognize as important and want to explore and change. Thus, during the initial stage of a group, contracts will be established with the members that clearly state why they are attending the group and what they expect from their participation in it.

One form of a *behavioral group* is the *multimodal* approach to therapy, which takes the whole person into consideration. Comprehensive group therapy entails the correction of irrational beliefs, deviant behaviors, unpleasant feelings, bothersome images, stressful relationships, negative sensations, and possible biochemical imbalances. The group process is characterized, from this perspective, by a broad assessment that may include questions such as the following: "What are your major strengths? What keeps you from getting what you want? What behaviors would you like to acquire, and what ones do you want to eliminate? What are some emotions that are a problem for you? How do you see yourself now? What are the values that give your life the most meaning? What are some ways that you satisfy your intellectual needs? What is the quality of your relationships with others? What do you give to others, and what do you get from them? What is the state of your health?" This process of initial assessment brings out some central and significant themes that can be productively explored in a group. It gets clients to think about what is going on in their life and encourages them to formulate personal goals that will give the group some direction.

THEME: CREATING AND MAINTAINING TRUST

Trust soon becomes an issue as the group gets under way. Members will often question their ability to trust the group leaders, the other members, and even themselves.

Judy, the professor, says: "I'm concerned that what I say to the group will not remain in the group. I have no reason to distrust anybody in here; still, I know that I have some reservations about revealing myself to the group."

Sharon expresses her lack of trust in herself: "I've never been in a group before, and I don't know if I'll fit in here or what is appropriate. I mean, I don't even know how to let others know what is going on within me, and I'm afraid that, if I do let people know, I'll just bore everybody."

Boyd doubts whether the leaders are competent to deal with what he calls his "heavy" feelings, such as suicidal impulses. "I'm afraid you guys will just try to cheer me up or maybe tell me I'm really crazy. Also, I'm worried about what the other people here will think about me."

Typically, groups focus on issues of trust, such as those illustrated by the examples just given, during the early stages of group process. It is clear that, if members are to drop their defenses and reveal themselves—as indeed they must if the group is to be effective—they need assurance that the group is a safe place to do this. More importantly, they need a *reason* to reveal themselves. Thus, members must see that, by being open and taking risks, they will understand themselves more fully.

Helping to build trust in the group is a vital task for group leaders, and the way in which they approach the group is of crucial importance. In the following section I've summarized some comments that might be made by practitioners of the various orientations during the early stages of a group. Note that the leaders try to promote trust by specifying what the group is designed to do and by indicating how the group process will work. Also note how their comments clearly reveal their different orientations.

Some Therapeutic Approaches

The following are summaries of what the leaders of the various group models might say to the group as they seek to establish a climate of trust at the opening session.

Psychoanalytic group. "This group is a place where you can safely explore feelings, events, and experiences that you have buried. We are here to assist you in working through unfinished business from your past, which will manifest itself through the interactions in the group. It is our job to facilitate group interaction by creating an accepting and tolerant climate that will promote active participation."

Adlerian group. "In this group we will be focusing on your style of life as it becomes evident through your behavior in here. We will also be giving attention to some of your early recollections, your memories of what it was like for you to be in your family, and how your position in your family might still affect you now. A group is an ideal place to make changes in your life, for the group is a social microcosm that represents your social world. In here we will encourage you to try on new behaviors and to put your insights into action by testing them in this group and in your encounters in daily life."

Psychodrama group. "In this group you will act out—not just talk about—your conflicts, and you will reenact emotionally significant scenes. By releasing pent-up feelings, you'll gain more insight, and you'll experiment with more spontaneous ways of behaving."

Existential group. "Here each of you can discover the ways in which you have restricted your freedom. Our main task is to challenge you to assume the responsibility for your own choices and search for a more real existence. We hope to share ourselves with you in the process."

Person-centered group. "Our job is to facilitate, not direct, this group. In part this means helping to make it an accepting and caring group. Since we assume that each of you has the capacity to know what you want, we also assume that, once you see this as a safe place, you'll drop your pretenses and show your real selves. We believe that eventually you'll learn to trust yourselves and to rely on your own judgments."

Gestalt group. "We'll stay as much as possible in the here and now and deal with whatever prevents you from maintaining a present-centered awareness. Our focus will be on the *what* and *how*, rather than the *why*, of behavior. With this focus, which will assist you in giving expression to parts of yourselves that you have denied, we expect that you will eventually become more integrated and whole. Above all, we are here to assist you in identifying the unfinished business from your past that impedes your present functioning."

Transactional-analysis group. "Each of you is our colleague in your own therapy. We don't presume the right to special knowledge about you; rather, we assume that *you* will decide on the course of your work in here, largely by developing clear contracts that will specify what you want to change and how you will seek to effect a change."

Behavior-therapy group. "We assume that, if you've learned ineffective behavior, you can learn new, constructive behavior. The group will offer a context for this learning. Our task is to teach you new coping skills; your task is to practice these skills, both within and outside the group. The group is designed to give you the support needed to reinforce any changes you make, so that they become an integral part of you."

Rational-emotive group. "Although others may be largely responsible for indoctrinating you with self-defeating beliefs, we hold you responsible for maintaining such beliefs. Accordingly, we'll be highly directive and active in getting you to critically evaluate your processes of self-indoctrination. Group work will be directed toward replacing your current irrational belief systems with a rational philosophy of life."

Reality-therapy group. "Since we believe that each of you is seeking a success identity, our main goal in this group is to assist you in determining whether your current behavior promotes success. If you discover that it does not and if you decide to change, it will be your responsibility to formulate a plan of action designed to promote change. The group is designed to offer you a place to practice this plan for change, and outside homework assignments will help you carry these changes into your everyday behavior."

THEME: DEALING WITH FEARS AND RESISTANCES

During the early stages of the group, members typically express fears about getting involved and display resistance toward any attempt at delving into deeply personal concerns. Some members keep their fears about becoming involved in the group to themselves, whereas others seem eager to express their fears and put them to rest so that they can begin to work. Whether or not the fears are expressed, they tend to give rise to some ambivalence: the desire to reveal oneself is balanced by the reluctance to expose oneself. Following are some typical expressions of this ambivalance.

- Why do I have to reveal my private feelings in this group? What good will it do anyhow?
- I'm afraid to get involved, because I may make a fool of myself.
- I'm afraid that, if I say what I really think and feel, the group will reject me.
- If I see myself as I really am, I may find that there is nothing inside me.
- I'm afraid that, by becoming too involved in this group, I may make my problems bigger than they really are.
- If I get too involved in the group, I'm afraid I'll become too dependent on it for solving problems that I have to handle alone.
- Right now my life is rather comfortable; if I become too involved in the group, I may open up a can of worms that I can't handle.
- I'm afraid that the group will strip away my defenses and leave me vulnerable.
- I'm somewhat afraid of disclosing myself to others, not only because of what *they* may think but also because of what *I* might find out about myself.
- I want to protect myself by not letting myself care. If I get too close to people in the group, I'll feel a real loss when it ends.

Some Therapeutic Approaches

Psychodrama group. Using a psychodrama framework, the co-leaders may direct members to express and share their fears, with the aim of showing participants that they are not alone in these fears. The resulting sense of commonality helps the group develop cohesiveness.

Psychoanalytic group.   Psychoanalytically oriented leaders see resistance as a basic part of the group process. Since, in this model, resistance to self-knowledge often presents itself in the form of resistance to others, dealing with resistance to the group is an essential aspect of therapy. At appropriate times the leaders may interpret the individual members' resistance to the group. The aim is to help members learn about themselves by exploring their reactions to other group members, who, it is believed, serve as catalysts to evoke early memories.

Gestalt group.   Gestalt leaders tend to deal with resistance by rehearsing the associated fears. For example, Ed, who holds back because of his fear of being rejected by the group, may be asked to stand in front of each group member and complete the sentence "You could reject me by . . ." Next, he may be asked to make the rounds again, this time to finish the sentence "You would reject me if you knew . . ." By completing the sentence in a different way with each member, Ed can express the full spectrum of the fears of rejection that he normally keeps inside of himself. The goal is to render the fears less compelling and to take some steps toward dealing with them.

Rational-emotive group.   Taking the example of Ed again, leaders of this orientation may confront him with questions such as: What would be so terrible if everyone in here *did* reject you? Would you fall apart? Why do you tell yourself that rejection is such an awful thing? The attempt here is to show Ed that he has uncritically bought the irrational idea that he will not survive if he gets rejected. The leaders may then invite other members to express similar irrational fears and then proceed to teach the group members that they are responsible for making themselves emotionally disturbed by unquestioningly accepting such irrational notions.

Existential group.   During the early stages of a group, members may express their fears that, if they take a look at themselves, they may find that they are empty or that they are not the person they have convinced themselves they are. This confrontation with oneself can be terrifying for some, and in an existential group these fears are openly acknowledged and worked with. The group leaders may ask the members to close their eyes and imagine that these fears of theirs are actually occurring in this group. For example, Robert, who is afraid of women and closeness with them, can imagine his worst fears happening in the group. Judy may confront her fears that she is living without any values of her own. And Boyd can allow himself to imagine his panic over the times he has feared he might want to kill himself. This is the first step in making a commitment to themselves and the group to face and deal with their fears.

THEME: COPING WITH LONELINESS AND ISOLATION

Randy, the high school teacher who has been abandoned by his wife and children, is the exponent of this theme. He keeps asking himself: "Why did she leave me? Am I to blame for what happened? Will I ever be able to trust anyone again? Will I be able to get over the pain of this breakup?"

Some Therapeutic Approaches

Person-centered group. The person-centered co-leaders may invite Randy to tell his story in detail. While he does so, the leaders pay full attention not only to what Randy is saying but also to his nonverbal expressions of pain over his losses and his feelings of being utterly alone and abandoned. The leaders'attention and the support of the group stimulate Randy to fully experience and share the intensity of his feelings.

The group leaders may notice that Ed, who has had similar experiences, appears deeply moved, and they will ask Ed to express what he is feeling. Ed may reveal that he is identifying with Randy and that he still feels torn up over his second divorce—a revelation that may cause Ed and Randy to spontaneously talk with each other, which in turn may provoke other members to share what they are feeling and demonstrate that they care about the two men. The support of the leaders and of the group as a whole would tend to encourage a full and open expression of both men's feelings, which previously may have been bottled up.

Psychodrama group. The leaders using a psychodrama approach are likely to ask Randy what he would like to understand more fully about the breakup of his marriage. Randy replies "There are a lot of things that have gone unsaid— things that I feel stuck with, things that I'm afraid I won't ever say." Randy is then asked to go to the stage area and say what he fears he'll never be able to say. When he has done so, he is asked to "become his wife" and, in this role, to say all the things he imagines that she would say. This exchange of roles is continued until the group can get a feeling of how Randy sees his wife.

Next, Randy is asked to select a member to play his wife's role. He picks Joanne and begins by expressing his hurt—his feelings of loneliness and loss. Joanne (as his symbolic wife) responds. Eventually Randy's pain turns to anger; he begins to release the bottled-up anger yet keeps blocking it with self-deprecating remarks. At this point, Robert, the member who has difficulty with women, is selected as Randy's double and steps next to Randy, shouting many of the things that Randy seems to be cutting off with his guilt. By having someone speak in his behalf, Randy may be able to eventually release his most intense, deepest rage.

When this scene has finally served its purpose, the leader may ask Randy to fantasize a future as he would wish it, say, five years from now. In this fantasy Randy sees his wife and children reunited with him. He is then asked to act out a scene from this future as he would wish it to be, playing his wife's role as well as his own. During the course of this psychodrama Randy recalls how his wife's departure vividly reminded him of the scene when his mother left him after she divorced his father. The importance of this connection would be underscored by the leader, who might suggest to Randy that he could deal with his childhood experience later within the group.

Rational-emotive group. The approach of RET leaders to Randy's problems will focus on getting him to stop his vicious self-blaming. Members of an RET group are quickly taught what is called the A-B-C of therapy. In Randy's case, the Activating event (A—that is, his wife's leaving) is not, according to this approach, the cause of Randy's misery now. Rather, the cause of misery is Randy's response to the Activating event—namely, his irrational Beliefs (B). Specifically, his response is to keep telling himself that, because his wife left him, he is rotten; that, if his wife does not love him, nobody will or can; that, if he had not been basically worthless and *if only* he had been different, his wife would still be with him. Thus, the emotional Consequence (C) of his emotional pain is seen as due not to his wife's departure but to his faulty and illogical thinking. In the RET group other members will confront Randy with his self-destructive style and persuade him to consider changing his thinking.

In the course of this work it is discovered that Randy has been avoiding making contacts with other women because he has convinced himself that no woman could *ever* want anything to do with him. Thus, the leaders challenge him to attack this self-defeating notion of basic unworthiness. Randy is asked to role-play asking a woman in the group for a date, and the male co-therapist coaches him in this play by showing him how to be assertive. Randy is given an opportunity to discuss his fears of getting involved again, which can lead him to begin differentiating between realistic and unrealistic fears. He receives a homework assignment, such as the task of initiating and maintaining a conversation with some women at his place of work, and is asked to keep a written record of his reactions to these encounters and to report the results to the group at its next session.

Adlerian group.   In working with the theme of loneliness and isolation, the Adlerian group leaders may pay attention to Randy's family constellation and to his early recollections. From this perspective, it is assumed that he wants to belong, to fit in with others, and to have a place of prominence in his family of origin. Randy may be asked to describe each sibling as he remembers him or her. He may also be asked for specific information on the social groupings of the siblings, along with some rating of how he sees himself in relation to his brothers and sisters. He may say something like the following: "I can remember how alone I felt at home as a kid. My bigger brother got all the attention, and I was sure I'd never measure up to him. I often felt that I didn't belong in our family. Especially when he was around, I just couldn't seem to get any of the attention no matter what I did! Just saying all this brings back the feelings of loneliness that I so often felt as a child."

Randy can be encouraged to look for some themes in his life and identify some key characteristics that identify him. He may very well see connections between his childhood experiences and the feelings of isolation he now feels.

THEME: RESOLVING DEPENDENCE/INDEPENDENCE CONFLICTS

Emily, the group member who is living with her parents and going to college, discusses the resentment she feels toward her parents. According to Emily, her parents control her life, are responsible for her insecurity, and make it difficult for her to break away and live on her own. She has admitted that she finds living at home comfortable. As she begins delving further, she sees that she is frightened of taking increased responsibility for her own life and that her parents are scapegoats for her own inability to become independent. In the group she struggles with conflicting desires—a desire to remain secure by clinging to what is known and a desire to assume more responsibility for directing her own life. Emily is torn between wanting to become her own parent (doing for herself what she now expects her parents to do for her) and fearing the added responsibility of increased maturity.

Some Therapeutic Approaches

Reality-therapy group. If Emily discusses her problem in a reality-therapy group, the leaders may confront her tendency to blame her parents as follows: "You seem to be getting a lot of mileage from making your parents responsible for your dependency. Also, you seem to dwell on the past too much, almost as if you were clinging to it as an excuse for not being the free person you say you want to be. Using your past to justify your current 'inability' to make decisions keeps you from getting in touch with your power. As long as you hold onto your past and blame your parents, you never really have to take an honest look at yourself."

The aim of this approach is to get Emily to evaluate her current behavior and to accept the role she is playing now; exploring her feelings or discussing her changing attitudes is of little interest here. The pivotal question for Emily is: does she want to continue her dependent behavior, or does she want to change it? If Emily decides that she does want to change, she will then be asked to develop a plan of action, which will include definite steps toward behaving more independently and a contract to change, which will include a commitment to try new behavior outside the group.

Existential group. Assume now that Emily brings up her dependence/independence conflicts in an existentially oriented group. It is probable that one of the co-leaders will ask other group members if they can identify with Emily. In our model group Joanne, who has a desire to leave her secure but boring marriage, Sharon, who feels guilty for not living up to her parents' expectations, and Beth, who may see herself in the parental role with respect to Emily's conflict, can all identify with Emily. In the existential group Emily, Joanne, Sharon, and Beth may be asked to form an inner circle and sit in the center of the group. The leader may instruct this subgroup to "discuss all the ways that you are unfree now, talk about how it feels to not be in charge of your own lives, express your fears of giving up your security in order to gain independence, and examine the advantages of remaining dependent."

The purpose behind this exercise is to provide these four participants with an opportunity to fully explore how they feel and think about their practice of giving up their power to others. The aim is to assist them to clearly see what keeps them secure (and unfree) and to honestly determine the cost of this security.

Transactional-analysis group. If Emily's problems are raised in a TA group, the leaders may take one or more of several exploratory paths—for example:

• identifying and analyzing the games that Emily is playing

- working on Emily's life script to determine how she is following a plan for life drawn up by her parents
- assisting her in seeing the typical ego state in which she functions (probably the Child ego state, at least with respect to her parents)
- exploring the injunctions that Emily has lived by, as well as her early decisions

The exploration of Emily's injunctions can involve many group members who share similar injunctions, such as "Don't grow up"; "Don't disappoint your parents"; "Don't think for yourself"; "Don't trust yourself"; "Do what is expected of you." The sharing of Emily's injunctions can provide other members with a valuable catalyst for examining the ways in which they have incorporated parental messages without thinking about them. Similarly, the sharing of an early decision that Emily has apparently made—"Let your parents take care of you, because you are not able to take care of yourself"—will be used by the group to explore other instances of early decisions.

Behavior-therapy group.   In a group with a behavioral orientation Emily will probably be asked to specify ways in which she would like to change her relationship with her parents. Next, she may be invited to role-play herself with the co-leaders, who act as her parents. In this role play Emily is directed to tell her parents what she would like to change in their relationship.

Later, other members may be invited to give Emily feedback answers to questions such as: Was she assertive? Is her style effective for the purpose of having her parents listen to her? If the feedback indicates that Emily comes across as a whining apologizer, the female co-leader may step in to demonstrate a direct style for clearly stating desires without apologies. Emily may then be asked to replay her role with the symbolic parents, using the information that she has just received. If appropriate, the group may then offer positive feedback, pointing out and supporting assertive behavior on Emily's part.

THEME: OVERCOMING THE FEAR OF INTIMACY

Another theme is exemplified by Robert's difficulties in forming close relationships of any kind, particularly intimate relationships with women. As Robert describes his struggles, he mentions several times that often he feels numb and emotionally dead. He worries that something is basically wrong with him, because he finds it hard to care for fellow group members who express psychological pain. As he puts it: "As some of you go through 'heavy' stuff, I feel detached, sort of cold and isolated. I'm not letting myself identify with anybody in here, and that makes me wonder if I'd ever be able to care and if I have the capacity to get intimately involved with anyone. I feel sort of dead inside." The correlative themes that are evoked and explored in the group include the fear of intimacy (and the need for intimacy), feelings of isolation and deadness, and, to some extent, feelings of hopelessness.

Some Therapeutic Approaches

Existential group. Existentially oriented leaders may tend to focus on Robert's numbness, encouraging him to let these feelings of deadness intensify and then to tell the group what it is like to "feel dead." This rather uncheering approach is designed to offer Robert the opportunity to feel the depths of his deadness. He may then be asked to lie on the floor under a sheet and "be dead." Then the other members talk about the "departed" Robert—what they miss about him, how they were affected by him, and how they feel about his being dead.

The leaders may also invite the participants to talk about the feelings that are being evoked in them—a path that could lead them to share how their feelings are often similar to Robert's. At the end of the session Robert throws off his sheet and expresses how it felt to be "dead." At this point he may be able to see that he has never really allowed himself to feel his deadness before and begin to challenge the idea that it is better to be numb than to allow oneself to get involved with others.

Gestalt group. The Gestalt leaders will focus on Robert's ambivalence toward intimacy. First, he is asked to face each of the women in the group and state his worst fear about getting close to her. Next, he is asked to concentrate on his here-and-now fears toward the women in the group. Then, he is asked to conduct a dialogue between the two sides of himself from two chairs.

As he sits in one chair and plays the side of him that wants to care and get involved, he says: "It feels lonely and cold behind the walls that I build around myself. I work so hard to keep people out. I want to get out of the walls, but I'm afraid of what is out there." As he sits in the other chair and plays the side that wants to remain behind those walls, he says: "Stay behind those walls that you've worked so hard to build. You're isolated, but at least you're safe. You know what happens whenever you let yourself really care: you always get burned, and that pain isn't worth the effort of getting involved." This dialogue, which may continue for about 15 minutes, helps Robert become more aware of the polarities within him, without forcing him to choose between his two sides yet.

Behavior-therapy group. The behavior therapists will use relaxation and desensitization techniques to approach Robert's fear of intimacy. Relaxation techniques, which are taught to the entire group, consist essentially of systematically tensing and relaxing all the muscles in the body and are practiced daily by members at home.

A practical application of relaxation techniques to Robert's difficulties may proceed as follows. Robert is instructed to construct an imaginary hierarchy of interpersonal situations ranging from those that would produce the least amount of anxiety to those that would produce the most. Robert is then asked to use the techniques that he has learned to become extremely relaxed. Next, he is guided through a fantasy about an interpersonal situation that, according to his hierarchy, generates the least degree of anxiety—say, merely seeing a

woman that he is attracted to. This is followed by fantasies of situations involving greater and greater anxiety. As soon as Robert experiences anxiety, he is
instructed to "switch off" that scene and relax. In this manner Robert may
manage to work himself up to sustaining fantasies about a high-anxiety-pro-
ducing situation—for example, approaching a woman and initiating a conversation with her.

At another session Robert may practice behavioral rehearsal, putting himself
into a real-life situation in the group. For example, after inviting him to assume
that Sharon is a woman that he would like to date, the group leader may ask
Robert: "How would you let Sharon know that you are interested in her? Assume
that you and Sharon are actually on a date. What might your conversation be
like? Pretend that you are saying good-bye. What would you tell her about your
feelings concerning her and your evening with her? What is it that you hope
you could say?" After this rehearsal, the leader asks Robert to select a woman
in his everyday life that he would actually like to make contact with and, with
the help of other group members, to develop a homework assignment relating
to making that contact—an assignment that he is to practice during the week
and to report on during the following session.

The action-oriented behavior-therapy approach has Robert challenge his
fears of intimacy, not analyze their cause. He begins in the relative safety of his
fantasies as guided in the group situation, progresses to dealing with his feelings toward a female member of his group (Sharon) by role playing (behavior
rehearsal), and finally applies his newly acquired skills to his everyday life.

Rational-emotive group.   The description of the behavioral group could
easily fit the RET group. The RET leaders, however, are more likely to challenge
Robert's perceptions about the catastrophic consequences of becoming intimate. The emphasis here is on teaching Robert that he is stopping himself by
his fears, many of which are unfounded or based on irrational beliefs. The aim
is to have Robert put himself in situations where he has to critically appraise
his beliefs regarding emotional closeness. As in the behavioral approach, he is
expected to carry out homework assignments.

Transactional-analysis group.   The TA leaders may well focus on exposing
and working with an early decision that Robert made—for example, "If you
open yourself to being loved by others, or if you let yourself care about others,
you are bound to be hurt. Thus, it's best to seal off your feelings and become
emotionally numb, because then you won't feel the pain." After some initial
probing, the leaders may have Robert reconstruct a specific, relevant scene
with his parents when he was 10 years old. With the help of the leaders, who
would probably use a Gestalt technique (combined with some psychodrama),
Robert attempts to experience the scene as completely as possible, including
the feelings of helplessness that he felt as a child. In that manner, he may be
led to see that a decision concerning closeness that he made as a helpless
child served his survival needs *then* but is no longer an appropriate basis for
his actions *now*.

Following this reconstruction, wherein Robert can experience the intensity of his fear of closeness, the leaders have him engage his cognitive faculties by asking him to consider *when* and *why* he made his early decision and to think about how that decision impedes his relationships in the present. Finally, some of his injunctions—for example, "Don't get close"; "Never let people know what you're feeling"; "Don't trust women"; "Don't feel"—may be challenged in a group discussion.

Psychoanalytic group. The psychoanalytic leaders may use Robert's response to them as a therapeutic device, and the following scenes may ensue. The male leader points out that Robert typically avoids, and appears uncomfortable with, the female leader. Robert admits his discomfort, explaining that he sees her as a dynamic and insightful woman who, he feels, could use her power to hurt him. While maintaining the focus on Robert's feelings toward the woman leader, the therapists draw parallels between his responses in group and his relationships with his mother and sisters.

Assuming that the interpretations are apt and timely, Robert may make some fruitful associations between how he behaved in his mother's presence and how he behaves in the group. He may begin to see how he is transferring some of his childhood feelings for his mother to the female leader. (This transference is encouraged, because it provides useful material that will eventually allow Robert to work through some of his attitudes toward women.) At the same time Robert may become aware of the ways in which he is competing with the women in the group for the therapists' attention—a behavior that may relate to his childhood behavior of competing with his sisters for their parents' attention. Whatever the insights, they are merely the beginning of significant work in a psychoanalytic group. In Robert's case, awareness of a connection between his childhood experiences and his current fear of closeness would be followed by an effort to use the transferences that have occurred with respect to women in the group to work through his fears of closeness.

THEME: DEALING WITH DEPRESSION

One common theme that emerges is exemplified by Ed (the oldest person in the group), who is chronically depressed and, like Robert, feels isolated and incapable of breaking out of his isolation. After two divorces, Ed sees himself as a failure in maintaining relationships; thus, he lives alone rather than risk further failure. Ed, an admitted alcoholic, describes how his drinking has ruined his personal and professional life and how all these failures have left him feeling hopeless, helpless, and in great need of alcohol for comfort. After some limited success with Alcoholics Anonymous, Ed clearly sees that booze doesn't solve his problems and that he is guilt ridden by his failures in life and weakness for alcohol. Now he wants to probe deeper into the reasons that compel him to seek refuge in drinking—reasons that he realizes are merely symptomatic of personality problems. Ed also realizes the importance of coming to grips with his bouts of depression.

Some Therapeutic Approaches

Person-centered group.   Leaders of a person-centered group will work to develop a climate of acceptance and trust in which Ed can express his feelings. By providing an example of accepting attentiveness, the leaders let Ed know that he has permission to feel what he feels and share these feelings with the group. In this manner, someone like Ed, who punishes himself with disapproval and rejection and expects the same treatment from others, may for the first time feel that he is accepted and acceptable. Armed with this new view of himself, Ed is in a far better position to probe the reasons behind his drinking.

Psychoanalytic group.   The psychoanalytic leaders will focus on any dependencies that Ed may develop with respect to the group—for example, dependence on the leaders for decision making and dependence on other members for support and approval. The leaders may tend to direct Ed toward exploring how he views each therapist, what he wants from them, and how he uses them (as he used his parents) to get confirmation as a person. By examining his need for approval from the group leaders, Ed may become aware, for instance, that he never really felt loved by his parents and that he grew up believing that failure to achieve perfection meant that he was a failure.

By exploring his reactions within the group, particularly with respect to the group leaders, and with the help of some interpretations by them, Ed begins to draw parallels between his interactions with his parents and family and his interactions with the group leaders and other members. For several sessions this association is explored in greater depth, and Ed begins working through his feelings toward each therapist. Eventually Ed may find that in many ways he is making the leaders his symbolic parents (expecting them to respond to him as his parents did and keeping himself a helpless child waiting for their approval) and, more generally, that he is reliving his past in the group.

In future sessions Ed may work on his inordinate need for approval and love, on his extreme dependence on others to direct him, and on his taking refuge in drinking to blunt the anxiety of not feeling loved. Thus, he could fruitfully explore the roots of his excessive drinking and come to understand that it is both an escape from anxiety and an attempt to create the illusion of being the powerful person he would like to be.

Reality-therapy group.   A way of describing the reality-therapy approach to Ed's problem is to contrast it with the approach of the psychoanalytic group. The differences include:

• Since reality therapy focuses on future success, not on past failure, Ed is not allowed to dwell on his past.

• Whatever reactions Ed has toward the leaders, they are assumed to be generated by the present therapeutic relationship and not to be the result of transference or distortions from Ed's past.

• The co-therapists actively work at having Ed look at his current behavior and decide whether this behavior is getting him what he wants. If Ed decides that his behavior is dysfunctional, he is challenged to develop a plan for change.

• The reality-therapy leaders discourage Ed from focusing on his *feelings* of hopelessness, despair, isolation, and dependence; rather, he is encouraged and directed to examine what it is that he is doing now that contributes to these feelings. To direct this examination of how Ed's actions are contributing to his feelings, the leaders ask questions such as: "What exactly did you do today from the time you woke up to now? You say that you feel despair and isolation; taking the last week, could you tell us specifically *what* you did whenever you had such feelings? How did your behavior contribute to your feelings? What do you see that you *can* do before our next session to begin to change your pattern? Are you willing to take specific steps that involve behaving differently? What are some constructive things that you can do when you feel a need to drink?"

• Regarding Ed's stated desire to penetrate the reasons underlying his drinking problem, the reality therapists will probably say: "We don't go looking for causes from the past to explain what we view as current irresponsible behavior. Insight into the unconscious reasons for your behavior is *not* our concern. Rather, we want to talk about your current options for beginning to actually decide on a course of action that will lead to responsible behavior, which will ultimately lead to a success identity."

Transactional-analysis group. The TA approach to Ed's "theme" will probably include the following elements:

• Work focuses on Ed's life script, which in his case may be captured succinctly in the phrase "drinking myself to death," and his supporting injunctions such as "Don't think!" "Don't succeed!" "Don't be competent!" In the group Ed may work on his process of developing his life course, so that he can come to see that his current script, "drinking myself to death," may be a self-fulfilling prophecy.

• The therapists may also point out the ways in which Ed is slowly killing himself psychologically by keeping himself isolated. In the group, time is devoted to examining the games he plays, along with the payoffs for these games. Eventually, Ed is led to see that his games are related to a purposeful plan. (That is, if Ed plays his games long enough, he will eventually collect enough bad feelings to justify the final ending of his script, which could be suicide. This would fulfill his basic injunction "Don't be!")

• Ed would also be led to examine the connection between the games he plays and his basic life position "I'm not OK—you're OK." Eventually, Ed may come to see that his game is to put the responsibility for his self-worth on others.

The aim of the work in the TA group is to help Ed understand *how* and under *what conditions* he formulated his original decision—for example, "Don't trust yourself, because you'll always fail. Instead, expect others to decide for you, because you're incapable of directing your own life." Once Ed sees how he made his decision and once he becomes aware of the games he plays—even in his group—he can be led to see that he doesn't have to continue being the victim of an early decision and that he is now in a position to make a new decision.

THEME: SEARCHING FOR MEANING IN LIFE

Boyd, the 22-year-old college student who experiences much anxiety and entertains occasional suicidal thoughts, shares with the group the acute panic he feels because of his suicidal fantasies. He says that, even though he sees that he has a large quantity of life left, he cannot see that it has much quality, and he wonders why he should go on. Like Ed, Boyd feels anxiety about making choices, and, like Ed—who is taking the slower route of alcohol—he wants to "end it all." When Boyd reveals the emptiness of his life, Judy says that she identifies with his problem. Judy's success as a professor still leaves her concerned over the emptiness in her life and struggling to find meaning.

Some Therapeutic Approaches

Existential group.   In an existential group the leaders may well use the fact that Judy identifies with Boyd's problems and ask both of them to sit in the center of the group to discuss their perceptions of how their life has lost meaning and to explore their sense of emptiness in greater depth. When this dialogue has run its course, the leaders invite other members to talk about aspects of their own life that have grown stale. Using these discussions as a basis, the leaders may then work with Judy, Boyd, or any of the other members on a variety of themes:

- Life doesn't have meaning by itself; it is up to us to create meaning in our life.
- Feelings of emptiness and a sense that life has lost its meaning may signal the need to begin building new meanings. The sense of purposelessness can be a sign that we are ready for a change.
- If we don't like the direction in which we are moving, we need to ask what we can do to change the direction and what we are doing to prevent change.
- We must accept responsibility for our own capacities and limitations and for what we are becoming.

In working with Judy, existential group leaders may focus on some of the paths she is taking to find meaning in her life—for example, her work, her relationships with others, and her leisure-time activities. In the existential view the anxiety Judy is feeling over what she terms "emptiness" is not seen in negative terms; rather, it is viewed positively as a potential growth force. The fact that Judy is questioning her values—values that may have been useful in the past—to determine the extent to which they still hold meaning for her indicates that she is ready for change. Her anxiety is seen as a natural response to the contemplation of change.

In working with Boyd, the existential group leaders may look beyond the obvious implications of his suicidal thoughts to discover how alive or how dead he is feeling with respect to the life that he still has. Here again Boyd's anxiety over his death impulses may be seen as a positive sign, as though Boyd were actually saying: "I want more from life than I am receiving. No longer am

I content with merely existing; I want to be *alive!*" In short, his anxiety will probably be viewed as an impetus for changing his life in such a way that he will *want* to live.

Behavior-therapy group. Behaviorally oriented leaders approaching the themes exemplified by Boyd and Judy will first help the two members define in concrete and specific terms what they want to explore. General goals, such as trying to find meaning in life, coping with emptiness, or experiencing existential anxiety over outworn projects, are far too vague for these leaders. Their focus would be on specifics, as seen in the following dialogue between Judy and one of the co-leaders, who is helping Judy define a specific area to focus on in the group.

Judy: I have a vague feeling of hollowness, as if there were an absence of any unifying purpose in life. I question the meaning of my life.
Co-leader: This lack of meaning that you speak about is vague. Could you pinpoint what it is that you would like to change?
Judy: What I'd like to change is the sense of emptiness I often experience. I want to feel that what I'm doing matters, that my life has meaning.
Co-leader: Perhaps we can make this goal more concrete by identifying what it is that you do that causes you to question your meaning.
Judy: I feel that, when I'm needed and appreciated, there is meaning in my life. When I'm unrecognized, I feel that life is empty.
Co-leader: Right now, could you list some of your activities that evoke a sense of meaningfulness and also list specific things that lead you to feel unappreciated?
Judy: I think I could but not right now. Maybe before our next group meeting.
Co-leader: Fine. Let me make a suggestion. Before we meet again, try to pay attention to the conditions that tend to be associated with either a feeling of purpose or the sense of emptiness you describe. Carry a notebook, and jot down a few notes concerning what you actually *do* in situations attached to these feelings. In this way we'll have a better sense of what you are doing, and we can work on specific areas of change.

As can be seen, the behavior therapist is attempting to break down the task into manageable parts—to identify specific behaviors that can be observed and to develop specific goals that can be measured. Rather than working on broad existential concerns such as the meaning of life, the leader focuses on observable behaviors that contribute to the feelings of emptiness Judy talked about and teaches Judy how to observe such behaviors. One can readily see how a similar approach would be taken to Boyd's case.

Adlerian group. In the cases of Ed, Boyd, and Judy—all of whom are searching for meaning—Adlerian procedures are quite appropriate. Adlerians assume that people are motivated by goals; the function of a group is to help members identify their life goals. This is done by asking them to look at what they are striving toward. Questions that can be asked are: "What are you after? Where are you going? What is your image of the central goal that gives your life meaning?" For members such as Boyd, Judy, and Ed, attention is given to their life plan, including their fictional goals. For example, Ed probably developed in early childhood a fictional image of what he would like to be in order to be safe and to feel that he belonged. His assessment of his early experiences might well be inaccurate, and his life-style today could be based on his striving for goals that he had as a child. Ed may have learned that drinking was a way for him to escape from painful reality. When he drank, he felt strong and superior, and eventually his whole life became centered on drinking. With alcohol he could convince himself that he was all that he wanted to be. However, this style of life is now proving to be ineffective, and Ed is seeing how empty his life is. With the encouragement of the group, he begins to challenge his mistaken beliefs, gains more awareness of how he has deceived himself by living in fantasy, and starts talking about ways to find new goals that will provide him with meaning in life.

Gestalt group. In her Gestalt group, Judy's declaration that she feels empty will probably be met by a question on how she experiences this emptiness. Let's postulate that Judy answers such a question as follows: "Sometimes I feel like I'm alone and lost in a desert. In fact, last night I had a dream about just that, about being lost in a desert. I was dying for lack of water—all I could see was rocks, sand, and one cactus bush with thorns on it. Then I stumbled across a well, but when I dipped into it, the well was bone dry. I began to cry, but there were no tears."

The Gestalt leaders will probably focus on Judy's dream as a way of helping her experience her emptiness more fully. They don't interpret her dream; rather, they help her discover the meaning of her dream for herself by asking her to *become* selected parts of her dream, giving them a voice and speaking in the present. What follows is a sample of this dream work.

Co-leader: Judy, I'd like you to become the cactus with thorns and speak as if you were the cactus bush.

Judy: Nobody better get close to me; if you do, I'll stick you. I'm all alone here, and that's the way I want to be. It's taken me a long time to grow these thorns; so stay away!

Co-leader: Now let yourself become the rocks.

Judy: I'm hard; nothing can get to me. I'll last forever. Nothing can get inside me.

Co-leader: What are you experiencing now?

Judy: In many ways I'm like that rock and thorny bush. People can't really get to me. I'm hard and protected.

Co-leader: And how does it feel to be hard and protected?

Judy: Safe. Yet, at the same time I'm lonely out here on this empty desert.

Co-leader: Now I'd like you to become the well. Try to speak as if you were the well in your dream.

Judy: I look as if I could keep you from dying of thirst—as if I could nourish you. Yet, when you dip inside me, you'll find that I'm all dried up. There's really no water deep inside me—I'm just a bottomless pit, dried and empty.

This process of becoming various parts of her dream can enable Judy to make connections between the different parts of her dream and her own life. Judy apparently fears that, although people see her as a bright and talented person with much to offer (a full well), she actually has nothing of value to offer (an empty well). Although the Gestalt technique of dream interpretation doesn't solve Judy's problem of emptiness or end her quest for meaning, it does help her move closer to experiencing her emptiness and becoming aware of her fear that she is the one who is keeping people out of her life.

THEME: CHALLENGING AND CLARIFYING VALUES

Sharon, the 25-year-old executive secretary who is living with a man over her parents' objections, feels comfortable with her life-style yet is uncomfortable about her parents' strong disapproval. According to Sharon, her parents feel that she is letting them down and that, until and unless she gets married, she is not worthy of their respect. She is in pain over the loss of their esteem. She says: "I don't really expect them to agree with me, and I can accept their right to think as they do. What troubles me, however, is that I'm really hung up on their refusal to let me live my life as I see fit. In order to live life as I want to, I have to decide to be disowned by them."

Some Therapeutic Approaches

Psychodrama group. Psychodrama directors will probably want to know whether Sharon remembers any time as a child when she wanted parental approval and didn't receive it. Let's say that Sharon recalls a time when she decided not to go to church anymore—a decision her parents could not accept, although they had no way of forcing her to continue attending church. The directors help Sharon reenact this childhood scene with the help of two group members who play her parents. The following are a few possibilities for a psychodrama format:

- Playing herself as a child, Sharon may say all the things now that she thought and felt but never said when her parents withdrew their affection.
- Sharon can ask her parents (still as the child) to respect her and allow her to have her own life.
- The symbolic parents may play their roles as rejecting parents or as accepting parents.
- Other group members can stand in for Sharon and say things that she finds difficult to express.
- Sharon can project a scene with her parents in the present that incorporates an interaction with them as she would wish it to be. In that case, she coaches others to be the parents she would want.

Following the psychodrama, there is an effort to connect Sharon's present problem with the feelings she had as a child. The ways she now pleads with her parents for approval could be much like her dynamics as a child. The experience of the psychodrama could at least help her see how to deal with her parents in a more direct and mature way than she typically does.

Person-centered group.   The leaders of a person-centered group will give Sharon the freedom to express and explore her feelings about the pain she feels over the loss of her parents' esteem. If the members and facilitator can really understand Sharon's struggle between wanting to live her own life and wanting parental acceptance, she is likely to gain more clarity on this issue. The facilitator probably does not introduce any techniques; rather, Sharon is invited to talk about her feelings, values, and thoughts. The goal is not to get the group's validation, for this would be the same as Sharon's striving for her mother's and father's validation. Instead, it is hoped that, as Sharon explores her conflicts, she will come to trust her ability to find a direction in life that is acceptable to her. The primary goal in this type of group is to foster a climate in which the actualizing tendency can freely express itself. If the members and the facilitator can show Sharon respect and positive regard, if they can understand her struggle as she experiences it, and if they can show her warmth and caring, then it is likely that she will profit from the group experience and move forward in a constructive manner. With the support of the group, she will find within herself the answers she is searching for, and she will probably rely less upon others to confirm her worth as a person.

Psychoanalytic group.   From an analytic perspective, Sharon can be viewed as having a passive, dependent attitude toward her parents. In some ways, she is still keeping herself infantile by looking at them to feed her and nourish her as a person. Sharon has not given up the fantasy of being the young girl that her parents wanted; this frustration of her need to be seen as the "ideal daughter" by her parents may bring about feelings of insecurity, disillusionment, and anxiety. The analytic leaders, and other members as well, can interpret her behavior as seeking the parents she has always wanted. She may now be treating others in the group as she treated her parents. Sharon may look to the leaders and some members to tell her how she should live her life and how she could win their unconditional love.

At the working stage Sharon may regress and reexperience some old and familiar patterns, which would be seen as material to be worked through in the group. How she behaved in the group sessions could provide some clues to the historical determinants of her present behavior. The group therapists would make timely interpretations so that some of her past could be brought to the surface. Another focus would be guiding Sharon in working through her transferences with the leaders and other members. In the group situation it is probable that she has re-created her original family; this transference interferes with her accurate appraisal of reality, since she is now projecting onto others in the group feelings she had for her parents.

Adlerian group.   As in the psychoanalytic group, interpretation will probably be a central therapeutic technique in the Adlerian group. However, Adlerian interpretation is different from psychoanalytic interpretation in that it is done in relation to Sharon's life-style. No time is devoted to exploring the possible causes of her struggle to win her parents' approval. Instead, the focus is the here-and-now behavior that Sharon displays, on her expectations that arise from her goals, and on ways that she can begin to challenge her thinking and thus make changes in her behavior. In the Adlerian group, Sharon is invited to consider the leaders' interpretations of her striving for parental approval. She explores her style of life to see how searching for approval may be a theme. The interpretation is focused on her goals, purposes, and intentions, as well as on her private logic and how it works. As Sharon gains insight, through referring to her basic premises and to the ways these beliefs are mistaken, she can begin the process of modifying these cognitions and thus find ways of leading a more satisfying life. The focus of the work is typically of a *cognitive* nature, for it is assumed that, if she changes her beliefs, her actions will also change.

Gestalt group.   The Gestalt leaders will probably focus on a specific behavior related to Sharon's problems—say, the fact that she speaks in a soft and pleading voice. To help her get in touch with what she is doing, the leaders can ask her to exaggerate this mannerism—for example: "Go around to each group member, and be as apologetic as you can be. Keep your eyes fixed to the ground, and tell everyone how much you need them to approve of you; then apologize for being a bother to them."

Through this exercise Sharon may gain an awareness of how her general style expresses tentativeness and how her demeanor invites people to feel sorry for her. Since, as suggested by her statement above, Sharon would like to deny her apologetic aspect, this exercise is aimed at exposing this aspect by exaggerating it. The leaders may then ask Sharon to bring her parents into the room and speak to them openly and candidly, in the way she would like to. Next, she is asked to switch places and "become her parents," in order to answer what she has just told them and to disclose what they may be thinking of Sharon yet not saying. This shifting in and out of roles—Sharon playing herself and then "becoming her parents"—continues until she can identify unfinished business from her past that gets in her way now. In the process, she may work on her feelings of resentment, anger, and fear toward her parents.

THEME: DEALING WITH THE TERMINATION OF THE GROUP

Up to this point I've given examples of how the various approaches to group therapy might be practiced with respect to the themes that have emerged in the model group. Although I think that it is valuable to practice working within the framework of each theory as you learn about it, I also see value in developing your own style of group leadership. As I see it, this can be done by selectively incorporating (both conceptually and technically) aspects of every group model described. Rather than limiting yourself to practicing any one model exclusively, you can integrate various components from all these models and begin to develop your own leadership style—a style that suits your personality and the kind of group you may lead.

To assist you in thinking about ways to integrate these different group models into your personal style, I will now describe how I would use concepts and techniques from the various approaches in dealing with some typical issues that I observe in most groups during the last few sessions. These themes include wrapping up, saying good-bye, consolidating learning, terminating issues, applying group learning to daily life, and evaluating outcomes.

Feelings of Separation and Loss

The final stage of a group is a very difficult time. The members are aware that their community is about to dissolve, and they are beginning to mourn their impending separation. Some of them are pulling back; they are becoming less intense and are no longer contributing much new material to work on. Others wonder whether they'll be able to maintain the openness they have learned in the group once they can't count any longer on the group's encouragement and support. They fear that in their everyday lives they won't find people who give them the kind of support they need to keep experimenting with change and, as a consequence, that they may regress to old ways.

If I were leading our model group, I would want to give its members an opportunity to fully express their feelings about the termination of the group. The *person-centered* approach, which stresses listening actively and giving permission to explore whatever feelings are present, offers a useful model for this phase of group work. Here members don't need much direction; rather, they need to be encouraged to face the reality that they have shared in an intense experience and soon will be going their separate ways. It is necessary to allow members to talk about any unfinished business they may have concerning their own problems or other members. If participants can fully express their feelings about separation, the transition period between leaving the group and carrying what they've learned in the group into their day-to-day life will be made easier.

I have often observed what I consider to be an irrational conviction on the part of many group participants that they won't be able to create in their everyday life that which they have experienced within the group. Here I apply the concepts of the *rational-emotive* approach and encourage participants to substitute rational ideas for what appear to be unfounded beliefs about separation from the group. The following examples may shed light on this process:

- *Irrational belief No. 1:* In this group I can be open and trusting, but I don't think that this is possible in my everyday life.
  Rational belief No. 1: I can be open with selected others, and I am largely responsible for initiating trust in my relationships.

- *Irrational belief No. 2:* There is no way I can be in my everyday life the way I was in here.
  Rational belief No. 2: If I choose to, I can create in my daily life the kind of relationships I valued in this group; that will enable me to be the kind of person I want to be wherever I am.

- *Irrational belief No. 3:* In the group I received support for the changes I made and valued; in my everyday life most people won't like many of my changes, and they won't give me the support I need to maintain them.
  Rational belief No. 3: I probably won't receive support or even approval for the changes I have made and will make, but I am no longer in desperate need of support from everyone.

The process of helping members challenge their beliefs about separation and about incorporating what they've acquired in the group can be most valuable. My goal is to help participants see that their group has been a place where they could learn *how* to form meaningful interpersonal relationships—a process that is not restricted to the group but that can be applied in any setting.

In this regard there is some value in helping participants understand any connections that might exist between their past and their family on the one side and the relationships they have developed within the group on the other. For that purpose the *psychoanalytic* approach is useful. In some ways the group represents a new family for its members, and, by relating their behaviors in the group "family" to their behaviors in their actual families, members can learn much about themselves. To assist participants in their process of making connections among behaviors, I ask them to consider the following questions:

- To whom was I drawn in this group?
- With whom did I have the most conflict?
- In what ways did my feelings and actions in this group resemble the ways in which I felt and acted as a child in my family?
- Were my reactions to the group leaders in any way similar to my reactions to my parents?
- What did I want from them?
- How did I react toward them?
- Did I experience feelings of competitiveness or jealousy within the group?

Looking Ahead

Another tool I use as the group is drawing to a close is the development of fantasies. I find that too often group members don't allow themselves to creatively imagine how they would like to experience their life. To assist them in their endeavor, I ask members to picture themselves and their life in some ideal future circumstance—a technique that is used by both the *Gestalt* and the *psychodrama* approaches. Applying the fantasy technique to the case in point, I might suggest to members the following:

- Imagine that you are attending a reunion of the group five years from now and that we are meeting to discuss how our life has changed during the past five years. What do you *most* want to be able to say to us at this reunion?
- Let yourself fantasize about all the ways that you want to be different in your everyday life once you leave this group. Close your eyes, and carry on a silent dialogue between yourself and the people who are most special in your life. What are you telling them now? What are these people saying back to you?
- Imagine that one year has passed since we ended the group. Also imagine that nothing has changed in your life—that you have continued the way you have always been. Try to picture how you would feel if that actually occurred.

I have found that some members and the group in general might benefit by sharing fantasies. For this purpose a brief Gestalt exercise that has members be themselves in the future and carry on a dialogue with significant people is useful. (In this exercise the members themselves play all parts in the dialogue.) Role-playing exercises are also helpful. For example, I sometimes ask participants to select a member of the group to role-play a person in their life. The role play begins by having the participant briefly tell the person selected what it is that he or she would like to change in their relationship and *how* he or she intends to make those changes.

Also during the final stages of the group, I ask the members to review what they have learned about their early decisions as a result of participating in this group—an approach characteristic of both *transactional analysis* and *rational-emotive therapy.* To stimulate this review, I typically question the members as follows:

- Do you want to revise any of these early decisions?
- Are these decisions still appropriate for you now?
- What new decisions do you want to make?

In addition, I ask members to review what they've learned concerning the games they play, as well as the payoffs from these games, and to think about specific ways in which they might experiment with game-free behavior outside of the group. Further, I ask members to identify, even write down, the self-defeating statements that they continue to indoctrinate themselves with, to share them, and to offer one another feedback concerning the validity of these self-statements, as well as suggestions on how to combat self-destructive thinking.

Toward the final stages of the group I rely heavily on the cognitive and action-oriented approaches characteristic of the *behavior therapies, reality therapy, rational-emotive therapy,* and *transactional analysis.* I see the group as a learning laboratory in which, it is hoped, the members have identified the specific changes that they are willing to make and have experimented with new behaviors. Assuming that this has indeed occurred, it becomes extremely important that the members carry out their own action-oriented programs outside the group. During the last session I have members work in small groups to formulate a *specific* contract—a brief statement of the plans they have concerning behavioral changes to be effected once the group ends. The aim of this small-group work is to have members clearly define what they now want to do and how they specifically intend to do it. The results of the efforts are then shared with the entire group. Finally, I try to schedule a follow-up session—usually several months after the termination of the group—for the purpose of allowing members to discuss, from that perspective, what the group meant to each of them as well as to report on the extent to which they have fulfilled their contract.

My experience has taught me that, after they have left the group, members tend to forget some of what they learned and to discount the actual value of what they did in the group. To help prevent this from occurring and to help members retain whatever they have learned—about others, about human struggling, about life, and about themselves—at the final session I ask them to review specific insights they had throughout the course of the group. It is my contention that, unless one articulates and shares with others the specifics of what one has learned in the group, one's group experience may soon become an indistinct blur.

Here, again, I find the principles of the *behavioral* approaches useful during the final session—specifically, the application of feedback principles to help members strengthen the perceptions that they gained during the course of the group. For example, I often ask members to complete feedback sentences for every member in the group such as:

- One of the things I like best about you is . . .
- One way I see you blocking your strengths is . . .
- My hope for you is . . .
- My greatest concern or fear for you is . . .
- The way I'll remember you in this group is . . .
- A few things that I hope you'll remember are . . .

Focused feedback, whether verbal or written, can give the participants a good sense of the impact they had on others in the group.

As the final session draws to a close, I give members a message to take with them—a message grounded in the *existential* approach: "I hope that you have become aware of your role and of the responsibility you bear for who you are now and for who you are becoming, that you will no longer blame others for your problems, and that you will no longer see yourself as a victim of circumstances outside of yourself. Many of you have become aware of the choices that are open to you; thus, you can now reflect fruitfully on the decisions you will make. Even if you decide to remain largely as you are, you now are aware that you *can* choose, that you don't need to have others design your life for you. Although choosing for yourself can provoke anxiety, it does give you a sense that your life is yours and that you have the power to shape your own future."

Finally, and as mentioned earlier, I feel it is important to schedule a follow-up group meeting several months after the end of the group to allow members to evaluate the outcomes of the group experience for themselves and to evaluate the group as a whole. In this connection I offer members some guidelines for evaluating themselves and their group experience, as well as topics to discuss at the follow-up group meeting.

Behavioral approaches stress developing clear goals, working on these goals during the sessions, and then evaluating the degree to which these goals were met. I see that what members do after the group ends is as important as the group sessions. Therefore, I tend to devote ample time to suggesting ways in which members might consolidate their learnings and carry them into daily living. Specifically, I encourage members to develop the habit of keeping a journal—writing down the problems they are encountering, describing how they feel about themselves in specific situations, and listing their successes and difficulties in following through with their contracts. Because I feel that an appropriate book read at an appropriate time can be a powerful catalyst in helping people make the changes they want to make, I encourage members to read as a way of continuing to work on themselves and to grow.

17

COMPARISONS, CONTRASTS, AND INTEGRATION

INTRODUCTION

The purpose of this chapter is fourfold: (1) to compare and contrast the various models as they apply to issues special to group work; (2) to raise some basic questions that you'll need to answer now and throughout the course of your practice; (3) to challenge you to attempt an integration of the various perspectives that is consistent with your personality; and (4) to stimulate your thinking about ways of developing and refining group techniques that reflect your leadership style.

The questions that this chapter will help you answer include:

- Is it possible to achieve some integration of the diverse group models by focusing on their commonalities?
- How would an integrated view of the various perspectives actually help you define your own goals of group counseling?
- How do you go about blending concepts and techniques from several approaches to achieve your own definition of the leader's role and your own unique leadership style?
- How can you achieve an optimum balance between responsible leadership and responsible membership, whereby you accept your rightful share of responsibility for the direction of the group without usurping the members' responsibility?
- How much structure does a group need?

- How do you develop techniques that are consonant with your personality and style and are also appropriate for the kinds of group you lead?
- What are some of the possible abuses and misuses of group techniques?
- What are the advantages and the dangers of an eclectic approach to group practice?

THE GOALS OF GROUP COUNSELING: VARIOUS PERSPECTIVES

In order to impart meaningful direction to their groups, leaders need to address themselves to the issue of goals. What should be the specific goals of a given group, and who should determine them? How can the leader help group members develop meaningful goals for themselves? How does the leader's theoretical orientation influence the process of goal setting? Is it possible to set group goals based on a variety of theoretical orientations?

Beginning group leaders would have great difficulty in giving a positive answer to the last question above; the differences among theoretical approaches with regard to goals seem irreconcilable. For example, behaviorally oriented groups stress specific, concrete goals such as becoming more assertive, losing weight, or eliminating phobias. On the other hand, the relationship-oriented and existential groups focus on lofty, often unmeasurable, goals such as achieving self-actualization or becoming an autonomous person.

Extreme as these differences may appear, they shouldn't stand in your way as you attempt your own theoretical integration. Each group model stresses certain facets of the human experience, and what seems like a conflict can actually be reinterpreted in unifying terms.

Most theoretical perspectives agree on the importance of group members' formulating their own specific goals. When leaders decide that they know what is best for the participants and force their own goals on them, they typically encounter resistance and promote lack of motivation. To be sure, leaders need to have some overall goals for the group, but such goals should in no way infringe on the members' freedom to select personal goals that will give direction to their work in the group. This individual goal setting is an ongoing process that needs to be constantly reevaluated. The leader can be of invaluable assistance in this regard by encouraging members to formulate clear and specific goals for themselves and by helping them determine how they can work toward achieving these goals.

To help you find common denominators among the goals stressed by the various theoretical models and to guide you in your attempt to integrate these models, I've brought together in Table 17-1 the essential therapeutic goals of each of the group approaches discussed in the preceding chapters. As you read the table, keep in mind that the diversity of goals can be simplified by seeing the goals as existing on a continuum from general, global, and long-term objectives to specific, concrete, and short-term objectives. Humanistic and relationship-oriented group approaches tend to deal with broad goals, and behavioral and cognitively oriented systems focus on short-term, observable, and precise goals. The goals at opposite ends of the continuum are not

Table 17-1.   Comparative Overview of Group Goals

Model	Goals
Psychoanalytic groups	To provide a climate that helps clients reexperience early family relationships. To uncover buried feelings associated with past events that carry over into current behavior. To facilitate insight into the origins of faulty psychological development and to stimulate a corrective emotional experience.
Adlerian groups	To create a therapeutic relationship that encourages participants to explore their basic life assumptions and to achieve a broader understanding of life-styles. To help clients recognize their strengths and their power to change. To encourage them to accept full responsibility for their chosen life-style and for any changes they want to make.
Psychodrama groups	To facilitate the release of pent-up feelings, to provide insight, and to help clients develop new and more effective behaviors. To open up unexplored possibilities for solving conflicts and for experiencing dominant sides of oneself.
Existential groups	To provide conditions that maximize self-awareness and reduce blocks to growth. To help clients discover and use freedom of choice and assume responsibility for their own choices.
Person-centered groups	To provide a safe climate wherein members can explore the full range of their feelings. To help members become increasingly open to new experiences and develop confidence in themselves and their own judgments. To encourage clients to live in the present. To develop openness, honesty, and spontaneity. To make it possible for clients to encounter others in the here and now and to use the group as a place to overcome feelings of alienation.
Gestalt groups	To enable members to pay close attention to their moment-to-moment experiencing, so they can recognize and integrate disowned aspects of themselves.
Transactional-analysis (TA) groups	To assist clients in becoming script and game free in their interactions. To challenge members to reexamine early decisions and make new ones based on awareness.
Behavior-therapy groups	To help group members eliminate maladaptive behaviors and learn new and more effective behavioral patterns. (Broad goals are broken down into precise subgoals.)
Rational-emotive-therapy (RET) groups	To teach group members that they are responsible for their own disturbances and to help them identify and abandon the process of self-indoctrination by which they keep their disturbances alive. To eliminate the clients' irrational and self-defeating outlook on life and replace it with a more tolerant and rational one.
Reality-therapy groups	To guide members toward learning realistic and responsible behavior and developing a "success identity." To assist group members in making value judgments about their behaviors and in deciding on a plan of action for change.

necessarily contradictory; it is just a matter of how specifically the goals are defined. Thus, a convergence is possible if practitioners view concrete, short-term goals as components of broad, long-range goals.

ROLE AND FUNCTIONS OF THE GROUP LEADER: VARIOUS PERSPECTIVES

Should the leader be a facilitator? a therapist? a teacher? a catalyst? just another, albeit more experienced, group member? a technician? a director? an evaluator? some or all of these?

How you answer these questions will depend in part on your theoretical perspective, but ultimately your answers will be based on your own definition of the leader's role and on your own assessment of what the most significant functions of the leader are. There are also certain criteria that cut across all the theoretical approaches—for example, the goals and type of group, the setting, the nature of the participants, and the demands of your job.

Before discussing the various perspectives on the group leader's role and functions, let's briefly review some of the tasks that I consider essential to successful group leadership.

1. Group leaders initiate and promote interaction by the way they structure the group and model behaviors that are conducive to interaction. Thus, they demonstrate how to share, take risks, and be honest and how to involve others in interactions. They can also share their leadership functions so that group members are able to become increasingly independent and don't need to lean on the leader to initiate and direct every action in the group.

2. Group leaders have the task of orienting members to group process, teaching them how to get the most from their group, and helping them become aware of the group dynamics. These goals are achieved by encouraging members to look at the direction their group is taking, to determine whether there are barriers that prevent them from working effectively, and to become aware of any hidden agenda that could obstruct the flow of the group.

3. Group leaders must be capable of sensitive, active listening. Only by paying full attention to the members' verbal and nonverbal communication can they help participants move toward a deeper level of self-exploration and self-understanding. If attending skills are lacking, genuine empathy and understanding between group leader and participants is not possible.

4. Group leaders are responsible for creating a climate conducive to exploring personally significant issues. Trust needs to be established early in a group, and the leader has a crucial role in building an atmosphere in which people can reveal themselves, can behave in new ways, and can question their basic beliefs and assumptions.

5. Group leaders are responsible for setting limits, helping establish group rules, and protecting members. Although leaders don't have to prepare a lengthy list of "dos" and "don'ts," they do need to establish certain ground rules. They need to inform members of their rights and responsibilities, stress the importance of the issue of confidentiality throughout the group's life, and take the necessary steps to ensure the physical and psychological safety of the group members.

6. Finally, group leaders need to direct attention to ways in which people can profit as much as possible from the group experience. They can do this by clarifying, summarizing, and integrating what has gone on and what has been learned, by helping members crystallize their feelings and new insights, and by encouraging them to decide on action programs that will facilitate applying what they have learned in the group to their outside lives.

As we have seen, each therapeutic approach stresses different functions for the group leader. For example, the person-centered approach emphasizes the role of facilitator. Since in this model the group is seen as having the resources to direct itself, the leader is supposed to facilitate rather than direct group process. Other approaches see the leader as a teacher. Rational-emotive therapy, reality therapy, Adlerian therapy, behavior therapy, and transactional analysis are all based on the assumption that group counseling or therapy is essentially an educational and learning process, and consequently the leader's key function is that of teaching skills and providing a cognitive framework that will lead to reeducation and behavioral changes.

Other models, such as the psychoanalytic approach, focus on the role of the group leader as a technical expert who interprets intrapsychic and interpersonal processes as they manifest themselves in a group. Still other models, such as the existential, the person-centered, and the Gestalt approaches, stress the leader's role in helping members gain an experiential awareness of their conflicts through meaningful relationships with the leader and others in the group. As we have seen, your roles and functions as a group leader are many; which of them you choose to emphasize is partly determined by your theoretical orientation. As you review the different perspectives summarized in Table 17-2, consider what elements you want to incorporate from each of them in defining your own role as group leader.

DEGREE OF STRUCTURING AND DIVISION OF RESPONSIBILITY: VARIOUS PERSPECTIVES

Group leaders often struggle with the question of what constitutes the optimum degree of structure in a group. It should be clear that all groups have a structure. Even the least directive group leaders, who avoid imposing a format on the group, do make the choice of having an open structure and letting the participants determine the course of the group.

Group structuring exists on a continuum, from extremely nondirective to highly directive. On the nondirective end of the continuum are psychoanalytic groups, person-centered groups, and some existential groups. In these groups the leaders tend to assume a passive stance and encourage group members to give direction to the group. One aspect of the learning value of these groups is that the members assume much of the responsibility for defining their own structure.

At the opposite end of the continuum are those leaders who provide a high degree of structure for the group. They often use structured exercises to open the group sessions; also, they employ techniques to focus members on specific themes or problem areas and to intensify emotions and conflicts. Many behavior-modification groups are characterized by a very directive and active group leadership. Typically, these groups are highly structured; there is a progression from session to session, the meetings are organized in accordance with a predetermined agenda, and certain procedures are used to direct the group toward exploration and resolution of specific problem areas.

Like structuring, division of responsibility can be conceptualized in terms of a continuum. At one end are those group leaders who see themselves as experts and who believe that they should actively intervene to keep the group moving in ways that they deem productive. The group's outcomes are seen as very dependent on the leader's skills. Thus, explaining members' failures in terms of their insufficient motivation or lack of ego strength is considered a rationalization on the part of the leader, who, being the expert, is the one who has failed and is the one responsible for the failure of the treatment plan. Behaviorally oriented group leaders embrace this view in full.

The rational-emotive group approach, too, places a large share of responsibility on the group leader. Since therapy is considered an educative process, the group leader is seen mainly as a teacher in charge of the reeducation of the group members. For effective results, group therapists are expected to employ a rapid-fire, didactic, persuasive methodology aimed at cognitive restructuring. However, despite the highly directive role RET assigns to the leader, it also places a considerable share of responsibility for directing the group on the members, who are expected to be active, work hard, and practice between group sessions.

At the other end of the continuum are group leaders who expressly announce at the beginning of a group that the members are responsible for themselves and that what they get (or fail to get) from a group depends on them and on them alone. This type of leadership is characteristic of some encounter-group leaders, who place total responsibility for the direction and outcome of a group squarely with the members and refuse to hold themselves responsible for what members choose to do or not do in the group.

Another group approach that emphasizes the responsibility of the group participants is the person-centered model, which sees the participants as the ones who truly know what is best for them. The leader does not assume responsibility for actively directing the group process; he or she functions as a facilitator by attempting to create a trusting climate wherein members can safely explore deeply personal issues and search for the necessary resources within themselves.

Somewhat in the middle of the continuum are Gestalt group leaders. They are typically active, in that they intervene with action-oriented techniques that do provide the group with structure, but they also insist that group members are the ones who are responsible for whatever they experience. The group process is seen as a way of helping the participants become aware of how they deny personal responsibility and learn how to rely on themselves for their own support. Group leaders are responsible for being aware of their own experience throughout the group process and for introducing appropriate techniques to intensify group work. Members are responsible for bringing up issues that they

Table 17-2.   *Comparative Overview of Leader's Role and Functions*

Model	Leader's Role
Psychoanalytic groups	Facilitates group interaction by helping create an accepting and tolerant climate. Remains relatively anonymous and keeps an objective stance, so that members will develop projections toward him or her. Signals indications of resistance and transference and interprets their meanings. Helps members work through unfinished business from the past. Sets limits for the group.
Adlerian groups	Uses procedures such as confrontation, self-disclosure, interpretation, and analysis of prevailing patterns to challenge beliefs and goals. Observes social context of behavior. Models attentive caring. Helps members accept and utilize their assets. Encourages members to develop the courage needed to translate what is learned in the group to behavior outside of the group.
Psychodrama groups	Functions as both facilitator and director. Has the job of warming up the group, helping set up a psycho-drama, directing the enactment, and then processing the outcomes with the participants. Specific tasks include facilitating, observing, directing, producing, and summarizing.
Existential groups	Has the central role of being fully present and available to individuals in the group and of grasping their sub-jective being-in-the-world. Functions by creating a per-son-to-person relationship, by disclosing himself or herself, and by confronting members in a caring way.
Person-centered groups	Facilitates the group (as opposed to directing it)— deals with barriers to communication, establishes a climate of trust, and assists the group in functioning effectively. His or her central task is to be real in the sessions and demonstrate caring, respect, and under-standing. Has the primary role of creating a climate of tolerance and experimentation. Often becomes directly involved by sharing personal feelings and impressions about what is happening in the group or reactions to various group members.

want to investigate in group and for making their own interpretations. Table 17-3 gives you an idea of the variety of theoretical positions that are taken with regard to the issues of structuring and division of responsibility.

My view is that group leaders need to achieve a balance between assuming too much and assuming too little responsibility for the direction of the group. On the one hand, leaders who assume too much responsibility rob members of the responsibility that is rightfully theirs. If clients are perceived by the leader as not having the capacity to take care of themselves, they soon begin to live up to this expectation. Besides undermining members' independence, leaders who assume an inordinate amount of responsibility burden themselves greatly. They tend to blame themselves for whatever failures or setbacks the group suffers. If members do little productive work, these leaders see it as their fault. If the group remains fragmented, they view this as a reflection of their lack of

Table 17-2. ***Comparative Overview of Leader's Role and Functions*** (continued)

Model	Leader's Role
Gestalt groups	Suggests techniques designed to help participants intensify their experience and be alert to their body messages. Assists clients in identifying and working through unfinished business from the past that interferes with current functioning. Focuses on members' behaviors and feelings.
Transactional-analysis (TA) groups	Has a didactic role. Teaches clients how to recognize the games they play to avoid intimacy, the ego state in which they are functioning in a given transaction, and the self-defeating aspects of early decisions and adopted life plans.
Behavior-therapy groups	Functions as an expert in behavior modification; thus, must be active and directive and often functions as teacher or trainer. Imparts information and teaches coping skills and methods of self-modification of behavior, so that members can practice effective skills outside group sessions.
Rational-emotive-therapy (RET) groups	Functions didactically: explains, teaches, and reeducates. Helps members see and rigorously confront their illogical thinking and identify the connection between self-defeating behavior and irrational beliefs. Teaches them to change their patterns of thinking and behaving.
Reality-therapy groups	Encourages members to face reality and make choices that will allow them to fulfill their needs in socially acceptable ways. Helps members by establishing a personal relationship with them, by firmly expecting that they will formulate and implement a plan for change, and by rejecting excuses for irresponsible behavior.

skill. In short, this style of leadership is draining, and the leaders who use it may soon lose the energy required to lead groups.

On the other hand, leaders who place all the responsibility for the direction and outcomes of a group on the participants may simply be trying to avoid their own role in the success or failure of their groups. Thus, if a group seems to go nowhere, these leaders avoid asking themselves whether their leadership or lack of it is a contributing factor.

THE USE OF TECHNIQUES: VARIOUS PERSPECTIVES

Techniques are quite useful both as catalysts for group action and as devices to keep the group moving. But techniques are just tools, and like all tools they can be used properly or misused. When, for example, leaders fall into a pattern of employing techniques mechanically, they become technicians and are not responding to the needs of the particular group they are leading. Also, indiscriminate use of techniques tends to increase the resistance level of the group instead of facilitating deeper communication. Some leaders, overly eager to use

Table 17-3.   Comparative Overview of Degree of Structuring and Division of Responsibility

Model	Structuring and Responsibility
Psychoanalytic groups	*Leader:* shies away from directive leadership and allows the group to determine its own course; interprets the meaning of certain behavioral patterns. *Members:* raise issues and produce material from the unconscious; assume increasing responsibility for interacting spontaneously, making interpretations, and sharing insights about others; become auxiliary therapists for one another.
Adlerian groups	*Leader:* at the outset, works toward goal alignment; takes active steps to establish and maintain a thera-peutic relationship, to explore and analyze the individ-ual's dynamics, and to communicate a basic attitude of concern and hope. *Members:* develop insight about themselves; assume the responsibility for taking posi-tive measures to make changes; consider alternative beliefs, goals, and behaviors.
Psychodrama groups	*Director/leader:* suggests specific techniques designed to intensify feelings, recreate past situations, and pro-vide increased awareness of conflicts; makes sure that the psychodrama protagonist is not left hanging and that other members of the group have a chance to share what they experienced during the psychodrama. *Members:* produce the material for psychodramas and, when in the role of protagonist, direct their own psychodramas.
Existential groups	*Leader:* may structure the group along the lines of cer-tain existential themes such as freedom, responsibility, anxiety, and guilt; shares here-and-now feelings with the group. *Members:* are responsible for deciding the issues they want to explore, thus determining the direction of the group.
Person-centered groups	*Leader:* provides very little structuring or direction. *Members:* are seen as having the capacity to find a meaningful direction, of being able to help one another, and of moving toward constructive outcomes.

new techniques, treat them as if they were a bag of tricks. Others, out of anxiety over not knowing how to deal with certain problems that arise in a group, try technique after technique in helter-skelter fashion. In general, group leaders should have sound reasons for using particular methods of intervention, and an overreliance on technique is, in my view, questionable.

I like to stress to my students that techniques need to be an extension of who the leader is as a person and that group leaders should not force them-selves to use techniques that don't suit their personality and their unique leadership style. Techniques need to be employed sensitively, appropriately, and skillfully. In observing group leaders in action, I have often noticed that many of them rely too much on techniques. I've seen, for example, the leader of a group that had become stale and seemed to be going nowhere intervene with technique after technique to merely get activity going or to keep the

Table 17-3.   Comparative Overview of Degree of Structuring and Division of Responsibility (continued)

Model	Structuring and Responsibility
Gestalt groups	*Leader:* is responsible for being aware of his/her present-centered experience and for using it in the context of the group; brings structure to the group by introducing appropriate techniques to intensify emotions. *Members:* must be active and make their own interpretations.
Transactional-analysis (TA) groups	Because of the stress on an equal relationship between leader and members, responsibility is shared, as specified in a contract. *Members* and *leader* spell out in the contract what changes members want to make and what issues they want to explore in the group.
Behavior-therapy groups	*Leader:* is responsible for active teaching and for having the group proceed according to a predetermined set of activities. *Members:* are expected to be active, to apply what they learn in group to everyday life situations, and to practice new behaviors outside the group.
Rational-emotive-therapy (RET) groups	*Leader:* is responsible for hammering away at any signs of member behavior based on faulty thinking; structures the group experience so that members stay with the task of making constructive changes. *Members:* are responsible for attacking their own self-defeating thinking and that of fellow group members; are expected to carry out self-confrontation outside the group and work hard at changing illogical thoughts.
Reality-therapy groups	*Leader:* teaches members to assume responsibility for how they live their life; structures the group by focusing on present behavior and by indicating ways of making specific behavioral changes; influences members by modeling success-oriented behavior; confronts clients who are not living realistically. *Members:* decide on specific changes they want to make; make value judgments regarding present behavior; are held responsible for implementing desired changes.

members talking, even though the talk was of a nonproductive nature. Instead of dealing openly and directly with what was going on in the group and with his own reactions, this leader (probably out of anxiety) tried to solve the problem by relying on gimmicks. The countless techniques I saw him use one after the other may have given this leader the false impression that the group was moving, but in reality they reaffirmed the group's immobility.

My basic assumption is that techniques should facilitate group process, not artificially create action in a group. I also assume that techniques are most effective when the group leader learns how to pay attention to the obvious. Techniques can deepen feelings that are already present, and they should grow out of what is going on in the group at the time. There is always something going on in a group, and this material can suggest appropriate techniques. Although my colleagues and I sometimes use techniques to introduce material at the initial stage of a group and often use them to integrate what members have learned at the final stage, we generally do not have a preset agenda. We take our cues from what is occurring within the group and flow with that, rather than attempting to direct the group to pursue a specific theme. For example, if I notice that there is little energy in the room and that nobody appears willing to do significant work, I don't introduce an exercise designed to stir up feelings or promote interaction. Instead, I may let the group know that I am feeling strained from taking too much responsibility for keeping the group alive, and I try to get some assessment of what each person is experiencing.

In conducting a training workshop for group leaders, I typically stress the importance of maintaining flexibility in the use of techniques. When my colleagues and I introduce a technique to deepen the exploration of thoughts, feelings, or conflicts of an individual, we are never certain about where the technique will go. Again, it is essential to pay attention to what the group members are experiencing and take your cues from them on where to go next. In other words, it is helpful to let them provide the lead and at the same time suggest ways for them to keep the issue they are exploring in focus.

In choosing techniques to facilitate group process, you must consider several factors. Your theory, of course, will influence what techniques you employ. If it focuses on cognitive aspects, then your techniques are likely to encourage clients to look for the connection between their thought patterns and their actions. If you have a Gestalt orientation, your techniques will tend to promote an awareness of present feelings and an intensification of these feelings. If you are behaviorally oriented, many of your techniques will be geared to getting members to monitor their actions and experiment with specific behaviors. Your style of leadership also has much to do with what techniques you will use. Finally, the population with whom you are working, the purpose of your group, and the stage of development of the group are all factors to consider in the selection of techniques.

To avoid using techniques routinely, leaders must understand the relationship between techniques and theoretical concepts and be fully aware of why they are using certain techniques; that is, they must have an idea of what they expect to occur as a result of the techniques they are using. In addition to having a rationale for using group techniques, leaders need to continually assess their effects. Finally, as I said earlier, the techniques must be suited to the personality of the group leader. For example, some people feel very comfortable with the dramatic methods of psychodrama and others do not. Techniques that are not extensions and expressions of the leader simply won't work.

As illustrated by Table 17-4, the various group models offer a variety of strategies for initiating and maintaining group interaction. There is no reason why group practitioners should restrict themselves to the techniques of a single approach simply because that's the approach they favor. For example, group leaders with an existential orientation can comfortably draw on techniques from the behavioral and cognitively oriented models and easily incorporate them into their leadership style. There are imaginative ways of blending Gestalt and transactional analysis, both conceptually and technically. Many of the techniques that are characteristic of the behavior-modification approach can be fruitfully applied to any other kind of group. The point I'm making here is that leaders need to use their imagination to discover ways of adapting techniques from various theoretical models to the specific type of group they lead and of modifying them to suit their leadership style.

AN INTEGRATED ECLECTIC MODEL OF GROUP COUNSELING

The term *integrated eclectic model* refers to a model based on concepts and techniques from several theoretical approaches. It is the model I use in my own practice of group work. The following description of the model is meant to provide you with some basis for integrating the various approaches and to help you gain more understanding of the practical applications of some aspects of these models in group work. I shall describe my model by reviewing in brief the aspects of the various approaches that I've incorporated in it.

Psychoanalytic approach. In my group work I place emphasis on childhood experiences and on the influence of the past on present functioning. Whenever possible and appropriate, I explore past experiences with the goal of increasing the members' awareness of how these experiences have contributed to making them the person they are or how present conflicts are related to earlier ones that were never fully understood or resolved.

Other psychoanalytic concepts I have incorporated in my integrated eclectic model are resistance, transference, and countertransference. I strongly believe that members' resistances that get in the way of full participation need to be faced and worked through. Thus, at the beginning of a group I explore with the members the anxieties, fears, and defensive approaches that will keep them from becoming actively involved. When appropriate, I examine transference relationships as they are manifested in the group situation, so that participants can become aware of the link between past unfinished business with significant people and present ways of perceiving and relating to others. I also make every effort to be aware of my feelings toward various members, particularly when these feelings are responses to the members' own unresolved conflicts. The nature and functioning of defenses, as they become evident in the group situation, are also given a great deal of attention.

I believe that, unless group leaders have a clear understanding and appreciation of the major developmental tasks and crises that are associated with each stage of human development, they won't have the necessary perspective for working in depth with members' struggles. I find an integration of Freud's psychosexual stages with Erikson's psychosocial stages valuable in providing a basis for differentiating between healthy and unhealthy developmental patterns. This combined Freudian/Eriksonian view of human development gives me a conceptual framework for understanding trends in development, critical needs at each period of life, choice potentials, and critical turning points. It also offers me a useful perspective on the relationship between earlier developmental experiences and later personality and behavioral conflicts.

This developmental viewpoint helps me understand some of the common struggles I observe in group members—struggles that are related to a particular

Table 17-4.   *Comparative Overview of Group Techniques*

Model	Techniques
Psychoanalytic groups	Interpretation, dream analysis, free association, analysis of resistance, and analysis of transference—all designed to make the unconscious conscious and bring about insight.
Adlerian groups	Analysis and assessment, exploration of family constellation, reporting of earliest recollections, confrontation, interpretation, cognitive restructuring, challenging of one's belief system, and exploration of social dynamics and of one's unique style of life.
Psychodrama groups	Self-presentation, presentation of the other, interview in the role of the other and interview in the role of the self, soliloquy, role reversal, double technique and auxiliary egos, mirroring, multiple doubles, future projection, and life rehearsal.
Existential groups	Since this approach stresses understanding first and techniques second, no specific set of techniques is prescribed. However, leaders can borrow techniques from other therapies to better understand the world of clients and to deepen the level of therapeutic work.
Person-centered groups	The stress is on the facilitator's attitudes and behavior, and few structured or preplanned techniques are used. Basic techniques include active listening, reflection of feelings, clarification, support, and "being there" for the client.
Gestalt groups	Many action-oriented techniques are available to the Gestalt-oriented leader, all of which are designed to intensify immediate experiencing and awareness of current feelings. Techniques include confrontation, empty chair, game of dialogue, making the rounds, fantasy approaches, reversal procedures, rehearsal techniques, exaggerating a behavior, staying with feelings, dialogues with self or significant others in the present, and dream work. Exercises are designed to enable participants to become increasingly aware of bodily tensions and of the fear of getting physically and emotionally close, to give members a chance to experiment with new behavior, and to release feelings. Guided fantasy, imagery, and other techniques designed to stimulate the imagination are used.
Transactional-analysis (TA) groups	Techniques include the use of a script-analysis checklist or questionnaire to detect early injunctions and decisions, games, and life positions; family modeling; role playing; and structural analysis.
Behavior-therapy groups	The main techniques, which are based on behavioral and learning principles and are aimed at behavioral changes and cognitive restructuring, include systematic desensitization, implosive therapy, assertion training, aversive techniques, operant-conditioning methods, self-help techniques, reinforcement and supportive measures, behavioral research, coaching, modeling, feedback, and procedures for challenging and changing cognitions.

Table 17-4. Comparative Overview of Group Techniques (continued)

Model	Techniques
Rational-emotive-therapy (RET) groups	The essential technique is active-directive teaching. Leaders probe, confront, challenge, and forcefully direct. They model and teach rational thinking, and they explain, persuade, and lecture clients. They use a rapid-fire style that requires members to constantly use their cognitive skills. RET uses a wide range of behavioral techniques such as deconditioning, role playing, behavioral research, homework assignments, and assertion training.
Reality-therapy groups	A wide range of techniques is used, such as role playing, confrontation, modeling, use of humor, contracts, and formulation of specific plans for action.

period in life. Erikson's developmental approach is not a group approach per se, for there are no standard group techniques in this model. Rather, this model provides a global view of human development that can help practitioners make sense out of what they observe in group work.

Adlerian approach.   I especially like the philosophy underlying the Adlerian approach that we are creative beings motivated by goals and purposes. I also find the notion that our basic feelings of inferiority can spur us to strive for mastery and power intriguing. The view that adversity, feelings of inferiority, and even traumatic experiences can be incentives for growth is one that I embrace fully.

The concept of the uniqueness of each person's life-style makes a great deal of sense to me. My work as a group leader has offered me countless opportunities to observe that each individual has a distinctive approach to life, as well as unique personality characteristics, and that such an approach is in great part determined by the person's perceived feelings of inferiority and helplessness.

Another Adlerian concept I find valuable is the interest in exploring the place the client occupied in the "family constellation." By correctly interpreting the child's role in his or her family, the therapist can better assess key decisions made at an early age that still influence the client's life. Thus, I often ask group members to report and work with some of their earliest recollections.

Psychodrama.   The action-oriented approach characteristic of role playing and psychodrama encourages group members to make their personal struggles come alive and helps them become directly involved in experiencing their conflicts. As you know, role-playing techniques can be incorporated into all the other group models. When it appears that participants are detached from the problems they are talking about, I often ask them to act out these conflicts. For example, if an adolescent begins to lose touch with her feelings as she talks about the problems she has relating to her father, I might ask her to select a "father" in the group and show us *how* she attempts to talk to him. Others in the group can learn about their own conflicts in an indirect way, and they can also become involved in the role-playing situation by showing the girl different ways of approaching her father. Thus, this technique can suggest alternative ways of behaving and alternative frameworks for understanding a conflict in some interpersonal situation.

Existential approach. The existential model provides the philosophical foundation of the integrated eclectic model. One of my basic assumptions is that we have the capacity to become increasingly self-aware and that heightened self-awareness results in greater freedom. My goal as a group leader is to make participants realize that they are not passive victims of life, that they have the power to change, and that they have choices—as one of my clients once said to me, "I can see now something I never saw before. I have a choice, and I can change my life if I want to."

However, with this freedom comes responsibility. Early in the group I essentially tell participants: "You are responsible for how you are living your life. If you don't like the way you are living, don't try to dodge responsibility by blaming your past or others around you. You and only you can shape your own destiny." This philosophy underlies my leadership style and deeply influences the way my groups operate. For example, we spend much time talking about the anxiety that is associated with accepting the responsibility for the direction of one's life. In fact, I encourage participants to explore whether the changes they are contemplating are really worth the price involved.

Other concepts of the existential model that form the basis of my personal style of group leadership include examining one's value system, clarifying the sources of meaning in life and recognizing where and how we find a sense of purpose, reflecting on the idea that our awareness of death gives meaning to life, and approaching new decisions knowing that we don't have much time to accomplish our life goals. I find that most group members are vitally concerned with these existential issues, because these are issues related to the core struggles of the contemporary person.

Person-centered approach. The person-centered model provides me with several important concepts. Perhaps the most important is the view of the group as a place for authentic encounters. As the group unfolds, I expect to see members drop their defenses and reveal who they really are behind their masks and pretenses. In fact, one of the real joys of doing group work is to observe people becoming real and honest and attempting to be accepted for themselves. When members voice the fear of being rejected for revealing their true nature, I invariably respond that, when people take the risk of being genuine, they are very rarely rejected—in fact, they generally elicit feelings of respect and caring.

As I have said many times before, trust is the foundation on which group process rests. Therefore, in the initial stages of a group I devote a lot of time to exploring barriers to trust and ways of creating a climate of trust. I try to make clear, for example, that risk taking is essential to the goal of building a trusting community. In a way, risking and engaging in new behavior are what the group is all about. However, it is important to stress that no one can be forced to take risks and that each person in the group must make the choice to risk or not to risk.

Gestalt therapy. Because of its wide range of techniques, Gestalt is a very useful source of procedures designed to intensify experiencing and integrate conflicting emotions. So, whenever possible, I ask group members to relive a past experience as though it were happening right now and talk directly to the person or persons with whom they are having conflicts.

I have incorporated in my model the focus on hindrances to present-centered awareness, such as thinking about the future and dwelling on the past. One way of detecting these blocks is paying attention to nonverbal language. When I notice a discrepancy between someone's words and body message, I explore it in the group. I don't attempt an interpretation of the discrepancy. I try instead to get the participants to become more aware of what they really are feeling and to learn what messages they are sending besides the verbal ones.

The Gestalt approach to dream work can be fruitfully integrated. If a member of one of my groups wants to explore a dream, I ask that person first to relate the dream and then to "become" various parts of the dream and act out the different roles.

Gestalt practitioners often focus on one person in the group while the other members observe the interaction. This is one Gestalt approach I don't favor, because I prefer techniques that allow participation by as many group members as possible. Also, I consistently attempt to get members to relate to one another and to initiate interactions.

Transactional analysis. TA supplies the cognitive dimension that I find lacking in the experiential approach of Gestaltists. (Note, however, that TA concepts can be successfully combined with Gestalt concepts and techniques.) Like the leaders of TA groups, I devote a lot of group time to examining past decisions and the degree to which they are still appropriate in the present. If the conclusion is that they are not, I encourage participants to make new ones. Many people never really critically evaluate their early programming; in a group, these people can become aware of parental injunctions, early decisions, and life positions and choose to deprogram themselves.

The concept of games (and how they prevent intimacy) is another concept that I borrow from transactional analysis and fruitfully explore in my groups to make members aware of the games they play in group interactions and in their everyday lives. I then encourage them to experiment with game-free behavior in and out of group.

Behavior therapy. In the course of my practice I have become increasingly aware of the value of the behavioral approach for groups. Let me say, first of all, that I don't see the behavioral and the existential approaches as mutually exclusive. In fact, I think that some of the existential goals can be best achieved by relying on certain learning principles and specific behavioral techniques.

Some of the ways in which I use this approach in my integrated eclectic model are the following:

1. I ask members to determine the specific changes they want to make; more specifically, I ask them to formulate their own concrete goals and to state them in a contract.

2. Most of the groups' norms are shaped by principles of reinforcement. Thus, members soon learn that they are positively reinforced for disclosing themselves in appropriate ways, for taking risks, for experimenting with new behaviors in the group, for becoming active participants, for giving honest feedback, and for demonstrating caring and concern for others.

3. Because of many people's inability to communicate effectively with others, to let others know what they want from them, and to effectively confront others when necessary, I find the use of assertion-training exercises and other role-playing techniques most valuable. These techniques are especially appropriate for those who cannot express anger, are overly polite, allow others to take advantage of them, and, more generally, find it difficult to assert their rights. Thus, I use much role playing (which is basically behavioral rehearsal) as well as coaching and modeling.

Rational-emotive therapy. This approach is highly didactic, cognitive, and action oriented—characteristics that I find quite compatible with the humanistic foundations of my integrated eclectic model. I see merit in the assertion that we must take action if we hope to challenge and combat irrational beliefs that prevent growth. I also see merit in RET's emphasis on challenging irrational assumptions that cause personal misery and on helping members substitute rational ideas for faulty ones.

Another of RET's techniques that I like to employ is homework assignments. I believe that participants can have all sorts of insights about themselves and still maintain the same ineffective life-style. Change requires taking specific steps outside the group that will lead to the desired outcomes. Therefore, I encourage members to give themselves concrete assignments to implement in and out of group. I don't believe that members need to be given assignments by the leader or other members: if they are committed to change, they will eventually assign themselves their own homework.

Reality therapy. My experience has taught me that it is very important for the leader to emphasize accountability. Value judgments about one's behavior and specific plans for change—both essential components of the reality-therapy model—are most valuable in upholding the concept of accountability.

Reality therapy's emphasis on commitment and accountability is in accord with the existential view that we are responsible for ourselves and for the direction we take. Thus, in my groups I place a great deal of emphasis on responsibility and accountability, and, in line with the reality-therapy approach, I insist that members avoid excuses and the blaming of others. If members report that they are regressing or failing to follow through with their contract, I direct their attention to the degree to which they want what they say they want and to the possibility that they may have attempted to do more than they can handle. Thus, it becomes a group task to explore how realistic some of these plans are and what modifications may be needed to make them more feasible.

APPLICATIONS OF THE INTEGRATED ECLECTIC MODEL

Introduction

Having discussed those concepts and techniques that I find particularly valuable from each of the ten theories discussed in this book, I'd like now to work toward a synthesis of applications of these theories at each stage of a group's development. Such a synthesis will illustrate how all the theories can be fruitfully applied throughout the evolutionary process of the group. My goal is a conceptual framework that can address the three factors of thinking/feeling/doing. As you've seen, some theories focus on cognition, others on the experiencing of feelings, and others on behavior. What seems ideal to me is to blend the unique contributions of these approaches so that all three dimensions of human experiencing are given attention at each phase of a group.

Theories Applied to the Pregroup Stage

The preparatory period in the formation of a group may be the most critical of all the stages. If the group's foundation is weak, the group may never get off the ground. Effective groups do not simply "happen." The hard work and careful organization that go into planning a group are bound to have payoffs once the group gets under way.

The behavioral theories are particularly relevant at the pregroup stage, for they emphasize assessing the need for a group as well as assessing the participant's readiness for a group. It behooves group leaders to be clear about their expectations, to have a rationale for why and how a group is an effective approach, and to have a clear vision of ways to design a specific group tailored to the unique needs and interests of the members. As a leader, if you are clear about how a group can benefit a prospective member, then you'll be better able to help him or her decide whether to join. If members know in advance what they are getting into, the chances are increased that they will become active and committed participants. In this regard, the therapeutic approaches that structure a group on a contractual basis have much to offer. A contract can help demystify the group process, can increase the members' sense of responsibility to become active agents in their own change, and can structure the course a group takes. As you will remember, the cognitively and behaviorally oriented therapies stress contracts as a way of beginning the process. TA groups, Adlerian groups, behavior-therapy groups, and, sometimes, rational-emotive-therapy and reality-therapy groups work on a contractual basis. Whatever your theoretical leaning, open-ended and flexible contracts can be drawn up before the group actually meets as a whole.

The functions of the leader that I see as especially important at the pregroup phase are developing a clear proposal for a specific group; recruiting, screening, and selecting members; providing orientation to the members so that they can derive the maximum gains from the experience; and, ideally, arranging for a preliminary group session to help members get acquainted and provide some teaching about the nature and functioning of groups.

Theories Applied to the Initial Stage

Basic characteristics. The early phase of a group is a time for orientation and exploration. Some of the distinguishing characteristics at this time are the following: Members are attempting to find a place in the group. They are trying to get acquainted and learn what a group is all about. They are gradually learning the norms and what is expected. Interactions tend to be of a socially acceptable nature and somewhat on the surface, and there is a certain tentativeness within the group. Perhaps the most basic issue is that of trust versus mistrust, and the attitudes and behaviors of the group leader are directly related to the creation of a level of trust that will promote significant interaction.

Drawing upon theories. The relationship-oriented approaches, especially person-centered therapy and existential therapy, provide an excellent foundation for building a community characterized by trust and the willingness to take the risks that are necessary for change. The leader's modeling is especially important, for it is my belief that members learn more from what the leader does than from what he or she says. Here is where enthusiasm about groups can be communicated to the members by a dedicated, competent, and caring group leader. A basic sense of respect for what the members are experiencing as they approach a new group can best be demonstrated by a leader's willingness to allow members to express what they are thinking and feeling in the here and now. Typically, members do have some initial anxieties. They may fear an unfamiliar situation, rejection, or closeness. Some may fear opening up more than they can manage, disrupting their life outside the group, or incurring the disapproval of others in the group. A genuine interest in listening to these feelings sets the tone for caring, attentiveness, and compassion and goes a long way toward creating a climate in which members can be free to share what they feel and think.

Besides encouraging members to express their feelings, I draw upon the cognitive therapies. Thus, members come to a group with certain expectations of themselves and what they think a group can do for them. Some may expect others to provide them with answers to their problems, some may expect to get from the group what they see themselves as missing in their relationships at home and work, and some may be convinced that a group will not really help them. Such expectations need to be stated and addressed at the early sessions.

Defining personal goals. It is during the initial stage that the *behavioral* approaches and the *cognitive therapies* have special relevance. I like the behavioral emphasis on helping members identify concrete aspects of their behavior that they most want to change. From there the leader may do some teaching to show members how involvement in the group can be instrumental in attaining their goals. I see it as counterproductive for leaders to impose upon members specific goals they should work toward, for, unless the members really want to change, there is little hope that change can be forced upon them. For this reason I value the Adlerian concept of goal alignment. Adlerians make special efforts to negotiate an alignment of goals between the client and the therapist. TA groups are also characterized by mutually agreed-upon therapeutic goals. In reality-therapy groups, there is emphasis upon challenging members to look at their behavior and decide whether it is working for them. If members make the value judgment that their current behavior is not working, then the process of making specific behavioral changes is in progress. Although I am very sympathetic toward existential goals of learning how to live more creatively by accepting freedom and responsibility, I think such broad goals need to be narrowed down so members have a clear idea of what feelings, thoughts, and actions they are willing to change and can learn how to make such changes.

Theories Applied to the Transition Stage

Learning to deal with conflict and resistance.   One of the most challenging and often frustrating periods in the life of a group is the transition phase. Before a group can progress to the working stage, it typically must learn to recognize and deal with anxiety, defensiveness, resistance, conflict, the struggle for control, challenges to the leader, and various problematic behaviors. Some groups reach the transitional period only to remain stuck there. This impasse can be traced either to a failure to establish norms during the pregroup and initial phases or to inept handling of resistance and conflict within the group. It is essential that conflict be both recognized and then dealt with therapeutically if the group is to move forward. Again, the role of leader modeling is critical. The manner in which the group leader deals with the inevitable resistance that manifests itself in various avoidances and defensive maneuvers will determine how well the group meets the developmental tasks at the transition phase. I hope you will learn how to respect resistance by seeing it as a normal and healthy sign of a group's movement toward autonomy. Rather than viewing resistance as a nuisance to be gotten around, you can help members to deal with the sources of their resistance in a therapeutic way.

Ways of conceptualizing resistance.   Several theoretical perspectives shed some light on the dynamics of resistance and suggest methods of dealing with it constructively. From a psychoanalytic perspective, the basic concept *resistance* is seen as anything that prevents members from dealing with unconscious material. Resistance is the unconscious attempt to defend oneself from the anxiety that would arise if the unconscious were uncovered. It helps me to remember that members have to struggle with intrapsychic conflicts as well as interpersonal conflicts. Sensitivity on the leader's part to the ambivalence that members experience in both wanting to be a part of the process of self-discovery and fearing self-knowledge helps participants begin to look at their fears and defenses. If leaders can respect the natural reluctance of members to plunge in and take risks and at the same time encourage members to express any reluctance they experience, there is a better chance that participants will work through their personal fears.

I see ways of combining the psychoanalytic and Adlerian ways of thinking about resistance. Group members typically reexperience some of the old feelings they had in their original family. Sibling rivalry, position in the group, acceptance/rejection feelings, strivings for attention and success, dealing with authority issues, learning how to manage negative feelings, and recalling traumatic childhood memories and experiences are all parts of the group experience. Groups offer participants the opportunity to become aware of patterns of thinking, feeling, and behaving that they established in their own family. People are often stuck in a developmental sense because of certain unfinished situations that now intrude on their ability to function as effectively as they might. The group provides a context in which participants can become aware of dysfunctional patterns that they picked up as children and cling to as adults. By working with their projections, transferences, attractions, and other feelings toward others in the group, however, the members can experiment with new ways of thinking about themselves and others, can allow themselves to experience a wider range of feelings than is typical outside of a therapeutic group, and can practice with new ways of behaving during the sessions as well as at home and work.

A feeling/thinking/behaving perspective.   At a time when a group is in transition, I appreciate the freedom given by the person-centered approach to express any feelings and have this expression be acceptable. My hope is that members will allow themselves to *feel* the ways in which they are resisting and to intensify those feelings. Here is where I draw upon some of the action-oriented techniques of Gestalt therapy and psychodrama so that they will have a way to experience as fully as possible whatever they feel. At some point I would also want to work with their belief systems and their self-talk. Here is where I find TA and rational-emotive therapy of value. For example, a member might verbally participate very little in a group because she is following certain parental injunctions, such as: "Don't show other people what you feel." "Don't talk in public about your family and personal problems." "Don't trust others." "Be strong and don't give in to feelings of self-pity." I think TA provides a useful framework within which members can gain awareness of these parental messages and their early decisions. And RET is also of value in helping members challenge some of the self-defeating beliefs that lead to an entrenchment of their defensiveness in the group. A member might say very little because of his fear of disapproval or because he has convinced himself that he must say things "perfectly" so that others will understand him. Once members allow themselves to experience their resistance on a feeling level, I see them as being more available for genuinely challenging their cognitions. Related to this is their willingness to begin to behave in different ways. I like the emphasis of reality therapy on paying attention to what one is *doing* and RET's emphasis on the need to practice new behaviors as the basis for making lasting changes.

Theories Applied to the Working Stage

During the working stage there is a commitment by members to explore significant problems they bring to the sessions and to express their reactions to what is taking place within the group. I find that this stage requires the least degree of structuring. In part this is because members bring up issues they want to work on, freely interact with one another, have the feeling of being a group rather than a bunch of strangers, and assume responsibility to keep the sessions moving.

Concepts and techniques at the working stage. My preference is to let the members raise the issues they are willing to seriously pursue rather than taking the responsibility for calling on them, drawing them out, or telling them what they should talk about. This does not imply a passive stance, however, for during the working stage I am very willing to suggest experiments and to invite members to take part in a technique that is designed to heighten whatever it is that they are experiencing. Again, my concern is with the feeling/thinking/doing dimensions, and the techniques I suggest reflect this type of integration. Once members declare that they do want to work and we decide what it is they want to accomplish, then I typically ask them if they are willing to participate in an experiment.

Generally, I prefer to begin with helping members get into contact with what they are feeling in the here and now. Gestalt techniques are most useful in focusing on present-centered awareness and bringing any unfinished business from the past to the surface. I favor the approach that asks members to bring any past issue into the present, as is true of both psychodrama and Gestalt. There is a lively quality to the work, and members rather quickly begin to experience what they feel rather than talking abstractly about feelings and thoughts. For example, if a woman becomes aware that she fears she is growing up to be just like the mother she resents, a good place to begin is to ask her to "bring her mother into the group" symbolically so that she can deal with her. Again, Gestalt and psychodramatic techniques offer a rich range of techniques to help her get into focus and intensify her experience. She might experiment with assuming her mother's identity and actually speaking to others in the group "as her mother." Although I value the contact with feelings, I think it is pseudowork to stop with catharsis or the mere expression of her feelings. I am likely to suggest that she identify some of the beliefs that she has picked up from her mother. Perhaps she has uncritically accepted some irrational ideas that she stubbornly clings to and now is keeping herself upset by living by untested assumptions.

Coupled with her emotional work, some exploration of her cognitions is likely to reveal how her daily behavior is limiting her. Therefore, I see debates as productive in a group. Especially valuable are debates that members can learn to have with themselves. They can challenge untested assumptions, argue the pros and cons of a given issue, and think about how they sometimes set themselves up for defeat. Working at a *behavioral* level is an excellent way to correct faulty thinking and emotional disturbances. For example, Fritz says that he has a low estimation of his worth, that he feels depressed and anxious much of the time, and that he is afraid to ask for what he wants. Rather than waiting around until Fritz feels better and begins to think differently about himself, I favor suggesting ways that he might begin to behave differently. My assumption is that, if he begins to behave more assertively, he might begin to like himself more and eventually change his view of the person he is. Role playing, behavioral rehearsals, and other behaviorally oriented techniques can teach Fritz some of the social skills he needs to function effectively. Of course, during the working and final phases I'd encourage Fritz to practice new behaviors in a variety of social settings and bring the results back to the group.

Theories Applied to the Final Stage

Review of the tasks of the final stage.   The final stage of the group's evolution is critical, for members have an opportunity to clarify the meaning of their experiences in the group, to consolidate the gains they have made, and to revise their decisions about what newly acquired behaviors they want to transfer to their daily life. The major tasks facing members during this consolidation stage involve learning ways to maintain these changed behaviors in the outside world. My focus is on getting the members to review the nature of any changes on a feeling/thinking/behaving level. Have they learned the value of expressing negative feelings rather than swallowing them? Have they learned that repressing their feelings results in some indirect expression of them? What cognitions have they modified? Have they let go of some dysfunctional cognitions that lead to emotional upsets? Have they let go of certain injunctions that they bought wholesale? Have they challenged their beliefs and values and made them their own? What concrete behavioral changes have they made that they value? How did they make these changes? How can they continue to behave in ways that are productive? What kind of plan for action can they devise now that the group is coming to an end so that they can continue to make progress?

Theoretical perspectives during the final stage.   I tend to use the most structure during the beginning and ending phases of a group. It is not my style to hope that members will automatically transfer specific emotional, cognitive, and behavioral changes from the group to the outside world. Therefore, I provide a structure that I hope will promote this transfer of learning. Whereas I tend to lean toward experiential therapies and exploration of feelings during the working phase, I lean toward the cognitive/behavioral therapies and toward putting one's learning into some type of conceptual framework during the final stage. From the behavioral therapies I draw techniques such as practice and rehearsal for leaving a group, self-monitoring procedures, building a support system beyond the group, and learning methods of self-reinforcement. Since I see therapy as a teaching/learning process, I try to help members devise a conceptual framework that will ensure that they can make sense of what they have experienced in the course of the group. Both RET and reality therapy are relevant models at this point in a group's history, since both stress the importance of developing specific plans for change, making a commitment to do what is needed to bring about change, and evaluating the outcomes of the therapeutic process. Although members are urged to try out a plan of action during the working phase, it is during the final stage that such a plan is essential.

It should not be assumed, because of the emphasis I am placing on cognitive work and behavioral plans for action during the final stage, that feelings are unimportant at this time. I see it as critical that members deal with their feelings about separation and termination, that they express any fears or reservations they might have about making it in the world without the support of the group, and that they learn how to say good-bye. Also, the opportunity to complete any unfinished business is paramount at this time.

During the ending stage the leader needs to watch for certain dangers. Members might avoid reviewing their experience and fail to put it into some cognitive framework, thus limiting the generalization of their learning. And because of their anxiety over separation, some members might distance themselves and thus get less benefit from the group. There is also the danger that members will consider the group as merely an experience in itself and as an end rather than a means to continue growing. To avert these dangers, I value the role of the group leader as a teacher. These pitfalls can be pointed out so that members can decide what, if anything, they will do differently. Also at this time members can be taught how to evaluate the impact of the group on them as well as assess the progress they have made as a group.

Theories Applied to the Postgroup Stage

After the group comes to an end, the members' main task is applying their in-group learning to an action program in their daily life so that they can function in self-directed ways. Personally, I value setting aside time for individual interviews with each member if possible, along with arranging for a follow-up group session. Such procedures have a built-in accountability factor, for both members and the leader can more accurately assess the impact of the group. Again, the behavioral approaches stress this type of accountability and evaluation. If this is a part of the leader's style, then he or she can make modifications in future groups based on what seemed to work. Follow-up procedures also provide a safety valve, for if members left the group with unresolved or negative feelings, they can at least discuss them with the group leader.

I hope you will see that groups can be effective if there is careful planning and designing to bring about change. It should by now be obvious that changes in one's thinking, feeling, and behaving are the result of strategies designed to produce change. Once such changes have come about, it does not mean that they will be long-lasting; this is why I devote attention to ways of extending such changes beyond the life of a group.

The Pros and Cons of an Eclectic Model

Because of space limitations, I could give you only a rough outline of the integrated eclectic model of group. It is my hope that, no matter how cursory, the preceding description has succeeded in conveying the multifaceted nature of this model—both conceptually and technically. As I've said so many times before, I am convinced that each practitioner must find a style that fits him or her as a person; the model I've described is the result of my own search for an approach to groups that fits me both professionally and personally. It is a model that reflects my view of groups as entities that express in an integrated fashion the feeling, thinking, or doing dimensions of individual members. It is also a model that combines the didactic with the experiential, since I believe that what we experience in a group needs to be supported by a conceptual framework. Without such a framework, it would be impossible for us to make sense of the experience and to understand its implications for our daily existence. Finally, it is a model that brings together the action-oriented, the insight-oriented, and the experientially oriented approaches—that is, affective, cognitive, and behavioral dimensions—to pursue more effectively the basic goal of any therapeutic group—change.

As I've said before, I see serious dangers in subscribing totally to the tenets of a single model. If you become a rigid follower of any one approach, you may overlook valuable dimensions of human behavior and unduly limit your effectiveness with different clients by trying to force them to fit the confines of your theory. Group leaders do need a theory of group process on which to base their techniques and procedures. But they also need to keep in mind that each theoretical model has something unique to offer and that effective leaders are continually defining and refining a personalized group theory that guides them in their practice and allows them to make sense of what occurs in groups.

Having said all that, I also wish to say that there are dangers in encouraging an eclectic approach. At its worst, eclecticism can be an excuse for sloppy practice—a practice that lacks a systematic rationale for what you actually do in your work. If you merely pick and choose according to whims, it is likely that what you select is just the reflection of your biases and preconceived ideas. At its best, eclecticism can be a creative synthesis and a selective blending of the unique contributions of diverse theories—the dynamic integration of concepts and techniques that fit the uniqueness of the group leader's personality and style.

CONCLUDING COMMENTS

It has been my experience that, between the first and the last day of an introductory course in group counseling, students find that what seems at first to be an overwhelming mass of knowledge and a bewildering array of theories eventually becomes a manageable store of understanding about the basis of counseling. Although, as most students recognize, a survey course does not turn prospective counselors into accomplished group leaders, the survey course on the theory and practice of group counseling does give students a basis for selecting from the many models to which they were exposed those therapeutic procedures that may be most useful and practical for them.

It is my hope that this will be your experience and that, at this point in the course, you will begin putting the theories together for yourself. It is also my hope that you will be patient enough to recognize that much of the theoretical foundation you have received in this book will take on new meanings when you gain more practical experience in leading various groups. The same is true for the many professional and ethical issues that were discussed in the book.

I think it's essential that you reflect on these basic issues, that you begin to formulate your own position on them, and that you discuss them with fellow students and instructors. Keep in mind, though, that these issues will also assume different meanings and dimensions once you confront them in your own practice. I am convinced, however, that, even though experience will teach you many new lessons, you will be far better equipped to deal with these and related issues when you meet them if you have reflected on them now.

I hope that this book and the manual that accompanies it have stimulated you to think productively about group process, to read more and learn more about the topics we have explored together, and to seek group experience both as a member and as a leader. I am sincerely interested in getting feedback from you regarding this textbook and the accompanying manual as well as your experience in your own training program. I'll welcome and value any suggestions for making this book more useful in future revisions. You can use the tear-out evaluation at the end of this book or write to me in care of Brooks/Cole Publishing Company, Monterey, California 93940.

NAME INDEX

Ackerman, M., 341
Adler, A., 179, 181, 183
Alberti, R., 353, 355, 356
Allen, T., 176
Angel, E., 220
Ansbacher, H., 175, 180, 188
Arbuckle, D., 39, 220
Asbury, F., 13
Authier, J., 48, 249, 257, 258, 260

Baer, J., 353, 356
Balzer, F., 13
Bandura, A., 342, 347, 364, 385
Bednar, R., 42, 106
Berenson, B., 39, 42
Berkowitz, S., 338
Berne, E., 311, 313, 317, 318, 320,
    323–325
Bion, W., 147
Blatner, H., 194, 202–204, 205–206,
    207, 210, 211
Blumberg, A., 13
Booraem, C., 347, 353, 355
Bootzin, R., 337
Borman, L., 15
Bozarth, J., 261, 269
Brown, G., 288

Brunell, L., 362
Bugental, J., 39, 220, 229, 239
Burnside, I., 161, 162
Burton, A., 220

Callanan, P., 23, 27–28, 35–36, 98–99,
    113
Carkuff, R., 13, 39, 42, 249, 252, 257
Cautela, J., 337
Childers, W., 13
Coates, T., 340, 341
Cole, S., 15, 16, 17
Corey, G., 8, 23, 27–28, 30, 35–36,
    97–99, 113, 159, 162, 231–232
Corey, M., 8, 23, 27–28, 30, 35–36,
    97–99, 113, 159, 162
Corlis, R., 39
Cormier, L., 346, 348, 352
Cormier, W., 346, 348, 352
Corsini, R., 176, 178, 179–180, 188,
    197–198, 199–200, 207, 269
Cotler, S., 353, 354, 355
Coulson, W., 261
Craighead, W., 353

Davison, G., 338, 341, 344, 348,
    349–350, 364, 365, 367

SUBJECT INDEX

A-B-C theory, 377
Acceptance, as therapeutic factor in
    groups, 108
Active listening, 46, 54, 250–251
Adlerian approach, 175–192
    in eclectic model, 463
    evaluation of, 188–190
    family therapy, application to,
        186–187
    group work, application to, 179–180,
        181–182
    influence of, on other approaches,
        189
    key concepts of, 176–181
    social interest, concept of, 179–180
    techniques of, 182–186
Adlerian family counseling, 186–187
    goals of, 186–187
    responsibility of family members in,
        187
    techniques of, 187
Adlerian groups:
    illustration of, 426, 427–428, 432,
        441–442, 444–445
    phases of, 182–186
    principles of, 181–186
    rationale for, 181

Adlerian groups *(continued)*:
    role and functions of leader, 186
    therapeutic goals of, 182
Adolescence, in developmental model,
    158–159
Adolescents, groups for, 9
Advice giving, 80, 91
Aggression, 95
Aloneness, 237–238
Alternate session, 29, 166
American Association for Counseling
    and Development, 20, 25, 32
American Association for Marriage and
    Family Therapy, 20, 32
American Board of Examiners in
    Psychodrama, 215
American Group Psychotherapy
    Association, 20, 170
American Mental Health Counselors
    Association, 32
American Psychiatric Association, 20
American Psychological Association, 20,
    25, 26, 32, 69
American Society of Group
    Psychotherapy and Psychodrama,
    217
Anal stage, 155

To the owner of this book:

I hope that you have enjoyed *Theory and Practice of Group Counseling* (2nd Edition) as much as I enjoyed writing it. I'd like to know as much about your experiences with the book as you care to offer. Only through your comments and the comments of others can I learn how to make *Theory and Practice of Group Counseling* a better book for future readers.

School: _____

Your Instructor's Name: _____

1. What did you like *most* about *Theory and Practice of Group Counseling?* _____

_____

_____

2. What did you like *least* about the book? _____

_____

3. Were all of the chapters of the book assigned for you to read? _____

(If not, which ones weren't?) _____

4. How interesting and informative was Chapter 16? _____

_____

_____

5. What material do you think could be omitted in future editions? _____

_____

_____

_____

6. If you used the student manual, how helpful was it as an aid in understanding concepts and theoretical approaches? _____

_____

_____

7. In the space below or in a separate letter, please let me know what other comments about the book you'd like to make. (For example, were any chapters *or* concepts particularly difficult?) Please recommend specific changes you'd like to see in future editions. I'd be delighted to hear from you!

Optional:

Your Name: _____ Date: _____

May Brooks/Cole quote you, either in promotion for *Theory and Practice of Group Counseling* or in future publishing ventures?

Yes _____   No _____

Sincerely,

Gerald Corey

CUT PAGE OUT AND
FOLD HERE

NO POSTAGE
NECESSARY
IF MAILED
IN THE
UNITED STATES

BUSINESS REPLY MAIL

FIRST CLASS   PERMIT NO. 84   MONTEREY, CALIF.

POSTAGE WILL BE PAID BY ADDRESSEE

DR. GERALD COREY
BROOKS/COLE PUBLISHING COMPANY
MONTEREY, CA 93940